SwiftUI

for Masterminds

How to take advantage of SwiftUI
to create insanely great apps
for iPhones, iPads, and Macs

J.D Gauchat

www.jdgauchat.com

Cover Illustration by **Patrice Garden**

The source code for this book is available at **www.formasterminds.com**

Table of Contents

Introduction

Mobile devices and computers have existed for some time, but they were always part of two separate ecosystems. For most of their history, cellphones and handheld devices had limited functionality and could only perform common tasks, such as storing contacts or sending emails, while personal computers were used for work and surfing the web. But everything changed with the launch of the iPhone in 2007. This revolutionary device could process information at the level of desktop computers and was small enough to fit in a pocket. It was the first of its kind, and users loved it.

However, not everything was perfect. Despite having similar capabilities, the iPhone was not the same as a personal computer. It was less powerful, had less memory, less storage capacity, a smaller screen, and an interface that required users to operate the device with their fingers instead of the mouse. These unique features forced Apple to create a device-specific operative system, called iPhoneOS, and developers to use two different sets of tools if they wanted their applications to be available for both Mac computers and iPhones.

Apple's innovation did not stop with the iPhone. In 2010, they released the iPad. The two devices had similar characteristics and shared the same operative system for a while, called iOS, but the iPad had a larger screen and, therefore, developers had to adapt their applications to it. To make matters worse, later that year the company introduced a new generation of Apple TV that could run iOS and, consequently, iOS apps, and a few years later they launched the Apple Watch with its small screen, unusual features, and its own operative system, called watchOS.

Although there were some similarities in the way they worked, the differences between these devices deepened overtime and Apple had to provide a separate set of tools to program applications for each one of them, which also included new operative systems. Apple TV got its own system called tvOS in 2015, and in 2019 the growing distinctions between iPhones and iPads compelled the company to introduce iPadOS, an operative system designed specifically for iPads.

Having many devices with such distinctive features was excellent for users, but the situation was difficult for developers. Developing apps that could work on more than one type of device was demanding and involved a steep learning curve. This resulted in many apps being distributed exclusively for one system or another. It didn't take time for Apple engineers to realize that their tools were not prepared to meet the demands of modern developers, and in June 2019, they released SwiftUI.

SwiftUI is like an abstraction layer that sits on top of previous tools to simplify the construction of user interfaces and revamp the way developers create applications for Apple devices. With SwiftUI, we can easily develop apps that share data and work seamlessly on all device, including iPhones, iPads, Apple TV, Apple Watch, and Mac computers.

SwiftUI is a revolutionary tool that opens the door to a new generation of applications. The situation was never better for developers. The tools are ready. The future looks bright. And you can be part of it.

 IMPORTANT: This book explains how to build applications for iPhones, iPads and Mac Computers, but everything you learn here can be applied to create applications for Apple Watch and Apple TV as well.

 The Basics: Links with additional information, examples, projects, videos, and resources are available at **www.formasterminds.com**. Apple's official documentation is available at **developer.apple.com**. Frameworks and APIs references are available at **developer.apple.com/reference**.

Conventions

This book explores basic and advanced topics required for the development of professional applications. Depending on your current level of knowledge, you may find some of these topics easy or difficult to learn. To help you navigate the book, we have identified each section with a label. The following is a description of what these labels represent.

(Basic)   The Basic label represents topics you can ignore if you already know the basics of Swift and app development. If you are learning how to develop applications for Apple devices for the first time, these sections are mandatory.

(Medium)   The Medium label represents topics that are not always required for app development. You can ignore the information presented in these sections until they are applied in practical situations later or you need them in your own applications.

(Advanced)   The Advanced label represents topics that are only required in advanced applications or API development. The information presented in these sections is not required for the development of most applications, but it can be helpful if you want to improve your understanding of how Apple technologies work.

If you are new to app development, read all the Basic sections first and only read the Medium sections when you need it later to understand how the examples work.

Code Examples

Every single topic presented in this book is explained through examples that you can try yourself. We recommend that you open Xcode and try the examples as you learn, but you can download the codes and projects from our website to save time (**www.formasterminds.com**).

The examples in this book only apply the technologies you already know, so they not always represent best practices. There are several programming patterns and best practices you can follow. What applies to you depends on the characteristics of your application and what you want to achieve with it. We recommend you explore all the possibilities presented in this book and also experiment and try your own.

Additional Information

Apple's technologies are extensive, and a book cannot teach you everything. After each topic is introduced, you should read the official specifications provided by Apple and look for additional examples on the web. The links to the specifications, additional information, tutorials and videos for each chapter are available on our website (**www.formasterminds.com**).

Chapter 1
App Development

(Basic) **1.1 Overview**

No matter the technology we use to develop our applications, we must comply with Apple's strict control. Apple requires developers to use the software provided by the company to create apps for its devices, and this software only works on Apple computers. For this reason, the options are limited, but the good news is that most of the tools and accounts we need are provided by the company for free.

- **Mac Computer**. This in theory could be any Intel-based Mac computer, but the development software required to create applications with SwiftUI only works with the latest operative system, currently macOS Catalina, so we need a computer that can run this system version or newer.
- **Xcode**. This is the software provided by Apple for development. The latest version is number 11. It's free and the package comes with everything we need to create applications, including an editor, the SDK (Software Development Kit), and a simulator to test our applications.
- **App Developer Account**. This is a basic account we can get for free. From this account, we can manage our membership, create certificates, app identifiers and other information we need to test and publish our apps.
- **Apple Membership**. This is the membership we need to publish our apps in the App Store. As of this writing, the cost of this membership is $99 US dollars per year.
- **Mobile Device**. This could be any of the devices available in the market that support the current versions of Apple's mobile operative systems (SwiftUI only works on iOS 13, tvOS 13, watchOS 6, iPadOS, and macOS Catalina). Testing our applications on a real device is highly recommended and necessary before publishing.

The steps we must follow to be ready to work are relatively simple. We must obtain a Mac Computer capable of running the operative system required by SwiftUI (currently macOS Catalina), make sure that we have an Apple ID to access our Developer Account (**developer.apple.com**), and install the latest version of Xcode (currently 11).

(Basic) **1.2 Xcode**

Xcode is a general-purpose IDE (Integrated Development Environment). It includes a very powerful editor with graphic tools to help us write our code, the SDKs (Software Development Kits) for the creation of software for the iOS, iPadOS, macOS, watchOS, and tvOS operative systems, and compilers for the C, C++, Objective-C and Swift programming languages.

Xcode is available as an app on the Mac App Store. To download this application, we must open the App Store from Launchpad (the application organizer that comes with macOS) or double-click the App Store icon inside the Applications folder in Finder. From the App Store, we must search for the term "Xcode". The window will show Xcode's icon at the top (Figure 1-1, number 1). Then, we must click on the *GET* button to download and install the software.

Figure 1-1: Xcode in the Mac App Store

Once the application has been downloaded, it is automatically installed. To open Xcode, we have to go to Launchpad and click on the icon or search for the program inside the Applications folder in Finder. Figure 1-2 shows Xcode's welcome screen.

Figure 1-2: Xcode's welcome screen

The welcome screen offers a list of the recent projects on the right and buttons on the left to start a new project or find those already created and stored in a repository. The following are the options currently available.

- **Get started with a playground**. This option creates a single file and provides a simplified interface called *Playground* that we can use to experiment and learn about the Swift language and the basic frameworks included in the SDK.
- **Create a new Xcode project**. This is the option we choose when we want to create a new application. The option generates a new Xcode project from a template that provides basic files and settings to start from.
- **Clone an existing project**. This option allows us to open and work on a project stored on a server. It is used to download a project already initiated by other developers or shared online.

 IMPORTANT: The first two options are the ones we are going to use in this book. We will open a Playground to learn fundamental programming concepts in the following chapters and work with Xcode projects later to learn how to create real applications.

(Basic) **1.3 Development**

The development process requires that we master a set of tools. We need to learn how to create code with a programming language, implement preprogrammed code to access all the features available on a device, and how to compile and prepare the app for distribution.

Chapter 1 - App Development

(Basic) Programming Languages

Several years ago, Apple adopted and implemented a language called Objective-C to allow developers to create applications for their devices. Due to the technical level required to work with this language, the spectacular success of Apple's mobile devices did not impress developers the same way as consumers. The demand for more and better applications was growing fast, but the complicated nature of the system did not appeal to most developers who were used to working with more traditional tools. To solve this problem, the company introduced a new programming language called *Swift*. Swift presents a simpler syntax that developers find familiar but preserving that low-level nature necessary to take advantage of every aspect of Apple's devices. Swift was designed to replace Objective-C and, therefore, is the language recommended to new developers.

(Basic) Frameworks and APIs

Programming languages by themselves cannot do much. They provide all the elements we need to interact with the system but are basic tools for storing and processing data. Because of the complexity of the information required to control sophisticated technologies and access every part of a system, it could take years to develop an application from scratch working with just the instructions offered by a programming language. For this reason, the languages are always accompanied by sets of pre-programmed routines grouped in libraries and frameworks that through a simple interface called *API* (Application programming interface) allow programmers to incorporate to their apps amazing functionality with just a few lines of code.

Frameworks and APIs are critical for app development. As developers, we must learn and apply these tools if we want to create useful applications and, therefore, they will become the main subject of study in following chapters.

(Basic) Compiler

Computers do not understand Swift or any other programming language. These languages were created for us to give machines instructions we can understand. Our code must be converted to elemental orders that work at an electronic level, turning multiple switches on and off to represent the abstraction humans work with. The translation from the language humans understand to the language computers understand is done by a program called *compiler*.

Compilers have specific routines to translate instructions from programming languages to machine code. They are language and platform specific, which means that we need a specific compiler to program in one language and for one particular device. There are a few compilers available for Apple systems, but the one currently used by Xcode is called *LLVM*. LLVM is capable of compiling code written in Swift, C, C++, and Objective-C.

With the compiler, the machinery to build an app is complete. Figure 1-3, below, shows all the elements involved. There are three main sources of code the compiler uses to build the application: our code, the frameworks our program requires, and a set of basic routines necessary for the app to run (called Application Loop in Figure 1-3). The process starts from Xcode. In this program we write our code, access frameworks through their APIs, and configure the app to be compiled. Combining our code, the codes from the frameworks our app requires and the basic routines (Application Loop), the compiler creates an executable program that may be run in a simulator, a device, or submitted to the App Store for distribution.

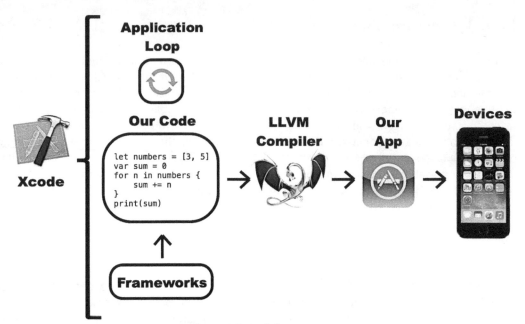

```
let numbers = [3, 5]
var sum = 0
for n in numbers {
    sum += n
}
print(sum)
```

Figure 1-3: *Building an App*

 The Basics: The Application Loop is a group of elemental routines, common to every program, that connects your app to the operative system and provides a loop (a code that executes itself over and over again) to constantly check for events produced by the user or coming from the system. Although you never work directly with these routines, they are connected to your code through the app's delegate to inform the state of the program, as we will see in further chapters.

Chapter 2
Introduction to Swift

Basic **2.1 Computer Programming**

Computers can't do anything unless we write a program. A program is a succession of instructions that the computer has to follow. We write the program using the instructions provided by a specific programming language, then a compiler translates these instructions into orders the computer can understand, and when we tell the computer to run the program, the orders are executed sequentially one by one.

The instructions are always listed in sequential order, but programming languages offer different ways to group them together and organize the code and the data that is going to be processed. Developing an app demands a deep understanding of these instructions and the combinations required to achieve the results we want. Since this may be daunting for those who want to create their first app, Xcode includes a tool called *Playground* to learn how to program and test our code.

Basic **Playground**

As the name suggests, Playground offers a place to experiment and play around with our code before including it in our applications. Although we could start an Xcode project to create an application right away, it is better to work with Playground first to learn how to program and how to take advantage of some of the fundamental frameworks included in the SDK.

Playground files are created from the *Get started with a playground* option on the Xcode's welcome window (Figure 1-2, below). The first window we see after we click on this option includes a few icons to select the template we want to use. These are files with pre-programmed code to help us get started with our project. The templates available at the moment are called Blank (with just a few lines of code to start from scratch), Game (with basic code to program a video game), Map (with the code to display a map), and Single View (with the same code required to create a view for an application).

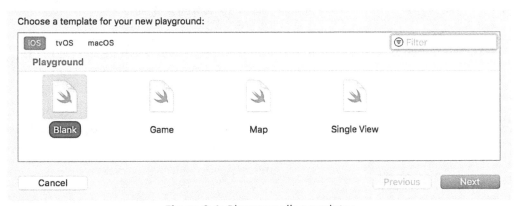

Figure 2-1: Playground's templates

After we select the template, Xcode asks for the name of the Playground file and the place on our hard drive where we want to store it. Once the file is created, Xcode shows the Playground's interface on the screen. Figure 2-2 illustrates what we see when we create a Blank template.

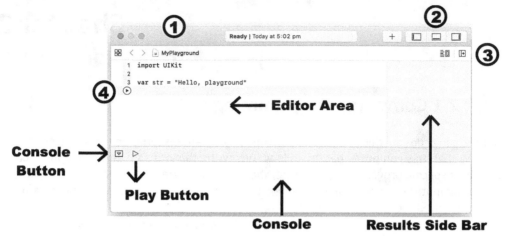

Figure 2-2: Playground's interface

 The Basics: The Xcode's menu at the top of the screen also includes the option to create the Playground file. If you cannot see Xcode's welcome window, open the *File* menu from the menu bar, select the option *New* and click on *Playground*.

Playground presents a simple interface with a toolbar at the top that includes a few buttons for configuration (number 1) and two main areas, the *Editor Area* where we write our code, and the *Results Side Bar* on the right where the results produced by our code are displayed. This interface can be expanded from the buttons on the toolbar (number 2). These buttons are used to open and close removable panels. The first button opens a panel on the left-hand side of the window called Navigator Area where we can see the resources included in our Playground project, the second button opens the Console at the bottom of the window, where we can read the errors produced by the code and print our own messages (as shown in Figure 2-2), and the third button opens a panel on the right-hand side of the window called Utilities Area, which contains information about the selected resource.

As illustrated in Figure 2-2, the Editor Area includes a button at the bottom of the panel to execute and stop the code (Play Button). Every time we insert a change in the code, we must press this button to execute it. There is also a play button on the left side of the Editor Area that we can press if we want to execute parts of the code instead (number 4). When this button is pressed, the code is executed up to the line in which the button is located.

 IMPORTANT: There are two more buttons on top of the Editor Area to set the editor's window (number 3). These are used to activate or deactivate the live preview and to add more areas to the editor when we are creating our applications with SwiftUI, as we will see in further chapters.

In the Editor Area, we can see the code we have programmed so far. When a new Playground file is created, Xcode offers a template that includes a few basic lines of code to start from. Listing 2-1 shows the code currently generated for the Blank template.

```
import UIKit
var str = "Hello, playground"
```

Listing 2-1: Playground template

A computer program is just text written in a specific format. Each line of text represents an instruction. Sometimes a single line includes several instructions, and therefore each line is

Chapter 2 - Introduction to Swift

usually called *statement*. Every statement is an order, or multiple orders, for the computer to perform a task. In the code of Listing 2-1, the first statement uses the instruction `import` to include in our code the pre-programmed codes from a framework called *UIKit* (an old frameworks used to create user interfaces before the introduction of SwiftUI), and the second statement uses the instruction `var` to store the text "Hello, playground" in memory.

If we press the Play Button to execute the code, we will see an indication of what the code does inside the Results Side Bar (in this case, it shows the text stored in memory by the `var` instruction). When we move the mouse over this indication, two small buttons show up, as illustrated in Figure 2-3.

Figure 2-3: *Quick Look and Show Result buttons*

The button on the left is called the *Quick Look*, and it shows a popup window with a visual representation of the final result of the execution of the code, such as the formatted text or an image (in this case, no visual effect is associated with the code so only the plain text is shown on that window).

Figure 2-4: *Quick Look window*

The button on the right is called *Show Result*, and what it does is to open a window within our code with a visual representation of the results of the execution of the code over time (in this case, nothing changes, so only the "Hello, playground" text is shown).

Figure 2-5: *Result window*

The code provided by Xcode for the Blank template is useless, but it shows the basic syntax of the Swift language and how to do elemental things in a program such as importing frameworks to add functionality and storing data in memory. The reason why one of the statements is storing data in memory is because this is the most important task of a program. A program's main functions are storing, retrieving, and processing data. Working with data in the computer's memory is a delicate process that demands meticulous organization. If we are not careful, data may be accidentally deleted, corrupted, or completely overwritten. To make sure this does not happen, programming languages introduce the concept of variables.

Basic 2.2 Variables

Variables are names representing values stored in memory. Once a variable is defined, its name remains the same but the value in memory they represent may change. This allows us to store and retrieve a value from memory without the need of remembering where in the memory the value was stored. With just mentioning the name of the variable created to store a value, we can get that value back or replace it with a new one. The system takes care of memory management in the background, but we still need to know how memory works to figure out what kind of values we can store.

(Basic) **Memory**

The computer's memory is like a huge honeycomb, with consecutive cells that can be in two possible states: activated or deactivated. They are electronic switches with on and off positions established by low and high energy levels.

Figure 2-6: Memory cells

Because of their two possible states, each cell is a small unit of information. One cell may represent two possible states (switch on or off), but by combining a sequence of cells we can represent more states. For example, if we combine two cells, we have four possible states.

Figure 2-7: Combining two cells

With these two cells, we can now represent up to four states (4 possible combinations). If we had used three cells instead, then the possible combinations would have been 8 (eight states). The number of combinations doubles every time we add another cell to the group. This can be extended to represent any number of states we want.

Because of its characteristics, this system of switches is used to represent binary numbers, which are numbers expressed by only two digits: 0 and 1. An on switch represents the value 1 and an off switch represents the value 0. Basic units were determined with the purpose of identifying parts of this endless series of digits. One cell was called a *bit* and a group of 8 bits was called a *byte*. Figure 2-8 shows how a byte looks like in memory, with some of its switches on representing the binary number 00011101.

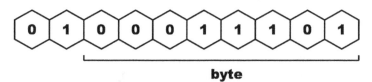

byte

Figure 2-8: Representation of one byte in memory

The possible combinations of 8 bits is 256, therefore, a byte can represent binary numbers of 8 digits, which in turn can be converted to numbers humans can understand, such as decimal numbers. With its 256 possible combinations, a byte can represent decimal numbers from 0 to 255. For instance, when the value of the byte in the example of figure 2-8 is converted to the decimal system, we get the number 29 (00011101 = 29).

 The Basics: Numbers of one numeral system, like binary, can be converted to any other numeral system, like decimal. The binary system is the one a computer can understand because it translates directly to the electronic

Chapter 2 - Introduction to Swift

switches they are built off, but humans find this is difficult to read, so we use other systems to express numbers. The decimal system is the one we use every day, but in computer programming you will often find numbers expressed in other systems, like hexadecimal (base-16).

To represent larger numbers, bytes are grouped together. For example, if we take two bytes from memory, we get a binary number composed of a total of 16 bits (16 zeros and ones). A binary number of 16 bits can represent decimal numbers from 0 to 65535 (a total of 65536 possible combinations). For coherence and to establish clearly defined data structures, each programming language declares its own units of data of a predetermined size. They are usually called *primitive types*.

(Basic) **Primitive Data Types**

Primitive data types are types of units of data defined by the language. They have always the same size, so when we store a value of one of these types the computer knows exactly how much memory to use. Of all the primitive types, probably the most useful is `Int`.

Int—This type is for integer numbers, which are numbers with no fractional component. In 64 bits systems, the size of this type is 8 bytes and therefore it can store values from -9,223,372,036,854,775,808 to 9,223,372,036,854,775,807.

Although it is recommended to always use the `Int` type to store integer numbers, there are frameworks that require a very specific type of integer. For this reason, Swift also defines the following types.

Int8—This type is for integer numbers of a size of 1 byte (8 bits). Because of its size, it can store values from -128 to 127.

Int16—This type is for integer numbers of a size of 2 bytes (16 bits). Because of its size, it can store values from -32,768 to 32,767.

Int32—This type is for integer numbers of a size of 4 bytes (32 bits). Because of its size, it can store values from -2,147,483,648 to 2,147,483,647.

Int64—This type is for integer numbers of a size of 8 bytes (64 bits). Because of its size, it can store values from -9,223,372,036,854,775,808 to 9,223,372,036,854,775,807.

If we check the size of each type presented so far and calculate the possible combinations of bits, we will discover that the maximum values don't match. For example, an `Int8` uses 1 byte, which means it is composed of 8 bits, and for this reason it should be able to store numbers from 0 to 255 (256 possible combinations). The reason why an `Int8` has a positive limit of 127 is because it only uses 7 bits to store its value, the first bit on the left is reserved to indicate the sign (positive or negative). Although these limits are not restrictive, the language also provides the unsigned versions of these types in case we need to store larger positive values.

UInt—This is the same as `Int` but for unsigned values. Because it does not reserve a bit for the sign, in 64-bit systems it can store values from 0 to 18,446,744,073,709,551,615.

The specific types for `UInt` are `UInt8`, `UInt16`, `UInt32`, and `UInt64`. These types work exactly like their equivalents for `Int`, but they are intended to store only positive numbers.

Although all these types are very useful, they are only good for storing binary values that can be used to represent integer numbers. Arithmetic operations also require the use of real numbers (e.g., 3.14 or 10.543). Computers cannot reproduce these types of values, but they can work with an approximation called floating-point numbers. The following are the floating-point data types defined in the Swift language.

Float—This type is for 32 bits floating-point numbers. It has a precision of 6 decimal digits.

Double—This type is for 64 bits floating-point numbers. It has a precision of at least 15 decimal digits.

Floating-point types can handle huge numbers using scientific notation, but because of their precision, it is recommended to declare a variable of type `Double` when performing calculations and use `Float` for minor tasks such as storing coordinates to position graphics on the screen.

(Basic) Declaration and Initialization

If we want to store data in memory, the first thing we need to do is to select the right type from the data types provided by the language and then create a variable of that type. This action is called *Declaration*, and it is done using the `var` instruction and the syntax `var name: type`.

```
var mynumber: Int
```

Listing 2-2: *Declaring variables*

The example of Listing 2-2 creates a variable called `mynumber` of type `Int`. When the system reads this statement, it reserves a space in memory of 8 bytes long (64 bits) and assigns the name `mynumber` to that space. After the execution of this statement, we can use the variable `mynumber` to store in memory any integer value from -9,223,372,036,854,775,808 to 9,223,372,036,854,775,807.

 IMPORTANT: According to the official specification, you can use almost any character you want to declare the name of a variable, except for spaces, mathematical symbols, and a few special Unicode characters. Also, they cannot start with a number. If you declare a variable with an illegal name, Xcode will show you an error. There are two things you should always remember: Swift distinguishes between lowercase and uppercase characters (`MyInt` is considered a different variable than `myint`), and also that to avoid conflict with reserved words you should declare complex names or define the names with a combination of two or more words (for example, `myint` instead of `int`).

Memory is a reusable resource. The space we reserve for a variable may have been used before by another variable that was deleted, or pieces of functional code could have been stored in that place, leaving incomprehensible data in the same space of memory we are now trying to use for the new variable. For this reason, after the declaration of a variable we always have to store a value in it. This action is called *Initialization*.

```
var mynumber: Int
mynumber = 5
```

Listing 2-3: *Initializing variables*

In the new example of Listing 2-3, we first declare the variable as we did before, and then initialize it with the value 5 (we store the number 5 in the space of memory reserved for this variable). To store the value, we use the = (equal) symbol and the syntax `name = value`, where `name` is the name of the variable and `value` is the value we want to store (once the variable was declared, we do not have to use the `var` instruction or specify its type anymore).

Most of the time, we know what the variable's initial value will be right away. In cases like this, Swift allows us to declare and initialize the variable in just one line of code.

Chapter 2 - Introduction to Swift

```
var mynumber: Int = 5
```

Listing 2-4: Declaring and initializing variables in the same statement

 Do It Yourself: If you haven't done it yet, create a new Playground file with the Blank template. Replace all the statements of the Xcode's template by the code of Listing 2-4 and press the Play button. You should see the value 5 on the Results Side Bar. Repeat this process for the following examples. Each example in this chapter replaces the previous one.

Variables are called variables because their values are not constant. We can change them any time we want. To store a new value in the space of memory reserved for a variable, we must implement the same syntax used for initialization.

```
var mynumber: Int = 5
mynumber = 87
```

Listing 2-5: Assigning a new value to a variable

The process of storing a new value is called *assignment*. In these terms, we can say that in the example of Listing 2-5 we "assign the value 87 to the variable `mynumber`". This new value replaces the old one in memory. After that second statement is executed, every time we read the `mynumber` variable from other statements in the code it will return the value 87 (unless another value is assigned to the variable later).

 IMPORTANT: Once a variable is declared, the values stored in that variable have to be of the same type. If we declare a variable of type `Int`, we cannot store floating-point values in it (e.g. 14.129).

Of course, we can create all the variables we want and of any type we need.

```
var mynumber: Int = 5
var myfavorite: Float = 14.129
```

Listing 2-6: Declaring variables of different types

The first statement of Listing 2-6 declares an integer variable and initializes it with the value 5. The second statement does the same but for a floating-point variable. When the values are of a clear type, Swift can infer them. If this is the case, the syntax may be simplified, as in the following example.

```
var mynumber = 5
var myfavorite = 14.129
```

Listing 2-7: Declaring variables without specifying the type

Swift infers the variable's type from the value we are trying to assign to it. In this last example, the value 5 is clearly an integer and the value 14.129 is clearly a floating-point value, so Swift creates the variable `mynumber` of type `Int` and the variable `myfavorite` of type `Double` (it selects the most comprehensive type).

 IMPORTANT: When the type is not clear, we must declare it explicitly. For example, if we are initializing a variable with the value 8, but we want to assign floating-point numbers to this variable in the future, we must declare it as `Float` or `Double` (as we did in Listing 2-6), otherwise Swift will infer an `Int`.

The Basics: Xcode offers a simple tool we can use to confirm the data type assigned to a variable and get additional information. All you have to do is click on the name of the variable while holding down the Option key on your keyboard. This opens a popup window with the full declaration of the variable, including its data type, and any information we may need to identify the function of the code. As we will see later, this not only works with variables but also with any type of instruction, including functions, properties, methods, etc.

An important feature of variables is that the value of one may be assigned to another.

```
var mynumber = 5
var myfavorite = mynumber
```

Listing 2-8: Assigning variables to variables

The second statement of Listing 2-8 reads the value of the `mynumber` variable and assigns it to the `myfavorite` variable. The type of `myfavorite` is inferred to be `Int` (the same of `mynumber`). After this code is executed, we have two integer variables, each with its own space in memory and the value 5 stored in them.

(Basic) Arithmetic Operators

Storing values in memory is what variables allow us to do, but those values do not have to be declared explicitly, they can also be the result of arithmetic operations. Swift supports the five basic arithmetic operations: + (addition), - (subtraction), * (multiplication), / (division) and % (remainder or modulus).

```
var mynumber = 5 + 10   // 15
```

Listing 2-9: Assigning the result of an operation to a variable

The Basics: The text added at the end of the statement of Listing 2-9 is a comment that we used to show the value produced by the statement. Comments are ignored by the compiler but useful for programmers to remember vital information that could help in further reviews of the code. They are introduced after the characters // (e.g., // `comment`) or in between the characters /* */ (e.g., /* `comment` */). Because they are frequently used to momentarily deactivate code, Xcode offers a shortcut to comment entire lines. You must select the lines of code you want to turn into a comment and press the keys Command and / (forward slash).

When the system reads the statement of Listing 2-9, it adds 10 to 5 and assigns the result to `mynumber` (15). Of course, we can use variables of any data type we need and perform any of the operations available.

```
var mynumber = 2 * 25   // 50
var anothernumber = 8 - 40 * 2   // -72
var myfraction = 5.0 / 2.0   // 2.5
```

Listing 2-10: Performing operations in variables of different type

The first two statements of Listing 2-10 are easy to read. They perform arithmetic operations over integer numbers that produce an integer value as result, so the variables `mynumber` and

Chapter 2 - Introduction to Swift

anothernumber will be of type **Int**. A problem arises when we work with operations that may produce floating-point numbers. That is why for the third statement we specifically declared the values as floating-point numbers (adding the fractional part .0). This forces Swift to infer the variable's type as **Double** and produce a result of that type.

 The Basics: Arithmetic operations are executed following an order of precedence determined by the operators. For example, multiplication and division have more precedence over addition and subtraction. This means that the multiplications and divisions will be performed before the additions and subtractions. If you want to change the order, you must enclose the values between parentheses (e.g., **var number = (8 - 40) * 2**).

When the compiler finds an operation with two or more numbers and has to infer the type of the result, it converts the number of the less comprehensive type to the most comprehensive type. For example, when we declare an **Int** and a **Double** in the same operation (e.g., 5 + 2.0), the **Int** value is converted and processed as **Double**, and therefore the result will also be **Double**. On the other hand, if all the values are integers, then the result will be an integer (unless the variable is explicitly declared as **Float** or **Double**).

```
var myfraction1 = 5.0 / 2.0   // 2.5
var myfraction2 = 5 / 2.0   // 2.5
var myfraction3 = 5 / 2   // 2
```

Listing 2-11: Inferring the type from an operation

Listing 2-11 declares and initializes three variables. In the first statement both numbers were declared as floating-point values, so the compiler infers a **Double** and creates the **myfraction1** variable of that type. In the second statement, we have an integer value and a floating-point value. Because of the floating-point value, the compiler interprets the integer (5) as a **Double** (5.0) and creates the **myfraction2** variable of type **Double**. But in the last statement there is no clear floating-point value. Both numbers were declared as integers (with no decimals). In this case, the compiler does not know what we want to do, so it interprets both numbers as integers and creates the **myfraction3** variable of type **Int**. When an operation produces a result that is expected to be an integer, any fractional part is discarded. In this example, the system gets rid of the decimal 5 from the result and only assigns the integer 2 to the variable. If we don't want to lose the fractional part, we must avoid inference and declare the data type ourselves as **Float** or **Double** (e.g., **var myfraction3: Double = 5 / 2**).

Dividing integer numbers may be pointless most of the time, except in some circumstances when we need to know the remainder. The remainder is the amount left over by a division between two numbers and it is calculated using the **%** symbol.

```
var remainder1 = 11 % 3   // 2
var remainder2 = 20 % 8   // 4
var remainder3 = 5 % 2   // 1
```

Listing 2-12: Calculating the remainder

Listing 2-12 shows three examples of how to calculate the remainder of a division. Each statement calculates the remainder of dividing the first number by the second number and assigns the result to the variable. For instance, the first statement produces the remainder 2. The system divides 11 by 3 and finds a quotient of 3. Then, to get the remainder, it calculates 11 minus the multiplication of 3 times the quotient (**11 - (3 * 3) = 2**).

The second statement produces a remainder of 4 and the third statement produces a remainder of 1. This last statement is particularly useful because it allows us to determine whether a value is odd or even. When we calculate the reminder of an integer number divided by 2, we get a result according to its parity (odd or even). If the number is even, the remainder is 0, and if the number is odd, the remainder is 1 (or -1 for negative numbers).

Performing arithmetic operations becomes useful when instead of numbers we use variables.

```
var mynumber = 5
var total = mynumber + 10   // 15
```

Listing 2-13: *Adding numbers to variables*

The example of Listing 2-13 declares the `mynumber` variable and initializes it with the value 5. In the next statement, the `total` variable is declared and initialized with the result of the addition of the current value of `mynumber` plus 10 (5 + 10).

In Listing 2-13, we used a new variable to store the result of the operation, but when the old value is not important anymore, we can store the result back into the same variable.

```
var mynumber = 5
mynumber = mynumber + 10   // 15
```

Listing 2-14: *Performing operations on the variable's current value*

In this example, the current value of `mynumber` is added to 10 and the result is assigned to the same variable. After the execution of the second statement, the value of `mynumber` is 15.

 The Basics: As in mathematics, the - sign may be used before the name of a variable to toggle its sign and get the opposite value. If the current value is positive, the result will be negative, and vice versa. For example, if the current value of `mynumber` is 20, the statement `var result = -mynumber` will assign the value -20 to `result`. Another useful application of this technique is to change the current sign of the value of a variable assigning to the variable its own value preceded by the - sign (e.g., `mynumber = -mynumber`).

Working with values previously stored in a variable allows our program to evolve and adapt to new circumstances. This is a good way to create a counter. We could add 1 to the current value of a variable and store the result in the same variable. Every time a statement like this is executed, the value of the variable is incremented by one unit. Recurrent increments and decrements of the values of variables are very important in computer programming. Because of this, Swift supports two operators that were specifically designed for this purpose.

- `+=` is a shorthand for `variable = variable + number`, where `number` is the value we want to add to the variable's current value.
- `-=` is a shorthand for `variable = variable - number`, where `number` is the value we want to subtract to the variable's current value.

With these operators, we can easily add or subtract a value to the current value of the variable and assign the result back to the same variable.

```
var mynumber = 5
mynumber += 4   // 9
```

Listing 2-15: *Modifying the variable's value using incremental operators*

Chapter 2 - Introduction to Swift

The process generated by the code of Listing 2-15 is straightforward. After the value 5 is assigned to the `mynumber` variable, the system reads the second statement, gets the current value of the variable, adds 4 to that value, and stores the result back to `mynumber` (9).

 IMPORTANT: Swift also offers Overflow operators (`&+`, `&-`, `&*`, `&/` and `&%`). These operators are useful when we think that an operation could produce a result that goes over the limit the data type can handle. For more information, visit our website and follow the links for this chapter.

(Basic) Constants

As mentioned before, the memory of a computer is a sequence of switches. There are millions and millions of switches, one after another, with no clear delimitations. To be able to know where the space occupied by a variable starts or ends, the system uses addresses. These addresses are just consecutive numbers that correspond to each byte of memory (8 bits). For example, if one byte is at the address 000000, the next byte will be at the address 000001, the next one at 000002, and so on. If we declare a variable of 4 bytes, the system has to reserve the four consecutive bytes and remember where they are so as not to overwrite them with the value of another variable. The task is easy when working with primitive types because their sizes are always the same, but the size of variables of more complex or custom data types depends on the values we assign to them. For example, the space in memory required to store the text "Hello" is smaller than the space required for the text "Hello World". A variable will occupy less space with the first value and more with the second one. Managing the memory for data of inconsistent size takes more time and consumes more resources than working with fixed sizes. This is one of the reasons why Swift includes the concept of constants.

Constants are the same as variables, but their values cannot change. Once a constant is declared and initialized, we cannot change its value. In fact, we will get an error if our code tries to do it, so we will know we made a mistake even before running our app. Constants provide a secure way to store a value and help the system manage the memory, improving the performance of our application and ensuring that a value does not change over time.

To declare a constant, we must apply the same syntax used for a variable but replace the `var` keyword by the `let` keyword.

```
let mynumber = 5
```

Listing 2-16: Declaring and initializing a constant

All the rules for variables also apply to constants; with the exception that we cannot assign a new value after the constant was already initialized. We can declare the constant first, specifying its type, and initialize it later, but we cannot assign new values to it. The `mynumber` constant declared in Listing 2-16 will always have the value 5.

 IMPORTANT: When to use constants or variables depends on your application. As guidance, you can follow what Apple recommends: if a stored value in your code is not going to change, always declare it as a constant with the `let` keyword. Use variables only for storing values that need to be able to change.

(Basic) 2.3 Data Types

Besides the primitive data types already studied, Swift defines additional data types to allow us to work not only with numbers but also more complex values such as logical values (true or false), characters, or text.

Characters

Because of their nature, computers cannot store decimal numbers, characters, or text. As we have seen in the previous section, the computer memory is only capable of storing 1s and 0s (switches on and off), but they can work with more complex values using tables that contain the information necessary to represent those values (numbers, letters, symbols, etc.). What the system stores in memory is not the character but the value corresponding to the index of the character on the table. For example, if we use the letter A, the value stored in memory will be the decimal number 65 (in its binary representation) because that's the position of the letter A on the table used by Swift to define these characters. When the value is stored, the system not only stores the value but also a reference to indicate that it represents a character and not just a number. That way, when we get the value back, the system reads the number 65, searches for the character in that position on the table and returns the letter or shows it on the screen.

There are several standard tables of characters available. Swift is compliant with a table called *Unicode*. This is a comprehensive table that includes every character from almost any language in the world, and also special characters, such as emojis. Due to its broad range, the space in memory required to store a single character varies from one character to another. For this reason, Swift provides the **Character** type to store these values.

```
var myletter: Character = "A"
```

Listing 2-17: Declaring and initializing a Character *variable*

A character is declared using the **Character** type and initialized with the value between double quotes. In Listing 2-17, we declare a variable called **myletter** with the character A as its value.

Besides the characters we can type from the keyboard, Unicode allows us to store emojis and symbols as characters, and Xcode offers a handy tool to select the graphics we want. By pressing the combination of keys Control + Command + Space, we can open a popup window and select a graphic with a click of the mouse.

Figure 2-9: Using emojis and symbols as characters

Strings

Individual characters are barely used in computer programming. Instead, we usually store strings of characters. The **string** type was created for this purpose.

```
let mytext: String = "My name is John"
```

Listing 2-18: Declaring and initializing a String *variable*

Chapter 2 - Introduction to Swift

A string is a sequence of **Character** values. It is declared with the **String** type and the value between double quotes. These types of variables are very flexible; we may replace the string by another one of different length, concatenate two or more, or even modify parts of them. Concatenation is a common operation and it is done with the **+** and **+=** operators.

```
var mytext = "My name is "
mytext = mytext + "John"   // "My name is John"
```

Listing 2-19: Concatenating strings

In Listing 2-19, the **mytext** variable is created with the value "My name is " and then the string "John" is added at the end of the current value to get the string "My name is John". The **+=** operator works in a similar way, and we can also combine them to get the string we want.

```
let smileyface = "😜"
var mytext = "My name is John "
mytext += smileyface   // "My name is John 😜"
```

Listing 2-20: Concatenating strings with the + and += operators

The example of Listing 2-20 adds a smiley face at the end of the current value of the **mytext** variable with the **+=** operator. Notice that the **smileyface** variable is considered by Swift to be a **String** value, not a **Character** value (as always, Swift selects the most comprehensive type).

With the **+** and **+=** operators we can only concatenate strings with strings. To concatenate strings with characters and numbers we must implement a procedure called *String Interpolation*. The variables must be included inside the string between parentheses and prefixed with a backslash.

```
let age = 44
let mytext = "I am \(age) years old"   // "I am 44 years old"
```

Listing 2-21: Including variables in strings

In the code of Listing 2-21, the **age** variable is read, and its current value is added to the string. The string "I am 44 years old" is then assigned to **mytext**. Using this tool, we can insert any variable we want inside a string, including **Character** and **String** variables, as well as the result of arithmetic operations. In the following example, the value of **age** is multiplied by 12 and the result is included in the string.

```
let age = 44
let mytext = "I am \(age * 12) months old"   // "I am 528 months old"
```

Listing 2-22: Performing operations inside strings

Sometimes we need to include special characters in the string, like backslashes or quotes. Swift offers two ways to achieve this purpose. We can prefix the special character with another backslash, or we can enclose the entire string in hash characters, as shown next.

```
let text1 = "This is \"my\" age"   // "This is "my" age"
let text2 = #"This is "my" age"#   // "This is "my" age"
```

Listing 2-23: Including special characters in a string

Another important feature of strings is the possibility to create multiple lines of text. Again, Swift offers two alternatives. We can include the special characters **\n** where we want to generate a new line or we can use triple quotes (**"""**) and the compiler will consider the original format of the text and automatically insert the **\n** characters when required, as shown next.

```
let twolines = "This is the first line\nThis is the second line"
let multiline = """
This is the first line
This is the second line
This is the third line
"""
```

Listing 2-24: Generating multiple lines of text

The `twolines` constant defined in the code of Listing 2-24 includes the **\n** characters in between the text, which tells the compiler to generate two lines of text instead of one. If we press the Show Result button on the Results Side Bar, Xcode introduces a box below the code showing the two lines of text, one on top of the other.

Something similar happens with the value of the `multiline` constant, although in this case the **"""** characters we used to define the text ask the compiler to add the **\n** characters at the end of each line to format the text as it was defined in the code.

(Basic) **Booleans**

Boolean variables are a type of variables that can only store two values: `true` or `false`. These variables are particularly useful when we want to execute an instruction or a set of instructions only if a condition is met. To declare a Boolean variable, we can specify the type as `Bool` or let Swift infer the type from its value, as in the following example.

```
var valid = true
```

Listing 2-25: Declaring a Boolean variable

The purpose of these variables is to simplify the process of identifying a condition. If we use an integer variable to indicate the state of a condition, we must remember which numbers we decided to use for the valid and the invalid states. Using a Boolean variable instead, we just have to check whether the value is equal to `true` or `false`.

 IMPORTANT: Booleans become useful when we use them along with instructions that allow us to perform a task or repetitive tasks according to a condition. We will study Conditionals and Loops later in this chapter.

(Basic) **Optionals**

As mentioned at the beginning of this chapter, after a variable is declared, we must provide its initial value. We cannot use a variable if it was not initialized. This means that a variable has a valid value all the time. But this is not always appropriate. Sometimes we do not have an initial value to assign to the variable during development or we need to indicate the absence of a value because the current one becomes invalid. For these situations, Swift defines a modifier that turns every data type into an optional type. This means that the variable marked as optional may have a value or be empty. To declare an optional, we add a question mark after the type's name.

Chapter 2 - Introduction to Swift

```
var mynumber: Int?
```

Listing 2-26: Declaring an optional variable of type Int

New values are assigned to optionals as we do with normal variables.

```
var mynumber: Int?
mynumber = 5
```

Listing 2-27: Assigning new values to optional variables

The empty state is represented by the keyword **nil**. Therefore, when an optional variable is declared but not initialized, as in previous examples, Swift assigns the **nil** keyword to the variable to indicate the absence of a value. If later we need to empty the variable, we can assign the keyword **nil** to it.

```
var mynumber: Int?
mynumber = 5
mynumber = nil
```

Listing 2-28: Using nil *to empty a variable*

The code of Listing 2-28 declares an optional integer, assigns the value 5 to it, and then declares the variable as empty with the keyword **nil**. Although optionals seem to work like regular variables, they do not expose their values. To read the value of an optional, we must unwrap it by adding an exclamation mark at the end of the name.

```
var mynumber: Int?
mynumber = 5
var total = mynumber! * 10   // 50
```

Listing 2-29: Unwrapping an optional variable

The last statement of Listing 2-29 unwraps **mynumber** to get its value, multiplies this value by 10, and assigns the result to the **total** variable. This is only necessary when we need to use the value. If we just want to assign an optional to another optional, the process is as always.

```
var mynumber: Int?
mynumber = 5
var total = mynumber
```

Listing 2-30: Assigning an optional to another optional

In this example, the system infers the type of the **total** variable to be an optional of type **Int** and assigns the value of **mynumber** to it. If we want to read the value of **total** later, we must unwrap it as we did with **mynumber** before.

 IMPORTANT: Before unwrapping an optional, we need to make sure it contains a value (it is not **nil**). If we try to unwrap an empty optional, the app will return an error and crash. Later in this chapter we will learn how to use conditional statements to check this condition.

There are times when we know that an optional will always have a value, but we do not know what the initial value is. For example, we could have a variable that receives a value from the system as soon as the application is executed. When the variable is declared in our code, we do not have a value to assign to it, but we know that the variable will have a value as soon as the user launches the app. For these situations, Swift provides the possibility to declare *implicitly unwrapped optionals*. These are optional variables declared with the exclamation mark instead of the question mark. The system reads these variables as optionals until we unwrap them with an exclamation mark or use the variable in a statement, as in the following example.

```
var mynumber: Int!
mynumber = 5
var total = mynumber * 10   // 50
```

Listing 2-31: Declaring implicitly unwrapped optionals

In Listing 2-31, the `mynumber` variable was declared as an implicitly unwrapped optional and it was later initialized with the value 5. Notice that it was not necessary to write the exclamation mark when reading its value anymore. The system unwraps the `mynumber` variable automatically to use its value in the multiplication (this is only available for implicitly unwrapped optionals).

(Basic) **Tuples**

A tuple is a type of variable that contains a group of one or more values of equal or different type. It is useful when we need to store values that are somehow related to each other. Tuples are declared with their values and types separated by a comma and between parentheses.

```
var myname: (String, String) = ("John", "Doe")
```

Listing 2-32: Declaring a tuple with two values

In this example, the `myname` variable is declared to be a tuple that contains two `String` values. The values of this tuple are of the same type, but we can use any combination of values we want and let Swift infer their types, as shown next.

```
var myname = ("John", "Doe", 44)
```

Listing 2-33: Declaring a tuple with values of different type

To be able to read the values later, an index is automatically assigned to each of the values of the tuple. Indexes start at the value 0, so the first value will be at index 0, the second at index 1, and so on. Using the corresponding index and dot notation we can access the value we want.

```
var myname = ("John", "Doe", 44)
var mytext = "\(myname.0) is \(myname.2) years old"  // "John is 44 years
old"
```

Listing 2-34: Reading a tuple

In Listing 2-34 we read the values of the `myname` tuple at index 0 and 2 to include them in a new string and assign the string to `mytext`. The same syntax may be used to modify a value.

```
var myname = ("John", "Doe", 44)
myname.0 = "George"
var mytext = "\(myname.0) is \(myname.2) years old"
```

Listing 2-35: Changing the value of a tuple

Chapter 2 - Introduction to Swift

The second statement of Listing 2-35 assigns a new string to the first value of the tuple. The new value has to be of the same type as the old one. If we had tried to assign an integer instead, we would have received an error. At the end, the value of `mytext` is "George is 44 years old".

Indexes are a quick way to access the values of a tuple, but they do not help us remember what the values represent. To facilitate the identification of the values in a tuple, we can assign a name to each one of them. The name must be declared before the value and separated with a colon, as shown next.

```
var myname = (name: "John", surname: "Doe", age: 44)
var mytext = "\(myname.name) is \(myname.age) years old"
```

Listing 2-36: Declaring names for the values of a tuple

Swift also provides a way to copy the values of the tuple into independent variables.

```
var myname = ("John", "Doe", 44)
var (name, surname, age) = myname
var mytext = "\(name) \(surname) is \(age) years old"
```

Listing 2-37: Creating multiple variables from the values of a tuple

The names of the variables are declared between parentheses and the tuple is assigned to this construction. The values are assigned to the variables in the same order they have in the tuple. These variables may be used later as we would do with any other variable. If only some of the values are required, the rest may be ignored writing an underscore in their place.

```
var myname = ("John", "Doe", 44)
var (name, _, age) = myname
var mytext = "\(name) is \(age) years old"
```

Listing 2-38: Ignoring some of the values of a tuple

Only the variables `name` and `age` are used in this last example (notice the underscore in the place of the second variable). The string assigned to `mytext` is "John is 44 years old".

 IMPORTANT: Tuples are particularly useful when working with functions, as we will see later. The use of tuples is only recommended when we need to share information between different pieces of code, but not to store persistent data. To store complex data structures, you should use collections (such as arrays or dictionaries). We will study functions and collections in Chapter 3.

(Basic) 2.4 Conditionals and Loops

Up to this point, we have been writing instructions in a sequence, one after another. In this programming pattern, the system executes each statement once and in the same order they were presented. It starts with the one at the top and goes on until it reaches the end of the list. The purpose of Conditionals and Loops is to break this sequential flow. Conditionals allow us to execute one or more instructions only when a condition is met, and Loops let us execute a group of instructions repeatedly.

(Basic) If and Else

A simple but handful conditional statement available in Swift is `if`. With `if` we can check a condition and execute a group of instructions only when the condition is true. The instructions that are going to be executed must be declared between braces after the condition.

```
var age = 19
var message = "John is old"
if age < 21 {
    message = "John is young"
}
```

Listing 2-39: Comparing two values with `if`

Two variables are declared in the code of Listing 2-39. The **age** variable contains the value we want to check, and the **message** variable is the one we are going to modify depending on the state of the condition. The **if** statement compares the value of **age** with the number 21 using the character < (less than). This comparison returns the state of the condition (true or false). If the condition is true (the value of **age** is less than 21), the instruction between braces is executed, assigning a new value to the **message** variable, otherwise the instruction is ignored, and the execution continues with the instructions after the braces. In this case, the value of **age** is less than 21 and therefore the string "John is young" is assigned to the **message** variable.

 The Basics: The instruction between braces in the example of Listing 2-39 is displaced to the right. The whitespace on the left is used to help us differentiate the statements between braces from the rest of the statements. This whitespace is automatically generated for you by Xcode, but you can add it yourself when necessary by pressing the Tab key on your keyboard.

The < symbol we used in the last example to compare values is part of a group of operators called *comparison operators*. The following is the list of comparison operators available in Swift.

- **==** checks whether the value on the left is equal to the value on the right.
- **!=** checks whether the value on the left is different than the value on the right.
- **>** checks whether the value on the left is greater than the value on the right.
- **<** checks whether the value on the left is less than the value on the right.
- **>=** checks whether the value on the left is greater or equal than the value on the right.
- **<=** checks whether the value on the left is less or equal than the value on the right.

All these operators are applied the same way we did in the previous example. For instance, the following code changes the value of **message** when the value of **age** is less or equal than 21.

```
var age = 21
var message = "John is old"
if age <= 21 {
    message = "John is young"
}
```

Listing 2-40: Comparing two values with the `<=` *operator*

 The Basics: Braces are applied in many constructions in Swift. They allow us to create independent processing units with their own instructions and variables. These constructions are usually called *blocks*. We will learn more about blocks in this and following chapters.

When only two results are required, we may define the condition using a Boolean. These values do not need to be compared with the expected value; they already return a state (true or false).

Chapter 2 - Introduction to Swift

```
var underage = true
var message = "John is allowed"
if underage {
    message = "John is underage"
}
```

Listing 2-41: Conditions with Boolean values

The code of Listing 2-41 checks whether the value of the **underage** variable is **true** or **false**. If it is **true** (which means the condition is true, as in this case), a new string of characters is assigned to the **message** variable.

If, on the other hand, we want to execute the statements when the value is **false**, Swift offers a logical operator to toggle the condition's state. All we have to do is to write an exclamation mark before the condition.

```
var underage = true
var message = "John is underage"
if !underage {
    message = "John is allowed"
}
```

Listing 2-42: Using logical operators

The original value of the **underage** variable in the code of Listing 2-42 is **true**, so when the **if** statement toggles the condition, the resulting condition is false and therefore the value of the **message** variable is not modified.

The exclamation mark is part of a group of logical operators provided by Swift.

- **!** (logical NOT) toggles the state of the condition. If the condition is true, it returns false, and vice versa.
- **&&** (logical AND) checks two conditions and returns true if both are true.
- **||** (logical OR) checks two conditions and returns true if one or both are true.

Logical operators work with any kind of conditions, not only Booleans. To work with complex conditions, it is recommended to enclose the condition between parentheses.

```
var smart = true
var age = 19
var message = "John is underage or dumb"
if (age < 21) && smart {
    message = "John is allowed"
}
```

Listing 2-43: Using logical operators to check several conditions

The **if** statement of Listing 2-43 compares the value of the **age** variable with 21 and checks the value of the **smart** variable. If **age** is less than 21 and **smart** is **true**, then the overall condition is true and a new string is assigned to **message**. If any of the individual conditions is false, then the overall condition is false and the block of instructions is not executed. In this case, both conditions are true and therefore the "John is allowed" string is assigned to **message**.

 The Basics: Using **&&** (AND) and **||** (OR) you can create a logical sequence. The system evaluates one condition at a time from left to right and compares the results. For example, a set of conditions that evaluate as **true && false || true**, return the value **true**. The first expression is evaluated as **false** (**true && false = false**), but the last value is evaluated against the first result, so the result is **true** (**false || true = true**). If you want to make sure that the expressions are evaluated in the correct order, you can declare them within parentheses, as in (**true && false**) || **true**. The expression within the parentheses is evaluated first, and the result is then evaluated against the rest of the expression.

Although we can use comparison operators and logical operators in most of the data types available, optionals are slightly different. Their values are wrapped, so we cannot compare them with other values or check their state as we do with Booleans. Optionals have to be compared against the keyword `nil` first and then unwrapped before working with their values.

```
var count = 0
var myoptional: Int? = 5
if myoptional != nil {
    let uvalue = myoptional!
    count = count + uvalue   // 5
}
```

Listing 2-44: Checking whether an optional contains a value or not

Listing 2-44 shows the process we must follow to read the value of an optional variable. The optional is checked first against `nil`. If it is different than `nil` (which means it contains a value), we unwrap the optional inside the block of statements using an exclamation mark, assign its value to a constant, and use the constant to perform any operation necessary (in this example, the value of the `count` variable is incremented by the value of the optional).

We always need to make sure that an optional has a value before unwrapping it. Because of this, Swift introduces a convenient syntax that checks the optional and unwraps its value at the same time. It is called *Optional Binding*.

```
var count = 0
var myoptional: Int? = 5
if let uvalue = myoptional {
    count = count + uvalue   // 5
}
```

Listing 2-45: Using optional binding to unwrap an optional variable

This new code is cleaner and easy to read. The optional is unwrapped as part of the condition checked by the `if` statement. If it is different than `nil`, its value is assigned to the `uvalue` constant and the statements in the block are executed, otherwise, the statements inside the block are ignored.

If we want to unwrap several optionals at the same time using Optional Binding, we must declare the expressions separated by a comma. This also applies when we want to check other conditions in the same statement. For instance, the following example unwraps an optional and only executes the code between angle brackets if its value is equal to 5.

```
var count = 0
var myoptional: Int? = 5
if let uvalue = myoptional, uvalue == 5 {
    count = count + uvalue   // 5
}
```

Listing 2-46: Checking multiple conditions with Optional Binding

Chapter 2 - Introduction to Swift

The **if** statement in Listing 2-46 unwraps the optional first and, if there is a value, compares it with the number 5. The statements in the block are executed only if both conditions are true.

There are times in which instructions have to be executed for either state of the condition (true or false). Swift includes the **if else** construction to help in this situation. The instructions are presented in two blocks. The first block will be executed when the condition is true, and the second block will be executed otherwise.

```
var mynumber = 6
if mynumber % 2 == 0 {
    mynumber = mynumber + 2   // 8
} else {
    mynumber = mynumber + 1
}
```

Listing 2-47: Using `if else` *to respond to both states of the condition*

The code of Listing 2-47 is a simple example that checks whether a value is odd or even using the remainder operator. The condition gets the remainder of the division between the value of the **mynumber** variable and 2 and compares the result against 0. If true, it means that the value of **mynumber** is even, so the first block is executed. If the value is different than 0, it means that it is odd and the condition is false, so the block corresponding to the **else** instruction is executed instead.

The statements **if** and **else** may be concatenated to check for as many conditions as we need. In the following example, we check the age of a customer. The first condition checks whether its age is less than 21. If this is not true, the second condition checks whether the age is over 21. And if this is not true, the final **else** block is executed.

```
var age = 19
var message = "The customer is "
if age < 21 {
    message += "underage"   // "The customer is underage"
} else if age > 21 {
    message += "allowed"
} else {
    message += "21 years old"
}
```

Listing 2-48: Concatenating `if else` *instructions*

If all we need from an **if** statement is to assign a value to a variable depending on a condition, we can use a shortcut provided by Swift called *ternary operator*. The ternary operator is a construction composed by the condition and the two values we want to return for each state, separated by the characters **?** and **:**, as in the following example.

```
var age = 19
var message = age < 21 ? "Underage" : "Allowed"   // "Underage"
```

Listing 2-49: Implementing the ternary operator

The first value is returned if the condition is true and the second value is returned if the condition is false. The advantage of using the ternary operator is that it reduces the code significantly, but the result is the same than using an **if else** statement.

Ternary operators can also be implemented to unwrap optionals. For instance, we can check whether an optional variable contains a value and assign it to another variable or give the variable a default value if the optional is empty.

```
var age: Int? = 19
var realage = age != nil ? age! : 0   // 19
```

Listing 2-50: Unwrapping an optional with a ternary operator

The code of Listing 2-50 defines an optional variable called **age** with the value 19. Next, we use a ternary operator to unwrap the variable and assign its value to a new variable called **realage**. If the optional contains a value, its value is assigned to the variable, otherwise, the value 0 is assigned instead.

Assigning values by default when the optional is empty is very common. To simplify our work, Swift offers the nil-coalescing operator, which is represented by the characters **??**. This operator works like the ternary operator implemented before; it unwraps the optional and returns its value or returns a default value if the optional is empty. In the following example, we create an empty optional called **age** and use the nil-coalescing operator to assign its value to the **maxage** variable or the value 100 if the optional is empty.

```
var age: Int?
var maxage = age ?? 100   // 100
```

Listing 2-51: Unwrapping an optional with the nil-coalescing operator

(Basic) Switch

We can repeat the **if** and **else** statements to check as many conditions as we need, but this pattern can make the code impossible to read and maintain. When several conditions must be verified, it is better to use the **switch** instruction. This instruction compares a value with a list of values and executes the statements corresponding to the value that matches. The possible values are listed between braces using the **case** keyword, as in the following example.

```
var age = 19
var message = ""
switch age {
   case 13:
      message = "Happy Bar Mitzvah!"
   case 16:
      message = "Sweet Sixteen!"
   case 21:
      message = "Welcome to Adulthood!"
   default:
      message = "Happy Birthday!"   // "Happy Birthday!"
}
```

Listing 2-52: Checking conditions with switch

The cases must be exhaustive; every possible value of the variable being checked has to be contemplated. If we do not include a **case** statement for every possible value, we must add a **default** statement at the end that is executed when no match is found.

In Listing 2-52, we compare the value of the **age** variable with a small set of values corresponding to special dates. If no **case** matches the value of the variable, as in this case, the **default** statement is executed and the string "Happy Birthday!" is assigned to **message**.

When we need to execute the same set of instructions for more than one value, we can declare the values separated by comma.

```
var age = 6
var message = "You go to "
switch age {
   case 2, 3, 4:
      message += "Day Care"
   case 5, 6, 7, 8, 9, 10, 11:
      message += "Elementary School"   // "You go to Elementary School"
   case 12, 13, 14, 15, 16, 17:
      message += "High School"
   case 18, 19, 20, 21:
      message += "College"
   default:
      message += "Work"
}
```

Listing 2-53: *Checking multiple conditions per case*

The `switch` statement can also work with more complex data types, such as strings and tuples. In the case of tuples, `switch` provides additional options to build complex matching patterns. For example, the following code checks the second value of a tuple to determine the difference in age.

```
var message = ""
var ages = (10, 30)

switch ages {
   case (10, 20):
      message = "Too close"
   case (10, 30):
      message = "The right age"   // "The right age"
   case (10, 40):
      message = "Too far"
   default:
      message = "Way too far"
}
```

Listing 2-54: *Matching a tuple in a* `switch` *statement*

This example always compares the first value of the tuple against 10 but checks different matches for the second value. If a value does not matter, we can use an underscore on its place to ignore it.

```
var message = ""
var ages = (10, 30)

switch ages {
   case (_, 20):
      message = "Too close"
   case (_, 30):
      message = "The right age"   // "The right age"
   case (_, 40):
      message = "Too far"
   default:
      message = "Way too far"
}
```

Listing 2-55: *Matching only the second value of a tuple*

An alternative offered by the `switch` statement to create complex matching patterns is to capture a value in a constant to be able to access it from the instructions of the `case`.

```
var message = ""
var ages = (10, 20)
switch ages {
   case (let x, 20):
      message = "Too close to \(x)"   // "Too close to 10"
   case (_, 30):
      message = "The right age"
   case (let x, 40):
      message = "Too far to \(x)"
   default:
      message = "Way too far"
}
```

Listing 2-56: Capturing values with constants

In the example of Listing 2-56, when the `switch` statement checks the first and third cases, it creates a constant called `x` and assigns the tuple's first value to it. Because of this, we can access the value from the statements inside the `case` and use it to customize the result (in this example we just add the value to a string).

There is an even more complex matching pattern that involves the use of a clause called `where`. This clause allows us to check additional conditions. In the following example, we capture the values of the tuple with another tuple and compare them against each other.

```
var message = ""
var ages = (10, 20)
switch ages {
   case let (x, y) where x > y:
      message = "Too young"
   case let (x, y) where x == y:
      message = "The same age"
   case let (x, y) where x < y:
      message = "Too old"   // "Too old"
   default:
      message = "Not found"
}
```

Listing 2-57: Comparing values with `where`

Every time the `switch` statement tries to match a `case` in the example of Listing 2-57, it creates a tuple and assigns the values of `ages` to it. The `where` clause compares the values and when the condition returns true it executes the statements in the `case`.

(Basic) While and Repeat While

The conditionals studied so far execute the statements corresponding to each of the states of the condition only once. Sometimes the program requires executing a block of instructions several times until a condition is satisfied. The simplest alternative offered by Swift to create this kind of loop is the `while` statement (and its sibling `repeat while`).

The `while` statement checks a condition and executes the statements in its block while the condition is true. The following example initializes a variable with the value 0 and then checks its value in a `while` statement. If the value of the variable is less than 5, the statements inside the block are executed. After this, the condition is checked again. The loop keeps running until the condition becomes false (the value of the `counter` variable is equal or greater than 5).

```
var counter = 0
while counter < 5 {
    counter += 1
}
```

Listing 2-58: Using while *to create a loop*

If the condition returns false when it is checked for the first time, the statements in the block are never executed. If we want to execute the statements at least once, we must use the **repeat while** instruction.

```
var counter = 10
repeat {
    counter += 1
} while counter < 5
```

Listing 2-59: Using repeat while *to create a loop*

In this case, the initial value of the **counter** variable is declared as 10. This is greater than 5, but since we are using **repeat while**, the statements in the block are executed before the condition is checked, so the final value of **counter** will be 11 (its value is incremented once and then the condition returns false, ending the loop).

(Basic) **For In**

The purpose of the **for in** loop is to iterate over collections of elements, like the strings of characters studied before. During the execution of a **for in** loop, the system reads the elements of the collection one by one in sequential order and assigns their values to a constant that can be processed by the statements inside the block. The condition that has to be satisfied for this loop to be over is reaching the end of the collection.

The syntax of a **for in** loop is **for constant in collection {}**, where **constant** is the name of the constant that we are going to use to capture the value of each element, and **collection** is the name of the collection that we want to iterate over.

```
var mytext = "Hello"
var message = ""

for letter in mytext {
    message += message != "" ? "-" : ""
    message += "\(letter)"
}
```

Listing 2-60: Using for in *to iterate over a string*

The code of Listing 2-60 defines two **String** variables: **mytext** with the text "Hello" and **message** with an empty string. Next, we use a **for in** loop to iterate over the characters of the string in **mytext** and add each character to the current value of **message**. In each cycle of the loop, the instruction takes one character from the value of **mytext**, assigns it to the **letter** constant, and executes the statements in the block. The first statement uses a ternary operator to check whether the value of **message** is an empty string. If not, it adds the - character at the end of it, otherwise, it adds an empty string. Finally, the second statement adds the current value of **letter** at the end of the **message** string.

In this example, the code works as follows: in the loop's first cycle, the character "H" is assigned to the `letter` constant. Because at this moment the `message` string is empty, nothing is added by the first statement. Then, the second statement adds the value of `letter` to the current value of `message` and the next cycle is executed. In this new cycle, the character "e" is assigned to the `letter` constant. This time, the `message` string already contains the letter "H", so the character "-" is added at the end by the first statement ("H-"), and then the second statement adds the letter "e" at the end of this new string ("H-e"). This process continues until all the characters in the `mytext` variable are processed. The final value of `message` is "H-e-l-l-o".

As mentioned before, strings are a collection of `Character` values and therefore the value assigned to the `letter` constant in each cycle is of type `Character`. Values of type `Character` can't be added to values of type `String` directly, we have to convert them into strings first, and this is the reason why we used string interpolation to add the letter to the string in the second statement of the `for in` block (see Listing 2-21).

When the constant is not required inside the block, we can replace it with an underscore.

```
var mytext = "Hello"
var counter = 0
for _ in mytext {
    counter += 1
}
var message = "The string contains \(counter) letters"   // 5
```

Listing 2-61: Iterating over a string without reading the characters

In the example of Listing 2-61 we iterate over the value of `mytext` to count the number of characters in the string. The value of the `counter` variable is incremented by 1 each cycle of the `for in` loop giving a total of 5.

(Basic) ## Control Transfer Statements

Loops sometimes must be interrupted, independently of the state of the condition. Swift offers multiple instructions to break the execution of loops and conditionals, the following are the most frequently used.

continue—This instruction interrupts the current cycle and moves to the next. The system ignores the rest of the statements in the block after the instruction is executed.

break—This instruction interrupts the loop. The rest of the statements in the block and any pending cycles are ignored after the instruction is executed.

The `continue` instruction is applied when we do not want to execute the rest of the statements in the loop, but we want to keep the loop running. For instance, the following code counts the letters in a string but ignores the letters "l".

```
var mytext = "Hello"
var counter = 0
for letter in mytext {
    if letter == "l" {
        continue
    }
    counter += 1
}
var message = "The string contains \(counter) letters"   // 3
```

Listing 2-62: Jumping to the next cycle of the loop

Chapter 2 - Introduction to Swift

The `if` statement inside the **for in** loop of Listing 2-62 compares the value of `letter` with the letter "l". If the characters match, the `continue` instruction is executed, the last statement inside the loop is ignored, and the loop moves on to the next character of `mytext`. In consequence, the code counts all the characters that are different than "l" (H, e, and o).

Unlike the `continue` instruction, the `break` instruction interrupts the loop completely, moving the execution of the program to the statements after the loop. The following example only counts the characters in the string that are placed before the first letter "l".

```
var mytext = "Hello"
var counter = 0

for letter in mytext {
    if letter == "l" {
        break
    }
    counter += 1
}
var message = "The string contains \(counter) letters"   // 2
```

Listing 2-63: Interrupting the loop

Again, the `if` statement of Listing 2-63 compares the value of `letter` with the character "l", but this time it executes the `break` instruction when a match is found. If the character currently processed by the loop is "l", the `break` instruction is executed, and the loop is over, no matter how many characters are left in the string. In consequence, only the characters located before the first letter "l" are considered (H and e).

The `break` instruction is also useful to cancel the execution of a `switch` statement. The problem with the `switch` statement in Swift is that the cases have to be exhaustive, which means that every possible value has to be contemplated. When this is not possible or necessary, we can use the `break` instruction to ignore the values that are not applicable. For example, we can declare the cases for the values we need and then break the execution in the `default` case for the rest of the values that we do not care about.

```
var age = 19
var message = ""

switch age {
    case 13:
        message = "Happy Bar Mitzvah!"
    case 16:
        message = "Sweet Sixteen!"
    case 21:
        message = "Welcome to Adulthood!"
    default:
        break
}
```

Listing 2-64: Ignoring values in a switch *statement*

After the execution of the code of Listing 2-64, the **message** variable is empty because there is no **case** that matches the value of the **age** variable and therefore the code in **default** is executed and the **break** instruction returns the control to the statements after the **switch**.

Executing the **break** instruction in the **default** case of a **switch** statement is very common because it allows us to only consider the values we need and ignore the rest.

The **guard** instruction is intended to prevent the execution of the code that follows the statement. For example, we can break the execution of a loop when a condition is satisfied, as we do with an **if else** statement.

```
var mytext = "Hello"
var counter = 0

for letter in mytext {
   guard letter != "l" else {
      break
   }
   counter += 1
}
var message = "The string contains \(counter) letters"   // 2
```

Listing 2-65: Interrupting a loop with guard

The **guard** instruction works along with the **else** instruction and therefore it is very similar to the **if else** statement, but the code is only executed when the condition is false. In the example of Listing 2-65, the **for in** loop reads the characters of the string in **mytext** one by one, as we did before. If the characters are different than the letter "l", we increase the value of **counter** by 1, but when the value of **letter** is equal to "l", the condition of the **guard** instruction is false and therefore the **break** instruction is executed, interrupting the loop.

 The Basics: The advantage of **guard** over the **if else** statements is that the variable or constant defined in the condition outlives the statement, and therefore we can read its value outside the block. Although you can implement the **guard** instruction to break or continue a loop, the instruction was introduced to work along with the **return** instruction to interrupt the execution of a function. We will study the **return** instruction and functions in the next chapter.

Chapter 2 - Introduction to Swift

Chapter 3
Swift Paradigm

Basic **3.1 Programming Paradigms**

Programs wouldn't be very useful if we were only able to write them as a consecutive set of instructions. At first, this was the only way to write a program, but soon programming languages incorporated tools to allow programmers to group instructions together and execute them every time necessary. The way instructions are organized is called *paradigm*. Different paradigms are now available, with the most common being the Object-Oriented Programming paradigm, or OOP. This paradigm emerges from the construction and integration of processing units called *objects*. Swift adopts OOP, but it is not focused as much on objects as other languages do. Instead, it implements other types of processing units called *structures* and *enumerations* along with blueprints called *protocols* to conform a new paradigm called *Protocol-Oriented Programing*. The Swift paradigm unifies objects, structures, and enumerations through protocols that define how these units behave and the type of functionality they have.

 Do It Yourself: As with the examples in the previous chapter, the examples in this chapter were designed to be tested in Playground. You just have to create a Playground file with a Blank template and then replace the code with the example you want to try.

Basic **3.2 Functions**

The processing units that define the Swift paradigm (objects, structures, and enumerations) are capable of encapsulating data along with functionality. The data is stored in the same variables we studied before, but the functionality is provided by functions. Functions are blocks of code delimited by curly braces and identified by a name. The difference between functions and the block of codes used in loops and conditional statements is that there is no condition to satisfy; the statements inside a function are executed every time the function is called (executed). Functions are called by writing their names followed by parentheses. This call may be performed from anywhere in the code and every time necessary, which completely breaks the sequential processing of a program. Once a function is called, the execution of the program continues with the statements inside the function (no matter where it is located in the code), and only returns back to the code that called the function once the execution of the function is over.

Basic **Declaration of Functions**

Functions are declared using the `func` keyword, a name, parentheses, and the code between braces.

```
var mynumber = 5
func myfunction() {
   mynumber = mynumber * 2   // 10
}
myfunction()
```

Listing 3-1: Declaring and calling functions

The code in Listing 3-1 declares the `mynumber` variable, initializes it with the value 5, and then declares a function called `myfunction()`. The statements in a function are only processed when the function is called, so after its declaration we call our function with the instruction `myfunction()`. Every time the `myfunction()` function is called, it multiplies the current value of `mynumber` times 2 and assigns the result back to the variable. Once all the statements inside the function are processed, the execution continues from the statement after the call.

As we already mentioned, once the function is declared, we can call it any time necessary and from anywhere in the program. For example, the following code runs a `while` loop that calls `myfunction()` a total of 5 times (the loop runs while `counter` is less than 5). Every time the function is executed, `mynumber`'s current value is multiplied by 2, getting a result of 160.

```
var mynumber = 5
var counter = 0
func myfunction() {
    mynumber = mynumber * 2   // 160
}
while counter < 5 {
    myfunction()
    counter += 1
}
```

Listing 3-2: Calling functions from a loop

The functions in these examples are modifying the value of an external variable (a variable that was not declared inside the function). Creating a function that works with values and variables that do not belong to the function itself could be dangerous; some variables may be modified by accident from other functions, the function may be called before the variables were even declared or initialized, or the variables that the function tries to modify may not be accessible by the function (functions have limited scope, as we will see later). To make sure that a function processes the right values, they have to be sent to the function when it is called. The type of values the function can receive and the names they are going to take are specified within the function's parentheses separated by a comma. When the function is executed, these parameters are turned into constants that we can read inside the function to access their values.

```
func double(number: Int) {
    let total = number * 2
    let message = "Result: \(total)"   // "Result: 10"
}
double(number: 5)
```

Listing 3-3: Sending values to a function

In the example of Listing 3-3, we don't use external variables anymore. The value to be processed is sent to the function when it is called and received by the function through its parameter. The parameters are declared within the function's parentheses with the same syntax used for constants or variables. We must write the name and the data type separated by a colon. In this example, the function is declared with one parameter of type `Int` called `number`.

The call must include the name of the parameter and the value we want to send to the function. When the function of Listing 3-3 is called, the value between the parentheses of the call (5) is assigned to the `number` constant, the value of the constant is multiplied by 2, and finally the result is included in a string with string interpolation.

Of course, we can include as many parameters as we need. The following example multiplies two values and creates a string with the result.

```
func multiply(number1: Int, number2: Int) {
    let result = number1 * number2
```

Chapter 3 - Swift Paradigm

```
    let message = "The result is \(result)"  // "The result is 80"
}
multiply(number1: 20, number2: 4)
```

Listing 3-4: Sending different values to a function

Functions may not only be called every time we need them, but also the values we provide to the function in the call may be different each time. This makes functions reusable.

```
func double(number: Int) {
    let total = number * 2
    let message = "Result: \(total)"
}
double(number: 5)   // "Result: 10"
double(number: 25)  // "Result: 50"
```

Listing 3-5: Sending different values to a function

The constants and variables declared inside a function, like **total** and **message**, are not accessible from other parts of the code (they have different scopes, as we will see in the next section of this chapter). This means that a function can receive values, but the result produced by the processing of those values is trapped inside the function. To communicate this result to the rest of the code, functions can return a value using a special instruction called **return**. The **return** instruction finishes the processing of the function, so we must declare it after all the statements required have been processed, as in the following example.

```
func double(number: Int) -> Int {
    let total = number * 2
    return total
}
let result = double(number: 25)
let message = "The result is \(result)"  // "The result is 50"
```

Listing 3-6: Returning a value from a function

When we create a function that returns a value, the type of the value returned has to be specified in the declaration after the parentheses with the syntax **-> Type**, where **Type** is just the data type of the value that is going to be returned by the function. A function can only return values of the type indicated in its definition. For instance, the function in Listing 3-6 can only return integer values because we declared the returned type as **Int** (**-> Int**).

When a function returns a value, the system calls the function first and then the value returned is processed inside the statement that made the call. For instance, in the code of Listing 3-6, we create the **result** variable and assign to this variable a call to the **double()** function. When the system processes this statement, the function is executed first and then the value returned (50) is assigned to the variable.

The values received and returned by a function may be of any available type. The following example takes a string and returns a tuple containing the characters of the string separated by a space and an integer with the total number of characters.

```
func sumCharacters(word: String) -> (String, Int) {
    var characters = ""
    var counter = 0
    for letter in word {
        characters += "\(letter) "
        counter += 1
```

```
    }
    return (characters, counter)
}
var (list, total) = sumCharacters(word: "Hello")
var message = "There are \(total) characters (\(list))"
```

Listing 3-7: *Returning a tuple*

The **sumCharacters()** function of Listing 3-7 receives a string (**word: String**) and returns a tuple composed of a string and an integer (**-> (String, Int)**). The function adds the characters to the **characters** variable and counts them with the **counter** variable, as we did before. At the end, the tuple is returned, its values are assigned to the **list** and **total** variables, and then incorporated into a string ("There are 5 characters (H e l l o)").

 The Basics: Notice that the string returned by the function contains a space at the end. The code in the **for in** loop adds a space at the end of each character, which means that the last character will also have a space on the right and therefore the string will end with a space and not the letter o. To remove this space, you can check the content of the **characters** variable before adding the space, as in the example of Chapter 2, Listing 2-60, or use the methods designed for this purpose, as we will see later in this chapter.

Besides returning the result of an operation, the **return** instruction can also be used to interrupt the execution of a function. The **guard** instruction introduced in Chapter 2 is perfect for cases like this, as illustrated by the following example.

```
func double(number: Int) -> Int {
    guard number < 10 else {
        return number
    }
    return number * 2
}
let result = double(number: 25)
let message = "The result is \(result)"   // "The result is 25"
```

Listing 3-8: *Interrupting the execution of a function with* guard

The **double()** function of Listing 3-8 is similar to previous examples. It receives a number, multiplies it by 2, and returns the result, but this time we first check that the value received by the function is less than 10. If the value is equal or higher than 10, the **guard** instruction calls the **return** instruction with the received value, otherwise, the statements of the function are executed as normal. In this case, the value sent to the function is 25, therefore the condition is false, and the same value is returned.

Notice that in the example of Listing 3-8 we simplified our code including the multiplication in the **return** instruction. The **return** instruction can take single values or expressions like this. The instruction takes care of solving the expression (or operation, as in this case) and returning the result. For this reason, sometimes we may find functions with only one statement in charge of returning a value. If this is the case, we can remove the **return** keyword. In the following example, the call sends the number 25 to the function, the value is multiplied by 2, and returned, as in previous examples, but this time we didn't have to declare the **return** keyword because there is only one statement inside the function and therefore the compiler knows what to return.

```
func double(number: Int) -> Int {
    number * 2
}
let result = double(number: 25)
```

```
let message = "The result is \(result)"   // "The result is 50"
```

Listing 3-9: Removing the `return` *keyword*

Besides the **return** keyword, Swift offers the **inout** keyword to preserve a value after the function finish processing. When a function's parameter is marked with the **inout** keyword, any changes performed on the value will be stored in the original variable. This is useful when we call a function from another function (or block of code) and we want modifications introduced by the second function to persist.

```
func first() {
   var number = 25
   second(value: &number)
   print("The result is \(number)")   // "The result is 50"
}
func second(value: inout Int) {
   value = value * 2
}
first()
```

Listing 3-10: Modifying external variables from a function

The code of Listing 3-10 defines two functions, **first()** and **second()**. The **second()** function receives an **inout** parameter called **value**, which means that any modification on its value will be stored in the original variable. The **first()** function defines a variable called **number** and then executes the **second()** function with it, so when the **second()** function multiplies this value times 2, the result (50) is stored in **number**. At the end of the code, we execute the **first()** function to start the process. Notice that in the call to the **second()** function we have to include an ampersand before the variable's name (&). This tells the system that the variable is going to be modified by the function.

An important aspect of the definition of a function are the parameter's names. When we call a function, we must declare the names of the parameters. For example, the function **double()** of previous examples includes a parameter called **number**. Every time we call this function, we have to include the name of the parameter in the call (e.g., **double(number: 50)**). The names in the call are called *argument labels*. Swift automatically generates argument labels for every parameter using the parameters' names. Sometimes the names we assign to the parameters of a function may be descriptive enough for the statements of the function but may be confusing when we perform the call. For cases like these, Swift allows us to define our own labels in the function's definition; we just have to declare them before the parameter separated by a space.

```
func double(years number: Int) -> Int {
   number * 2
}
let result = double(years: 8)
let message = "The result is \(result)"   // "The results is 16"
```

Listing 3-11: Declaring argument labels

The **double()** function of Listing 3-11 declares an argument label called **years** for the **number** parameter. From now on, the name of the parameter (**number**) is the one used by the statements of the function to access the value received from the call, while the argument label (**years**) is used when calling the function to identify the value.

If what we want is to remove an argument label, we must define it with an underscore.

```
func multiply(number1: Int, _ number2: Int) -> Int {
    number1 * number2
}
let result = multiply(number1: 25, 3)
let message = "The result is \(result)"   // "The result is 75"
```

Listing 3-12: Removing argument labels

In this example, we preserved the behavior by default for the first parameter and removed the argument label for the second parameter. Now the call only has to include the argument label of the first parameter (`multiply(number1: 25, 3)`).

Every function we have defined so far requires the values to be specified in the call. We cannot omit any of the values that the function expects to receive, but Swift lets us declare a default value for any of the function's parameters and avoid this requirement.

```
func sayhello(name: String = "Undefined") -> String {
    return "Your name is " + name
}
let message = sayhello()   // "Your name is Undefined"
```

Listing 3-13: Declaring default values for parameters

The code of Listing 3-13 declares the function `sayhello()` with one parameter of type `String` called `name` and with the string "Undefined" as its value by default. When the function is called without a value, the string "Undefined" is assigned to `name`.

(Medium) ## Generic Functions

Although creating two or more functions with the same name is not allowed, we can do it if their parameters are not the same. This is called *overloading* and allows us to define multiple functions with the same name that process different types of values.

```
func getDescription(value: Int) -> String {
    let message = "The value is \(value)"
    return message
}
func getDescription(value: String) -> String {
    let message = "The value is \(value)"
    return message
}
let result1 = getDescription(value: 3)       // "The value is 3"
let result2 = getDescription(value: "John")  // "The value is John"
```

Listing 3-14: Declaring different functions with the same name

The functions in Listing 3-14 have the same name but one receives an integer and the other a string. We can say that the function that receives the string overloads the function that receives the integer. When we call the `getDescription()` function, Swift selects the function to execute depending on the value of the attribute (when we call the function with an integer, the first function is executed, and when we do it with a string, the second function is executed).

The advantage of creating functions with the same name is that there is only one name to remember. We call the function and Swift takes care of executing the right one depending on the values assigned to the attributes in the call. But when the functions perform the same task and only differ in the type of value received, we end up with two or more pieces of code to maintain,

Chapter 3 - Swift Paradigm

which can introduce errors. In cases like this, we can replace both functions with a generic function using a generic data type.

Generic data types are placeholders for real data types. When the function is called, the generic data type is turned into the data type of the received values. If we send an integer, the generic data type turns into an `Int` data type, if we send a string, it turns into a `String`. To define a generic function, we must declare the generic data type using a custom name between angle brackets after the function's name, as in the following example.

```
func getDescription<T>(value: T) -> String {
    let message = "The value is \(value)"
    return message
}
let result1 = getDescription(value: 3.5)   // "The value is 3.5"
let result2 = getDescription(value: "George")   // "The value is George"
```

***Listing 3-15:** Defining generic functions*

The function of Listing 3-15 is a generic function. The generic data type was called T (this is a standard name for a generic data type, but we can use any name we want). The function performs the same task and it has the same name than the two functions from the previous example, but now we have reduced the amount of code in our program. When the function is called, the `T` generic data type is converted into the data type received and the value is processed (The first time the function is called in our example, `T` is turned into a `Double` and the second time into a `String`).

 IMPORTANT: Although we can send any value of any type we want to a generic function, the operations we can perform on them are very limited due to the impossibility of the compiler to know the nature of the received values. For example, we can add two integers, but we can't add two Boolean values. To solve these issues, we can constrain the generic data types with protocols. We will study how to define protocols and how to use them later in this chapter.

 The Basics: In our example, both parameters are of type `T` and therefore both must be of the same data type, but we can declare two or more generic data types separated with commas if necessary (e.g., `<T, U>`).

(Basic) **Standard Functions**

The main advantage of functions is that we can call them from any part of the program that has access to them, and they will always perform the same operations. We don't even need to know how the function does it, we just have to send to the function the values we want to process and read the result. Because of these features, functions can be shared, and programmers can implement pre-programmed functions provided by libraries and frameworks to incorporate additional functionality that would take them too long to develop themselves.

All the features of the Swift language we have implemented so far are included in a library called *Standard Library*. The Standard Library includes everything, from operators to primitive data types, as well as predefined functions. These functions are global and therefore they are accessible from anywhere in our code. The following are some of the most frequently used.

print(String**)**—This function prints a string on the Xcode's console.

abs(Value**)**—This function returns the absolute value of an integer (inverts negative values to always get a positive number).

max(Values**)**—This function compares two or more values and returns the largest.

min(Values)—This function compares two or more values and returns the smallest.

There are also functions available to stop the execution of the application in case of an unrecoverable error.

fatalError(String)—This function stops the execution of the application and prints the message provided by the argument on the console.

precondition(Bool, String)—This function stops the execution of the application and prints a message on the console if a condition is false. The first argument is the condition to be checked and the second argument is the message we want to print on the console.

Of all the functions in the Swift Standard Library, `print()` is probably the most useful. Its purpose is to print messages on the Xcode's console that may help us solve the errors in our code. In the following example, we use it to print the result of multiple operations.

```
let absolutenumber = abs(-25)
let minnumber = min(absolutenumber, 100)
print("The number is: \(minnumber)")   // "The number is: 25"
```

Listing 3-16: Printing values on the console with `print()`

The code of Listing 3-16 uses the **abs()** function to calculate the absolute value of -25, then gets the minimum value of **absolutenumber** and the number 100 with the **min()** function, and finally prints a message on the console with the result.

 The Basics: If you don't see the Xcode's console at the bottom of the Playground's editor, press the Console button at the bottom left of the editor or the middle button on the right side of the toolbar (Chapter 2, Figure 2-2, number 2).,Alternatively, you can select the options View/Debug Area/Activate Console from the menu at the top of the screen.

Sequences or collections of values are very important in computer programming. The strings studied in Chapter 2 are a clear example. A string is a sequence of values of type **Character**. As we will see later in this chapter, the Swift Standard Library includes several types of collections to store sequence of values that are important to the application or the user, but it also offers a few global functions to create sequences of values our application may need temporarily to process information. The following are some of the most frequently used.

stride(from: Value, **through:** Value, **by:** Value)—This function returns a collection of values from the value specified by the **from** attribute to the value specified by the **through** attribute in intervals specified by the **by** attribute.

stride(from: Value, **to:** Value, **by:** Value)—This function returns a collection of values from the value specified by the **from** attribute to the value specified by the **through** attribute in intervals specified by the **by** attribute. The last value is not included.

repeatElement(Value, **count:** Int)—This function returns a collection containing the number of elements specified by the **count** attribute, each one with the value specified by the first attribute.

zip(Collection, Collection)—This function returns a collection of tuples containing the values of the collections provided by the attributes in sequential order.

The following example applies some of these functions to create a list of tuples that contain a string and an integer.

```
let sequencetext = repeatElement("Hello", count: 5)
let sequencenumbers = stride(from: 0, to: 10, by: 2)
let finalsequence = zip(sequencetext, sequencenumbers)

for (text, number) in finalsequence {
    print("\(text) - \(number)")
}
```

Listing 3-17: Creating collections of values

The code of Listing 3-17 calls the **repeatElement()** function to create a sequence of 5 elements, all of them with the string "Hello" ("Hello", "Hello", "Hello", "Hello", "Hello"). Next, the **stride()** function creates another collection with integers from 0 to 10, increased by 2, and without including the last one (0, 2, 4, 6, 8). Next, the **zip()** function merges these two collections in one collection of tuples, where each tuple has the corresponding value of each collection; the first tuple contains the first value of the **sequencetext** collection along with the first value of the **sequencenumbers** collection, and so on. Finally, we use a **for in** loop to iterate over the values of the **finalsequence** collection and print the values of each tuple on the console ("Hello - 0", "Hello - 2", "Hello - 4", "Hello - 6", "Hello - 8").

(Basic) Scopes

The conditionals and loops studied in Chapter 2 and the functions studied in this chapter have a thing in common: they all use blocks of code (statements between braces) to enclose their functionality. Blocks are independent processing units; they contain their own statements and variables. To preserve their independence and avoid conflicts between these units and the rest of the code, their variables and constants are isolated. Variables and constants declared inside a block are not accessible from other parts of the code; they can only be used inside the block in which they were created.

The space in the code where a variable is accessible is called *scope*. Swift defines two types of scopes: the global scope and the local scope (also referred as global space or local space). The variables and constants outside a block have global scope, while those declared inside a block have local scope. The variables and constants with global scope are accessible from any part of the code, while those with local scope are only accessible from the statements inside the block in which they were created (and also the statements from blocks created inside their block). For better understanding, here is a practical example.

```
var multiplier = 1.2
var total = 0.0

func first() {
    let base = 10.0
    total += base * multiplier
}
func second() {
    let multiplier = 5.0
    let base = 3.5
    total += base * multiplier
}
first()
second()
print("Total: \(total)")   // "Total: 29.5"
```

Listing 3-18: Using variables and constants of different scopes

The example of Listing 3-18 declares two variables in the global space, `multiplier` and `total`, and two functions with some local constants. The `multiplier` and `total` variables are global and therefore they are accessible from anywhere in the code, but the constants defined inside the functions are available only to the statements inside the function in which they were created. Therefore, the `base` constant declared inside the `first()` function is only accessible from this function (neither the statements in the global space nor other functions or blocks outside `first()` have access to it), but we can modified the value of `total` from this function because it is a global variable.

The next function, `second()`, declares a new constant called `multiplier`. This constant has the same name as the `multiplier` variable declared before in the global space, but they have different scopes and therefore they are different. When we read the value of `multiplier` in the `second()` function to add a new value to the `total` variable, the `multiplier` that the system reads is the one declared inside the function because in that space this constant has precedence over the global variable with the same name.

 Do It Yourself: Replace the code in your Playground file with the code of Listing 3-18. Check the values on the Results Side Bar to understand how the variables are accessed and what variable is used each time.

As demonstrated by the example of Listing 3-18, we can declare variables and constants with the same name as long as they have different scopes. Another example is the `base` constant declared inside the `second()` function. This constant has the same name as the one declared in the `first()` function, but it has a different scope and therefore it is a different constant.

(Medium) ## Closures

Blocks of code, such as those used to create functions, conditionals, and loops, have their own scope and know the variables that are available to them. Because of this, we can generate independent processing units that do not interfere with the operations of other units. This feature is so important in computer programming that Swift offers the possibility to create independent blocks called *Closures* to take advantage of it.

Closures are simple blocks of code with the syntax `{ (parameters) -> Type in statements }`. They are similar to functions (functions are actually closures with a name), but everything goes between the braces and the `in` keyword is included to separate the closure's data types from the statements.

Closures can be assigned to variables and then executed using the name of the variable and parentheses, as we do with functions. The name of the variable becomes the name of the closure. The following example creates and executes a closure that multiplies two numbers and returns the result.

```
let multiplier = { (number: Int, times: Int) -> Int in
    let total = number * times
    return total
}
print("The result is \(multiplier(10, 5))")   // "The result is 50"
```

Listing 3-19: Assigning closures to variables

The code of Listing 3-19 defines a closure and assigns it to the `multiplier` constant. From that moment on, the name of the constant may be used to execute the closure. Notice that the parameters of the closure and the return type are declared with the same syntax as functions (`(number: Int, times: Int) -> Int`), but the parameters' names are not turned into argument labels and therefore they are ignored in the call.

Chapter 3 - Swift Paradigm

An advantage of being able to assign closures to constants or variables is the possibility to initialize them with the result of complex processes or operations. The closure is assigned to the constant or variable and executed right away adding parentheses at the end of the declaration. When the system reads the statement, it executes the closure first and then assigns the value returned by the closure to the constant or variable.

```
let myaddition = { () -> Int in
    var total = 0
    let list = stride(from: 1, through: 9, by: 1)
    for number in list {
        total += number
    }
    return total
}()
print("The total is \(myaddition)")   // "The total is 45"
```

Listing 3-20: Initializing a variable with the value returned by a closure

The closure declared in Listing 3-20 doesn't receive any value and returns an integer (`()  ->  Int`). The code in the closure adds the values of a collection and returns the result, but because we included the parentheses at the end of the definition, the value assigned to the **myaddition** constant is the one returned by the closure (45), not the closure itself.

The task performed in this example is simple, the numbers from 1 to 9 are added one after another in a **for in** loop and the result of the addition is returned and assigned to the **myaddition** variable, but executing a closure as soon as it is declared is a technique usually implemented for more complex processes such as loading a file or opening a database.

If the closure does not receive any parameter, as in the last example, we can simplify its syntax declaring the type of the constant or variable and letting Swift infer the type of the value returned by the closure. Notice that when the closure doesn't receive a value, we can also remove the **in** keyword.

```
let myaddition: Int = {
    var total = 0
    let list = stride(from: 1, through: 9, by: 1)
    for number in list {
        total += number
    }
    return total
}()
print("The total is \(myaddition)")   // "The total is 45"
```

Listing 3-21: Simplifying a closure

Closures cannot only be assigned to variables but also sent and returned from functions, as any other value. When a function receives a closure, the parameter's data type only has to include the data types the closure receives and returns, as in the following example.

```
let multiplier = { (number: Int, times: Int) -> Int in
    let total = number * times
    return total
}
func processclosure(myclosure: (Int, Int) -> Int) {
    let total = myclosure(10, 2)
    print("The total is: \(total)")   // "The total is: 20"
}
```

```
processclosure(myclosure: multiplier)
```

Listing 3-22: Sending a closure to a function

The first statement of Listing 3-22 defines a closure that multiplies two integers and returns the result. A function that receives a closure of this type is defined next. Notice that the data type of the value received by the function was declared as `(Int, Int) -> Int`. This indicates to the compiler that the `processclosure()` function can receive a closure that in turn receives two integer values and return another integer. When the `processclosure()` function is called in the last statement, the value of the `multiplier` variable is sent to the function. The function assigns the closure to the `myclosure` constant and the closure is executed inside the function using this name and the values 10 and 2, producing the result 20.

The closure was defined in the global space and was executed inside the `processclosure()` function, but we don't really need to assign the closure to a global variable, we can just define it in the function's call.

```
func processclosure(myclosure: (Int, Int) -> Int) {
    print("The total is: \(myclosure(10, 2))")   // "The total is: 20"
}
processclosure(myclosure: { (number: Int, times: Int) -> Int in
    return number * times
})
```

Listing 3-23: Assigning the closure to the function's argument

The code of Listing 3-23 works the same way as the previous example, but it was simplified by assigning the closure directly to the function's argument. This can be simplified even further by using a pattern called *Trailing Closures*. When the final argument of a function is a closure, we can declare the closure at the end of the call, as in the following example.

```
func processclosure(myclosure: (Int, Int) -> Int) {
    print("The total is: \(myclosure(10, 2))")   // "The total is: 20"
}
processclosure() { (number: Int, times: Int) -> Int in
    number * times
}
```

Listing 3-24: Using Trailing Closures

When we pass the closure this way, the call does not include the attribute `myclosure` anymore. The closure declared after the parentheses is considered as the last argument of the function and therefore the label is not necessary.

The code of Listing 3-24 works the same way as previous examples, the only advantage is the reduction of the amount of code we had to write. And that can be simplified even more. In the last example we already removed the `return` keyword. As explained before, when the content of a function (or in this case a closure) includes only one statement, the compiler implies that the value produced by that statement is the one that has to be returned and therefore the `return` keyword is not required anymore. But when we are passing the closure to a function, Swift can also infer the data types of the values received by the closure and therefore we don't have to declare that either. Instead, we can represent these values using shorthand argument names. These are special placeholders composed by the $ symbol and an index starting from 0. The first value received by the closure is represented by $0, the second value by $1, and so on.

```
func processclosure(myclosure: (Int, Int) -> Int) {
```

Chapter 3 - Swift Paradigm

```
   print("The total is: \(myclosure(10, 2))")   // "The total is: 20"
}
processclosure() { $0 * $1 }
```

Listing 3-25: Inferring the closure's data types

Again, the code is the same, but now the closure is extremely simple. When it is executed from the **processclosure()** function, it receives the values 10 and 2 and assigns them to the placeholders $0 and $1, respectively. Then, it multiplies their values and returns the result.

In the previous examples, we have executed the closure received by the function inside the same function, but there are situations in which a closure has to be executed outside the function. This usually applies to asynchronous operations, as we will see later. If we want to execute a closure received by the function from outside the function, we must declare it as an *escape* closure. Escape closures are closures that remain in memory after the execution of the function is over. They are declared by preceding them with the keyword **@escaping**.

```
var myclosure: () -> Void = {}

func passclosure(closure: @escaping () -> Void) {
   myclosure = closure
}
passclosure() { () -> Void in
   print("Closure Executed")
}
myclosure()
```

Listing 3-26: Declaring escaping closures

In the code of Listing 3-26, we declare a variable called **myclosure** that stores a closure that doesn't receive or return any values (**() -> Void**) and then we assign an empty closure to it. After that, we define a function called **passclosure()** that receives an escaping closure and all it does is assign that closure to the **myclosure** variable. Next, we call the **passclosure()** function with a trailing closure that prints a message on the console. Up to this point, all we are doing is passing the closure to the function and the function is assigning that closure to the **myclosure** variable, so at the end we execute the closure in **myclosure** and the message is printed on the console.

 The Basics: When we define the data type of a closure, we must declare the data types of the values it receives and the data type of the values it returns. Therefore, if the closure doesn't return any value, we must declare the return type as **Void**, as we did in the example of Listing 3-26.

(Basic) **3.3 Structures**

Structures are an essential part of the organizational paradigm proposed by Swift. They are custom data types that include not only the data but also the code in charge of processing that data. When we define a structure, what we are doing is declaring a data type that may contain variables and constants (called *properties*) and functions (called *methods*). Later we can declare variables and constants of this type to store information with the characteristics defined by the structure. These values (called *instances*) will be unique, with its own properties and methods.

(Basic) **Definition of Structures**

To define a new structure, we must use the **struct** keyword and enclose the data and functionality between braces.

```
struct Item {
    var name: String = "Not defined"
    var price: Double = 0
}
```

Listing 3-27: Defining a structure

Listing 3-27 defines a structure called `Item` with two properties (variables): `name` and `price`. The definition by itself does not create anything; it is just delineating the elements of the type (also called *members*), like a blueprint used to create the real structures. What we have to do to store values of this new data type in memory, as we would do with any other data type, is to declare a variable or constant of this type. The declaration is done as before, but the type is the name of the structure and the initialization value is a special initializer with the syntax `Name()` (where `Name` is, again, the name of the structure).

```
struct Item {
    var name: String = "Not defined"
    var price: Double = 0
}
var purchase: Item = Item()
```

Listing 3-28: Declaring a variable of type `Item`

The code of Listing 3-28 creates a variable of type `Item` that stores an instance of the `Item` structure containing the properties `name` and `price`. The instance is created by the `Item()` initializer and then assigned to the `purchase` variable.

 The Basics: It is advisable to write the names of custom data types, such as structures and classes, capitalized (e.g., `Item`, `TheItem`, `TheRedItem`, etc.). This syntax helps us differentiate the names of data types from other elements such as functions and variables.

The properties of a new instance always take the values declared in the structure's definition (`"Not Defined"` and 0), but we can change them as we do with any other variable. The only difference is that the properties are inside a structure, so every time we want to access them, we must mention the structure they belong to. The syntax implements dot notation, as in `variable.property`, where `variable` is the name of the variable that contains the instance of the structure and `property` is the name of the property we want to access.

```
struct Item {
    var name = "Not defined"
    var price = 0.0
}
var purchase = Item()
purchase.name = "Lamps"
purchase.price = 10.50
print("Product: \(purchase.name) $ \(purchase.price)")
```

Listing 3-29: Assigning new values to the properties of a structure

In Listing 3-29, the structure and `purchase` variable are declared as before, but this time we let Swift infer their types. After the instance is created, new values are assigned to its properties using dot notation. Dot notation is not only used to assign new values but also to read the current ones. At the end, we read and print the values of the `name` and `price` properties on the console ("Product: Lamps $ 10.5").

Chapter 3 - Swift Paradigm

Do It Yourself: Replace the code in your Playground file with the code of Listing 3-29. Create another variable and assign to it the initializer of the `Item` structure to create another instance. Assign different values to the properties of each instance to learn how to work with copies of the same structure.

Structures may be instantiated inside other structures, as many times as necessary, in an unlimited chain. The dot notation is extended in these cases to reach every element.

```
struct Price {
    var USD = 0.0
    var CAD = 0.0
}
struct Item {
    var name: String = "Not defined"
    var price: Price = Price()
}
var purchase = Item()
purchase.name = "Lamps"
purchase.price.USD = 10.50
```

Listing 3-30: Structures inside structures

Listing 3-30 defines two structures: `Price` and `Item`. The `price` property of the `Item` structure was defined as a property of type `Price`. Instead of storing a single value, now it can store a structure with two properties, `USD` and `CAD`, for American and Canadian dollars. When the `Item` structure is created and assigned to the `purchase` variable, the `Price` structure for the `price` property is also created with its values by default (`var price: Price = Price()`). By concatenating the names of the variables and properties containing these structures we can read and modify any value we want. For instance, the last statement in the code of Listing 3-30 accesses the `USD` property of the `price` structure inside the `purchase` structure to assign a price to the item in American Dollars (`purchase.price.USD = 10.50`).

In this example, the `price` object is created during instantiation, but this is not usually the case. Sometimes the values of the properties containing objects are defined after the instance is created and therefore those properties must be declared as optionals. The problem with optionals is that we always have to check whether the variable or property has a value before we use it. To simplify this task, Swift introduces Optional Chaining.

Optional Chaining is a simple tool to access objects, properties and methods in a hierarchical chain that contains optional components. As always, the access to these components is done through dot notation, but a question mark is added to the names of the variables and properties that have optional values. When the system finds an optional, it checks whether it contains a value and continues processing the expression only in case of success, as shown next.

```
struct Price {
    var USD = 0.0
    var CAD = 0.0
}
struct Item {
    var name: String = "Not defined"
    var price: Price?
}
var purchase = Item()
purchase.name = "Lamps"
purchase.price?.USD = 10.50   // nil
```

Listing 3-31: Accessing optional properties

The `price` property in the code of Listing 3-31 is an optional (its initial value is not defined). Every time we read this property, we must unwrap its value, but if we use Optional Chaining, we just have to concatenate the values with dot notation and add a question mark after the name of the optional (`purchase.price?.USD`). The system reads every component in the instruction and checks their values. If any of the optionals have no value, it returns `nil`, but when all the optionals have values, the instruction performs the task.

(Medium) ## Key Paths

Besides using dot notation to read and write a property, we can use key paths. A key path is a reference to a property that we can use to read and modify its value. The advantage of using key paths instead of dot notation is that they are stored in structures and therefore we can pass them to other parts of the code and then use them to access the values of the properties they are referencing without even knowing what those properties are. This can be useful when we need to interact with libraries and frameworks, or when we are extending code to include our own functionality.

Swift defines several structures to store key paths. For instance, a read-only key path is stored in an instance of a structure of type `KeyPath` and read-and-write key paths are stored in a structure of type `WritableKeyPath`.

The syntax to define a key path includes a backward slash and the name of the data type followed by the name of the property we want to reference. To access the value of a property using a key path, Swift offers a syntax that includes square brackets after the instance's name and the keyword `keypath`, as illustrated in the following example.

```
struct Item {
   let name: String
   let price: Double
}
var purchase: Item = Item(name: "Lamps", price: 27.50)
let keyPrice = \Item.price
print(purchase[keyPath: keyPrice])   // "27.5"
```

Listing 3-32: Creating key paths

The code of Listing 3-32 defines a structure with two properties: `name` and `price`. Next, we create a key path to reference the `price` property. Because the properties are defined as constants, the key path is created of type `KeyPath` (a read-only key path). In the last statement, we access the value of the `price` property of the `purchase` instance using this key path and print it on the console.

We can easily create a read-and-write key path by defining the structure's properties as variables. In the following example, we turn the `name` and `price` properties into variables and modify the value of `price` using our `keyPrice` key path.

```
struct Item {
   var name: String
   var price: Double
}
var purchase: Item = Item(name: "Lamps", price: 27.50)
let keyPrice = \Item.price
purchase[keyPath: keyPrice] = 30.00
print(purchase.price)
```

Listing 3-33: Using read and write key paths

Chapter 3 - Swift Paradigm

(Basic) **Methods**

If we could only store properties, structures would be just a complex data type, like a tuple, but as we mentioned before, code may also be defined as part of the structure. This is done through functions. Functions inside structures are called *methods*, but their definition is the same.

The syntax to execute a method is **variable.method()**, where **variable** is the name of the variable that contains the instance of the structure and **method** is the name of the method we want to call inside that structure, as shown in the following example.

```
struct Item {
   var name = "Not defined"
   var price = 0.0

   func total(quantity: Double) -> Double {
      return quantity * price
   }
}
var purchase = Item()
purchase.name = "Lamp"
purchase.price = 10.50
print("Total: \(purchase.total(quantity: 2))")   // "Total: 21.0"
```

Listing 3-34: Defining methods

In Listing 3-34, a method was declared as part of the definition of the **Item** structure. The method receives a value representing the number of items sold and calculates the total money spent in the transaction. We could have performed this operation outside the structure by reading the value of the **price** property but having a method in the structure itself presents two advantages. First, we don't have to worry about how the method calculates the value; we just call the method with the right value and let its statements perform the task, no matter how complex it is. And second, we do not have to write the operation over and over again, because it is always part of the instance of the structure we are working with.

A method can read the values of the instance's properties but cannot assign new values to them. If we want a method to be able to modify the values of the properties of its own instance, we must use a special keyword called **mutating**. The **mutating** keyword goes before the **func** keyword in the method's definition.

```
struct Item {
   var name = "Not defined"
   var price = 0.0
   mutating func changename(newname: String) {
      name = newname
   }
}
var purchase = Item()
purchase.changename(newname: "Lamps")
print("Product: \(purchase.name)")   // "Product: Lamps"
```

Listing 3-35: Assigning new values to properties from inside the structure

The **changename()** method of the **Item** structure in Listing 3-35 is declared as a mutating method to be able to assign a new value to the **name** property from its statements. Therefore, we do not need to modify the **name** property directly, we can just call this method with the value we want to store in the property, as we do in this example, and the method takes care of assigning the value to the property.

Chapter 3 - Swift Paradigm

Every instance we create from the structure's definition has the purpose to store and process specific data. For example, we can create multiple instances of the `Item` structure defined in previous examples to store information about several products. Each product will have its own name and price, so the properties of each instance must be initialized with the proper values. The initialization of an instance is a very common process, and it is difficult to do if we have to assign the values one by one after the instances are created. For this reason, Swift provides different alternatives to initialize values. The most convenient is called *memberwise initializer*.

Memberwise initializers detect the properties of the structure and declare their names as argument labels. Using these argument labels, we can provide the values for initialization between the parentheses of the initializer. The following code implements the memberwise initializer to initialize an instance of the `Item` structure declared in previous examples.

```
struct Item {
    var name = "Not defined"
    var price = 0.0
}
var purchase = Item(name: "Lamp", price: 10.50)
print("Purchase: \(purchase.name) $ \(purchase.price)")
```

Listing 3-36: Initializing properties

Memberwise initializers reduce the amount of code and simplify initialization. Also, if we use the memberwise initializer, we can ignore the values by default declared in the definition.

```
struct Item {
    var name: String
    var price: Double
}
var purchase = Item(name: "Lamp", price: 10.50)
print("Purchase: \(purchase.name) $ \(purchase.price)")
```

Listing 3-37: Using memberwise initializers to provide the initial values of a structure

The two forms of initialization we have seen so far are not customizable enough. Some structures may have multiple properties to initialize or even methods that must be executed right away to get the proper values for the instance to be ready. To add more alternatives, Swift provides a method called `init()`. The `init()` method is called as soon as the instance is created, so we can use it to assign values to the properties or perform operations and initialize the properties with the results.

```
struct Price {
    var USD: Double
    var CAD: Double

    init() {
        USD = 5
        CAD = USD * 1.29
    }
}
var myprice = Price()
```

Listing 3-38: Initializing properties from the `init()` method

Chapter 3 - Swift Paradigm

When the instance is generated by the initializer, the properties are created first and then the init() method is executed. Inside this method we can perform any operation we need to get the properties' initial values. In the example of Listing 3-38, we assign an initial value of 5 to the USD property and then multiply this value by the corresponding exchange rate to get the value of the CAD property (the same price in Canadian dollars).

As well as any other method or function, the init() method may include parameters. These parameters are included to be able to specify initial values from the initializer.

```
struct Price {
    var USD: Double
    var CAD: Double
    init(americans: Double) {
        USD = americans
        CAD = USD * 1.29
    }
}
var myprice = Price(americans: 5)
```

Listing 3-39: *Declaring the parameters of the* init() *method*

This is similar to what Swift creates for us in the background when we use memberwise initializers, but the advantage of declaring the init() method ourselves is that we can specify only the parameters we need (as in the last example) or even declare multiple init() methods to present several alternatives for initialization, as shown next.

```
struct Price {
    var USD: Double
    var CAD: Double
    init(americans: Double) {
        USD = americans
        CAD = USD * 1.29
    }
    init(canadians: Double) {
        CAD = canadians
        USD = CAD * 0.7752
    }
}
var myprice = Price(canadians: 5)
```

Listing 3-40: *Declaring multiple* init() *methods*

As we mentioned when we were studying functions, Swift identifies each function by its name and parameters, so we can declare several functions with the same name as long as they have different parameters. Of course, this also applies to methods, including the init() method. In the example of Listing 3-40, two init() methods were declared to initialize the instance of the structure. The first method receives a **Double** value with the name **americans** and the second method also receives a **Double** value but with the name **canadians**. The right method will be executed according to the attribute included in the initializer. In this example, we use the attribute **canadians** with the value 5, so the instance is initialized by the second method.

(Medium) **Computed Properties**

The properties we have declared up to this point are called *Stored Properties*. Their function is to store a value in memory. But there are other types of properties called *Computed Properties*.

These properties do not store a value of their own, instead they have access to the rest of the properties of the structure and can perform operations to set and retrieve their values.

Two special methods were included for computed properties to be able to set and retrieve a value: `get` and `set`. These methods are also called *getters* and *setters* and are declared between braces after the property's name. Although both methods are useful, only the `get` method is mandatory. Here is a simple example.

```
struct Price {
    var USD: Double
    var ratetoCAD: Double
    var canadians: Double {
        get {
            return USD * ratetoCAD
        }
    }
}
var purchase = Price(USD: 11, ratetoCAD: 1.29)
print("Price in CAD: \(purchase.canadians)")   // "Price in CAD: 14.19"
```

Listing 3-41: Declaring computed properties

The structure defined in Listing 3-41 contains a stored property called `USD` to store the price in American dollars, a stored property called `ratetoCAD` to store the exchange rate for Canadian dollars, and a computed property called `canadians` that converts the US dollars into Canadian dollars and returns the result. Computed properties are like methods, they calculate the value every time the property is read. No matter if the value of the `ratetoCAD` property changes, the `canadians` property will always return the right price in Canadian dollars.

Including the `set` method for the `canadians` property we can, for example, set a new price using the same currency.

```
struct Price {
    var USD: Double
    var ratetoCAD: Double
    var ratetoUSD: Double
    var canadians: Double {
        get {
            return USD * ratetoCAD
        }
        set {
            USD = newValue * ratetoUSD
        }
    }
}
var purchase = Price(USD: 11, ratetoCAD: 1.29, ratetoUSD: 0.7752)
purchase.canadians = 500
print("Price: \(purchase.USD)")   // "Price: 387.6"
```

Listing 3-42: Adding the `set` method to set a new value

The new structure defined in Listing 3-42 can retrieve and set a price in Canadian dollars. When we set a new value for the `canadians` property, the value is stored in a constant called `newValue` (the constant is created automatically for us). Using this constant, we can process the value received and perform the operations we need. In this example, the value of `newValue` is multiplied by the exchange rate to turn the price in Canadian dollars into American dollars. The price is always stored in American dollars but using the `canadians` property we can set it and retrieve it in Canadian dollars.

Chapter 3 - Swift Paradigm

If we want to use a different name for the new value, we can set the parameter's name between parentheses. In the following example the parameter was called `CAD` and used instead of `newValue` to calculate the value for the `USD` property.

```
struct Price {
    var USD: Double
    var ratetoCAD: Double
    var ratetoUSD: Double
    var canadians: Double {
        get {
            return USD * ratetoCAD
        }
        set(CAD) {
            USD = CAD * ratetoUSD
        }
    }
}
var purchase = Price(USD: 11, ratetoCAD: 1.29, ratetoUSD: 0.7752)
```

Listing 3-43: *Using a different name for the parameter of the* set *method*

Computed properties with only a getter are called read-only properties, because we can only read their values. When we declare a read-only property, we can omit the **get** method.

```
struct Price {
    var USD: Double
    var ratetoCAD: Double
    var canadians: Double {
        return USD * ratetoCAD
    }
}
var purchase = Price(USD: 11, ratetoCAD: 1.29)
print(purchase.canadians)   // "14.190000000000001"
```

Listing 3-44: *Defining real-only properties*

(Medium) **Property Observers**

Properties are accessible from every part of the code that has access to the instances they belong to. Therefore, they may be modified at any moment by different processes, such as in response to user interaction or events produced by the system. To inform an instance that one of its properties was modified, Swift introduces Property Observers.

Property Observers are special methods, similar to the `get()` and `set()` methods we have just studied, that can be added to a property to execute code before and after a value is assigned to it. The methods are called `willSet()` and `didSet()`, and are declared between braces after the properties declaration.

```
struct Price {
    var increment: Double = 0
    var oldprice: Double = 0
    var price: Double {
        willSet {
            increment = newValue - price
        }
        didSet {
            oldprice = oldValue
```

```
        }
    }
}
var product = Price(price: 15.95)
product.price = 20.75
print("New price: \(product.price)")   // "New price: 20.75"
print("Old price: \(product.oldprice)")  // "Old price: 15.95"
```

Listing 3-45: Adding observers to a property

The `Price` structure of Listing 3-45 includes three properties: `increment`, `oldprice`, and `price`. We use the `price` property to store the value of an item, the `oldprice` property to store the previous price, and the `increment` property to store the difference between the old price and the new one. To set up this last value, we declare property observers for the `price` property. Every time a new value is assigned to this property, the `willSet()` and `didSet()` methods are executed. Swift automatically creates a parameter called `newValue` for the `willSet()` method to provide access to the value that is going to be assigned to the property, and a parameter called `oldValue` for the `didSet()` method to provide access to the property's old value after the new value was assigned (we can change the names of these parameters as we did for the `set()` method in Listing 3-43). In our example, when the `willSet()` method is executed, the current value of `price` is subtracted from `newValue` to get the difference between the current price and the new one, and the result is assigned to the `increment` property. And in the `didSet()` method, we assign the old price provided by `oldValue` to the `oldprice` property to have access to the item's previous price.

(Basic) ## Type Properties and Methods

The properties and methods declared above are accessible on the instances created from the definition of the structure. This means that we must create an instance of the structure to be able to access those properties and methods. But there are times when being able to execute properties and methods from the definition itself makes sense. We might need, for example, to get some information that affects all the instances, set some values to create instances with a specific configuration, or call methods to create instances with standard values. In Swift, this is possible by declaring type properties and methods (properties and methods accessible from the type, not the instance created from that type).

Type properties and methods for structures are declared adding the `static` keyword to their definition. Once a property or method is declared with this keyword, they are only accessible from the definition itself. In the following example, we include a type property called `currencies` to inform how many currencies the structure can handle.

```
struct Price {
    var USD: Double
    var CAD: Double
    static var currencies = 2
}
print(Price.currencies)   // 2
```

Listing 3-46: Defining type properties

As illustrated by the code of Listing 3-46, there is no need to create an instance to access a type property or method. After the definition, the `currencies` property is read using the name of the structure and dot notation (`Price.currencies`). If we create an instance from this definition, the only properties accessible from the instance will be `USD` and `CAD`. The `currencies` property is a type property, only accessible from the type itself. The same happens with methods.

Chapter 3 - Swift Paradigm

```
struct Price {
    var USD: Double
    var CAD: Double
    static func reserve() -> Price {
        return Price(USD: 10.0, CAD: 11.0)
    }
}
var reserveprice = Price.reserve()
print("Price in USD: \(reserveprice.USD) CAD: \(reserveprice.CAD)")
```

Listing 3-47: Defining type methods

The structure in the example of Listing 3-47 includes a type method called **reserve()**. The method creates and returns an instance of the structure it belongs to with standard values. This is a common procedure and another way to create our own initializer. If we use the initializer by default, the values have to be provided every time the instance is created, but with a type method the only thing we have to do is call the method on the type to get in return an instance already configured with specific values. In our example, the values correspond to a reserved price. We call the **reserve()** method on the **Price** type, the method creates an instance of the **Price** structure with the values 10.0 and 11.0, and then the instance returned is assigned to the **reserveprice** variable. At the end, the values of both properties are printed on the console to confirm that their values were defined by the **reserve()** method.

(Advanced) Generic Structures

At the beginning of this chapter, we explained how to create generic functions. These are functions that can process values of different data types. The function defines a placeholder for the data type and then adopts the data type of the received value. But generics data types are not exclusive to functions, we can also turn data types themselves, such as structures, into generic types. The advantage is that we can create independent processing units that can handle different types of values. To create a generic structure, we must declare the generic data type after the name of the structure and between angle brackets, as we did for functions.

```
struct MyStructure<T> {
    var myvalue:T
    func description() {
        print("The value is: \(myvalue)")   // "The value is: 5"
    }
}
let instance = MyStructure<Int>(myvalue: 5)
instance.description()
```

Listing 3-48: Defining generic structures

The code of Listing 3-48 defines a generic structure called **MyStructure** with one generic type called **T**. The structure contains a generic property called **myvalue** and a method that prints a message with its value. After the definition, we create an instance of this structure with an integer. The system replaces the **T** with the **Int** type, creates the instance, and assigns the value 5 to the **myvalue** property. In the last statement, we call the **description()** method to print the message on the console.

Notice that when we create an instance of a generic structure, the data type we want the structure to work with is included after the name and between angle brackets, but this is only required when the initialization doesn't include any value. For example, the following code creates an instance of the same structure but with a string and lets Swift infer the generic type from the value.

```swift
struct MyStructure<T> {
   var myvalue:T

   func description() {
      print("The value is: \(myvalue)")   // "The value is: Hello"
   }
}
let instance = MyStructure(myvalue: "Hello")
instance.description()
```

Listing 3-49: Using generic structures

 The Basics: These are basic examples of how to create generic data types. As with functions, generics only become useful when we constrain the data using protocols. We will learn more about generics in the following sections and study protocols at the end of this chapter.

(Basic) Primitive Type Structures and Casting

Including several properties and methods inside a structure and then assigning an instance of that structure to a variable is a simple way to wrap data and functionality together in a single portable unit of code. Structures are usually used this way, as practical wrappers of code, and Swift takes advantage of this feature extensively. In fact, all the primitive data types defined in Swift are structures. The syntax `variable: Int = value`, for example, is a shortcut provided by Swift for the initializer `variable = Int(value)`. Every time we assign a new value to a primitive variable, we are assigning a structure that contains that value (all the conversions are done for us in the background). The following are the initializers of some of the primitive types studied in Chapter 2.

Int(Value)—This is the initializer of the `Int` data type. The attribute is the value we want to assign to the instance. If no value is provided, the value 0 is assigned by default. Initializers for similar types are also available (`Int8()`, `Int16()`, `Int32()`, and `Int64()`).

UInt(Value)—This is the initializer of the `UInt` data type. The attribute is the value we want to assign to the instance. If no value is provided, the value 0 is assigned by default. Initializers for similar types are also available (`UInt8()`, `UInt16()`, `UInt32()`, and `UInt64()`).

Float(Value)—This is the initializer of the `Float` data type. The attribute is the value we want to assign to the instance. If no value is provided, the value 0.0 is assigned by default.

Double(Value)—This is the initializer of the `Double` data type. The attribute is the value we want to assign to the instance. If no value is provided, 0.0 is assigned by default.

The structures for these types were already defined for us in the Swift Standard Library. All we have to do to get an instance is to call its initializer with the value we want to store.

```swift
var mynumber = Int(25)
var myprice = Double(4.99)
```

Listing 3-50: Initializing variables with standard initializers

Chapter 3 - Swift Paradigm

The variables `mynumber` and `myprice`, declared in Listing 3-50, are inferred to be of type `Int` and `Double`. The initializers create a structure for each value and assign the instances to the variables. This is the same as assigning the values directly to the variable (e.g., `var myprice = 4.99`). There is no advantage in the use of initializers for primitive types except when the value provided is of a different data type. The definitions of these structures include several initializers that convert the value to the corresponding type. This is usually called *casting*, and we can use it to turn a variable of one type into another when required. For example, when we divide numbers, the system converts those numbers to the right type and performs the operation, but variables are already of a specific type and therefore they have to be explicitly converted before the operation is performed or we get an error (The process does not really convert the variable; it just creates a new value of the right type).

```
var number1: Int = 10
var number2: Double = 2.5
var total = Double(number1) / number2   // 4.0
```

Listing 3-51: Casting a variable

The variables `number1` and `number2` of Listing 3-51 are of type `Int` and `Double`. To perform a division between these two variables we must cast one of them to the data type of the other (arithmetic operations cannot be performed on values of different type). Using the `Double()` initializer, we create a new value of type `Double` from the value of `number1` and perform the operation (the value 10.0 created by the initializer is divided by the value 2.5 of `number2` to get the result 4.0). The process is described as "casting the `number1` variable to a `Double`".

These initializers are also useful when working with `String` values. Sometimes the characters of a string represent numbers that we need to process. The problem is that strings cannot be processed as numbers. We cannot include a string in an arithmetic operation without first converting the string into a value of a numeric data type. Fortunately, the initializers for numeric types such as `Int` and `Double` can convert a value of type `String` into a number. If the operation cannot be performed, the initializer returns `nil`, so we can treat it as an optional value. In the following example, we convert the string "45" into the integer 45 and add it to the value 15.

```
var units = "45"
if let number = Int(units) {
    let total = number + 15
    print("The total is \(total)")   // "The total is 60"
}
```

Listing 3-52: Extracting numbers from strings

Just as any other structure, the structures defined for primitive types also have their own properties and methods. This includes type properties and methods. For instance, the following are the most frequently used properties and methods provided by the structures that process integer values, such as `Int` or `Int8`.

min—This type property returns the minimum value the type can handle.

max—This type property returns the maximum value the type can handle.

random(in: Range)—This type method returns a random number. The value is calculated from a range of integers provided by the `in` attribute.

negate()—This method inverts the sign of the value.

isMultiple(of: Int)—This method returns `true` if the value is a multiple of the value provided by the **of** attribute (this is similar to what we can achieve with the % operation).

The `min` and `max` properties are especially useful because they allow us to determine whether an operation could overflow a variable (produce a result that is greater or less than the minimum and maximum allowed).

```
var mynumber: Int8 = 120
let increment: Int8 = 10

if (Int8.max - mynumber) >= increment {   // (127 - 120) >= 10
    mynumber += increment
}
print(mynumber)   // "120"
```

Listing 3-53: Checking the maximum possible value for the `Int8` *type*

The code of Listing 3-53 takes advantage of the `max` property to make sure that incrementing the value of a variable will not overflow the variable (the result will not be greater than the maximum the variable can handle). The code starts by defining a variable of type `Int8` to store the result of the operation and another to store the number we want to add. Then, we calculate how far the current value of **mynumber** is from the maximum value admitted by an `Int8` type variable (`Int8.max - mynumber`) and compare this result with the value of **increment**. If the number of units we have left is greater or equal than the value of **increment**, we know that the operation can be performed without going over the limit (in this example the operation is not performed because the addition of 120 + 10 produces a result greater than the limit of 127 admitted by the `Int8` data type).

 Do It Yourself: Replace the code in your Playground file with the code of Listing 3-53. Print the values of the `min` and `max` properties of other integer types, such as `Int16`, `Int32`, and `Int64` to see their limitations.

The type `Double` also includes its own selection of properties and methods. The following are the most frequently used.

pi—This type property returns the value of the constant Pi.

infinity—This type property returns an infinite value.

minimum(Double, Double)—This type method compares the values provided by the attributes and returns the minimum.

maximum(Double, Double)—This type method compares the values provided by the attributes and returns the maximum.

random(in: Range)—This type method returns a random number. The value is calculated from a range of values of type `Double` provided by the `in` attribute.

negate()—This method inverts the sign of the value.

squareRoot()—This method returns the square root of the value.

remainder(dividingBy: Double)—This method returns the remainder produced by dividing the value by the value specified by the `dividingBy` attribute.

rounded(FloatingPointRoundingRule)—This method returns the value rounded according to the rule specified by the attribute. The attribute is an enumeration with the values `awayFromZero`, `down`, `toNearestOrAwayFromZero`, `toNearestOrEven`, `towardZero` and `up`.

Chapter 3 - Swift Paradigm

In this case, the most useful method is probably `rounded()`. With this method, for instance, we can round a floating-point value to the nearest integer.

```
var mynumber: Double = 2.890
mynumber = mynumber.rounded(.toNearestOrAwayFromZero)
print("The round number is \(mynumber)")   // "The round number is 3.0"
```

Listing 3-54: Rounding floating-point values

Of course, Boolean values are also structures. Among others, the `Bool` data type offers the following methods.

toggle()—This method toggles the value. If the value is `true`, it becomes `false` and vice versa.

random()—This type method returns a random `Bool` value.

The following example checks the current value of a variable and changes the value to `false` if it is `true`.

```
var valid: Bool = true
if valid {
    print("It is Valid")
    valid.toggle()
}
print(valid)   // false
```

Listing 3-55: Changing the value of a `Bool` variable

(Basic) **Range Structures**

The `random()` method provided by some of the structures introduced above work with ranges of values. These are structures included in the Swift Standard Library that can manage open and close ranges of values. For instance, we can create a range between 1 and 5. If the range is open, it will include the values 1, 2, 3, and 4, but if the range is closed, it will include the values 1, 2, 3, 4, and 5. Swift includes two operators to generate these ranges.

- ... (three dots) creates a range from the value on the left to the value on the right, including both values in the range (e.g., 1...5 creates a range that includes the values 1, 2, 3, 4 and 5). The value on the right can be ignored to create a one-sided range. A one-sided range goes from the value on the left to the maximum value allowed for the data type.
- ..< (two dots and the less than character) creates a range from the value on the left to the value before the value on the right (e.g., 1..<5 creates a range that includes the values 1, 2, 3 and 4).

When we declare a range using these operators, Swift creates the proper structure according to the operator involved. A structure of type `Range` is created for an open range and a structure of type `ClosedRange` is created for a closed range. These structures provide common properties and methods to work with the range. The following are the most frequently used.

lowerBound—This property returns the range's lower value (the value on the left).

upperBound—This property returns the range's upper value (the value on the right). This property is not available for partial ranges.

contains(Element)—This method returns a Boolean value that determines if the value specified by the attribute is inside the range.

clamped(to: Range)—This method compares the original range with the range specified by the **to** attribute and returns a new range with the part of the ranges that overlap.

reversed()—This method returns a collection with the values of the range in reversed order.

Ranges are useful in a variety of situations. For instance, if we need a loop with a fixed number of cycles, we can implement a `for in` loop with a range. The following example iterates over a closed range of integers from 0 to 10, generating a total of 11 cycles.

```
var total = 0
for value in 0...10 {
    total += value
}
print("The total is \(total)")   // "The total is 55"
```

Listing 3-56: Using `for in` to iterate over a range

Of course, we can also invert that loop.

```
var message = ""
var range = 0..<10

for item in range.reversed() {
    message += "\(item) "
}
print(message)   // "9 8 7 6 5 4 3 2 1 0 "
```

Listing 3-57: Inverting a range

The code of Listing 3-57 creates a range from 0 to 9 with the `..<` operator and then calls the `reversed()` method to invert it. This method creates a collection with the values of the range in reverse order, so we can read it with a `for in` loop. The statement inside the loop adds the values to the **message** string, and this string is printed on the console at the end to confirm that the values were effectively reversed.

With ranges, we can also simplify **switch** statements that have to consider multiple values per case.

```
var age = 6
var message = "You have to go to "

switch age {
    case 2...4:
        message += "Day Care"
    case 5...11:
        message += "Elementary School"
    case 12...17:
        message += "High School"
    case 18..<22:
        message += "College"
    case 22...:
        message += "Work"
    default:
        message += "Breastfeeding"
}
```

Chapter 3 - Swift Paradigm

```
print(message)   // "You have to go to Elementary School"
```

Listing 3-58: Using range operators in a `switch` *statement*

In the example of Listing 3-58 we compare an age with several ranges of ages (integers). If the value of **age** is within one of the ranges, the instructions for that **case** are executed. As illustrated by this example, we can also declare only one side of a range and let the system determine the other. The last case in Listing 3-58 creates a one-sided close range from the value 22 to the maximum value allowed for the type.

As mentioned before, ranges are used by the **random()** method of primitive data types to get a random value. The following example generates a loop that calculates multiple random values from 1 to 10. The condition stops the loop when the number returned by the method is equal to 5. Inside the loop, we also increment the value of the **attempts** variable to calculate the number of cycles required for the **random()** method to return our number.

```
var mynumber: Int = 0
var attempts = 0

while mynumber != 5 {
    mynumber = Int.random(in: 1...10)
    attempts += 1
}
print("It took \(attempts) attempts to get the number 5")
```

Listing 3-59: Calculating random numbers

(Basic)   **String Structures**

Not only primitive data types and ranges are structures, but also the rest of the data types defined in the Swift Standard Library, including the **String** data type. As we have seen in Chapter 2, we can initialize a **String** structure by simply assigning a string (a text between double quotes) to a constant or a variable. This is another shortcut. In the background, instances of the **String** structure are created from the initializer included in the structure's definition.

String(Value**)**—This initializer creates a string from the value provided by the attribute. The **String** structure defines multiple versions of this initializer to create strings from different types of values, including other strings, characters, and numbers.

Once the string is created, we can manipulate it with the properties and methods provided by the **String** structure. The following are the most frequently used.

isEmpty—This property returns a Boolean that indicates whether the value is an empty string or not. This is the same as comparing the string with an empty string.

count—This property returns the total number of characters in the string.

first—This property returns the first character in the string.

last—This property returns the last character in the string.

lowercased()—This method returns a copy of the string in lowercase letters.

uppercased()—This method returns a copy of the string in uppercase letters.

hasPrefix(String**)**—This method returns a Boolean value that indicates whether the string begins with the text specified by the attribute or not.

hasSuffix(String**)**—This method returns a Boolean value that indicates whether the string ends with the text specified by the attribute or not.

append(String)—This method adds a character or a string of characters at the end of the original string. This is the same as concatenating strings with the + operator.

contains(Character)—This method returns a Boolean value that indicates whether the character specified by the attribute exists in the string or not.

Most of the time, we will assign a string directly to a variable as we have done so far, but the `String()` initializer may be useful when we need to convert values into strings. For instance, the following example converts the number 44 into a string and counts the number of characters in the string.

```
var age = String(44)
var mytext = "Total digits \(age.count)"   // "Total digits 2"
```

Listing 3-60: Converting a number into a string

An important characteristic of Swift's strings is that they are composed of Unicode characters. The particularity of these types of characters is that they can occupy different amounts of memory, even when the characters look the same. Because of this, it is not possible to establish the position of a character using integer values. The index of the first character is always 0, but the index of the consecutive characters depends on the size of their predecessors. Swift solves this problem by defining a data type called `Index`. This is another structure defined inside the `String` structure specifically designed to manage string indexes. The `String` structure includes properties and methods to work with these indexes and access the characters. The following are the most frequently used.

startIndex—This property returns the index value of the first character of the string.

endIndex—This property returns the index value of one position after the last character of the string. It is useful to manipulate range of characters, as we will see later.

firstIndex(of: Character)—This method returns the index where the character specified by the **of** attribute appears for the first time in the string.

insert(Character, at: Index)—This method inserts into the string the character provided by the first attribute at the position determined by the **at** attribute.

insert(contentsOf: String, at: Index)—This method inserts into the string the value of the **contentsOf** attribute at the position determined by the **at** attribute.

remove(at: Index)—This method removes and returns the character at the position determined by the **at** attribute.

prefix(through: Index)—This method returns a string created from the first character of the original string to the character at the index indicated by the **through** attribute.

prefix(upTo: Index)—This method returns a string created from the first character of the original string to the character at the index indicated by the **upTo** attribute, but without including this last character.

replaceSubrange(Range, with: String)—This method replaces the characters in the position determined by the range provided as the first attribute with the string provided by the **with** attribute.

removeSubrange(Range)—This method removes the characters in the positions determined by the range specified by the attribute.

The indexes created by the `Index` structure are used to access specific characters in a string, but strings don't use dot notation like tuples, the index of the character we want to read has to be declared after the string's name, enclosed in square brackets. For instance, the following code reads the `startIndex` property to access the first character of a string.

```
var text = "Hello World"
if !text.isEmpty {
   let start = text.startIndex
   let firstChar = text[start]
   print("First character is \(firstChar)")   // "First character is H"
}
```

Listing 3-61: Processing the string's characters

The first thing we do in the example of Listing 3-61 is to check the value of the `isEmpty` property to make sure the string is not empty and there are characters to read (notice the `!` operator to invert the condition). Once we know we can proceed, we get the index of the string's first character from the `startIndex` property and read the character in that position using square brackets.

If we want to access a character in a different position, we must increment the value returned by `startIndex`. The trick is that, since `Index` values are not integers, we cannot add a simple number to them. Instead, we must use the methods provided by the `String` structure.

index(after: Index)—This method increments the index specified by the **after** attribute one unit and returns a new `Index` value with the result.

index(before: Index)—This method decrements the index specified by the **before** attribute one unit and returns a new `Index` value with the result.

index(Index, **offsetBy:** Int)—This method increments the index specified by the first attribute the amount of units specified by the **offsetBy** attribute and returns a new `Index` value with the result.

The following example advances the initial index 6 positions to get a different character.

```
var text = "Hello World"
if text != "" {
   let start = text.startIndex
   let newIndex = text.index(start, offsetBy: 6)
   print("The character is \(text[newIndex])")   // "The character is W"
}
```

Listing 3-62: Calculating a specific index

The `index()` method applied in Listing 3-62 takes an integer to calculate the new index. The original index is increased the number of units indicated by the integer and the resulting `Index` value is returned. With this index, we get the character at the position 6 (indexes start from 0).

If we wanted to get the previous index, we could have specified a negative number of units for the offset value, but another way to move forward and backward is to implement the other versions of the `index()` method. The following example gets the next index after the initial index and prints the corresponding character on the screen.

```
var text = "John"
let start = text.startIndex
var next = text.index(after: start)
print("Second letter is \(text[next])")   // "Second letter is o"
```

Listing 3-63: Getting the next index

Once the right index is calculated, we can call some of the **string** methods to insert or remove characters. The **insert()** method, for instance, inserts a single character at the position indicated by its second attribute. In the following example, we call it with the value of the **endIndex** property to add a character at the end of the string (**endindex** points to the position after the last character).

```
var text = "Hello World"
text.insert("!", at: text.endIndex)
print("New string is \(text)")   // "New string is Hello World!"
```

Listing 3-64: Inserting a character in a string

If we do not know exactly where the character we are looking for is located, we can find a specific index with the **index()** method. The value returned by this method is an optional containing the **Index** value of the first character that matches its attribute or **nil** in case of failure. In the following example, we implement this method to find the first space character and remove it with the **remove()** method.

```
var text = "Hello World"
var findIndex = text.firstIndex(of: " ")
if let index = findIndex {
    text.remove(at: index)
    print("New string is \(text)")   // "New string is HelloWorld"
}
```

Listing 3-65: Removing a character

If we want to work with groups of characters, we must implement ranges of **Index** values. In previous examples we created ranges of integers, but the operators can take any type of values we need, including **Index** values.

```
var text = "Hello World"
var start = text.startIndex
var findIndex = text.firstIndex(of: " ")
if let end = findIndex {
    print("First word is \(text[start..<end])") //"First word is Hello"
}
```

Listing 3-66: Getting a range of characters

The **firstIndex()** method in Listing 3-66 looks for a space character and returns its index. With this value, we can create a range from the first character to the space character and get the first word. But we have to be careful because the **end** index is pointing to the space character, not to the last character of the word. To get the word without the space, we have to create an open range with the **..<** operator, so the character on the right is not included.

We can also use ranges to replace or remove parts of the text. The **String** structure offers the **replaceSubrange()** and **removeSubrange()** methods for this purpose.

```
var text = "Hello World"
var start = text.startIndex
var findIndex = text.firstIndex(of: " ")
if let end = findIndex {
    text.replaceSubrange(start..<end, with: "Goodbye")   // "Goodbye World"
}
```

Chapter 3 - Swift Paradigm

```
findIndex = text.firstIndex(of: " ")
if let start = findIndex {
    text.removeSubrange(start...)   // "Goodbye"
}
```

Listing 3-67: Working with ranges of characters

Listing 3-67 implements both methods. The `replaceSubrange()` method replaces the characters from the beginning of the string up to the character before the space character (the word "Hello") with the string "Goodbye", getting the sentence "Goodbye World", and the `removeSubrange()` method uses an open range to remove the characters of this sentence from the space character to the end of the string (" World"), getting the final string "Goodbye". Notice that after applying the methods over the same string, the indexes are lost and therefore they must be calculated again. That is why before calling the `removeSubrange()` method we search for the position of the space character once more and update the `findIndex` variable.

The rest of the methods provided by the `String` structure are straightforward. For instance, the following example implements two of them to check if a string contains the word "World" at the end and converts all the letters into uppercase letters.

```
let text = "Hello World"

if text.hasSuffix("World") {
    print(text.uppercased())   // "HELLO WORLD"
}
```

Listing 3-68: Implementing `String` methods

(Basic) Array Structures

The strings studied before and the values we have created in previous examples with functions such as `stride()` or `repeatElement()` are collections of values. Collections do not represent a value; they are containers for other values. A value of type `String` does not contain the string "Hello", it contains a collection of variables of type `Character`, with the values H, e, l, l, and o. Swift includes several collections like this, some were defined to contain specific values, like `String`, and others are generic (they are defined with a generic data type that can be turn into any other data type we need). One of those generic data types for collections, and probably the most frequently used, is `Array`.

Arrays are collections that contain an ordered list of values. They are generic structures that have the capacity to store all the values we need of any data type we want, but with the condition that once a data type is selected, all the values must be of that same type. For example, if we create an array of type `Int`, we will only be able to store values of type `Int` in it.

Swift offers multiple syntaxes to create an array, including the structure's initializers.

Array<Type>()—This initializer returns an empty `Array` structure of the data type indicated by the value of **Type**.

Array(repeating: Value, count: Int)—This initializer returns an `Array` structure with copies of the same value. The **repeating** attribute determines the value to copy and the **count** attribute determines how many copies the array will contain.

Another way to create an array is to declare the data type between square brackets followed by parentheses (e.g., `var list = [Int]()`), but the most frequently used is declaring the array with some initial values enclosed in square brackets and separated by comma, as in the following example.

```
var list: [Int] = [15, 25, 35]
```

Listing 3-69: *Declaring arrays*

As with any other variable, Swift may infer the type from the values.

```
var list = [15, 25, 35]
```

Listing 3-70: *Declaring arrays with type inference*

The `list` array declared in these examples was initialized with three integer values, 15, 25 and 35. The values of an array are usually called *elements* or *items*. On these terms, we can say that the code of Listing 3-70 declares an array of three elements of type `Int`.

An index is assigned to each value automatically, starting from 0, and as with strings, we must specify the index of the value we want to read surrounded by square brackets.

```
var list = [15, 25, 35]
print(list[1])   // 25
```

Listing 3-71: *Reading the array's elements*

The last statement of Listing 3-71 prints the value of the second element of the `list` array (the element at index 1) on the console. We can also use indexes to modify the values of an array, as we did with tuples.

```
var list = [15, 25, 35]
list[0] = 400
print(list)   // [400, 25, 35]
```

Listing 3-72: *Assigning a new value to an element*

Assigning new values is only possible for elements that already exist in the array. To add a new element, or several, we can use the += operator.

```
var list = [15, 25, 35]
list += [45, 55]
print(list)   // [15, 25, 35, 45, 55]
```

Listing 3-73: *Adding new elements to an array*

The += operator adds an array at the end of another array. In Listing 3-73 we use it to add two more elements to the array declared in the first statement. The final array contains the values 15, 25, 35, 45, and 55, in that order.

What the += operator does is to concatenate two arrays and assign the result back to the same variable. If we want to combine two or more arrays, we can apply the + operator.

```
var list1 = [15, 25, 35]
var list2 = [45, 55, 65]
var final = list1 + list2   // [15, 25, 35, 45, 55, 65]
```

Listing 3-74: *Concatenating two arrays*

It is possible to declare arrays of arrays. These types of arrays are called multidimensional arrays. Arrays inside arrays are listed separated by comma.

Chapter 3 - Swift Paradigm

```
var list: [[Int]] = [[2, 45, 31], [5, 10], [81, 12]]
```

Listing 3-75: Creating multidimensional arrays

The example of Listing 3-75 creates an array of arrays of integers (notice the declaration of the array [Int] inside another array [[Int]]). To access the values, we must declare the indexes of each level between square brackets, one after another. The following example returns the first value (index 0) of the second array (index 1). The instruction looks for the array at index 1 and then it gets the number at index 0.

```
var list: [[Int]] = [[2, 45, 31], [5, 10], [81, 12]]
print(list[1][0])   // 5
```

Listing 3-76: Reading values from a multidimensional array

To remove all the elements from an array, we can assign to the variable one of the initializers introduced before or just square brackets with no values.

```
var list = [15, 25, 35]
list = []
```

Listing 3-77: Removing the elements of an array

Arrays are collections of values and therefore we can iterate over their values with a **for in** loop, as we did with strings before.

```
var total = 0
let list = [15, 25, 35]
for value in list {
    total += value
}
print("The total is \(total)")   // "The total is 75"
```

Listing 3-78: Reading an array with a for in loop

The code of Listing 3-78 uses a **for in** loop to add the numbers of the **list** array to the **total** variable. At the end we print the result. Although this is a legit way to do it, arrays offer multiple properties and methods to read and process their values. Here is a list of the most frequently used.

count—This property returns the total number of elements in the array.

isEmpty—This property returns a Boolean value that indicates if the array is empty.

first—This property returns the first element of the array or **nil** if the array is empty.

last—This property returns the last element of the array or **nil** if the array is empty.

append(Element)—This method adds the value specified by the attribute at the end of the array.

insert(Element, at: Int)—This method adds a new element in a specific position of the array. The first attribute is the value we want to assign to the new element, and the **at** attribute represents the position of the array in which we want to insert the element.

remove(at: Int)—This method removes an element from the array in the index specified by the **at** attribute.

removeFirst()—This method removes the first element of the array. It returns the value of the element deleted.

removeLast()—This method removes the last element of the array. It returns the value of the element deleted.

removeAll(where: Closure)—This method removes the elements in the array that meet the condition established by the closure assigned to the `where` attribute.

removeSubrange(Range)—This method removes a range of elements from the array. The attribute is a range of integers representing the indexes of the elements to remove.

replaceSubrange(Range, **with:** Array)—This method replaces a range of elements with the elements of the array provided by the **with** attribute. The first attribute is a range of integers corresponding to the indexes of the elements we want to replace.

dropFirst(Int)—This method removes the number of elements specified by the attribute from the beginning of the array. If no amount is declared, the method removes only the first element.

dropLast(Int)—This method removes the number of elements specified by the attribute from the end of the array. If no amount is declared, the method removes only the last element.

enumerated()—This method is used to iterate over the elements of the array. It returns a tuple containing the index and the value of the current element.

min()—This method compares the values of the elements in the array and returns the smallest.

max()—This method compares the values of the elements in the array and returns the largest.

sorted()—This method returns a new array with the elements of the original array sorted in ascending order.

sorted(by: Closure)—This method returns a new array with the elements of the original array in the order determined by the attribute. The attribute is a block of code (closure or function) that determines the order.

randomElement() —This method randomly selects an element from the array and returns it. If the array is empty, the value returned is `nil`.

shuffled()—This method returns an array with the elements of the original array in random order.

reversed()—This method returns a new array with the elements of the array in reverse order.

swapAt(Int, Int)—This method exchanges the values of the elements at the indexes specified by the attributes.

joined(separator: String)—This method returns a string that includes all the values in an array of strings joined by the string specified by the **separator** attribute.

filter(Closure)—This method filters an array and returns another array with the values that passed the filter. The attribute is a block of code (closure or function) that processes the elements and returns a Boolean indicating whether the value passed the test or not.

map(Closure)—This method returns a new array containing the results of processing each of the values of the array. The attribute is a block of code (closure or function) that process the elements one by one.

reduce(Value, Closure)—This method sends the values of the array to the closure one by one and returns the result of the operation. The first attribute is the value that is going to be processed with the first value of the array, and the second attribute is the closure we want to use to process the values.

contains(where: Closure)—This method returns a Boolean value that determines if the array contains an element that meets the condition in the closure specified by the `where` attribute.

allSatisfy(Closure)—This method returns a Boolean value that determines if all the elements of the array comply with the requisites of a closure.

difference(from: Array)—This method returns a `CollectionDifference` structure containing all the changes that has to be performed to synchronize the array with the array provided by the **from** method. This method can work in conjunction with the `applying()` method to apply all the changes in the array at once (see Listing 3-141).

In the previous example we have seen how to iterate over the elements of an array with the `for in` loop, but that iteration only returns the value of the element, not its index. An alternative is provided by the `enumerated()` method, designed to work with these types of loops. Each cycle returns a tuple with the index and the value of the current element.

```
let fruits = ["Banana", "Orange", "Apple"]
var message = "My fruits:"

for (myindex, myfruit) in fruits.enumerated() {
    message += " \(myindex + 1)-\(myfruit)"
}
print(message)   // "My fruits: 1-Banana 2-Orange 3-Apple"
```

Listing 3-79: Reading indexes and values of an array

The example of Listing 3-79 uses the constants **myindex** and **myfruit** to capture the values produced by the **enumerated()** method and generate a string. Notice that since the array's indexes start from 0, we added 1 to **myindex** to start counting from 1.

Another useful member of arrays is the **count** property. As mentioned before, we can access each element of the array with the index between square brackets. But trying to read a value in an index that has not yet been defined will return an error. To make sure that the index exists, we can check whether it is greater than 0 and less than the total amount of elements in the array using the **count** property.

```
let ages = [32, 540, 12, 27, 54]
let index = 3
if index > 0 && index < ages.count {
    print("The value is: \(ages[index])")   // "The value is: 27"
}
```

Listing 3-80: Checking whether an array contains a value in a specific index

The methods to add and remove elements from an array are straightforward. The following example illustrates how to implement them.

```
var fruits = ["Banana", "Orange"]
if !fruits.isEmpty {
    fruits.append("Apple")   // ["Banana", "Orange", "Apple"]
```

```
fruits.removeFirst()   // "Banana"
fruits.insert("Pear", at: 1)   // ["Orange", "Pear", "Apple"]
fruits.insert(contentsOf: ["Cherry", "Peach"], at: 2)
   // ["Orange", "Pear", "Cherry", "Peach", "Apple"]
}
```

Listing 3-81: Adding and removing elements

 The Basics: Every time an array is modified, its indexes are reassigned. For instance, if you remove the first element of an array of three elements, the index 0 is reassigned to the second element and the index 1 to the third element. The system makes sure that the indexes of every array are always consecutive and start from 0.

A more complex method is **removeAll(where:)**. This method allows us to remove several elements of the array at once, but only those that meet a condition. The condition is established by a closure that processes each of the values in the array and returns **true** or **false** depending on whether the value meets the condition or not. In the following example, we compare each value with the string "Orange" and therefore all the values "Orange" are removed from the array.

```
var fruits = ["Banana", "Orange", "Apple", "Orange"]
fruits.removeAll(where: { (value) in
   value == "Orange"
})
print(fruits)   // ["Banana", "Apple"]
```

Listing 3-82: Removing all the elements that meet a condition

Another method that can receive a closure to determine a condition is **contains(where:)**. In the following example, we use this method to determine whether an array contains a value greater than 60 or not.

```
var list = [55, 12, 32, 5, 9]
let found = list.contains(where: { (value) in
   value > 60
})
print(found)   // false
```

Listing 3-83: Finding if an element meets a condition

Besides reading values one by one, we can also select a random value with the **randomElement()** method. This method selects a value from the array and returns an optional, so we must compare it against **nil** or use optional binding before processing it, as in the following example.

```
let fruits = ["Banana", "Orange", "Apple"]
if let randomValue = fruits.randomElement() {
   print("The selected value is: \(randomValue)")
}
```

Listing 3-84: Selecting a random value from an array

Another random operation is performed by the **shuffled()** method. With this method we can randomly order the elements of an array.

```
var fruits = ["Banana", "Orange", "Apple"]
fruits = fruits.shuffled()
print(fruits)   // e.g.: ["Orange", "Apple", "Banana"]
```

Listing 3-85: Changing the order of the elements of an array

Besides working with all the elements of an array, we can do it with a range of elements. Ranges work with arrays the same way they work with strings. They offer an easy way to create new arrays with some of the elements of another.

```
var fruits = ["Banana", "Orange", "Apple", "Cherry"]
var someFruits = fruits[0..<2]   // ["Banana", "Orange"]
print("The new selection has \(someFruits.count) fruits")
```

Listing 3-86: Reading a range of elements

The code of Listing 3-86 gets the elements at the indexes 0 and 1 from the **fruits** array and assigns them to the new **someFruits** array. Now we have two arrays: **fruits** with 4 elements and **someFruits** with 2.

Arrays created from a range of indexes are of type **ArraySlice**. This is another collection type provided by Swift to store temporary arrays that are composed of elements taken from other arrays. We can iterate over these types of arrays with a loop or read its elements as we do with normal arrays, but if we want to assign them to other array variables or use them for persistent storage, we have to cast them as **Array** types using the **Array()** initializer. The initializer takes the values of the **ArraySlice** variable and returns a normal array. The following example uses the initializer to cast the **someFruits** array created before.

```
var fruits = ["Banana", "Orange", "Apple", "Cherry"]
var someFruits = fruits[0..<2]   // ["Banana", "Orange"]
var newArray = Array(someFruits)
```

Listing 3-87: Casting arrays of type ArraySlice

As well as the **String** structure, the **Array** structure also offers the **removeSubrange()** and **replaceSubrange()** methods to remove and replace a range of elements.

```
var fruits = ["Banana", "Orange", "Apple", "Banana", "Banana"]
fruits.removeSubrange(1...2)
fruits.replaceSubrange(0..<2, with: ["Cherry", "Cherry"])
print(fruits)   // "["Cherry", "Cherry", "Banana"]"
```

Listing 3-88: Removing and replacing elements

In Listing 3-88, we call the **removeSubrange()** method to remove the range of elements from index 1 to 2, getting an array filled with the value "Banana", and then we call the **replaceSubrange()** method to replace the elements from index 0 to 1 with another array filled with "Cherries". This is a simple example that illustrates how the methods work, but it shows a recurrent situation in app development where sometimes we need to fill a collection with elements of the same value. When working with arrays, this is simple to achieve. The **Array** structure includes an initializer that takes two attributes called **repeating** and **count** and generates an array filled with the number of elements indicated by **count** and with the value indicated by **repeating**.

```
var fruits = ["Banana", "Orange", "Apple"]

let total = fruits.count
let newArray = Array(repeating: "Cherry", count: total)
fruits.replaceSubrange(0..<total, with: newArray)

print(fruits)   // "["Cherry", "Cherry", "Cherry"]"
```

Listing 3-89: Initializing an array with elements of the same value

The advantage of this initializer is that we do not have to know how many elements we need during development. We can calculate the number during execution and create an array filled with all the elements we need and values by default. In the example of Listing 3-89, we create an array with the same amount of elements as the **fruits** array and then use the **replaceSubrange()** method to replace every single element with a new one.

The methods to remove and replace elements of an array are not selective enough; they affect the elements in a specific index or a range of indexes without considering their values. If we want to perform a more specific job, we have to use the **filter()** method. This method takes a function or a closure as an attribute, iterates over the array, and sends each element to the block of code for processing. If the function or closure returns **true**, the element is included in the new array, otherwise it is ignored. The following example calls the **filter()** method with a function called **myfilter()**. What the function does is to return **true** if the value received is different than the string "Grape". As a result, the new array returned by **filter()** will contain only the elements "Apple" and "Banana".

```
var fruits = ["Apple", "Grape", "Banana", "Grape"]

func myfilter(fruit: String) -> Bool {
   if fruit != "Grape" {
      return true
   } else {
      return false
   }
}
var filteredArray = fruits.filter(myfilter)   // ["Apple", "Banana"]
```

Listing 3-90: Filtering the elements of an array

If we prefer, instead of a function we can take advantage of the flexibility of closures and greatly simplify our code.

```
var fruits = ["Apple", "Grape", "Banana", "Grape"]
var filteredArray = fruits.filter({ $0 != "Grape" })
print(filteredArray)   // "["Apple", "Banana"]"
```

Listing 3-91: Using closures

The **filter()** method now uses a closure to process the values. The method sends the values one by one to the closure, the closure replaces the placeholder ($0) with the current value, compares it with the value "Grape", and returns a Boolean value with the result (see Closures in this chapter, Listing 3-25).

If what we need is to modify the elements of an array all at once, we can use the **map()** method. This method sends to a closure the values of the array one by one and returns another array with the results produced by the closure.

Chapter 3 - Swift Paradigm

```
let list = [2, 4, 8, 16]
let half = list.map({ $0 / 2 })
print(half)  // "[1, 2, 4, 8]"
```

Listing 3-92: Mapping an array

The example of Listing 3-92 defines a list of integers and then calls the **map()** method on the array to divide each value by 2. The **map()** method sends the values of the array to the closure one by one, the closure replaces the **$0** placeholder with the current value, divides it by 2, and returns the result. All the results are stored in a new array and that array is returned by the **map()** method when the process is over.

Of course, we can perform any kind of operations on the values in the closure. For instance, the following code converts the values into strings with the **String()** initializer.

```
let list = [1, 2, 3, 4, 5]
let listtext = list.map({ String($0) })
print(listtext)  // "["1", "2", "3", "4", "5"]"
```

Listing 3-93: Converting the elements of an array into strings

When all we want to do is to initialize a new structure with the value received by the closure, instead of a closure, Swift allows us to provide the structure's initializer. The value received by the closure is sent to the initializer and a new structure of that type is returned, as illustrated in the following example.

```
let list = [1, 2, 3, 4, 5]
let listtext = list.map(String.init)
print(listtext)  // "["1", "2", "3", "4", "5"]"
```

Listing 3-94: Using a structure initializer with the map() *method*

This example produces the same result as before, but instead of using a closure, we use a reference to the **String** initializer. The **map()** method sends the values to the initializer, the initializer returns a new **String** structure with that value, and the process continues as always.

Another way to process all the values of an array at once is with the **reduce()** method. This method works in a similar way than **map()**, but instead of storing the results in an array, it sends the result back to the closure to get only one value in return. For instance, the following code uses the **reduce()** method to get the result of the addition of all the numbers in an array.

```
let list = [2, 4, 8, 16]
let total = list.reduce(0, { $0 + $1 })
print(total)  // "30"
```

Listing 3-95: Reducing an array

The code of Listing 3-95 defines the same list of integers as before, but this time it calls the **reduce()** method on the array. This method sends two values at a time to the closure. In the first cycle, the values sent to the closure are the one provided by the first attribute **(0)** and the first value of the array **(2)**. In the second cycle, the values sent to the closure are the value returned by the closure in the first cycle (0 + 2 = **2**), and the second value of the array **(4)**. The loop goes on until all the values of the array are processed.

When it comes to sorting the elements of an array, there are several options available. The most frequently used are **reversed()** and **sorted()** (and its variant **sorted(by:)**). The **reversed()** method takes the elements of an array and returns a new array with the same elements in reversed order. The value returned by the method is stored in a structure of type **ReversedCollection**. As we did before with the **ArraySlice** type, we can cast these values as **Array** structures with the **Array()** initializer.

```
var fruits = ["Apple", "Blueberry", "Banana"]
var array = Array(fruits.reversed())   // ["Banana", "Blueberry", "Apple"]
```

Listing 3-96: Reversing the elements of an array

The **sorted()** method sorts the array in ascending order and returns a new array with the values in order.

```
var fruits = ["Blueberry", "Apple", "Banana"]
let basket = fruits.sorted()
print(basket)   // ["Apple", "Banana", "Blueberry"]
```

Listing 3-97: Sorting the elements of an array

If we want to sort the elements in a custom order, we have to use the **sorted(by:)** method. This method works in a similar fashion to the **filter()** method studied before. It takes a function or a closure that receives the value of two elements and returns **true** if the first element should appear before the second element, or **false** otherwise. From this value, the method establishes the order of the elements and generates the new array.

```
var fruits = ["Apple", "Raspberry", "Banana", "Grape"]
var newArray = fruits.sorted(by: { $0 > $1 })
print(newArray[0])   // "Raspberry"
```

Listing 3-98: Sorting the elements of an array in a custom order

The closure provided to the **sorted()** method in Listing 3-98 receives two values, replaces the placeholders with those values, and returns the result of the comparison. When the **sorted()** method is executed, it performs a loop. On each cycle, two values of the **fruits** array are sent to the closure. The closure compares the values and returns **true** or **false** accordingly. This indicates to the **sorted()** method which value should appear before the other in the new array, effectively sorting the elements.

Unlike the example we programmed for the **filter()** method, this one does not compare the attribute against a specific value. This allows us to order arrays of any data type. For example, we can use the same closure to sort an array of integers.

```
var numbers = [55, 12, 32, 5, 9]
var newArray = numbers.sorted(by: { $0 < $1 })
print(newArray[0])   // 5
```

Listing 3-99: Sorting an array of integers

If we decide to work with specific data types, we can perform custom tasks. For example, we can process **String** values to count the characters and order the strings according to their length.

Chapter 3 - Swift Paradigm

```
var fruits = ["Apple", "Blueberry", "Banana", "Grape"]
var newArray = fruits.sorted(by: { $0.count < $1.count })
print(newArray)  // ["Apple", "Grape", "Banana", "Blueberry"]
```

Listing 3-100: Sorting strings according to the number of characters

Arrays also include two powerful methods to compare elements: **min()** and **max()**. These methods compare the values and return the smallest or largest, respectively.

```
let ages = [32, 540, 12, 27]

if let older = ages.max() {
    let digits = String(older)
    print("The maximum age is \(digits.count) digits long")
}
```

Listing 3-101: Getting the largest element

The code of Listing 3-101 takes the largest value from an array of integers and counts the number of digits in the returned value. Because the **max()** method returns an optional, we use optional binding to get its value. The rest of the code turns this value into a string and counts its characters to print the number of digits on the console.

Besides selecting the largest or smallest value with the **max()** and **min()** methods, we can also fetch values from the array using the **first** and **last** properties.

```
let ages = [32, 540, 12, 27]
if let firstAge = ages.first {
    print("The first person is \(firstAge) years old")  // 32
}
```

Listing 3-102: Getting the first value of an array

The value returned by the **first** property is also an optional, so we must use optional binding again to get its value and store it in the **firstAge** constant. The **first** and **last** properties only get the first and last value, respectively. To search for any value in the array or its index, the **Array** structure offers the following methods.

firstIndex(of: Element)—This method performs a search from the beginning of the array and returns the index of the first element found that is equal to the value of the **of** attribute.

lastIndex(of: Element)—This method performs a search from the end of the array and returns the index of the first element found that is equal to the value of the **of** attribute.

firstIndex(where: Closure)—This method returns the index of the first value that meets the condition in the closure assigned to the **where** attribute.

lastIndex(where: Closure)—This method returns the index of the last value that meets the condition in the closure assigned to the **where** attribute..

first(where: Closure)—This method returns the first value that meets the condition in the closure assigned to the **where** attribute.

last(where: Closure)—This method returns the last value that meets the condition in the closure assigned to the **where** attribute.

If we only need the index of a particular element, we can use the `firstIndex(of:)` method. For instance, the following example looks for the first appearance of the number 540 in the `ages` array and prints its index.

```
let ages = [32, 540, 12, 27, 54]
if let index = ages.firstIndex(of: 540) {
   print("The value is at the position \(index)")   // 1
}
```

Listing 3-103: Getting the index of a specific value

If what we need instead is to get the index of a value that meets certain condition, we can use methods like `firstIndex(where:)` or `lastIndex(where:)` depending whether we want to search from the beginning or the end of the array.

```
let ages = [32, 540, 12, 27, 54]
let first = ages.firstIndex(where: { $0 < 30 })
if first != nil {
   print("The first value is at index \(first!)")   // 2
}
```

Listing 3-104: Getting the index of a value that meets a condition

In the example of Listing 3-104, we look for the index of a value that is smaller than 30. The `firstIndex(where:)` method reads every value of the array from the beginning and sends them to the closure assigned to the `where` attribute. This closure assigns the current value to the placeholder and compares it against the number 30, if the value is greater than 30, the closure returns `false`, otherwise it returns `true` and the index of that value is assigned to the `first` variable. In this case, the first number in the array smaller than 30 is 12, and therefore the index assigned to the variable is 2.

(Basic) Set Structures

If we store two elements in an array, one element will automatically receive the index 0 and the other the index 1. This correlation between indexes and values never changes, allowing elements to be listed always in the right order and have elements with the same value at different indexes. Sets are like arrays, but they do not assign an index to their values and therefore there is no order and no duplicated values. This makes accessing values in sets much faster than arrays, but also makes them only useful in very specific circumstances.

Sets are created from the `Set` structure and the declaration is like arrays, but we must specify the type as `Set`.

```
var ages: Set = [15, 25, 35, 45]
```

Listing 3-105: Creating a set of integers

The set's data type is inferred by Swift from the values assigned to it. If we need to declare the type explicitly, for instance, to create an empty set, we must specify it between angle brackets, like with any other generic type.

```
var ages: Set<Int> = []
```

Listing 3-106: Creating an empty set of integers

Chapter 3 - Swift Paradigm

Because elements in a set are not associated with an index, if we want to know whether an element exists or not, we must search for its value. One way to do it is with a **for in** loop.

```
var ages: Set = [15, 25, 35, 45]
for age in ages {
    if age == 35 {
        print("There is a 35")   // "There is a 35"
        break
    }
}
```

Listing 3-107: *Looking for a value in a set*

Working with loops is slow and time consuming, so sets also provide their own properties and methods to process their values. The following are the most frequently used.

count—This property returns the number of elements in the set.

isEmpty—This property returns a Boolean that indicates whether the set is empty or not.

contains(Element)—This method returns a Boolean that indicates whether or not there is an element in the set with the value specified by the attribute.

contains(where: Closure)—This method returns a Boolean that determines if the set contains an element that meets the condition in the closure specified by the **where** attribute.

min()—This method compares the elements in the set and returns the smallest.

max()—This method compares the elements in the set and returns the largest.

sorted()—This method returns an array with the elements of the set in ascending order.

sorted(by: Closure)—This method returns an array with the elements of the set in the order determined by the closure specified by the **by** attribute.

randomElement()—This method randomly selects an element from the set and returns it. If the set is empty, the value returned is **nil**.

shuffled()—This method returns an array with the elements of the set in random order.

insert(Element)—This method inserts a new element in the set with the value provided by the attribute.

union(Collection)—This method returns a new set created with the values of the original set plus the values provided by the attribute. The attribute may be an array or another set.

subtract(Collection)—This method returns a new set created by subtracting the elements provided by the attribute to the original set. The attribute may be an array or another set.

intersection(Collection)—This method returns a new set created with the values of the original set that match the values provided by the attribute. The attribute may be an array or another set.

remove(Element)—This method removes from the set the element with the value provided by the attribute.

isSubset(of: Set)—This method returns a Boolean that indicates whether or not the set is a subset of the set specified by the **of** attribute.

isSuperset(of: Set)—This method returns a Boolean that indicates whether or not the set is a superset of the set specified by the **of** attribute.

isDisjoint(with: Set)—This method returns a Boolean that indicates whether or not the original set and the set specified by the **with** attribute have elements in common.

Using these methods, we can easily access and modify the values of a set. For instance, we can implement the `contains()` method to search for a value.

```
var fruits: Set = ["Apple", "Orange", "Banana"]
if fruits.contains("Apple") {
    print("Apple exists!")
}
```

Listing 3-108: *Using* `contains()` *to find an element in a set*

To insert a new element we just have to execute the `insert()` method.

```
var fruits: Set = ["Apple", "Orange", "Banana"]
if !fruits.contains("Grape") {
    fruits.insert("Grape")
}
print("The set has \(fruits.count) elements")   // 4
```

Listing 3-109: *Inserting a new element*

In listing 3-109, we use the `contains()` method again to check if an element with the value "Grape" already exists in the set. If no element is found, we insert the element with the `insert()` method (Checking the value is not really necessary in this case; if the value is already part of the set, the `insert()` method does not perform any action).

To remove an element we have to call the `remove()` method.

```
var fruits: Set = ["Apple", "Orange", "Banana"]
if let removed = fruits.remove("Banana") {
    print("\(removed) was removed")   // "Banana was removed"
}
```

Listing 3-110: *Removing an element from a set*

The `remove()` method removes the element which value matches the value of its attribute and returns an optional with the value removed or `nil` in case of failure. In the code of Listing 3-110, we get the value returned by the method and print a message if it was removed successfully.

Sets are collections without order. Every time we read a set, the order in which its values are returned is not guaranteed, but we can use the `sorted()` method to create an array with the values of the set in order. The following example sorts the elements of the **fruits** set in alphabetical order, creating a new array we called **orderFruits**.

```
var fruits: Set = ["Apple", "Orange", "Banana"]
var orderFruits = fruits.sorted()
if let lastItem = orderFruits.last {
    print(lastItem)   // "Orange"
}
```

Listing 3-111: *Sorting the elements of a set*

The rest of the methods available to manipulate the set are straightforward. The following example joins two sets with the `union()` method and then subtracts elements from the result with the `subtract()` method.

Chapter 3 - Swift Paradigm

```
var fruits: Set = ["Apple", "Banana"]
var newSet = fruits.union(["Grapes"])    // "Banana", "Grapes", "Apple"
newSet.subtract(["Apple", "Banana"])     // "Grapes"
```

Listing 3-112: Combining sets

The **Set** structure also offer methods to compare sets. We can determine if a set is a subset or a superset of another set with the **isSubset()** and **isSuperset()** methods or check if two sets have elements in common with the **isDisjoint()** method. The following example implements the **isSubset()** method to check if the fruits in a basket come from the store. The code checks if the elements in the **basket** set are found in the **store** set and returns **true** in case of success.

```
var store: Set = ["Banana", "Apple", "Orange", "Pear"]
var basket: Set = ["Apple", "Orange"]
if basket.isSubset(of: store) {
    print("The fruits in the basket are from the store")
}
```

Listing 3-113: Comparing sets

 The Basics: Use a set instead of an array every time you do not need an ordered list of elements and you are worried about performance. Sets are faster than arrays and dictionaries, and that is usually the only advantage they have to offer.

Basic Dictionary Structures

There is only one way to access the elements of an array and that is through their numeric indexes. Dictionaries offer a better alternative. With dictionaries, we can define the indexes ourselves using any custom value we want. Each index, also known as *key*, has to be explicitly declared along with its associated value. Swift offers multiple syntaxes to create a dictionary, including the structure's initializers.

Dictionary<Type1: Type2>()—This initializer returns an empty **Dictionary** structure with the keys and values of the data type indicated by the value of **Type1** and **Type2**, respectively.

Dictionary(grouping: Collection, by: Closure)—This initializer returns a **Dictionary** structure with the values provided by the **grouping** attribute grouped in arrays according to the keys returned by the closure provided by the **by** attribute.

If the data types are explicitly defined, we can also declare an empty dictionary with a simplified syntax, as in **var list: [String: String] = Dictionary()**, or use square brackets with a colon, as in **var list: [String: String] = [:]**. This shortcut is also used to define a dictionary with initial values. In this case, the keys and values are separated by a colon and the items are separated by comma, as in the following example.

```
var list: [String: String] = ["First": "Apple", "Second": "Orange"]
```

Listing 3-114: Declaring a dictionary with initial values

The first value of each item is the key and the second is the value. Of course, if the keys and the values are of a clear type, Swift can infer them.

```
var list = ["First": "Apple", "Second": "Orange"]
```

Listing 3-115: Declaring a dictionary with type inference

As with arrays, if we want to read or replace a value, we just have to declare its key (index) in square brackets after the name of the dictionary.

```
var list = ["First": "Apple", "Second": "Orange"]
list["Second"] = "Banana"
```

Listing 3-116: Assigning a new value to an element of a dictionary

The second statement of Listing 3-116 assigns a new value to the element identified with the keyword "Second". Now the dictionary contains two elements with the values "Apple" and "Banana". If the keyword used to assign the new value exists, the system updates the value, but if the keyword does not exist, a new element is created, as shown next.

```
var list = ["First": "Apple", "Second": "Orange"]
list["Third"] = "Banana"
print(list)  // "["Second": "Orange", "First": "Apple", "Third":
"Banana"]"
```

Listing 3-117: Adding a new element to a dictionary

In this last example, the second statement assigns the value "Banana" to a keyword that does not exist. The system creates the new element with the specified keyword and value.

Dictionaries return optional values. If we try to read an element with a keyword that does not exist, the value returned is **nil**.

```
var list = ["First": "Apple", "Second": "Orange"]
print(list["Third"])  // nil
```

Listing 3-118: Reading an element that does not exist

The code of Listing 3-118 tries to read a value with the keyword "Third" that does not exist in the **list** dictionary. As a result, the value **nil** is printed on the console. If the element exists and we want to read its value, we must unwrap it.

```
var list = ["First": "Apple", "Second": "Orange"]
if let first = list["First"], let second = list["Second"] {
    print("We have \(first) and \(second)")  // "We have Apple and Orange"
}
```

Listing 3-119: Reading the values

Since dictionary elements are optionals, we can assign the value **nil** to remove them. The following example removes the element with the keyword "First".

```
var list = ["First": "Apple", "Second": "Orange"]
list["First"] = nil
```

Listing 3-120: Removing an element from a dictionary

Chapter 3 - Swift Paradigm

As with arrays and sets, we can also iterate over the values of a dictionary with a `for in` loop. Albeit the iteration over dictionaries is a bit different. Dictionaries return a tuple containing the index and the value of each element, so we must apply the same syntax used in previous examples to store the values of the tuple in constants.

```
var fruits = ["First": "Apple", "Second": "Orange"]
var message = "My fruits:"
for (myindex, myfruit) in fruits {
    message += " \(myindex)-\(myfruit)"
}
print(message)   // "My fruits: First-Apple Second-Orange"
```

Listing 3-121: Using `for in` *to iterate over a dictionary*

The `for in` loop in Listing 3-121 reads the elements of the **fruits** dictionary one by one, assigns the index and the value of the current element to the **myindex** and **myfruit** constants, and adds their values to the **message** variable, so at the end we get a string with all the keys and values of the dictionary.

Of course, dictionaries may also contain arrays as values. The declaration is simple, the key is declared as always, and the single value is replaced by an array.

```
var fruits: [String: [String]] = ["A": ["Apple", "Apricot"], "B":
["Banana", "Blueberries"]]
```

Listing 3-122: Combining dictionaries with arrays

Reading the values of a dictionary like this is a little bit more complicated. Because dictionaries return optionals, we cannot just specify the indexes as we do for multidimensional arrays (see Listing 3-76). The value returned by the dictionary has to be unwrapped before accessing its values.

```
var fruits: [String: [String]] = ["A": ["Apple", "Apricot"], "B":
["Banana", "Blueberries"]]
if let list = fruits["A"] {
    print(list[0])   // "Apple"
}
```

Listing 3-123: Reading arrays inside dictionaries

In Listing 3-123, we create a dictionary with two values. The values are arrays of strings with a string as key. The code gets the array corresponding to the "A" key, unwraps it, and stores it in a constant. The **list** constant now contains the array assigned to the "A" key, and therefore when we read the element at index 0 of that array, we get the value "Apple".

This is how the **Dictionary(grouping:, by:)** initializer works. It takes the values of a collection and groups them together in arrays according to the value of a key returned by the closure, as in the following example.

```
let list = [15, 25, 38, 55, 42]
let group5 = Dictionary(grouping: list, by: {$0 % 5 == 0 ? "Yes" : "No"})
print(group5)   // "["No": [38, 42], "Yes": [15, 25, 55]]"
```

Listing 3-124: Grouping values by a key

The **Dictionary** initializer implemented in Listing 3-124 takes the values of the **list** array, sends them to the closure one by one, and creates a new dictionary with the keys returned by the closure. The closure receives the value and returns the strings "Yes" or "No" depending on whether the current value is multiple of 5. If the value is multiple of 5, it is included in an array with the key "Yes", otherwise it is included in an array with the key "No".

Dictionaries incorporate plenty of functionality by themselves, but they also include properties and methods to manage their values. The following are the most frequently used.

count—This property returns the total number of elements in the dictionary.

isEmpty—This property returns a Boolean value that indicates if the dictionary is empty.

keys—This property returns a collection with the keys of the elements in the dictionary.

values—This property returns a collection with the values of the elements in the dictionary.

sorted(by: Closure)—This method returns an array of tuples containing each element of the dictionary (key and value) in the order determined by the closure specified by the **by** attribute.

randomElement()—This method randomly selects an element from the dictionary and returns a tuple with its key and value. If the dictionary is empty, the value returned is **nil**.

shuffled()—This method returns an array of tuples containing the keys and values of each element of the dictionary in random order.

updateValue(Value, **forKey:** Key)—This method updates the value of an element with the value and key specified by its attributes. If the key does not exist, the method creates a new element. It returns the previous value when the key already exists or **nil** otherwise.

removeValue(forKey: Key)—This method removes the element with the key equal to the value of the **forKey** attribute. It returns an optional containing the value of the deleted element or **nil** if no element with the specified key was found.

contains(where: Closure)—This method returns a Boolean value that determines if the dictionary contains an element that meets the condition in the closure specified by the **where** attribute.

Some of the methods provided by the **Dictionary** structure are similar to those included in the **Array** and **Set** structures, but others are more specific. For example, the **updateValue()** and **removeValue()** methods require the element's key to process the values.

```
var fruits = ["one": "Banana", "two": "Apple", "three": "Pear"]
fruits.updateValue("Banana", forKey: "three")   // "Pear"
fruits.removeValue(forKey: "one")   // "Banana"
print(fruits)   // "["three": "Banana", "two": "Apple"]"
```

Listing 3-125: Adding and removing elements from a dictionary

The **updateValue()** method updates the value of an element when there is already an element with that key or creates a new one if the key does not exist. This is the same as assigning a value directly to an element (see Listings 3-116 and 3-117), but the method returns the previous value, which may be useful sometimes.

As sets, dictionaries are an unordered collection of values, but we can create an array with their elements in a specific order using the **sorted()** method. The method processes and returns the values as tuples, with the element's key as the first value and the element's value as the second value of the tuple.

```
var fruits = ["one": "Banana", "two": "Apple", "three": "Pear"]
var list = fruits.sorted(by: { $0.1 < $1.1 })
print(list)
```

Listing 3-126: Sorting the values of a dictionary

As with arrays, the **sorted()** method sends to the closure two values at a time, but when working with dictionaries, the values are sent as tuples containing the key and value of each element. For instance, the first values sent to the closure in the example of Listing 3-126 are ("one", "Banana") and ("two", "Apple"). These values take the place of the placeholders **$0** and **$1**, so if we want to order the elements according to their values (the names of the fruits), we must compare the values of the tuples at the index 1 (**$0.1 < $1.1**). The array returned is a collection of tuples in alphabetical order, with every element containing the keys and values of the original dictionary (**[(key: "two", value: "Apple"), (key: "one", value: "Banana"), (key: "three", value: "Pear")]**).

Earlier, we saw how to iterate over the elements of a dictionary with a **for in** loop (see Listing 3-121). The loop gets each element and generates a tuple with the key and value. But there are times when we only need the element's key or the element's value. The **Dictionary** structure provides two properties for this purpose: **keys** and **values**. The properties return a collection containing only the keys or the values of the elements, respectively.

```
var fruits = ["one": "Banana", "two": "Apple", "three": "Pear"]
for key in fruits.keys {
   if key == "two" {
      print("We have an element with the key 'two'")
   }
}
```

Listing 3-127: Iterating over the dictionary's keys

The collections returned by the **keys** and **values** properties are structures of type **Keys** and **Values** defined inside the **Dictionary** structure. As we did before with other collection types, to work with their values we can turn them into arrays with the **Array()** initializer.

```
var fruits = ["one": "Banana", "two": "Apple", "three": "Pear"]
let keys = Array(fruits.keys)
print(keys)
```

Listing 3-128: Reading a dictionary key

 IMPORTANT: The order in which the elements of a dictionary are stored and returned is not guaranteed. The **for in** loop and the **keys** and **values** properties may return the values in a different order than the one they were declared. If you need an ordered list, use an array or turn the dictionary into an array with the **sorted()** method.

Basic 3.4 Enumerations

Enumerations are a way to create custom data types with their own limited set of values. An enumeration type is like the Boolean type but with the possible values defined by the programmer. They are declared with the keyword **enum** and the values between braces. Each value is defined using the **case** keyword.

```
enum Number {
    case one
    case two
    case three
}
```

Listing 3-129: Defining an enumeration type

The example of Listing 3-129 defines an enumeration type we call **Number** with three possible values: **one, two,** and **three**. We can assign any names we want for the enumeration and its values. The values may also be declared just in one **case** statement separated by comma.

```
enum Number {
    case one, two, three
}
```

Listing 3-130: Declaring the enumeration values in one statement

An enumeration is a custom data type. As we did with structures, we must create a variable of this type and assign to that variable one of the possible values using dot notation.

```
enum Number {
    case one, two, three
}
var mynumber: Number = Number.one
```

Listing 3-131: Declaring a variable of type Number

Variables declared of this type may only have the values allowed by the type (**one, two,** or **three**). To assign a value, we must use the name of the enumeration and dot notation. The **mynumber** variable declared in Listing 3-131 is of type **Number** and has the value **one**.

Once the type of the variable was already defined, only the dot and the value are necessary to modify its value.

```
enum Number {
    case one, two, three
}
var mynumber = Number.one
mynumber = .two
```

Listing 3-132: Assigning a new value to a variable of type Number

In the last statement of Listing 3-132, we assign a new value to **mynumber**. The value **.two** may have been written as **Number.two**. Both syntaxes are valid, but Swift infers that the value provided is of the same type as the variable's type, so it is not necessary to declare the name of the enumeration anymore.

Like Booleans, enumeration types may be used as signals to indicate a state that can be checked later to decide whether to perform a certain task. Therefore, they are frequently used with conditionals and loops. The following example checks the value of an enumeration variable with a **switch** statement. This statement is particularly useful when working with enumerations because these data types have a limited set of values, making it easy to define a **case** for each one of them.

Chapter 3 - Swift Paradigm

```
enum Number {
    case one
    case two
    case three
}
var mynumber = Number.two
switch mynumber {
    case .one:
        print("The number is 1")
    case .two:
        print("The number is 2")    // "The number is 2"
    case .three:
        print("The number is 3")
}
```

Listing 3-133: Using `switch` *with an enumeration type*

In Listing 3-133, the enumeration type **Number** is defined and then the **mynumber** variable is declared of this type and the value **two** is assigned to it. Next, a **switch** statement compares the value of this variable with the three possible values of its type and prints a message on the console. Notice again that Swift can infer the type of the enumeration inside the **switch** statement, so specifying the type **Number** is not required anymore.

(Medium) ## Raw Values

The cases of an enumeration type can have values by default. These values are called *raw values*. Swift assigns values by default to every case, starting from 0, but we can assign our own to each case, as we do with normal variables.

```
enum Number: String {
    case one = "Number One"
    case two = "Number Two"
    case three = "Number Three"
}
var mynumber = Number.one
```

Listing 3-134: Assigning raw values to enumeration values

Enumerations behave like structures. We can define our own properties and methods inside an enumeration, and they also include initializers, properties and methods by default. The most useful property is called **rawValue**, which lets us read the raw values of each **case**.

```
enum Number: String {
    case one = "Number One"
    case two = "Number Two"
    case three = "Number Three"
}
var mynumber = Number.one
print("The value is \(mynumber.rawValue)")    // "The value is Number One"
```

Listing 3-135: Reading raw values

Additionally, enumerations include a member initializer to create an instance from a raw value. Instead of declaring the variable using the name of the member, as we did in previous examples (**one**), we can use the initializer and the raw value. The initializer includes the **rawValue** attribute to specify the value used to create the instance.

```
enum Number: String {
    case one = "Number One"
    case two = "Number Two"
    case three = "Number Three"
}
var mynumber = Number(rawValue: "Number Two")
if mynumber == .two {
    print("Correct Value")   // "Correct Value"
}
```

Listing 3-136: Creating an enumeration from a raw value

In Listing 3-136, we create an instance of **Number** with the raw value "Number Two" and then check that the variable contains the proper value with an **if** statement. We can compare the case value or the raw value to identify an instance of an enumeration type. It doesn't really matter what value we use as long as we know what we are looking for.

What makes enumerations part of the programming paradigm proposed by Swift is not their capacity to store different types of values but the possibility to include custom methods and computed properties. The following example adds a method to our **Number** enumeration that prints a message depending on the current value of the instance.

```
enum Number: Int {
    case one
    case two
    case three

    func printMessage() -> String {
        switch self {
            case .one:
                return "We are the best"
            case .two:
                return "We have to study more"
            case .three:
                return "This is just the beginning"
        }
    }
}
var mynumber = Number.two
print(mynumber.printMessage())   // "We have to study more"
```

Listing 3-137: Adding methods to an enumeration

When we need to check the current value of the instance from inside a method, we must use the **self** keyword. This keyword refers to the instance where the method is being executed (in our case, **mynumber**), and this is how we can check for the instance's current value and return the right message (we will learn more about the **self** keyword later).

(Medium) ## Associated Values

Enumerations include the possibility to associate values to a case. These are values we can attach to a case when variables of that type are initialized. For instance, in the following example we create an enumeration that can store information about a character, but it provides the possibility to differentiate between letters and numbers.

```
enum MyCharacters {
    case number(Int, String)
```

Chapter 3 - Swift Paradigm

```
        case letter(Character, String)
}
var character = MyCharacters.number(1, "Number One")
switch character {
    case .number(let value, let description):
        print("\(description) - \(value)")   // "Number One - 1"
    case .letter(let letter, let description):
        print("\(description) - \(letter)")
}
```

Listing 3-138: Associating values

The code of Listing 3-138 defines an enumeration called **MyCharacters** that includes two cases. The first case is called **number** and it takes two associated values: an integer and a string. The second case is called **letter** and it also takes two associated values: a character and a string. When we create a value of this type, we must select the case value, as always, but in this case, we also must specify the corresponding associated values. If the value of the enumeration is **number**, we must provide an integer and a string, and if the value is **letter**, we must provide a character and a string. In this example, we create an instance with the value **number** and the associated values 1 and "Number One".

In each case of the **switch** statement, we test whether the value is **number** or **letter** and extract their associated values with constants between parenthesis, like what we did with tuples before (see Listing 2-37). If we need to test a single case, we can use an **if** or a **guard** statement and assign the value to the case we want to test.

```
enum MyCharacters {
    case number(Int, String)
    case letter(Character, String)
}
var character = MyCharacters.number(1, "Number One")

if case .number(let number, let text) = character {
    print("Number: \(number)")   // "Number: 1"
    print("Text: \(text)")   // "Text: Number One"
}
```

Listing 3-139: Reading associated values from an `if` statement

The syntax includes the **case** keyword and the necessary constants to receive the values. The statement is saying something like "Assign the value to this case, if not possible, return false". In our example, if the **character** variable doesn't contain a **MyCharacters** enumeration with the value **number**, the statement returns **false** and nothing is done, otherwise, the associated values in the **character** variable are assigned to the constants and printed on the console.

(Advanced) **Collection Difference**

Associated values are commonly implemented by libraries and frameworks to share data with our code. For instance, the **Array** structure defined in the Swift Standard Library includes the **difference()** method. We have introduced this method before. Its purpose is to compare two arrays and return a structure of type **CollectionDifference** that contains a collection of values that represent the difference between the arrays. These values are of type **Change**, an enumeration defined by the **CollectionDifference** structure that includes the following values and their associated values to represent single changes.

insert(offset: Int, **element:** Element, **associatedWith:** Int?)—This enumeration value represents the insertion of an element. It includes three associated values. The **offset** value indicates the index in which the element is inserted, the **element** value is the inserted element, and the **associatedWith** value is the index of the element that is associated with this change.

remove(offset: Int, **element:** Element, **associatedWith:** Int?)—This enumeration value represents the removal of an element. It includes three associated values. The **offset** value indicates the index from which the element was removed, the **element** value is the removed element, and the **associatedWith** value is the index of the element that is associated with this change.

As we will see later, the code that comprises an application is usually divided into separate units that take care of very specific tasks, like storing the user's data and showing it on the screen. This means that sometimes we may have two sets of data that represent the same information and therefore we must keep them synchronized. For instance, we may have data stored in an array that represents the information saved by the user on a file, and another array with a copy of that data that we are using to show the information on the screen. If the data from the file changes, we must update the data that is shown to the user. If that data is stored in ordered collections, such as arrays, we can synchronize them with the `difference()` method, as in the following example.

```
var list1 = [1, 2, 3, 4, 5]
var list2 = [2, 4, 8, 16, 32]

let diff = list1.difference(from: list2)
for change in diff {
   switch change {
   case .insert(let offset, let element, _):
      list2.insert(element, at: offset)
   case .remove(let offset, _, _):
      list2.remove(at: offset)
   }
}
print(list2)   // "[1, 2, 3, 4, 5]"
```

Listing 3-140: Synchronizing arrays

The code of Listing 3-140 defines two arrays: `list1` and `list2`. In this example, we are assuming that `list2` is the array that has to be synchronized with the changes in `list1`, so we determine the current differences by calling the `difference()` method on `list1`. This gives us a collection of `Change` values that tell us which elements of the `list2` array we must remove or add. Next, we create a `for in` loop to iterate over the collection. Because these values are enumeration values with associated values, we must use a `switch` statement to process them. In the case the value is `insert()`, we insert a new element in the `list2` array with the `insert()` method (see Listing 3-81), but if the value is `remove()`, we remove the element with the `remove()` method. Notice that if we are not going to use an associated value, instead of declaring a constant we can just write an underscore.

At the end of this process, the array stored in the `list2` variable will be the same as the one stored in the `list1` variable. Of course, we could have simplified this process by assigning `list1` to `list2`, but knowing exactly which elements change in one array with respect to the other is useful when we need to perform tasks after a change is applied. If we don't need to process the changes one by one but still want to modify the array with the values returned by the `difference()` method, we can call the `applying()` method offered by the `Array` structure to perform all the changes at once.

Chapter 3 - Swift Paradigm

```
var list1 = [1, 2, 3, 4, 5]
var list2 = [2, 4, 8, 16, 32]

let diff = list1.difference(from: list2)
if let newlist = list2.applying(diff) {
   list2 = newlist
}
print(list2)  // "[1, 2, 3, 4, 5]"
```

Listing 3-141: Applying all the changes at once

The **applying()** method returns the array with all the changes applied, or **nil** if it can't apply the difference to the array, so we have to check this value and then assign the result back to **list2**. The result is the same as before, the array in **list2** contains the same values as **list1**, but with the difference that all the changes were performed at once.

(Basic) # 3.5 Objects

Objects are data types that encapsulate data and functionality in the form of properties and methods, but unlike the structures and enumerations introduced before they are stored by reference, which means that more than one variable can refer to the same object. This makes objects suitable for situations where the same piece of data has to be shared by different parts of the code.

(Basic) ## Definition of Objects

Like structures and enumerations, objects are defined first and then instances are created from their definition. The definitions of objects are called *classes*, and what we called objects are the instances created from those classes. Classes are declared the same way as structures or enumerations, but instead of the **struct** or **enum** keywords we must use the **class** keyword.

```
class Employee {
   var name = "Undefined"
   var age = 0
}
```

Listing 3-142: Defining a class

The code of Listing 3-142 defines a simple class called **Employee** with two properties: **name** and **age**. As always, this does not create anything, it is just defining a new custom data type. To store data in memory in this format, we must declare a constant or a variable of this type and assign to it an instance of the class created with an initializer.

```
class Employee {
   var name = "Undefined"
   var age = 0
}
let employee1 = Employee()
employee1.name = "John"
employee1.age = 32
```

Listing 3-143: Creating an object from a class

In Listing 3-143, the **Employee()** initializer creates a new instance of the class **Employee**. Since in this case the words instance and object are synonyms, we can say that we have created a new object called `employee1` containing two properties, `name` and `age`, and then use dot notation to modify their values.

Another way to modify the values of the properties of an object is from its methods. In contrast to structures, the object's methods can modify the properties of their own object without adding anything to the definition (they do not need to be declared as `mutating`).

```
class Employee {
   var name = "Undefined"
   var age = 0
   func changename(newname: String, newage: Int) {
      name = newname
      age = newage
   }
}
let employee1 = Employee()
employee1.changename(newname: "Martin", newage: 32)
print("Name: \(employee1.name)")   // "Name: Martin"
```

Listing 3-144: Modifying properties from the object's methods

In Listing 3-144, the `changename()` method is added to the `Employee` class to modify the values of its properties. After the instance is created, we call this method to assign the values "Martin" and 32 to the `name` and `age` properties, respectively.

 IMPORTANT: As well as structures, we can create all the objects we need from the same definition (class). Each object will have its own properties, values, and methods.

(Basic) Type Properties and Methods

We have studied type properties and methods before with structures. These are properties and methods that are accessible from the data type and not from the instances created from that type. They work in classes the same way as in structures, but instead of the `static` keyword we must use the `class` keyword to define them.

```
class Employee {
   var name = "Undefined"
   var age = 0
   class func description() {
      print("This class stores the name and age of an employee")
   }
}
Employee.description()
```

Listing 3-145: Declaring a type method for a class

The code of Listing 3-145 defines a simple `Employee` class with two properties: `name` and `age`. The type method declared next is just describing the purpose of the class. Every time the `description()` method is executed on the class, a description is printed on the console. Again, we don't have to create an instance because the method is executed on the class itself.

(Basic) Reference Types

The data types we have studied before, including structures and enumerations, are value types. This means that every time we assign a variable of any of these types to another variable, the

Chapter 3 - Swift Paradigm

value is copied. For example, if we create an instance of a structure and then assign that instance to another variable, the instance is copied, and we end up with two instances of the same structure (two copies in memory). Here is an example.

```
struct Employee {
    var name = "Undefined"
}
var employee1 = Employee()
var employee2 = employee1
employee2.name = "George"

print("Employee1 Name: \(employee1.name)")   // "Undefined"
```

Listing 3-146: Creating a copy of an instance

The code of Listing 3-146 defines a simple structure called **Employee** with just one property called **name**. After the definition, a new instance is created with the **Employee()** initializer and assigned to the **employee1** variable. Next, the **employee1** variable is assigned to a new variable called **employee2**. At this moment, the system makes a copy of the structure contained in the **employee1** variable and assigns that copy to **employee2**. Both variables, **employee1** and **employee2**, have a copy of the structure. Therefore, when we assign the value "George" to the property of the instance in the **employee2** variable, the value of the property in **employee1** is still "Undefined". The following figure illustrates this process.

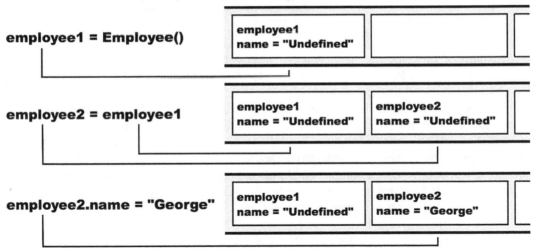

Figure 3-1: Value types stored in memory

Figure 3-1 shows how two different copies of the **Employee** structure, one referenced by the **employee1** variable and the other referenced by the **employee2** variable, are stored in memory. Any modification to the values of one of the instances will not affect the other, because they occupy different spaces in memory.

Objects, on the other hand, are passed by reference. This means that when we assign an existing object to a constant or a variable, a reference to the object is assigned to it, not a copy of the object. Here is the same example, this time applied to objects.

```
class Employee {
    var name = "Undefined"
}
let employee1 = Employee()
```

```
let employee2 = employee1
employee2.name = "George"
print("Employee1 Name: \(employee1.name)")   // "George"
```

Listing 3-147: Creating a new reference to an object

The object in `employee2` is the same as the object in `employee1`. Any change in the `name` property is reflected in the other because both constants point to the same object in memory (they refer to the same instance). Figure 3-2 next illustrates this process.

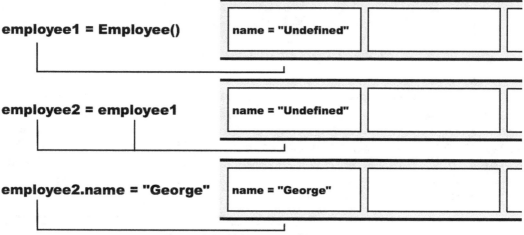

Figure 3-2: Objects stored in memory

Constants or variables that were assigned an object do not store the object; they store the value of the memory address where the object is located. When a constant or variable containing this address is assigned to another constant or variable, only the address is copied, and therefore the object is not duplicated. This is the most important characteristic of objects, and what makes them suitable for situations in which data in memory has to be accessed and shared by different parts of the code. A common example is when we need to define a data type to control the device's screen. The screen is only one, so we shouldn't generate multiple copies of the data that controls it. Instead, we create an object and pass the reference of that object to the rest of the code. Each part of the code accesses the same object and works with the same properties and methods. Every change on its properties is always reflected on the screen.

 IMPORTANT: Because constants and variables store a reference to an object (a memory address), two or more variables in your code may reference the same object. If you need to know whether this is the case, you can compare the variables with the operators `===` (identical to) and `!==` (not identical to) provided by Swift. If what you need is to know whether two objects contain different information, you can use the basic operators `==` and `!=`, but you can only do this when the objects conform to the `Equatable` protocol; a protocol that determines how the objects will be compared. We will study protocols and the `Equatable` protocol later in this chapter.

 The Basics: When you modify the properties of an object, its properties are modified but not its reference. That is why objects are usually stored in constants and only their properties are defined as variables. Unless we plan to replace one object by another later, it is always recommended to store objects in constants.

Chapter 3 - Swift Paradigm

Because the same object may be referenced by multiple constants or variables, every language that works with objects offers a way for the object to reference itself. In Swift this is done automatically, but there are situations in which this reference has to be declared explicitly. For this purpose, Swift defines a special keyword called `self`. We have introduced this keyword earlier in this chapter to be able to read the current value of an enumeration from inside the instance (see Listing 3-137). In structures and objects, the `self` keyword works the same way; it references the instance in which the code is being executed.

The most common situation in which the use of this keyword is required is when we need to declare the names of the parameters of a method equal to the names of the object's properties. If the names are the same, the system doesn't know whether we are referring to the property or the parameter. The `self` keyword clarifies the situation.

```
class Employee {
    var name = "Undefined"

    func changename(name: String) {
        self.name = name
    }
}
let employee1 = Employee()
employee1.changename(name: "Martin")

print("Name: \(employee1.name)")   // "Name: Martin"
```

Listing 3-148: Referring to the object with `self`

The `self` keyword in the `changename()` method of Listing 3-148 represents the object created from the `Employee` class and helps the system understand what we are referring to when we use the word `name`. When we call the `changename()` method in the `employee1` object, the value of the `name` parameter is assigned to the `name` property (`self.name`) of the object. The `self` keyword in this example is a reference to the object stored in the `employee1` variable. This would be the same as declaring `employee1.name`, but since we do not know the name of the variable that is going to store the instance when the class is defined, we must use `self` instead.

Another useful application of the `self` keyword is to reference the data type itself. The value generated by reading the `self` keyword on a data type is called *metatype*. A metatype refers to the type itself, not an instance of it. For example, the value `Int.self` refers to the definition of the `Int` data type, not an integer number created from that type, as shown in the following example.

```
let reference = Int.self
let newnumber = reference.init(20)
print(newnumber)   // "20"
```

Listing 3-149: Referring to the data type with `self`

The code in Listing 3-149 stores a reference to the `Int` data type in a constant and then uses that constant to create an instance of `Int` with the value 20. Notice that when working with metatypes we must declare the `init()` method implicitly to create an instance. Metatypes are widely used to pass references of data types to methods and initializers of other types, as we will see in further chapters.

(Medium) Memory Management

As we explained before, because objects are stored by reference, they can be referenced by several variables at the same time. If a variable is erased, the object it references cannot be erased from memory because another variable could still be using it. This creates a situation in which the device's memory is filled with objects that are no longer necessary. The solution provided by Apple was to create an automatic system that counts the number of variables referencing an object and only removes the object from memory when all the references are erased (all the variables were erased, set to **nil**, or they were assigned a reference to another object). The system is called *ARC* (Automatic Reference Counting) and it was integrated into Objective-C and now Swift. Thanks to ARC, we do not have to worry about the memory; the objects are automatically erased when there is no longer a constant or a variable containing a reference to that space in memory.

In an ideal scenario, this system works like magic, counting how many references we create to the same object and erasing that object when none of those references exist anymore. But there are situations in which we can create something called *Strong Reference Cycle*. This happens when two objects have a property that references the other object.

```
class Employee {
    var name: String?
    var location: Department?
}
class Department {
    var area: String?
    var person: Employee?
}
var employee: Employee? = Employee()
var department: Department? = Department()

employee?.name = "John"
employee?.location = department

department?.area = "Mail"
department?.person = employee
```

Listing 3-150: *Referencing one object from another*

The code of Listing 3-150 defines two classes: **Employee** and **Department**. Both classes contain a property that references an object of the other class (**location** and **person**). After the definition, objects of each class are created and stored in the **employee** and **department** variables. The reference in the **department** variable is assigned to the **location** property of the **employee** object, and the reference in the **employee** variable is assigned to the **person** property of the **department** object. After this, each object contains a reference to the other, as shown in Figure 3-3.

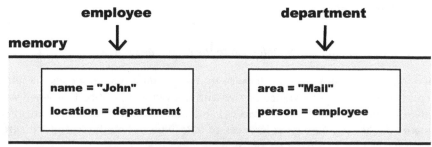

Figure 3-3: *Objects referencing each other*

Chapter 3 - Swift Paradigm

At this point, each object is referenced by a variable and a property. The object of the `Employee` class is referenced by the `employee` variable and the `person` property, and the object of the `Department` class is referenced by the `department` variable and the `location` property. If, for some reason, we do not need to access these objects from our code anymore and erase or modify the values of the `employee` and `department` variables, ARC will not erase the objects from memory because their properties still have a reference that keeps them alive. This is illustrated in Figure 3-4.

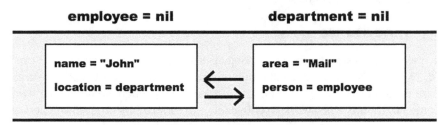

Figure 3-4: *Objects preserved in memory*

In this example, we assume that the value `nil` was assigned to the `employee` and `department` variables, and in consequence the objects are not accessible anymore, but they are preserved in memory because ARC has no way to know that they are no longer required.

Swift has solved this problem classifying the references into three categories: strong, weak, and unowned. Normal references are strong; they are always valid and the objects they point to are preserved in memory for as long as they exist. These are the kind of references we have been using so far, and that is why the cycle created by our example is called Strong Reference Cycle. The solution to break this cycle is to define one of the references as `weak` or `unowned`. When ARC encounters one of these types of references to be the last reference to an object, the object is erased from memory as if the reference had never existed.

```
class Employee {
    var name: String?
    var location: Department?
}
class Department {
    var area: String?
    weak var person: Employee?
}
var employee: Employee? = Employee()
var department: Department? = Department()

employee?.name = "John"
employee?.location = department
department?.area = "Mail"
department?.person = employee
```

Listing 3-151: *Assigning weak references*

In the code of Listing 3-151, the `person` property was declared as `weak`. Now, when the references from the variables are erased, the object created from the `Employee` class is erased from memory because the only reference left is the weak reference from the `person` property. After this object disappears, the object created from the `Department` class does not have any other strong reference either, so it is also erased from memory.

What the weak reference does is to reference an object without affecting ARC's counting. Weak references are not considered by ARC to determine whether an object should be erased or not. The unowned reference works the same way, but it differs with the weak reference on the type of values it applies to. Weak references apply to variables and properties with optional values (they can be empty at some point) and unowned references apply to non-optional values (they always have a value).

 IMPORTANT: Closures can create strong reference cycles if we try to access properties or methods defined outside the closure. If we need to reference properties or methods with `self`, we can declare the reference to `self` as weak with the syntax `[weak self]`. The expression must be declared before the closure's parameters.

Medium **Inheritance**

One of the main purposes of structures and objects is to define pieces of code that can be copied and shared. The code is defined once and then instances (copies) of that code are created every time they are required. This programming pattern works well when we define our own code but presents some limitations when working with code programmed by other developers and shared through libraries and frameworks. The programmers creating the code for us cannot anticipate how we are going to use it and all the possible variations required for every specific app. To provide a solution to this problem, classes incorporate inheritance. A class can inherit properties and methods from another class and then improve it adding some properties and methods of its own. This way, programmers can share classes and developers can adapt them to their needs.

To illustrate how inheritance works, the following examples present a situation in which a class has to be expanded to contain additional information that was not initially contemplated.

```
class Employee {
    var name = "Undefined"
    var age = 0
    func createbadge() -> String {
        return "Employee \(name) \(age)"
    }
}
```

Listing 3-152: Defining a basic class

The **Employee** class declared in Listing 3-152 is a normal class, like those we have defined before. It has two properties and a method called **createbadge()** that returns a string containing the values of those properties. This class would be enough to create objects that generate the string of text necessary to print a badge for every employee showing its name and age. But for the sake of argument, let's say that some of the employees require a badge that also displays the department they work in. One option is to define another class with the same properties and methods and add what we need, but this produces redundant code and it is difficult to do when the class was taken from a library (they are usually too complex to modify or duplicate). The solution is to create a new class that inherits the characteristics of the basic class and adds its own properties and methods to satisfy the new requirements. To indicate that a class inherits from another class, we must write the name of the basic class after the name of the new class separated by a colon.

```
class Employee {
    var name = "Undefined"
    var age = 0
    func createbadge() -> String {
        return "Employee \(name) \(age)"
    }
}
```

Chapter 3 - Swift Paradigm

```
class OfficeEmployee: Employee {
   var department = "Undefined"
}
```

Listing 3-153: Inheriting properties and methods from another class

The `OfficeEmployee` class added to our code in Listing 3-153 only has one property called `department`, but it inherits the **name** and **age** properties, and also the `createbadge()` method from the `Employee` class. All these properties and methods are available in any of the objects created from the `OfficeEmployee` class, as shown next.

```
class Employee {
   var name = "Undefined"
   var age = 0

   func createbadge() -> String {
      return "Employee \(name) \(age)"
   }
}
class OfficeEmployee: Employee {
   var department = "Undefined"
}
let employee = OfficeEmployee()
employee.name = "George"
employee.age = 25
employee.department = "Mail"

var badge = employee.createbadge()
print("Badge: \(badge)")   // "Badge: Employee George 25"
```

Listing 3-154: Creating objects from a subclass

A class like `Employee` is called *superclass*, and a class that inherits from another class like `OfficeEmployee` is called *subclass*. In these terms, we can say that the `OfficeEmployee` class is a subclass that inherits the properties and methods of its superclass `Employee`. A class can inherit from a superclass that already inherited from another superclass in an infinite chain. When a property is accessed, or a method is called, the system looks for it on the object's class and, if it is not there, it keeps looking in the superclasses up the hierarchical chain until it finds it.

 IMPORTANT: Inheritance does not work the other way around. For example, considering the code of Listing 3-154, objects created from the class `OfficeEmployee` have access to the `department` property of this class and the properties and methods of the `Employee` class, but objects created from the `Employee` class do not have access to the `department` property.

Because of this hierarchical chain, sometimes a method does not have access to all the properties available for the object. For example, the `createbadge()` method called on the `employee` object created in Listing 3-154 have access to the properties declared on the `Employee` class but not to those declared in the `OfficeEmployee` class. If we want the method to also print the value of the `department` property, we must implement it again in the `OfficeEmployee` class with the appropriate modifications. This is called *method overriding*. To override a method of a superclass, we prefix it with the **override** keyword.

```
class Employee {
   var name = "Undefined"
   var age = 0
```

```
    func createbadge() -> String {
        return "Employee \(name) \(age)"
    }
}
class OfficeEmployee: Employee {
    var department = "Undefined"

    override func createbadge() -> String {
        return "Employee \(department) \(name) \(age)"
    }
}
let employee = OfficeEmployee()
employee.name = "George"
employee.age = 25
employee.department = "Mail"

var badge = employee.createbadge()
print("Badge: \(badge)")   // "Badge: Employee Mail George 25"
```

Listing 3-155: Overriding an inherited method

The new **OfficeEmployee** subclass of Listing 3-155 overrides the **createbadge()** method of its superclass to generate a string that includes the value of the **department** property. Now, when the method is executed from an object of this class, the method called is the one declared in **OfficeEmployee** (the old method from the superclass is ignored), and the badge generated includes the values of the three properties.

Using inheritance, we have created a new class without modifying previous classes or duplicating any code. The **Employee** class can create objects to store the name and age of an employee and generate a badge with this information, and the **OfficeEmployee** class can create objects to store the name, age, and also the department of the employee and generate a more complete badge with the values of all these properties.

As explained before, when we call the **createbadge()** method on the **employee** object created from the **OfficeEmployee** class in Listing 3-155, the method executed is the one defined in the **OfficeEmployee** class. If we want to execute the method on the superclass instead, we must use a special keyword called **super**. The **super** keyword is like the **self** keyword, but instead of referring to the object, **super** refers to the superclass. It is often used when we have overridden a method, but we still need to execute the method of the superclass. Here is an example.

```
class Employee {
    var name = "Undefined"
    var age = 0
    func createbadge() -> String {
        return "Employee \(name) \(age)"
    }
}
class OfficeEmployee: Employee {
    var department = "Undefined"

    override func createbadge() -> String {
        let oldbadge = super.createbadge()
        return "\(oldbadge) \(department)"
    }
}
let employee = OfficeEmployee()
employee.name = "George"
employee.age = 25
employee.department = "Mail"
```

```
var badge = employee.createbadge()
print("Badge: \(badge)")    // "Badge: Employee George 25 Mail"
```

Listing 3-156: Calling a method on the superclass

This is the same as the previous example, but now, when the `createbadge()` method of an object created from the `OfficeEmployee` class is called, the method calls the `createbadge()` method of the superclass first and assigns the result to the `oldbadge` constant. The value of this constant is later added to the value of the `department` property to generate the final string.

(Medium) Type Casting

Inheritance not only transfers functionality from one class to another but also connects the classes together. The superclasses and their subclasses are linked together in a hierarchical chain. Because of this, whenever we declare a variable of the type of the superclass, objects of the subclasses can be assigned to that variable too. This is a feature that allows us to do things like creating arrays of objects that are of different classes but belong to the same hierarchy.

```
class Employee {
    var name = "Undefined"
    var age = 0
}
class OfficeEmployee: Employee {
    var deskNumber = 0
}
class WarehouseEmployee: Employee {
    var area = "Undefined"
}
var list: [Employee] = [OfficeEmployee(), WarehouseEmployee(),
OfficeEmployee()]
```

Listing 3-157: Creating an array of objects from different subclasses

The code of Listing 3-157 defines a superclass called `Employee` and then two subclasses of `Employee` called `OfficeEmployee` and `WarehouseEmployee`. The purpose is to have the common information for every employee in one class and then have classes for specific types of employee. Following this organization, we can create objects that only contain the `name`, `age`, and `deskNumber` properties to represent employees working at the office and objects that only contain the `name`, `age`, and `area` properties to represent employees working at the warehouse.

No matter the differences between one object and another, they all represent employees of the same company, so sooner or later we will have to include them on the same list. The class hierarchy allows us to do that. We can declare a collection, such as an array, of the data type of the superclass and then store objects of the subclasses in it. In Listing 3-157, we did exactly that with the `list` array.

This is all good until we try to read the array. The elements of the array are all considered to be of type `Employee`, so we can only access the properties defined in the `Employee` class. Also, there is no way to know what type of object each element is. We could have an `OfficeEmployee` object at index 0 and later replace it by a `WarehouseEmployee` object. The indexes and the array itself do not provide any information that allow us to identify the objects. Swift solves both problems with the `is` and `as` operators.

is—This operator returns a Boolean indicating whether the value is of a certain data type.

as—This operator converts a value of one class to another class when possible.

Identifying an object is easy with the **is** operator. This operator returns a Boolean value that we can use in an **if** statement to check the object's class.

```
var countOffice = 0
var countWarehouse = 0

for obj in list {
   if obj is OfficeEmployee {
      countOffice += 1
   } else if obj is WarehouseEmployee {
      countWarehouse += 1
   }
}
print("We have \(countOffice) employees working at the office")   //2
print("We have \(countWarehouse) employees working at the warehouse") //1
```

Listing 3-158: Identifying the object's data type

In Listing 3-158, we create the **list** array again with objects from the same classes defined in the previous example, but this time we add a **for in** loop to iterate over the array and count how many objects of each class we have found. The **if** statement inside the loop uses the **is** operator to check if the current object stored in the **obj** constant is of type **OfficeEmployee** or **WarehouseEmployee** and increments the counter respectively (**countOffice** or **countWarehouse**). At the end, the values of the counters are printed on the screen to show how many objects of each class are in the array.

 Do It Yourself: The example of Listing 3-158 and the following examples, omit the definitions of the structures and the **list** array introduced in Listing 3-157. If you want to test these examples, you must include those definitions in your code.

Counting objects is not really what these operators are all about. The idea is to figure out the type with the **is** operator and then convert the object with the **as** operator to be able to access their properties and methods. The **as** operator converts a value of one type to another. The conversions are not always guaranteed, and that is why this operator comes in two more forms: **as!** and **as?**. These versions of the **as** operator work similarly to optionals. The **as!** operator forces the conversion and returns an error if the conversion is not possible, and the **as?** operator tries to convert the object and returns an optional with the new object or **nil** in case of failure.

```
for obj in list {
   if obj is OfficeEmployee {
      let temp = obj as! OfficeEmployee
      temp.deskNumber = 100
   } else if obj is WarehouseEmployee {
      let temp = obj as! WarehouseEmployee
      temp.area = "New Area"
   }
}
```

Listing 3-159: Casting an object

When we use the **as!** operator we are forcing the conversion, so we need to make sure that the conversion is possible or otherwise the app will crash (this is the same that happens when we unwrap optionals with the exclamation mark). In the code of Listing 3-159, we only use this operator after we have already checked with the **is** operator that the object is of the right class. Once the object is casted (converted) into its real type, we can access its properties and

Chapter 3 - Swift Paradigm

methods. In this example, the objects returned by the `as!` operator are stored in the `temp` constant and then new values are assigned to the `deskNumber` and `area` properties, respectively.

Checking for the type before converting is a little bit redundant. To simplify this code, we can use the `as?` operator. Instead of forcing the conversion and crashing our app in case of failure, this version of the `as` operator tries to perform the conversion and returns an optional with the result of the operation.

```
for obj in list {
    if let temp = obj as? OfficeEmployee {
        temp.deskNumber = 100
    } else if let temp = obj as? WarehouseEmployee {
        temp.area = "New Area"
    }
}
```

Listing 3-160: Casting an object with the `as?` operator

In this example, we use optional binding to cast the object and assign the result to the `temp` constant. First, we try to cast `obj` as an `OfficeEmployee` object. If we are successful, we assign the value 100 to the `deskNumber` property, but if the value returned is `nil`, then we try to cast the object to the `WarehouseEmployee` class to modify its `area` property.

Casting can also be performed on the fly if we are sure that the conversion is possible. The statement to cast the object is the same but it must be declared between parentheses.

```
let myarea = (list[1] as! WarehouseEmployee).area
print("The area of employee 1 is \(myarea)")   // "Undefined"
```

Listing 3-161: Casting an object on the fly

In this example, we do not assign the object to any variable; we just cast the element of the `list` array at index 1 as a `WarehouseEmployee` object inside the parentheses and then access its `area` property. The value of this property is stored in the `myarea` constant and then printed on the console. Remember that conversions performed with the `as!` operator are only possible when we are sure it is going to be successful.

 IMPORTANT: The `as!` operator is applied when the conversion is guaranteed to be successful, and the `as?` operator is used when we are not sure about the result. But we can also use the basic `as` operator when the Swift compiler can verify that the conversion will be successful. There are two circumstances when this is possible: when we are converting an object of a subclass into its superclass and when we are casting some primitive data types (e.g.: `String` values into `NSString` objects).

The `as` operator works on objects that belong to the same class hierarchy. Because sometimes the objects that require casting are not in the same hierarchy, Swift defines several generic data types to represent values of any kind. The most frequently used is `AnyObject`, which was defined to represent objects of any type. Taking advantage of this generic type, we can create collections with values that are not associated with each other.

```
class Employee {
    var name = "Undefined"
}
```

```
class Department {
    var area = "Undefined"
}
var list: [AnyObject] = [Employee(), Department(), Department()]

for obj in list {
    if let temp = obj as? Employee {
        temp.name = ""
    } else if let temp = obj as? Department {
        temp.area = ""
    }
}
```

Listing 3-162: Working with objects of AnyObject *type*

The **list** array declared in Listing 3-162 is of type **AnyObject** and therefore it can contain objects of any type (any class). To populate the array, we created two simple and independent classes: **Employee** and **Department**. A few objects are created from these classes and included in the array. The objects are later casted by the **as?** operator inside a **for in** loop and their corresponding properties are modified following the same procedure used in previous examples.

 IMPORTANT: The **AnyObject** type represents any object, but there is also a type available called **AnyClass** that can be used to represent any class. This is a protocol to which all classes conform, so we can use it to represent any class we want.

(Basic) Initialization

We have been initializing the properties during definition in every class declared so far. This is because classes do not provide memberwise initializers as structures do. The properties of a class have to be initialized explicitly in the definition or during instantiation by the **init()** method. This is the same method previously introduced for structures and we can use it in our classes to create our own initializers.

```
class Employee {
    var name: String
    var age: Int

    init(name: String, age: Int) {
        self.name = name
        self.age = age
    }
}
let employee1 = Employee(name: "George", age: 28)
```

Listing 3-163: Declaring a Designated Initializer

The **init()** method declared for the **Employee** class in Listing 3-163 initializes every property of the class with the values specified in the **Employee()** initializer. This type of initializer is called *Designated Initializer*. When we declare a Designated Initializer, we need to make sure that all the properties are initialized. If we know that in some circumstances our code will not be able to provide all the values during initialization, we can also declare a Convenience Initializer. A Convenience Initializer is an initializer that offers a convenient way to initialize an object with default values for some or all its properties. It is declared as an **init()** method but preceded with the **convenience** keyword. A Convenience Initializer must call the Designated initializer of the same class with the corresponding values.

```
class Employee {
   var name: String
   var age: Int

   init(name: String, age: Int) {
      self.name = name
      self.age = age
   }
   convenience init() {
      self.init(name: "Undefined", age: 0)
   }
}
let employee1 = Employee()
```

Listing 3-164: Declaring a Convenience Initializer

When we create an instance of **Employee**, the system detects the number and type of attributes provided and executes the corresponding initializer. For example, if we provide the values for the **name** and the **age** parameters in the code of Listing 3-164, the system executes the Designated Initializer because this is the initializer that contains the necessary parameters to receive those values, but if the initialization does not include any attribute, as in this example, the Convenience Initializer is executed instead and then the Designated Initializer is called with values by default ("Undefined" for the **name** parameter and 0 for the **age** parameter).

This process is similar to what we have done with structures. The difference is inheritance. Classes can inherit properties and methods from other classes, and this includes the **init()** method. When a subclass does not provide its own Designated Initializer, the initializer of its superclass is executed.

```
class Employee {
   var name: String
   var age: Int

   init(name: String, age: Int) {
      self.name = name
      self.age = age
   }
}
class OfficeEmployee: Employee {
   var department: String = "Undefined"
}
let employee1 = OfficeEmployee(name: "George", age: 29)
```

Listing 3-165: Inheriting the Designated Initializer

The code of Listing 3-165 defines the subclass **OfficeEmployee** that inherits from the **Employee** class. The **OfficeEmployee** class does not provide any initializer, so the only initializer available is the one provided by its superclass. This initializer only initializes the properties **name** and **age** of the superclass. The **department** property of **OfficeEmployee** is explicitly initialized with the value "Undefined" (every object created from this class has this value by default). To provide an initializer that also includes this property, we must declare a new Designated Initializer in the **OfficeEmployee** class.

```
class Employee {
   var name: String
   var age: Int
```

```
    init(name: String, age: Int) {
        self.name = name
        self.age = age
    }
}
class OfficeEmployee: Employee {
    var department: String
    init(name: String, age: Int, department: String) {
        self.department = department
        super.init(name: name, age: age)
    }
}
let employee1 = OfficeEmployee(name: "John", age: 24, department: "Mail")
```

Listing 3-166: Declaring a Designated Initializer for the subclass

The Designated Initializer of a subclass must initialize the properties of its own class first and then call the initializer of its superclass. This is done by calling the `init()` method on **super**. The **super** keyword refers to the superclass, so when the system executes the **super.init()** statement in the code of Listing 3-166, the `init()` method of the superclass is executed and the **name** and **age** properties of this class are initialized.

 IMPORTANT: If you need to declare the same initializer of the superclass in the subclass, you have to overwrite the initializer in the subclass with the **override** keyword, as in **override init()**, and call the initializer of the superclass with **super** (**super.init()**).

 The Basics: There are different ways to combine Designated and Convenience initializers. The possibility of classes to inherit from other classes in an unlimited chain can turn initialization into a very complex process. This book does not explore all the possibilities provided by Swift for initialization. For more information, visit our website and follow the links for this chapter.

(Advanced) **Deinitialization**

There is a counterpart of the initialization process called *Deinitialization*. Despite its name, this process is not directly related to the initialization process but rather to the ARC system. ARC, as we studied previously in this chapter, is an automatic system adopted by Swift to manage memory. Letting the system manage the memory and take care of removing the objects our program does no longer need presents a huge advantage, but it also means that we do not always know when an object is going to be removed. There are times when an object is using resources that must be closed, information that has to be stored, or we just have to report to other objects that the object is not available anymore. Whatever the task, Swift offers the **deinit** method to execute any last-minute instructions we need before the object is erased from memory.

```
class Item {
    var quantity = 0.0
    var name = "Not defined"
    var price = 0.0

    deinit {
        print("This instance was erased")
    }
}
```

```
var purchase: Item? = Item()
purchase = nil
```

Listing 3-167: Declaring a deinitializer

The code of Listing 3-167 defines a simple class with a deinitializer. The object is created and assigned to an optional variable. Right after that, the **nil** value is assigned to the same variable to erase the reference and test the **deinit** method, which prints a message on the console.

(Advanced) ## Access Control and Modifiers

Swift defines keywords (also called *modifiers*) that can be applied to entities (classes, structures, properties, methods, etc.) to confer them special attributes. We have already seen the **override** keyword required to overwrite methods of a superclass, but there are more available.

lazy—This keyword defines a property whose initial value is not assigned until the property is used for the first time.

final—This keyword is used on a class when we don't want to allow the code to create subclasses of it. It must be declared before the **class** keyword.

The **lazy** keyword is frequently used when the property's value may take time to be determined and we do not want the initialization of the structure or the class to be delayed. For example, we may have a property that stores the name of an employee retrieved from a server. This is a resource intensive task that we should perform when the value is required and not every time an object is created from this class.

```
class Employee {
    lazy var name: String = {
        // Loading name from a server
        print("Loading...")

        return "Undefined"
    }()
    var age = 0
}
let employee = Employee()
```

Listing 3-168: Defining `lazy` *properties*

The **Employee** class of Listing 3-168 defines two properties, **name** and **age**, but this time a closure is assigned to the **name** property to get the employee's name from a server (we will see how to retrieve information from the web in Chapter 16). Because we declared that property as **lazy**, the closure will only be executed when we try to read the property's value. If we execute the example as it is, we get nothing in return, but if we read the **name** property with a statement at the end, we will see the text "Loading..." printed on the console, which shows that the closure assigned to the property was executed to generate the property's value.

 Do It Yourself: Replace the code in your Playground file with the code of Listing 3-168 and press the play button to run it. You shouldn't see anything on the console. Now add the statement **print(employee.name)** at the end of the code and run it again. You should see the text "Loading..." printed by the closure followed by the text "Undefined" printed by the statement.

The Swift language also includes keywords in charge of defining the level of access for each entity in our code. Access control in Swift is based on modules and source files, but it also applies to single properties and methods. Source files are the files we create for our application, the properties and methods are the ones we have created for our structures and classes in previous examples, and modules are units of code that work together. For instance, a single application and each of the frameworks included in it are considered modules (we will introduce frameworks in Chapter 4). Considering this classification, Swift defines a total of five keywords to determine accessibility.

open—This keyword determines that an entity is accessible from the module it belongs to and other modules.

public—This keyword determines that an entity is accessible from the module it belongs to and other modules. The difference between `public` and `open` is that we can't create subclasses of `public` classes outside the module in which they were defined. This also applies to methods and properties (e.g., `public` methods can't be overridden outside the module in which they were declared).

internal—This keyword determines that an entity is accessible only inside the module in which it was created. This is the default access mode for applications. By default, every entity defined in our application is only accessible from inside the application.

private—This keyword determines that an entity is accessible only from the context in which it was created (e.g., a `private` property in a class will only be accessible from methods of the same class).

fileprivate—This keyword determines that an entity is accessible only from the file in which it was declared (e.g., a `fileprivate` property in a class will only be accessible by other entities defined inside the file in which it was declared).

As we will see later, most of these keywords apply to frameworks and are rarely used in single applications. By default, the properties and methods we include in our classes and structures are declared `internal`, which means that our classes and structures are only available from inside our application (module). Unless we are creating our own frameworks, this is all we need for our applications, and is the reason why we didn't have to specify any keyword when we defined our structures and classes before. All our classes and structures are accessible by the rest of the code inside our application, but if we want to have a level of control in our data types or avoid modifying values by mistake, we can declare some of them as `private`, as in the following example.

```
class Employee {
    private var name = "Undefined"
    private var age = 0

    func showValues() {
        print("Name: \(name)")
        print("Age: \(age)")
    }
}
let employee = Employee()
employee.showValues()
```

Listing 3-169: *Declaring* `private` *properties*

The code of Listing 3-169 defines the **name** and **age** properties of our **Employee** class as **private** and adds a method called **showValues()** to access their values. Due to access control,

Chapter 3 - Swift Paradigm

these properties are only accessible through the method in the class. If we try to read their values from outside the object using dot notation, Xcode will return an error (`employee.name`).

(Basic) 3.6 Protocols

The two main characteristics of classes, and therefore objects, are the capacity to encapsulate data and functionality and the possibility to share and improve code through inheritance. This introduced a huge advantage over previous paradigms and turned Object-Oriented Programming into the industry standard for a while. But that changed with the introduction of protocols in Swift. Protocols define properties and methods that structures can have in common. This means that Swift's structures not only can encapsulate data and functionality, just like objects, but by conforming to protocols they can also share code. Figure 3-5 illustrates the differences between these two paradigms.

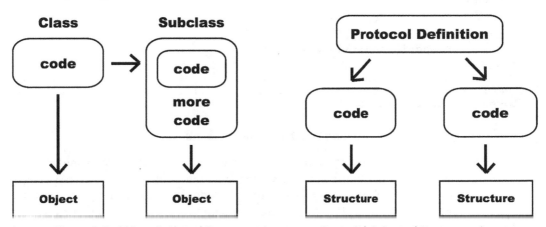

Figure 3-5: Object-Oriented Programming versus Protocol-Oriented Programming

In OOP, the code is implemented inside a class and then objects are created from that class. If we need to create objects with additional functionality, we must define a subclass that inherits the code from the superclass and adds some of its own. Protocols offer a slightly different approach. The properties and methods we want the structures to have in common are defined in the protocol and then implemented by the structures' definitions. This lets us associate different structures together through a common pattern. The code implemented by each structure is unique, but they follow a blueprint set by the protocol. If we know that a structure uses a protocol, we can always be sure that besides its own definitions, it will also include the properties and methods defined by the protocol. In addition, protocols can be extended to provide their own implementations of the properties and methods we want the structures to have in common, allowing the paradigm to completely replace classes and objects.

 IMPORTANT: The Swift paradigm is built from the combination of structures and protocols, but protocols may also be adopted by enumerations and classes. For instance, Objective-C and the frameworks programmed in this language use protocols to offer a programming pattern called *Delegation*. We will study how to conform to protocols from classes and how to implement delegation later in this chapter.

(Basic) Definition of Protocols

Protocols are defined with the `protocol` keyword followed by the name and the list of properties and methods between braces. No values or statements are assigned or declared inside a protocol, only the names and the corresponding types; the structure that conforms to the protocol takes care of the implementation. Because of this, methods are defined as always, but they omit the braces and the statements, and properties have to include the **get** and **set** keywords between braces to indicate whether they are read-only properties, or we can read and also assign values to them (see Listing 3-42 for an example of getters and setters). To indicate that the structure conforms to the protocol, we must include the protocol's name after the structure's name separated by a colon, as shown in the following example.

```
protocol Printer {
    var name: String { get set }
    func printdescription()
}
struct Employees: Printer {
    var name: String
    var age: Int

    func printdescription() {
        print("Description: \(name) \(age)")   // "Description: John 32"
    }
}
let employee1 = Employees(name: "John", age: 32)
employee1.printdescription()
```

Listing 3-170: Defining protocols

The protocol is only a blueprint; it tells the structure what properties and methods are required, but the structure has to provide its own implementations. In the example of Listing 3-170, we define a protocol called **Printer** that includes the **name** property and the **printdescription()** method. The **Employees** structure defined next conforms to this protocol, and along with the protocol's property and method it also implements its own property called **age**. Although this property was not defined in the protocol, we can read it inside the **printdescription()** method and print its value.

The advantage of this practice is evident when structures of different types conform to the same protocol, as shown in the following example.

```
protocol Printer {
    var name: String { get set }
    func printdescription()
}
struct Employees: Printer {
    var name: String
    var age: Int

    func printdescription() {
        print("Description: \(name) \(age)")
    }
}
struct Offices: Printer {
    var name: String
    var employees: Int

    func printdescription() {
        print("Description: \(name) \(employees)") // "Description: Mail 2"
    }
}
let employee1 = Employees(name: "John", age: 32)
```

```
let office1 = Offices(name: "Mail", employees: 2)
office1.printdescription()
```

Listing 3-171: Defining multiple structures that conform to the same protocol

Although the structures created in Listing 3-171 from the **Employees** and **Offices** definitions are different (they have different properties), they both conform to the **Printer** protocol and provide their own implementation of the **printdescription()** method. The common functionality defined by the protocol ensures that no matter what type of structure we are working with, it will always have an implementation of **printdescription()**.

Protocols not only act as blueprints, they are also considered to be data types. We can treat a structure as if it is of the data type of the protocol it conforms to. This lets us associate structures by their common functionality.

```
let employee1 = Employees(name: "John", age: 32)
let office1 = Offices(name: "Mail", employees: 2)

var list: [Printer] = [employee1, office1]
for element in list {
   element.printdescription()
}
```

Listing 3-172: Using protocols as data types

Listing 3-172 uses the same protocol and structures defined in the previous example, but this time it stores the instances in an array. The type of the array was defined as **Printer**, which means the array may contain structures of any type as long as they conform to the **Printer** protocol. Because of this, no matter the element's data type (**Employees** or **Offices**) we know that they always have an implementation of the **name** property and the **printdescription()** method.

When we process a structure or an object as a protocol type, we can only access the properties and methods defined by the protocol. If we need to access the instance's own properties and methods, we must cast it using the **as** operator introduced before. The following example prints the value of the **age** property if the element of the array is of type **Employees**.

```
let employee1 = Employees(name: "John", age: 32)
let office1 = Offices(name: "Mail", employees: 2)

var list: [Printer] = [employee1, office1]
for element in list {
   if let employee = element as? Employees {
      print(employee.age)   // "32"
   }
   element.printdescription()
}
```

Listing 3-173: Accessing the instance's own properties

Because protocols are data types, we can use them as any other type, define variables, send and receive them from functions, etc. The following example declares a function that returns a value of type **Printer**.

```
func getFile(type: Int) -> Printer {
   var data: Printer!
   if type == 1 {
      data = Employees(name: "John", age: 32)
```

```
    } else if type == 2 {
        data = Offices(name: "Mail", employees: 2)
    }
    return data
}
let file = getFile(type: 1)
file.printdescription()   // "Description: John 32"
```

Listing 3-174: Returning values of a protocol data type

The **getFile()** function of Listing 3-174 creates an instance of a structure depending on the value received. If the **type** parameter is equal to 1, it returns an instance of **Employees**, but if the value is equal to 2, it returns an instance of **Offices**. But because the value returned by the function is of type **Printer** we know it will always include the **printdescription()** method.

 Do It Yourself: The last three examples use the protocol and structures defined in Listing 3-171. Copy the definitions of Listing 3-171 in your Playground file and add the code of the example you want to try.

(Advanced) Generic Protocols

Protocols can also define generic properties and methods, but they work slightly different than the generic types studied before. When we want to define a protocol with a generic property or method, we first must define the name of the generic type with the **associatedtype** keyword, as in the following example.

```
protocol Printer {
    associatedtype protype
    var name: protype { get set }
}
struct Employees: Printer {
    var name: String
}
let employee = Employees(name: "John")
print(employee.name)   // "John"
```

Listing 3-175: Defining generic protocols

The code of Listing 3-175 defines a generic protocol called **Printer** and a simple structure that conforms to that protocol called **Employees**. The protocol defines a generic type with the name **protype** and then a property of that type. The property's real data type is defined by the structure or the class that conforms to the protocol. In this case, the **Employees** structure defines the **name** property to be of type **String**, and that's the type of values we can use in the instances of this structure, but we could have declared the property as an integer or any other data type we needed.

(Medium) Swift Protocols

The Swift language makes use of protocols extensively. Almost every API includes protocols that define common features and behavior for their data types, including enumerations, structures and classes. But there are also important protocols defined in the Swift Standard Library that we can use to improve our custom data types. The following are some of the protocols provided by Swift to define basic behavior.

Chapter 3 - Swift Paradigm

Equatable—This protocol defines a data type which values can be compared with other values of the same type using the operators `==` and `!=`.

Comparable—This protocol defines a data type which values can be compared with other values of the same type using the operators `>`, `<`, `>=`, and `<=`.

Numeric—This protocol defines a data type that only works with values that can participate in arithmetic operations.

Hashable—This protocol defines a data type that provides the hash value required for the value to be included in sets and as index of dictionaries.

CaseIterable—This protocol defines a data type, usually an enumeration without associated values, that includes a property called `allCases` that contains the collection of all the cases included in the type.

These protocols are responsible of elemental processes performed by the system and the Swift language. For example, when we compare two values with the `==` or `!=` operators, the system checks whether the values conform to the `Equatable` protocol and then calls a type method in the values' data types to compare them and solve the condition (true or false, depending on whether the values are equal or not). Because these operations are common, by default, Swift primitive data types conform to the `Equatable` protocol and implement its methods, but we can also implement them in our own data types to compare their values. For this purpose, we must declare that the data type conforms to the protocol and implement the methods required by it. The `Equatable` protocol requires only one method called `==` to check for equality (the system infers that if two values are not equal, they are different, and therefore the method for the != operator is optional). This method must have a name equal to the operator (`==`), receive the two values to compare, and return a Boolean value to communicate the result of the comparison. For instance, we can make our `Employees` structure conform to the `Equatable` protocol and implement a method with the name `==` to be able to compare two different instances of the same structure.

```
struct Employees: Equatable {
   var name: String
   var age: Int

   static func == (value1: Employees, value2: Employees) -> Bool {
      return value1.age == value2.age
   }
}
let employee1 = Employees(name: "John", age: 32)
let employee2 = Employees(name: "George", age: 32)

let message = employee1 == employee2 ? "Equal" : "Different"
print(message)   // "Equal"
```

Listing 3-176: Conforming to the `Equatable` *protocol*

In this example, we use the `==` method to compare the values of the `age` properties and therefore the structures are going to be equal when the employees are the same age. In this case, both instances are created with the value 32 and therefore the value "Equal" is assigned to the `message` constant when we compare the objects with the ternary operator.

If what we want is to compare each of the properties in the structure, then we can omit the method. When we conform to the `Equatable` protocol, the compiler automatically generates the method for us to compare all the values of the structure (in this case, `name` and `age`).

```
struct Employees: Equatable {
   var name: String
   var age: Int
}
let employee1 = Employees(name: "John", age: 32)
let employee2 = Employees(name: "George", age: 32)
let message = employee1 == employee2 ? "Equal" : "Different"
print(message)  // "Different"
```

Listing 3-177: Letting the compiler create the protocol methods for us

Because we did not declare the `==` method in the example of Listing 3-177, the system creates the method for us and compares the values of both properties. As a result, the objects are considered different (the ages are the same, but the names are different).

Of course, we could have compared the properties directly (`employee1.name == employee2.name`) but being able to compare the objects instead simplifies the code and allow us to use our structures (or objects) in APIs that require the values to be comparable. For example, when we created a generic function earlier in this chapter, we could not perform any operations on the values received by the function (see Listing 3-15). Because the data type we used in those functions is generic, Swift is incapable of knowing the capabilities of the data type and therefore Xcode returns an error if we try to perform operations on the values, but we can easily change the situation by making the generic type conform to a protocol. This feature is called *type constraint* because it constrains the generic type to a data type with certain capabilities. For instance, the function in the following example receives two generic values, but only of a data type that conforms to the `Equatable` protocol, and therefore we can compare the values inside the function.

```
struct Employees: Equatable {
   var name: String
   var age: Int
}
func compareValues<T: Equatable>(value1: T, value2: T) -> String {
   let message = value1 == value2 ? "equal" : "different"
   return message
}
let employee1 = Employees(name: "George", age: 55)
let employee2 = Employees(name: "Robert", age: 55)

let result = compareValues(value1: employee1, value2: employee2)
print("The values are \(result)")  // "The values are different"
```

Listing 3-178: Adding a type constraint to a generic function

The conformance to the protocol is specified inside the angle brackets after the name of the generic type. The `compareValues()` function of Listing 3-178 declares the `T` type to conform to `Equatable` and then compares the values with a ternary operator and returns the result. In this case, the ages of the employees are the same (55), but the names are different ("George" and "Robert"), and therefore the system considers the structures to be different.

Another protocol used as a type constraint is `Numeric`. This protocol determines that the data types of the values received by the function must support arithmetic operations.

```
func calculateResult<T: Numeric>(value1: T, value2: T) {
   print(value1 + value2)  // 7.5
}
```

Chapter 3 - Swift Paradigm

```
calculateResult(value1: 3.5, value2: 4)
```

Listing 3-179: Using the `Numeric` *protocol to set a type constraint*

The `calculateResult()` function of Listing 3-179 is a generic function and therefore it can receive any value of any type, but because we set a type constraint with the **Numeric** protocol, the function can only receive values of data types that can participate in arithmetic operations.

Besides comparing for equality with the **Equatable** protocol, we can also compare magnitudes with the **Comparable** protocol. This protocol is similar to **Equatable**, but the system does not offer a default implementation of the type methods, we have to implement them ourselves. The protocol requires four methods to represent the operations >, <, >= and <=. In the following example, we compare the ages of the employees.

```
struct Employees: Comparable {
   var name: String
   var age: Int
   static func > (value1: Employees, value2: Employees) -> Bool {
      return value1.age > value2.age
   }
   static func < (value1: Employees, value2: Employees) -> Bool {
      return value1.age < value2.age
   }
   static func >= (value1: Employees, value2: Employees) -> Bool {
      return value1.age >= value2.age
   }
   static func <= (value1: Employees, value2: Employees) -> Bool {
      return value1.age <= value2.age
   }
}
let employee1 = Employees(name. "George", age: 32)
let employee2 = Employees(name: "Robert", age: 55)

if employee1 > employee2 {
   print("\(employee1.name) is older")
} else {
   print("\(employee2.name) is older")   // "Robert is older"
}
```

Listing 3-180: Conforming to the `Comparable` *protocol*

This protocol works in a similar way than the **Equatable** protocol. When we compare two instances of the **Employees** structure, the system calls the corresponding type method and the method returns **true** or **false** according to the values of the **age** properties of each instance. Because in this example the value of **age** in the **employee1** structure is not greater than the value of **age** in the **employee2** structure, we get the message "Robert is older".

Another useful protocol is **Hashable**. Every time we include a structure or an object in a set or use them as the index of a dictionary, the system requires the data type to provide a hash value that can be used to uniquely identify each item. This is a random integer that is created based on the values of the properties. The function of the **Hashable** protocol is to define properties and methods to handle this value. Most of the data types defined by Swift conform to this protocol and that is why we do not have any problems when including these values in a set or as the index of dictionaries, but for custom structures and objects we have to provide the hash value ourselves. Fortunately, as well as with the **Equatable** protocol, if we do not need a specific property to be used to create the hash value, we just have to conform to the protocol and the system creates the value for us. The following example makes the **Employees** structure conform to the **Hashable** protocol, so we can include the instances in a set.

```
struct Employees: Hashable {
   var name: String
   var age: Int
}
let employee1 = Employees(name: "John", age: 32)
let employee2 = Employees(name: "Robert", age: 55)
let list: Set<Employees> = [employee1, employee2]

for item in list {
   print(item.name)
}
```

Listing 3-181: Conforming to the `Hashable` *protocol*

Hash values are random integers but are created based on the values of the properties. If we just conform to the protocol, the system used the values of all the properties in the instance to create it, but we can declare a specific property to be included by implementing a method defined by the protocol. The protocol defines a method to set the value and a property to read it.

hashValue—This property returns the instance's hash value. It is of type `Int`.

hash(into: inout Hasher)—This method defines the properties that are going to be included in the hasher to create the hash value.

To calculate the hash value, the Swift Standard Library includes a structure called **Hasher**. This is the structure received by the **hash(into:)** method and it contains a method called **combine()** to tell to the hasher which properties should be fed to the hasher to create the value. The following example illustrates how to implement the **hash(into:)** method and call the **combine()** method on the hasher to create a hash value from the **name** property.

```
struct Employees: Hashable {
   var name: String
   var age: Int

   func hash(into hasher: inout Hasher) {
      hasher.combine(name)
   }
}
let employee = Employees(name: "George", age: 32)
print(employee.hashValue)   // e.g., 7722685913545470055
```

Listing 3-182: Defining our own hash value

At the end of the code of Listing 3-182, we print the value of the **hashValue** property. Because the resulting value is always an integer that is calculated randomly every time the app is executed, we won't notice any difference from when both properties were used to create it, but this procedure may be useful for applications that manage sensitive information.

The last protocol mentioned above is called **CaseIterable**. This is a simple protocol that defines a property called **allCases** to store a collection with all the cases in an enumeration. Again, the system automatically initializes this property, so all we have to do is to declare that the enumeration conforms to the protocol. In the following example, we define an enumeration with three cases and then iterate through the collection in the **allCases** property to print their names.

```
enum Departments: CaseIterable {
    case mail
    case marketing
    case managing
}
var message = ""
for department in Departments.allCases {
    message += "\(department) "
}
print(message)   // "mail marketing managing "
```

Listing 3-183: Conforming to the `CaseIterable` *protocol*

(Medium) **Extensions**

Protocols only define the properties and methods that the data types will have in common, but they do not include any implementation. However, we can implement properties and methods that will be common to all the data types that conform to the protocol by taking advantage of a feature of the Swift language called *extensions*. Extensions are special declarations that add functionality to an existent data type. We can use them with structures, enumerations, and classes, but they are particularly useful with protocols because this is the way protocols can provide their own functionality. The syntax includes the **extension** keyword followed by the name of the data type we want to extend. The following example recreates the **Printer** protocol we used in previous examples and extends it with a method called **printdescription()**.

```
protocol Printer {
    var name: String { get set }
}
extension Printer {
    func printdescription() {
        print("The name is \(name)")
    }
}
struct Employees: Printer {
    var name: String
    var age: Int
}
struct Offices: Printer {
    var name: String
    var employees: Int
}
let employee = Employees(name: "John", age: 45)
let office = Offices(name: "Mail", employees: 2)

employee.printdescription()   // "The name is John"
office.printdescription()   // "The name is Mail"
```

Listing 3-184: Extending the protocol

In the example of Listing 3-184, we define a **Printer** protocol with just the **name** property and then extend it to include a common implementation of the **printdescription()** method. Now, the **Employees** and **Offices** structures in our example share the same implementation and produce the same result when their **printdescription()** methods are executed.

As we already mentioned, extensions are not only available for protocols but also for any other data type. We can use them to extend structures, enumerations, or classes. This is particularly useful when we do not have access to the definitions of the data types and need to add some functionality (like when they are part of a library or framework). In the following example, we extend the **Int** structure to provide a method that prints a description of its value.

```
extension Int {
    func printdescription() {
        print("The number is \(self)")
    }
}
let number = 25
number.printdescription()   // "The number is 25"
```

Listing 3-185: Extending other data types

The **Int** type is a structure defined in the Swift Standard Library. We cannot modify its definition, but we can extend it to add more functionality. In this last example, we add a method called **printdescription()** to print a message with the current value (notice the use of the **self** keyword to refer to the instance). This method is not included in the original definition, but it is now available for our code.

Of course, we can also extend our own data types if we consider that appropriate. The following example extends our **Employees** structure to add a new method.

```
struct Employees {
    var name: String
    var age: Int
}
extension Employees {
    func printbadge() {
        print("Name: \(name) Age: \(age)")
    }
}
let employee = Employees(name: "John", age: 50)
employee.printbadge()   // "Name: John Age: 50"
```

Listing 3-186: Extending custom data types

Extensions can also be conditional. For instance, if we have a generic structure, we can add an extension only for specific types of values. The condition is determined by the **where** clause This is the same clause used in **switch** statements in Chapter 2, but now applied to extensions (see Listing 2-57). The clause works like an **if** statement, so the extension is only applied if the condition is met, as in the following example.

```
struct Employees<T> {
    var value: T
}
extension Employees where T == Int {
    func doubleValue() {
        print("\(value) times 2 = \(value * 2)")
    }
}
let employee = Employees(value: 25)
employee.doubleValue()   // "25 times 2 = 50"
```

Listing 3-187: Defining a conditional extension

Chapter 3 - Swift Paradigm

In the example of Listing 3-187, we define a generic structure called `Employees` with a generic property called `value` and then define an extension for this structure with a method called `doubleValue()`, but this method will only be added to the instance if the data type used to create the instance is `Int` (the method is only available for integers). At the end, we create an instance with the value 25 and call the method, which multiplies the value by 2 and prints a string with the result. This works because we created the instance with an integer, but if we try to do it with another type of value, Xcode will show an error.

Another useful implementation of extensions is the customization of string interpolation. We have introduced string interpolation in Chapter 2 and have been using it in almost every example to insert values into strings (e.g., `print("My name is \(name)")`). What we haven't mentioned is that these values are managed by a structure called `String.StringInterpolation` (a typealias of `DefaultStringInterpolation`) and that by extending this structure we can customize how the system processes the values. The `StringInterpolation` structure includes the following methods for this purpose.

appendInterpolation(Value**)**—This method interpolates the value provided by the attribute into the final string.

appendLiteral(String**)**—This method adds the string provided by the attribute to the interpolation.

To customize the interpolation, we have to extend the `StringInterpolation` structure with an overload of the `appendInterpolation()` method, process the value inside this method, and finally append the result to the interpolation with the `appendLiteral()` method, as in the following example.

```
extension String.StringInterpolation {
    mutating func appendInterpolation(celsius value: Double) {
        let fahrenheit = ((value * 9)/5) + 32
        appendLiteral(String(fahrenheit))
    }
}
print("Temperature in Fahrenheit \(celsius: 25)")
```

Listing 3-188: Customizing string interpolation

The `appendInterpolation()` method can take as many parameters as we need. In this example, we define only one parameter with the name `value` and the label `celsius`. When we create a string with this label and a number, the method is executed. Inside, we use the formula to turn Celsius degrees into Fahrenheit and then add the result to the interpolation with the `appendLiteral()` method to get the string "Temperature in Fahrenheit 77.0".

Medium **Delegates**

As we have already seen, an instance of a structure or an object can be assigned to the property of another instance. For example, we could have an instance of a structure called `Employees` with a property that contains an instance of a structure called `Offices` to store information about the office where the employee works. This opens the door to new programming patterns where the instances adopt different roles. The most useful pattern is called *delegation*. A structure or object delegates responsibility for the execution of certain tasks to another structure or object.

```
struct Salary {
    func showMoney(name: String, money: Double) {
        print("The salary of \(name) is \(money)")
    }
}
struct Employees {
    var name: String
    var money: Double
    var delegate: Salary

    func generatereport() {
        delegate.showMoney(name: name, money: money)
    }
}
let salary = Salary()
var employee1 = Employees(name: "John", money: 45000, delegate: salary)

employee1.generatereport()   // "The salary of John is 45000.0"
```

Listing 3-189: Delegating tasks

The **Employees** structure of Listing 3-189 contains three properties. The properties **name** and **money** store the employee's data, while the **delegate** property stores the instance of the **Salary** structure in charge of printing that data. The code creates the **Salary** instance first and then uses it to create the **Employees** instance. When we call the **generatereport()** method on the **employee1** structure at the end, the method calls the **showmoney()** method on **delegate**, effectively delegating the task of printing the data to this structure.

This pattern presents two problems. First, the structure that is delegating has to know the data type of the structure that is going to become the delegate (in our example, the **delegate** property had to be declared of type **Salary**). Following this approach, not every structure can be a delegate, only the ones specified in the definition (only structures of type **Salary** can be delegates of structures of type **Employee**). The second problem is related to how we know which are the properties and methods that the delegate has to implement. If the structure is too complex or Is taken from a library, we could forget to implement some methods or properties and get an error when the structure tries to access them. Both problems are solved by protocols. Instead of declaring a specific structure as the delegate, we define a protocol and declare the **delegate** property to be of that type, as shown in the following example.

```
protocol SalaryProtocol {
    func showMoney(name: String, money: Double)
}
struct Salary: SalaryProtocol {
    func showMoney(name: String, money: Double) {
        print("The salary of \(name) is \(money)")
    }
}
struct Employees {
    var name: String
    var money: Double
    var delegate: SalaryProtocol
    func generatereport() {
        delegate.showMoney(name: name, money: money)
    }
}
let salary = Salary()
```

```
let employee1 = Employees(name: "John", money: 45000, delegate: salary)
employee1.generatereport()   // "The salary of John is 45000.0"
```

Listing 3-190: Delegating with protocols

The **delegate** property of the **Employees** structure is now of type **SalaryProtocol**, which means that it can store any instance of any type providing that it conforms to the **SalaryProtocol** protocol. As shown by this example, the advantage of protocols is that we can use structures of different types to perform the task. It doesn't matter what type they are as long as they conform to the delegate's protocol and implement its properties and methods. For example, we could create two different structures to print the data of our last example and assign to the delegate one instance or another depending on what we want to achieve.

```
protocol SalaryProtocol {
    func showMoney(name: String, money: Double)
}
struct Salary: SalaryProtocol {
    func showMoney(name: String, money: Double) {
        print("The salary of \(name) is \(money)")
    }
}
struct BasicSalary: SalaryProtocol {
    func showMoney(name: String, money: Double) {
        if money > 40000 {
            print("Salary is over the minimum")
        } else {
            print("The salary of \(name) is \(money)")
        }
    }
}
struct Employees {
    var name: String
    var money: Double
    var delegate: SalaryProtocol

    func generatereport() {
        delegate.showMoney(name: name, money: money)
    }
}
let salary = Salary()
var employee1 = Employees(name: "John", money: 45000, delegate: salary)

employee1.delegate = BasicSalary()
employee1.generatereport()   // "Salary is over the minimum"
```

Listing 3-191: Using different delegates

The **BasicSalary** structure added in Listing 3-191 conforms to the **SalaryProtocol** protocol and implements its **showMoney()** method, but unlike the **Salary** structure, it produces two different results depending on the employee's salary. The output produced by the execution of the **generatereport()** method on the **Employees** structure now depends on the type of structure we previously assigned to the **delegate** property.

(Medium) ## 3.7 Errors

Simple frameworks and classes usually work as expected. If we call a method, the method performs its task without failure. If it does fail, it usually returns a neutral value like 0 or **nil** to indicate that there was a problem. But this is not always enough. More complex frameworks cannot guarantee success and may encounter multiple problems while trying to fulfill their purpose. For this reason, Swift introduces a systematic process to report and handle errors called *Error Handling*.

(Medium) Throwing Errors

When a method reports an error, it is said that it *throws* an error. Several frameworks provided by Apple are already programmed to throw errors, as we will see in further chapters, but we can also do it from our own structures and classes. To throw an error, we must use the `throw` and `throws` keywords. The `throw` keyword is used to throw the error and the `throws` keyword is specified in the method's declaration to indicate to the rest of the code that the method can throw errors.

Because a method can throw multiple errors, we also must indicate the type of error found with values of an enumeration type. This is a custom enumeration that conforms to the `Error` protocol. For instance, let's consider the following example.

```
struct Stock {
   var totalLamps = 5
   mutating func sold(amount: Int) {
      totalLamps = totalLamps - amount
   }
}
var mystock = Stock()
mystock.sold(amount: 8)
print("Lamps in stock: \(mystock.totalLamps)")   // "Lamps in stock: -3"
```
Listing 3-192: Producing an error inside a method

The code of Listing 3-192 defines a structure called `Stock` that manages the stock of lamps available in the store. The class includes the `totalLamps` property to store the number of lamps we still have available and the `sold()` method to process the lamps sold. The method updates the stock by subtracting the number of lamps we have sold from the value of the `totalLamps` property. If the number of lamps sold is less than the number of lamps in stock, everything is fine, but when we sell more lamps than we have, as in this example, there is clearly a problem.

To throw an error, we have to declare the types of errors available for the method, declare the method as a throwing method adding the `throws` keyword in the declaration (between the attributes and the returning data types), detect the error, and throw it with the `throw` keyword.

```
enum Errors: Error {
   case OutOfStock
}
struct Stock {
   var totalLamps = 5
   mutating func sold(amount: Int) throws {
      if amount > totalLamps {
         throw Errors.OutOfStock
      } else {
         totalLamps = totalLamps - amount
      }
   }
}
var mystock = Stock()
```
Listing 3-193: Throwing errors

Chapter 3 - Swift Paradigm

In Listing 3-193, we declare an enumeration called `Errors` that conforms to the `Error` protocol and includes a case called `OutOfStock`. By declaring `sold()` as a throwing method with the `throws` keyword, we can now throw the `OutOfStock` error every time we try to sell more lamps than we have. If the lamps sold are more than the number of lamps in stock, the method throws the error, otherwise the stock is updated.

(Medium) **Handling Errors**

Now that we have a method that can throw errors, we must handle the errors when the method is executed. Swift includes the `try` keyword and the `do catch` statements for this purpose. The `do catch` statements create two blocks of code. If the statements inside the `do` block return an error, the statements in the `catch` block are executed. To execute a method that throws errors, we must declare these statements and call the method inside the `do` statement with the `try` keyword in front of it, as shown in the following example.

```
enum Errors: Error {
    case OutOfStock
}
struct Stock {
    var totalLamps = 5
    mutating func sold(amount: Int) throws {
        if amount > totalLamps {
            throw Errors.OutOfStock
        } else {
            totalLamps = totalLamps - amount
        }
    }
}
var mystock = Stock()
do {
    try mystock.sold(amount: 8)
} catch Errors.OutOfStock {
    print("We do not have enough lamps")
}
```
Listing 3-194: Handling errors

The code of Listing 3-194 expands the previous example to handle the error thrown by the `sold()` method. Because of the addition of the `try` keyword, the system tries to execute the `sold()` method in the `mystock` structure and check for errors. If the method returns the `OutOfStock` error, the statements inside the `catch` block are executed. This pattern allows us to respond every time there is an error and report it to the user or correct the situation without having to crash the app or produce unexpected results.

 Do It Yourself: Create a new Playground file. Copy the code of Listing 3-194 inside the file. You should see the message "We do not have enough lamps" printed on the console. Replace the number 8 with the number 3. Now the message should not be printed because there are enough lamps in stock.

 The Basics: You can add as many errors as you need to the `Errors` enumeration. The errors can be checked later with multiple `catch` statements in sequence. Also, you may add all the statements you need to the `do` block. The statements before `try` are always executed, while the statements after `try` are only executed if no error is found.

If we do not care about the error returned, we can force the `try` keyword to return an optional with the syntax `try?`. If the method throws an error, the instruction returns `nil`, and therefore we can avoid the use of the `do catch` statements.

```
enum Errors: Error {
    case OutOfStock
}
struct Stock {
    var totalLamps = 5
    mutating func sold(amount: Int) throws {
        if amount > totalLamps {
            throw Errors.OutOfStock
        } else {
            totalLamps = totalLamps - amount
        }
    }
}
var mystock = Stock()
try? mystock.sold(amount: 8)   // nil
```

Listing 3-195: Catching errors with `try?`

The instruction at the end of Listing 3-195 returns the value `nil` if the method throws an error, or an optional with the value returned by the method if everything goes right.

Sometimes, we know beforehand that a throwing method is not going to throw an error and therefore we want to avoid writing unnecessary code. In cases like this, we can use the syntax `try!`. For instance, the following code checks if there are enough lamps before calling the `sold()` method, so we know that the instruction will never throw the `OutOfStock` error.

```
enum Errors: Error {
    case OutOfStock
}
struct Stock {
    var totalLamps = 5
    mutating func sold(amount: Int) throws {
        if amount > totalLamps {
            throw Errors.OutOfStock
        } else {
            totalLamps = totalLamps - amount
        }
    }
}
var mystock = Stock()

if mystock.totalLamps > 3 {
    try! mystock.sold(amount: 3)
}
print("Lamps in stock: \(mystock.totalLamps)")
```

Listing 3-196: Ignoring the errors

 IMPORTANT: Like optionals, if the method throws an error and we declare the `try` keyword with an exclamation mark, the app crashes, so we have to be sure that the method is not going to throw an error before creating instructions with `try!`.

Chapter 3 - Swift Paradigm

Chapter 4
Introduction to Frameworks

Basic ## 4.1 Frameworks

The programming tools introduced in previous chapters are not enough to build professional applications. Creating an app requires accessing complex technologies and performing repetitive tasks that involve hundreds or thousands of lines of code. Given this situation, developing systems always include preprogrammed codes that perform common tasks, which allows developers to focus on more meaningful goals. These pieces of code (classes, structures, etc.) are organized according to their purpose and constitute what we know as frameworks.

Frameworks are collections of libraries and APIs (Application Programming Interfaces) that we can use to add functionality to our applications. This includes managing databases, creating graphics on the screen, storing files, accessing resources on the web, sharing data online, and more. Apple has been developing these frameworks since the production of the first personal computer, offering a very diverse set of tools, with old and new frameworks that sometimes overlap and even replace each other. These frameworks are essential for creating professional applications for Apple devices and therefore are part of the SDK (Software Development Kit) that is included with Xcode.

Basic ### Importing Frameworks

The Swift Standard Library we have been using in previous chapters is automatically loaded for us and available everywhere in our code, but when we require the use of other frameworks, we must indicate it to the system. This is done by adding the `import` instruction at the beginning of each file followed by the name of the framework we want to include (e.g., `import Foundation`). Once the framework is imported, it is automatically included in our file, giving us access to all the structures, classes, functions and any of the values defined in its code.

Basic ## 4.2 Foundation

Foundation is one of the oldest frameworks provided by Apple. It was written in Objective-C and developed by Steve Jobs's second company NeXT. The framework was created to manage basic tasks but also to store data. Data storage is one of its most important functions. Foundation provides its own data types (structures and classes) to store numbers and strings of characters, to create arrays and dictionaries, and even a primary class called `NSObject` with basic behavior that every other class inherits from. Most of these definitions are now obsolete, replaced by Swift's data types, but others remain useful, as we will see next.

Basic ### Standard Functions

No matter the language, there are simple operations that are always required by any program. Functions for performing tasks such as calculating the power of a number or generating a random value were always provided through standard libraries. Some of these basic features are included in the Swift Standard Library, but other are provided by frameworks like Foundation. The following are some of the basic functions offered by the Foundation framework.

pow(Float, Float)—This function returns the result of raising the first value to the power of the second value. The attributes may be numbers of type `Float` or `Double`.

sqrt(Float)—This function returns the square root of the value of its attribute. The attribute may be of type `Float` or `Double`.

log(Float)—This function returns the natural logarithm of the value of its attribute. Other related functions are `log2()`, `log10()`, `log1p()`, and `logb()`. The attribute may be of type `Float` or `Double`.

sin(Float)—This function returns the sine of the value of its attribute. Other related functions are `asin()`, `sinh()`, and `asinh()`. The attribute may be of type `Float` or `Double`.

cos(Float)—This function returns the cosine of the value of its attribute. Other related functions are `acos()`, `cosh()`, and `acosh()`. The attribute may be of type `Float` or `Double`.

tan(Float)—This function returns the tangent of the value of its attribute. Other related functions are `atan()`, `atan2()`, `tanh()`, and `atanh()`. The attribute may be of type `Float` or `Double`.

The application of these functions is straightforward, as shown in the following example.

```
import Foundation

let square = sqrt(4.0)
let power = pow(2.0, 2.0)
let maximum = max(square, power)

print("The maximum value is \(maximum)")   // "The maximum value is 4.0"
```

Listing 4-1: Applying math functions

The first thing we do in the code of Listing 4-1 is to import the Foundation framework. After this, we can implement any of the tools defined inside the framework, including the basic functions introduced above. This example gets the square root of 4.0, calculates 2.0 to the power of 2.0, and compares the results using the `max()` function from the Swift Standard Library.

(Basic) **Strings**

Foundation defines a class called `NSString` to store and manage strings of characters. The `String` structure offered by the Swift Standard Library for this same purpose adopts most of its functionality, turning the class obsolete, but because Swift coexists with old frameworks and data types, `NSString` objects are still required in some circumstances. The `NSString` class includes several Initializers to create these objects. The one usually implemented in Swift takes an attribute called `string` with the string of characters we want to assign to the object.

```
import Foundation

var text: NSString = NSString(string: "Hello")
print(text)   // "Hello"
```

Listing 4-2: Creating an `NSString` object

If we already have a `String` value in our code, we can cast it into an `NSString` object with the `as` operator.

Chapter 4 - Introduction to Frameworks

```
import Foundation
var text = "Hello World"
var newText = text as NSString
print(newText)    // "Hello World"
```

Listing 4-3: Casting a `String` *value into an* `NSString` *object*

A `String` structure can be turned into an `NSString` object with the `as` operator because they are interconnected. It is said that the `String` structure bridges with the `NSString` class. This means that we can access the functionality offered by the `NSString` class from the `String` structure, including the following properties and methods.

capitalized—This property returns a string with the first letter of every word in uppercase.

length—This property returns the number of characters in the string of an `NSString` object (If the string was created as a `String` value, we should use the `count` property instead).

localizedStringWithFormat(String, Values**)**—This type method creates a string from the string provided by the first attribute and the values provided by the second attribute. The first attribute is a template used to create the string, and the second attribute is the list of values we want to include in the string separated by comma.

contains(String**)**—This method returns a Boolean value that indicates whether or not the string specified by the attribute was found inside the original string.

trimmingCharacters(in: CharacterSet**)**—This method erases the characters indicated by the **in** attribute at the beginning and the end of the string and returns a new string with the result. The attribute is a `CharacterSet` structure that includes type properties to select the type of characters we want to remove. The most frequently used properties are `whitespaces` (selects spaces) and `whitespacesAndNewlines` (selects spaces and new line characters).

compare(String, **options:** CompareOptions, **range:** Range?, **locale:** Locale?**)**— This method compares the original string with the string provided by the first attribute and returns an enumeration of type `ComparisonResult` with a value corresponding to the lexical order of the strings. The `orderedSame` value is returned when the strings are equal, the `orderedAscending` value is returned when the original string precedes the value of the first attribute, and the `orderedDescending` value is returned when the original string follows the value of the first attribute. The **options** attribute is a property of the `CompareOptions` structure. The properties available are `caseInsensitive` (it considers lowercase and uppercase letters to be the same), `literal` (performs a byte-to-byte comparison), `diacriticInsensitive` (ignores diacritic marks such as the visual stress on vowels), `widthInsensitive` (ignores the width difference in characters that occurs in some languages), and `forcedOrdering` (the comparison is forced to return `orderedAscending` or `orderedDescending` values when the strings are equivalent but not strictly equal). The **range** attribute defines a range that determines the portion of the original string we want to compare. Finally, the **locale** attribute is a `Locale` structure that defines localization. Except for the first attribute, the rest of the attributes are optional.

caseInsensitiveCompare(String**)**—This method compares the original string with the string provided by the attribute. It works exactly like the `compare()` method but with the option `caseInsensitiveSearch` set by default.

range(of: String, **options:** CompareOptions, **range:** Range?, **locale:** Locale?**)**— This method searches for the string specified by the first attribute and returns a range to indicate where the string was found or `nil` in case of failure. The **options** attribute is a property of the `CompareOptions` structure. The properties available for this method are the same we have for the `compare()` method, with the difference that we can specify three more: `backwards` (searches from the end of the string), `anchored` (matches characters only at the beginning or the end, not in the middle), and `regularExpression` (searches with a regular expression). The **range** attribute defines a range that determines the portion of the original string where we want to search. Except for the first attribute, the rest of the attributes are optional.

As we already mentioned, the `String` structure is bridged to the `NSString` class and therefore we can call these methods from `string` values, but because they are defined in the `NSString` class, we still must import the Foundation framework to be able to use them. Some of them are like those offered by the `String` structure but allow us to perform additional operations on the values. For instance, we can incorporate values into strings with string interpolation, but the `localizedStringWithFormat()` method offers a different approach. This method takes a string with placeholders and replaces the placeholders with a list of values. The placeholders are declared with the % symbol followed by a character that represents the type of value we want to include. For example, if we want the placeholder to be replaced by an integer, we must use the characters %d.

```
import Foundation

var age = 44
var mytext = String.localizedStringWithFormat("My age is %d", age)
print(mytext)   // "My age is 44"
```

Listing 4-4: Creating a formatted string

The code of Listing 4-4 replaces the %d characters in the string with the value of the **age** variable, stores the resulting string in the **mytext** variable, and prints it on the console.

There are different placeholders available. The most frequently used are %d for integers, %f for floating-point numbers, %g to remove redundant 0 (zeros), and %@ for objects and structures. We can use any of these characters and as many times as necessary. This is very similar to what we would get with string interpolation, but with this method we can also format the values. For instance, we can determine the number of digits a value will have by adding the amount before the letter, as in the following example.

```
import Foundation

let length = 12.3472
let total = 54
let decimals = String.localizedStringWithFormat("Decimals: %.2f", length)
let digits = String.localizedStringWithFormat("Digits: %.5d", total)
print(decimals)   // "Decimals: 12.35"
print(digits)   // "Digits: 00054"
```

Listing 4-5: Formatting numbers

The code of Listing 4-5 formats two numbers, a double and an integer. The double is processed with the %.2f placeholder, which means that the value has to be rounded to two decimals after the point, and the integer is processed with the %.5d placeholder, which means that it has to contain a total of five digits. It there are not enough digits in the value, the method completes the number with 0 (zeros).

Other methods provided by the `NSString` class perform operations that are already available for `String` values, but they produce a more comprehensive result. For example, the `compare()` method compares two strings the same way we do with the `==` operator, but the value returned is not just `true` or `false`.

```
import Foundation
var fruit = "Orange"
var search = "Apple"

var result = fruit.compare(search)
switch result {
   case .orderedSame:
      print("Fruit and Search are equal")
   case .orderedDescending:
      print("Fruit follows Search")   // "Fruit follows Search"
   case .orderedAscending:
      print("Fruit precedes Search")
}
```

Listing 4-6: Comparing `String` *values*

The `compare()` method takes a string, compares it to the original string, and returns a value of the `ComparisonResult` enumeration type to indicate the order. The `ComparisonResult` enumeration contains three values: `orderedSame`, `orderedDescending`, and `orderedAscending`. After comparing the values of the `fruit` and `search` variables in our example, the `result` variable contains one of these values according to the lexical order of the strings. In this case, the value "Orange" assigned to `fruit` is bigger (follows alphabetically) the value "Apple" assigned to `search`, so the value returned is `orderedDescending` (the order is descending from `fruit` to `search`). We check this value with a `switch` statement and print a message according to the result.

The `compare()` method implemented in Listing 4-6 and the `==` operator studied in Chapter 2 consider a lowercase string different than an uppercase string. Adding an option to the `compare()` method we can compare two strings without considering lower or uppercase letters.

```
import Foundation
var fruit = "Orange"
var search = "ORANGE"

var result = fruit.compare(search, options: .caseInsensitive)
switch result {
   case .orderedSame:
      print("The values are equal")   // "The values are equal"
   case .orderedDescending:
      print("Fruit follows Search")
   case .orderedAscending:
      print("Fruit precedes Search")
}
```

Listing 4-7: Comparing `String` *values with options*

The strings stored in the `fruit` and `search` variables in Listing 4-7 are different, but because of the `caseInsensitive` option, they are considered equal. This type of comparison is very common, which is why the class includes the `caseInsensitiveCompare()` method that all it does is calling the `compare()` method with the `caseInsensitive` option already set.

Despite this being the most common scenario, we can perform more precise comparison by providing a range to the `compare()` method. The option specifies the range of characters in the original string we want to compare.

Chapter 4 - Introduction to Frameworks

```
import Foundation

var phone = "905-525-6666"
var search = "905"

var start = phone.startIndex
var end = phone.firstIndex(of: "-")

if let endIndex = end {
   let result = phone.compare(search, options: .caseInsensitive, range:
start..<endIndex)
   if result == .orderedSame {
      print("The area code is the same")   // "The area code is the same"
   } else {
      print("The area code is different")
   }
}
```

Listing 4-8: Comparing only a range of characters

The example of Listing 4-8 compares only the initial characters of a string to check the area code of a phone number. The code defines a range that goes from the first character of the **phone** variable to the position before the - character. This range is provided to the **compare()** method and in consequence the value of the **search** variable is compared only against the first three characters of the **phone** variable.

Besides comparing strings we can also search for strings using the **range()** method. This method searches for a string inside another string and returns a range that determines where the string was found.

```
import Foundation

var text = "The Suitcase is Black"
var search = "black  "
search = search.trimmingCharacters(in: .whitespacesAndNewlines)

var range = text.range(of: search, options: .caseInsensitive)
if let rangeToReplace = range {
   text.replaceSubrange(rangeToReplace, with: "Red")
}
print(text)   // "The Suitcase is Red"
```

Listing 4-9: Searching and replacing characters in a string

The **range()** method returns an optional value that contains the range where the string was found or **nil** in case of failure. In Listing 4-9, we search for the value of the **search** variable inside the **text** variable and check the optional value returned. When we have a range to work with (which means that the value was found) we use it to call the **replaceSubrange()** method of the **String** structure (see Listing 3-67). With this method, we replace the characters inside the range by the string "Red". Notice that because search values are usually provided by the user, we trim the value of the **search** variable with the **trimmingCharacters()** method to make sure that there are no space characters at the beginning or the end of the string (the two spaces after the word "black" are removed).

(Basic) **Ranges**

Although Swift includes range structures to store ranges of values, some frameworks programmed in Objective-C still implement an old Foundation class called **NSRange**. The

NSRange class is slightly different than the Swift's Range structure. Instead of storing the initial and final values of the range, NSRange objects store the initial value and the length of the range. The following are the initializers each data type includes to convert one value to another.

NSRange(Range)—This initializer creates an NSRange object from a Range value.

NSRange(Range, **in:** String)—This initializer creates an NSRange object to represent a Range structure with string indexes.

Range(NSRange)—This initializer creates a Range structure from an NSRange value.

Range(NSRange, **in:** String)—This initializer creates a Range structure to represent an NSRange object with string indexes.

The NSRange class also includes two properties to retrieve its values: location and length. The following example initializes an NSRange object from a Swift range and prints its values.

```
import Foundation

let range = NSRange(4..<10)
print("Initial: \(range.location)")   // "Initial: 4"
print("Length: \(range.length)")   // "Length: 6"
```

Listing 4-10: Creating and reading an NSRange value

The initializer implemented in this example is for countable ranges. If we work with string indexes, we must use the initializer defined for strings. This is because the String structure works with Unicode characters while NSString objects work with a more specific character encoding called *UTF-16*. Working with different character encodings means that the space the characters occupy in memory varies. A range that represents a series of characters in a String value may differ from a range that represents the same series of characters in an NSString value. The following example illustrates how to work with this initializer.

```
import Foundation

let text = "Hello World"
if let start = text.firstIndex(of: "W") {
    let newRange = NSRange(start..., in: text)
    print("Initial: \(newRange.location)")   // "Initial: 6"
    print("Length: \(newRange.length)")   // "Length: 5"
}
```

Listing 4-11: Converting a range of string indexes

(Basic) **Numbers**

Foundation offers a class called NSNumber to represent and store different types of numbers. With the introduction of the Swift's primitive types, the use of this class is no longer necessary, but there are a few old frameworks that still require these types of values. To create an NSNumber object from a Swift data type, we must use the following initializer.

NSNumber(**value:** Value)—This initializer creates an NSNumber object with the value specified by the **value** attribute. The attribute may be a value of any of the data types available in Swift for numbers.

The class also provides properties to perform the opposite operation; getting Swift data types from `NSNumber` objects. The following are the most frequently used.

intValue—This property returns an `Int` value with the object's number.

floatValue—This property returns a `Float` value with the object's number.

doubleValue—This property returns a `Double` value with the object's number.

The following example shows how to create `NSNumber` objects and how to get them back as Swift data types to perform operations.

```
import Foundation

var number = NSNumber(value: 35)
var double = number.doubleValue * 2   // 70
```

Listing 4-12: Working with NSNumber *objects*

As well as Swift primitive data types, `NSNumber` objects use the maximum number of digits allowed for the type. Every time we print one of these values, all the digits are shown on the screen. Earlier in this chapter we showed how to customize the number of digits presented for a number with an `NSString` type method and placeholders (e.g., `%.2f`), but Foundation offers its own class for this purpose called `NumberFormatter`. This class allows us to create strings that contain numbers in a specific format. The class offers properties and methods to work with standard formats or create our own.

numberStyle—This property sets or returns a value that determines the style used to format the number. It is an enumeration of type `Style` with the values `none` (default), `decimal`, `currency`, `percent`, `scientific`, and `spellOut`.

roundingMode—This property sets or returns the rounding mode. It is an enumeration of type `RoundingMode` with the values `ceiling`, `floor`, `down`, `up`, `halfEven` (default), `halfDown`, and `halfUp`.

minimumIntegerDigits—This property sets or returns an integer value that determines the minimum number of digits included in the number's integer part.

maximumIntegerDigits—This property sets or returns an integer value that determines the maximum number of digits included in the number's integer part.

minimumFractionDigits—This property sets or returns an integer value that determines the minimum number of digits included after the decimal point.

maximumFractionDigits—This property sets or returns an integer value that determines the maximum number of digits included after the decimal point.

string(from: NSNumber)—This method returns a string that includes the number provided by the **from** attribute in the format specified by the properties of the object.

The default configuration of a `NumberFormatter` object sets the style as `none` and the rounding mode as `halfEven`, which means that the string produced by the `string()` method will be composed of a number with the decimal part rounded to the nearest integer, but we can change this behavior assigning new values to the object's properties.

```
import Foundation

var money = NSNumber(value: 5.6897)
```

```
let format = NumberFormatter()
format.numberStyle = .currency
format.roundingMode = .floor
var price = format.string(from: money)   // $5.68
```

Listing 4-13: Formatting a number to represent money

To format a number, we must create the `NumberFormatter` object with the `NumberFormatter()` initializer, then configure its properties, and finally execute the `string()` method to get the formatted number in a string. In the example of Listing 4-13, we create a `NumberFormatter` object and then set its style as `currency` and its rounding mode as `floor`. The number stored in the `money` variable is sent to the `string()` method of this object to get the string in the specified format. The result is a string with the currency symbol and the number of decimal digits corresponding to the device's configuration. For example, if the device was set in the United States, the string produced by this example will be "$5.68".

If we want to format a number with a specific number of digits, we can take advantage of the `minimumFractionDigits` and `maximumFractionDigits` properties.

```
import Foundation

var money = NSNumber(value: 5.68)

let format = NumberFormatter()
format.numberStyle = .decimal
format.minimumFractionDigits = 3
format.maximumFractionDigits = 3
var price = format.string(from: money)   // $ 5.680
```

Listing 4-14: Specifying the number of digits

Once the `NumberFormatter` object is created, it can be used to format all the numbers we want. In the following example, we create two strings to represent the price and total price of a transaction. Notice that, to be able to perform operations with the numbers, this time we use Swift data types and convert them to `NSNumber` objects at the end.

```
import Foundation

var money = 5.6897
var total = money * 4

let format = NumberFormatter()
format.numberStyle = .currency
format.roundingMode = .ceiling
var price = format.string(from: NSNumber(value: money))   // $5.69
var result = format.string(from: NSNumber(value: total))   // $22.76
```

Listing 4-15: Formatting multiple values

We can also change the style and the rounding mode to get the format we need. The most common styles are `currency` to represent money, `percent` to represent percentages, and `spellOut` to describe the number in words ("five point six eight nine seven"). The rounding modes used more often are `ceiling`, `floor`, and `halfEven`, to round the last digit up, down, or to the closest integer.

 IMPORTANT: Besides the standard configurations, the `NumberFormatter` class offers multiple properties to set any custom format necessary. For example, instead of relying on the system to provide the symbol for the currency, you can specify it explicitly by assigning a new value to the `currencySymbol` property. To see all the properties available, visit our website and follow the links for this chapter.

(Basic) Dates

Foundation defines multiple classes and structures to create and process dates, including `Date`, `Calendar`, `DateComponents`, `DateInterval`, `DateFormatter`, `Locale`, and `TimeZone`. The data type that creates the structure to store the actual date is `Date`. The following are some of its initializers.

Date()—This initializer creates a `Date` structure with the system's current date.

Date(timeIntervalSinceNow: TimeInterval)—This initializer creates a `Date` structure with a date calculated from the addition of the current date plus the time specified by the `timeIntervalSinceNow` attribute. The attribute is a value of type `TimeInterval` (a type alias of `Double`) that indicates how many seconds the date is from the initial date.

Date(timeInterval: TimeInterval, since: Date)—This initializer creates a `Date` structure with a date calculated from the addition of the date specified by the **since** attribute plus the time specified by the **timeInterval** attribute. The attribute is a value of type `TimeInterval` (a type alias of `Double`) that indicates how many seconds the date is from the initial date.

The following example shows different ways to initialize a date.

```
import Foundation

var currentdate = Date()
var nextday = Date(timeIntervalSinceNow: 24 * 60 * 60)
var tendays = Date(timeInterval: -10 * 24 * 3600, since: nextday)
```

Listing 4-16: Storing dates with `Date` *structures*

If the initializer requires an interval, as those in the code of Listing 4-16, the value is specified in seconds. An easy way to calculate the seconds is multiplying every component. For example, the date for the **nextday** object created in our example is calculated adding 1 day to the current date. The number of seconds in 1 day are calculated multiplying the 24 hours of the day by the 60 minutes in an hour and by the 60 seconds in a minute (24 * 60 * 60). There are 86400 seconds in a day, but it is much easier to remember the values of the components. For the **tendays** object, we apply the same technique. The initializer used to get this object adds the interval to a specific date (**nextday**). The seconds are calculated by multiplying the components, albeit this time it multiplies the previous result by -10 to get a date 10 days before **nextday** (we will see better ways to add components to a date later).

 IMPORTANT: These methods require a value of type `Double` to declare the interval in seconds, but instead of `Double` the framework calls it `TimeInterval`. This is a type alias (an alternative name for an existing type). Once defined, aliases are used exactly like regular data types. To create your own type aliases, you can use the instruction **typealias** (e.g., **typealias myinteger = Int**).

Besides the initializers, the class also includes two type properties that return special dates. These properties produce values that are useful to set limits and sort lists.

Chapter 4 - Introduction to Frameworks

distantFuture—This type property returns a `Date` structure with a value that represents a date in a distant future.

distantPast—This type property returns a `Date` structure with a value that represents a date in a distant past.

The `Date` structure also includes properties and methods to calculate and compare dates. The following are the most frequently used.

timeIntervalSinceNow—This property returns a `TimeInterval` value representing the difference in seconds between the date in the `Date` structure and the current date.

compare(Date)—This method compares the date in the `Date` structure with the date specified by the attribute and returns an enumeration of type `ComparisonResult` with a value corresponding to the temporal order of the dates. The possible values are `orderedSame` (the dates are equal), `orderedAscending` (the date is earlier in time than the value of the attribute), and `orderedDescending` (the date is later in time than the value of the attribute).

timeIntervalSince(Date)—This method compares the date in the `Date` structure with the date specified by the attribute and returns the interval between both dates in seconds. The value returned is of type `TimeInterval`.

addingTimeInterval(TimeInterval)—This method adds the seconds specified by the attribute to the date in the `Date` structure and returns a new `Date` structure with the result.

addTimeInterval(TimeInterval)—This method adds the seconds specified by the attribute to the date in the `Date` structure and stores the result in the same structure.

Comparing dates and calculating the intervals between dates is a constant requirement in app development. The following example compares the current date with a date calculated from a specific number of days. If the resulting date is later in time than the current date, the code prints a message on the console to show the time remaining in seconds.

```
import Foundation

var days = 7

var today = Date()
var event = Date(timeIntervalSinceNow: Double(days) * 24 * 3600)

if today.compare(event) == .orderedAscending {
   let interval = event.timeIntervalSince(today)
   print("We have to wait \(interval) seconds")
}
```

Listing 4-17: Comparing two dates

The dates in `Date` structures are not associated to any calendar. This means that to be able to interpret the components in a date (year, month, day, etc.) we must decide first in the context of which calendar the date is going to be interpreted. The calendar for a date is defined by a structure called `Calendar`. This structure provides properties and methods to process a date according to a specific calendar (Gregorian, Buddhist, Chinese, etc.). To initialize a `Calendar` structure, we have the following initializer and type property.

Calendar(identifier: Identifier)—This initializer creates a `Calendar` structure with the calendar specified by the attribute. The **identifier** attribute is a property of a structure called `Identifier` defined inside the `Calendar` structure. The properties available are gregorian, buddhist, chinese, coptic, ethiopicAmeteMihret, ethiopicAmeteAlem, hebrew, ISO8601, indian, islamic, islamicCivil, japanese, persian, republicOfChina, islamicTabular and islamicUmmAlQura.

current—This type property returns a structure with the current calendar set in the system.

A `Calendar` structure includes the following properties and methods to manage the calendar and to get and set new dates.

identifier—This property returns the value that identifies the calendar.

locale—This property sets or returns the `Locale` structure used by the `Calendar` structure to process dates. The value by default is the `Locale` structure defined by the system.

timeZone—This property sets or returns the `TimeZone` structure used by the `Calendar` structure to process dates. The value by default is the `TimeZone` structure defined by the system.

dateComponents(Set, from: Date)—This method returns a `DateComponents` structure with the components indicated by the first attribute from the date indicated by the **from** attribute. The first attribute is a set with properties of a structure called `Unit` that represent each component. The most frequently used are year, month, day, hour, minute, and second.

dateComponents(Set, from: Date, to: Date)—This method returns a `DateComponents` structure with the components indicated by the first attribute, which values represent the difference between the dates specified by the from and to attributes. The first attribute is a set with properties of a structure called `Unit` that represent each component. The most frequently used are year, month, day, hour, minute, and second.

date(byAdding: DateComponents, to: Date)—This method returns a `Date` structure with the value obtained by adding the components indicated by the **byAdding** attribute to the date indicated by the **to** attribute.

date(from: DateComponents)—This method returns a date created from the components provided by the **from** attribute. The value returned is a `Date` structure.

The `Calendar` structure works along with the `DateComponents` structure to read and return components from a date. The instances created from the `DateComponents` structure include the properties year, month, day, hour, minute, second, and weekday to read and set the values of the components. The following example combines all these elements to get the year of the current date.

```
import Foundation
var today = Date()
let calendar = Calendar.current
var components = calendar.dateComponents([.year], from: today)
print("The year is \(components.year!)")
```

Listing 4-18: Extracting components from a date

In Listing 4-18, we get a reference to the calendar set in the system by reading the `current` property and then the `dateComponents()` method is executed to get the year component of the current date.

Several components may be retrieved at once by adding the corresponding properties to the set. The following example gets the year, month and day of the current date.

```
import Foundation

var today = Date()
let calendar = Calendar.current
var comp = calendar.dateComponents([.year, .month, .day], from: today)
print("Today \(comp.day!)-\(comp.month!)-\(comp.year!)")
```

Listing 4-19: Extracting multiple components from a date

DateComponents structures are used to retrieve the components of existing dates and to set the values for new dates. In the following example, a new **Date** structure is created from the values of a **DateComponents** structure.

```
import Foundation

let calendar = Calendar.current
var comp = DateComponents()
comp.year = 1970
comp.month = 8
comp.day = 21

var birthday = calendar.date(from: comp)   // "Aug 21, 1970, 12:00 AM"
```

Listing 4-20: Creating a new date from single components

The **date(from:)** method of the **Calendar** structure returns a new date with the values provided by the **DateComponents** structure. The components which values are not explicitly defined take values by default (e.g., 12:00 AM).

Generating a new date demands the use of a specific calendar. For example, in the code of Listing 4-20, the values of the components are declared with the format established by the Gregorian calendar. In this case, we relied on the calendar returned by the system, but if we want to use the same calendar no matter where the app is executed, we must set it ourselves from the **Calendar** initializer.

```
import Foundation

let id = Calendar.Identifier.gregorian
let calendar = Calendar(identifier: id)

var comp = DateComponents()
comp.year = 1970
comp.month = 8
comp.day = 13
var birthday = calendar.date(from: comp)   // "Aug 13, 1970 at 12:00 AM"
```

Listing 4-21: Using a Gregorian calendar

Declaring a specific calendar is not only recommended when creating new dates but also when calculating dates by adding components, as in the following example.

```
import Foundation

let id = Calendar.Identifier.gregorian
let calendar = Calendar(identifier: id)
var comp = DateComponents()
```

```
comp.day = 120
var today = Date()
var appointment = calendar.date(byAdding: comp, to: today)
```

Listing 4-22: Adding components to a date

The `date()` method implemented in Listing 4-22 adds components to a date and returns a new `Date` structure with the result. In this example, the component `day` was set to a value of 120. The `date()` method takes this value and adds it to the date in the `today` structure (the current date), and returns the result.

A common task when working with multiple dates is getting the lapse of time between dates, such as the remaining hours for a process to end or the remaining days for an event. The `Calendar` structure includes a version of the `dateComponents()` method that allows us to compare two dates and get the difference expressed in a specific component.

```
import Foundation

let calendar = Calendar.current
var comp = DateComponents()
comp.year = 1970
comp.month = 8
comp.day = 21

var today = Date()
var birthdate = calendar.date(from: comp)

if let olddate = birthdate {
   let components = calendar.dateComponents([.day], from: olddate, to:
today)
   print("Days between dates: \(components.day!)")
}
```

Listing 4-23: Comparing dates

This example calculates the days between a birthdate and the current date. The value returned by the `date()` method used to generate the birthdate returns an optional, so we have to unwrap it before trying to calculate the difference. In Listing 4-23, we assign this value to the `olddate` constant and then compare it with the current date in the `today` structure. The number of days between the dates is returned and printed on the console.

Another way to specify intervals between dates is with the `DateInterval` structure. This structure allows us to create an interval with `Date` values. The following are its initializers.

DateInterval(start: Date, end: Date)—This initializer creates a `DateInterval` structure with the interval between the values provided by the **start** and **end** attributes.

DateInterval(start: Date, duration: TimeInterval)—This initializer creates a `DateInterval` structure with an interval that starts at the date specified by the **start** attribute and last as long as the time specified by the **duration** attribute.

The `DateInterval` structure also offers the following properties and methods to access the values of the interval.

start—This property sets or returns the initial `Date` of the interval.

end—This property sets or returns the final `Date` of the interval.

duration—This property sets or returns the duration of the interval in seconds.

Chapter 4 - Introduction to Frameworks

contains(Date)—This method returns a Boolean value that indicates whether or not the date specified by the attribute is inside the interval.

intersects(DateInterval)—This method returns a Boolean value that indicates if the interval intersects with the interval specified by the attribute.

intersection(with: DateInterval)—This method returns a `DateInterval` value with the interval in which the original interval and the interval provided by the **with** attribute overlap.

A typical use of the `DateInterval` structure is to create an interval from two dates and check if a specific date falls within the interval, as in the following example.

```
import Foundation

let calendar = Calendar.current
var components = DateComponents()
components.year = 1970
components.month = 8
components.day = 21
var birthday = calendar.date(from: components)

components.year = 2020
components.month = 8
components.day = 21
var future = calendar.date(from: components)

if birthday != nil && future != nil {
    let today = Date()
    let interval = DateInterval(start: birthday!, end: future!)
    if interval.contains(today) {
        print("You still have time")   // "You still have time"
    }
}
```

Listing 4-24: Finding a date in an interval

The code of Listing 4-24 creates two dates, **birthday** and **future**, and then generates an interval from one date to another. The **contains()** method is used next to check whether the current date is within the interval or not.

Printing independent components, as we did in previous examples, is not a problem because they are just integer values, but a complete date requires a format that will vary depending on the requirements of the app. For example, sometimes the limited space available on the screen to print the date demands expressing it just with basic values, but in other circumstances the application may require a full description, including the names of the month and the day of the week. Foundation provides the **DateFormatter** class to produce a textual representation of dates and times. The following are some of its properties and methods.

dateStyle—This property sets or returns the style of the date. It is an enumeration of type **Style** with the values **none**, **short**, **medium**, **long**, and **full**.

timeStyle—This property sets or returns the style of the time. It is an enumeration of type **Style** with the values **none**, **short**, **medium**, **long**, and **full**.

dateFormat—This property sets or returns a custom format for the date and time. Its value is a string with characters that specify the position of the components of the date.

monthSymbols—This property returns an array of strings with the names of the months in correlative order (index 0 returns "January", index 1 "February", and so on). Other related properties are **shortMonthSymbols** (returns an abbreviation of the names) and **veryShortMonthSymbols** (returns the initials).

locale—This property sets or returns the **Locale** structure used by the **DateFormatter** object to process the date. The value by default is the **Locale** structure defined by the system.

timeZone—This property sets or returns the **TimeZone** structure used by the **DateFormatter** object to process the date. The value by default is the **TimeZone** structure defined by the system.

string(from: Date)—This method returns a string with the date provided by the **from** attribute in the format specified by the properties of the object.

date(from: String)—This method interprets the value of the **from** attribute as a date and returns a **Date** structure containing the value or **nil** when no date is found in the string.

The process to format a date is simple. The **DateFormatter** object is created first, then the **dateStyle**, **timeStyle**, or **dateFormat** properties are initialized to set the format we want, and finally the **string()** method is called to get the string.

```
import Foundation

var today = Date()
let formatter = DateFormatter()
formatter.dateStyle = DateFormatter.Style.medium
formatter.timeStyle = DateFormatter.Style.medium

var mydate = formatter.string(from: today) // "Aug 6, 2019 at 7:36:50 PM"
```

Listing 4-25: Formatting dates

In the code of Listing 4-25, the style is declared as **medium** for the date and time, but we can specify other values to produce a different result. If only the date or the time are required, we can declare the style **none** for the one we want to hide or leave the property with the value by default, as in the following example.

```
import Foundation

var today = Date()
let formatter = DateFormatter()
formatter.dateStyle = DateFormatter.Style.full
var mydate = formatter.string(from: today)   // "Tuesday, August 6, 2019"
```

Listing 4-26: Formatting only the date

The **string()** method in Listing 4-26 returns a string containing the full date without the time (the style for the time was not declared). The full date includes the names of the day and the month. If we want to design a custom format, we can use the **dateFormat** property.

```
import Foundation

var today = Date()
let formatter = DateFormatter()
formatter.dateFormat = "(yyyy) MM dd"
var mydate = formatter.string(from: today)   // "(2019) 08 06"
```

Listing 4-27: Defining a custom format

Chapter 4 - Introduction to Frameworks

The `dateFormat` property uses specific characters to represent date components. The `string()` method replaces those characters by the values of the date and returns the formatted string.

 Do It Yourself: Replace the code in your Playground file with the codes of Listings 4-25, 4-26, or 4-27. Try different values and combinations for the `dateStyle`, `timeStyle`, and `dateFormat` properties to see the strings they produce.

 IMPORTANT: In the example of Listing 4-27, we used the characters for the year (`yyyy`) the month (`MM`), and the day (`dd`) to define the format, but there are also characters available for the hour (`HH`), minutes (`mm`), seconds (`ss`), and more. For a complete list, visit our website and follow the links for this chapter.

The `Calendar` structure and `DateFormatter` class process dates according to local conventions, including the language, symbols, etc. This means that the components of a date are going to be interpreted according to the conventions currently set on the device. For example, the same date will look like this "Tuesday, August 6, 2019" for a user in the United States and like this "2019年8月6日 星期二" for a user in China. How dates are going to be processed is determined by an object of the `Locale` structure. Every device has a `Locale` structure assigned by default, and our code will work with it unless we determine otherwise. To get a reference to the current structure or create a new one, the `Locale` structure includes the following initializer and type property.

Locale(identifier: String)—This initializer creates a `Locale` structure configured for the region determined by the value of the attribute. The attribute is a string that represents a language and a region (e.g., en_US for the United States, zh_CN for China).

current—This type property returns the `Locale` structure assigned by default to the device or defined by the user in the Settings app.

The structure also offers properties to get information from an instance or the class itself. The following are the most frequently used.

identifier—This property returns a string with the locale's identifier.

languageCode—This property returns a string with a code that identifies the locale's language.

regionCode—This property returns a string with a code that identifies the locale's region.

calendar—This property returns a `Calendar` structure with the locale's calendar.

decimalSeparator—This property returns a string with the locale's decimal separator.

currencyCode—This property returns a string with a code that identifies the locale's currency.

currencySymbol—This property returns a string with the symbol that represents the locale's currency.

usesMetricSystem—This property returns a Boolean value that determines whether the locale is using the metric system.

availableIdentifiers—This type property returns an array of strings with the locale identifiers available in the system.

preferredLanguages—This type property returns an array with the languages preferred by the user.

Although it is recommended to use the `Locale` structure set by the system and keep the values by default, there are times when our application has to present the information with a specific configuration. For example, we may need to create an application that always shows dates in Chinese, no matter where the user is located. We can do this by assigning a `Locale` structure to the `locale` property of the `DateFormatter` object used to format the date.

```
import Foundation

var today = Date()
let formatter = DateFormatter()
formatter.dateStyle = DateFormatter.Style.full

let chinaLocale = Locale(identifier: "zh_CN")
formatter.locale = chinaLocale
let displayDate = formatter.string(from: today) // "2018年8月30日 星期三"
```

Listing 4-28: Defining a different location

The code of Listing 4-28 creates a new `Locale` structure with the zh_CN identifier, which corresponds to China and the Chinese language, and assigns it to a `DateFormatter` object. Now, every string generated by this object will contain a date formatted according to Chinese conventions.

 IMPORTANT: The list of identifiers you can use to create a `Locale` structure is extensive. You can print the type property `availableIdentifiers` from the `Locale` structure to get an array with the values available (e.g., `print(Locale.availableIdentifiers)`).

 The Basics: The `Locale` structure is not only used to define date formats but also multiple linguistic and cultural norms that apply to a region. For this reason, the class is used to prepare the app for international distribution.

The date stored in a `Date` structure is not a date but the number of seconds between the date represented by the object and an arbitrary date in the past (January 1st, 2001). To process these values and get the actual date, the `Calendar` structure and the `DateFormatter` class need to know the time zone the date belongs to. Foundation includes the `TimeZone` structure to manage time zones. An object is assigned by default to the system containing the time zone where the device is located (that is why when we display a date it coincides with the date on our device), but we can create a different one as we did with the `Locale` structure. To get a reference to the current structure or create a new one, the `TimeZone` structure includes the following initializer and type property.

TimeZone(identifier: String)—This initializer creates a `TimeZone` structure configured for the time zone determined by the value of the **identifier** attribute. The attribute is a string that represents the name of the time zone (e.g., "Europe/Paris", "Asia/Bangkok").

current—This type property returns the `TimeZone` structure assigned by default to the device or defined by the user in the Settings app.

Time zones are a very complex subject, but usually the applications are quite simple. For example, we can calculate the time in different parts of the world from the same date using different `TimeZone` structures.

```
import Foundation

let tokyoTimeZone = TimeZone(identifier: "Asia/Tokyo")
let madridTimeZone = TimeZone(identifier: "Europe/Madrid")
```

Chapter 4 - Introduction to Frameworks

```
var today = Date()   // "Aug 6, 2019 at 7:52 PM"
let formatter = DateFormatter()
formatter.dateStyle = DateFormatter.Style.short
formatter.timeStyle = DateFormatter.Style.short

formatter.timeZone = tokyoTimeZone
let tokyoDate = formatter.string(from: today)   // "8/7/19, 8:52 AM"

formatter.timeZone = madridTimeZone
let madridDate = formatter.string(from: today)   // "8/7/19, 1:52 AM"
```

Listing 4-29: *Working with different time zones*

The code of Listing 4-29 creates two **TimeZone** structures, one for Tokyo's time zone and another for Madrid's time zone, and then assigns the structures to a **DateFormatter** object to generate the strings from the current date and get the current times in Tokyo and Madrid.

 IMPORTANT: The list of names for the time zones is stored in a database. The **TimeZone** structure offers the **knownTimeZoneIdentifiers** type property to get an array with the values available. You can print this property to see the whole list (e.g., **print(TimeZone.knownTimeZoneIdentifiers)**).

Medium **Measurements**

Other types of data some applications need are units of measurement, such as pounds, miles, etc. Defining our own units present some challenges, but Foundation includes the **Measurement** structure to simplify our work. This structure includes two properties, one for the value and another for the unit. The initializer requires these two values to create the structure.

Measurement(value: Double, unit: Unit)—This initializer creates a **Measurement** structure with the values specified by the **value** and **unit** attributes. The **unit** attribute is a property of a subclass of the **Dimension** class.

The value declared for the **Measurement** structure is the number that determines the magnitude, like 55 in 55 km, and the unit is a property of a subclass of the **Dimension** class that represents the unit of measurement, like km in 55 km. The **Dimension** class contains all the basic functionally required for measurement but is through its subclasses that the units of measurement are determined. Foundation offers multiple subclasses to define units for different types of dimensions. The following are the most frequently used.

UnitDuration—This subclass of the **Dimension** class defines the units of measurement for duration (time). The subclass includes the following properties to represent the units: **seconds**, **minutes** and **hours**, with **seconds** defined as the basic unit.

UnitLength—This subclass of the **Dimension** class defines the units of measurement for length. The subclass includes the following properties to represent the units: **megameters**, **kilometers**, **hectometers**, **decameters**, **meters**, **decimeters**, **centimeters**, **millimeters**, **micrometers**, **nanometers**, **picometers**, **inches**, **feet**, **yards**, **miles**, **scandinavianMiles**, **lightyears**, **nauticalMiles**, **fathoms**, **furlongs**, **astronomicalUnits**, and **parsecs**, with **meters** defined as the basic unit.

UnitMass—This subclass of the **Dimension** class defines the units of measurement for mass. The subclass includes the following properties to represent the units: **kilograms**, **grams**, **decigrams**, **centigrams**, **milligrams**, **micrograms**, **nanograms**, **picograms**, **ounces**, **pounds**, **stones**, **metricTons**, **shortTons**, **carats**, **ouncesTroy**, and **slugs**, with **kilograms** defined as the basic unit.

UnitVolume—This subclass of the `Dimension` class defines the units of measurement for volume. The subclass includes the following properties to represent the units: `megaliters`, `kiloliters`, `liters`, `deciliters`, `centiliters`, `milliliters`, `cubicKilometers`, `cubicMeters`, `cubicDecimeters`, `cubicMillimeters`, `cubicInches`, `cubicFeet`, `cubicYards`, `cubicMiles`, `acreFeet`, `bushels`, `teaspoons`, `tablespoons`, `fluidOunces`, `cups`, `pints`, `quarts`, `gallons`, `imperialTeaspoons`, `imperialTablespoons`, `imperialFluidOunces`, `imperialPints`, `imperialQuarts`, `imperialGallons`, and `metricCups`, with `liters` defined as the basic unit.

The `Measurement` structure includes the following properties and methods to access the values and convert them to different units.

value—This property sets or returns the structure's value. It is of type `Double`.

unit—This property sets or returns the structure's unit of measurement. It is represented by a property of a subclass of the `Dimension` class.

convert(to: Unit)—This method converts the values of the `Measurement` structure to the unit specified by the **to** attribute. The attribute is a property of a subclass of the `Dimension` class.

converted(to: Unit)—This method converts the values of the `Measurement` structure to the unit specified by the **to** attribute and returns a new `Measurement` structure with the result. The attribute is a property of a subclass of the `Dimension` class.

The initialization of a `Measurement` structure is simple, we just have to provide the value for the magnitude and the property that represents the unit of measurement we want to use. The following example creates two structures to store a measure of 30 centimeters and another of 5 pounds.

```
import Foundation

var length = Measurement(value: 30, unit: UnitLength.centimeters) // 30.0
cm
var weight = Measurement(value: 5, unit: UnitMass.pounds)  // 5.0 lb
```

Listing 4-30: Initializing `Measurement` *structures*

If the measures are of the same dimension (e.g., length), we can perform operations with their values. The `Measurement` structure allows the operations `+`, `-`, `*`, `/`, and also the use of the comparison operators `==`, `!=`, `<`, `>`, `<=`, and `>=` to compare values. The following example adds two measures in centimeters.

```
import Foundation

var length = Measurement(value: 200, unit: UnitLength.centimeters)
var width = Measurement(value: 800, unit: UnitLength.centimeters)

var total = length + width  // 1000.0 cm
```

Listing 4-31: Adding the values of two `Measurement` *structures*

If the units are different, the `Measurement` structure returned by the operation is defined with the dimension's basic unit. For example, if we are working with lengths, the basic unit is `meters`.

```
import Foundation

var length = Measurement(value: 300, unit: UnitLength.meters)
var width = Measurement(value: 2, unit: UnitLength.kilometers)

var total = length + width   // 2300.0 m
```

Listing 4-32: Adding two values of different units

The code of Listing 4-32 adds two lengths of different units (meters and kilometers). The system converts kilometers to meters and then performs the addition, returning a **Measurement** structure with a value in meters (the default unit).

If we want everything to be performed in the same unit, we can convert a value to a different unit using the **convert()** or **converted()** methods. In the following example, we convert the unit of the **length** variable to kilometers and perform the addition again in kilometers.

```
import Foundation

var length = Measurement(value: 300, unit: UnitLength.meters)
var width = Measurement(value: 2, unit: UnitLength.kilometers)
length.convert(to: UnitLength.kilometers)

var total = length + width   // 2.3 km
```

Listing 4-33: Converting units

The values of a **Measurement** structure are printed as they are stored and with the units they represent, but this is usually not what we need to display to our users. Foundation offers the **MeasurementFormatter** class to format these values. This class works in a similar way than the **DateFormatter** class studied in the previous section. The class can determine how the value and the unit are going to be displayed (e.g., cm, centimeters) and adapt them to the location and configuration of the device (the user's country and language). The following are all the properties and methods available in the **MeasurementFormatter** class to format a value.

unitStyle—This property sets or returns the style used to display the measure. It is an enumeration of type **UnitStyle** defined in a superclass of the **MeasurementFormatter** class. The possible values are **short**, **medium** and **long**.

unitOptions—This property sets or returns options that determine how the values are going to be presented. It is a property of a structure called **UnitOptions** defined inside the **MeasurementFormatter** class. The properties available are **providedUnit** (uses the provided unit instead of the local unit), **naturalScale** (expresses the numbers in a natural format, like in kilometers instead of meters when the numbers are big enough), and **temperatureWithoutUnit** (shows the value of the temperature without the unit).

numberFormatter—This property sets or returns a custom format for the number. It is a value of type **NumberFormatter**.

locale—This property sets or returns the **Locale** structure used by the **MeasurementFormatter** object to process the value. The value by default is the **Locale** structure defined by the system.

string(from: Measurement)—This method returns a string with the measure provided by the **from** attribute in the format specified by the properties of the object.

As with the **DateFormatter** class, the **MeasurementFormatter** class has to be initialized first and then configured with the type of format we want to use. The final string is generated with the **string()** method, as in the following example.

```
import Foundation

var length = Measurement(value: 40, unit: UnitLength.kilometers)

var formatter = MeasurementFormatter()
formatter.unitStyle = MeasurementFormatter.UnitStyle.long
formatter.unitOptions = MeasurementFormatter.UnitOptions.naturalScale

var newValue = formatter.string(from: length)   // "24.855 miles"
```

Listing 4-34: Formatting a measure

One of the advantages of using a formatter to present a measure is that the value and the unit are automatically adapted to the location and language of the user. If the code is executed in a location where the unit of measurement is miles instead of kilometers, the values of the **Measurement** structure will be converted to miles, as shown in Listing 4-34 ("24.855 miles").

If our application has to present the same unit of measurement independently of the device's location, we can set a specific locale with the **locale** property, as we did before for dates. The following example formats the measures in Chinese, no matter where the app is executed.

```
import Foundation

var length = Measurement(value: 40, unit: UnitLength.kilometers)

var formatter = MeasurementFormatter()
formatter.unitStyle = MeasurementFormatter.UnitStyle.long
formatter.unitOptions = MeasurementFormatter.UnitOptions.naturalScale
formatter.locale = Locale(identifier: "zh_CN")

var newValue = formatter.string(from: length)   // 40公里
```

Listing 4-35: Formatting a measure for a specific locale

We can also specify a format for the number. The **MeasurementFormatter** class offers the **numberFormatter** property to assign a **NumberFormatter** object to the formatter. For example, we can format the value of a measure to always include 6 digits.

```
import Foundation

var length = Measurement(value: 40, unit: UnitLength.kilometers)

var formatter = MeasurementFormatter()
formatter.unitStyle = MeasurementFormatter.UnitStyle.long
formatter.unitOptions = MeasurementFormatter.UnitOptions.naturalScale

var formatNumber = NumberFormatter()
formatNumber.minimumIntegerDigits = 6
formatter.numberFormatter = formatNumber

var newValue = formatter.string(from: length)   // "000025 miles"
```

Listing 4-36: Formatting the value

 IMPORTANT: The **Measurement** class also allows you to define your own units of measurement. The topic is beyond the scope of this book. For more information, visit our website and follow the links for this chapter.

Chapter 4 - Introduction to Frameworks

Timers are objects created from the `Timer` class that perform an action after a specific period. There are two types of timers: repeating and non-repeating. Repeating timers perform the action and then reschedule themselves to do it again in an infinite loop. Non-repeating timers, on the other hand, perform the action once and then invalidate themselves. The class includes the following properties and methods to create and manage timers.

isValid—This property returns a Boolean value that indicates if the timer can still be fired or it was invalidated.

timeInterval—This property returns the time interval in seconds for repeating timers. It is a value of type `TimeInterval`.

tolerance—This property sets or returns a period of tolerance in seconds to provide the system with more flexibility. It is a value of type `TimeInterval`. The value by default is 0.

scheduledTimer(withTimeInterval: TimeInterval, **repeats:** Bool, **block:** Closure)—This type method returns repeating and non-repeating timers depending on the values of its attributes. The **withTimeInterval** attribute represents the seconds the timer has to wait before performing the action, the **repeats** attribute is a Boolean value that determine if the timer is repeating (`true`) or non-repeating (`false`), and the **block** attribute is a closure to be execute when the time is up.

fire()—This method fires the timer without considering the time remaining.

invalidate()—This method invalidates the timer (stops the timer).

The `scheduledTimer()` method creates a timer according to the value of its attributes and automatically adds it to an internal loop that will process it when the time is up. The time is set in seconds with a `TimeInterval` value (a typealias of `Double`) and we can declare the closure as a trailing closure to simplify the code, as in the following example.

```
import Foundation
print("Wait 5 seconds...")
Timer.scheduledTimer(withTimeInterval: 5.0, repeats: false) { (timer) in
    print("The time is up")
}
```

Listing 4-37: Creating a non-repeating timer

The example of Listing 4-37 creates a non-repeating timer. The code prints a message and then initializes a timer with the `scheduleTimer()` method. The timer is set to 5 seconds, non-repeating, and the closure just prints another message on the console. When we execute the code, the first message appears on the console and after 5 seconds the message "The time is up" is displayed.

The closure receives a reference to the `Timer` object that we can use to access the timer's properties or invalidate it. It was not required in the last example, but it may be useful when we work with repeating timers, as in the following example.

```
import Foundation

var counter = 0
func startTimer() {
```

```
Timer.scheduledTimer(withTimeInterval: 1.0, repeats: true) {
(timerref) in
    report(timer: timerref)
  }
}
func report(timer: Timer) {
  print("\(counter) times")
  counter += 1
  if counter > 10 {
    print("Finished")
    timer.invalidate()
  }
}
startTimer()
```

Listing 4-38: Creating a repeating timer

In Listing 4-38, we define two functions. The **startTimer**() function schedules the timer, and the **report**() function is executed when the time is up. In this last function, we count how many times the code is executed with the **counter** variable and each time we print a message on the console with that number. If the value is greater than 10, we print the message "Finished" and invalidate the timer, so the function is not executed anymore (repeating timers keep running indefinitely until they are invalidated).

Do It Yourself: Replace the code in your Playground with the example you want to try. With the example of Listing 4-37, you should see a message printed on the console after 5 seconds, and with the example of Listing 4-38, you should see a total of 10 messages and the text "Finished" at the end.

(Advanced) ## Operation Queues

Apple systems can take advantage of the multiple cores in modern processors to execute different pieces of code simultaneously, increasing the amount of work the application can perform at any given time. For example, we may have a code that downloads a file from the Internet and another code that shows the progress on the screen. In cases like this, we cannot wait for one code to finish to execute the other; we need the two pieces of code to work at the same time. The system allows our applications to create multiple path of execution to run these tasks simultaneously. These paths are called *threads*. When the app is launched, the system defines one thread for our code to run, usually refer to as the main thread, and then the application creates more threads as needed.

Threads can make our app run faster, but they also add complexity to our code that is hard to handle. We not only have to decide when it is appropriate to create a new thread but also to which cores the threads are going to be assigned to and control the conflicts that multiple threads accessing the same data can cause. Because of the complexity of threads, Apple offers two simple ways to schedule tasks: Operations and Grand Central Dispatch (GCD). With these systems we can focus on the tasks at hand and let the system manage the threads.

The simplest system is Operations. Foundation includes the **Operation** class to create operation objects. The class provides all the necessary functionality to configure an operation, but we must create a subclass to include the statements the operation is required to perform. For simple operations, the framework defines a standard subclass of **Operation** called **BlockOperation**. This subclass can create an operation from the statements provided by a closure. The following is its initializer.

BlockOperation(block: Closure)—This initializer creates an operation with the statements specified by the closure assigned to the **block** attribute.

Chapter 4 - Introduction to Frameworks

Because the `BlockOperation` class is a subclass of `Operation`, it has access to its properties and methods. The following are the most useful.

completionBlock—This property sets a closure with the statements we want to execute after the operation is completed.

queuePriority—This property sets the operation's priority. It is an enumeration called `QueuePriority` included in the `Operation` class. The values available are `veryLow`, `low`, `normal`, `high`, and `veryHigh`.

cancel()—This method asks the system to cancel the operation.

The operations have to be added to a queue to be scheduled for execution. For this purpose, Foundation includes the `OperationQueue` class. Once an instance of this class is created, we can use the following methods to manage the operations in the queue.

addOperation(Operation)—This method adds the operation specified by the operation attribute to the queue. The attribute is an object created from an `Operation` subclass.

addOperations([Operation], waitUntilFinished: Bool)—This method adds the operations specified by the first attribute to the queue. The **waitUntilFinished** attribute determines whether the thread will be blocked until the operations are finished or not.

addOperation(Closure)—This method creates an `Operation` object from the statements provided by the attribute and adds it to the queue. The attribute is a closure with the statements we want to include in the operation.

cancelAllOperations()—This method cancels all the operations in the queue.

addBarrierBlock(Closure)—This method executes a closure after all the operations in the queue have finished and don't allow other operations added to the queue later to be executed until the execution of the closure has been completed.

By default, the code is executed in the main thread created by the system for our application. In terms of the operations, this is called the *main queue*. If we want some code to be executed in a different queue, we must create an operation and add it to a new queue.

```
import Foundation

let operation = BlockOperation(block: {
    var total: Double = 1
    for f in 1..<100 {
        total = log(total + Double(f))
    }
    print("Total: \(total)")
})
let queue = OperationQueue()
queue.addOperation(operation)
print("Printed in the Main Queue")
```

Listing 4-39: Adding operations to a queue

The operation is created by the `BlockOperation()` initializer. This initializer takes a closure with the statements we want to execute (in this case, a loop to calculate the logarithm of a sequence of values) and creates the operation. With the operation ready, we initialize a new `OperationQueue` object to represent the queue and add the operation to it.

When the code of Listing 4-39 is executed, the system creates the operation, adds it to a new queue, and runs it as soon as it can. At this point, the system is running two codes at the same time, the code in the main queue and the code in the new queue we have just created. As a

Chapter 4 - Introduction to Frameworks

result, we will see the message "Printed in the Main Queue" on the console first, and then the message produced by the operation, because the operation takes more time to complete.

This code guarantees that the code in the main queue is executed, no matter how much time the statements in the operation take to finish the process. If we hadn't created the operation and added it to a new queue, the system would have had to wait until the execution of the loop was over to execute the last statement and print the message on the console.

 Do It Yourself: Replace the code in your playground file with the code of Listing 4-39 and press the play button. The Xcode's console should print the message "Printed in the Main Queue" first and then another message with the result of the operation.

Some frameworks, like SwiftUI, can only work in the main queue. If we try to access the elements of the interface from a different queue, the application will produce unexpected results. The `OperationQueue` class offers the following type property to get a reference to the main queue.

main—This type property returns a reference to the `OperationQueue` object representing the main queue.

Code inside a closure may sometimes be executed in a different queue. Every time we execute code inside an operation or a block of code, we must consider whether that code can be executed in any queue or it only works properly in the main queue. If the code is required to be executed in the main queue, we must insert it in an operation, get a reference to the main queue from the **main** property, and add the operation to it, as in the following example.

```
import Foundation

let operation = BlockOperation(block: {
    var total: Double = 1
    for f in 1..<100 {
        total = log(total + Double(f))
    }
    let main = OperationQueue.main
    main.addOperation({
        print("Printed in the Main Queue")
    })
})
let queue = OperationQueue()
queue.addOperation(operation)
```

Listing 4-40: Adding operations to the main queue

In Listing 4-40, we get a reference to the main queue inside an operation and then add an operation to it that prints a message on the console. Because we assign it to the main queue, this operation is executed in the main thread, even when it was defined inside another operation.

The operations are performed asynchronously and therefore the order in which they are executed is not determined by the Operation Queue but rather by the system. Some operations are executed simultaneously and others in an order different than the one established by the queue. If our code requires the operations to be executed in a specific order, we must declare dependencies between them. A dependency makes an operation dependent on the execution of another. For instance, if we have an operation One and add a dependency to operation Two, the operation One won't be executed until the operation Two's execution is over. The **Operation** class includes two methods to add and remove dependencies.

addDependency(Operation**)**—This method adds a dependency to the operation. The attribute is a reference to the operation to which the original operation depends on.

removeDependency(Operation**)**—This method removes a dependency. The attribute is a reference to the operation to which the original operation depends on.

The following example illustrates how to add a dependency between two operations.

```
import Foundation

let firstoperation = BlockOperation(block: {
    print("First Operation Executed")
})
let secondoperation = BlockOperation(block: {
    print("Second Operation Executed")
})
firstoperation.addDependency(secondoperation)

let queue = OperationQueue()
queue.addOperations([firstoperation, secondoperation], waitUntilFinished:
false)
```

Listing 4-41: Adding a dependency

The process is simple, we define the operations and then call the **addDependency**() method on the operation we want to make dependent on another. In Listing 4-41, we create two operations called **firstoperation** and **secondoperation** and then make the **firstoperation** dependent on the **secondoperation**. Because of this, the **firstoperation** is only executed after the execution of the **secondoperation** is over.

 Do It Yourself: Replace the code in your playground file with the code of Listing 4-41 and press play. You should see the message "Second Operation Executed" on the console before the message "First Operation Executed".

As we already mentioned, Operations are the high-level system offered by Foundation to schedule simultaneous tasks, but there is another system that we can also implement for this purpose called Grand Central Dispatch (GCD). GCD is an old system programmed in the C language that works like Operations in Foundation but at a lower level, offering a deeper access to the system. This system is not defined in Foundation but in its own framework called *Dispatch*.

Dispatch is a new framework that replaces the old GCD programmed in the C language. It includes an extensive list of classes to provide access to all the original features of GCD, but with a friendly API. To schedule an operation, all we need to do is to create an instance of the **DispatchQueue** class. The following is the class initializer.

DispatchQueue(label: String**)**—This initializer creates a queue identified with the value specified by the **label** attribute.

Once the **DispatchQueue** instance is created, we must call its methods to add a task to the queue. The class includes two methods to dispatch tasks synchronously (the operation must finish before others are initiated) or asynchronously (multiple operations are executed simultaneously).

async(execute: Closure**)**—This method asynchronously executes the statements in the closure specified by the **execute** attribute.

sync(execute: Closure**)**—This method synchronously executes the statements in the closure specified by the **execute** attribute.

The Dispatch framework is just another way to perform multiple tasks simultaneously. The following example repeats the code we used before with Operations, but this time the task is performed by a `DispatchQueue` object.

```
import Foundation

let queue = DispatchQueue(label: "myqueue")
queue.async(execute: {
   var total: Double = 1
   for f in 1..<100 {
      total = log(total + Double(f))
   }
   print("Total: \(total)")
})
print("Printed in the Main Queue")
```

Listing 4-42: Dispatching tasks with GCD

The `DispatchQueue` class also offers a type property to access the main queue.

main—This type property returns the `DispatchQueue` object referencing the main queue.

As we did before, the following example updates a previous code to perform a task in the main queue from a secondary queue.

```
import Foundation

let queue = DispatchQueue(label: "myqueue")
queue.async(execute: {
   var total: Double = 1
   for f in 1..<100 {
      total = log(total + Double(f))
   }
   let main = DispatchQueue.main
   main.sync(execute: {
      print("Printed in the Main Queue")
   })
})
```

Listing 4-43: Working on the main queue with GCD

When the code of Listing 4-43 is executed, it creates a queue with a closure to calculate the logarithm of a series of values. When the operation is over, the task gets a reference to the main queue and performs a second task to print a message on the console. This last operation is performed synchronously since we are already inside an asynchronous queue.

 Do It Yourself: These examples work the same way as the examples introduced for Foundation's Operations. Replace the code in your playground file with the example you want to try and press play. The results should be the same as before.

Like Operations, the tasks we assign to a queue are not performed in order. They can be executed simultaneously or in an order different than the one established by the queue. To control the situation, the Dispatch framework offers the `DispatchGroup` class that we can use to track the completion of multiple operations. With an object of this class, we can indicate when a task begins and finishes and then execute a closure when they are all over. The class includes the following methods for this purpose.

Chapter 4 - Introduction to Frameworks

enter()—This method indicates that a task has enter the group of tasks to be monitored.

leave()—This method indicates that a task in the group has finished.

notify(queue: DispatchQueue, **execute:** Closure)—This method executes a closure when all the tasks in the group are over. The **queue** attribute determines the queue in which the closure will be processed, and the **execute** attribute is the closure to be executed.

The following example adds two tasks to a queue called "myqueue", but unlike previous examples, we include each one of them in a dispatch group and print a message when all the tasks are over.

```
import Foundation

let group = DispatchGroup()
let queue = DispatchQueue(label: "myqueue")

group.enter()
queue.async(execute: {
   print("First Task Executed")
   group.leave()
})
group.enter()
queue.async(execute: {
   print("Second Task Executed")
   group.leave()
})
group.notify(queue: .main, execute: {
   print("The tasks are over")
})
```

Listing 4-44: Adding tasks to a Dispatch Group

A dispatch group is created from an instance of the `DispatchGroup` class and the tasks are added to the group with the `enter()` and `leave()` methods. In the example of Listing 4-44, we create the `DispatchGroup` object and then add two tasks to the queue. Before adding each task, we call the `enter()` method, and after the task is over we call the `leave()` method to communicate the state of the task to the group. At the end, we call the `notify()` method to print a message when the execution of all the tasks is over.

Threads usually work along with a code that generates a loop to process events. Foundation defines a class called `RunLoop` to create these loops. The system automatically generates a `RunLoop` object for the main thread that takes care of processing the events for our application. This is the application loop we mentioned in Chapter 1. The `RunLoop` class includes the following type property and instance method to access the main loop and to perform tasks in the queue.

main—This type property returns a reference to the `RunLoop` object assigned to the main queue.

perform(Closure)—This method assigns a task to the main loop. The attribute is a closure with the code we want to execute in the main queue.

The `RunLoop` object assigned by the system to the main thread is used by some frameworks to reference the main queue, as we will see in later chapters, but we can also add tasks manually with the `perform()` method, as in the following example.

```
import Foundation
let operation = BlockOperation(block: {
```

```
    var total: Double = 1
    for f in 1..<100 {
        total = log(total + Double(f))
    }
    let main = RunLoop.main
    main.perform {
        print("Printed in the Main Queue")
    }
})
let queue = OperationQueue()
queue.addOperation(operation)
```

Listing 4-45: Adding tasks to the main queue with RunLoop

(Basic) **4.3 Core Graphics**

Core Graphics is an old framework programmed in the C language. It was developed to provide a platform-independent two-dimensional drawing engine for Apple systems. The framework is composed of basic drawing tools and its own specific data types. Due to its characteristics, instead of being replaced, the framework was integrated with newer frameworks and, therefore, is still in use.

(Basic) **Data Types**

What modern applications require the most from this old framework are its data types. In Swift, Core Graphics data types are implemented as structures, with their own initializers, properties and methods. Each one of them was defined to store values that represent attributes of elements on the screen, such as position or size. The following is a structure included in the framework to specify independent values.

CGFloat—This structure is used to store values of type `Double` for drawing purposes.

A more complex structure is `CGSize`, designed to store values that represent dimensions. This data type includes the following initializer, properties and method.

CGSize(width: CGFloat, height: CGFloat)—This initializer creates a `CGSize` structure with the values specified by the **width** and **height** attributes. The structure defines initializers to create instances from values of type `Int`, `CGFloat`, and `Double`.

zero—This type property returns a `CGSize` structure with its values set to zero.

width—This property sets or returns the structure's width.

height—This property sets or returns the structure's height.

equalTo(CGSize)—This method returns a Boolean value that indicates whether the `CGSize` structure is equal to the value of the attribute.

Another structure is `CGPoint`, which is used to define points in a two-dimensional coordinate system. This data type includes the following initializer, properties and method.

CGPoint(x: CGFloat, y: CGFloat)—This initializer creates a `CGPoint` structure with the coordinates specified by the **x** and **y** attributes. The structure defines initializers to create instances from values of type `Int`, `CGFloat`, and `Double`.

zero—This type property returns a `CGPoint` structure with its values set to zero.

x—This property sets or returns the structure's x coordinate.

y—This property sets or returns the structure's y coordinate.

equalTo(CGPoint)—This method returns a Boolean value that determines whether the `CGPoint` structure is equal to the value of the attribute.

There is also a similar structure called `CGVector` to manage a two-dimensional vector. This data type includes the following initializer and properties.

CGVector(dx: CGFloat, **dy:** CGFloat)—This initializer creates a `CGVector` structure with the vector's coordinates specified by the **dx** and **dy** attributes. The structure defines initializers to create instances from values of type `Int`, `CGFloat`, and `Double`.

zero—This type property returns a `CGVector` structure with its values set to zero.

dx—This property sets or returns the structure's x coordinate.

dy—This property sets or returns the structure's y coordinate.

Finally, there is a more complex structure called `CGRect` that we can use to define and work with rectangles. This data type includes the following initializers, properties and methods.

CGRect(origin: CGPoint, **size:** CGSize) —This initializer creates a `CGRect` structure to store the origin and size of a rectangle. The **origin** attribute is a `CGPoint` structure with the coordinates of the rectangle's origin, and the **size** attribute is a `CGSize` structure with the rectangle's width and height.

CGRect(x: CGFloat, **y:** CGFloat, **width:** CGFloat, **height:** CGFloat) —This initializer creates a `CGRect` structure to store the origin and size of a rectangle. The **x** and **y** attributes define the coordinates of the rectangle's origin, and the **width** and **height** attributes its size. The structure defines initializers to create instances from values of type `Int`, `CGFloat`, and `Double`.

zero—This type property returns a `CGRect` structure with its values set to zero.

origin—This property sets or returns a `CGPoint` structure with the coordinates of the rectangle's origin.

size—This property sets or returns a `CGSize` structure with the rectangle's width and height.

minX—This property returns the minimum value of the rectangle's **x** coordinate.

minY—This property returns the minimum value of the rectangle's **y** coordinate.

maxX—This property returns the maximum value of the rectangle's **x** coordinate.

maxY—This property returns the maximum value of the rectangle's **y** coordinate.

midX—This property returns the value of the rectangle's **x** coordinate located at the horizontal center of the rectangle.

midY—This property returns the value of the rectangle's **y** coordinate located at the vertical center of the rectangle.

equalTo(CGRect)—This method returns a Boolean value that determines if the `CGRect` structure is equal to the value specified by the attribute.

contains(CGPoint)—This method returns a Boolean value that determines if the value specified by the attribute is contained inside the `CGRect` structure. The attribute may be of type `CGPoint` (to detect if a point is inside the rectangle) or `CGRect` (to detect if another rectangle is inside the original rectangle).

intersects(CGRect)—This method returns a Boolean value to indicate if the rectangle specified by the attribute intersects with the original rectangle.

intersection(CGRect)—This method returns a **CGRect** structure with the coordinates and size of the rectangle formed by the intersection of the original rectangle with the rectangle specified by the attribute.

union(CGRect)—This method returns a new **CGRect** structure with the coordinates and size of a rectangle that includes the original rectangle and the rectangle specified by the attribute.

The structures provided by Core Graphics are declared and initialized as any other structures in Swift, but we must import the Core Graphics framework first for the types to be recognized.

```
import CoreGraphics

var myfloat: CGFloat = 35
var mysize: CGSize = CGSize(width: 250, height: 250)
var mypoint: CGPoint = CGPoint(x: 20, y: 50)
var myrect: CGRect = CGRect(origin: mypoint, size: mysize)
var myvector: CGVector = CGVector(dx: 30, dy: 30)
```

Listing 4-46: Initializing Core Graphics' structures

 The Basics: The values in a coordinate system are identified with the letters **x** and **y**. Core Graphics follows this convention and assigns these names to the parameters of the structures that store coordinate values.

The **CGSize**, **CGPoint**, and **CGVector** structures may be initialized with their member initializers, but the **CGRect** structure provides an additional initializer to create the instance from the values of its internal structures.

```
import CoreGraphics

var myrect = CGRect(x: 30, y: 20, width: 100, height: 200)

print("The origin is at \(myrect.origin.x) and \(myrect.origin.y)")
print("The size is \(myrect.size.width) by \(myrect.size.height)")
```

Listing 4-47: Using the CGRect convenience initializer

The **origin** and **size** properties of a **CGRect** value are **CGPoint** and **CGSize** structures, respectively, so they can be copied into other variables or properties as any other values.

```
import CoreGraphics

var myrect = CGRect(x: 30, y: 20, width: 100, height: 200)

var mypoint = myrect.origin
var mysize = myrect.size
print("The origin is at \(mypoint.x) and \(mypoint.y)")
print("The size is \(mysize.width) by \(mysize.height)")
```

Listing 4-48: Accessing the structures inside a CGRect structure

When we don't have initial values for the coordinates or the size, we can use the **zero** type property to create a structure with all the values initialized to 0.

```
import CoreGraphics

var myrect = CGRect.zero
```

```
print("The origin is at \(myrect.origin.x) and \(myrect.origin.y)")
print("The size is \(myrect.size.width) by \(myrect.size.height)")
```

Listing 4-49: Assigning empty structures to a CGRect *variable*

The **myrect** variable of Listing 4-49 is a **CGRect** structure with all its properties initialized with the value 0. Assigning the value of the **zero** property to a variable is the same as using the initializer **CGRect(x: 0, y: 0, width: 0, height: 0)**.

The **CGRect** structure also includes properties to calculate values from its coordinates and size. For example, the **midX** and **midY** properties return the coordinates at the center of each side.

```
import CoreGraphics

var rect = CGRect(x: 0, y: 0, width: 100, height: 100)
print("The horizontal center is \(rect.midX)")   // 50.0
```

Listing 4-50: Calculating the coordinate at the center of the rectangle

The rest of the methods included in the **CGRect** structure are easy to implement as well. The following example creates a rectangle and a point and then checks whether the point is inside the rectangle or not with the **contains()** method.

```
import CoreGraphics

var rect = CGRect(x: 0, y: 0, width: 100, height: 100)
var point = CGPoint(x: 10, y: 50)
if rect.contains(point) {
   print("The point is inside the rectangle")
}
```

Listing 4-51: Detecting if a point is inside a rectangle

(Basic) ## 4.4 UIKit

UIKit (User Interface Kit) is the framework provided by Apple to define the elements of the graphic interface. From text to buttons and switches, all the standard elements that users interact with on the screen to insert, select and process information are defined by the classes in this framework. Although its primary function is to create the user interface, the framework also includes several classes to create the objects the application needs to work and connect with the rest of the system. Figure 4-1 shows the main elements involved.

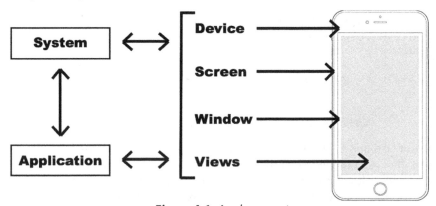

Figure 4-1: App's ecosystem

⟨ Basic ⟩ Application

When the user presses the icon to run an application, the first step performed by the system is to create an object of a class provided by the UIKit framework called `UIApplication` (the prefix UI stands for UIKit). This object starts a loop, a code that executes itself over and over again, to keep the application running (see Chapter 1, Figure 1-3), it also checks for events generated by the user or the system, reports changes in the state of the app, and provides access to the open windows and the user interface.

The `UIApplication` object is automatically created as soon as our app is launched and works along with the system to keep the application responsive. There is nothing we need to do to set up this object, but there are times when we must access the object to configure the app or respond to changes reported by the system, like when a remote notification is received, or the app is closed. For this purpose, the class includes the following type property to access it.

shared—This type property returns a reference to the instance of the `UIApplication` class that was created for our application.

The `UIApplication` object designates a delegate and calls methods on it that we can use to perform custom tasks. The object includes the following property to access this delegate.

delegate—This property returns a reference to the object assigned as the delegate of the `UIApplication` object.

Mac computers and iPads can work with multiple windows. As we will see later, what users call windows, in UIKit are called *Scenes*. Each window is a scene and the scenes are associated to scene sessions for configuration. The `UIApplication` class includes the following properties to manage the scenes and the scene sessions of our application.

supportsMultipleScenes—This property returns a Boolean to indicate if the application supports multiple scenes (multiple windows).

connectedScenes—This property returns a set with references to the scenes that are currently connected to the application.

openSessions—This property returns a set with references to the scene sessions currently active or archived by the system.

windows—This property returns an array with references to all the windows opened by the application.

The following example illustrates how to access the `UIApplication` object.

```
import UIKit

let app = UIApplication.shared
if app.supportsMultipleScenes {
   print("Multiple Windows App")
} else {
   print("Single Window App")   // "Single Window App"
}
```

Listing 4-52: Accessing the UIApplication *object*

In the code of Listing 4-52, we first import UIKit to have access to all the tools defined in this framework and then read the **shared** property to get a reference to the `UIApplication` object created for our app. With this reference, we check whether the application allows the user to open multiple windows or not by reading the **supportsMultipleScenes** property (We will learn how to work with multiple windows in Chapter 9).

Chapter 4 - Introduction to Frameworks

The UIKit framework also includes specific classes to manage the device in which the app is running and its screen. For the device, UIKit defines the **UIDevice** class. We can use an object of this class to access the device and read its configuration. The following is the type property that returns the **UIDevice** object representing the current device.

current—This type property returns an instance of the **UIDevice** class that represents the device in which the app is currently running.

The following are some of the properties and methods provided by the **UIDevice** class to read the device's configuration and activate or deactivate some of its features.

systemName—This property returns a string with the name of the operative system running in the device (e.g., "iOS").

systemVersion—This property returns a string with the version of the operative system running in the device (e.g., "13.0").

userInterfaceIdiom—This property returns the type of device running the application. The value returned is an enumeration of type **UIUserInterfaceIdiom** with the values **unspecified**, **phone**, **pad**, **TV**, and **carPlay**.

The implementation of this class is simple. We get an instance of the object that represents the current device and then read its properties. The following example checks whether the application is running on an iPhone or not.

```
import UIKit

let current = UIDevice.current
let device = current.userInterfaceIdiom

if device == .phone {
   print("This is an iPhone")
} else {
   print("This is not an iPhone")  // "This is not an iPhone"
}
```

Listing 4-53: Getting information from the device

The device's screen is represented by an object of the **UIScreen** class. This class allows us to get information that describes the main screen and external screens connected to the device. It includes two type properties to get these objects and some instance properties to return information about the screen.

main—This type property returns a **UIScreen** object to manage the main screen.

bounds—This property returns a **CGRect** value with the dimensions of the screen expressed in points. The values vary according to the device's orientation.

nativeBounds—This property returns a **CGRect** value with the dimensions of the screen expressed in pixels. The values are always returned considering a portrait orientation.

scale—This property returns a **CGFloat** value representing the scale of the screen. This is a value that translates between points and real pixels on the screen, as we will see next.

brightness—This property sets or returns a **CGFloat** value that determines the brightness of the screen. It takes values from 0.0 to 1.0.

The screen of a device is composed of a grid of hundreds of dots called *pixels*, ordered in rows and columns. The number of pixels varies from one device to another. To compensate for the disparities between devices, Apple adopted the concept of points (sometimes called *logical pixels*). The goal was to have a unit of measurement that is independent of the device and the density of the pixels on the screen. A point occupies a square of one or more pixels, depending on the device, but the developer does not need to know how many, it is all managed by the system.

At this moment, points in Apple mobile devices may represent a square of up to three pixels, depending on the device and the technology. The following is the list of the number of points and the corresponding pixels for some of the devices available.

- iPhone 5   320 x 568 points   640 x 1136 pixels   2x scale
- iPhone 6/7/8   375 x 667 points   750 x 1334 pixels   2x scale
- iPhone 6/7/8 Plus   414 x 736 points   1242 x 2208 pixels   3x scale
- iPhone X   375 × 812 points   1125 × 2436 pixels   3x scale
- iPad, iPad 2 and Mini 768 x 1024 points   768 x 1024 pixels   1x scale
- iPads with Retina   768 x 1024 points   1536 x 2048 pixels   2x scale
- iPad Pro   1366 x 1024 points   2732 x 2048 pixels   2x scale

The difference between points and pixels represents the scale. iPhones 3 and older have a scale of 1 (1 point represents 1 pixel), while iPhones 4, 5, 6, 7 and 8 have a scale of 2 (1 point represents a square of 2 pixels). Some iPhones and iPads share a grid with the same amount of points, independently of the scale, but with the introduction of the iPhones Plus and X, the scale was expanded to 3 (1 point represents 3 pixels). This allows developers to create graphic interfaces that adapt to every device, no matter how many pixels they have.

To determine the location of each point, Apple uses a coordinate system. The system counts the columns and rows from the top-left corner to the bottom-right corner, as illustrated next.

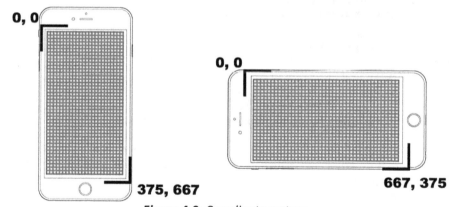

Figure 4-2: Coordinate system

The properties **bound**, **nativeBounds**, and **scale** included in the **UIScreen** class return the values corresponding to the screen of the device where the app is running. The **bound** and **nativeBounds** properties contain **CGRect** structures, while **scale** is just a **CGFloat** value.

```
import UIKit
let screen = UIScreen.main
let pointsWidth = screen.bounds.size.width
let pointsHeight = screen.bounds.size.height
print("Width: \(pointsWidth) x Height: \(pointsHeight)")

let pixelsWidth = screen.nativeBounds.size.width
```

```
let pixelsHeight = screen.nativeBounds.size.height
print("Width: \(pixelsWidth) x Height: \(pixelsHeight)")
print("Scale: \(screen.scale)")
```

Listing 4-54: Getting information from the screen

The native resolution in pixels is always returned considering a portrait orientation, but the size in points is returned according to the current orientation. For example, the dimensions of the iPhone X's screen are 375 points wide and 812 points tall in portrait, but 812 points wide and 375 points tall in landscape.

(Basic) Scenes

The **UIApplication** object runs the application, a **UIDevice** object provides information about the device, and a **UIScreen** object describes and configures the screen. The next step is to control the content of the screen. And for this purpose, the UIKit framework defines scenes.

Scenes are what users call windows. Some devices, such as iPhones and iPods Touch, can only work with one scene at a time (one window), but iPads and Mac computers can work with multiple scenes (multiple windows). UIKit defines the **UIWindowScene**.class to control each scene. An object of this class is created per scene and then a **UIWindow** object is created to control the area in which the user interface is displayed. Inside this window, in a hierarchical order, graphic containers called *views* are generated to represent each element of the interface. Figure 4-3 shows what this hierarchy looks like.

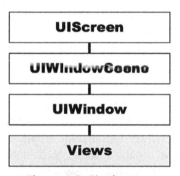

Figure 4-3: Single scene

When the application runs on an iPad or a Mac computer, the system generates one scene for each of the windows opened by the user or the app.

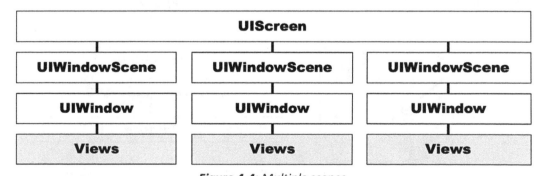

Figure 4-4: Multiple scenes

No matter if the app is showing one scene or multiple, the process to define the content of each one of them is the same. We must configure a window for the scene and then add all the views inside with the content we want to show to the user.

Basic **Windows**

A window is a space on the screen where the elements of the user interface are laid out. UIKit includes the `UIWindow` class to create the object that manages the window for each scene in our app. When the system creates a new scene, either because the app was just launched or because the user requested a new window, we must create a `UIWindow` object and connect it to the scene. The class includes the following initializer for this purpose.

UIWindow(windowScene: UIWindowScene)—This initializer returns a `UIWindow` object that represent the window for the scene specified by the **windowScene** attribute.

The `UIWindow` object defines the area of the screen where the user interface is going to be displayed. Inside this window, we include all the views that represent our interface. Therefore, once the `UIWindow` object for the scene is initialized, we must tell the system which view is going to be shown first. The following is the property included by the class for this purpose.

rootViewController—This property sets or returns a reference to the app's initial view.

After the window and its initial view were defined, we must inform the system that this is the window we want to show for this scene. The `UIWindow` class includes the following method for this purpose.

makeKeyAndVisible()—This method positions the window in from of any other windows that may exist for the scene and makes it visible.

> ⚠️ **IMPORTANT:** When we use SwiftUI to create our interfaces, we must take care of initializing and configuring the window every time a new scene is requested. We will learn how to do this in Chapter 5.

 Basic **Views**

The window is the space where the graphics are displayed, but it does not generate any visible content by itself. As mentioned before, the user interface is built inside the window from similar containers called *views*. These views are rectangular areas of custom size, designed to display graphics on the screen. Some views are used just as containers or empty space while others are used to present graphic tools, such as buttons or switches, and graphic content, such as images and text. These views are organized in a hierarchy, one inside another, as illustrated next.

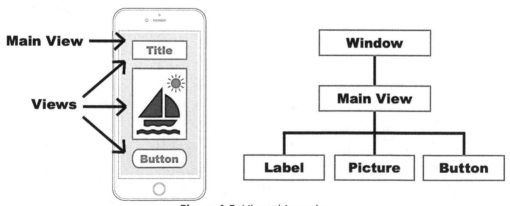

Figure 4-5: Views hierarchy

> ⚠️ **IMPORTANT:** Views in SwiftUI can be containers for other views or provide their own content. We will learn more about SwiftUI and how to create and organize these views in the following chapters.

Chapter 4 - Introduction to Frameworks

Chapter 5
Xcode

(Basic) **5.1 Interface**

Up to this point, we have been working with a simplified interface called Playground. Playground was designed to reduce the learning curve and for testing, but to build full applications we must move to the Xcode's main interface. This is a toolset that comprises an editor, a canvas to show previews, resource managers, configuration panels, and debugging tools, all integrated into a single working space where we can create and modify our applications.

(Basic) **Xcode Projects**

Applications are built from several files and resources, including our own codes, frameworks, images, databases, etc. Xcode organizes this information in projects. An Xcode project comprises all the information and resources necessary to create one application. The welcome window, illustrated in Figure 1-2, presents a button called *Create a new Xcode project* to initiate a project. When this button is clicked, a window appears to select the template we want to use.

Figure 5-1: Selecting the type of project

The selection screen organizes all the options in several categories: iOS, watchOS, tvOS, macOS, and Cross-Platform. Once we select the platform, Xcode presents a list of icons that represent the templates available. Templates include basic files with pre-programmed code that help us organize our project. To develop applications with SwiftUI for iPhones, iPads and Mac computers, we must select the Single View App option under the iOS category, as shown in Figure 5-1, above. After selecting the template, the next step is to insert information about the project. Figure 5-2 shows all the values required for the Single View App template.

Figure 5-2: Project's configuration window

The Product Name is the name of the project. By default, this is the name of our app, so we should write a name that is appropriate for our application, but we can change it later. Next is the Team's account. This is the developer account created with our Apple ID or our company's account. If we haven't yet registered our account with Xcode, we will see the Add Account button to add it (we explain how to add an account to Xcode below). After the team, we must insert the Organization Name. This is just a text with our name or the name of our company. The next value is the Organization Identifier. Xcode uses this value to create a unique identifier for our app and therefore it is recommended to declare it with an inverted domain, as we did in our example (com.formasterminds). Using the inverted domain ensures that only our app will have that identifier. Next, we must select the programming language we want to use to program our application. In this example, we have selected Swift because this is the language used to create apps with SwiftUI, but Objective C is also available. After the language, we must select the technology we are going to use to design the user interface. There are two options available, SwiftUI and an old system called *Storyboards*. SwiftUI is the technology we apply in this book, but Storyboards are still available for those that want to develop applications for older systems. And finally, there is a list of options we can select to incorporate additional functionality to our project, such as Core Data and Tests (We will study these options in further chapters).

As mentioned above, the Team's field shows a list of developer accounts registered with Xcode. If we haven't yet inserted our developer account in Xcode, we will see the Add Account button instead. Pressing this button, we open a window to insert our Apple ID.

Figure 5-3: *Registering our Apple account in Xcode*

 The Basics: The Apple ID is the identification you used to initialize your computer. If you don't have an Apple ID or want to create an additional one for development, you can press the Create Apple ID button or go to developer.apple.com and select the option Account.

Once we insert our Apple ID, the account is configured to work with our copy of Xcode and we can select it from the list. With the account selected and all the information inserted in the form, we can now press the Next button to select the folder where are project is going to be stored. Xcode creates a folder for each project, so we only have to designate the destination folder where we are going to store all our projects and everything else is generated for us.

 Do It Yourself: Open Xcode. In the welcome screen, click on the option Create a new Xcode project (Figure 1-2). You can also go to the File menu at the top of the screen and select the options New/Project. After this, you should see the templates window (Figure 5-1). Select the iOS tab, click on the Single View App icon, and press Next. Now you should see the form of Figure 5-2. In Product Name, Insert the name of your project. In the Team option, select your developer account or press the Add Account button to add your account to Xcode. In Organization Name, write your name or the name of your company. In Organization Identifier insert the inverted domain of your website or blog. Next, select the Swift language from the Language option and activate the option Use SwiftUI. Make sure that the rest of the options are deactivated. Finally, press Next and select a folder where to store your project.

Chapter 5 - Xcode

IMPORTANT: Although it's not mandatory, you should get your own domain and website. Apple not only recommends the use of an inverted domain to generate the Bundle Identifier, but at the time of submitting your app to the App Store you will be asked to provide the web page used for promotion and where the users should go for support (see Chapter 17).

Once the project is created, Xcode generates the initial files according to the selected template and presents the main interface on the screen. Figure 5-4 shows what this interface looks like.

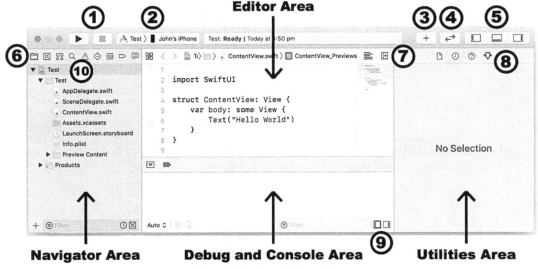

Figure 5-4: Xcode's interface

There are four main areas on this interface, the Navigation Area on the left, the Editor Area in the middle, the Console Area at the bottom, and the Utilities Area on the right. The window also includes a toolbar at the top to provide additional information. From this bar, we can run or stop the application (Figure 5-4, number 1), select the destination, such as a simulator or a device (Figure 5-4, number 2), incorporate views or modifiers to the user interface (Figure 5-4, number 3), review code in repositories (Figure 5-4, number 4), and show or hide the removable panels on the left, right, and bottom (Figure 5-4, number 5).

Each area also includes buttons to select the type of information we want to see. For instance, the Navigator Area on the left includes multiple buttons at the top to select between panels where we can get the list of files created for our application, perform a search, get a list of warnings and errors, see the resources consumed by our app, and more. The Utilities Area on the right presents a similar arrangement, with buttons at the top to select the content we want to see, although in this case only the last option called the Attribute Inspector panel is useful when we are developing applications with SwiftUI (Figure 5-4, number 8). And finally, the Console Area at the bottom of the Editor Area also includes some buttons for configuration. The most relevant are the two in the lower right corner (Figure 5-4, number 9). These buttons show and hide two panels, one with information about the values processed by our app, and another with the console. This is the same console we used in Playground to see the errors our code produces and print messages.

The Navigator Area, the Console Area, and the Utilities Area can be removed from the buttons on the upper right corner (Figure 5-4, number 5). The Editor Area is permanent and shows the content of the selected file, but we can modify its configuration with the two buttons in the upper right corner (Figure 5-4, number 7). The button on the right is called *Add Editor* and what it does is to add more editor panels to the Editor Area. By default, new editors are placed on the right side of previous editors, but we can place them on top of each other by pressing and holding the Option key. We can keep dividing each editor as long as we want, we can resize them by dragging the lines between them and close them by pressing the x button in the upper left corner. These divisions are useful when we need to edit two or more files at the same time. We can click on an editor and then select the file we want to show in that editor. Figure 5-5 shows what we see when we press the Add Editor button. Two editors are shown side by side.

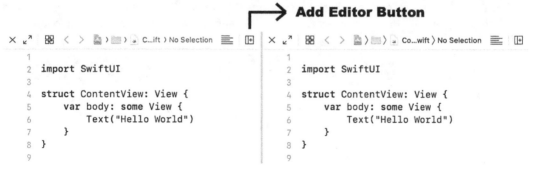

Figure 5-5: Multiple editors in the Editor Area

On the other hand, the button on the left is called Adjust Editor Options and it shows a popup menu with options to expand the editor, as shown in Figure 5-6.

Figure 5-6: Adjust Editor Options

The most useful options in SwiftUI are the Canvas, the Layout, and the Minimap. The Canvas option displays a panel where we can see a preview of each view (screen) and also run the application for testing, the Layout option allows us to place this preview on the right or at the bottom of the code, and the Minimap option shows a visual representation of our code that we can use for reference and navigation.

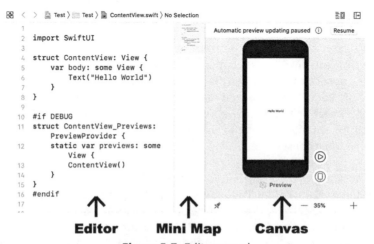

Figure 5-7: Editor panel

Chapter 5 - Xcode

The Basics: If you want to hide the canvas, you just have to select the option Show Editor Only from this same menu, and the code editor will expand to take up all the space in the Editor Area.

In addition to the previews offered by the Canvas, there are two other ways to run and test our application from Xcode: the simulator and a real device. The buttons to select these options, run and stop the application are located on the left side of the toolbar.

Figure 5-8: Buttons to execute the app

Applications always run on a specific destination and can have different configurations. The destination could be multiple things, from real devices to windows or simulators, and the configuration defines things like the region where the device is located, or the human language used by the app to display the information on the screen. To store this information, Xcode uses targets and schemes. Every time we create a new project, Xcode automatically generates a target with a scheme for it. The target determines how the app is going to be built and all the resources it will include, while a scheme defines the configuration used to run or test the application. When we want to run our application, we must tell Xcode which target we want to use and the destination (a simulator or a device). The target is selected from the button on the left of the Scheme section and the destination is selected from the button on the right (Figure 5-8, right). Usually, the target and the scheme provided by Xcode is all we need, so we just have to press the destination button, and select a simulator or a device from the list.

Figure 5-9: Options available to run the app

After the target and the destination are selected, we can press the Play button to run the application (Figure 5-8, left). If we use a simulator, a new window opens where we can see our app and interact with it, as shown in Figure 5-10.

Figure 5-10: App running in simulator

 Do It Yourself: If you haven't done it yet, create a new Single View App project following the steps described above. After the Xcode's interface opens, press the destination button (Figure 5-8, right) and select one of the iPhone's simulators. Press the Play button to run the app. You should see the simulator's window on the screen with the text "Hello World" at the center (Figure 5-10).

 IMPORTANT: The devices are automatically available after they are connected to the computer with a USB cable, but you can also use Wi-Fi. At the bottom of the destination list, there is an option called Add Additional Simulators. This opens a window to configure devices and simulators. If you select a device, you will see the option Connect via network. Activating this checkbox allows you to deploy your application to the device via Wi-Fi.

 The Basics: Pressing the Play button on the toolbar runs the app on the simulator or a device, but we can also build our code without running the app. This is useful when we want to check if the code contains errors. The option is available in the Product menu or by pressing the keys Command + B.

The scheme can be configured from the options we get when we press the target button (Figure 5-8, right), but to configure the target, we must click on the first item in the Navigator Area (Figure 5-4, number 10). This opens a series of configuration panels in the Editor Area, as shown in Figure 5-11.

Figure 5-11: Target configuration

Chapter 5 - Xcode

From here, we can configure the project or the target. If the options are not visible, we must click the button on the upper left corner (Figure 5-11, number 1). Once we select the target, we can click on the different panels to find the option we want to modify. The most useful is the General panel. In this panel we can specify things like the version of our app and the build (Figure 5-11, number 2). These are values we need to declare before submitting our app to Apple. Every time we build our app and submit it to Apple for review, we have to specify a new build, and every time we publish a new version of our app that is already available to users we have to declare the new version number (We will learn more about how to submit an app in Chapter 17).

In the General panel we also have the options to select the system and the platforms for which we want to develop our app. Applications programmed with SwiftUI require iOS 13 or later, but we can develop for any device, including iPhones, iPads, or Mac computers, as we will see later. By default, the iPhone and iPad options are activated.

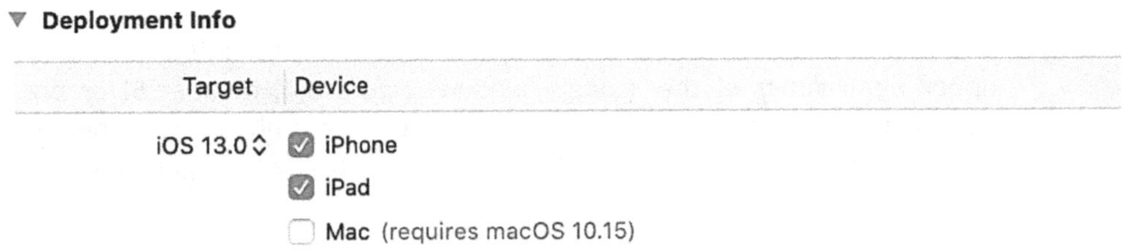

Figure 5-12: *Deployment systems and devices*

Something else we can control from the General panel is the app's orientation. In the Device Orientation section, we can select the orientations we want the app to have. By default, Portrait (vertical) and Landscape (horizontal) are activated, but the option Upside Down is deactivated. This is to prevent the user from trying to answer a phone call with the phone upside down.

Device Orientation ☑ Portrait
☐ Upside Down
☑ Landscape Left
☑ Landscape Right

Figure 5-13: *Device orientation*

Another useful panel is called Signing & Capabilities. From this panel we can declare the developer account we want to use to build the app, but most importantly, we can add capabilities by pressing the Capability button on the upper left corner (Figure 5-14, number 1). Capabilities are additional functionality we can incorporate to our app, such as access to iCloud, Background Modes, Sign in with Apple, and more. We will see how to add and work with some of these systems in further chapters.

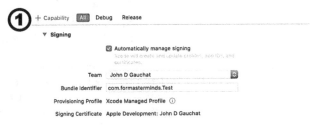

Figure 5-14: *Capability*

(Basic) **5.2 Template**

The Single View App template used to develop an application with SwiftUI includes the minimum files and code the application needs to run. Figure 5-15 shows the Navigator Area with all the items created by this template.

Figure 5-15: Files created by the Single View App template

 The Basics: If you cannot see the Navigator Area, press the left button on the upper right corner of the Xcode's window (Figure 5-4, number 5) or press Command + 1 on your keyboard. If the Navigator Area is not showing the list of files, click on the first button at the top of the panel (circled in Figure 5-15).

Medium Application Delegate

The first file on the list is called AppDelegate.swift and contains a class called `AppDelegate`. As we already mentioned, when the app is launched, the system creates an object of the `UIApplication` class to provide the basic functionality necessary for the app to process information and respond to the user. The object created from the `AppDelegate` class is assigned as the delegate of the `UIApplication` object. Every time the system has to report a change to our code, it calls methods on this delegate. For this purpose, the `AppDelegate` class conforms to the `UIApplicationDelegate` protocol. The following are the protocol methods we need to implement on this delegate when working with SwiftUI.

application(UIApplication, **didFinishLaunchingWithOptions:** Dictionary**)**—This is the first method to be called by the `UIApplication` object. It is called to let us know that all the necessary objects were already instantiated, and the app is ready to work.

application(UIApplication, **configurationForConnecting:** UISceneSession, **options:** UIScene.ConnectionOptions**)**—This method is called when a new scene (window) is requested by the system or the user. The method must return a `UISceneConfiguration` object with the configuration for the scene.

application(UIApplication, **didDiscardSceneSessions:** Set**)**—This method is called when the user discards a scene (closes a window). The **didDiscardSceneSessions** attribute is a set with `UISceneSession` objects representing the sessions for each scene.

As soon as the app is launched, the `UIApplication` object calls the `application(UIApplication, didFinishLaunchingWithOptions:)` method. In this method, we can write all the code we need to prepare our application, such as declaring initial values, creating or opening a database, checking the current settings, etc. A common practice is to define properties that contain values or references we will need to access from the rest of the application. The following example shows how to define and initialize a property from this class.

```
import UIKit

@UIApplicationMain
```

```
class AppDelegate: UIResponder, UIApplicationDelegate {
    var basicSalary: Double!

    func application(_ application: UIApplication,
didFinishLaunchingWithOptions launchOptions:
[UIApplication.LaunchOptionsKey: Any]?) -> Bool {
        basicSalary = 30000.0
        return true
    }
}
```

Listing 5-1: Adding some properties to the app's delegate object

The code of Listing 5-1 adds a property called **basicSalary** to the **AppDelegate** class. When the **application(UIApplication, didFinishLaunchingWithOptions:)** method is called, we initialize this property with the value 30000.0. This is a simple but practical example that illustrates how we can add properties to the application delegate and initialize them when the app is launched. After the property is implemented in the delegate, we can access it from any part of our code through the **delegate** property of the **UIApplication** object. If we store a new value in this property, it will be preserved while the app is running. The delegate object offers a safe place to store common values required by the application, and therefore it is used to set up databases, manage user data and files, as we will see later.

The other two methods defined in the **UIApplicationDelegate** protocol that are useful for applications developed with SwiftUI are called when a scene is created or discarded. When the system or the user generates a new window, the **application(UIApplication, configurationForConnecting:, options:)** method is called in the delegate. From this method, we must return the configuration of the scene, which is defined with an object of the **UISceneConfiguration** class. The class includes the following initializer.

UISceneConfiguration(name: String?, sessionRole: UISceneSession.Role)—This initializer returns a **UISceneConfiguration** object configured with the values provided by the attributes. The **name** attribute is a string with the name that identifies the configuration. The **sessionRole** attribute is a constant from a structure called **Role** that specifies the role of the scene. There are three constants available **windowApplication** (windows on the main screen), **windowExternalDisplay** (windows on an external display), and **carTemplateApplication** (windows on a vehicle screen). Applications for iPhones, iPads and Mac computers work with the **windowApplication** role.

The initializer provides the name of the configuration and the role of the scene, but we also must declare the name of the class that is going to be assigned as the scene's delegate. For this purpose, the **UISceneConfiguration** class includes the following property.

delegateClass—This property sets or returns the class that is going to be used to create the scene's delegate.

There are two ways to define this object. We can use the initializer to define the name of the configuration and the role, and then assign the name of the class we are going to use to create the scene's delegate to the **delegateClass** property, or we can define this value in a file called *info.plist*. The Single View App template uses this last approach. It defines the name of the configuration and the delegate class in the info.plist file, and then calls the initializer with that name, as shown next.

```
func application(_ application: UIApplication, configurationForConnecting
connectingSceneSession: UISceneSession, options:
UIScene.ConnectionOptions) -> UISceneConfiguration {
```

```
return UISceneConfiguration(name: "Default Configuration",
sessionRole: connectingSceneSession.role)
}
```

Listing 5-2: Configuring a scene

After a scene is requested by the system or the user, the method of Listing 5-2 is called. This method creates a `UISceneConfiguration` object using the configuration defined in the info.plist file with the name "Default Configuration" and the role received by the method (`connectingSceneSession.role`), which is usually the `windowApplication` value for windows in the main screen.

This configuration is enough for most applications, so all we have to do is to leave the method as it is declared by the template and the scene will be properly configured, but later we will learn more about the info.plist file and how to work with multiple scenes.

(Medium)   ## Scene Delegate

The next file generated by the Single View App template is called SceneDelegate.swift and it defines the delegate of the scene (window). As we just mentioned, every time a scene is created, we must return a `UISceneConfiguration` object to configure the scene. This configuration defines the class that is going to be used to create the scene's delegate, and the SceneDelegate.swift file is where the Single View App template defines this delegate class.

Like the `UIApplication` object, the `UIWindowScene` object calls methods on its delegate to report to our code changes in the scene. From these methods, we can perform custom tasks every time a new scene is created or the state of a scene changes. The methods are defined by the `UIWindowSceneDelegate` protocol, which inherits from the `UISceneDelegate` protocol. The following are the most useful.

scene(UIScene, willConnectTo: UISceneSession, **options:** UIScene-.ConnectionOptions)—This method is called when a new scene is added to the app. In this method, we must create a window for the scene and assign it to the delegate's `window` property.

sceneDidDisconnect(UIScene)—This method is called when a scene was removed from the app.

sceneDidBecomeActive(UIScene)—This method is called when a scene becomes active and therefore it is responding to user events.

sceneWillResignActive(UIScene)—This method is called when a scene is about to be moved to the background and stop responding to user events.

sceneWillEnterForeground(UIScene)—This method is called when a scene is about to become visible and respond to user events.

sceneDidEnterBackground(UIScene)—This method is called when a scene is no longer visible and does not respond to user events anymore.

There are three states we can identify for the scene: foreground, background, and disconnected. The foreground state is when the scene is visible and ready to receive input from the user, the background state is when the scene is not visible but still running, and the disconnected state is when the scene was terminated. Every time the state changes, the system calls one of the methods defined in the `UIWindowSceneDelegate` protocol to communicate to our code what's going on, so we can respond to the change (see Listing 14-4).

Besides these methods, the `UIWindowSceneDelegate` protocol also defines a property we must implement to store a reference to the windows assigned to the scene.

Chapter 5 - Xcode

window—This property sets or returns a reference to the `UIWindow` object assigned to the scene.

When a scene is created, the system calls the `scene(UIScene, willConnectTo:, options:)` method on the scene's delegate. In this method, we must create the window for the scene and assign it to the `window` property, as shown in the following example.

```
import UIKit
import SwiftUI

class SceneDelegate: UIResponder, UIWindowSceneDelegate {
    var window: UIWindow?

    func scene(_ scene: UIScene, willConnectTo session: UISceneSession,
options connectionOptions: UIScene.ConnectionOptions) {
        let contentView = ContentView()
        if let windowScene = scene as? UIWindowScene {
            let window = UIWindow(windowScene: windowScene)
            window.rootViewController = UIHostingController(rootView:
contentView)
            self.window = window
            window.makeKeyAndVisible()
        }
    }
}
```

Listing 5-3: Creating the window for the scene

This is more or less the code that the template provides to create the window. The first thing we have to do is to cast the `UIScene` object received by the method to a `UIWindowScene` object with the `as?` operator. This is because the scenes are defined by the `UIWindowScene` class, but the method receives a value of type `UIScene`, a basic class from which the `UIWindowScene` class inherits. Once we get this object, we have to initialize a new `UIWindow` object with it (`UIWindow(windowScene: windowScene)`). The next step is to tell the window which is the initial view (screen) to show. For this purpose, the UIKit framework provides the `UIHostingController` class. This is a class that transforms a view created with SwiftUI into a view controller that the UIKit framework can process. As we will see later, SwiftUI generates a layer of abstraction to simplify the creation of user interfaces and the organization of an application, but the user interface is still created with classes defined in the UIKit framework and therefore we have to use the `UIHostingController` class to turn one type of view into another. The class includes the following initializer.

UIHostingController(rootView: View)—This initializer returns a `UIHosting-Controller` object configured with the SwiftUI view provided by the **rootView** attribute.

The view assigned to the `UIHostingController` object must be an instance of a structure that conforms to the `View` protocol. As we will see later, the Single View App template creates one of these structures for us with the name `ContentView`, and that's why in the example of Listing 5-3 we initialize a structure with this name and use it to create the `UIHostingController` object. After this object is initialized, we must assign it to the `rootViewController` property of the `UIWindow` object to define it as the initial view of our application. With this value, the window is configured, so the next step is to assign it to the `window` property of the delegate object and then call the `makeKeyAndVisible()` method on it to make it visible.

Another file created by the Single View App template is called ContentView.swift and takes care of defining the initial view of our application. As explained in Chapter 4, views are rectangular areas that display and organize content on the screen. Defining views is how we create the user interface. There are different kinds of views. some provide their own content, such as text or images, and others act as containers to organize the rest of the views in the interface. Views in SwiftUI are defined by a structure that conforms to a protocol called `View` and implement a computed property defined by the protocol called `body`, as in the following example.

```
import SwiftUI

struct ContentView: View {
    var body: some View {
        Text("Hello World")
    }
}
```

Listing 5-4: Defining the view

This is the same code generate by the template. It defines a structure called `ContentView` that conforms to the `View` protocol and therefore implements a computed property called `body` that returns a view of type `Text` to show a text on the screen (Notice that because there is only one statement in the block, we didn't have to include the `return` keyword).

Although the `ContentView` structure abides by the requirements of the `View` protocol, its name is arbitrary. We can assign any name we want to our views and create as many as we need, but in this case is relevant because `ContentView` is declared by the template as the root view of the window in the scene's delegate (see Listing 5-3). If we change the name of this structure or decide to create another structure to use as the initial view, we need to make sure that the name in the scene's delegate is replaced by the new one.

SwiftUI files include the definition of two structures, one that declares the views and another that creates the preview on the canvas. This second structure conforms to the `PreviewProvider` protocol which defines a type property called `previews` that returns the view or the group of views to display on the canvas. The following is the structure defined by Xcode for the `ContentView` view included in the template.

```
struct ContentView_Previews: PreviewProvider {
    static var previews: some View {
        ContentView()
    }
}
```

Listing 5-5: Defining the preview

When a preview structure is present in our file, Xcode compiles the application and shows a preview on the canvas. The content of the preview is defined by the value of the `previews` property. The templates provided by Xcode define the content of this property as an instance of the view, so what we see on the canvas is the content generated by the view (in this case, the `ContentView` view), but we can include in the preview any content we want.

Previews are automatically generated by Xcode, but Xcode cannot always determine when our code is ready to generate the preview. If we insert large changes to the code, we must tell Xcode when it can resume the previews. For this purpose, the canvas displays a banner at the top with a Resume button that we must press after all the modifications are done.

Chapter 5 - Xcode

Figure 5-16: Canva's Resume button

(Basic) **Assets Catalog**

The next item in the Navigator Area is not a file but a folder with the name Assets.xcassets. This is called the Assets Catalog and takes care of storing and managing images, icons, colors, symbols and more, but it is mostly used for images.

Images are used for everything in mobile applications, from backgrounds and patterns to the creation of customized controls. But before incorporating images into our projects, we must consider that images are stored in files with a resolution in pixels, while the user interface is defined in points.

The screens of Apple devices have different resolutions and scales. In some devices, one point represents one pixel and in others more. At this moment, three scales have been defined: 1x, 2x, and 3x (see Chapter 4). The 1x scale defines one point as one pixel, the 2x scale defines 1 point as a square of 2 pixels, and the 3x scale defines one point as a square of three pixels. For this reason, every time we want to show images in our interface, we must consider the conversion between pixels and points. For example, if we have an image of 300 pixels wide and 400 pixels tall, in a device with a scale of 1x the image will almost occupy the whole screen, but in a device with a scale of 2x the image will look half its size. The image is occupying the same space, 300 by 400 pixels, but because of the higher resolution this number of pixels represents a smaller area on the screen in devices with scales of 2x or 3x, as shown in Figure 5-17.

Figure 5-17: Same image in devices with different scale

There are multiple solutions to this problem. The simplest are to scale up a small image in devices with higher resolution or scale down a big image in devices with lower resolution. For example, we can expand an image of 300 x 400 pixels to 600 x 800 pixels and make it look like the same size in a screen with a scale of 2x (a space of 300 x 400 points represents 600 x 800 pixels at this scale), or we could start with an image of 600 x 800 pixels and reduce it to 300 x 400 pixels for devices with half the scale. One way or another, we have a problem. If we expand a small image to fit in a bigger screen, it loses quality, and if we reduce it, it occupies unnecessary space in memory because the image is never shown in its original resolution. Fortunately, there is a more efficient solution. It requires us to include in our project three versions of the same image, one for every scale. Considering the image of our example, we will need one picture of the husky in a size of 300 x 400 pixels for devices with a scale of 1x, another of 600 x 800 pixels for devices with a scale of 2x, and a third one of 900 x 1200 for devices with a scale of 3x. When we take this approach, the images can be shown in the same size and with the same quality no matter the device, as illustrated in Figure 5-18.

Figure 5-18: *Different images for specific scales*

Providing the same image in different resolutions solves the problem but introduces some complications. We must create three versions of the same image and then select which one is going to be shown depending on the scale of the device. To help us select the right image, Apple systems were designed to detect the scale that corresponds to the image by reading a suffix on the file's name. What we have to do is to provide three files with the same name but with suffixes that determine the scale they correspond to. The file containing the image for the 1x scale (300 x 400 pixels in our example) only requires the name and the extension (e.g., **husky.png**), the name of the file with the image for the 2x scale (600 x 800) has to contain the suffix @2x (e.g., **husky@2x.png**), and the name of the file with the image for the 3x scale (900 x 1200) has to contain the suffix @3x (e.g., **husky@3x.png**). Every time the interface requires an image, the system reads the suffixes and loads the file corresponding to the scale of the screen.

The Basics: There is a very useful app available on the App Store for Mac computers called Prepo that can take an image of one size and expand it or reduce it to generate the images required for the rest of the scales. It can also help you generate the icons for your app.

There are two ways to incorporate images into our project. One is to drag the files to the Navigator Area and the second alternative is to use the Assets Catalog. The first option is simple. We must create the images for the resolutions we want to provide and then drag them from Finder, as shown in Figure 5-19.

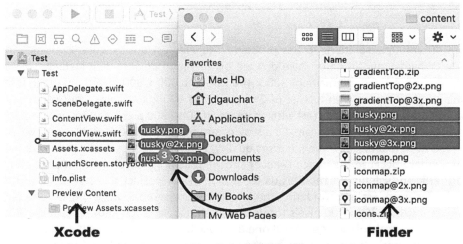

Figure 5-19: *Dragging files from Finder to our Xcode's project*

Chapter 5 - Xcode

When we drop the files into our Xcode's project, a window asks for information about the destination and the target. If we want the files to be copied to the project's folder (recommended), we must activate the option *Copy items if needed*, as shown in Figure 5-20 below. We also must indicate that the files are going to be added to the target created for our project selecting the target in the *Add to targets* option (the project used in Figure 5-20 was called *Test*).

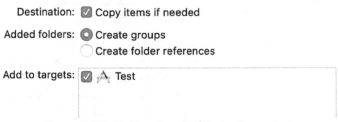

Destination: ☑ Copy items if needed
Added folders: ⦿ Create groups
               ◯ Create folder references
Add to targets: ☑ Ⓐ Test

Figure 5-20: *Options to add files to the project*

Once we select these options and click the Finish button, Xcode adds the files to our project.

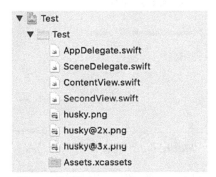

Figure 5-21: *Images in our project*

IMPORTANT: When we select the option to copy the files into our project's folder, we end up with two copies of the same files, one in the original folder and another in our project's folder. If we modify the original files and try to add them again to the project, instead of overwriting the files Xcode shows an error. To add the updated files to our project, we must remove the old ones by selecting the files in the Navigator Area and pressing the Delete key on the keyboard. Xcode asks if we want to remove the reference or remove the files. Selecting the option *Move to Trash*, the files are completely removed from the project and we can add them again.

After the files are added, we can use their names to load the images from code, as we will see later. With this technique, we can add as many resources to the project as needed, including images, videos, sounds, and data. But as we already mentioned, for images there is a better way called Assets Catalog. The images are added to the Assets Catalog and then we must ask for the one we want by mentioning its name. This is similar to what we have done so far, but the advantage is that Xcode provides a visual interface to manage the catalog, so we can see a quick preview of the image, and load and organize the versions for each scale and appearance (light and dark modes). The interface opens in the Editor Area when we click on the Assets.xcassets item, as shown in Figure 5-22.

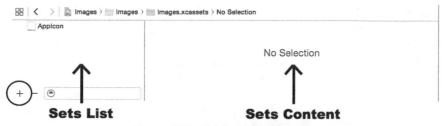

Sets List   **Sets Content**

Figure 5-22: Empty Assets Catalog

The interface includes two columns: the column on the left presents a list of sets of resources, such as images, colors, or symbols, and the column on the right displays the content of the selected set. An image set is composed of the three versions of an image, one for each scale, and additional images that we want to present for different appearances (light or dark mode) and devices (iPhone, iPad, Mac, etc.). The list also includes a permanent set called AppIcon that contains the images for the icons necessary to publish our app in the App Store.

New sets can be added from the + button in the lower left corner (circled in Figure 5-22) or the Editor menu at the top of the screen. If we open the Editor menu and click on the option Add Assets / *New Image Set*, a new empty set is created.

Figure 5-23: New set of images

The name of the set is the name we are going to use to get the image from code. Xcode calls the new set *Image* but we can click on it and rename it. Once the set is created, we can drag the file to the corresponding squares on the right column of the interface. For example, the file husky.png from our previous example goes inside the 1x square, the file husky@2x.png goes inside the 2x square, and the file husky@3x.png goes inside the 3x square. Figure 5-24 shows the Editor Area after the images are dragged from Finder to the Assets Catalog and the name of the set is changed to "husky".

Figure 5-24: Husky set is ready

Once the images are included in the catalog, the set is ready to use. We do not need to copy the files to the project's folder anymore or anything like it. All we have to do is to load the image from our app using the name defined for the set (in this case, "husky"). But this process is still a little bit tedious. An easy way to create a new set is to drag the three images for the set to the Assets Catalog. Xcode creates a new set with the images and assigns their names as the name of the set. The creation and configuration of the set is done automatically when we drag the files and drop them inside the Assets Catalog. In fact, we can drag several files together and Xcode takes care of extracting the information and creating all the sets for us.

Chapter 5 - Xcode

Do It Yourself: The images of the husky are available on our website. Download the files to your hard drive, click on the Assets.xcassets item in your project, and drag and drop the pictures into the Assets Catalog. You should see something similar to Figure 5-24.

Besides the possibility of including a version of the image for every scale, we can also add versions for different devices and appearances. With SwiftUI, we can develop applications for every Apple device, and each device possess unique characteristics. By default, the set of images is assigned to a Universal device, which means that the images of the set are going to be display on any device, but we can add to the set images for a specific device by selecting the options in the Attributes Inspector panel, as shown in Figure 5-25.

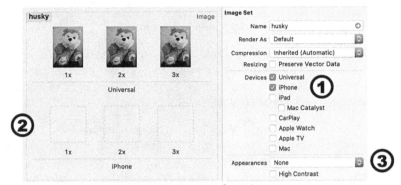

Figure 5-25: *Images for iPhones*

When a set is selected, the Attributes Inspector panel on the right shows a list of properties assigned to the set, including Devices and Appearance. If we check the box of a device or select a different value for the appearance (Dark or Light), the interface adds placeholders where we can drag and drop the images for that specific attribute. For instance, in Figure 5-25, we checked the box for iPhones and now we have three placeholders to add images for that specific device. After the images are incorporated into the Assets Catalog, we can load the image from our code using its name and the system will pick the right version according to the characteristics of the device.

The Assets Catalog is not only used for images but also other resources, like colors or symbols. For instance, if we want to specify different colors for the light and dark modes, we can add a Color Set and then select the mode from the Appearance option. The set is added from the Editor menu (Add Assets / New Color Set) and the appearance is selected from the Attribute Inspector panel (Figure 5-26, number 1). Xcode adds placeholders to the interface for each of the selected options (Figure 5-26, number 2). Clicking on a placeholder adds options at the bottom of the Attributes Inspector panel to select the color we want for the mode.

Figure 5-26: *Color for Dark mode*

One more thing we can do from the Assets Catalog is to define our app's icons. Icons are the little images that the user taps on the home screen to launch the app. The Assets Catalog includes a set called *AppIcon* to manage the icons we must provide for the application. The set includes placeholders for every icon we need and for every scale to cover all the devices and screens available. It even includes information about their size in points that we can use to design the images. The sizes required depend on the versions of the system and the type of devices our app is prepared for.

Figure 5-27: AppIcon set for icons

As any other image, the icons may be created from any image editor software available in the market. A file has to be created for every size required. For example, the first two placeholders require images of 20 points, which means that we must create an image of a size of 40 pixels for the 2x scale and an image of a size of 60 pixels for the 3x scale.

 IMPORTANT: The Single View App template includes an additional Assets Catalog to incorporate images into the project that are only going to be used for previews during development. The item is called *Preview Assets.xcassets* and is inside a group called *Preview Content*. The resources loaded into this Assets Catalog are available during development but not for the final app. We will learn more about previews in further chapters.

(Medium) ## Launching Screen

The next item in the Navigator Area is a file responsible for generating the launching screen called LaunchScreen.storyboard. The launching screen is what is shown when the app is loading. No matter how small, an app always takes a few seconds to load and be responsive. This screen is necessary to show the user that the app is responding to the action of tapping its icon and give the impression that it is already running.

The LaunchScreen.storyboard is a Storyboard. Storyboards use a different system from SwiftUI to create the interface. Instead of defining the views in structures, as we did with the `ContentView` structure in Listing 5-4, the interface is created visually by dragging the elements from the Library to an area of the screen that represents the device, and their position and size are determined with constraints. Figure 5-28 shows the representation of an iPhone that we see on the Editor Area when we click on this file.

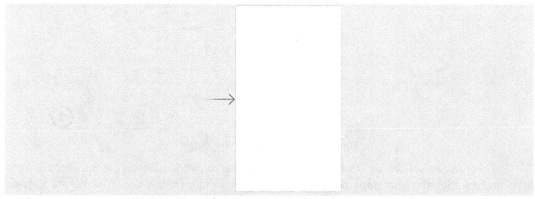

Figure 5-28: Storyboard

Chapter 5 - Xcode

Storyboards show a different toolbar at the bottom of the Editor Area with buttons to configure the storyboard and set constraints to define the position and the size of the elements on the interface.

Figure 5-29: Storyboard's toolbar

From the button on the left (number 1), we can select the device we want to be represented in the storyboard, including style and orientation. The - and + buttons in the middle (number 2) zoom the storyboard in and out. And the rest of the buttons on the right (number 3) open menus to select and apply constraints that determine the position and size of each element on the interface.

A common launching screen consists of an image that anticipates what the interface is going to look like or presents the company's or the application's logo. Inserting an image in the view in the storyboard is easy. We must open the Library (Figure 5-4, number 3) and drag the object called Image View to the storyboard, as shown in Figure 5-30.

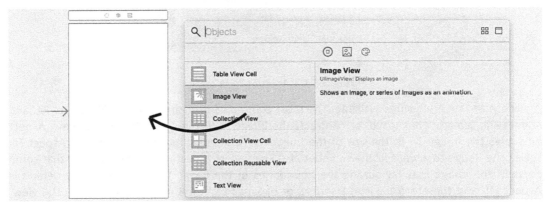

Figure 5-30: Image View in the Library

The Image View is represented by a gray rectangle. When selected, the rectangle shows little handles on the corners that we can drag to change its size. In Figure 5-31, next, we expand the Image View to occupy the entire screen.

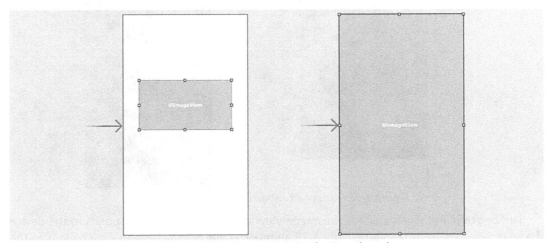

Figure 5-31: Image view in the Storyboard

The Image View will show an image on the screen. To assign this image, we must open the Attributes Inspector panel on the Utilities Area and select the image from the Image option. In the example of Figure 5-32, we assign the husky image included before in our Assets Catalog.

Figure 5-32: Option to assign an image to the Image View

Image Views have their own size, independent of the size of the image they contain. When we load an image, we must tell the system how it has to accommodate that image inside the view. This is called the Content Mode and the option is available in the Attributes Inspector panel as well.

Figure 5-33: Content Mode option

There are several values available. The most commonly used are Scale to Fill, Aspect Fit, and Aspect Fill. Scale to Fill expands or contracts the image to fit the size of the Image View, Aspect Fit scales the image to fit the size of the Image View, keeping its aspect ratio, and Aspect Fill scales the image to always fill the view but also keeping its aspect ratio, which means that some parts of the image may lay outside the boundaries of the Image View. The value by default is Aspect Fit, and therefore the image shrinks or expands to fit in the area occupied by the view. Figure 5-34 shows what we see by default (left) and what we get when we select the Aspect Fill option.

Figure 5-34: Aspect Fit mode and Aspect Fill mode

The position and size we set for the Image View in the storyboard corresponds to the device we have selected on the toolbar (Figure 5-29, number 1), but we still have to determine how the view is going to adapt when it is shown on a device with a different screen. This is done with

Chapter 5 - Xcode

constraints. Constraints are rules that establish the relationship between elements and between the elements and their containers. These rules are simple statements that determine things like how far a view should be from another view, or how a view should adapt its size to the space available. Although we could set these constraints one by one from the buttons in the toolbar (Figure 5-29, number 3), Xcode offers a simplified system to attach constraints called *Autoresizing*. The system can be accessed from the Size Inspector panel in the Utilities Area, as shown in Figure 5-35.

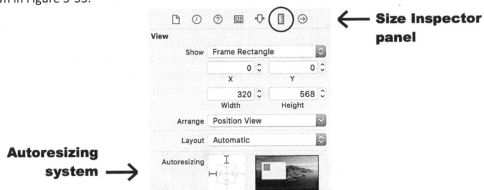

Figure 5-35: Autoresizing system

To assign the rules, the Autoresizing tool presents four lines on each side of a square and two double arrows inside. The lines pin the element to the sides and the arrows determine if the element will expand proportionally to the space available or preserve its original size.

When we select an element in the storyboard, the tool shows the rules already applied to that element. By default, the left and top lines are activated, and the double arrows are deactivated (Figure 5-35). This means that the element will stay in its position and always keep the original size (the one we set in the storyboard), but we can deactivate those rules or assign new ones by clicking on the lines. For example, if we want the width of a view to increment proportionally to the space available, we can click on the horizontal double arrow to activate it, as shown in Figure 5-36.

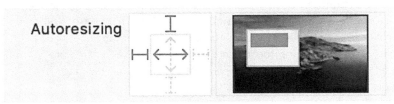

Figure 5-36: Resizing rules

After this, the view will be reduced or expanded along with the available space when the device is rotated, or the window takes up more space on the screen. For the launching screen of Figure 5-34 (right), we need the image to stick to the sides and to expand to occupy the whole screen. To achieve this, we must activate the four lines (left, right, top, and bottom) and the two double arrows (width and height), as shown in Figure 5-37.

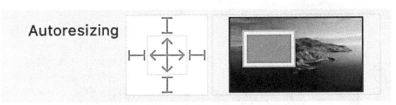

Figure 5-37: Expanding the Image View

With these rules, the sides of the Image View are pinned to the sides of its container (the window) and its width and height are allowed to change, so the image will cover the whole screen.

Do It Yourself: Click on the LaunchScreen.storyboard item in your project to open the storyboard in the Editor Area. Click on the + button in the Xcode's toolbar to open the Library (Figure 5-4, number 3). Drag an Image View to the storyboard (Figure 5-30). You should see something similar to Figure 5-31, left. Drag the corners of the Image View to the corners of the device's screen, as shown in Figure 5-31, right. Go to the Utilities Area on the right, select the Attributes Inspector panel (Figure 5-32, left), and select the husky image in the Image field (Figure 5-32, right). You should see something similar to Figure 5-34, left (the husky image is available in our website). In the Attributes Inspector panel, find the Content Mode option and select the value Aspect Fit (Figure 5-33). You should see something similar to Figure 5-34, right. Click on the image in the storyboard and open the Size Inspector panel in the Utilities Area (Figure 5-35). Activate all the lines and the arrows in the Autoresizing tool (Figure 5-37). Click on the View As button at the bottom of the storyboard (Figure 5-29, number 1) and select a different device to see how the image expands to occupy the device's entire screen.

The Basics: An image pinned to the center or the sides of the window is usually all we need for a launching screen. If your app requires something more sophisticated, you will have to apply individual constraints from the menus in the toolbar (Figure 5-29, number 3). The system of constraints is called Auto Layout and it is explained in detail in our book iOS Apps for Masterminds. For more information, visit our website and follow the links for this chapter.

(Medium) **Info.plist File**

There is one more item provided by the Single View App template we need to examine. It is a file called info.plist. We mentioned this file before. It takes care of storing the configuration of the target. In it, we will find the configuration options available in the General panel (Figure 5-11) plus others we can change or add to modify the behavior of our app.

The info.plist file orders the information in a hierarchy. The values are identified with keys and may contain other values inside. When we select it from the Navigator Area, Xcode shows an editor in the Editor Area with the current values.

Key		Type	Value
▼ Information Property List		Dictionary	(14 items)
Localization native development re...	⇕	String	$(DEVELOPMENT_LANGUAGE)
Executable file	⇕	String	$(EXECUTABLE_NAME)
Bundle identifier	⇕	String	$(PRODUCT_BUNDLE_IDENTIFIER)
InfoDictionary version	⇕	String	6.0
Bundle name	⇕	String	$(PRODUCT_NAME)
Bundle OS Type code	⇕	String	$(PRODUCT_BUNDLE_PACKAGE_TYPE)
Bundle versions string, short	⇕	String	1.0
Bundle version	⇕	String	1
Application requires iPhone enviro...	⇕	Boolean	YES
▶ Application Scene Manifest	⇕	Dictionary	(2 items)
Launch screen interface file base...	⇕	String	LaunchScreen
▶ Required device capabilities	⇕	Array	(1 item)
▶ Supported interface orientations	⇕	Array	(3 items)
▶ Supported interface orientations (i...	⇕	Array	(4 items)

Figure 5-38: Content of the info.plist file

Chapter 5 - Xcode

If we move the mouse over an item, the editor shows a + button on the right to add another item to the hierarchy. For example, to add a new option to the main list, we must click on the + button of the root item called "Information Property List" (Figure 5-38, number 1). When we click this button, the editor shows a list of possible options to choose from.

The values of each item are listed on the right column and can be edited just by clicking on them. If this column shows the number of items instead of a value, it means that the item is a container for other items. To see the rest of the items in the hierarchy, we must click the arrow on the left. For instance, the info.plist file defines two items that contains the orientations allowed for iPhones and iPads, if we click in the arrow of the iPad option, we will see something similar to Figure 5-39.

▼ Supported interface orientations (iPad)	Array	(4 items)
Item 0	String	Portrait (bottom home button)
Item 1	String	Portrait (top home button)
Item 2	String	Landscape (left home button)
Item 3	String	Landscape (right home button)

Figure 5-39: Option to define the orientations allowed for iPads

If we want to remove one of the options, we just have to click on it and press Delete and that option won't be available anymore. For instance, removing the item 0 of the Supported interface orientation (iPad) option will disable one of the portraits orientations when our application runs on an iPad.

Items can contain other items in an infinite chain. For example, the option Application Scene Manifest contains multiple items that define the configuration of a scene (window). If we keep opening the items, we get to see an item that specifies the configuration of the initial scene provided by the template, as shown in Figure 5-40.

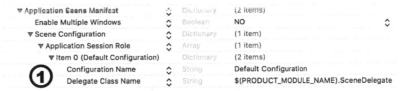

Figure 5-40: Scene configuration

The configuration of a scene for SwiftUI requires two values, the name of the configuration and the name of the class that is going to be the delegate for the scene. The configuration included by the template, defines a configuration with the name "Default Configuration" and a delegate class called SceneDelegate. That is why, when the delegate method for the application creates a `UISceneConfiguration` object with the name "Default Configuration", the `SceneDelegate` class is assigned as the delegate of the scene.

The Basics: The configuration provided in the info.plist file by the Single View App template is more than enough for most applications, but there are applications that require the configuration of multiple scenes and also frameworks that require authorization from this file to work properly, as we will see later.

Chapter 5 - Xcode

(Basic) **6.1 User Interface**

The user interface is the most important aspect of an application. Apple offers two ways to create it: Storyboards and SwiftUI. We have already introduced Storyboards in Chapter 5. A Storyboard is a visual tool that allows us to design the interface by dragging and dropping elements from the library to the Editor Area. We used it to design the launching screen of our app, but it is also required when the application is developed with the UIKit framework. SwiftUI, on the other hand, defines the views in code with a declarative syntax, replacing Storyboards altogether. The interface is declared in the definition of a structure, one view at a time, and then the compiler takes care of generating all the code necessary to display it on the screen and adapt it to every device. We declare exactly what we need and then the compiler takes care of the rest.

(Basic) **View Protocol**

In SwiftUI, the user interface is built by combining and nesting views. These views are defined by structures that conform to the **View** protocol. The protocol's only requirement is the implementation of a computed property called **body** that returns at least one view. Within the closure assigned to this property is where we declare all the views we need to design the interface, as shown in the following example.

```
import SwiftUI

struct ContentView: View {
    var body: some View {
        Text("Hello World")
    }
}
```

Listing 6-1: *Defining a structure that conforms to the* View *protocol*

When the system processes a **View** structure, it creates a view called *root view*, and then determines its size from the size of its container. This container can be the window or another view. For instance, the **ContentView** view created by the Single View App template is assigned as the window's root view from the scene's delegate, and therefore its size is going to be determined by the size of the window (see Listing 5-3).

The views defined in the **body** property follow a different path. They determine their size from the size of their container, but then they propose that size to their content and is the content who finally determines the size of the view. We can see this at work when we preview the interface produced by the **ContentView** structure created by the template. The structure creates a white view that occupies the whole screen and then a small view with the text "Hello World" at the center, as shown in Figure 6-1.

```
1
2   import SwiftUI
3
4   struct ContentView: View {
5       var body: some View {
6           Text("Hello, World!")
7       }
8   }
9
10  struct ContentView_Previews:
        PreviewProvider {
11      static var previews: some View {
12          ContentView()
13      }
14  }
```

Root View ←

Text View ←

Hello, World!

Figure 6-1: Views created by the Single View App template

Do It Yourself: Create a SwiftUI project with the Single View App template, as explained in Chapter 5 (see Figure 5-2). Click on the ContentView.swift file to see its content in the editor. If the canvas is not visible, click on the Adjust Editor button and activate the Canvas option (Chapter 5, Figure 5-6). If necessary, press the Resume button to resume the preview (Chapter 5, Figure 5-16). After a few seconds, you should see the representation of a device on the canvas with the text generated by the `ContentView` view at the center, as shown in Figure 6-1. To change the type of device used by the canvas, you can select it from the Destination button in the toolbar (Chapter 5, Figure 5-8). If instead of the canvas you want to run the application on the simulator or a device, after selecting the destination press the Play button on the left.

(Advanced) **Opaque Types**

The value produced by the **body** property is a view, a structure that conforms to the **View** protocol, but because the views assigned to the property may be different each time, it is declared as an opaque type (**some View**). Opaque types are data types that hide the value's data type from the programmer. They are usually required when working with generic data types, like the generic structures introduced before (see Listing 3-48). For example, the **reversed()** method included in **Array** structures returns a **ReversedCollection** structure, and this structure is generic, so the definition of the type depends on the type of values we are processing. An array of strings will generate a structure of type **ReversedCollection<Array<String>>** and an array of integers will return a structure of type **ReversedCollection<Array<Int>>**, as in the following example.

```
func reverseit(mylist: [Int]) -> ReversedCollection<Array<Int>> {
   let reversed = mylist.reversed()
   return reversed
}
let reversedlist = reverseit(mylist: [1, 2, 3, 4, 5])
print(Array(reversedlist))   // "[5, 4, 3, 2, 1]"
```

Listing 6-2: Returning values of complex data types

The code of Listing 6-2 defines a function called **reverseit()** that receives an array of integers and returns a **ReversedCollection** value with the values in reverse order. Once the function returns the collection, we turn it into an array and print it on the console.

This code runs and there are no issues with it, until we decide to work with different value types, such as strings. Instead of **ReversedCollection<Array<Int>>**, the return data type would have to be defined as **ReversedCollection<Array<String>>**. Although in this case it may seem easy to switch types, the generic data types used to create SwiftUI views can be complex and replacing them repeatedly in generic properties or methods can be time consuming and error prone. But if we know that the values we want to return conform to the same protocol, we can declare the return type as opaque and let the compiler figure out the data type for us. When the compiler finds an opaque type, it takes care of detecting the real data type of the value and process it as such.

Opaque types are declared with the **some** keyword followed by the name of the protocol the type conforms to. For instance, collections such as the one returned by the **reversed()** method, conform to a protocol called **Collection**, so we can define the return type as **some Collection** and let the compiler do the work for us.

```
func reverseit(mylist: [String]) -> some Collection {
    let reversed = mylist.reversed()
    return reversed
}
let reversedlist = reverseit(mylist: ["One", "Two", "Three", "Four",
"Five"])
print(Array(reversedlist))   // "["Five", "Four", "Three", "Two", "One"]"
```

Listing 6-3: Returning opaque types

The example of Listing 6-3 defines the same **reverseit()** function, but this time the function receives an array of strings and returns the opaque type **some Collection**. The value returned by the function is of type **some Collection**, but the compiler detects the value's data type as **ReversedCollection<Array<String>>** and process it as such, which means that we are still able to turn it into an **Array** and print its values on the console.

 IMPORTANT: Functions, methods or closures that return an opaque type must always return a value of a specific type. When the compiler finds an opaque type, it determines the value's real data type from the value returned. If we, for instance, use an **if else** statement to select the view we want to assign to the **body** property, the compiler won't be able to determine the right data type of the value returned and will show an error.

(Basic) **Text View**

The views declared in the **body** property are also structures that conform to the **View** protocol. SwiftUI defines several structures to produce standard views. The **Text** view used by the template is one of them. This structure takes a string and returns a view that displays the text on the screen. The following are two common initializers used with this view.

Text(String)—This initializer creates a **Text** view with the text defined by the attribute.

Text(LocalizedStringKey, comment: String?)—This initializer creates a **Text** view with a localizable text (a text used for internationalization). The first attribute is a **LocalizedStringKey** structure that defines the text we want to translate, and the **comment** attribute is an optional string with a comment to help the translator.

Because of text being the primary means of communication, **Text** views are implemented all the time in SwiftUI applications, and that is why the **ContentView** view generated by the Single View App template includes one. As shown in Listing 6-1, the **Text** view included in the template is created with a **String** value to display the text "Hello World" on the screen (see Figure 6-1), but a **Text** view can also take a **LocalizedStringKey** structure. This structure receives a string and includes it in a table that can later be used for translation. The advantage of this type of strings over a normal `String` value is that the structure defines two custom string interpolations (see Listing 3-188). A value of type `LocalizedStringKey` can include a string interpolation with one of two parameters to format the text: `formatter` and `specifier`. The `specifier` parameter accepts a string with placeholders to specify the format.

```
import SwiftUI
struct ContentView: View {
   var number: Float = 30.87512

   var body: some View {
      Text("My Number: \(number, specifier: "%.2f")")
   }
}
```

Listing 6-4: Formatting the content of a Text *view with a specifier*

In the code of Listing 6-4, we format the value of the `number` property to have only two digits after the decimal point (see Listing 4-5). This view displays the text "My Number: 30.88".

On the other hand, the `formatter` parameter specifies the format with a subclass of the `Formatter` class, like the `NumberFormatter` class studied in Chapter 4.

```
import SwiftUI
struct ContentView: View {
   var number: Float = 30.87512

   var formatter: NumberFormatter {
      let format = NumberFormatter()
      format.numberStyle = .currency
      return format
   }
   var body: some View {
      Text("My Number: \(NSNumber(value: number), formatter: formatter)")
   }
}
```

Listing 6-5: Formatting the content of a Text *view with a* Formatter *subclass*

The example of Listing 6-5 defines a computed property that returns a `NumberFormatter` class configured with the `currency` style and then applies this format to the `number` property to define the text for the view. Notice that `Formatter` subclasses only work with Foundation values, so we had to convert the property into an `NSNumber` object. The string displayed by the `Text` view is "My number: $30.88".

 Do It Yourself: Update the ContentView.swift file in your project with the example you want to try. If the canvas is not visible, click on the Adjust Editor button and activate the Canvas option. If necessary, press the Resume button to resume the preview. You should see the text produced by the `Text` view on the canvas, as before.

(Basic) ## Modifiers

Views are presented with attributes by default, such as a standard font and color, but the `View` protocol defines methods to modify their aspect. These methods are called *modifiers*, and they are executed right after the instance is created, as in the following example.

Chapter 6 - SwiftUI Framework

```
import SwiftUI

struct ContentView: View {
    var body: some View {
        Text("Hello World")
            .font(.largeTitle)
    }
}
```

Listing 6-6: Applying modifiers to a view

When the system reads the **body** property of the example in Listing 6-6 to build the interface, it creates an instance of the **Text** structure with the string "Hello World", and then calls the **font** method on this structure. This method creates a new view with the **largeTitle** attribute applied to the text and returns that view. As a result, the **body** property produces a view with a large title. If we have the canvas activated, we can see the change in real time.

```
1
2   import SwiftUI
3
4   struct ContentView: View {
5       var body: some View {
6           Text("Hello, World!")
7               .font(.largeTitle)
8       }
9   }
10
11  struct ContentView_Previews:
        PreviewProvider {
12      static var previews: some View {
13          ContentView()
14      }
15  }
16
```

Hello, World!

Figure 6-2: Modifiers

 Do It Yourself: Update the ContentView.swift file with the code of Listing 6-6. Press the Resume button on the canvas to resume the preview. You should see something similar to Figure 6-2.

 The Basics: Modifiers are usually declared below the view, one per line, but they may be written in one line, as in **Text("Hello World").font(.largeTitle)**.

Our code and the canvas are interconnected. For instance, we can click on the representation of the **Text** view on the canvas to select it, and the code that generates that view is highlighted in the editor. Or we can perform a change in the code or the canvas, replace content or add modifiers, and everything will be reflected on the other side.

Xcode offers two ways to modify our views from the canvas. One alternative is to click on the view and open the Attributes Inspector panel in the Utilities Area on the right to see a list of all the attributes we can change for that view.

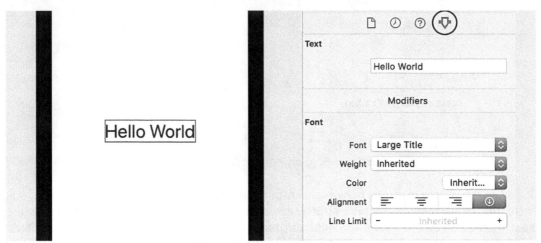

Figure 6-3: View's attributes

The Attributes Inspector panel shows the attributes currently assigned to the view. In our example, the option Large Title is already selected because we added the `font()` modifier in Listing 6-6. If we remove the modifier, the panel is updated to show the current values. The same happens the other way around. if we change any value on this panel, the change is reflected in the canvas and the corresponding modifier is added to the code.

Another way to modify our views is with a context menu. If we move the mouse over a view in the canvas or in our code and click on it while holding down the Command key, we will see a menu with multiple options to modify the view. One of those options is called *Show SwiftUI Inspector* and it opens a panel with all the same options we can find in the Attributes Inspector panel. Changing the options in this window produces the same effect as before.

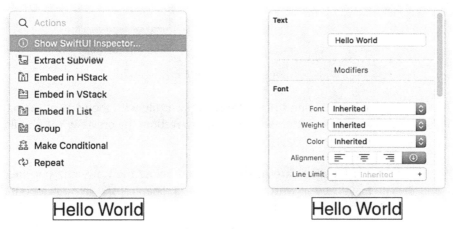

Figure 6-4: View's context menu

Additionally, Xcode offers a library with a list of views and modifiers that we can incorporate to our interface by dragging and dropping them onto the canvas or the code. The library is activated from the Library button in the toolbar (Chapter 5, Figure 5-4, number 3), and the lists of views and modifiers are selected from the buttons in the window's toolbar. The first button presents a list with all the views and the second button opens a list with all the modifiers available. We can also use the search bar at the top of the window for a quick search. Figure 6-5, next, illustrates how to add a modifier from this library to change the color of the text.

Chapter 6 - SwiftUI Framework

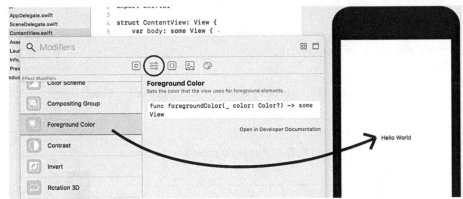

Figure 6-5: Adding a modifier from the Library

 Do It Yourself: With the ContentView.swift file selected, and the canvas opened, move the mouse to the "Hello World" text on the canvas, press and hold the Command key and click on it. You should see a context menu (Figure 6-4, left). Click on the Show SwiftUI Inspector option. In the next window, click on the Text field, change the text to "Goodbye World", and press Enter. You should see the text changing on the canvas and the code.

Most modifiers are defined by the `View` protocol and then implemented by the structures that conform to it. There are common modifiers that apply to most views and others that are more specific. The following are some common modifiers used to determine the size of the view.

frame(width: CGFloat?, **height:** CGFloat?, **alignment:** Alignment)—This modifier assigns a new size and alignment to the view. The **alignment** attribute determines the alignment of the view's content. It is a structure of type `Alignment` with the type properties `bottom`, `bottomLeading`, `bottomTrailing`, `center`, `leading`, `top`, `topLeading`, `topTrailing`, and `trailing`.

frame(minWidth: CGFloat?, **idealWidth:** CGFloat?, **maxWidth:** CGFloat?, **minHeight:** CGFloat?, **idealHeight:** CGFloat?, **maxHeight:** CGFloat?, **alignment:** Alignment)—This modifier assigns a minimum and a maximum size to the view. We can also define an ideal width and height that will be taken into consideration when the available space is distributed among the views. The **alignment** attribute determines the alignment of the view's content. It is a structure of type `Alignment` with the type properties `bottom`, `bottomLeading`, `bottomTrailing`, `center`, `leading`, `top`, `topLeading`, `topTrailing`, and `trailing`.

padding(CGFloat)—This modifier adds padding between the view's content and its frame. The attribute determines the width of the padding. We can provide a `CGFloat` value to specify the padding for all sides (No value assigns a standard padding that adapts to each device), an `EdgeInsets` value to specify a padding for each side, or a set of `Edge` values along with a `CGFloat` value to declare which sides we want to modify and for how much (`padding([Edge], CGFloat)`). The `Edge` type is an enumeration with the values `bottom`, `leading`, `top`, `trailing`, `horizontal` (left and right), and `vertical` (top and bottom).

The size of a view is usually determined by the size of its content. For instance, the size of a `Text` view is determined by the size of its text. If we want the view to extend beyond the area occupied by the text, we can use these modifiers to add a padding or set a specific size. In the following example, we give the `Text` view a fixed size and align the content to the left.

```
import SwiftUI

struct ContentView: View {
    var body: some View {
        Text("Hello World!")
            .frame(width: 250, height: 100, alignment: .leading)
    }
}
```

Listing 6-7: Assigning a fixed size to a view

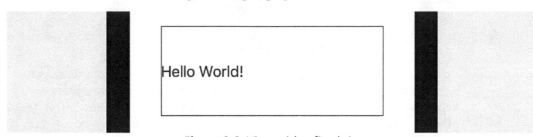

Figure 6-6: View with a fixed size

 Do It Yourself: Update the code of the ContentView.swift file with the code of Listing 6-7. If necessary, press the Resume button to resume the preview. Click on the `Text` view in the code or in the canvas to select it. You should see a blue rectangle indicating the area occupied by the view, as illustrated in Figure 6-6.

The attributes in the `frame()` modifiers are optional. We can declare only the width or the height, and the rest of the attributes will be defined with the values set by the view. This is particularly useful when we want to turn one side of the view flexible. Flexible views are defined with the **maxWidth** and **maxHeight** attributes. For instance, we can assign the value `infinity` to the **maxWidth** attribute to extend the view to the left and right side of the window.

```
import SwiftUI

struct ContentView: View {
    var body: some View {
        Text("Hello World!")
            .frame(minWidth: 0, maxWidth: .infinity)
    }
}
```

Listing 6-8: Creating flexible containers

The value `infinity` is a type property defined in the `CGFloat` structure that asks the system to expand the view to occupy all the space available in its container. In our example, we only defined the **maxWidth** attribute, so the `Text` view extends to the edge of the screen on each side but adopts the height of the text.

Figure 6-7: Flexible view

Chapter 6 - SwiftUI Framework

IMPORTANT: Notice that for a flexible view to work properly it is recommended to always declare the minimum size as well. If you are declaring a flexible width, you should set the `minWidth` attribute, and if you are declaring a flexible height, you should also include the `minHeight` attribute, as in the example of Listing 6-8.

Another way to specify a custom size is with the `padding()` modifier. The padding is generated between the content and the edges of the view. There are different ways to determine the padding's width. For instance, if we don't specify any value, the system assigns one by default, but we can also provide a `CGFloat` value to declare a specific width.

```
import SwiftUI

struct ContentView: View {
    var body: some View {
        Text("Hello World")
            .padding(25)
    }
}
```

Listing 6-9: Adding a padding to the view

The code of Listing 6-9 assigns a padding of 25 points to the `Text` view. The padding is applied between the text and the view's frame.

Figure 6-8: View with padding

The `View` protocol defines a structure called `EdgeInsets` that we can use to specify a width for each side of the view. The structure includes the following initializer.

EdgeInsets(top: CGFloat, **leading:** CGFloat, **bottom:** CGFloat, **trailing:** CGFloat)—This initializer returns an `EdgeInsets` structure with the values specified by the attributes.

The leading and trailing values are assigned to the left or the right side depending on the language. For instance, if the language set on the device is left-to-right, like English, the leading value is assigned to the left side of the view and the trailing value to the right. The following example assigns a padding of 40 points to only the left and right sides.

```
import SwiftUI

struct ContentView: View {
    var body: some View {
        Text("Hello World")
            .padding(EdgeInsets(top: 0.0, leading: 40.0, bottom: 0.0,
trailing: 40.0))
    }
}
```

Listing 6-10: Assigning a specific padding for each side

Figure 6-9: Padding on the sides

The code of Listing 6-10 assigns padding to specific sides of the view. Another way to do it is with the values of an enumeration provided by SwiftUI called **Edge**. This enumeration includes the values **bottom, leading, top,** and **trailing** to represent each side. We must declare a set with the values that represent the sides we want to affect and a second attribute with the width we want to assign to the padding.

```
import SwiftUI
struct ContentView: View {
    var body: some View {
        Text("Hello World")
            .padding([.top, .bottom], 50)
    }
}
```

Listing 6-11: Assigning padding with Edge values

The example of Listing 6-11 adds a padding of 50 points at the top and bottom of the view.

Figure 6-10: Padding at the top and bottom

In addition to the view, we can also style its content. For instance, the **View** protocol defines modifiers that are especially useful for **Text** views. The following are the most frequently used.

font(Font)—This modifier assigns a font to the text. The attribute is a **Font** structure that provides type properties and methods to select the font we want, including custom fonts.

bold()—This modifier assigns the bold style to the text.

italic()—This modifier assigns the italic style to the text.

fontWeight(Weight)—This modifier assigns a weight to the text. The possible values are defined by a structure inside the **Font** structure called **Weight**. The properties available are **black, bold, heavy, light, medium, regular, semibold, thin,** and **ultraLight.**

underline(Bool, color: Color)—This modifier underlines the text. The first attribute is a Boolean value that indicates whether the text has an underline or not, and the second attribute defines the color of the line.

strikethrough(Bool, color: Color)—This modifier draws a line through the text. The first attribute is a Boolean value that indicates whether the text is strikethrough or not, and the second attribute defines the color of the line.

shadow(color: Color, radius: CGFloat, x: CGFloat, y: CGFloat)—This modifier assigns a shadow to the text. The attributes define the color of the shadow, its size, and the horizontal and vertical offsets.

The most important aspect of a text is the font. The system defines standard fonts and sizes to show the text produced by a `Text` view, but we can specify our own with the `font()` modifier. The `font()` modifier assigns the font to the view, but the font is defined by an instance of the `Font` structure. With this structure, we can create custom and dynamic fonts. Custom fonts are fonts provided by the system or the developer, and dynamic fonts are the fonts Apple recommends using because they adapt to the font size selected by the user from Settings.

The easiest to implement are dynamic fonts. They are defined by type properties provided by the `Font` structure, so all we have to do is to apply the `font()` modifier with the property that represents the font type we want to assign to the text. We have done this before with the `largeTitle` property (see Listing 6-6), but the structure also includes the properties `title`, `headline`, `subheadline`, `body`, `callout`, `caption`, and `footnote`.

```
import SwiftUI

struct ContentView: View {
    var body: some View {
        Text("Hello World")
            .font(.body)
    }
}
```

Listing 6-12: Assigning dynamic font types

The `body` property produces a font similar to the standard font provided by the system, but we can use other properties to get fonts with different styles and sizes. Figure 6-11 shows some of the fonts returned by these properties compared to the system's standard font.

Hello World   Hello World   Hello World   Hello World

Standard / Body   **footnote**   **title**   **headline**

Figure 6-11: Dynamic font types

 Do It Yourself: Dynamic fonts have a predefine size, but they change according to the size defined by the user from Settings. If you want to see how your text looks like in different sizes, run the app in the simulator or a device, open the Settings app, go to Accessibility / Display & Text Size / Large Text, activate Large Accessibility Sizes, and then change the size from the slider at the bottom. Later, we will see how to test dynamic fonts on the canvas.

Although it is recommended to use dynamic fonts, the `Font` structure also includes the following type methods to implement the font defined by the system or to load custom fonts when necessary.

system(size: CGFloat)—This type method returns the system font with the size defined by the **size** attribute.

custom(String, **size:** CGFloat)—This type method returns a font of the type specified by the first attribute and with the size specified by the **size** attribute.

With the `system()` method we can get the standard font provided by the system but of any size we want. The font and size defined by this method are not affected by the choices the user makes from Settings.

```
import SwiftUI
```

```
struct ContentView: View {
    var body: some View {
        Text("Hello World")
            .font(Font.system(size: 50))
    }
}
```

Listing 6-13: Using the system font

The example of Listing 6-13 displays a text with a size of 50 points that always remains at that size no matter the changes performed by the user, but the font type is the one defined by the system. If we want to use a custom font, we have to implement the `custom()` method.

Operative systems come with a set of standard fonts. If the font we want to use is already included in the system, we just have to specify its name and size, as in the following example.

```
import SwiftUI

struct ContentView: View {
    var body: some View {
        Text("Hello World")
            .font(Font.custom("Georgia", size: 50))
    }
}
```

Listing 6-14: Using standard fonts

Hello World

Figure 6-12: Text with the Georgia font

If the font we want to include is not provided by the system, we must copy the file into the project and add an option to the info.plist file with the name of the font. Including the file in our project is easy; we must drag it from Finder into the Navigator Area, as we did before for images (see Chapter 5, Figure 5-19). We just have to make sure that the option "Copy items if necessary" and the target are selected (see Chapter 5, Figure 5-20). The next step is to ask the system to include the font in our application by adding the option "Fonts provided by application" in the info.plist file, as shown in Figure 6-13.

Figure 6-13: Custom fonts declared in the info.plist file

The option is added from the + button (circled in Figure 6-13). The option already includes an item (Item 0), so all we have to do to add the font is to press the arrow on the left to expose the item (Figure 6-13, number 1) and then replace its value with the name of the file that contains our font (Figure 6-13, number 2).

In this example, we include the horsepower.ttf file, which defines a font called *Horse Power*. Now, we can use this font from our application, as shown next.

Chapter 6 - SwiftUI Framework

```
import SwiftUI
struct ContentView: View {
    var body: some View {
        Text("Hello World")
            .font(Font.custom("Horsepower-Regular", size: 50))
    }
}
```

Listing 6-15: Using custom fonts

Figure 6-14: Text with a custom font

 Do It Yourself: Download the horsepower.ttf file from our website or provide your own. Drag the file from Finder to the Navigator Area of your project (Figure 5-19). Make sure to check the option "Copy items if necessary" and the target (Figure 5-20). Open the info.plist file, click on the + button in the Information Property List option, and select the option "Fonts provided by the application". Click on the arrow at the left of the option to reveal its items. You should see the Item 0 with no value. Click on the value field to change it. Copy and paste the name of your font's file, including the extension. Modify the `ContentView` structure with the code of Listing 6-15. Press the Resume button to see the text with the new font on the canvas.

 IMPORTANT: The names we have to provide to the `custom()` method are the PostScript names. To find the PostScript name of the font you want to add to your project, open the Font Book application from the Applications folder, go to the View menu, and select the option Show Font Info. Click on the font. The PostScript name is shown on the right panel.

Applying the rest of the modifiers available for `Text` views is straightforward, as shown next.

```
import SwiftUI
struct ContentView: View {
    var body: some View {
        Text("Hello World")
            .font(.largeTitle)
            .underline()
            .fontWeight(.heavy)
            .shadow(color: Color.gray, radius: 1, x: 1, y: 1)
    }
}
```

Listing 6-16: Applying multiple styles to a text

The structure of Listing 6-16 defines a `Text` view with a `largeTitle` font, a weight of type **heavy**, a shadow, and underlines the text. In this example, we define the **radius, x,** and **y** attributes of the **shadow()** modifier to 1 to cast a subtle shadow that extends to the right and bottom of the text.

Hello World

Figure 6-15: Multiple styles applied to a text

`Text` views can process the + operator and combine themselves into one view. Applying this feature, we can assign the styles to each view independently but make them look like they are one single text.

```swift
import SwiftUI

struct ContentView: View {
    var body: some View {
        Text("Hello ")
            .font(.largeTitle)
        + Text("World")
            .underline()
        + Text("!!!")
            .fontWeight(.heavy)
    }
}
```

Listing 6-17: Joining `Text` *views*

The first `Text` view in the example of Listing 6-17 is displayed with a `largeTitle` font, the second view is underlined, and a weight of type `heavy` was assigned to the third view, but they all look like one single line of text.

Hello World!!!

Figure 6-16: Multiple `Text` *views with different styles*

If what we want is to show multiple lines of text, a single `Text` view is enough. By default, a `Text` view adjusts its size to display the full text, but we can implement modifiers provided by the `View` protocol to set a limit on the number of lines allowed or to format the text.

lineLimit(Int**)**—This modifier determines how many lines the text can contain. The attribute is an optional of type `Int` that indicates the number of lines we want. By default, the value is set to `nil`, which means the view will extend to include the number of lines necessary to show the full text.

multilineTextAlignment(TextAlignment**)**—This modifier defines the alignment of multiline texts. The attribute is an enumeration of type `TextAlignment` with the values `center`, `leading`, and `trailing`.

lineSpacing(CGFloat**)**—This modifier determines the space between lines.

truncationMode(TruncationMode**)**—This modifier determines how the text is truncated when it doesn't fit inside the view's frame. The attribute is an enumeration of type `TruncationMode` with the values `head`, `middle`, and `tail`.

The following example displays a text aligned to the center and with a space of 5 points between lines.

```
import SwiftUI

struct ContentView: View {
    var body: some View {
        Text("Monsters are real, and ghosts are real too. They live inside
us, and sometimes, they win. Stephen King.")
            .padding()
            .multilineTextAlignment(.center)
            .lineSpacing(5)
    }
}
```

Listing 6-18: Formatting text

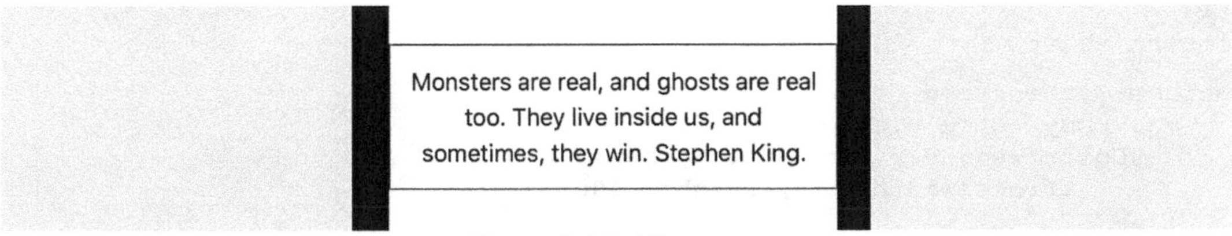

Monsters are real, and ghosts are real
too. They live inside us, and
sometimes, they win. Stephen King.

Figure 6-17: Alignment

If we limit the number of lines, we must consider how the text is going to be displayed to the user when it is too long, or it doesn't fit within the view. By default, the system truncates the text and adds ellipsis at the end to indicate that part of the text is missing, but we can move the ellipsis to the beginning or the middle with the `truncationMode()` modifier.

```
import SwiftUI

struct ContentView: View {
    var body: some View {
        Text("Monsters are real, and ghosts are real too. They live inside
us, and sometimes, they win. Stephen King.")
            .padding()
            .lineLimit(1)
            .truncationMode(.middle)
    }
}
```

Listing 6-19: Truncating text

Monsters are real...in. Stephen King.

Figure 6-18: Truncation mode

(Basic)   ## Color View

Some modifiers change the colors of the view. Colors in SwiftUI are defined by a `Color` view. The following are some of the structure's initializers.

Color(red: Double, **green:** Double, **blue:** Double, **opacity:** Double)—This
initializer returns a `Color` view with the color and opacity defined by the attributes. The attributes determine the levels of red, green, blue, and opacity that define the color with values from 0.0 to 1.0. The opacity value can be ignored.

Color(hue: Double, **saturation:** Double, **brightness:** Double)—This initializer returns a `Color` view with the color defined by the attributes. The attributes determine the level of hue, saturation and brightness of the color with values from 0.0 to 1.0.

The `Color` structure also offers an extensive list of type properties that return a `Color` view with a predefined color that adapts to the interface mode (light or dark). The properties available are `black`, `blue`, `gray`, `green`, `orange`, `pink`, `primary`, `purple`, `red`, `white`, and `yellow`. There is also a property to make the view transparent called `clear`, and two properties called `primary` and `secondary` that return predefined colors that also change depending on the mode set for the interface (light or dark).

Most of the time, `Color` views are used to define a color for the content of other views, but they are views and therefore they can be included in the interface like any other.

```
import SwiftUI

struct ContentView: View {
   var body: some View {
      Color(red: 0.9, green: 0.5, blue: 0.2)
         .frame(width: 250, height: 100)
   }
}
```

Listing 6-20: Implementing `Color` *views*

Figure 6-19: `Color` *view*

The code of Listing 6-20 creates a `Color` view of color orange and a size of 250 by 100 points. In this case, the `Color` initializer was implemented with values from 0.0 to 1.0 to determine the levels of red, green and blue, but RGB colors (Red, Green, Blue) are usually determined with integer values from 0 to 255. If we want to work with these values, we can convert them dividing the number by 255. For instance, the following initializer assigns an RGB color with the values 100, 228, 255 (cyan).

```
import SwiftUI

struct ContentView: View {
   var body: some View {
      Color(red: 100/255, green: 228/255, blue: 255/255)
         .frame(width: 250, height: 100)
   }
}
```

Listing 6-21: Defining the color with RGB values

Colors defined with the initializers are static colors, which means they are always the same, independent of the interface mode (light or dark), but we can assign dynamic colors with the structure's properties. Dynamic colors adapt to the current mode. The following example creates a `Color` view with the `red` property. In dark mode this color will look slightly different than in light mode.

```
import SwiftUI

struct ContentView: View {
    var body: some View {
        Color.red
            .frame(width: 250, height: 100)
    }
}
```

Listing 6-22: Assigning a dynamic color

If we want to define our own colors for light and dark modes, we can include a dynamic color in the Assets Catalog, as we did in Chapter 5, Figure 5-26, and then load it from code. In the following example, we assume that there is a color in the Assets Catalog with the name MyColor.

```
import SwiftUI

struct ContentView: View {
    var body: some View {
        Color("MyColor")
            .frame(width: 250, height: 100)
    }
}
```

Listing 6-23: Assigning a dynamic color from the Assets Catalog

Do It Yourself: Open your project and click on Assets.xcassets in the Navigator Area to open the Assets Catalog. Click on the + button and select the option New Color Set (Chapter 5, Figure 5-22). Click on the set to select it, open the Attributes Inspector panel and change its name to MyColor and the Appearance to Any, Dark (Chapter 5, Figure 5-26, number 1). Click on the squares that represent the colors in the Editor Area and select a different color for each one of them from the Attributes Inspector panel. Modify your ContentView structure with the code of Listing 6-23 and press Resume on the canvas, if necessary, to see what the interface looks like. Later, we will see how to test this in previews, but for the moment you can run the application in the simulator or a device and select the interface mode from Settings (light or dark) to see both colors applied to the text.

As we already mentioned, the most common application of Color views is to define the colors of other views. The following are some of the modifiers that require a Color view to define the color or are useful when working with these types of views.

foregroundColor(Color**)**—This modifier assigns a color to the view's content. The attribute is a view of type Color.

background(View, **alignment:** Alignment**)**—This modifier assigns a view as the view's background. The first attribute is a view, including Color views, and the **alignment** attribute determines how the view is going to be aligned within the bounds of the view.

border(Color, **width:** CGFloat**)**—This modifier assigns a border to the view. The first attribute is a Color view that determines the border's color and the **width** attribute determines its width.

cornerRadius(CGFloat**)**—This modifier rounds the corners. The attribute determines the radius of the corners.

overlay(View, **alignment:** Alignment)—This modifier displays a view in front of the view that is being modified. The first attribute is a SwiftUI view, including `Color` views, and the **alignment** attribute determines how the view is going to be aligned within the bounds of the view.

Using these modifiers, we can apply colors to different parts of the view. For instance, the `foregroundColor()` modifier assigns a color to the view's content. In the following example, we use it to change the color of the text in a `Text` view.

```
import SwiftUI

struct ContentView: View {
    var body: some View {
        Text("Hello World")
            .font(.largeTitle)
            .foregroundColor(Color.red)
    }
}
```

Listing 6-24: *Assigning a color to the text of a* Text *view*

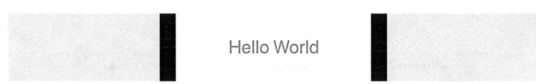

Figure 6-20: *Text in different color*

Besides changing the color of the text, we can assign a color to the view's background. The `background()` modifier can take any view, but it is usually applied with a `Color` view.

```
import SwiftUI

struct ContentView: View {
    var body: some View {
        Text("Hello World")
            .font(.largeTitle)
            .background(Color.gray)
    }
}
```

Listing 6-25: *Assigning a background color to a* Text *view*

Figure 6-21: *View's background*

As we have seen earlier, the area occupied by the view is determined by a rectangular frame. In `Text` views, the size of this rectangle is determined by the size of the text. If we want to extend the background, we can set the frame's size with the `frame()` modifier or add a padding with the `padding()` modifier (see Listings 6-7 and 6-9).

```
import SwiftUI
```

Chapter 6 - SwiftUI Framework

```
struct ContentView: View {
    var body: some View {
        Text("Hello World")
            .font(.largeTitle)
            .padding(20)
            .background(Color.gray)
    }
}
```

Listing 6-26: Assigning a background color to the view and the padding

Notice that the padding was applied before the background. This is important because the order of the modifiers matters. Every time a modifier is executed, a new view is created with the characteristics of the previous view and the changes requested by the modifier. For example, the code of Listing 6-26 creates a `Text` view with the text "Hello World", then the `font()` modifier creates a new view with a large text, after that the `padding()` modifier creates another view with the characteristics of the previous one but with a padding of 20 points, and finally the `background()` modifier creates another view with a background that covers the whole area occupied by the previous view, which includes the padding. If we had declared the background before the padding, the background color would have been applied to the view generated by the `font()` modifier, which didn't include the padding, as illustrated in Figure 6-22.

Figure 6-22: Background applied before and after the padding

In addition to the background, we can assign a border to the view with the `border()` modifier. This modifier takes a view that represents the style of the border and its width and adds a border with those characteristics.

```
import SwiftUI

struct ContentView: View {
    var body: some View {
        Text("Hello World")
            .font(.largeTitle)
            .padding(20)
            .background(Color.gray)
            .border(Color.yellow, width: 10)
    }
}
```

Listing 6-27: Assigning a border

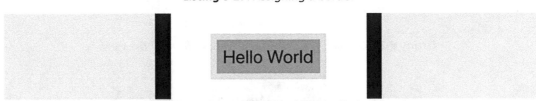

Figure 6-23: Background and border applied to the view

If we have a view with a background or content that fills the view's frame, such as a `Color` view or an image, we can round its corners with the `cornerRadius()` modifier.

```
import SwiftUI

struct ContentView: View {
    var body: some View {
        Text("Hello World")
            .font(.largeTitle)
            .padding(20)
            .background(Color.gray)
            .cornerRadius(20)
    }
}
```

Listing 6-28: Rounding corners

Figure 6-24: Round corners

 The Basics: The `cornerRadius()` modifier clips the content of the view to its frame, which means that any content that extends beyond the limits of the view is going to be hidden. This includes the border. One way to create a round border is to include the text inside a container, such as a stack, and give the views different background colors. We will learn how to work with stacks and containers later in this chapter.

The `overlay()` modifier works like the `background()` modifier but instead of displaying the view in the background, it does so on the front. For instance, the following code adds a translucent yellow view in front of the view generated by the previous example.

```
import SwiftUI

struct ContentView: View {
    var body: some View {
        Text("Hello World")
            .font(.largeTitle)
            .padding(20)
            .background(Color.gray)
            .cornerRadius(20)
            .overlay(
                Color(red: 1, green: 1, blue: 0.3, opacity: 0.2)
                    .frame(width: 160, height: 40)
            )
    }
}
```

Listing 6-29: Displaying an additional view in front of the view

Figure 6-25: Overlay

Chapter 6 - SwiftUI Framework

We have already learned how to incorporate images into our project (see Chapter 5). Of course, we can show these images in our application. SwiftUI includes the `Image` view for this purpose. The following are some of its initializers.

> **Image(**String**)**—This initializer creates an `Image` view with the image indicated by the attribute. The attribute is a string with the name of the file or the set in the Assets Catalog (the extension is not required).

> **Image(systemName:** String**)**—This initializer creates an `Image` view with an SF symbol. The **systemName** attribute is the name of the symbol.

An `Image` view can load and display any image that was incorporated to our project or added to the Assets Catalog. All we need is to specify its name. For instance, the following example creates an `Image` view with an image we put in the Assets Catalog called *Toronto*.

```
import SwiftUI
struct ContentView: View {
    var body: some View {
        Image("Toronto")
    }
}
```

Listing 6-30: Displaying an image

Do It Yourself: Download the Toronto.jpg file from our website or provide your own image. Drag the files to the Assets Catalog in your project (Figure 5-22). Modify the **ContentView** structure with the code of Listing 6-30. You should see a picture of Toronto on the canvas.

By default, `Image` views are the size of their content. If the image is larger than the window, as in this case, the view will extend beyond the limits of the screen.

Figure 6-26: Image view larger than the screen

The image is independent of the view. If we try to resize it with the **frame()** modifier, the view adopts the size determined by the modifier, but the image remains in its original size. To determine how the image adapts to the space provided by the view, we must apply the following modifiers implemented by the `Image` structure.

clipped()—This modifier clips the image to the view's frame.

resizable()—This modifier resizes the image to fit in the view's frame.

aspectRatio(CGSize, **contentMode:** ContentMode**)**—This modifier changes the image's aspect ratio to the values specified by the first attribute and resizes the image according to the mode specified by the **contentMode** attribute. This attribute is an enumeration of type `ContentMode` with the values `fill` and `fit`. If we want to use the original aspect ratio, we can declare the first attribute as `nil` or just ignore it.

scaledToFit()—This modifier scales the image to fit the view. It works like the `aspectRatio()` modifier with the aspect ratio set to `nil` and the mode to `fit`.

scaledToFill()—This modifier scales the image to fill the view. It works like the `aspectRatio()` modifier with the aspect ratio set to `nil` and the mode to `fill`.

There are several transformations we can apply to the image with these modifiers. One alternative is to clip the image to the view's frame with the `clipped()` modifier.

```
import SwiftUI

struct ContentView: View {
    var body: some View {
        Image("Toronto")
            .frame(width: 250, height: 100)
            .clipped()
    }
}
```

Listing 6-31: Clipping the image

The `clipped()` modifier creates a new view that only shows the part of the image that is within the view's frame.

Figure 6-27: Image clipped

This reduces the size of the visible image, but the image is still presented in its original size, independent of the size of the view. To adapt the size of the image to the size of the view, we have to make the image flexible with the `resizable()` modifier.

```
import SwiftUI

struct ContentView: View {
    var body: some View {
        Image("Toronto")
            .resizable()
            .frame(width: 250, height: 100)
    }
}
```

Listing 6-32: Resizing the image

The `resizable()` modifier creates a view that adjusts the size of the image to fit the space available within the view's frame.

Figure 6-28: Image resized

The Basics: As we already mentioned, modifiers return a new view and therefore the order in which they are applied matters. The `resizable()` modifier applied in the example of Listing 6-32 is implemented by the `Image` structure and therefore it must be applied first. If we try to declared this modifier after the `frame()` modifier, we will get an error because the `frame()` modifier does not return an `Image` view, it returns a view of type `some View`.

In the example of Listing 6-32, we didn't have to clip the image because the `resizable()` modifier resizes the image to the size of the view. But this creates another problem. The image is squashed. If we want to resize the image but keeping its original aspect ratio, we have to define the content mode with the `aspectRatio()` modifier. This content mode is the same we set for the image in our launching screen in Chapter 5 (see Figure 5-34). The values available are `fit` (Aspect Fit) and `fill` (Aspect Fill).

```
import SwiftUI
struct ContentView: View {
    var body: some View {
        Image("Toronto")
            .resizable()
            .aspectRatio(contentMode: .fit)
            .frame(width: 250, height: 100)
    }
}
```

Listing 6-33: Resizing an image to fit the view

In the example of Listing 6-33, we create an `Image` view with the same image as before, but this time we resize it with the `resizable()` modifier and make it fit in the space available preserving its original aspect ratio with the `aspectRatio()` modifier. The same effect can be achieved with the `scaledToFit()` modifier.

```
import SwiftUI
struct ContentView: View {
    var body: some View {
        Image("Toronto")
            .resizable()
            .scaledToFit()
            .frame(width: 250, height: 100)
    }
}
```

Listing 6-34: Resizing an image to fit the view with the `scaledToFit()` modifier

There are two modes available: `fit` and `fill`. Figure 6-29 shows what happens when we apply these content modes to the image of our example.

Chapter 6 - SwiftUI Framework

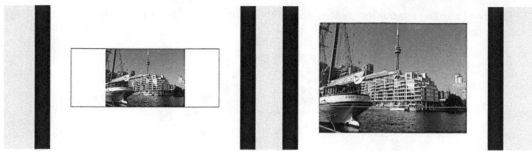

Figure 6-29: *Aspect fit (left) and aspect fill (right)*

In `fit` mode, the image is resized to fit inside the view, even when that leaves some parts of the frame empty (Figure 6-29, left). In `fill` mode, the image is resized to fill the view, even when parts of the image may lie outside the view (Figure 6-29, right). If we want to use the `fill` mode to fill the view but don't want the image to extend outside the view, we can clip it with the `clipped()` modifier.

```
import SwiftUI

struct ContentView: View {
    var body: some View {
        Image("Toronto")
            .resizable()
            .scaledToFill()
            .frame(width: 250, height: 100)
            .clipped()
    }
}
```

Listing 6-35: *Resizing image to fill the view*

Figure 6-30: *Clipped image*

Often, the user interface must include an image that adapts to the space available. An easy way to achieve this is to make the image resizable and set its mode to `fit`.

```
import SwiftUI

struct ContentView: View {
    var body: some View {
        Image("Toronto")
            .resizable()
            .scaledToFit()
    }
}
```

Listing 6-36: *Resizing image to fill the container*

When the size of the frame is not declared, the view works along with the content to set its final size. At first, the view takes all the space available in its container, but then it asks the image

Chapter 6 - SwiftUI Framework

what size to take. Because the image mode was set to `fit`, the image allows the view to extend as much as it can but adjusts the view's height to its own height to preserve the original aspect ratio. The result is shown in Figure 6-31.

Figure 6-31: *Flexible* `Image` *view*

If instead of the `fit` mode, we set the aspect ratio to `fill`, the image adapts to the width and height of the screen. If the image is wider or taller than the screen, the view will expand beyond the limits of the screen, as illustrated in Figure 6-26 above, but we can force the view to take the size of the screen with the `frame()` modifier and flexible values.

```
import SwiftUI

struct ContentView: View {
    var body: some View {
        Image("Toronto")
            .resizable()
            .scaledToFill()
            .frame(minWidth: 0, maxWidth: .infinity, minHeight: 0,
maxHeight: .infinity)
    }
}
```

Listing 6-37: *Adjusting the* `Image` *view to the size of the screen*

Now the `Image` view takes the size of the screen and the image fills the view, as shown in Figure 6-32, below. This is useful when we use an image to define the interface's background. But notice that the area occupied by the image doesn't include the status bar at the top or any tool bar at the bottom. This area is called the Safe Area. We will learn more about this area and how to remove this limitation later.

Figure 6-32: *Image of the size of the screen*

Of course, we can also apply common modifiers to an `Image` view. Some modify the view, others the image. The following example adds a padding, round corners, and a shadow to our image.

```
import SwiftUI
struct ContentView: View {
    var body: some View {
        Image("Toronto")
            .resizable()
            .scaledToFit()
            .cornerRadius(25)
            .padding(20)
            .shadow(color: Color.black, radius: 5, x: 5, y: 5)
    }
}
```

Listing 6-38: Applying style modifiers to an Image *view*

Again, the order is important. In this example, we applied the `padding()` after the `cornerRadius()` to make sure the rounded corners are generated on the image, not the padding.

Figure 6-33: Image view with common modifiers

The `View` protocol also defines modifiers that are particularly useful with `Image` views. The following are the most frequently used.

blur(radius: CGFloat, **opaque:** Bool)—This modifier applies a blur effect to the view. The **radius** attribute determines how diffuse the blur effect is, and the **opaque** attribute determines whether the blur effect is going to be opaque or transparent.

colorMultiply(Color**)**—This modifier multiplies the view's colors with a specific color. As a result, the view's original colors tend toward the color defined by the attribute.

saturation(Double**)**—This modifier increases or decreases the intensity of the colors.

contrast(Double**)**—This modifier applies contrast to the view.

opacity(Double**)**—This modifier defines the view's level of opacity. The attribute takes values from 0.0 (fully transparent) to 1.0 (fully opaque).

scaleEffect(CGSize**)**—This modifier changes the horizontal and vertical scales of the view to the values specified by the attribute. The modifier only affects the view's content.

The implementation of these modifiers is straightforward. We must select the modifier according to the effect we want to apply and assign it to the view. The following example scales the image to half its size and makes it blurry.

```
import SwiftUI

struct ContentView: View {
   var body: some View {
      Image("Toronto")
          .resizable()
          .scaledToFit()
          .padding()
          .scaleEffect(CGSize(width: 0.5, height: 0.5))
          .blur(radius: 5)
   }
}
```

Listing 6-39: Applying visual effects to an Image *view*

The size of the view is still the one calculated by the interface, but the image's size is reduced to half by the **scaleEffect()** modifier.

Figure 6-34: Visual effects applied to the image

Apple systems provide predefined images we can use in our applications. We have introduced emojis in Chapter 2 (see Figure 2-9). They can be included in strings and displayed on the screen with a **Text** view, as shown next.

```
import SwiftUI

struct ContentView: View {
   var body: some View {
      Text("🍔")
          .font(Font.system(size: 100))
   }
}
```

Listing 6-40: Displaying emojis

The example of Listing 6-40 displays an emoji of a hamburger with a size of 100 points. The idea behind emojis is to quickly convey information or mood, so they don't scale well and should only be used to establish a connection with the user or between users. To incorporate icons that represent functionality, such as a button to send an email, add an item to a list, or share data, Apple recommends using symbols designed specifically for this purpose called *SF Symbols*. These symbols are scalable, come in different versions, and adapt to the current font, making it easy to integrate them with the rest of the interface.

Symbols are loaded and displayed with an **Image** view, but we must create the view with the initializer **Image(systemName:)** and the name of the symbol, as in the following example.

```
import SwiftUI

struct ContentView: View {
    var body: some View {
        Image(systemName: "envelope.circle")
    }
}
```

Listing 6-41: Displaying SF symbols

SF symbols were designed to work with text and therefore their size can be determined by a font and their style by the font's weight. But unlike **Text** views, **Image** views don't include a modifier to change the weight of the font, so we must implement the following method provided by the **Font** structure.

weight(Weight**)**—This modifier assigns a weight to the font. The attribute is a structure of type **Weight** with the properties **black, bold, heavy, light, medium, regular, semibold, thin,** and **ultraLight**.

```
import SwiftUI

struct ContentView: View {
    var body: some View {
        Image(systemName: "envelope.circle")
            .font(Font.system(size: 100).weight(.semibold))
    }
}
```

Listing 6-42: Styling a symbol

In the example of Listing 6-42, we apply the **font()** modifier with the system font, a size of 100 points, and a weight of type **semibold**. Notice that we declare the modifiers all in one line, but we could have defined the **Font** in a constant and use that constant to apply it to the **Image** view, as in the following example.

```
import SwiftUI

struct ContentView: View {
    let myfont = Font.system(size: 100)

    var body: some View {
        Image(systemName: "envelope.circle")
            .font(myfont.weight(.semibold))
    }
}
```

Listing 6-43: Storing the font in a constant

The code of Listing 6-43 initializes a **Font** structure with the system's font and a size of 100, and then modifies an **Image** view with this font and a weight of type **semibold**. This is the same we did before, but this time the **weight()** modifier is applied to the value of the **myfont** constant, making our code easier to read.

No matter how we organize our code, the view always shows the symbol of an envelope on the screen.

Figure 6-35: SF Symbol

 IMPORTANT: The system assigns a unique name to each symbol. Apple offers an application called SF Symbols that presents a list of all the symbols available and their names. The application is available in the App Store.

(Basic) **Event Modifiers**

Besides the modifiers to change the styles and format of the views, SwiftUI includes modifiers to respond to events. These events can be produced by the user, such as when the user touches the screen with a finger, or by the system, such as when information is received from the network. There are multiple modifiers available to process events, some are more specific, others more generic. For instance, the `View` protocol defines the following modifiers to perform a task when a view appears or disappears.

onAppear(perform: Closure)—This modifier executes the closure specified by the **perform** attribute when the view appears.

onDisappear(perform: Closure)—This modifier executes the closure specified by the **perform** attribute when the view disappears.

These modifiers are applied like any other, but unlike the rest, they are executed when the event they respond to is detected by the system. For instance, in the following example we print a message on the console with the `onAppear()` modifier, but the text is not printed until the view appears on the screen.

```
import SwiftUI
struct ContentView: View {
   let fontSize: CGFloat = 100

   var body: some View {
      Image(systemName: "envelope.circle")
         .font(Font.system(size: fontSize))
         .onAppear(perform: {
            print("Current font size: \(self.fontSize)")
         })
   }
}
```

Listing 6-44: Performing a task when the view appears

The code in Listing 6-44 prints a message on the console with the value of a constant used to determine the size of the font. It is not a very useful example, but it shows how to implement these modifiers. Besides the `onAppear()` and `onDisappear()` modifiers, SwiftUI includes others to process gestures, like the `onTapGesture()` modifier used to detect a tap on the view, and others even more specific, like the `onReceive()` modifier used to receive data emitted by a publisher, but all of them work in a similar way; they perform a task when the event is detected by the system. We will see more practical examples of the `onAppear()` modifier and work with the rest of the modifiers in later chapters.

Do It Yourself: Update the `ContentView` structure with the code of Listing 6-44. Run the application on the simulator or a real device, as explained in Chapter 5, Figure 5-8. You should see the message "Current font size: 100.0" printed on the console. Later in this chapter, we will learn how to work with the console from the canvas.

IMPORTANT: SwiftUI syntax makes extensive use of closures. Properties inside a closure must be referenced from `self` (as we did with the `fontSize` property in Listing 6-44) This is a requirement of Swift to remind us that referencing a property from inside the closure could create a strong reference cycle, as we have seen in Chapter 3 (see Memory Management).

(Medium) ## Custom Modifiers

Interfaces with single views, like those we have created so far, are the exception. User interfaces are created by the combination of multiple views. This means that often we will find ourselves applying the same modifiers repeatedly. In cases like this, we can avoid repetition by implementing custom modifiers. Custom modifiers encapsulate multiple modifiers in a single structure that we can apply later to the views with the `modifier()` modifier. The structure must conform to the `ViewModifier` protocol and implement a method called `body` that receives a parameter of type `Content`. The parameter represents the views we want to modify and, therefore, it is to this parameter that we apply the actual modifiers, as shown next.

```
import SwiftUI

struct MyModifiers: ViewModifier {
   func body(content: Content) -> some View {
       content
          .font(Font.system(size: 100).weight(.semibold))
          .foregroundColor(Color.blue)
   }
}
struct ContentView: View {
   var body: some View {
       Image(systemName: "envelope.circle")
          .modifier(MyModifiers())
   }
}
```

Listing 6-45: Applying custom modifiers

In the example of Listing 6-45, we define a structure that conforms to the `ViewModifier` protocol and then apply the `font()` and `foregroundColor()` modifiers to the `content` parameter of its `body` method. This defines a custom modifier called `MyModifiers` that then we can apply to the views in our interface. The result is the same as applying the modifiers directly to the views, but it makes our code less repetitive.

Figure 6-36: Custom modifiers

The `ViewModifier` structure is a structure like any other, so we can include properties and initialize those properties with different values every time the modifier is applied. For instance, we can include a property to store a `CGFloat` value, so every time the custom modifier is applied, we can select the size to be assigned to the font.

```
import SwiftUI

struct MyModifiers: ViewModifier {
   var size: CGFloat

   init(size: CGFloat) {
      self.size = size
   }
   func body(content: Content) -> some View {
      content
         .font(Font.system(size: size).weight(.semibold))
         .foregroundColor(Color.blue)
   }
}
struct ContentView: View {
   var body: some View {
      Image(systemName: "envelope.circle")
         .modifier(MyModifiers(size: 50))
   }
}
```

Listing 6-46: Customizing a custom modifier

(Basic) **6.2 Layout**

The closure assigned to the `body` property must return one view. We haven't had any issues so far because all our examples return only a `Text` view or an `Image` view, but the user interface is composed of multiple views, some work as containers, others display content, and there are several views in charge of processing the user's input. Therefore, to create the interface, we must be able to group multiple views in one single view and arrange them on the screen. The solution proposed by SwiftUI is to work with stacks.

(Basic) **Stacks**

Views can be arranged in three different ways, side by side, on top of each other, or overlapping. SwiftUI defines the following views to create these stacks.

VStack(alignment: HorizontalAlignment, **spacing:** CGFloat?, **content:** Closure)—This initializer creates a `VStack` view that arranges views vertically. The **alignment** attribute determines the horizontal alignment of the views. It is a structure of type `HorizontalAlignment` with the type properties `center`, `leading`, and `trailing`. The **spacing** attribute determines the space between views, and the **content** attribute is a closure that defines the list of views we want to show in the stack.

HStack(alignment: VerticalAlignment, **spacing:** CGFloat?, **content:** Closure)— This initializer creates an `HStack` view that arranges views horizontally. The **alignment** attribute determines the vertical alignment of the views. It is a structure of type `VerticalAlignment` with the type properties `bottom`, `center`, `firstTextBaseline`, `lastTextBaseline`, and `top`. The **spacing** attribute determines the space between views, and the **content** attribute is a closure that defines the list of views we want to show in the stack.

ZStack(alignment: Alignment, **content:** Closure)—This initializer creates a `ZStack` view that overlays the views. The **alignment** attribute determines the horizontal and vertical alignment of the views. It is a structure of type `Alignment` with the type properties `bottom`, `bottomLeading`, `bottomTrailing`, `center`, `leading`, `top`, `topLeading`, `topTrailing`, and `trailing`. The **content** attribute is a closure that defines the list of views we want to show in the stack.

Stacks are created with values by default. For instance, a `VStack` aligns its views to the center and with a standard space in between. If that's all we need, we just have to declare its content.

```
import SwiftUI

struct ContentView: View {
   var body: some View {
      VStack(content: {
         Text("City")
         Text("New York")
      })
   }
}
```

Listing 6-47: Creating a vertical stack

The closure assigned to the **content** attribute is a `Content` closure. `Content` closures are processed by a property wrapper called `@ViewBuilder` which job is to construct views from closures. This means that all we have to do to create the content of a stack is to list the views one after another, as we did in the example of Listing 6-47, and the compiler takes care of creating the code to present them on the screen in that same order (We will learn more about property wrappers in the next chapter).

Because the **content** attribute is a closure, we can declare its value as a trailing closure and simplify the code.

```
import SwiftUI

struct ContentView: View {
   var body: some View {
      VStack {
         Text("City")
         Text("New York")
      }
   }
}
```

Listing 6-48: Creating a vertical stack with a trailing closure

The result is the same. The `Text` views take the size of their content and are displayed one on top of the other, and the `VStack` view takes the width of its largest child and the height from the sum of the height of its children.

Figure 6-37: Vertical stack

Chapter 6 - SwiftUI Framework

By default, the views inside a `VStack` are aligned to the center, but we can change that with the `alignment` attribute. Besides `center`, the attribute can take the values `leading` and `trailing`, which mean left and right when the device is configured with a left-to-right language like English.

```
import SwiftUI

struct ContentView: View {
    var body: some View {
        VStack(alignment: .leading) {
            Text("City")
            Text("New York")
        }
    }
}
```

Listing 6-49: Aligning views in a vertical stack

Another value defined by default is the space between the views. If we don't specify any value, the views are placed on top of each other with no space in between. There are multiple ways to include a space between the views. One is with the `padding()` modifier introduced before. But if the stack contains multiple views, we will have to assign the modifier to each one of them. An easier way to do this is to declare the **spacing** attribute, as in the following example.

```
import SwiftUI

struct ContentView: View {
    var body: some View {
        VStack(alignment: .leading, spacing: 20) {
            Text("City")
            Text("New York")
        }
    }
}
```

Listing 6-50: Adding a space between the views

The space is added only between the views, not at the top or the bottom. The purpose is to separate the views, as shown in Figure 6-38.

Figure 6-38: Vertical stack aligned to the left with a space of 20 points in between

The `HStack` view works in a similar way. The views are declared on a list, one after another, and the compiler takes care of creating the code to display them side by side.

```
import SwiftUI

struct ContentView: View {
    var body: some View {
        HStack {
            Image(systemName: "cloud")
                .font(.system(size: 80))
```

Chapter 6 - SwiftUI Framework

```
        Text("New York")
      }
   }
}
```

By default, the views in a horizontal stack are aligned to the center and positioned with a standard space in between (usually 8 points).

Figure 6-39: *Horizontal stack aligned to the center*

An **HStack** view includes the same attributes as a **VStack** for alignment and spacing, but the **alignment** attribute specifies the vertical alignment. This is useful when the stack is composed of views of different heights. The height of the stack is determined by the height of its tallest view and the rest of the views are aligned according to the attribute's value. Figure 6-40 shows all the possible vertical alignments. In this example, we reduce the width of the stack to force the **Text** view to display the text in two lines and show how the **firstTextBaseline** and the **lastTextBaseline** alignments work.

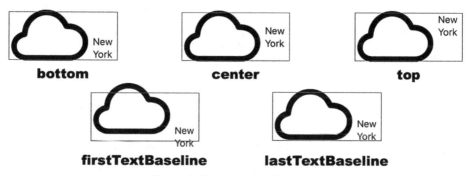

Figure 6-40: HStack *alignments*

Besides the vertical and horizontal stacks, SwiftUI also provides the **ZStack** view to overlay the views. The views appear on the screen in front of each other in the same order they are declared inside the stack.

```
import SwiftUI

struct ContentView: View {
   var body: some View {
      ZStack {
         Image(systemName: "cloud")
            .font(.system(size: 80))
         Text("New York")
      }
   }
}
```

Listing 6-52: Creating a ZStack

Chapter 6 - SwiftUI Framework

Figure 6-41: Views in a ZStack

By default, the views are aligned to the center, but as we did with the horizontal and verticals stacks, we can include the **alignment** attribute to define a different alignment. The possible values are `bottom`, `bottomLeading`, `bottomTrailing`, `center`, `leading`, `top`, `topLeading`, `topTrailing`, and `trailing`.

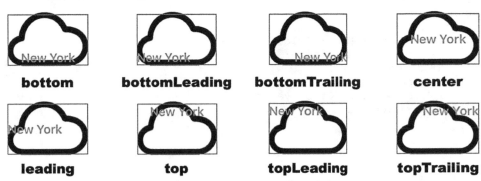

Figure 6-42: ZStack *alignments*

The following example aligns the content of the **zstack** to the bottom. The stack takes the size of its biggest element, the cloud, so the text is moved to the bottom.

```
import SwiftUI
struct ContentView: View {
    var body: some View {
        ZStack(alignment: .bottom) {
            Image(systemName: "cloud")
                .font(.system(size: 80))
            Text("New York")
                .font(.system(size: 14))
        }
    }
}
```

Listing 6-53: Aligning views in a ZStack

Figure 6-43: Bottom alignment in a ZStack

When views overlap, like those included in a **zstack** view, the system determines the order in which they appear on the screen from the order they are declared in the code. The first view is drawn first, then the second view is drawn in front of it, and so on. The View protocol defines the following modifier to change this order.

zIndex(Double)—This modifier sets the order of the view in the Z axis (the axis perpendicular to the screen).

By default, all the views are assigned the index 0, which means they are all at the same level, and that is why the system draws the views according to the order in which they are declared in the code, but we can move a view to the back by assigning a negative Z index or to the front with a value greater than 0. When views have different indexes, they are drawn in the order determined by those values, starting from the view with the smallest index. In the following example, we include the same `Image` view and `Text` view used before, but because we set an index of -1 for the `Text` view, it is drawn in the back.

```swift
import SwiftUI

struct ContentView: View {
    var body: some View {
        ZStack {
            Image(systemName: "cloud")
                .font(.system(size: 80))
            Text("New York")
                .padding(8)
                .background(Color.yellow)
                .zIndex(-1)
        }
    }
}
```

Listing 6-54: Setting the Z index of a view

The `Text` view in Listing 6-54 includes a yellow background, so we can see its position in the Z axis. The `Image` view should be drawn first, and then the `Text` view should cover most of the image, but because the index for the `Image` view is set by default to 0 and we set an index of -1 for the `Text` view, the `Text` view is drawn behind the `Image` view.

Figure 6-44: Custom Z index

When we group views with a stack, we can apply modifiers to all the views at the same time by assigning the modifiers to the stack instead of individual views. For instance, if we want to assign the same color to the `Text` view and the `Image` view of the previous example, we can apply the `foregroundColor()` modifier to the `ZStack` view.

```swift
import SwiftUI

struct ContentView: View {
    var body: some View {
        ZStack(alignment: .bottom) {
            Image(systemName: "cloud")
                .font(.system(size: 80))
            Text("New York")
                .font(.system(size: 14))
        }.foregroundColor(Color.red)
    }
}
```

Listing 6-55: Assigning modifiers to the stack and its content

Chapter 6 - SwiftUI Framework

Figure 6-45: Shared modifiers

Stacks can be combined and nested as required by the interface. For instance, we can incorporate a **VStack** inside the previous stack to include more text next to the image.

```
import SwiftUI

struct ContentView: View {
    var body: some View {
        HStack {
            Image(systemName: "cloud")
                .font(.system(size: 80))
            VStack(alignment: .leading) {
                Text("City")
                    .foregroundColor(.gray)
                Text("New York")
                    .font(.title)
            }
        }
    }
}
```

Listing 6-56: Nesting stacks

The code of Listing 6-56 defines a **VStack** view inside an **HStack** view. The **VStack** includes two **Text** views aligned to the left and with different styles. The result is shown in Figure 6-46.

Figure 6-46: Nested stacks

 The Basics: When you decide to include a view in a stack, you can write the code yourself or get Xcode to do it for you by selecting the option from the context menu. We used this menu before to add modifiers to a **Text** view (Figure 6-4). If you press the Command key and click on the view, the context menu appears with the options to embed the view in a **VStack** or an **HStack**.

(Basic)   **Spacer**

The alignment options available for **VStack** and **HStack** views align the views in the opposite axis. A vertical stack can align the views horizontally, and a horizontal stack can align the views vertically. To align the views on the same axis, we must add a flexible space with a **Spacer** view.

Spacer(minLength: CGFloat**)**—This initializer creates a **Spacer** view that generates a flexible space. The **minLength** attribute determines the minimum size in points the space can take. If the attribute is not declared, the minimum length is 0.

A **Spacer** view can be declared any time we need to add a flexible space. It provides a more customizable way to align the views or extend them to the sides of its container. For instance, in the following example we add a flexible space between the image and the **VStack** of our view to move the views to the left and right side of their container.

```
import SwiftUI

struct ContentView: View {
    var body: some View {
        HStack {
            Image(systemName: "cloud")
                .font(.system(size: 80))
            Spacer()
            VStack(alignment: .leading) {
                Text("City")
                    .foregroundColor(.gray)
                Text("New York")
                    .font(.title)
            }
        }
    }
}
```

Listing 6-57: Aligning the views with a flexible space

The system calculates the widths of the image and the stack, and then assigns the rest of the space available to the **Spacer** view, as shown in Figure 6-47.

Figure 6-47: Flexible space in between views

A **Spacer** view can be positioned anywhere on the list, not only between views. This is useful when we want the views to be at the top or the bottom of the screen. For instance, we can embed the **HStack** of previous examples in a **VStack** and add a **Spacer** at the bottom to move our views to the top of the screen.

```
import SwiftUI

struct ContentView: View {
    var body: some View {
        VStack {
            HStack {
                Image(systemName: "cloud")
                    .font(.system(size: 80))
                VStack(alignment: .leading) {
                    Text("City")
                        .foregroundColor(.gray)
                    Text("New York")
                        .font(.title)
                }
                Spacer()
            }
            Spacer()
        }
    }
}
```

Listing 6-58: Aligning the views to the left and the top

Chapter 6 - SwiftUI Framework

In the example of Listing 6-58, we use two `Spacer` views, one at the end of the `HStack` to move the views to the left, and another at the end of the main `VStack` to move the `HStack` up. This `Spacer` view takes all the space available at the bottom, effectively moving the rest of the views up.

Figure 6-48: Views at the top of the safe area

(Basic) ## Safe Area

The system defines a layout guide called *Safe Area* where we can place the content of our interface. This is the area determined by the space remaining in the window after all the toolbars and special views are displayed by the system (including the notch at the top of modern iPhones). That's the reason why there is a space between the view or our previous example and the top of the screen (Figure 6-48). The white bar at the top is the space occupied by the system's toolbar. Although it is recommended to always build the interface inside the safe area, the `View` protocol provides the following modifier to ignore it.

edgesIgnoringSafeArea(Edge)—This modifier creates a view that ignores the safe area. The attribute is a value or a set of values that indicates the sides to be ignored. This is an enumeration with the values `all`, `bottom`, `leading`, `top`, and `trailing`.

This modifier must be applied to any view we want to extend to the edges of the screen, such as backgrounds or images. For instance, if we want the interface of our previous example to extend to the top, we can apply the modifier to the main `VStack` view.

```
import SwiftUI

struct ContentView: View {
    var body: some View {
        VStack {
            HStack {
                Image(systemName: "cloud")
                    .font(.system(size: 80))
                VStack(alignment: .leading) {
                    Text("City")
                        .foregroundColor(.gray)
                    Text("New York")
                        .font(.title)
                }
                Spacer()
            }
            Spacer()
        }.edgesIgnoringSafeArea(.all)
    }
}
```

Listing 6-59: Ignoring the safe area

Figure 6-49: Views at the top of the screen

(Medium) **Priorities**

Stacks divide the space equally among the views, but we must decide what to do when there is not enough room to show them all. By default, the system assigns a fixed size to images and reduces the size of `Text` views to make them fit, as in the following example.

```
import SwiftUI

struct ContentView: View {
    var body: some View {
        HStack {
            Text("Manchester")
                .font(.title)
                .lineLimit(1)
            Image(systemName: "cloud")
                .font(.system(size: 80))
            Text("New York")
                .font(.title)
                .lineLimit(1)
        }
    }
}
```

Listing 6-60: Arranging the views with priorities by default

The code of Listing 6-60 creates an `HStack` with three views: a text, an image, and another text. In an iPhone SE in portrait mode, where there is no room to display them all, the system retains the image's original size but compresses the `Text` views to make them fit in the remaining space, as shown in Figure 6-50.

Figure 6-50: Priorities by default

In this example, we limited the `Text` views to only one line and therefore the system truncates the texts. If this is not what we want, we must decide which `Text` view is going to have priority. The `View` protocol defines the following modifiers for this purpose.

layoutPriority(Double)—This modifier sets the view's priority. A higher priority determines that the view will get as much space as possible. The value by default is 0.

fixedSize(horizontal: Bool, **vertical:** Bool)—This modifier fixes the view to its ideal horizontal or vertical size. If no attributes are specified, the size is fixed on both dimensions.

Chapter 6 - SwiftUI Framework

All the views have a priority of 0 by default. If we want the system to reserve more space for a view, we must declare its priority higher than 0, as in the following example.

```
import SwiftUI

struct ContentView: View {
    var body: some View {
        HStack {
            Text("Manchester")
                .font(.title)
                .lineLimit(1)
            Image(systemName: "cloud")
                .font(.system(size: 80))
            Text("New York")
                .font(.title)
                .lineLimit(1)
                .layoutPriority(1)
        }
    }
}
```

Listing 6-61: Assigning a higher priority for a view

The code of Listing 6-61 assigns a priority of 1 to the second **Text** view. Now the system calculates the space required by this view first and therefore the "New York" text is shown in full.

Figure 6-51: Custom priorities

When we assign a higher priority to a view and there is no space to show them all, the system lays out the views with lower priority first and gives them the minimum possible size, and then assigns the remaining space to the view with the higher priority. So, if there is still no room to show the entire view, its content is clipped. If what we want is to force the view to take the size of its content no matter what, we must apply the **fixedSize()** modifier.

```
import SwiftUI

struct ContentView: View {
    var body: some View {
        HStack {
            Text("Manchester")
                .font(.title)
                .lineLimit(1)
                .fixedSize()
            Image(systemName: "cloud")
                .font(.system(size: 80))
            Text("New York")
                .font(.title)
                .lineLimit(1)
                .layoutPriority(1)
        }
    }
}
```

Listing 6-62: Defining a view with a fixed size

This is the same code as before, but now we assign the `fixedSize()` modifier to the first `Text` view. In consequence, this view is going to adopt the size of its content and the "Manchester" text will be shown in full, no matter the priority of the rest of the views.

Figure 6-52: View with a fixed size

(Medium) ## Alignment Guides

There are two possible alignments, horizontal and vertical. Horizontal stacks align the views vertically and vertical stacks align the views horizontally. This is because SwiftUI expects the views in the stack to be of different sizes and therefore it needs to know how they are going to be aligned in the stack's perpendicular axis. Usually, this is enough to build a simple interface, but professional applications require more flexibility. The `View` Protocol defines the following modifiers to customize alignment.

alignmentGuide(HorizontalAlignment, **computeValue:** Closure**)**—This modifier defines the values of the horizontal alignment. The first attribute determines the type of alignment we want to customize. It is a structure of type `HorizontalAlignment`, with the type properties `center`, `leading`, and `trailing`. The **computeValue** attribute is a closure that receives the current dimensions of the view and returns a `CGFloat` type with the new value for the alignment.

alignmentGuide(VerticalAlignment, **computeValue:** Closure**)**—This modifier defines the values of the vertical alignment. The first attribute determines the type of alignment we want to customize. It is a structure of type `VerticalAlignment`, with the type properties `bottom`, `center`, `firstTextBaseline`, `lastTextBaseline`, and `top`. The **computeValue** attribute is a closure that receives the current dimensions of the view and returns a `CGFloat` type with the new value for the alignment.

The following example aligns three images of different sizes. They are all 100 points wide, but the signbus.png image is 200 points tall, the signplane.png image is 170 points tall, and the signphone.png image is 220 points tall (the images are available on our website).

```
import SwiftUI
struct ContentView: View {
    var body: some View {
        HStack(alignment: .center) {
            Image("signbus")
            Image("signplane")
            Image("signphone")
        }.border(Color.blue, width: 2)
    }
}
```

Listing 6-63: Aligning images to the center with standard values

A stack view establishes a common point of alignment according to its alignment type and the dimensions of its views. For instance, if the alignment of a vertical stack is `center`, the stack gets the position of the `center` alignment of each view and from that value it calculates a common point of alignment (usually the point of alignment of its tallest view) and then repositions all the views to match that common point.

Chapter 6 - SwiftUI Framework

Figure 6-53: *Images aligned to the center*

Figure 6-53 shows our three images aligned to the center. In this example, we applied a blue border to the stack to make it easy to see the changes produced by the alignment and added a yellow line on top of the picture to visualize the common point of alignment chose by the stack.

 Do It Yourself: Download the signbus.png, signplane.png and signphone.png files from our website and add them to the Assets Catalog. Update the `ContentView` structure in your project with the code of Listing 6-63. You should see on the canvas something similar to Figure 6-53. Use this project to try the rest of the examples in this section.

The alignment values are determined by the stack's coordinates system, starting from the top-left corner. The value at the top is 0 and the value at the bottom of the view depends on the children's height. Every view has an alignment guide with values that determine their points of alignment. The value associated with the `top` alignment is 0, the value associated with the `bottom` alignment is equal to the view's height, and the value associated with the `center` alignment is the height divided by two (the formula is: `top` + (`bottom` - `top`) / 2).

The views return these alignment guides by default, but we can change them with the modifiers introduced above. For instance, the wheels of the bus in our example are below the common point of alignment (see Figure 6-53, above). This image is 200 points tall, so the center alignment returned by the image is at 100 points, but the wheels are 18 points below.

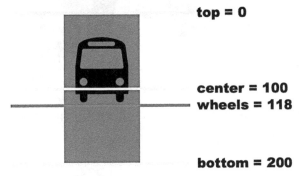

Figure 6-54: *Alignment guides for the bus*

As illustrated in Figure 6-54, the `center` alignment by default for the bus is 100 points (half its height), but the wheels are positioned at 118 points. If we want to center the image at this point, we must add 18 points to the image's natural center.

```
import SwiftUI

struct ContentView: View {
    var body: some View {
        HStack(alignment: .center) {
            Image("signbus")
                .alignmentGuide(VerticalAlignment.center, computeValue: {
dimension in
                    return dimension[VerticalAlignment.center] + 18
                })
            Image("signplane")
            Image("signphone")
        }.border(Color.blue, width: 2)
    }
}
```

Listing 6-64: Aligning images to the center with custom values

The **alignmentGuide**() modifier requires two values. The first one is a value that represents the type of alignment we want to modify. In this case, we are aligning the views to the center, so we modify the **VerticalAlignment.center** type. The second value is a closure that must return the new value for this type of alignment. The closure receives a value of type **ViewDimensions**. This is a structure with two properties, **width** and **height**, to return the current width and height of the image, and also includes the definition of a subscript, which allows us to get the values for each alignment guide using square brackets and the alignment as the key (as in a dictionary). In the example of Listing 6-64, we get the current value of the **VerticalAlignment.center** key for the view, add 18 to it and return the result. From that moment on, the **center** alignment for this view will return 118 instead of 100, so the view is aligned 18 points higher.

Figure 6-55: Bus aligned with custom values

If we want to align all the images to the bottom of their graphics, we must modify the alignment guide for each **Image** view.

```
import SwiftUI

struct ContentView: View {
    var body: some View {
        HStack(alignment: .center) {
            Image("signbus")
                .alignmentGuide(VerticalAlignment.center) { dimension in
                    dimension[VerticalAlignment.center] + 18 }
```

Chapter 6 - SwiftUI Framework

```
        Image("signplane")
            .alignmentGuide(VerticalAlignment.center) { dimension in
                dimension[VerticalAlignment.center] + 68 }
        Image("signphone")
            .alignmentGuide(VerticalAlignment.center) { dimension in
                dimension[VerticalAlignment.center] + 89 }
    }.border(Color.blue, width: 2)
  }
}
```

Listing 6-65: Aligning all images to the center with custom values

The code of Listing 6-65 declares the closures as trailing closures and omits the **return** keyword to simplify the code, but the process is the same. The image of the bus is 200 points tall, its default center is at 100 points, but the base of the bus is at 118 points, so we add 18 points to the current center alignment (118 - 100). The image of the plane is 170 points tall, its default center is at 85 points, but the base of the plane is at 153 points, so we add 68 points to the current center alignment (153 - 85). And we do the same for the phone. The image is 220 points tall, its default center is at 110 points, but the base of the phone is at 199 points, so we add 89 points to the current center alignment (199 - 110). As a result, we get all the images aligned by the base of their graphics.

Figure 6-56: Images aligned by their baselines

So far, we have modified the alignment guides of views that belong to the same stack. If our interface requires us to align views from different containers (stacks), we must define custom alignment types. Custom alignment types are defined as extensions of the alignment structures (**VerticalAlignment** and **HorizontalAlignment**). We worked with extensions before in Chapter 3. They add functionality to an existing data type (see Listing 3-186). In this case, we use an extension to add a custom alignment guide. For this purpose, the extension must include an enumeration that conforms to the **AlignmentID** protocol, which only requirement is a method called **defaultValue** that returns the alignment's default value. The extension must also include a type property which sole purpose is to simplify the declaration of the alignment, as shown in the following example.

```
import SwiftUI

extension VerticalAlignment {
    enum BusAlignment: AlignmentID {
        static func defaultValue(in dimension: ViewDimensions) -> CGFloat {
```

```
        return dimension[VerticalAlignment.center]
      }
   }
   static let alignBus = VerticalAlignment(BusAlignment.self)
}
struct ContentView: View {
   var body: some View {
      HStack(alignment: .alignBus) {
         VStack {
            Image("signbus")
         }
         VStack(alignment: .leading) {
            Text("Transportation")
            Text("Bus")
                .font(.largeTitle)
         }
      }.border(Color.blue, width: 2)
   }
}
```

Listing 6-66: *Defining custom alignment guides*

The code in Listing 6-66 defines an extension for the `VerticalAlignment` structure. We call the enumeration `BusAlignment` because we are going to use it to align the image of the bus. Its default value was defined as the current value of the `center` alignment. After this, we define a type property called `alignBus` that returns an alignment of this type. Notice that the value provided to the `VerticalAlignment`'s initializer is a reference to the definition of the `BusAlignment` enumeration, not an instance of it (see Listing 3-149).

Our view includes two `VStack` views, one for the image of the bus and another with two `Text` views, embedded in an `HStack`. The custom `alignBus` alignment defined before was assigned to the `HStack`, and therefore the `VStacks` are aligned to the center.

Figure 6-57: *Views aligned with custom alignment guides*

The yellow line drawn in front of the picture in Figure 6-57 shows the common point of alignment. The `HStack` calls the `defaultValue` method for each `VStack` view, gets in return the value of their current `center` alignment, and therefore it aligns the `VStacks` to the center.

Of course, we can change this alignment by modifying the alignment guides of the views. For instance, if we want to position the "Bus" text in line with the bus's window, we must move the `alignBus` alignment for those views. The alignment for the bus image has to be at the center of the bus's window and the alignment for the text has to be at the center of the word.

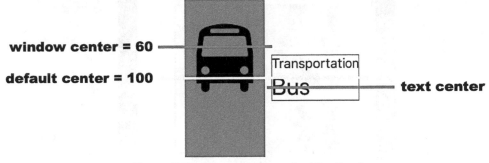

Figure 6-58: *Alignments required for the views*

The `center` alignment of the bus image is at the position 100, and the center of the bus's window is at the position 60, so to move the alignment point to the center of the window we must subtract 40 to this view's `center` alignment. For the text is simpler, we just have to return the value of the current `center` alignment, as in the following example.

```
import SwiftUI

extension VerticalAlignment {
    enum BusAlignment: AlignmentID {
        static func defaultValue(in dimension: ViewDimensions) -> CGFloat {
            return dimension[VerticalAlignment.center]
        }
    }
    static let alignBus = VerticalAlignment(BusAlignment.self)
}
struct ContentView: View {
    var body: some View {
        HStack(alignment: .alignBus) {
            VStack {
                Image("signbus")
                    .alignmentGuide(.alignBus) { dimension in
dimension[VerticalAlignment.center] - 40 }
            }
            VStack(alignment: .leading) {
                Text("Transportation")
                Text("Bus")
                    .font(.largeTitle)
                    .alignmentGuide(.alignBus) { dimension in
dimension[VerticalAlignment.center] }
            }
        }.border(Color.blue, width: 2)
    }
}
```

Listing 6-67: *Aligning views with custom alignment guides*

The definition of the custom alignment is the same as before, but now we modify the values for each view we want to move with the `alignmentGuide()` modifier. The alignment for the image of the bus is moved 40 points up the center line and the alignment for the **Text** view is moved to its center alignment, so we get the views right where we want them.

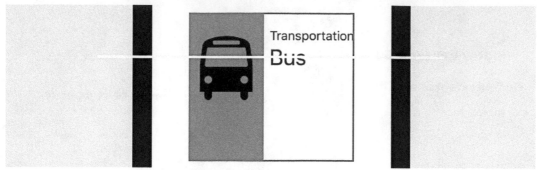

Figure 6-59: Views with a custom alignment

 Do It Yourself: Getting used to how SwiftUI aligns the views takes time. Try different values and alignments to learn how the system works. For more information, visit our website and follow the links for this chapter.

(Basic) **Groups**

Stack views create a structure of type `TupleView` to organize their content. This structure can manage up to 10 views and therefore that's the maximum number of views a stack can contain. Although is not common to find this issue in a professional application, we can avoid it by using `Group` views. The following is the view's initializer.

Group(content: Closure)—This initializer creates a `Group` view that contains the views defined by the closure assigned to the attribute.

The purpose of `Group` views is to group views together. We can use them to split large lists of views into groups of 10 or less to avoid the issue mentioned above, but also for other purposes, such as applying styles to many views at a time, as in the following example.

```
import SwiftUI

struct ContentView: View {
    var body: some View {
        VStack {
            Group {
                Text("This is the list of")
                Text("Cities")
            }.foregroundColor(Color.gray)
            Group {
                Text("Manchester")
                Text("Viena")
            }.font(.largeTitle)
        }
    }
}
```

Listing 6-68: Arranging the views in groups

Each `Group` view defined in Listing 6-68 contains two `Text` views. To style these views, we apply modifiers to the `Group` views, not their content, so all the views within each group are affected by the same modifier.

Chapter 6 - SwiftUI Framework

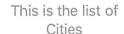

This is the list of
Cities

Manchester
Viena

Figure 6-60: Modifiers applied to groups of views

The closure assigned to the `body` property can only return one view, so the compiler can determine the data type of the view and process the value correctly. If we try to return different views depending on a condition, we will get an error, but we can use a `Group` view to solve this issue. The solution is to insert the conditional statement inside a `Group` view and return that view instead.

```
import SwiftUI

struct ContentView: View {
    var body: some View {
        let device = UIDevice.current.userInterfaceIdiom
        return Group {
            if device == .phone {
                Text("iPhone")
            } else {
                Image(systemName: "keyboard")
            }
        }
    }
}
```

Listing 6-69: Assigning different views to the body *property*

The first thing we do in the example of Listing 6-69 is to read the value of the `userInterfaceIdiom` property of the `UIDevice` object representing the current device (see Chapter 4, Listing 4-53). If the device is an iPhone, we create a `Text` view with the text "iPhone", and if it is something else, we create an `Image` view with the symbol of a keyboard. Therefore, the view displayed on the screen is selected at run time, depending on the value of the `userInterfaceIdiom` property, but because we embedded this view in a `Group` view, the compiler can identify the value returned and therefore the code is valid.

The Basics: A `Group` view can also be used to simplify the code or even to present multiple previews of the same view on the canvas. We will study how to configure previews at the end of this chapter.

(Medium) ## Additional Views

Views can be passed around in our code and returned from methods by wrapping them in `Group` views, but there is a better alternative. SwiftUI includes a structure called `AnyView` that we can use to create a view that wraps other views. The following is the structure's initializer.

AnyView(View**)**—This initializer creates an `AnyView` view that contains the views specified by the attribute. The attribute can be a single view or a hierarchy of views.

In the following example, we detect the device in a method and return an `AnyView` view with the content for the `body` property.

```
import SwiftUI

struct ContentView: View {
    var body: some View {
        getView()
    }
    func getView() -> AnyView {
        let device = UIDevice.current.userInterfaceIdiom
        var myView: AnyView!

        if device == .phone {
            myView = AnyView(Text("iPhone"))
        } else {
            myView = AnyView(Image(systemName: "keyboard"))
        }
        return myView
    }
}
```

Listing 6-70: Wrapping views in an `AnyView` *view*

The `ContentView` structure of Listing 6-70 includes a method called `getView()` that returns a structure of type `AnyView`. This structure is defined according to the value returned by the `userInterfaceIdiom` property of the `UIDevice` object. As we did before, if the value is `phone`, we create a `Text` view, otherwise, we create an `Image` view. But both views are inside an `AnyView` view, so we always return the same type of view. When the content of the `body` property is processed, the method is called, and the view returned by the method is displayed on the screen. This wrapper is useful when we must include different views in our interface depending on the space available on the screen, the device where the app is running, or its orientation (see Chapter 9).

The `AnyView` structure, as well as many other views defined by SwiftUI, requires another view to be instantiated. In the example of Listing 6-70, we used a `Text` view and an `Image` view to create the `AnyView` views, but sometimes these views may be defined dynamically, which means that we may not always have a view to provide to the initializer. For cases like this, SwiftUI includes the `EmptyView` view.

EmptyView()—This initializer creates an `EmptyView` view with no content and no size.

The `EmptyView` view works like any other, but it doesn't provide any content and it has no size, so it is not going to affect the interface. The following example shows an empty view when the device is not an iPhone.

```
import SwiftUI

struct ContentView: View {
    var body: some View {
        VStack {
            getView()
        }
    }
    func getView() -> AnyView {
        let device = UIDevice.current.userInterfaceIdiom
        var myView: AnyView!

        if device == .phone {
            myView = AnyView(Text("iPhone"))
        } else {
```

Chapter 6 - SwiftUI Framework

```
            myView = AnyView(EmptyView())
        }
        return myView
    }
}
```

Listing 6-71: Returning an empty view

(Basic) Custom Views

The code required to define the user interface can grow considerably as we build our application. When we reach a certain level of complexity, we must think about refactoring (reorganizing our code). The pattern proposed by SwiftUI involves breaking down the views into smaller pieces. For instance, we can define a view that displays a background image and then initializes custom views to present the rest of the content. The following example illustrates how to split the interface into custom views by creating what is generally known as a *Detail view*; a view that presents the information selected by the user.

Figure 6-61: Detail view

We begin by defining a custom alignment guide that we need to align the flag with the name of the city, and then define the basic layout required to contain the rest of the views.

```
import SwiftUI

extension VerticalAlignment {
    enum FlagAlignment: AlignmentID {
        static func defaultValue(in dimension: ViewDimensions) -> CGFloat {
            return dimension[VerticalAlignment.center]
        }
    }
    static let alignFlag = VerticalAlignment(FlagAlignment.self)
}
struct ContentView: View {
    var body: some View {
        ZStack {
            Image("newyork")
                .resizable()
                .aspectRatio(contentMode: .fill)
                .frame(minWidth: 0, maxWidth: .infinity, minHeight: 0,
maxHeight: .infinity)
```

```
        VStack {
            Spacer()
            TitleView()
                .padding()
            DescriptionView()
                .padding([.leading, .trailing, .bottom])
        }
    }.edgesIgnoringSafeArea(.all)
  }
}
```

Listing 6-72: Creating the basic layout for a detail view

Our main container is a **ZStack** view, so we can display an image in the background and the rest of the interface at the front. The **edgesIgnoringSafeArea()** modifier is applied to this view to let the background image occupy the whole screen. To create this background, we define an **Image** view with a picture of New York city. The image is forced to adopt the size of its view with the **resizable()** modifier, but because we set the image's mode as **fill**, we declare the size of the view with the **frame()** modifier, which forces the **Image** view to adopt the size of the screen and the image to fill all the space available (see Figure 6-29, right).

On top of the background image, we define a **VStack** to contain the rest of the views. Because we want the views in the stack to be aligned to the bottom, we include a **Spacer** view at the top, and then initialize our custom views (**TitleView** and **DescriptionView**).

Custom views are incorporated to the interface the same way we do with standard SwiftUI views. We just have to create an instance of the structure and the system includes all its content in that place. The way they are defined is also the same. We must create a structure that conforms to the **View** protocol and then implement the **body** property. The first view initialized after the spacer is called **TitleView**.

```
struct TitleView: View {
    var body: some View {
        HStack(alignment: .alignFlag) {
            Text("US")
                .font(.system(size: 40))
                .alignmentGuide(.alignFlag) { d in
                    d[VerticalAlignment.center] }
            VStack(alignment: .leading) {
                HStack {
                    Text("New York")
                        .font(.largeTitle)
                        .fontWeight(.bold)
                        .alignmentGuide(.alignFlag) { d in
                            d[VerticalAlignment.center] }
                    Spacer()
                    Text("♥")
                }
                HStack {
                    Text("☆☆☆☆☆")
                        .shadow(color: Color.black, radius: 1, x: 1, y: 1)
                    Spacer()
                }
            }
        }
        .padding()
        .background(Color(red: 0.7, green: 0.8, blue: 0.7))
```

Chapter 6 - SwiftUI Framework

```
        .cornerRadius(20)
        .shadow(color: Color.black, radius: 5, x: 1, y: 1)
    }
}
```

Listing 6-73: Defining a custom view for the title

The container for this view is an **HStack** that uses our custom alignment to align the flag with the name of the city. This view was styled with a padding, a green background, round corners and a shadow. The content is divided in two sections, a **Text** view to show the flag, and a **VStack** with the rest of the information. Notice the **Spacer** views in each **HStack** used to align the texts.

After instantiating the **TitleView** view, the main view creates an instance of a view called **DescriptionView**. We use this view to display a long text with the description of the city.

```
struct DescriptionView: View {
    var body: some View {
        VStack {
            Text("New York City comprises 5 boroughs sitting where the
Hudson River meets the Atlantic Ocean. Its iconic sites include
skyscrapers such as the Empire State Building and Central Park. Broadway
theater is staged in neon-lit Times Square.")
                .font(.body)
                .fixedSize(horizontal: false, vertical: true)
        }
        .padding()
        .background(Color(red: 1, green: 1, blue: 1, opacity: 0.8))
        .cornerRadius(20)
    }
}
```

Listing 6-74: Defining a custom view for the description

This is also a simple view with styles that are familiar to us, but there is something important that we should mention. We gave the **Text** view with the description of the city a fixed size on the vertical axis with the **fixedSize()** modifier. This causes the **Text** view to take the vertical space required to display the entire text, but it also causes the stack containing the **Text** view to grow taller. If later we insert a longer text, this can make the rest of the views move beyond the boundaries of the screen. Of course, this is not what our interface should do. Instead, the stack view should have a fixed size and the user should be able to scroll the text to read it in its entirety. We will learn how to work with **ScrollView** views to scroll content in Chapter 10.

 Do It Yourself: Download the newyork.jpg file from our website or provide your own. Add the image to the Assets Catalog. Replace the code in the ContentView.swift file with the code of Listing 6-72. Add the codes of Listings 6-73 and 6-74 below. You should see the interface of Figure 6-61 on the canvas.

When the views are defined by multiple structures, we can declare them in the same file, as we suggested doing it for this example, or in separate files. The option to create a new file is available from the File menu (File/New/File) or by pressing the keys Command + N. Xcode offers two templates to create Swift files, one for common Swift files and another for SwiftUI views. We can find them in the iOS tab, under the names Swift File and SwiftUI view.

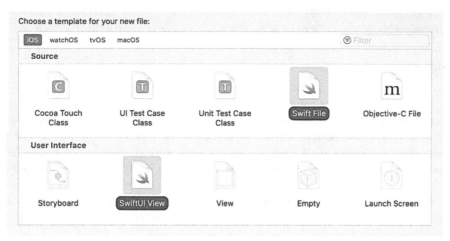

Figure 6-62: File templates

Although they have different names, they are both Swift files and are created with the same extension (.swift). The only difference between the two is the code included by Xcode. A common Swift file only includes an `import` statement for the `Foundation` framework, while a SwiftUI file includes a `View` structure with a `Text` view inside and a `PreviewProvider` structure to create the preview on the canvas. The `View` structure takes the name assigned to the file. For instance, if we want to create a SwiftUI file to store the `DescriptionView` structure from the previous example, we must call the file DescriptionView.swift, so Xcode will create the structures with the right name (It is recommended to write the name in capital letters to match the structure's name). Notice that if we store a view in a separate file, we must import the SwiftUI framework again or the SwiftUI views won't be recognized.

 The Basics: Xcode organizes the files in groups. Groups are not real directories. All the files are stored in the same directory, but they can be organized in groups to help us find them in the Navigator Area. Groups are created from the File menu. Click on the main group at the top of the list (yellow folder with the name of the project) and select the option File/New/Group to create a new one. Then you can assign the group a name and drag files inside.

(Basic) **6.4 Previews**

Xcode automatically builds the app and shows on the canvas a preview of the view we are currently working on. If we introduce large changes to the code, we must press the Resume button at top of the canvas to tell Xcode to resume the preview, but otherwise the process is automatic. With that said, there are things we can do to customize the preview or change its configuration. Figure 6-63 shows the buttons available.

Figure 6-63: Buttons to configure the canvas

The two buttons at the lower-right corner of the canvas activate or deactivate different types of previews. The button at the top (number 1) generates a live preview when activated, which means that the preview can process our input, like a real application. This is useful when we want to check that the elements the user can interact with are working correctly. The second button (number 2) activates the preview on a device. With this button activated, we can run the application on a device and all the changes in the code are going to be reflected on the device's screen.

The buttons at the bottom of the canvas allow us to adjust the previews. The - and + buttons on the right (number 4) change the scale of the preview, and the button on the left (number 3) pins the current preview on the canvas. Since every view can include its own preview, being able to pin a preview to the canvas can be useful when we need to work on a view while seeing the preview of another.

If we need to check for errors or print messages on the console, the Live Preview button includes an additional option for debugging. To select it, we have to click on the button while pressing and holding the Control key. Figure 6-64 shows the options available.

Figure 6-64: *Live Preview menu*

If we select the option Live Preview, we will see the app running on the canvas, but if we select the option Debug Preview, we can also open the console and see the messages printed by the system or our code. For instance, the following example prints a text on the console when the instance of the view is initialized.

```
import SwiftUI

struct ContentView: View {
    init() {
        print("The instance was initialized")
    }
    var body: some View {
        Text("Hello World")
    }
}
```

Listing 6-75: *Printing messages on the console*

The example of Listing 6-75 adds an initializer to the `ContentView` structure defined by the template. The initializer prints a message on the console as soon as the structure is initialized.

 Do It Yourself: Create a SwiftUI project with the Single View App template. Update the `ContentView` structure with the code of Listing 6-75. Press and hold the Control key and then click on the Live Preview button (Figure 6-63, number 1). Select Debug Preview (Figure 6-64) and open the Xcode's console. You should see messages from the system along with the message printed by the code.

 IMPORTANT: There are some restrictions on where you can execute code and print messages from the definition of the structure. You can do it inside the closure assigned to the `body` property (you just have to remember to prefix the view's initializer with the `return` keyword to tell the system what is the view you want to return), but you can't do it from the closures assigned to stack views or groups. Those closures are of type `Content`, which means they expect only a list of views, not executable code. If you need to run code or print a message on the console when a view appears on the screen, you can use the `onAppear()` modifier introduced before (see Listing 6-44).

(Medium) Preview Modifiers

The `View` protocol defines modifiers that are applicable when views are displayed in preview mode. The following are the ones that are currently available.

previewDevice(PreviewDevice)—This modifier determines the device used for the preview. The attribute is a structure of type `PreviewDevice`. The structure includes an initializer that takes a string that represents the device we want to use. Some possible strings are "iPhone 8", "iPhone 8 Plus", "iPhone SE", "iPhone X", "iPhone Xs Max", "iPad (6th generation)", "iPad Pro (9.7-inch)", "Apple TV", and "Mac".

previewDisplayName(String)—This modifier assigns a name to the preview. The attribute is the string we want to display on the canvas, below the preview.

previewLayout(PreviewLayout)—This modifier defines the size of the preview. The attribute is an enumeration of type `PreviewLayout` with three values: `device` (default), `fixed(width: CGFloat, height: CGFloat)`, and `sizeThatFits` (adapts the size to the size of the view).

The preview is set to work with the type of device selected in the scheme from the Xcode's toolbar (see Figure 5-8), but we can overwrite that configuration with the `previewDevice()` modifier.

```
struct ContentView_Previews: PreviewProvider {
    static var previews: some View {
        ContentView()
            .previewDevice(PreviewDevice(stringLiteral: "iPhone SE"))
    }
}
```

Listing 6-76: Configuring the preview

This example configures the preview to represent an iPhone SE, but we can include additional previews in the canvas for different devices by embedding the views in a `Group` view.

```
struct ContentView_Previews: PreviewProvider {
    static var previews: some View {
        Group {
            ContentView()
                .previewDevice(PreviewDevice(stringLiteral: "iPhone SE"))
                .previewDisplayName("iPhone SE")
            ContentView()
                .previewDevice(PreviewDevice(stringLiteral: "iPhone Xs Max"))
                .previewDisplayName("iPhone Xs Max")
        }
    }
}
```

Listing 6-77: Configuring the preview to represent multiple devices

The example of Listing 6-77 also includes the `previewDisplayName()` modifier to display a name below each preview to identify the device that the preview is representing.

Chapter 6 - SwiftUI Framework

Do It Yourself: Update the `ContentView_Previews` structure in your ContentView.swift file with the code of Listing 6-77. Scroll the canvas to see the preview in both devices. A link to see the list of strings you can use with the `PreviewDevice` structure is available on our website.

Besides representing a device, a preview can have a free form. The `previewLayout()` modifier uses a value of the `PreviewLayout` enumeration to determine the preview's type. The value by default is `device`, which configures the preview to represent a device, but there are two more. The `fixed(width: CGFloat, height: CGFloat)` value sets a fixed size, and the `sizeThatFits` value adapts the size of the preview to the size of the view. For instance, the following example applies the `sizeThatFits` value to the preview for the `ContentView` view created by the template.

```
struct ContentView_Previews: PreviewProvider {
    static var previews: some View {
        ContentView()
            .previewLayout(.sizeThatFits)
    }
}
```

Listing 6-78: Adapting the size of the preview to the size of the view

Because the `ContentView` view generated by the template only contains a `Text` view with the text "Hello World", the preview adopts the size of that view.

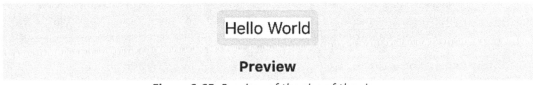

Preview

Figure 6-65: Preview of the size of the view

(Medium) **Environment**

The environment is a data structure that belongs to the application and contains data about the application and the views. It is accessible from anywhere in our code and its values can be modified or more data can be added to it. Because of its characteristics, the environment is also used to provide access to the user's data, as we will see in the next chapter, or to access databases and files from any part of the application. But we can also modify its values to change the configuration of a view to simulate different conditions, such as setting the light or dark interface mode or the font type, and this is why it is useful in previews.

The environment stores the configuration for the views in properties, so changing the values of these properties affects how the views look or behave. The following is the modifier defined by the `View` protocol for this purpose.

environment(KeyPath, Value)—This modifier processes the view and returns a new one with the characteristics defined by the attributes. The first attribute is a key path to the environment property we want to modify, and the second attribute is the value we want to assign to that property.

There are several properties available in the environment to control the behavior of the application and the views. The following are the most frequently used.

colorScheme—This property sets or returns the color scheme. It is an enumeration of type `ColorScheme` with the values `light` and `dark`.

sizeCategory—This property sets or returns the size category for the text. It is an enumeration with the values `small`, `medium`, `large`, `extraSmall`, `extraLarge`, `extraExtraLarge`, `extraExtraExtraLarge`, `accessibilityMedium`, `accessibilityLarge`, `accessibilityExtraLarge`, `accessibilityExtraExtraLarge`, and `accessibilityExtraExtraExtraLarge`.

font—This property sets or returns the font by default. It is a value of type `Font`.

accessibilityEnabled—This property sets or returns a Boolean value that determines whether Accessibility is enabled on the device.

layoutDirection—This property sets or returns the layout's direction. It is an enumeration of type `LayoutDirection` with the values `leftToRight` and `rightToLeft`.

calendar—This property sets or returns the calendar used by the view to process dates. It is a value of type `Calendar`.

locale—This property sets or returns the locale used by the view to process local data, such as language, currency, etc. It is a value of type `Locale`.

timeZone—This property sets or returns the time zone used by the view to calculate dates. It is a value of type `TimeZone`.

 The Basics: These are just some of the properties included in the environment but are the ones we normally used to configure previews. As we will see in further chapters, these properties can also be used to update the user interface, and there are additional properties to connect our application to a database, enable or disable user interaction, and more.

The implementation is simple. We must apply the `environment()` modifier to the view, and provide the key path of the property we want to modify and the new value. The key path is declared as we did before (see Chapter 3, Listing 3-32), but this time we can omit the data type because Swift can infer it, as in the following example.

```
import SwiftUI

struct ContentView: View {
    var body: some View {
        Text("Hello World")
            .foregroundColor(Color("MyColor"))
    }
}
struct ContentView_Previews: PreviewProvider {
    static var previews: some View {
        ContentView()
            .environment(\.colorScheme, .dark)
    }
}
```

Listing 6-79: Activating dark mode

In the code of Listing 6-79, we assign a dynamic color called MyColor to the `Text` view, and then activate dark mode for the preview. The example assumes that we have added a Color Set to the Assets Catalog called MyColor and assigned different colors for the modes Any/Dark, as we did in Chapter 5 (see Figure 5-26). The `environment()` modifier assigns the value `dark` to the environment's `colorScheme` property, changing the view's environment to dark mode, so the preview displays the text in the color we have selected for that mode.

 Do It Yourself: Create a Color Set in the Assets Catalog with the name MyColor and assign different colors for the Any and Dark appearances, as we did in the example of Figure 5-26. Update the ContentView.swift file with the code of Listing 6-79. On the canvas, you should see the text in the color selected for dark mode. Remove the `environment()` modifier and resume the preview. Now, you should see the text in the color selected for Any.

If we need to compare configurations, we can group multiple views with a `Group` view and modify different properties for each one of them, as we did in Listing 6-77. The following example tests three different size categories for the text. The `sizeCategory` property is where the environment stores the value that represents the size for the text selected by the user from Settings. By modifying this property, we can see what our interface looks like when the user selects different sizes of text.

```
import SwiftUI

struct ContentView: View {
    var body: some View {
        Text("Hello World")
    }
}
struct ContentView_Previews: PreviewProvider {
    static var previews: some View {
        Group {
            ContentView()
                .environment(\.sizeCategory, .small)
            ContentView()
                .environment(\.sizeCategory, .large)
            ContentView()
                .environment(\.sizeCategory, .extraExtraLarge)
        }.previewLayout(PreviewLayout.sizeThatFits)
    }
}
```

Listing 6-80: Comparing environments

In the example of Listing 6-80, we also apply the `previewLayout()` modifier to adjust the previews to the size of the `Text` views. Figure 6-66 shows the previews displayed on the canvas by this code.

Figure 6-66: Multiple previews with different environment configurations

 Do It Yourself: Replace the code in your ContentView.swift file with the code of Listing 6-80. Assign other values to the `sizeCategory` property to see what the text looks like on those sizes. We will see how to implement additional environment properties in practical situations in further chapters.

Chapter 6 - SwiftUI Framework

Basic) **7.1 States**

In the previous chapter, we introduced SwiftUI's main feature, its declarative syntax. With SwiftUI we can declare the views the way we want them to appear on the screen and let the system take care of creating the code necessary to make it happen. But a declarative syntax is not just about organizing the views, it is also about how they are updated when the state of the app changes. For instance, we may have an interface like the one in Figure 7-1, below, with a `Text` view displaying a title, an input field for the user to insert a new title, and a button to replace the old title with the new one.

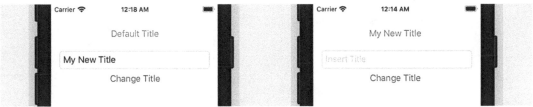

Figure 7-1: *User Interface*

The view with the title by default represents the initial state of our interface. The state is updated with each character the user types in the input field (Figure 7-1, left), and when the button is pressed, the interface moves to an additional state in which the title inserted by the user has replaced the title by default and changed color (Figure 7-1, right).

Every time there is a change of state, the views must be updated to reflect it. In previous systems, this involved extensive codes to keep the data and the interface synchronized, but in a declarative syntax all we have to do is to declare what the configuration of the views should be in each state and the system takes care of generating all the code necessary to perform the changes.

The possible states the interface can go through are determined by the information stored by the app. For instance, the characters inserted by the user in the input field and the color used in our example are values stored by the app. Every time these values change, the app is in a new state and therefore the interface must be updated to reflect it. Establishing this dependency between the app's data and the interface demands a lot of code, but SwiftUI keeps it simple using property wrappers.

Advanced) **Property Wrappers**

Property wrappers are a tool provided by the Swift language that allows us to encapsulate functionality in a property. They are like the computed properties introduced in Chapter 3 (see Listing 3-41), but applicable to multiple properties. As other Swift features, they were designed to simplify our code. For instance, we can define a property wrapper that limits the value of a property to a certain range. All the properties declared with it will only accept values between those limits.

A property wrapper is just a structure, but it must be preceded by the `@propertyWrapper` keyword and include a property with the name `wrappedValue` to process and store the value. The structure must also include an initializer for the `wrappedValue` property. The following is a Playground example that illustrates how to define a property wrapper that performs the aforementioned task; it limits the value of a property to a minimum of 0 and a maximum of 255.

```
import Foundation
@propertyWrapper
struct ClamppedValue {
    var storedValue: Int = 0
    var min: Int = 0
    var max: Int = 255

    var wrappedValue: Int {
        get {
            return storedValue
        }
        set {
            if newValue < min {
                storedValue = min
            } else if newValue > max {
                storedValue = max
            } else {
                storedValue = newValue
            }
        }
    }
    init(wrappedValue: Int) {
        self.wrappedValue = wrappedValue
    }
}
```

Listing 7-1: *Defining a property wrapper*

Listing 7-1 defines a property wrapper called `ClamppedValue`. The structure contains three properties to store and control the value. The `storedValue` property stores the current value of the property, and the `min` and `max` properties determine the minimum and maximum values allowed for the properties defined with this property wrapper. There is also the required `wrappedValue` property, defined as a computed property with a getter and a setter. The getter returns the current value of the `storedValue` property, but the setter checks whether the new value is within the minimum and maximum allowed before storing it. If the new value exceeds a limit, the values of the `min` or `max` properties are assigned to the `storedValue` property accordingly.

The code of Listing 7-1 defines the property wrapper, but it doesn't define any property of this kind. Implementing a property wrapper is easy, we must declare the properties as we always do but preceded with the name of the property wrapper prefixed with the @ character.

```
struct Price {
    @ClamppedValue var firstPrice: Int
    @ClamppedValue var secondPrice: Int

    func printMessage() {
        print("First Price: \(firstPrice)")   // "First Price: 0"
        print("Second Price: \(secondPrice)")   // "Second Price: 255"
    }
}
var purchase = Price(firstPrice: -42, secondPrice: 350)
purchase.printMessage()
```

Listing 7-2: *Using a property wrapper*

The `Price` structure in Listing 7-2 includes two properties that use the `ClampedValue` property wrapper, `firstPrice` and `secondPrice`, and a method to print their values. The instances of the structure are initialized with the values -42 and 350. Both values exceed the limits established by the property wrapper, so the value stored for each property is the limit they exceeded; 0 for `firstPrice` and 255 for `secondPrice`.

 Do It Yourself: Create a new Playground file and replace the code in the template with the codes of Listings 7-1 and 7-2. Press play. You should see the messages " First Price: 0" and " Second Price: 255" printed on the console.

(Basic) @State

Property wrappers can store and process values, and that is why SwiftUI implements them to store and keep track of the states of our app's interface. The one designed to store the states of a single view is called `@State`. This property wrapper stores a value and notifies the system when that value changes, so the views are updated to show the change to the user. We define a property of this type and then use it when we need to display its value or assign a new one.

The `@State` property wrapper was designed to store the states of a single view, so we should declare the properties of this type as part of the view structure and as `private` (the access is restricted to the structure in which they were declared).

```
import SwiftUI

struct ContentView: View {
   @State private var title: String = "Default Title"

   var body: some View {
      VStack {
         Text(title)
            .padding(10)
         Button(action: {
            self.title = "My New Title"
         }, label: {
            Text("Change Title")
         })
         Spacer()
      }.padding()
   }
}
```

Listing 7-3: Defining a state

In the code of Listing 7-3, we declare a `@State` property called `title` of type `String` and initialize it with the value "Default Title". In the `body` of the view, we show the value of this property with a `Text` view within a vertical stack. Below the text, we include a `Button` view. We will study `Button` views in Chapter 8, but for now all we need to know is that a `Button` view displays a label and performs an action when the label is tapped by the user. We defined the label as a `Text` view with the text "Change Title", so the user knows that it has to press that button to change the title, and in the closure assigned to the action we change the value of the `title` property to "My New Title".

The `title` property is used in two places, first in the `Text` view to show the current value to the user, and then in the `Button` view to modify its value. In consequence, every time the button is pressed, the value of the `title` property changes, the `@State` property wrapper notifies the system, and the content of the `body` property is refreshed to display the new value on the screen.

Figure 7-2: Initial state (left) and state after the button is pressed (right)

 Do It Yourself: Create a SwiftUI project. Update the `ContentView` structure with the code of Listing 7-3. Press the Live Preview button on the canvas to activate the live preview (Figure 6-63, number 1). Wait a few seconds for the interface to be ready and press the Change Title button to assign the text to the `Text` view. You should see something similar to Figure 7-2, right.

All this process works automatically. We don't have to assign the new value to the `Text` view or tell the view that a new value is available, it's all done by the `@State` property wrapper. And we can include all the `@State` properties we need to store every state of the interface. For instance, in the interface of Figure 7-1, we not only change the text of the title but also its color. The following example adds a `@State` property of type `Bool` to our view to determine whether the user already inserted a new title or not and assign the proper color to the text.

```
import SwiftUI
struct ContentView: View {
   @State private var title: String = "Default Title"
   @State private var titleActive: Bool = false

   var body: some View {
      VStack {
         Text(title)
            .padding(10)
            .foregroundColor(titleActive ? Color.red : Color.gray)
         Button(action: {
            self.title = "My New Title"
            self.titleActive = true
         }, label: { Text("Change Title") })
         Spacer()
      }.padding()
   }
}
```

Listing 7-4: Defining multiple states

The `titleActive` property contains a Boolean that determines the color of the text, so we have to check its value to assign the appropriate color. In the example of Listing 7-4, we use a ternary operator for this purpose (see Listing 2-49). This is the recommended practice because it allows the system to determine all the possible states the view can respond to and produce a smooth transition from one state to another. if the value of `titleActive` is `true`, we assign the red color to the `foregroundColor()` modifier, otherwise, we assign the gray color.

In the button's action, besides assigning a new value to the `title` property, we now assign the value `true` to the `titleActive` property to activate this state. The `titleActive` property informs the system that there is a new value available, the system refreshes the views, the ternary operator is evaluated again, and in consequence the red color is assigned to the text.

 The Basics: There are two states in the example of Listing 7-4, and both change at the same time, but the system takes into consideration these situations and makes sure that the interface is updated only when necessary.

A `@State` property creates a dependency between itself and the view and therefore the view is updated every time its value changes. It is said that the view is *bound* to the property. The binding we have used so far is unidirectional. If the property is modified, the view is updated. But there are views which values are modified by the user and therefore they must be able to store the value back into the property without the code's intervention. For this purpose, SwiftUI allows us to define a bidirectional binding. Bidirectional bindings are declared by prefixing the name of the property with the $ sign.

The views that usually require bidirectional binding are control views, such as those that create switches the user can turn on and off, or input fields to insert text. The following example implements a **TextField** view to illustrate this feature. A **TextField** view creates an input field. The values required by its initializer are a string with the text we want to show as placeholder and the **Binding** property we are going to use to store the value inserted by the user (we will learn more about **TextField** views and other control views in Chapter 8).

```
import SwiftUI

struct ContentView: View {
    @State private var title: String = "Default Title"
    @State private var titleActive: Bool = false
    @State private var titleInput: String = ""

    var body: some View {
        VStack {
            Text(title)
                .padding(10)
                .foregroundColor(titleActive ? Color.red : Color.gray)
            TextField("Insert Title", text: $titleInput)
                .textFieldStyle(RoundedBorderTextFieldStyle())
            Button(action: {
                self.title = self.titleInput
                self.titleActive = true
                self.titleInput = ""
            }, label: { Text("Change Title") })
            Spacer()
        }.padding()
    }
}
```

Listing 7-5: *Defining bidirectional binding*

In this example, we add to our code the **@State** property we need to store the text inserted by the user, and then define a **TextField** view between the title and the button. The **TextField** view was initialized with the placeholder "Insert Title", and the new **titleInput** property was provided as the binding property for the view ($titleInput). This creates a permanent connection between the view and the property, so every time the user types or removes a character in the input field, the new value is assigned to the property.

In the action for the **Button** view, we introduced two modifications. First, we assign the value of the **titleInput** property to the **title** property. This effectively updates the title of the view with the text inserted by the user. And finally, we assign an empty string to the **titleInput** property to clear the input field and leave it ready for the user to start typing again.

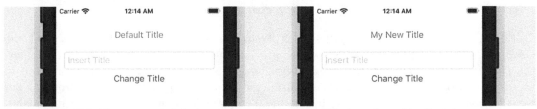

Figure 7-3: *The* TextField *view is cleared after the title is assigned to the* Text *view*

Do It Yourself: Update the `ContentView` structure with the code of Listing 7-5. Press the Live Preview button on the canvas to activate the live preview. Click on the text field and insert a text. Press the Change Title button. You should see something similar to Figure 7-3, right.

As we have already learned, property wrappers are defined as structures and therefore they contain their own properties. SwiftUI allows us to access the underlying structure of a property wrapper by prefixing the property's name with an underscore (e.g., `_title`). Once we get the structure, we can access its properties. The structure that defines the `@State` property wrapper is called `State`. This is a generic structure and therefore it can process values of any type. The following are the properties defined by this structure to store the state's values.

wrappedValue—This property returns the value managed by the `@State` property.

projectedValue—This property returns a structure of type `Binding` that creates the bidirectional binding with the view.

The value stored by the `wrappedValue` property stores the value we assign to the `@State` property, like the "Default Title" string assigned to the `title` property in the last example, and the `projectedValue` property stores a structure of type `Binding` that creates the bidirectional binding we need to store a value back to the property from a control. As we have seen from the examples of this chapter, SwiftUI provides an easy way to access these properties. If we read the `@State` property directly (e.g., `title`), the value returned is the one stored in the `wrappedValue` property, and if we prefix the property's name with a `$` sign (e.g., `$title`), we access the `Binding` structure stored in the `projectedValue` property. This is how SwiftUI proposes we work with `@State` properties, but in theory we can also access the properties directly, as in the following example.

```
import SwiftUI

struct ContentView: View {
    @State private var title: String = "Default Title"
    @State private var titleInput: String = ""

    var body: some View {
        VStack {
            Text(_title.wrappedValue)
                .padding(10)
            TextField("Insert Title", text: _titleInput.projectedValue)
                .textFieldStyle(RoundedBorderTextFieldStyle())
            Button(action: {
                self._title.wrappedValue = self._titleInput.wrappedValue
                self._titleInput.wrappedValue = ""
            }, label: { Text("Change Title") })
            Spacer()
        }.padding()
    }
}
```

Listing 7-6: Accessing the properties of a `State` *structure*

Notice that instead of using the SwiftUI shortcuts, as we did before, we read the `wrappedValue` and `projectedValue` properties of the `State` structure directly. Of course, this is not necessary, but may be required sometimes. For example, SwiftUI doesn't allow us to access and work with `@State` properties outside the closure assigned to the `body` property, but we can replace one `State` structure by another. For example, if we want to initialize the input

Chapter 7 - Declarative User Interface

field in our previous example with the default value of the `title` property, we can access the `State<String>` structure inside the `title` property with an underscore (`_title`) and assign it as the `State` structure of the `titleInput` property when the view is initialized.

```
init() {
    _titleInput = _title
}
```

Listing 7-7: Initializing `@State` *properties*

The `title` property is defined with a `State` structure that can process `String` values. Therefore, when the `ContentView` structure is initialized, the `title` property is a `State` structure of type `State<String>` with the value "Default Title" assigned to its `wrappedValue` property. All we do in the initializer of Listing 7-7 is to assign a copy of this structure to the `titleInput` property, so the value stored in this property will also be "Default Title".

 Do It Yourself: Update the `ContentView` structure with the code of Listing 7-6. Add the initializer of Listing 7-7 to the `ContentView` structure (bellow the `@State` properties). Activate the live preview. You should see the input field initialized with the value "Default Title". An easier way to initialize a `@State` property is with the `onAppear()` modifier introduced in Chapter 6 (see Listing 6-44), or storing the states in an observable object, as we will see later.

Basic @Binding

A `@State` property belongs to the structure in which it was declared and should only be accessed from the views assigned to the `body` property of that structure (that is why we declare them `private`), but, as we have seen In Chapter 6, when our views grow significantly, It Is advisable to consolidate them into smaller structures. The problem with organizing the views this way is that the additional structures lose the reference to the `@State` properties and therefore we are not able to read or modify their values anymore. Defining new `@State` properties inside these additional views is not a solution because all we are doing is to create new states. What we need is to create a bidirectional connection between the `@State` properties defined in one structure and the code from the other. For this purpose, SwiftUI includes the `@Binding` property wrapper.

The following view is the same as previous examples, but this time we move the `Text` view that displays the title to a custom view called `HeaderView` and define a `@Binding` property in this view to access one of the `@State` properties of the `ContentView` structure.

```
import SwiftUI

struct ContentView: View {
    @State private var title: String = "Default Title"
    @State private var titleInput: String = ""

    var body: some View {
        VStack {
            HeaderView(title: $title)
            TextField("Insert Title", text: $titleInput)
                .textFieldStyle(RoundedBorderTextFieldStyle())
            Button(action: {
                self.title = self.titleInput
                self.titleInput = ""
            }, label: { Text("Change Title") })
            Spacer()
```

```
      }.padding()
   }
}
struct HeaderView: View {
   @Binding var title: String

   var body: some View {
      Text(title)
         .padding(10)
   }
}
```

Listing 7-8: Using @Binding *properties*

The **body** property of **ContentView** now contains the **VStack** view with the input field and the button, but the title is managed by an instance of the new **HeaderView** structure defined at the bottom. In this custom view, we include the same **Text** view as before, but add a **@Binding** property to be able to access the **title** property of **ContentView**.

A **@Binding** property always receives its value from a **@State** property, so we don't have to assign a default value to it, but the connection created between them is bidirectional, so we have to remember to prefix the **@State** property with the **$** sign to connect the **@Binding** property with the **Binding** value inside the **@State** property (**HeaderView(title: $title)**).

Because of the bidirectional binding created between the **@Binding** property and the **Binding** value inside the **@State** property, every time the button is pressed, the changes are detected by the system, and the **body** property of the **HeaderView** structure is processed again to show the new values on the screen.

 Do It Yourself: Update the ContentView.swift file with the code of Listing 7-8. Remember to keep the **ContentView_Previews** structure at the bottom to be able to see the preview on the canvas. Press the Live Preview button to activate the live preview, insert a text in the text field and press the Change Title button. Everything should work as before.

We can access the values of a **@Binding** property the same way we do with a **@State** property. If we just read the property, as we did in Listing 7-8, the value returned is the value stored in it, and if we prefix the name with a **$** sign, the value returned is the **Binding** structure the property wrapper uses to establish the bidirectional binding with the view. But if we prefix the name of the **@Binding** property with an underscore (e.g., **_title**), the value returned is not a **State** structure but another **Binding** structure. This is because a **@Binding** property wrapper is defined by a structure of type **Binding**. Of course, the structure also includes properties to access its values.

wrappedValue—This property returns the value managed by the **@Binding** property.

projectedValue—This property returns a structure of type **Binding** that creates the bidirectional binding with the view.

As we did with the **State** structure, we can access and work with the values stored in the **@Binding** property from these properties. The following code defines a new **HeaderView** for our example that gets the value stored in the structure from the **wrappedValue** property, counts the total number of characters in the string, and displays the result along with the title.

```
struct HeaderView: View {
   @Binding var title: String
   var counter: Int = 0
```

Chapter 7 - Declarative User Interface

```
init(title: Binding<String>) {
    self._title = title

    let sentence = self._title.wrappedValue
    counter = sentence.count
}
var body: some View {
    Text("\(title) (\(counter))")
        .padding(10)
}
}
```

Listing 7-9: *Accessing the values of a* `@Binding` *property*

In Listing 7-9, we define a normal variable called `counter` to store the number of characters in the string and a custom initializer to be able to count the characters and store the number in this variable before the view is shown on the screen. Because the `@Binding` property doesn't have an initial value, we also must initialize this property from our initializer. The value received by the `HeaderView` structure is a `Binding` structure that can manage values of type `String`, so the data type for the attribute must be declared as `Binding<String>`. Notice that to pass this value to the `@Binding` property we apply the same technique as before. We use the underscore to access the underlying `Binding` structure of the `@Binding` property and replace it with the structure received from `ContentView` (`self._title = title`). In the view, we now display the values of the `title` and `counter` properties.

Figure 7-4: *Title defined with the values of the* `@Binding` *property*

 Do It Yourself: Update the `HeaderView` structure from the previous example with the code of Listing 7-9. Activate the live preview. You should see the title by default with the number of characters on the side, as show in Figure 7-4.

The `@Binding` property of the `HeaderView` view is connected to the `@State` property of the `ContentView` view and therefore it receives its value from this property, but there are times when instances of structures like these are created independently and therefore, they require a `Binding` value. To define this value, the `Binding` structure includes the following initializer and type method.

Binding(get: Closure, **set:** Closure)—This initializer creates a `Binding` structure. The **get** attribute is a closure that returns the current value, and the **set** attribute is a closure that receives a new value for storage or processing.

constant(Value**)**—This type method creates a `Binding` structure with an immutable value. The attribute is the value we want to assign to the structure.

There are many circumstances in which we may need a `Binding` value. For instance, if we want to create a preview of the `HeaderView`, we must provide a value for the `title` property. The following example illustrates how to create a new `Binding` structure to provide this value and how to define the preview for this view.

```
struct HeaderView_Previews: PreviewProvider {
    static var previews: some View {
        let constantValue = Binding<String>(
            get: { return "My Preview Title"},
            set: { value in
                print(value)
            })
        return HeaderView(title: constantValue)
    }
}
```

Listing 7-10: Creating a Binding *structure*

The code of Listing 7-10 instantiates a new **Binding** structure. The initializer works like a computed property. It includes a getter and a setter. The getter returns the current value and the setter receives the values assigned to the structure. In this example, we always return the same string and since we are not assigning new values to the structure, we just print the value on the console. The instance is assigned to the **constantValue** constant and then sent to the **HeaderView** structure, so the view has a value to show on the canvas.

There is no much use for the **Binding** structure of this example other than provide the value required by the **HeaderView** structure. In cases like this, we can take advantage of the **constant()** method. This type method creates and returns a **Binding** structure with an immutable value, exactly what we need in this case, so we can simplify our code by creating the structure with this method instead.

```
struct HeaderView_Previews: PreviewProvider {
    static var previews: some View {
        HeaderView(title: .constant("My Preview Title"))
    }
}
```

Listing 7-11: Creating a Binding *structure with an immutable value*

 Do It Yourself: Add the structure of Listing 7-11 to the ContentView.swift file. You should see the preview of the **HeaderView** view along with the preview of the **ContentView** view on the canvas. We will see more examples of how to implement the **constant()** method in further chapters.

(Basic) **@Environment**

Besides custom states, we can also respond to states set by the system in the environment. We have worked with the environment before to configure previews (see Environment in Chapter 6), but some of its properties, like **colorScheme** and **sizeCategory**, represent states that can change while the app is being executed, so we can read their values and update the views accordingly. For this purpose, SwiftUI includes the **@Environment** property wrapper. This property wrapper works in a similar way than **@State** but it is designed to report to the system changes in the environment's properties. The **@Environment** property wrapper is created with the **Environment** structure. The following is the structure's initializer.

Environment(KeyPath)—This initializer creates an **Environment** structure that provides access to an environment property. The attribute is the key path of the property we want to access.

Chapter 7 - Declarative User Interface

Because the initializer of the `Environment` structure receives an attribute to specify the property's key path, connecting the property wrapper with the property we want to monitor is easy, as illustrated in the following example.

```
import SwiftUI

struct ContentView: View {
    @Environment(\.colorScheme) var mode

    var body: some View {
        Text("Mode: \(mode == .dark ? "Dark" : "Light")")
            .padding(30)
            .background(mode == .dark ? Color.black : Color.yellow)
            .foregroundColor(mode == .dark ? Color.white : Color.black)
    }
}
```

Listing 7-12: Responding to updates in the states of the environment

In Listing 7-12, we define a property called `mode` to create a binding between the view and the environment's `colorScheme` property, and then assign different values to the modifiers of a `Text` view depending on the current mode (`dark` or `light`). When the user changes the scheme mode for the device from Settings, the value of the `colorScheme` property in the environment changes, this changes the value of the `mode` property in our view, and the view is updated to reflect the new state.

Figure 7-5: Light and dark modes

Do It Yourself: Create a new SwiftUI project. Update the `ContentView` structure with the code of Listing 7-12. Run the application in a device. Press the Home button, open the Settings app, select the Display & Brightness option, and click on Dark or Light to select the mode. Open the app again. You should see something similar to Figure 7-5. You can also test the modes in the canvas by modifying the value of the `colorScheme` property from the preview, as we did in Listing 6-79. We will work with other environment properties in further chapters.

(Basic) 7.2 Model

Professional applications are composed of several views that represent all the screens the user can navigate through. These views need to access the same data and respond to the same states to update the interface and stay synchronized. Therefore, the app must provide a unique source of data and the views must be able to read and modify it. This unique source of data is usually called the *model*.

The model is part of the basic organization of an application. In this paradigm, a group of structures or objects define the model (the app's data and states) and the views access the model to present the data to the user.

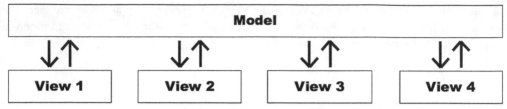

Model

View 1 View 2 View 3 View 4

Figure 7-6: App's model

This organization cannot be created with @State properties. The @State property wrapper used in previous examples can only store values that control the states of a single view. What we need is to create an object that we can pass to the views and that will inform the system when its values change. SwiftUI defines the following protocol and property wrappers for this purpose.

ObservableObject—This protocol defines the tools required by an object to inform the system every time its values change.

@ObservedObject—This property wrapper listens to changes in an observable object and receives the new values.

@Published—This property wrapper turns any property into a publisher, which means that the changes on the property's values are going to be reported to the system.

(Basic) **Observable Object**

To create the model and keeps the view up to date, we must define a class that conforms to the ObservableObject protocol, define the properties we want to use to store the states with the @Published property wrapper, and then include a property defined with the @ObservedObject property wrapper inside every view we want to connect to this model.

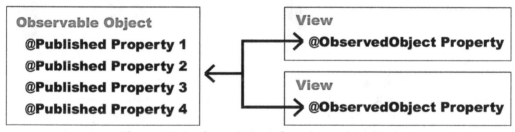

Figure 7-7: Implementation of an observable object

The advantage of working with an observable object and @Published properties instead of @State properties is that the states can now be managed from all the views of our application (all the screens the user can navigate through). The @ObservedObject property contains a reference to the observable object, so we can modify its values, and the @Published properties will inform the system when their values change, so the views, and therefore the entire interface, is synchronized with the data.

The following is an example of how to define this class. We called it AppData. The AppData class conforms to the ObservableObject protocol and includes four @Published properties to store the data.

```
import SwiftUI

class AppData: ObservableObject {
   @Published var title: String = "Default Title"
   @Published var author: String = "Unknown"
   @Published var titleInput: String = ""
```

Chapter 7 - Declarative User Interface

```
    @Published var authorInput: String = ""
}
```

Listing 7-13: Storing our data in an observable object

The purpose of this application is to store the title and author of a book. The `title` and `author` properties store the final values, and the `titleInput` and `authorInput` properties are going to be used by the view to receive the input from the user.

 The Basics: The classes defined to store the data are a central part of our application and can be large, so it is recommendable to store them in a separate file. For this example, we have created a Swift file called AppData.swift (see Figure 6-62).

Because the source of data (also called the source of truth) has to be unique, we can't create one object for each view, we have to create one instance from the class and then pass a reference of that object to all the views. Figure 7-8, below, illustrates this scheme. We pass a reference of our model to the view that defines the initial screen, and then pass that reference to the rest of the views that conform the interface, so all the views work on the same object.

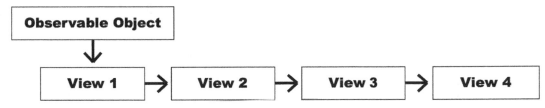

Figure 7-8: Observable object model

The first view to receive a reference to the model should be the view assigned as the root view of the window. In our examples, this is the `ContentView` view, which is instantiated in the `SceneDelegate` object (see Listing 5-3). We could use the `SceneDelegate` object to instantiate the observable object, but because a delegate is created for every scene (window), it is recommendable to manage the model from the `AppDelegate` object instead (see Listing 5-1). In the following example, we adopt this pattern and create the instance of our `AppData` class in the `AppDelegate` class.

```
import UIKit

@UIApplicationMain
class AppDelegate: UIResponder, UIApplicationDelegate {
    var myData: AppData!

    func application(_ application: UIApplication,
didFinishLaunchingWithOptions launchOptions:
[UIApplication.LaunchOptionsKey: Any]?) -> Bool {
        myData = AppData()
        return true
    }
    func application(_ application: UIApplication,
configurationForConnecting connectingSceneSession: UISceneSession,
options: UIScene.ConnectionOptions) -> UISceneConfiguration {
        return UISceneConfiguration(name: "Default Configuration",
sessionRole: connectingSceneSession.role)
    }
}
```

Listing 7-14: Initializing the observable object in the AppDelegate *class*

Listing 7-14 is the `AppDelegate` class of our project. Here, we define an optional property of type `AppData` called `myData` to store an instance of our observable object, and then create that instance in the `application(UIApplication, didFinishLaunchingWithOptions:)` method. This method is executed as soon as the app is launched, which means that our model is going to be ready by the time the views try to access the data.

The advantage of storing the app's data in the `AppDelegate` object is that we can access it from anywhere in our code through the `UIApplication` object. We have introduced this class in Chapter 4 (see Listing 4-52). The class includes the `shared` property to return the `UIApplication` object created for our app, and this object includes the `delegate` property to return a reference to the `AppDelegate` object. From this object, we can access the `myData` property with our model and send a reference to the initial view.

The following is the `SceneDelegate` class of our project. Here, we access the `myData` property from the `AppDelegate` object and send a reference to the `ContentView` view (Notice that the object returned by the `delegate` property is of type `UIResponder` and our `AppDelegate` class is a subclass of `UIResponder`, so we cast it with the `as!` operator).

```
import UIKit
import SwiftUI

class SceneDelegate: UIResponder, UIWindowSceneDelegate {
    var window: UIWindow?

    func scene(_ scene: UIScene, willConnectTo session: UISceneSession,
options connectionOptions: UIScene.ConnectionOptions) {
        let app = UIApplication.shared
        let delegate = app.delegate as! AppDelegate
        let contentView = ContentView(appData: delegate.myData)

        if let windowScene = scene as? UIWindowScene {
            let window = UIWindow(windowScene: windowScene)
            window.rootViewController = UIHostingController(rootView:
contentView)
            self.window = window
            window.makeKeyAndVisible()
        }
    }
}
```

Listing 7-15: Sending a reference of the observable object to the initial view

After these modifications, we have an instance of our observable object stored in the `AppDelegate` object, and a reference of this object was passed to the `ContentView` structure. Now, we must add to `ContentView` the `@ObservedObject` property to store this reference.

```
import SwiftUI

struct ContentView: View {
    @ObservedObject var appData: AppData

    var body: some View {
        VStack(spacing: 8) {
            Text("\(appData.title) - \(appData.author)")
                .padding(10)
            TextField("Insert Title", text: $appData.titleInput)
                .textFieldStyle(RoundedBorderTextFieldStyle())
            TextField("Insert Author", text: $appData.authorInput)
                .textFieldStyle(RoundedBorderTextFieldStyle())
            Button(action: {
```

```
            self.appData.title = self.appData.titleInput
            self.appData.author = self.appData.authorInput
        }, label: { Text("Save") })
        Spacer()
    }.padding()
    }
}
struct ContentView_Previews: PreviewProvider {
    static var previews: some View {
        ContentView(appData: AppData())
    }
}
```

Listing 7-16: Working with the observable object from the views

This is very similar to what we have done before, but instead of reading and storing the values in @**State** properties, we do it in the @**Published** properties of our observable object. The process is the same. When we store a value in a @**Published** property, the property tells the system that new values are available, and the views our automatically updated.

The interface is also similar, although this time we have to access the properties inside the observable object referenced by the **appData** property. The view of Listing 7-16 defines a **Text** view to display the values of the **title** and **author** properties, and then two **TextField** views to let the user insert a new title and author. These views store the values in the **titleInput** and **authorInput** properties, so at the end, we added a **Button** view to assign the values of these properties to the **title** and **author** properties and update the text on the screen with the new values inserted by the user.

The major difference presented by this example is in the preview structure. The **AppData** object that represents our model is passed to the instance of the **ContentView** structure created for the application, but the **ContentView_Previews** structure creates a separate instance of the **ContentView** structure to show on the canvas, so we have to provide an additional **AppData** object to this instance, as we did in Listing 7-16 (**ContentView(appData: AppData())**). Now, the preview on the canvas works as always.

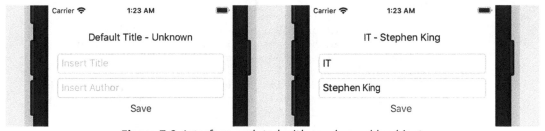

Figure 7-9: Interface updated with an observable object

 Do It Yourself: Open the File menu at the top of the screen and click on the New/File options to create a new Swift file (Figure 6-62). Assign the name AppData.swift to the file and replace the code defined by the template with the code of Listing 7-13. Update the code of your AppDelegate.swift file with the code of Listing 7-14, and the code of your SceneDelegate.swift file with the code of Listing 7-15. Finally, update the **ContentView** structure with the code of Listing 7-16 and press the Live Preview button to run the application on the canvas. You should see something similar to Figure 7-9.

In the model of Listing 7-13, we define four properties, **title** and **author** to store the actual information and **titleInput** and **titleAuthor** to receive input from the user. Multiple views that may be added later to our application will have to access the **title** and **author** properties to show their values to the user, but the `titleInput` and `authorInput` properties are only required by the view that contains the `TextField` views. This means that we are storing the private state of a view in the app's model. Although there is nothing wrong with this approach, it is recommendable to use the model to store the app's data but manage the states of the views from the views themselves. There are different patterns we can implement to organize our application. One approach is to create additional observable objects to manage the states of each view. The following is the model we need for this example.

```
import SwiftUI

class AppData: ObservableObject {
    @Published var title: String = "Default Title"
    @Published var author: String = "Unknown"
}
```

Listing 7-17: Storing only the app's data in the model

Our model now only stores the title and author of the book. To manage the states of the view and provide the binding properties for the `TextField` views, we can define an additional observable object for the `ContentView` view, as in the following example.

```
import SwiftUI

class ContentViewData: ObservableObject {
    @Published var titleInput: String = ""
    @Published var authorInput: String = ""
}
struct ContentView: View {
    @ObservedObject var contentData = ContentViewData()
    @ObservedObject var appData: AppData

    var body: some View {
        VStack(spacing: 8) {
            Text("\(appData.title) - \(appData.author)")
                .padding(10)
            TextField("Insert Title", text: $contentData.titleInput)
                .textFieldStyle(RoundedBorderTextFieldStyle())
            TextField("Insert Author", text: $contentData.authorInput)
                .textFieldStyle(RoundedBorderTextFieldStyle())
            Button(action: {
                self.appData.title = self.contentData.titleInput
                self.appData.author = self.contentData.authorInput
            }, label: { Text("Save") })
            Spacer()
        }.padding()
    }
}
struct ContentView_Previews: PreviewProvider {
    static var previews: some View {
        ContentView(appData: AppData())
    }
}
```

Listing 7-18: Defining an observable object for a view

Everything is the same as before, but we have defined an additional observable object for the `ContentView` view called `ContentViewData`, and now the characters inserted by the user are stored in the `@Published` properties of this object. When the user presses the Save button, we assign the values of these properties to the `title` and `author` properties to store the data in the model.

If we want to initialize the `titleInput` and `authorInput` properties with the values stored in the model, we can provide a custom initializer for the `ContentView` structure.

```
init(appData: AppData) {
    self.appData = appData
    contentData.titleInput = self.appData.title
    contentData.authorInput = self.appData.author
}
```

Listing 7-19: *Initializing the view's observable object*

The initializer passes the reference of the model to the `appData` property and then assigns the values of the model's `title` and `author` properties to the `titleInput` and `authorInput` properties of the `contentData` object, so the `TextField` views show the current values.

Figure 7-10: *Text fields initialized with the model's values*

 Do It Yourself: Update the AppData.swift file with the code of Listing 7-17 and your ContentView.swift file with the code of Listing 7-18. Run the application. You should see something similar to Figure 7-9. Add the initializer of Listing 7-19 to the `ContentView` structure (below the `@ObservedObject` properties) and run the application. You should see something similar to Figure 7-10.

Basic @EnvironmentObject

Our application may have a view that presents a menu, another view that displays a list of items, and another one that shows information pertaining to the item selected by the user. All these views need to access the app's data and therefore all of them must contain a reference to the model. But passing this reference from one view to another until we reach the one that requires its values, as illustrated in Figure 7-8, can be cumbersome and error prone. A better alternative is to pass the reference of the model to the environment and then read it from the environment whenever we need it.

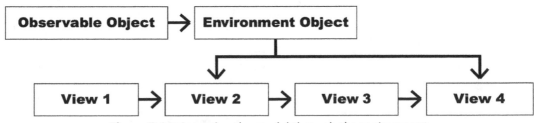

Figure 7-11: *Accessing the model through the environment*

As we already mentioned, the environment is a general-purpose container that stores information about the app and the views, but it can also store custom data, including references to observable objects. The `View` protocol includes the following modifier to add an observable object to the environment of a view.

environmentObject(Object)—This modifier assigns an object to the environment of a view hierarchy. The attribute is a reference to the object we want to share with the views.

The `environmentObject()` modifier assigns an object to the environment of a view's hierarchy, so we must apply it to the window's root view if we want the initial view and all the views on its hierarchy to have access to the model. The following code shows the modifications we must introduce to our application to pass the reference of our `AppData` object to the environment of the `ContentView` structure.

```
import UIKit
import SwiftUI

class SceneDelegate: UIResponder, UIWindowSceneDelegate {
   var window: UIWindow?

   func scene(_ scene: UIScene, willConnectTo session: UISceneSession,
options connectionOptions: UIScene.ConnectionOptions) {
      let app = UIApplication.shared
      let delegate = app.delegate as! AppDelegate
      let contentView = ContentView()
         .environmentObject(delegate.myData)

      if let windowScene = scene as? UIWindowScene {
         let window = UIWindow(windowScene: windowScene)
         window.rootViewController = UIHostingController(rootView:
contentView)
         self.window = window
         window.makeKeyAndVisible()
      }
   }
}
```

Listing 7-20: Assigning the observable object to the view's environment

This code passes a reference of the model to the `ContentView`'s environment, so we don't need to pass the reference to every view anymore, we just have to get the reference from the environment only when it is required by the view. SwiftUI includes the `@EnvironmentObject` property wrapper for this purpose.

```
import SwiftUI

class ContentViewData: ObservableObject {
   @Published var titleInput: String = ""
   @Published var authorInput: String = ""
}
struct ContentView: View {
   @ObservedObject var contentData = ContentViewData()
   @EnvironmentObject var appData: AppData

   var body: some View {
      VStack(spacing: 8) {
         Text("\(appData.title) - \(appData.author)")
            .padding(10)
```

```
                TextField("Insert Title", text: $contentData.titleInput)
                    .textFieldStyle(RoundedBorderTextFieldStyle())
                TextField("Insert Author", text: $contentData.authorInput)
                    .textFieldStyle(RoundedBorderTextFieldStyle())
                Button(action: {
                    self.appData.title = self.contentData.titleInput
                    self.appData.author = self.contentData.authorInput
                }, label: { Text("Save") })
                Spacer()
            }.padding()
        }
}
struct ContentView_Previews: PreviewProvider {
    static var previews: some View {
        ContentView().environmentObject(AppData())
    }
}
```

Listing 7-21: Getting a reference to the observable object from the environment

There are two changes in this code from the previous example. Instead of storing the reference of the model in an @ObservedObject property, we use an @EnvironmentObject property. The reference works the same way, but by using the environment we don't have to pass it to every view anymore, we can just read it from the environment only when it is required (see Figure 7-11). And second, an instance of our model was assigned to the environment of the ContentView view created for the preview. This is because this ContentView view does not belong to the hierarchy of the ContentView view created for the application, and therefore they work with different environments.

Do It Yourself: Update the SceneDelegate.swift file with the code of Listing 7-20, and the ContentView.swift file with the code of Listing 7-21. The application works as before, but now the values are taken from the observable object through the environment and therefore they are available to all the views that belong to the ContentView's hierarchy. We will learn how to add more views to this hierarchy in Chapter 9.

IMPORTANT: The environment stores key/value pairs. These types of values are like dictionary values, they have a key and a value associated to that key. When we apply the environmentObject() modifier with an instance of our observable object, the environment stores an item with the key AppData (the object's data type) and the object as the value. When an @EnvironmentObject property is defined, the property wrapper looks for an item which key is the property's data type and assigns its value to the property.

The Basics: Like the values of @State properties, the values in the observable object referenced by the @EnvironmentObject property can only be read and modified within the closure assigned to the body property. If you try to read these values from a custom initializer, as we did in Listing 7-19, you will get an error. An alternative is to access the values from the body property after the views were created using the onAppear() modifier introduced in Chapter 6 (see Listing 6-44).

Working with the values as they are provided by the model may cause some issues. Something we must consider is that views usually transform the values before presenting them to the user, but views in SwiftUI should only be responsible of defining the interface. We have found this situation before, when we had to combine the values of the title and author of the book to create the screen's title (see the Text view in Listing 7-21). In addition, multiple views may need to perform the same transformations on the data but doing so from different views can be error prone.

There are different patterns we can adopt to improve the organization of our application. The one recommended by Apple is called Model View View-Model (MVVM). In this pattern, there is a model with the basic information, a view-model that prepares that information for the view, and the view that presents the information to the user.

Figure 7-12: MVVM

To implement this pattern in our example, we need three elements: a structure with the basic information (the model), a structure that prepares that information to be presented by the views (the view model), and an observable object to keep the model and the views synchronized.

```
import SwiftUI

struct Book {
    var title: String
    var author: String
}
struct BookViewModel {
    var book: Book
    var header: String {
        return book.title + " " + book.author
    }
}
class AppData: ObservableObject {
    @Published var userData: BookViewModel

    init() {
        userData = BookViewModel(book: Book(title: "Default Title", author:
"Unknown"))
    }
}
```

Listing 7-22: Defining an MVVM pattern

The code of Listing 7-22 replaces the model introduced before (Listing 7-17). First, we define a structure called **Book** with properties to store the title and the author of a book. This is now our model. Next, we define a structure called **BookViewModel** to prepare the information for the view. This structure contains two properties: the **book** property to store an instance of the **Book** structure and a computed property called **header** to return a string that combines the values of the book's **title** and **author** properties. Lastly, we define the observable object. This object must provide access to the user's data, so we define a **@Published** property to store this data (a single book in this example), and an initializer to provide the initial data.

Chapter 7 - Declarative User Interface

Usually, the data is loaded from the web or a file, but in this case, we are working with temporary data, so we initialize the observable object with a new instance of the `BookViewModel` structure that contains an instance of the `Book` structure with values by default. Now, we can access the model from the views.

```swift
import SwiftUI

class ContentViewData: ObservableObject {
    @Published var titleInput: String = ""
    @Published var authorInput: String = ""
}
struct ContentView: View {
    @ObservedObject var contentData = ContentViewData()
    @EnvironmentObject var appData: AppData

    var body: some View {
        VStack(spacing: 8) {
            Text(appData.userData.header)
                .padding(10)
            TextField("Insert Title", text: $contentData.titleInput)
                .textFieldStyle(RoundedBorderTextFieldStyle())
            TextField("Insert Author", text: $contentData.authorInput)
                .textFieldStyle(RoundedBorderTextFieldStyle())
            Button(action: {
            self.appData.userData.book.title =
self.contentData.titleInput
            self.appData.userData.book.author =
self.contentData.authorInput
            }, label: { Text("Save") })
            Spacer()
        }.padding()
    }
}
struct ContentView_Previews: PreviewProvider {
    static var previews: some View {
        ContentView().environmentObject(AppData())
    }
}
```

Listing 7-23: Accessing the model in an MVVM pattern

The view of Listing 7-23 now accesses the model through the observable object and the view model structure. For instance, the title of the book is stored in the `title` property of the `Book` structure. This structure is available from the `book` property of the `BookViewModel` structure, which was assigned to the `userData` property of the `AppData` object. So, to modify the title, we have to write `appData.userData.book.title` as we did in the action for the `Button` view.

Another thing different from the previous example is how we show the title. Instead of combining the values of the model's `title` and `author` properties, we read the `header` property in the instance of the `BookViewModel` structure (`appData.userData.header`). We don't have to create a new string anymore, we just read the `header` property and the view model takes care of reading the values from the model and create the string for us. All the work of formatting and processing the values was transferred from the view to the view model.

The function of the model in this pattern doesn't change much. Instead of the observable object, the information is stored in the instance of the `Book` structure, but because that instance is assigned to the instance of the `BookViewModel` structure, which in turn is assigned to a `@Published` property of the observable object, every time a value in the model is modified, the `@Published` property reports the change to the system, the views are updated, and the new values are displayed on the screen.

Do It Yourself: Update the AppData.swift file in your project with the code of Listing 7-22, and the ContentView.swift file with the code of Listing 7-23. If you start a new project instead, remember to create an instance of the observable object from the `AppDelegate` class (Listing 7-14) and pass a reference to the environment from the `SceneDelegate` class (Listing 7-20). Run the application. You should see something like Figure 7-9, left.

IMPORTANT: This is a basic example to illustrate how the MVVM pattern is organized, but in practical applications the observable object stores a collection of view models and it takes care of loading, adding, modifying and removing the elements of that collection. We will create applications that implement a more realistic MVVM pattern in further chapters.

Medium 7.4 Combine Framework

The `@Published` property wrapper and the `ObservableObject` protocol introduced in this chapter are defined in a framework called *Combine*. The Combine framework includes protocols and data types we can use to process values over time. If a change is introduced to the data from one part of the code, we can automatically notify the other parts that a new value is available. There are two main responsibilities the elements of this system can take: they can be publishers or subscribers. A publisher determines how the values and errors are produced and sends those values to subscribers when they change, and a subscriber receives the values produced by a publisher over time.

Figure 7-13: *Combine*

There are many ways to create publishers and subscribers and many types available. For instance, the Combine framework defines the `@Published` property wrapper to turn any property into a publisher and the `ObservableObject` protocol to define a publisher that emits the values of an object before they change. SwiftUI, in turn, allows us to connect to these publishers with the `@ObservedObject` and `@EnvironmentObject` property wrappers. When a new value is assigned to a `@Published` property of an observable object, the `@ObservedObject` and `@EnvironmentObject` properties receive the new values and the system updates the views. We don't have to do anything; all the code to create the publishers and the subscribers is produced by the Combine and SwiftUI frameworks in the background, but there are additional tools we can use to create our own publishers and subscribers, customize them, and apply them to other parts of our application.

Medium Publishers

Combine defines the `Publisher` protocol to create publishers, but we don't have to create the publishers ourselves, the framework includes predefined data types that conform to this protocol and provide all the functionality we need to emit values. The two most frequently used are `Just` and `Future`. The following are their initializers.

Just(Value)—This initializer creates a `Just` publisher that sends the value specified by the attribute just once and then finishes.

Future(Closure)—This initializer creates a `Future` publisher that can be used to send a value downstream when an asynchronous operation is over. The attribute is a closure that receives another closure that must be called with a value of type `Result` to indicate whether the operation was successful or not.

Publishers receive the values from a source and then send them downstream to the subscribers. These values are usually produced by asynchronous operations, like a scrip that downloads data from the web, or by controls that receive input from the user. But if we just need to send a single value, we can create a `Just` publisher.

```
import Foundation
import Combine

let myPublisher = Just("55")
```

Listing 7-24: Creating a `Just` publisher

Publishers are generic, so they can emit different types of values, and they can also include a value of type `Error` to report the error occurred in the transmission. The `Just` publisher never produces an error, so its data type is defined as `Just<Type>`, where `Type` is the data type of the value to be sent. For instance, the publisher created in the code of Listing 7-24 is of type `Just<String>` (see Listing 3-48).

The `Just` publisher defined in Listing 7-24 sends the string "55" downstream. Of course, this code doesn't do anything, it just creates the publisher and assigns it to the `myPublisher` constant. To receive the value, we must define a subscriber that subscribes to this publisher.

 Do It Yourself: Create a new Playground file and replace the code generated by the template with the code of Listing 7-24. The code doesn't produce any result, but you can use this file to test the following examples.

(Medium) Subscribers

As with publishers, the Combine framework defines a protocol for creating subscribers. This protocol is called `Subscriber`. The Combine framework includes two classes that conform to this protocol and create convenient subscribers called `Sink` and `Assign`. The following are their initializers.

Sink(receiveCompletion: Closure, **receiveValue:** Closure)—This initializer creates a `Sink` subscriber that subscribes to a publisher and can receive an unlimited number of values. The **receiveCompletion** attribute is a closure that is executed when the publisher finishes emitting values. The closure receives a value of type `Completion`, an enumeration with the values `finished` and `failure`. The **receiveValue** attribute is also a closure that is executed when a value arrives. This closure receives the value to be processed.

Assign(object: Reference, **keyPath:** KeyPath)—This initializer creates an `Assign` subscriber that assigns the received value to a property of an object. The **object** attribute is a reference to the object we want to modify, and the **keyPath** attribute is a key path that points to the property we want to use to store the value.

After creating the subscriber, we must assign it to the publisher. The `Publisher` protocol defines the following method for this purpose.

subscribe(Subscriber)—This method assigns the subscriber specified by the attribute to the publisher.

The process is straightforward. We create the publisher, create the subscriber, and then assign the subscriber to the publisher with the `subscribe()` method.

```
import Foundation
import Combine

let myPublisher = Just("55")

let mySubscriber = Subscribers.Sink<String, Never>(receiveCompletion: {
completion in
   if completion == .finished {
      print("Complete")
   }
}, receiveValue: { value in
   print("Value: \(value)")
})
myPublisher.subscribe(mySubscriber)
```

Listing 7-25: Assigning a subscriber to a publisher

Subscribers are also generic and therefore we must specify the data type they can receive and the type of error they can process. In this example, the `Just` publisher is emitting a value of type `String` with no error. To declare the return type of a value that doesn't exist, the Swift Standard Library defines an enumeration called `Never`, so the data type of our subscriber is `<String, Never>`.

In the example of Listing 7-25, we define closures for the two attributes of the `Sink` initializer. The **receiveCompletion** attribute receives a value of type `Completion`. This is an enumeration with the values `finished` and `failure`. If the operation is successful, the value received by the closure is equal to `finished`, but if the process fails, the value is `failure`, which is an associated value that contains the type of error received. In this case, the `Just` publisher does not produce any error, so we only check for the `finished` value. On the other hand, the **receiveValue** attribute receives the value emitted by the publisher, so we print it on the console to confirm it arrived correctly.

Once the subscriber is assigned to the publisher, the process begins. The subscriber asks for values to the publisher and the publisher emits those values downstream. The publisher of our example sends the value "55" to the subscriber and then it sends the completion signal to finish the connection, so we see the texts "Value: 55" and "Complete" printed on the console.

(Medium) **Transforming Values**

The publisher and subscriber defined in the previous example work with the same type of value. The publisher sends a string and the subscriber receives a string. If the value produced by the publisher is not of a data type the subscriber can process, we must transform it and then publish it again. The Combine framework defines several structures that conform to the `Publisher` protocol to receive a value for processing and create a new publisher. The following are the initializers of the most frequently used.

Map(upstream: Publisher, **transform:** Closure)—This initializer creates a `Map` publisher to transform values. The **upstream** attribute is a reference to the upstream publisher, and the **transform** attribute is a closure that transforms the values received from that publisher. The closure receives the value emitted by the upstream publisher and must return the value we want the `Map` publisher to emit.

Filter(upstream: Publisher, isIncluded: Closure)—This initializer creates a `Filter` publisher to filter values. The **upstream** attribute is a reference to the upstream publisher, and the **isIncluded** attribute is a closure that filters the values received from that publisher. The closure receives the value emitted by the upstream publisher and must return a Boolean value that indicates whether the current value is valid or not.

Debounce(upstream: Publisher, dueTime: SchedulerTimeIntervalConvertible, scheduler: Queue)—This initializer creates a `Debounce` publisher to delay the stream. The **upstream** attribute is a reference to the upstream publisher. The **dueTime** attribute is a method defined by the `SchedulerTimeIntervalConvertible` protocol that determines the time the publisher is going to wait before processing the next value. The methods available are `seconds()`, `microseconds()`, `milliseconds()`, and `nanoseconds()`. Finally, the **scheduler** attribute is a `DispatchQueue`, `OperationQueue`, or `RunLoop` value that determines in which queue the operation that controls the delay is going to be executed.

RemoveDuplicates(upstream: Publisher, predicate: Closure)—This initializer creates a `RemoveDuplicates` publisher to remove duplicated values. The **upstream** attribute is a reference to the upstream publisher, and the **predicate** attribute is a closure that receives the last two values emitted by the publisher and must return a Boolean value that determines whether the values are equal or not.

ReceiveOn(upstream: Publisher, scheduler: Queue)—This initializer creates a `ReceiveOn` publisher to indicate the queue in which the value should be received by the subscriber. The **upstream** attribute is a reference to the upstream publisher, and the **scheduler** attribute is a `DispatchQueue`, `OperationQueue`, or `RunLoop` value that determines in which queue the value is going to be received by the subscriber.

TryMap(upstream: Publisher, transform: Closure)—This initializer creates a `TryMap` publisher. This publisher works like the `Map` publisher, but it can return `nil` values that won't be sent downstream and return errors. The **upstream** attribute is a reference to the upstream publisher, and the **transform** attribute is a closure that receives the values to process and returns the result.

FlatMap(upstream: Publisher, maxPublishers: Demand, transform: Closure)—This initializer creates a `FlatMap` publisher that allows us to return a new custom publisher for each value; useful to process asynchronous operations. The **upstream** attribute is a reference to the upstream publisher. The **maxPublishers** attribute determines the maximum number of values sent by the publisher. It is a structure of type `Demand` with the `unlimited` and `none` properties, and also the `max()` method to declare a specific number. Finally, the **transform** attribute is a closure that receives the current value and returns a publisher.

Catch(upstream: Publisher, handler: Closure)—This initializer creates a `Catch` publisher to process errors. The **upstream** attribute is a reference to the upstream publisher, and the **handler** attribute is a closure that receives the error and returns a publisher to replace the one that failed.

CombineLatest(Publisher, Publisher)—This initializer creates a `CombineLatest` publisher to process values from two publishers at a time. The attributes are references to the publishers we want to combine. The framework also defines the `CombineLatest3` and `CombineLatest4` publishers to combine three and four publishers respectively.

Merge(Publisher, Publisher)—This initializer creates a `Merge` publisher to merge two publishers into one. The attributes are references to the publishers we want to merge.

The framework also defines the **Merge3**, **Merge4**, **Merge5**, **Merge6**, **Merge7** and **Merge8** to merge up to 8 publishers.

Zip(Publisher, Publisher)—This initializer creates a **zip** publisher that waits for new values from two publishers and emits a tuple with the latest values received. The attributes are references to the publishers we want to combine. The framework also defines the **zip3** and **zip4** publishers to work with three and four publishers respectively.

Decode(upstream: Publisher, decoder: Coder)—This initializer creates a **Decode** publisher to decode data. It is frequently used to decode JSON data downloaded from the web. The **upstream** attribute is a reference to the upstream publisher, and the **decoder** attribute is an object in charge of decoding the data. The framework also defines a publisher called **Encode** to encode data.

Autoconnect(upstream: Upstream)—This initializer creates an **Autoconnect** publisher to activate publishers that wait for the order to connect before sending data.

We can chain these publishers to perform as many transformations as we need to get values the subscriber can process, as illustrated in Figure 7-14.

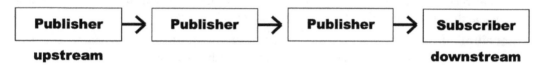

upstream   downstream

Figure 7-14: Publisher chain

The most common publisher used to transform a value is **Map**. For instance, we can use **Map** to turn the string "55" emitted by the **Just** publisher in the previous example into an integer we can use in an arithmetic operation.

```
import Foundation
import Combine

let myPublisher = Just("55")

let processPublisher = Publishers.Map<Just<String>, Int>(upstream:
myPublisher, transform: { value in
   return Int(value) ?? 0
})
let mySubscriber = Subscribers.Sink<Int, Never>(receiveCompletion: {
completion in
   if completion == .finished {
      print("Complete")
   }
}, receiveValue: { value in
   print("Value: \(value * 100)")
})
processPublisher.subscribe(mySubscriber)
```

Listing 7-26: Transforming a value with a publisher

As any other publisher, the **Map** publisher is generic, which means it can receive values of any type. The publisher takes a reference to the upstream publisher, in our case a **Just** publisher that process a string, and generates a value to send downstream, which in our example is an integer, so the type of this publisher must be declared as **<Just<String>, Int>**.

Chapter 7 - Declarative User Interface

In the closure assigned to the **transform** attribute, we cast the value into an integer with the `Int()` initializer, and if not possible, we return the value 0 instead. This result is sent downstream to the subscriber, so now the subscriber must be declared of type `<Int, Never>` to be able to process an integer.

The completion closure for the subscriber is the same as before, but because we are receiving an integer instead of a string, we can perform arithmetic operations on the value. In this example, we multiply the value by 100, getting the string "Value: 5500".

 Do It Yourself: Replace the code in your Playground file with the code of Listing 7-26 and press play. You should see the messages "Value: 5500" and "Complete" printed on the console.

(Medium)   **Operators**

Defining and connecting publishers and subscribers one by one as we did so far can be cumbersome, but the `Publisher` protocol defines methods that do all the work for us. These methods are called *operators* and can create all the publishers defined by the framework. The following are the operators available for the publishers listed above.

map(Closure)—This operator creates a `Map` publisher to transform values. The attribute is a closure that receives the values emitted by the upstream publisher and must return the value we want the `Map` publisher to emit.

filter(Closure)—This operator creates a `Filter` publisher to filter values. The attribute is a closure that receives the values emitted by the upstream publisher and must return a Boolean value that indicates whether the current value is valid or not.

debounce(for: SchedulerTimeIntervalConvertible, **scheduler:** Queue)—This operator creates a `Debounce` publisher to delay the stream. The **for** attribute is a method defined by the `SchedulerTimeIntervalConvertible` protocol that determines the time the publisher is going to wait before processing the next value. The methods available are `seconds()`, `microseconds()`, `milliseconds()`, and `nanoseconds()`. And the **scheduler** attribute is a `DispatchQueue`, `OperationQueue`, or `RunLoop` value that determines in which queue the operation that controls the delay is going to be executed.

removeDuplicates()—This operator creates a `RemoveDuplicates` publisher to remove duplicated values.

receive(on: Queue)—This operator creates a `ReceiveOn` publisher to indicate the queue in which the value should be received by the subscriber. The **on** attribute is a `DispatchQueue`, `OperationQueue`, or `RunLoop` value that determines in which queue the value is going to be received by the subscriber.

tryMap(Closure)—This operator creates a `TryMap` publisher. This publisher works like the `Map` publisher, but it can return `nil` values that won't be sent downstream. The attribute is a closure that receives the values to process and returns the result.

flatMap(maxPublishers: Demand, Closure)—This operator creates a `FlatMap` publisher that allows us to return a new custom publisher for each value; useful to process asynchronous operations. The **maxPublishers** attribute determines the maximum number of values sent by the publisher. It is a structure of type `Demand` with the `unlimited` and `none` properties, and also the `max()` method to declare a specific number. And the second attribute is a closure that receives the current value and returns a publisher.

catch(Closure)—This operator creates a `Catch` publisher to process errors. The attribute is a closure that receives the error and returns a publisher to replace the one that failed.

combineLatest(Publishers, Closure)—This operator creates a `CombineLatest` publisher to process values from multiple publishers at a time. The first attribute is a list of references to the publishers we want to combine, and the second attribute is a closure we can use to transform the values and return the result.

merge(with: Publishers)—This operator creates a `Merge` publisher to merge multiple publishers into one. The **with** attribute is a list of references to the publishers we want to merge.

zip(Publishers)—This operator creates a `Zip` publisher that waits for new values from multiple publishers and emits a tuple with the latest values received. The attribute is a list of references to the publishers we want to combine.

decode(type: Type, decoder: Coder)—This operator creates a `Decode` publisher to decode data. It is frequently used to decode JSON data downloaded from the web. The **type** attribute is the data type we want to turn the data into, and the **decoder** attribute is an object in charge of decoding the data. The framework also defines the `encode(encoder: Coder)` operator to encode data.

autoconnect()—This operator creates an `Autoconnect` publisher to connect the a connectable publisher. These are publishers defined by a protocol that inherits from the `Publisher` protocol called `ConnectablePublisher`. These types of publishers emit values only after they are connected. The protocol also defines the `connect()` operator to connect the publisher manually.

The `Publisher` protocol also defines operators to create the `Sink` and `Assign` subscribers, so we can define the whole chain of events with operators.

sink(receiveCompletion: Closure, receiveValue: Closure)—This operator creates a `Sink` subscriber that subscribes to a publisher and can receive an unlimited number of values. The **receiveCompletion** attribute is a closure that is executed when the publisher finishes emitting values. The closure receives a value of type `Completion`, an enumeration with the values `finished` and `failure`. The **receiveValue** attribute is also a closure that is executed when a value arrives. This closure receives the value to be processed.

assign(to: KeyPath, on: Object)—This operator creates an `Assign` subscriber that assigns the received value to a property of an object. The **to** attribute is a key path that point to the property we want to use to store the value, and the **on** attribute is a reference to the object we want to modify.

The advantage of using operators is that they simplify our code. We can compose multiple operators in the same statement with a syntax like the one we use to apply modifiers in SwiftUI.

```
import Foundation
import Combine

let myPublisher = Just("55")
    .map({ value in
        return Int(value) ?? 0
    })
```

```
    .sink(receiveValue: { value in
       print("Value: \(value * 100)")
    })
```

Listing 7-27: Defining publishers and subscribers with operators

This code performs the same operation on the values than before, but it is clear and concise. We only need to define the publisher that initiates the chain and the rest of the publishers and subscribers are defined by operators, one after another, in an order that represents the steps taken to transmit and transform the values. For instance, in the example of Listing 7-27, we create the `Just` publisher, apply the `map()` operator to turn the value emitted by this publisher into an integer, and finally apply the `sink()` operator to create the subscriber, assign it to the publisher, and process the received value.

(Medium) ## Subjects

There is one more type of publishers defined by the Combine framework called *Subjects*. Subjects are defined by the `Subject` protocol and they differ from other publishers in that they provide a method that we can call to emit a value. The framework includes the following two classes to create a publisher of this type.

PassthroughSubject()—This subject publishes the value it receives from the method or another publisher.

CurrentValueSubject(Value**)**—This subject stores and publishes the last value received from the method or another publisher, so new subscribers always have a value to work with. The attribute is the initial value we want the publisher to emit.

The `Subject` protocol defines the following methods to publish values.

send(Value**)**—This method tells the publisher to send the value specified by the attribute.

send(completion: Completion**)**—This method tells the publisher to send a completion signal.

Subjects are also generic, so we must specify the data type of the value and the error in the initialization. In the following example, we create a `PassthroughSubject` instance that works with values of type `String` and doesn't produce any errors (`<String, Never>`).

```
import Foundation
import Combine

let myPublisher = PassthroughSubject<String, Never>()

let subscriber = myPublisher
    .filter({
       return $0.count < 5
    })
    .sink(receiveValue: { value in
       print("Value: \(value)")
    })
myPublisher.send("This")
myPublisher.send("is")
myPublisher.send("Amazing")
myPublisher.send("!")
```

Listing 7-28: Creating a `PassthroughSubject`

Chapter 7 - Declarative User Interface

Once we have the instance of the subject, we can apply operators to it. In the example of Listing 7-28, we apply the `filter()` operator to filter out the values that are five characters or more, and then assign to the publisher a `Sink` subscriber that prints the values on the console (Notice that to read the value received by the closure of the `filter()` operator we use the placeholder `$0`, as we explained in Listing 3-25).

Every time we call the publisher's `send()` method, the value is emitted by the publisher, filtered, and if it has less than five characters, it is printed on the console. In our example, we call this method four times, but only the values "This", "is" and "!" are printed, because the value "Amazing" has more than five characters and therefore it does not reach the subscriber.

Do It Yourself: Replace the code in your Playground file with the code of Listing 7-28 and press play. You should see the messages "Value: This", "Value: is", and "Value: !" printed on the console.

With `PassthroughSubject` subjects is easy to pass errors. We must define an enumeration that conforms to the `Error` protocol, as we did in Listing 3-193, and declare this data type as the type of errors the publisher can handle.

```
import Foundation
import Combine

enum MyErrors: Error {
    case wrongValue
}
let myPublisher = PassthroughSubject<String, MyErrors>()

let subscriber = myPublisher
    .filter({
        return $0.count < 5
    })
    .sink(receiveCompletion: { completion in
        if completion == .failure(.wrongValue) {
            print("Publisher failed")
        }
    }, receiveValue: { value in
        print("Value: \(value)")
    })
myPublisher.send("Car")
myPublisher.send(completion: .failure(.wrongValue))
```

Listing 7-29: Sending completion errors

The example of Listing 7-29 defines an enumeration called `MyErrors` with only one value called `wrongValue`, and then initializes a `PassthroughSubject` subject that can pass this type of errors (`PassthroughSubject<String, MyErrors>`). To process the error, we assign a closure to the **receiveCompletion** attribute of the `sink()` operator that checks if the received value is of type `failure` with the associated value `wrongValue`. Finally, we test this code at the end by sending an error with the `send(completion:)` method.

Do It Yourself: Replace the code in your Playground file with the code of Listing 7-29 and press play. You should see the messages "Value: Car", and "Publisher failed" printed on the console.

As we have already seen, SwiftUI implements all the tools we need to create publishers and subscribers and keep the interface up to date, but we can expand these features using Combine. For this purpose, the `View` protocol defines the following modifier to turn any view into a subscriber and receive values from external publishers.

> **onReceive(Publisher, perform:** Closure)—This modifier adds a subscriber to a view. The first attribute is a reference to the publisher to which the view is going to subscribe, and the **perform** attribute is the closure to be executed when a value is received.

As we will see in further chapters, with this modifier, we can subscribe to our own publishers, but also to additional publishers defined by frameworks. In addition to SwiftUI, other frameworks are also integrated with Combine and provide their own tools for creating publishers. For instance, the `Timer` class, defined in the Foundation framework, includes the following type method to generate a publisher.

> **publish(every:** TimeInterval, **on:** RunLoop, **in:** Mode)—This type method creates a publisher that emits the current date. The **every** attribute determines the time the publisher has to wait before sending the next value. The **on** attribute determines the queue in which the process is going to be executed. And the **in** attribute determines the mode of the `RunLoop`. This is a structure of type `Mode` with the properties `default`, `common`, `eventTracking`, `modalPanel`, and `tracking`.

The publisher returned by this method is of type `TimerPublisher`; a class that conforms to the `ConnectablePublisher` protocol. As mentioned above, these types of publishers don't emit any value until they are connected with the `connect()` or `autoconnect()` operators. In the following example we use `autoconnect()` to start sending values from the publisher as soon as it is created.

```
import SwiftUI

class ContentViewData: ObservableObject {
    @Published var counter: Int = 0

    let timerPublisher = Timer.publish(every: 2, on: RunLoop.main, in:
.common)
        .autoconnect()
}
struct ContentView: View {
    @ObservedObject var contentData = ContentViewData()

    var body: some View {
        Text("Counter: \(contentData.counter)")
            .onReceive(contentData.timerPublisher, perform: { value in
                self.contentData.counter += 1
            })
    }
}
```

Listing 7-30: Generating a publisher from a `Timer`

The interface created by the code of Listing 7-30 is just a `Text` view that displays the value of a `@Published` property on the screen, but we apply the `onReceive()` modifier to the view to modify the value of this property. The timer is created as soon as the observable object is initialized and emits the current date right away and then again, every two seconds. We do nothing with this value in the `onReceive()` modifier, but we increase the value of the `counter` property by 1 every time a new value is received, so we see the value on the screen increasing every two seconds.

Counter: 0   Counter: 10

Figure 7-15: Counter created with a `TimerPublisher` *publisher*

 Do It Yourself: Update the ContentView.swift file with the code of Listing 7-30 and run the application. You should see the counter increasing by one unit every two seconds, as illustrated in Figure 7-15.

 IMPORTANT: There are more publishers and subscribers available, some we have been working with already without known it, like the `AnyCancelable` subscriber returned by some of the operators applied in this chapter (see Chapter 16, Listing 16-31). There is also a wrapper publisher called `AnyPublisher` and another for subjects called `AnySubject`. The topic is extensive, and exploring the Combine framework requires a separate book, but there are plenty of resources on the web to learn about it. For more information, visit our website and follow the links for this chapter.

8.1 Control Views

In previous chapters, we introduced two controls: `Button` views and `TextField` views. Controls are visual tools the user interacts with to change the state of the interface, select options, or insert, modify or delete information. SwiftUI defines several structures to create these control views and add them to the interface.

Button View

As we have already seen, the `Button` view creates a simple control that performs an action when pressed. The following are some of the structure's initializers.

Button(String, **action:** Closure**)**—This initializer creates a `Button` view. The first attribute is a string that defines the button's label, and the **action** attribute is a closure with the code to be executed when the button is pressed.

Button(action: Closure, **label:** Closure**)**—This initializer creates a `Button` view. The **action** attribute is a closure with the code to be executed when the button is pressed, and the **label** attribute is a closure that returns the views to be displayed as the button's label.

We have already implemented the second initializer to create our buttons, but if we only want to use a string for the label, we can simplify the code using the first initializer and a trailing closure for the action.

```
import SwiftUI
struct ContentView: View {
   @State private var colorActive: Bool = false

   var body: some View {
      VStack(spacing: 10) {
         Text("Default Title")
            .padding()
            .background(colorActive ? Color.green : Color.clear)
         Button("Change Color") {
            self.colorActive.toggle()
         }
         Spacer()
      }.padding()
   }
}
```

Listing 8-1: Implementing Button *views*

The example of Listing 8-1 includes a `Text` view and a `Button` view in a `VStack`. The `Text` view displays always the same string with a background color defined by the `colorActive` property. If the value of this property is `true`, we assign the `green` color to the background, otherwise the color assigned is `clear` (transparent). When the button is pressed, we toggle the value of this property, the `body` property is evaluated again, and the text's background changes to the next color (for more information on the `toggle()` method, see Listing 3-55).

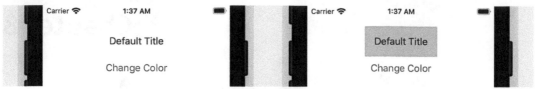

Figure 8-1: Button's action

 Do It Yourself: Create a SwiftUI project. Update the `ContentView` structure with the code of Listing 8-1. Activate the Live Preview on the canvas and press the Change Color button. You should see the interfaces of Figure 8-1. Use this project to test the following examples.

In this last example, we used a ternary operator to select the value for the `background()` modifier depending on the value of the `colorActive` property (see Listing 2-49). But we can also use an `if else` statement to change the interface when a state changes. For instance, sometimes, controls like buttons are used to show or hide a view in the interface.

```
import SwiftUI

struct ContentView: View {
    @State private var showInfo = false

    var body: some View {
        VStack(spacing: 10) {
            Button("Show Information") {
                self.showInfo.toggle()
            }.padding()
            if showInfo {
                Text("This is the information")
            }
            Spacer()
        }
    }
}
```

Listing 8-2: Adding and removing views from the interface

The button in the view of Listing 8-2 toggles the value of a `@State` property called `showInfo`. Below the button, we check the value of this property. If the value is `true`, we show a `Text` view, otherwise, we do nothing. Therefore, when the button is pressed, the value of the `showInfo` property changes, the content of the `body` property is drawn again, and the `Text` view appears or disappears, depending on the value of the property.

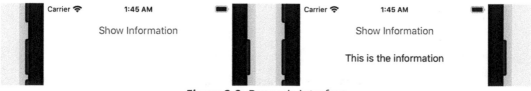

Figure 8-2: Dynamic interface

The `View` protocol defines a few modifiers that are useful for control views, including buttons.

accentColor(Color**)**—This modifier defines the color of the elements in the control.

disabled(Bool**)**—This modifier determines whether the control responds to the user interaction or not.

Chapter 8 - Controls

labelsHidden()—This modifier hides the labels assign to the controls.

The following example applies these two modifiers to change the label's color and disable the button after it is pressed.

```
import SwiftUI

struct ContentView: View {
    @State private var title: String = "Default Title"
    @State private var color = Color.clear
    @State private var buttonDisabled = false

    var body: some View {
        VStack(spacing: 10) {
            Text(title)
                .padding()
                .background(color)
            Button("Change Color") {
                self.color = Color.green
                self.buttonDisabled = true
            }
            .accentColor(Color.green)
            .disabled(buttonDisabled)
            Spacer()
        }.padding()
    }
}
```

Listing 8-3: Disabling a button

The view of Listing 8-3 defines an additional **@State** property called **buttonDisabled** to control the state of the button. When the button is pressed, the code assigns the value **false** to the **buttonDisabled** property and the button stops working, so the user can press it only once.

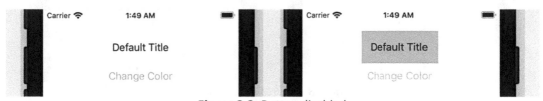

Figure 8-3: Button disabled

The **accentColor()** modifier assigns a color to the elements of the control, in this case the button's label, but we can use views to define the label, as we did in previous examples, and assign the styles to those views instead. The **label** attribute is very flexible. It can include views like **Text** views and **Image** views. We can even organize multiple views in stacks. The only thing we must consider is that the **Button** view creates a template from the images in the label. If we want to display images in their original colors, we must apply the following modifier.

renderingMode(TemplateRenderingMode)—This modifier defines the rendering mode for an **Image** view. The attribute is an enumeration defined by the **Image** structure with the values **original** and **template**. By default, **Image** views use the **original** mode and **Button** views use the **template** mode.

The following example defines a button with an image and a text. The **renderingMode()** modifier was applied to the **Image** view to show the image in its original colors.

```
import SwiftUI
struct ContentView: View {
    @State private var title: String = "Default Title"
    @State private var expanded: Bool = false

    var body: some View {
        VStack(spacing: 10) {
            Text(title)
                .frame(width: expanded ? 300 : 150, height: 50)
                .background(Color.yellow)
            Button(action: {
                self.expanded.toggle()
            }, label: {
                VStack {
                    Image("expand")
                        .renderingMode(.original)
                    Text("Expand")
                }
            })
            Spacer()
        }.padding()
    }
}
```

Listing 8-4: Defining the label of a button with an Image *view*

The view in Listing 8-4 includes a **@State** property called **expand** to control the width of the **Text** view. If the value of the property is **true**, the number 300 is assigned to the view's width, otherwise, the width takes the value 150. Every time the user presses the button, the value of the **expand** property is toggled with the **toggle()** method and therefore the width of the **Text** view changes.

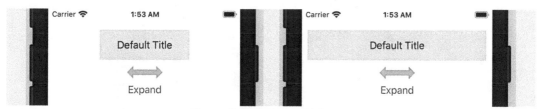

Figure 8-4: Button with image

 Do It Yourself: Download the expand.png image from our website and add it to the Assets Catalog. Update the **ContentView** structure with the code of Listing 8-4, activate the Live Preview, and press the Expand button. You should see the interface of Figure 8-4. Remove the **renderingMode()** modifier. You should see the template of the image in color blue. You can assign the **accentColor()** modifier to change the template's color if you want.

Besides these options, we can define a completely new style for the button. The **View** protocol includes the following modifier for this purpose.

buttonStyle(ButtonStyle**)**—This modifier defines the style of the bottom. The attribute is a structure that conforms to the **ButtonStyle** protocol.

There are a few structures defined by the system that conform to the **ButtonStyle** protocol and provide some options for styling, such as **DefaultButtonStyle** (default), **PlainButtonStyle**, and **BorderlessButtonStyle**. These styles do not change the

Chapter 8 - Controls

appearance of the buttons but define their behavior. For instance, the `PlainButtonStyle` removes the behavior by default allowing us to include the button in the rows of a `List` view, as we will see in Chapter 10. If we want to define a style that deviates from the one applied by the system, we must create our own structure. The protocol's only requirement is for the structure to implement the following method.

makeBody(configuration: Configuration)—This method defines and returns a view that replaces the body of the button. The **configuration** attribute is a value of type `Configuration` that contains information about the button.

This method receives a value of type `Configuration`, a typealias of `ButtonStyleConfiguration`, which contains properties that return information about the button. The following are the properties available.

isPressed—This property returns a Boolean value that indicates whether the button was pressed or not.

label—This property returns the view or views that define the button's current label.

The following example defines a button that expands when pressed. The styles include a padding and a green border. To apply these styles, we must create a structure that conforms to the `ButtonStyle` protocol, implement the `makeBody()` method, and return from this method the view we want to assign as the body of the button.

The current views that make up the body of the button are provided by the `label` property of the `Configuration` structure, so we can read and modify the value of this property to apply the new styles, as shown next.

```
import SwiftUI

struct MyStyle: ButtonStyle {
    func makeBody(configuration: MyStyle.Configuration) -> some View {
        let pressed = configuration.isPressed
        return configuration.label
            .padding()
            .border(Color.green, width: 5)
            .scaleEffect(pressed ? 1.5 : 1.0)
    }
}
struct ContentView: View {
    @State private var title: String = "Default Title"
    @State private var color = Color.gray

    var body: some View {
        VStack {
            Text(title)
                .padding()
                .foregroundColor(color)
            Button("Change Color") {
                self.color = Color.green
            }.buttonStyle(MyStyle())
            Spacer()
        }.padding()
    }
}
```

Listing 8-5: Defining custom styles for the button

In Listing 8-5, we define a structure called `MyStyle` and implement the required `makeBody()` method. This method gets the current configuration of the button from the type properties and then proceeds to modify and return the label. First, we read the value of the `isPressed` property to know if the button was pressed or not, and then apply the new styles to the `label` property. This property returns a copy of the views that create the button's current label, and therefore by modifying its value we are effectively modifying the label. In this case, we apply a padding, a border, and then assign a scale depending on the value of the `isPressed` property. If the value is `true`, which means the button is being pressed, we assign a scale of 1.5 to expand it, but if the value is `false`, we bring the scale back to 1.

In the view, we create an instance of this structure and assign it to the `Button` view with the `buttonStyle()` modifier. The result is shown in Figure 8-5.

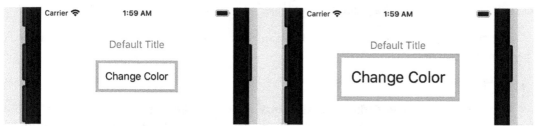

Figure 8-5 *Button with custom styles*

Do It Yourself: Update the ContentView.swift file with the code of Listing 8-5. Activate the live preview and press the button. You should see the button expanding, as show in Figure 8-5, right.

(Basic) **TextField View**

The `TextField` view is another control we introduced in Chapter 7. The view creates an input field the user can interact with to insert a value. The following is the structure's initializer with its most useful attributes.

TextField(String, **text:** Binding, **onEditingChanged:** Closure, **onCommit:** Closure**)**—This initializer creates an input field. The first attribute defines the field's placeholder. The **text** attribute is a `Binding` property that stores the value inserted by the user. The **onEditingChanged** attribute is a closure that is executed when the editing state changes. This closure receives a Boolean value that is `true` when editing begins and `false` when editing ends (the focus moves to another element). And the **onCommit** attribute is a closure that is executed when the user presses the Done (Return) key.

The `View` protocol defines a few modifiers that are particularly useful with `TextField` views.

textFieldStyle(TextFieldStyle**)**—This modifier defines the style of the text field. The attribute is a structure that conforms to the `TextFieldStyle` protocol. The framework includes three structures that conform to this protocol: `DefaultTextFieldStyle`, `PlainTextFieldStyle`, and `RoundedBorderTextFieldStyle`.

disableAutocorrection(Bool**)**—This modifier enables or disables the system's autocorrection feature. By default, the value is `true` (enabled).

autocapitalization(UITextAutocapitalizationType**)**—This modifier defines the capitalization type used to format the text. The attribute is an enumeration with the values `none`, `words`, `sentences`, and `allCharacters`.

keyboardType(UIKeyboardType**)**—This modifier defines the keyboard type. The attribute is an enumeration with the values **default**, **asciiCapable**, **numbersAndPunctuation**, **URL**, **numberPad**, **phonePad**, **namePhonePad**, **emailAddress**, **decimalPad**, **twitter**, **webSearch**, **asciiCapableNumberPad**, and **alphabet**.

The most frequently used style is the **RoundedBorderTextFieldStyle** because it delimits the text field with a classic border and round corners.

```
import SwiftUI

struct ContentView: View {
    @State private var title: String = "Default Title"
    @State private var titleInput: String = ""

    var body: some View {
        VStack(spacing: 15) {
            Text(title)
                .lineLimit(1)
                .padding()
                .background(Color.yellow)
            TextField("Insert Title", text: $titleInput)
                .textFieldStyle(RoundedBorderTextFieldStyle())
                .autocapitalization(.words)
            Button("Save") {
                self.title = self.titleInput
                self.titleInput = ""
            }
            Spacer()
        }.padding()
    }
}
```

Listing 8-6: Configuring a text field

In Listing 8-6, we apply the **RoundedBorderTextFieldStyle** style to the **TextField** view and capitalize each word. As a result, the area occupied by the input field is visible, and all the words inserted by the user are capitalized.

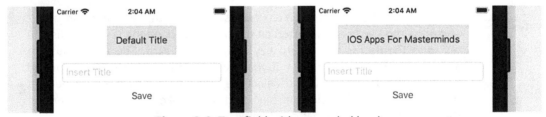

Figure 8-6: Text field with a rounded border

 Do It Yourself: Update the **ContentView** structure with the code of Listing 8-6 and activate the Live Preview. Insert a text in the input field and press the Save button. You should see the interface of Figure 8-6.

Besides a button, the user normally expects to be able to save the value by pressing the Done/Return button on the keyboard. This is controlled by the **onCommit** attribute of the **TextField** view initializer. The attribute takes a closure and executes it when the Done/Return button is pressed. Because the actions for the **Button** view and the **onCommit** attribute are usually the same, is better to move the code to a method and call the method when the user performs any of those actions, as in the following example.

```
import SwiftUI
struct ContentView: View {
   @State private var title: String = "Default Title"
   @State private var titleInput: String = ""

   var body: some View {
      VStack(spacing: 15) {
         Text(title)
            .lineLimit(1)
            .padding()
            .background(Color.yellow)
         TextField("Insert Title", text: $titleInput, onCommit: {
            self.assignTitle()
         }).textFieldStyle(RoundedBorderTextFieldStyle())
         HStack {
            Spacer()
            Button("Save") {
               self.assignTitle()
            }
         }
         Spacer()
      }.padding()
   }
   func assignTitle() {
      self.title = self.titleInput
      self.titleInput = ""
   }
}
```

Listing 8-7: Responding to the Done button

The code of Listing 8-7 adds a method to the structure called `assignTitle()` that performs the same action as before. The method is called from two places: the closure assigned to the **onCommit** attribute and the action of the **Button** view. If the button in the interface is pressed, the `assignTitle()` method is executed, and the same happens when the Done/Return button in the keyboard is pressed. The value inserted in the text field is always stored in the `title` property, regardless of the action the user decides to perform.

 Do It Yourself: Update the `ContentView` structure with the code of Listing 8-7 and press the Live Preview button on the canvas. Click on the text field, insert a text and then press the Return key on your keyboard. The text should be assigned to the title, as before. If you test this example in the simulator and don't see the device's keyboard, select the Hardware option from the menu at the top of the screen, click on Keyboard, and make sure that the Connect Hardware Keyboard option is deactivated.

 IMPORTANT: As mentioned in Chapter 3, functions are closures with a name. This means that every time an attribute requires a closure and that closure's only statement calls a function, we can provide the function itself as the attribute's value, as in `Button("Save", action: assignTitle)`. If we specify the function with parentheses, the value returned by the function is assigned to the attribute, but if we specify only the function's name, a reference to the function is assigned instead, so the function is only executed when the action is performed (in this case, the function is only executed when the button is pressed). The result is the same, but it simplifies our code.

Chapter 8 - Controls

Another attribute included in the `TextField` initializer is **onEditingChanged**. We can use this attribute to provide a closure that will be executed when the user begins editing the field and when the edition is over (the focus moves to another element). The closure receives a Boolean value; `true` means the user began editing and `false` means the user finished editing.

In the following example, we implement this attribute to change the background color of the text fields when the user starts typing on them. For this purpose, we need to control a few more states that determine the current colors, so this time we decided to manage the view's states from an observable object.

```
import SwiftUI

class ContentViewData: ObservableObject {
    @Published var title: String = "Default Name"
    @Published var nameInput: String = ""
    @Published var surnameInput: String = ""
    @Published var colorName: Color = Color.white
    @Published var colorSurname: Color = Color.white
}
struct ContentView: View {
    @ObservedObject var contentData = ContentViewData()
    var colors = [Color.white, Color(red: 0.9, green: 0.9, blue: 0.9)]

    var body: some View {
        VStack(spacing: 10) {
            Text(contentData.title)
                .lineLimit(1)
                .padding()
                .background(Color.yellow)
            TextField("Insert Name", text: $contentData.nameInput,
onEditingChanged: { self.contentData.colorName = $0 ? self.colors[1] :
self.colors[0] })
                .padding(8)
                .background(contentData.colorName)
            TextField("Insert Surname", text: $contentData.surnameInput,
onEditingChanged: { self.contentData.colorSurname = $0 ? self.colors[1] :
self.colors[0] })
                .padding(8)
                .background(contentData.colorSurname)
            HStack {
                Spacer()
                Button("Save") {
                    self.contentData.title = self.contentData.nameInput + " "
+ self.contentData.surnameInput
                    self.contentData.colorName = self.colors[0]
                    self.contentData.colorSurname = self.colors[0]
                }
            }
            Spacer()
        }.padding()
    }
}
```

Listing 8-8: Responding to the editing state

The observable object in Listing 8-8 defines a **@Published** property to store the title of the screen (`title`), two **@Published** properties to store the text inserted by the user in each text field (`nameInput` and `surnameInput`), and two more **@Published** properties to store their current colors (`colorName` and `colorSurname`). After defining the **@ObservedObject** property to connect the view to this observable object, we also define an array with the two possible colors for the text fields (`colors`). The first element is the color **white**, and the second is a custom gray.

The views are similar than before. All the work is done by the closures assigned to the **onEditingChanged** attributes of each text field. Every time the user taps on a text field, the code in the closure for that **TextField** view is executed. If the value received by the closure is **true**, it means that the user is editing the text, so the color in index 1 is assigned to the property. But if the value is **false**, the color in index 0 is assigned instead. As a result, when the user taps on a text field the background color turns gray, and when the user taps on the other text field, the previous text field's background turns white again.

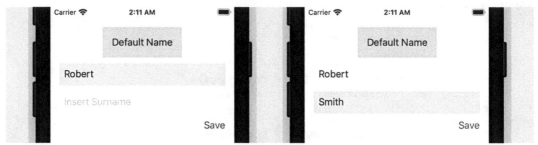

Figure 8-7: *Editing states*

In the last example, we didn't check whether the properties contain a value or not, but usually the application has to prevent the user from saving invalid or empty values. There are different ways we can control this. One alternative is to check the values before storing them. We let the users type whatever they want but only store the values that we consider valid.

```
Button("Save") {
    let tempName = self.contentData.nameInput.trimmingCharacters(in:
.whitespaces)
    let tempSurname = self.contentData.surnameInput.trimmingCharacters(in:
.whitespaces)

    if !tempName.isEmpty && !tempSurname.isEmpty {
        self.contentData.title = tempName + " " + tempSurname
        self.contentData.colorName = self.colors[0]
        self.contentData.colorSurname = self.colors[0]
    }
}
```

Listing 8-9: *Checking the values before storing*

In this example, we first trim the **nameInput** and **surnameInput** properties to remove spaces at the beginning or the end (see Strings in Chapter 4) and then check that the resulting values are not empty before storing them in the **title** property. The Save button is still enabled, but the values are not stored until the user inserts a text in both fields.

 Do It Yourself: Replace the **Button** view of the example in Listing 8-8 with the **Button** view of Listing 8-9. You shouldn't be able to modify the title until you have inserted a name and a surname.

Another alternative is to disable the button with the **disabled()** modifier if the values inserted by the user are not what the application is expecting.

Chapter 8 - Controls

```
Button("Save") {
    let tempName = self.contentData.nameInput.trimmingCharacters(in:
.whitespaces)
    let tempSurname = self.contentData.surnameInput.trimmingCharacters(in:
.whitespaces)

    if !tempName.isEmpty && !tempSurname.isEmpty {
        self.contentData.title = tempName + " " + tempSurname
        self.contentData.colorName = self.colors[0]
        self.contentData.colorSurname = self.colors[0]
    }
}.disabled(contentData.nameInput.isEmpty ||
contentData.surnameInput.isEmpty)
```

Listing 8-10: Disabling the button

In this example, we implement the `disabled()` modifier introduced before to disable the button until the user types a text in both fields. If one text field or both are empty, the button doesn't work.

 Do It Yourself: Replace the `Button` view of the previous example with the `Button` view of Listing 8-10. You shouldn't be able to press the Save button until you have inserted a name and a surname.

Besides checking whether the properties contain a valid value, we can also limit what the user can type on the fields. For instance, we could only accept numbers or a specific amount of characters. This is easy to achieve when we work with an observable object and `@Published` properties. All we have to do is to add the `didSet` property observer to the properties we want to control (see Listing 3-45). If the new value is not valid, we can assign the old value back to the property.

```
class ContentViewData: ObservableObject {
    @Published var title: String = "Default Name"
    @Published var nameInput: String = "" {
        didSet {
            if nameInput.count > 10 {
                nameInput = oldValue
            }
        }
    }
    @Published var surnameInput: String = "" {
        didSet {
            if surnameInput.count > 15 {
                surnameInput = oldValue
            }
        }
    }
    @Published var colorName: Color = Color.white
    @Published var colorSurname: Color = Color.white
}
```

Listing 8-11: Controlling user's input

The code of Listing 8-11 defines a new observable object for our example. A `didSet` observer was added to the `nameInput` and the `surnameInput` properties to control their values. When the user types or deletes a character in an input field, the `didSet` observer is executed and we can process the value. In the `didSet` observer assigned to the `nameInput` property, we check whether the new value has more than 10 characters. If it does, we assign the old value to the property, limiting the number of characters the user can insert to 10. We do something similar to the `surnameInput` property, but the limit this time is 15 characters. As a result, the user can type up to 10 character for the name and 15 characters for the surname.

 Do It Yourself: Update the `ContentViewData` structure from the previous example with the code of Listing 8-11. Run the application. Type characters in the fields. You shouldn't be able to type more than 10 characters for the name and 15 characters for the surname.

Of course, besides the number of characters we can establish other conditions. The following example only accepts integer numbers for the name.

```
class ContentViewData: ObservableObject {
    @Published var title: String = "Default Name"
    @Published var nameInput: String = "" {
        didSet {
            if Int(nameInput) == nil && oldValue.count <= nameInput.count {
                nameInput = oldValue
            }
        }
    }
    @Published var surnameInput: String = ""
    @Published var colorName: Color = Color.white
    @Published var colorSurname: Color = Color.white
}
```

Listing 8-12: Accepting only integer numbers

The `didSet` observer applied to the `nameInput` property in Listing 8-12 tries to cast the current value into an integer with the `Int()` initializer. If the value returned by the initializer is `nil`, it means that the value is not a number, so we assign the old value to the property. Notice that If the user erases the characters, when the last character is removed, the value of the `nameInput` property is an empty string and therefore the `Int()` initializer returns `nil`. This means that the last character will be assigned back to the property and therefore the user won't be able to erase it. To solve this issue, we also check that the number of characters in the `oldValue` constant is less or equal than the number of characters in the property before assigning the old value to the property.

 Do It Yourself: Update the `ContentViewData` structure from the previous example with the code of Listing 8-12. Run the application. You should only be able to type numbers for the name.

When we filter the values like this, it is a good idea to guide the user by providing the appropriate keyboard. The `TextField` view defines the `keyboardType()` modifier for this purpose. In the following example, we define the keyboard of the first `TextField` view as `numberPad`, so the user can only see numbers.

```
TextField("Insert Name", text: $contentData.nameInput, onEditingChanged:
{ self.contentData.colorName = $0 ? self.colors[1] : self.colors[0] })
    .padding(8)
    .background(contentData.colorName)
    .keyboardType(.numberPad)
```

Listing 8-13: Configuring the keyboard

Chapter 8 - Controls

Do It Yourself: Replace the first `TextField` view in your `ContentView` structure with the `TextField` view of Listing 8-13 and run the application on the simulator or a device. Tap on a text field. You should see the number pad keyboard on the screen. If you are in the simulator and the keyboard doesn't appear, remember to deactivate the Connect Hardware Keyboard option from the Hardware menu.

(Basic) SecureField View

SwiftUI also includes a view to create a secure text field. The view replaces the characters inserted by the user with dots to hide the text. The structure includes the following initializer.

SecureField(String, **text:** Binding, **onCommit:** Closure**)**—This initializer creates a secure input field. The first attribute defines the text field's placeholder, the **text** attribute is a `Binding` property that stores the value inserted by the user, and the **onCommit** attribute is a closure that is executed when the user presses the Done (Return) key.

The implementation is the same as with `TextField` views, and we can also apply some of the modifiers available for text fields.

```
import SwiftUI
struct ContentView: View {
   @State private var title: String = ""

   var body: some View {
      VStack(spacing: 15) {
         Text(title)
             lineLimit(1)
            .padding()
         SecureField("Insert Title", text: $title)
            .textFieldStyle(RoundedBorderTextFieldStyle())
         Spacer()
      }.padding()
   }
}
```

Listing 8-14: Using a secure text field

The `SecureField` view looks the same as the `TextField` view. The only difference is that the characters are hidden.

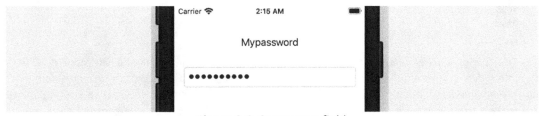

Figure 8-8: Secure text field

 Do It Yourself: Create a SwiftUI project and update the `ContentView` structure with the code of Listing 8-14. Press the Live Preview button and insert characters in the input field. You should see the characters being replaced by black dots, as illustrated in Figure 8-8. Use this project to test the rest of the examples in this chapter.

Toggle View

The `Toggle` view creates a control to switch between two states. In mobile devices it is presented as a switch the user can turn on and off, and in a computer, it is shown as a checkbox. The view includes the following initializers.

Toggle(String, isOn: Binding)—This initializer creates a `Toggle` view. The first attribute defines the control's label, and the **isOn** attribute is the `Binding` property that stores the current state.

Toggle(isOn: Binding, label: Closure)—This initializer creates a `Toggle` view. The **isOn** attribute is a `Binding` property that stores the current state, and the **label** attribute is a closure that returns a view or a group of views to show as the control's label.

The view requires a `Binding` property to store the current value. In the following example, we provide a `@State` property for this purpose and use the value of this property to select the proper label.

```
import SwiftUI

struct ContentView: View {
   @State private var currentState: Bool = true

   var body: some View {
      VStack {
         Toggle(isOn: $currentState, label: {
            Text(currentState ? "On" : "Off")
         })
         Spacer()
      }.padding()
   }
}
```

Listing 8-15: Using a `Toggle`

The code of Listing 8-15 uses a ternary operator to check the value of the `currentState` property and display the corresponding text ("On" or "Off"). By default, we set the value of the property to `true`, so the switch is activated and the "On" label is displayed on the screen, but if we touch the switch, it is turned off, the view is updated, and the "Off" label is shown instead.

Figure 8-9: Switch on and off

The `Toggle` view creates a horizontal stack to contain the label and the control with a flexible space in between, so by default, the view occupies all the horizontal space available in its container and the label and the control are displaced to the sides. If we want to have absolute control on the position and size of the view, we can apply the `fixedSize()` modifier to reduce the view to its ideal size or hide the label with the `labelsHidden()` modifier.

```
import SwiftUI

struct ContentView: View {
   @State private var currentState: Bool = true
```

Chapter 8 - Controls

```
var body: some View {
    HStack {
        Toggle("", isOn: $currentState)
            .labelsHidden()
        Text(currentState ? "On" : "Off")
            .padding()
            .background(Color(currentState ? .yellow : .gray))
    }.padding()
    }
}
```

Listing 8-16: Defining a custom label for the Toggle *view*

In this example, we apply the **labelsHidden()** modifier to the switch. The view is now of the size of the control and centered on the screen. The label is not shown anymore, so an empty string is enough, but we include a **Text** view on the side to display the current value.

Figure 8-10: Custom size and label for the switch

Like **Button** views, **Toggle** views also implement a modifier to define the style of the control.

toggleStyle(ToggleStyle**)**—This modifier defines the style of the toggle. The attribute is a structure that conforms to the **ToggleStyle** protocol.

As with the **ButtonStyle** protocol for buttons, there are some system-designed structures that conform to the **ToggleStyle** protocol and provide options for styling, such as **DefaultToggleStyle** (default) and **SwitchToggleStyle**, but they are not very useful. To create our own style, we must define a custom structure. The protocol's only requirement is for the structure to implement the following method.

makeBody(configuration: Configuration**)**—This method defines and returns a view that replaces the body of the toggle. The **configuration** attribute is a value of type **Configuration** that contains information about the control.

This method receives a value of type **Configuration**, a typealias of **ToggleStyleConfiguration**, which contains properties that return information about the control. The following are the properties available.

isOn—This property returns a Boolean value that indicates whether the toggle is on or off.

label—This property returns the view that defines the toggle's current label.

The **isOn** property is a **@Binding** property that creates a bidirectional binding with the view and therefore we can read and modify its value to activate or deactivate the control. In the following example, we create a **Toggle** view that looks like a checkbox. When the control is tapped, the graphic changes color indicating the current state (gray deactivated and green activated).

```
import SwiftUI

struct MyStyle: ToggleStyle {
    func makeBody(configuration: MyStyle.Configuration) -> some View {
```

```
            HStack(alignment: .center) {
                configuration.label
                Spacer()
                Image(systemName: "checkmark.rectangle.fill")
                    .font(.largeTitle)
                    .foregroundColor(configuration.isOn ? Color.green : Color.gray)
                    .onTapGesture {
                        configuration.$isOn.wrappedValue.toggle()
                    }
            }
        }
    }
}
struct ContentView: View {
    @State private var currentState: Bool = false

    var body: some View {
        VStack {
            HStack {
                Toggle("Enabled", isOn: $currentState)
                    .toggleStyle(MyStyle())
            }
            Spacer()
        }.padding()
    }
}
```

Listing 8-17: Defining a custom `Toggle` *view*

There are a few things we must consider before customizing a `Toggle` view. First, the `label` property of the `Configuration` structure contains a copy of the view that represents the control's current label, so if we want to keep this label, we must include the value of this property in the new content. Second, a `Toggle` view is designed with an `HStack` view and a `Spacer` view between the label and the control. If we want to stick to the standard design, we must preserve this arrangement. And third, we are responsible of responding to user interaction and update the state of the control, so we must check for a gesture and change the control's state by modifying the value of the `isOn` property when the gesture is performed by the user.

In the example of Listing 8-17, we define a structure called `MyStyle` and implement the required `makeBody()` method to provide the new design for the `Toggle` view. To preserve the standard design, we wrap the views with an `HStack` view and separate the label and the control with a `Spacer` view. We first read the value of the `label` property to include the current label, then declare the `Spacer` view, and finally define an `Image` view that presents an SF Symbol that looks like a checkbox. To turn this `Image` view into a control, we apply a few modifiers. First, we define its size with a `font()` modifier. Next, we apply the `foregroundColor()` modifier to change the color of the symbol depending on the current value of the `isOn` property. And finally, we use the `onTapGesture()` modifier to detect when the user taps on the `Image` view. We will learn more about gesture modifiers in Chapter 12. For now, all we need to now is that this modifier adds a gesture recognizer to the view and executes a closure every time the view is tapped. In the closure, we access the `Binding` value of the `isOn` property and toggle its value by applying the `toggle()` modifier to the Boolean value stored in its `wrappedValue` property. This modifies the current value, which changes the state of the control, turning it on and off. The result is shown in Figure 8-11.

Figure 8-11: Custom styles for the `Toggle` *view*

Do It Yourself: Update the ContentView.swift file with the code of Listing 8-17. Activate the live preview and click on the checkbox. You should see the symbol changing colors, as show in Figure 8-11.

(Basic) **Slider View**

A `Slider` view creates a control that allows the user to select a value from a range of values. It is displayed as a horizontal bar with a knob that indicates the selected value. The structure includes the following initializer.

> **Slider(value:** Binding, **in:** Range, **step:** Float, **onEditingChanged:** Closure**)**—This initializer creates a `Slider` view. The **value** attribute is the `Binding` property we want to use to store the current value, the **in** attribute is a range that specifies the minimum and maximum values the user can choose from, the **step** attribute indicates the number by which the current value will be increased or decreased, and the **onEditingChanged** attribute is a closure that is executed when the user starts or finishes moving the slider.

To create a slider, we must provide at least a `@State` property to store the value and a range to determine the minimum and maximum values.

```
import SwiftUI

struct ContentView: View {
    @State private var currentValue: Float = 5

    var body: some View {
        VStack {
            Text("Current Value: \(currentValue)")
            Slider(value: $currentValue, in: 0...10)
            Spacer()
        }.padding()
    }
}
```

Listing 8-18: Creating a slider

The code of Listing 8-18 creates a slider from the value 0 to 10 and displays the current value with a `Text` view. Because we initialize the `currentValue` property with the number 5, the knob of the slider is positioned in the middle.

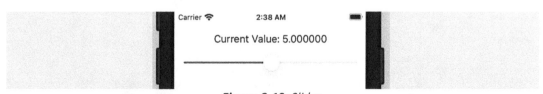

Carrier 🗼   2:38 AM   🔋

Current Value: 5.000000

Figure 8-12: Slider

The `Slider` view takes values of type `Float` or `Double`, and therefore it allows us to select a floating-point value. If we want to work with integers, we can specify a step of 1.0.

```
import SwiftUI

struct ContentView: View {
    @State private var currentValue: Float = 5
```

```
var body: some View {
    VStack {
        Text("Current Value: \(currentValue, specifier: "%.0f")")
        Slider(value: $currentValue, in: 0...10, step: 1.0)
        Spacer()
    }.padding()
}
}
```

Listing 8-19: Creating a slider to select an integer value

In the example of Listing 8-19 we specify a step of 1.0 for the slider and format the current value with a specifier to remove all the digits after the decimal point (see Listing 6-4). Now, the knob doesn't slide smoothly, it jumps from one position to another by 1 point, and the current value is displayed on the screen without the decimal digits.

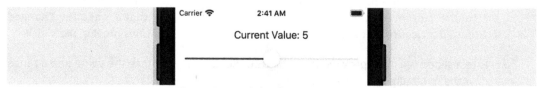

Figure 8-13: Slider for integer values

The **Slider** view's initializer also includes the **onEditingChanged** attribute. We have seen this attribute before in **TextField** views. The attribute takes a closure that receives a Boolean value to indicate whether the user begins or finishes moving the slider. We can use it to highlight the value that is been edited, as in the following example.

```
import SwiftUI

struct ContentView: View {
    @State private var currentValue: Float = 5
    @State private var textActive: Bool = false

    var body: some View {
        VStack {
            Text("Current Value: \(currentValue, specifier: "%.0f")")
                .padding()
                .background(textActive ? Color.yellow : Color.clear)
            Slider(value: $currentValue, in: 0...10, step: 1.0,
onEditingChanged: { self.textActive = $0 })
            Spacer()
        }.padding()
    }
}
```

Listing 8-20: Responding to the slider state

Listing 8-20 includes a new **@State** property called **textActive**. The closure assigned to the **onEditingChanged** attribute assigns the value **true** to this property when the user begins moving the slider and the value **false** when the user let the knob go. The **background()** modifier of the **Text** view reads the value of this property to assign a different background color to the view depending on the current state. Because of this, the text that displays the slider's current value has a yellow background while the user is moving the slider, or no color otherwise.

Chapter 8 - Controls

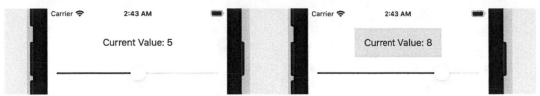

Figure 8-14: Slider states

(Basic) Stepper View

The `Stepper` view creates a control with two buttons that allow us to increase or decrease a value. The structure provides multiple initializer with several combinations of attributes for configuration. The following are the most frequently used.

Stepper(String, **value:** Binding, **in:** Range, **step:** Float)—This initializer creates a `Stepper` view. The first attribute defines the control's label, the **value** attribute is the `Binding` property we want to use to store the current value, the **in** attribute is a range that determines the minimum and maximum values allowed, and the **step** attribute is a `Float` or a `Double` (depending on the `Binding` value) that determines the amount by which the value is going to be increased or decreased.

Stepper(String, **onIncrement:** Closure?, **onDecrement:** Closure?)—This initializer creates a `Stepper` view. The first attribute defines the control's label, the **onIncrement** attribute is a closure that is executed when the user taps on the + button, and the **onDecrement** attribute is a closure that is executed when the user taps on the - button.

To implement a `Stepper` view, we need a `@State` property to store the current value and define the range of values we want the user to choose from.

```swift
import SwiftUI

struct ContentView: View {
    @State private var currentValue: Float = 0

    var body: some View {
        VStack {
            Text("Current Value: \(currentValue, specifier: "%.0f")")
            Stepper("Counter", value: $currentValue, in: 0...100)
            Spacer()
        }.padding()
    }
}
```

Listing 8-21: Creating a stepper

The `Stepper` view works with floating-point values of type `Float` or `Double`, so we must use a specifier again to remove the digits after the decimal point (`%.0f`).

Figure 8-15: Stepper

By default, the value is increased or decreased by one unit, but we can change that with the **step** attribute. The following example defines a `Stepper` view that increases or decreases the value by 5 units.

Chapter 8 - Controls

```
import SwiftUI

struct ContentView: View {
    @State private var currentValue: Double = 0

    var body: some View {
        VStack {
            Text("Current Value: \(currentValue, specifier: "%.0f")")
            Stepper("Counter", value: $currentValue, in: 0...100, step: 5)
            Spacer()
        }.padding()
    }
}
```

Listing 8-22: Defining the steps of a stepper

Like the `Toggle` view, the `Stepper` view is implemented with a horizontal stack and a flexible space between the label and the control. If we want to provide our own label and define a custom position for the control, we have to apply the `labelsHidden()` modifier, as we did in Listing 8-16. The following example defines a custom label and creates the view with the **onIncrement** and **onDecrement** attributes to display an arrow on the screen that tells the user whether the last value was increased or decreased.

```
import SwiftUI

struct ContentView: View {
    @State private var currentValue: Float = 0
    @State private var goingUp: Bool = true

    var body: some View {
        VStack {
            HStack {
                Text("\(currentValue, specifier: "%.0f")")
                Text(goingUp ? "↑" : "↓")
                    .foregroundColor(goingUp ? Color.green : Color.red)
                Stepper("", onIncrement: {
                    self.currentValue += 5
                    self.goingUp = true
                }, onDecrement: {
                    self.currentValue -= 5
                    self.goingUp = false
                }).labelsHidden()
            }
            Spacer()
        }.padding()
    }
}
```

Listing 8-23: Modifying the interface when the value is increased or decreased

In the example of Listing 8-23, we define two `@State` properties: `currentValue` to store the current value of the stepper, and a Boolean property called `goingUp` to indicate whether the last value was increased or decreased. The views are included in an `HStack` to show them side by side. The first one is the same `Text` view we used before to display the stepper's current value. After this view, we include a second `Text` view that checks the `goingUp` property to show an arrow pointing up or down, depending on the property's value. The same property is used to determine the color of the arrows. Finally, we define the `Stepper` view with the **onIncrement** and **onDecrement** attributes. In the closures assigned to these attributes, we increase or

Chapter 8 - Controls

decrease the value by 5 and change the value of the `goingUp` property to indicate whether the last value was increased or decreased. As a result, the user can see a green arrow pointing up when the + button is pressed and a red arrow pointing down when the - button is pressed.

Figure 8-16: Custom stepper

 Do It Yourself: Update the `ContentView` structure with the code of Listing 8-23. To insert the arrows, open the emojis selector by pressing the keys Control, Command and Space at the same time (see Figure 2-9). Press the Live Preview button and click on the stepper's buttons. You should see the values go up and down and the arrows change color.

Chapter 8 - Controls

Chapter 9
Navigation

Basic **9.1 Multiple Views**

Apps that only require one view and a simple interface are hard to find. Due to the small size of the screen, developing apps for mobile devices demands the creation of multiple views to represent virtual screens that replace one another in response to the user or the system. Practical applications contain several views connected with each other in a predetermined path that users can follow to navigate throughout the content. Figure 9-1 illustrates how these views work together to expand the interface.

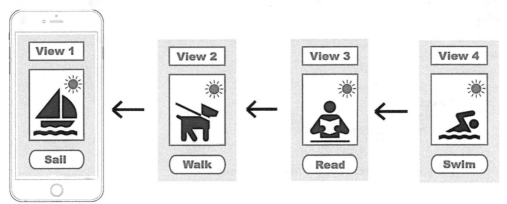

Figure 9-1: Multiple views to expand the interface

Basic **NavigationView View**

The SwiftUI template generated by Xcode includes the initial view, but we are responsible for creating the rest. The definition of these additional views is always the same. We must declare a structure that conforms to the **View** protocol and implement the **body** property. But there are different ways to present these views to the user. The mechanism recommended by Apple introduces the views by moving them from right to left, as illustrated in Figure 9-1. If the user wants to go back to the previous view, the current view is removed with a transition in the opposite direction. To create this navigation system, SwiftUI defines the **NavigationView** structure. The following is the structure's initializer.

NavigationView(content: Closure)—This initializer creates a **NavigationView** view. The **content** attribute is a closure that contains the initial view of the navigation hierarchy.

A **NavigationView** view incorporates a bar at the top of the interface to provide tools for navigation. The following are the modifiers defined by the **View** protocol to configure this bar.

navigationBarTitle(String, **displayMode:** TitleDisplayMode)—This modifier assigns a title to the view. The title is displayed in the navigation bar with a format that depends on the display mode. The first attribute is a string with the title we want to assign to the view, and the **displayMode** attribute is an enumeration that defines the mode for the title. The values available are **automatic** (the same mode as the previous view), **inline** (adapts to the normal size of the bar), and **large** (expands the bar to show a large title).

navigationBarItems(leading: View, **trailing:** View)—This modifier adds items to the navigation bar. The **leading** attribute defines the view that is displayed on the leading side of the bar (the left side in English), and the **trailing** attribute defines the view that is displayed on the trailing side of the bar (the right side in English).

navigationBarBackButtonHidden(Bool)—This modifier hides the Back button that is automatically generated by the `NavigationView` view.

navigationBarHidden(Bool)—This modifier shows or hides the navigation bar.

statusBar(hidden: Bool)—This modifier hides the status bar for all the views in the navigation hierarchy. The **hidden** attribute determines if the status bar is hidden or not.

A `NavigationView` view creates a hierarchy of views. Therefore, the first step we need to take to create this navigation hierarchy is to define the hierarchy's initial view and embed it in a `NavigationView` view. In our examples, this is the `ContentView` view created by the template.

```
import SwiftUI

struct ContentView: View {
    var body: some View {
        NavigationView {
            VStack {
                Text("Hello World")
                Spacer()
            }.padding()
            .navigationBarTitle("Home Screen")
        }
    }
}
```

Listing 9-1: Initiating a navigation hierarchy

The code of Listing 9-1 creates a `VStack` with a `Text` view that shows the message "Hello World". This is the initial view of our navigation hierarchy, so we embed it in a `NavigationView` view and give it the title "Home Screen".

Notice that the `navigationBarTitle()` modifier is applied to the `VStack`, not to the `NavigationView` view. This is because we only must declare the `NavigationView` view for the initial view, the rest of the views are not declared inside a `NavigationView`, they are implicitly considered to be part of the navigation hierarchy, so the modifiers are always applied directly to them.

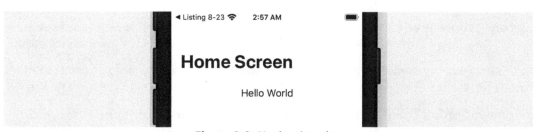

Figure 9-2: Navigation view

 Do It Yourself: Create a SwiftUI project and update the `ContentView` structure with the code of Listing 9-1. Activate the live preview in the canvas. You should see the interface in Figure 9-2. Use this project to test the following examples.

The size of the navigation bar created by the `NavigationView` view depends on the title mode. By default, the mode is defined as **automatic** and therefore all the views in the navigation hierarchy show a large title (Figure 9-2), but we can change that by assigning the **inline** mode instead.

```
import SwiftUI

struct ContentView: View {
    var body: some View {
        NavigationView {
            VStack {
                Text("Hello World")
                Spacer()
            }.padding()
            .navigationBarTitle("Home Screen", displayMode: .inline)
        }
    }
}
```

Listing 9-2: Setting the title mode

Now the title is shown in a standard size and with a predefined style, and all the views in the hierarchy will inherit this mode.

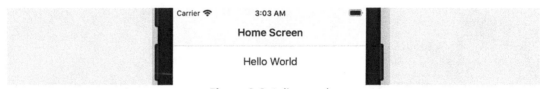

Figure 9-3: Inline mode

The `NavigationView` structure also includes the `statusBar()` modifier to hide the status bar. Because the modifier affects the system, not the `NavigationView` view, it must be applied to the `NavigationView` itself.

```
import SwiftUI

struct ContentView: View {
    var body: some View {
        NavigationView {
            VStack {
                Text("Hello World")
                Spacer()
            }.padding()
            .navigationBarTitle("Home Screen")
        }.statusBar(hidden: true)
    }
}
```

Listing 9-3: Hiding the status bar

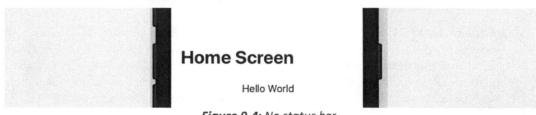

Figure 9-4: No status bar

Besides the title, the navigation bar can include other elements. The `NavigationView` structure implements the `navigationBarItems()` modifier for this purpose. The modifier includes two attributes, one to define the elements on the left (`leading`) and another to define the elements on the right (`trailing`). The modifier can be declared only once, so if we want to include buttons on the left and right, we must declare both attributes in the same modifier. The following example shows how to add a button to the right side of the bar.

```
import SwiftUI
struct ContentView: View {
    @State private var setColor: Bool = true

    var body: some View {
        NavigationView {
            VStack {
                Text("Hello World")
                    .foregroundColor(setColor ? Color.black : Color.green)
                Spacer()
            }.padding()
            .navigationBarTitle("Home Screen")
            .navigationBarItems(trailing: Button("Change Color") {
                self.setColor.toggle()
            })
        }
    }
}
```

Listing 9-4: Adding buttons to the navigation bar

The view defines a `@State` property of type `Bool` called `setColor` to determine the color of the text, and then adds a `Button` view to the navigation bar that toggles the value of this property. If the button is pressed, the value of the property changes and therefore the text is shown in a different color.

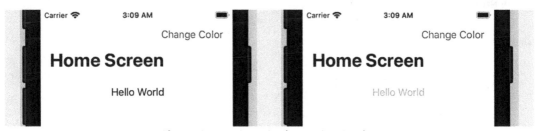

Figure 9-5: Buttons in the navigation bar

Basic **NavigationLink View**

There is no view hierarchy if we only have one view. To allow the user to open additional views, SwiftUI defines the `NavigationLink` view. This is a control view that creates a button the user can press to open another view. The following are the structure's initializers.

NavigationLink(String, destination: View)—This initializer creates a `NavigationLink` view. The first attribute is the text we want to assign to the button's label, and the **destination** attribute is the view we want to open when the button is pressed. If we want to define a complex label for the button, we can use the initializer `NavigationLink(destination: Destination, label: Closure)` instead.

Chapter 9 - Navigation

NavigationLink(String, **destination:** View, **isActive:** Binding)—This initializer creates a `NavigationLink` view. The first attribute is the text we want to assign to the button's label, the **destination** attribute is the view we want to open when the button is pressed, and the **isActive** attribute is a `Binding` property of type `Bool` that allows us to control whether the view opened by the button remains open or not. If we want to define a complex label for the button, we can use the initializer `NavigationLink(destination: View, isActive: Binding, label: Closure)` instead.

NavigationLink(String, **destination:** View, **tag:** Value, **selection:** Binding)—This initializer creates a `NavigationLink` view. The first attribute is the text we want to assign to the button's label, the **destination** attribute is the view we want to open when the button is pressed, the **tag** attribute is a value that identifies the button, and the **selection** attribute is an optional `Binding` property of the same type as the value assigned to the **tag** attribute that allows us to control whether the view opened by the button remains open or not (the property receives the same value assigned to the tag). If we want to define a complex label for the button, we can use the initializer `NavigationLink(destination: View, tag: Value, selection: Binding, label: Closure)` instead.

The following example includes a `NavigationLink` view to provide a button for the user to open another view called `SecondView`.

```
import SwiftUI
struct ContentView: View {
    var body: some View {
        NavigationView {
            VStack(spacing: 15) {
                Text("Hello World")
                NavigationLink("Show Second Screen", destination:
SecondView())
                Spacer()
            }.padding()
            .navigationBarTitle("Home Screen")
        }
    }
}
```

Listing 9-5: Including a navigation link

Now, we must define the `SecondView` view that is going to be opened when the user presses the button. When a view represents an entire screen, as in this case, it is recommendable to define it in a separate file. We called this file SecondView.swift.

```
import SwiftUI
struct SecondView: View {
    var body: some View {
        VStack(spacing: 5) {
            Text("This is the content of the")
            Text("second screen")
            Spacer()
        }.padding()
        .navigationBarTitle("Second Screen")
    }
}
```

```
struct SecondView_Previews: PreviewProvider {
    static var previews: some View {
        NavigationView {
            SecondView()
        }
    }
}
```

Listing 9-6: Defining the second view (screen)

The `SecondView` view defined in Listing 9-6 includes two `Text` views to show a message at the top of the screen. This view is opened from the `ContentView` view and therefore it is part of its hierarchy, so we don't have to embed it in a `NavigationView` view, but we have to declare its title with the `navigationBarTitle()` modifier, as we did for the initial view. We call this one "Second Screen".

When the user taps the button in the `ContentView` view, an instance of the `SecondView` view is created and presented on the screen transitioning from right to left. The result is shown in Figure 9-6.

Figure 9-6: Initial and second screen

 Do It Yourself: Update the `ContentView` structure with the code of Listing 9-5. Press Command + N or select the options New/File from the File menu to create a new file. Click on the SwiftUI icon to create a SwiftUI file. Assign the name SecondView.swift to the file. Update the code created by the template with the code of Listing 9-6. Select the ContentView.swift file again and activate the live preview in the canvas. You should see the interface on the left side of Figure 9-6. Click on the Show Second Screen button. The interface should transition to the second view shown on the right side of Figure 9-6. At the time of writing, `NavigationLink` views do not work property on the canvas or the simulator. If you find any issues, we recommend you run this examples on a device, as explained in Chapter 5 (see Figure 5-8).

 IMPORTANT: The views defined by the `SecondView` structure of Listing 9-6 are not embedded in a `NavigationView` view because the `SecondView` view is opened from the `ContentView` view and therefore it is already part of a navigation hierarchy, but the instance of this view created for the preview is not part of that hierarchy and therefore if we want to see on the canvas what this view is going to look like when it is presented to the user, we have to embed it in a `NavigationView` view, as we did in this example.

The view opened by a `NavigationLink` view includes a button in the navigation bar that the user can tap to go back to the previous view. This button is automatically generated by SwiftUI and it is part of the basic tools provided for navigation. In the example of Figure 9-6, the button was named "Back", but this label changes according to the title of the previous view. If the title is short enough, it is assigned to the button's label, but if it is too long, the text "Back" is shown instead. For instance, if we change the title of the `ContentView` view of Listing 9-5 to "Home", the button will read "Home" instead of "Back". This helps the user identify the view that is going to appear on the screen if the button is pressed. But that is about all the configuration options we have for this button. If we need something different, we must remove the back button and create our own.

The `NavigationView` structure defines the `navigationBarBackButtonHidden()` modifier to remove the back button. Once we hide this button, we must provide our own to remove the view. One way of removing the view is by modifying the state of the presentation from the environment. For this purpose, the environment includes the following property.

> **presentationMode**—This property returns a `Binding` value with a `PresentationMode` structure, which includes a Boolean property called `isPresented` that determines whether the view is being presented or not, and a method called `dismiss()` that we can call to dismiss the view.

We have worked with properties from the environment before (see Listing 7-12). All we have to do is to add an `@Environment` property to the view and then read or modify its values. The `presentationMode` property is a `Binding` structure that in turn stores another structure of type `PresentationMode` that includes the method `dismiss()` to remove the view. This structure is accessible from the `wrappedValue` property of the `Binding` structure, as shown next.

```
import SwiftUI

struct SecondView. View {
    @Environment(\.presentationMode) var presentation

    var body: some View {
        VStack(spacing: 5) {
            Text("This is the content of the")
            Text("second screen")
            Spacer()
        }.padding()
        .navigationBarTitle("Second Screen")
        .navigationBarBackButtonHidden(true)
        .navigationBarItems(leading: Button("Go Back") {
            self.presentation.wrappedValue.dismiss()
        })
    }
}
```

Listing 9-7: Dismissing the view from the environment

The `SecondView` in Listing 9-7 defines a property called `presentation` that is connected to the `presentationMode` property in the environment. Using this reference, we can create a button to dismiss the view. First, we apply the `navigationBarBackButtonHidden()` modifier with the value `true` to remove the Back button included by default. After this, we add a new button with the `navigationBarItems()` modifier. This modifier can take one or two attributes to define buttons for the left or the right side of the navigation bar. In this case, we assign the new button to the **leading** attribute to place our back button on the left. The button is created with the "Go Back" label and an action that calls the `dismiss()` method offered by the `presentationMode` value to remove the view. If the button is pressed, the method is executed, and the view is removed as before.

Figure 9-7: Custom back button

Do It Yourself: Update the `SecondView` structure in the SecondView.swift file with the code of Listing 9-7. Select the ContentView.swift file and activate the live preview on the canvas. Press the button to open the `SecondView` view and then press the Go Back button to go back. You should see the interface in Figure 9-7. Remember to test these projects on a device if you find any issues with the navigation.

Although we can dismiss any view with the environment's `presentationMode` property, the `NavigationLink` view provides its own tools to dismiss a view. One alternative is to define a `@State` property to control the state of the view and initialize the `NavigationLink` with it. When the navigation button is pressed, the system assigns the value `true` to this property and the view is presented on the screen. Later, when we want to close the view, all we have to do is to assign the value `false` to it and the view is removed. The following is the code we need for the `ContentView` structure.

```
import SwiftUI

struct ContentView: View {
    @State private var activeLink: Bool = false

    var body: some View {
        NavigationView {
            VStack(spacing: 15) {
                Text("Hello World")
                NavigationLink("Show Second Screen", destination:
SecondView(active: $activeLink), isActive: $activeLink)
                Spacer()
            }.padding()
            .navigationBarTitle("Home Screen")
        }
    }
}
```

Listing 9-8: Controlling the state of the view opened by a navigation link

In the code of Listing 9-8, we introduce a new `@State` property called `activeLink` to control the state of the view opened by the `NavigationLink` button (`true` means that the view must be shown, `false` that the view must be removed). The `activeLink` property must be assigned to the **isActive** attribute of the `NavigationLink` initializer, so the system knows where to get the current state of the view, and also it must be passed to the `SecondView` structure, so we can change its value to `false` and close the view when necessary. This means that the `SecondView` structure must include a **@Binding** property to receive this value.

```
import SwiftUI

struct SecondView: View {
   @Binding var active: Bool

   var body: some View {
      VStack(spacing: 5) {
         Text("This is the content of the")
         Text("second screen")
         Spacer()
      }.padding()
      .navigationBarTitle("Second Screen")
      .navigationBarBackButtonHidden(true)
      .navigationBarItems(leading: Button("Go Back") {
         self.active = false
      })
   }
}
struct SecondView_Previews: PreviewProvider {
   static var previews: some View {
      NavigationView {
         SecondView(active: .constant(true))
      }
   }
}
```

Listing 9-9: *Dismissing the view by modifying a state*

The view of Listing 9-9 includes a `@Binding` property called `active` that creates a bidirectional binding with the `activeLink` property of the `ContentView` structure. We need this bidirectional binding to close the view. For this purpose, we remove the Back button again with the `navigationBarBackButtonHidden()` modifier and create our own, as we did in the previous example. The process is the same, but instead of calling the `dismiss()` method on the `presentationMode` value, we assign the value `false` to the `active` property. This changes the value of the `activeLink` property of the `ContentView` structure to `false`, which deactivates the navigation link and in consequence the `SecondView` view is removed.

 Do It Yourself: Update the `ContentView` structure with the code of Listing 9-8 and the content of the SecondView.swift file with the code of Listing 9-9. Select the ContentView.swift file and activate the live preview. You should see the interface in Figure 9-7. Click the buttons to open and close the second view.

Navigation links can be activated from other parts of the code, including control views. All we have to do is to assign the value `true` to the `@State` property that controls the link, as in the following example.

```
import SwiftUI

struct ContentView: View {
   @State private var activeLink: Bool = false

   var body: some View {
      NavigationView {
         VStack(spacing: 15) {
            Text("Hello World")
            Button("Show Second Screen") {
               self.activeLink = true
            }
```

```
            NavigationLink(destination: SecondView(active: $activeLink),
isActive: $activeLink, label: {
                    EmptyView()
                })
                Spacer()
            }.padding()
            .navigationBarTitle("Home Screen")
        }
    }
}
```

Listing 9-10: Activating a navigation link programmatically

The view in Listing 9-10 includes a `Button` view and a `NavigationLink` view. An `EmptyView` view was assigned to the label of the `NavigationLink` view, so the view is not shown on the screen and doesn't take any space in the interface (see Listing 6-71). When the button is pressed, the value `true` is assigned to the `activeLink` property. In consequence, the navigation link is activated and the `SecondView` view is shown on the screen.

Of course, navigation links can also be added to the navigation bar, as any other button. The following example updates the `SecondView` view to add a navigation button on the right side of the bar to open a third view.

```
import SwiftUI

struct SecondView: View {
    @Binding var active: Bool

    var body: some View {
        VStack(spacing: 5) {
            Text("This is the content of the")
            Text("second screen")
            Spacer()
        }.padding()
        .navigationBarTitle("Second Screen")
        .navigationBarBackButtonHidden(true)
        .navigationBarItems(leading: Button("Go Back") {
            self.active = false
        }, trailing: NavigationLink(destination: ThirdView(), label: {
            Image(systemName: "plus.circle")
        }))
    }
}
struct SecondView_Previews: PreviewProvider {
    static var previews: some View {
        SecondView(active: .constant(false))
    }
}
```

Listing 9-11: Adding more views to the hierarchy

The code is the same as before, but we added the **trailing** attribute to the `navigationBarItems()` modifier to add a `NavigationLink` button on the right side of the navigation bar. For the label, we declare an `Image` view initialized with an SF Symbol called plus.circle (a + sign inside a circle), and the destination is a new view called `ThirdView`. We called this file ThirdView.swift.

Chapter 9 - Navigation

```
import SwiftUI

struct ThirdView: View {
    var body: some View {
        VStack(spacing: 5) {
            Text("This is the content of the")
            Text("third screen")
            Spacer()
        }.padding()
        .navigationBarTitle("Third Screen")
    }
}
struct ThirdView_Previews: PreviewProvider {
    static var previews: some View {
        NavigationView {
            ThirdView()
        }
    }
}
```

Listing 9-12: Including more views in the navigation hierarchy

Now, we have a total of three views that generate three screens for our application. The Home Screen created by the `ContentView` structure, the Second Screen, created by the `SecondView` structure, and the Third Screen, created by the `ThirdView` structure. When we tap the navigation button in the Home Screen, the Second Screen is opened, and when we tap the + button in the Second Screen, the Third Screen opens. Notice that the back button must be defined for each view, so the button for the Third Screen view is created with the label by default.

Figure 9-8: More views in the hierarchy

 Do It Yourself: Update the `SecondView` structure with the code of Listing 9-11. Create a new SwiftUI file called ThirdView.swift and update the code generated by the template with the code of Listing 9-12. Test the application on the canvas. You should be able to navigate to the Third Screen and back.

 IMPORTANT: At the time of writing, the `NavigationLink` view does not work properly when it is included in a navigation bar. If you find any issues, you can always add a regular button to the navigation bar with a `Button` view to activate the link and then include the `NavigationLink` view in the interface, as we did in the example in Listing 9-10.

In the last example, we added the navigation button to the right side of the navigation bar, but we can include a list of buttons on one side or the other. All we have to do is to define the buttons inside an `HStack` view, as in the following example.

```
import SwiftUI

struct SecondView: View {
    @Binding var active: Bool

    var body: some View {
        VStack(spacing: 5) {
            Text("This is the content of the")
            Text("second screen")
            Spacer()
        }.padding()
        .navigationBarTitle("Second Screen")
        .navigationBarBackButtonHidden(true)
        .navigationBarItems(leading:

        HStack {
            Button("Go Back") {
                self.active = false
            }
            Text("|")
            NavigationLink(destination: ThirdView(), label: {
                Text("Go Forward")
            })
        })
    }
}
struct SecondView_Previews: PreviewProvider {
    static var previews: some View {
        SecondView(active: .constant(false))
    }
}
```

Listing 9-13: Adding multiple buttons on one side of the navigation bar

The code of Listing 9-13 updates the `SecondView` of our example to create two buttons on the left side of the navigation bar. The view assigned to the **leading** attribute is an `HStack`, so we can include inside all the buttons and views we need. The first view is our custom back button, next there is a `Text` view with the string "|" to separate the buttons, and finally we include the navigation button to open the `ThirdView` view, but this time we assigned the text "Go Forward" to the label. The result is shown in Figure 9-9.

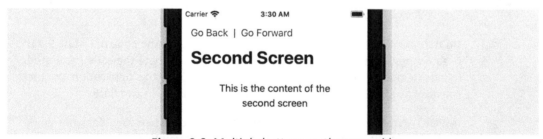

Figure 9-9: Multiple buttons on the same side

If we need to display two or more navigation buttons in the same view, we cannot use the same `@State` property for every navigation link because once we assign the value `true` to the property all the views are opened at once. Every navigation link requires its own `@State` property to manage its state. A better alternative is to assign a tag to identify the `NavigationLink` buttons and manage their states from a single optional property that stores this value. If the property contains a value different than `nil`, the view identified with that value is opened, and when the value `nil` is assigned to the property, the view is closed. To illustrate

Chapter 9 - Navigation

how this works, we are going to create an application that stores pictures and show the selected picture on the screen. The following is the model we need to store information about the pictures (Notice that we are going to access this model from the environment, so we also need the `AppDelegate` class of Listing 7-14 and the `SceneDelegate` class of Listing 7-20).

```
import SwiftUI

struct Picture {
   var image: String
   var rating: Double
}
struct PictureViewModel {
   var picture: Picture

   var rating: Int {
      return Int(picture.rating)
   }
}
class AppData: ObservableObject {
   @Published var userData: [PictureViewModel]

   init() {
      userData = [
         PictureViewModel(picture: Picture(image: "nopicture", rating:
0)),
         PictureViewModel(picture: Picture(image: "spot1", rating: 0)),
         PictureViewModel(picture: Picture(image: "spot2", rating: 0)),
         PictureViewModel(picture: Picture(image: "spot3", rating: 0))
      ]
   }
}
```

Listing 9-14: Defining the model for the pictures

The first structure defined in Listing 9-14, called `Picture`, is our model. This structure stores a string with the name of the image and a `Double` value with the rating assigned to the picture by the user. The next structure, called `PictureViewModel`, is the view model. This is the structure that prepares the information for the views. Here, we have a property called `picture` to store an instance of the `Picture` structure and a computed property called `rating` to return the picture's rating as an integer. Finally, we have the observable object we need to store the data and provide it to the view. The object defines a `@Published` property called `userData` to store an array with all the pictures available and a custom initializer to fill this array with initial data. This information is usually loaded from a database or the internet, but in this case we just create four permanent pictures, one called nopicture with an image to use as placeholder, and three more called spot1, spot2, and spot3 with pictures of landscapes (the files are available on our website).

Next, we must define the buttons in the initial view. The purpose of these buttons is to open a view that shows the picture corresponding to the button that was pressed.

```
import SwiftUI

struct ContentView: View {
   @State private var selectedLink: Int? = nil

   var body: some View {
      NavigationView {
         VStack(alignment: .leading, spacing: 15) {
```

```
            NavigationLink("🖼 Picture 1", destination:
DetailView(selected: 1), tag: 1, selection: $selectedLink)
            NavigationLink("🖼 Picture 2", destination:
DetailView(selected: 2), tag: 2, selection: $selectedLink)
            NavigationLink("🖼 Picture 3", destination:
DetailView(selected: 3), tag: 3, selection: $selectedLink)
               Spacer()
         }.padding()
         .frame(minWidth: 0, maxWidth: .infinity, alignment: .leading)
         .navigationBarTitle("Menu")
      }
   }
}
```

Listing 9-15: Managing multiple navigation buttons in one view

The **ContentView** view of Listing 9-15 defines three **NavigationLink** buttons. The first button is identified with the label "Picture 1" and the tag 1, the second button with the label "Picture 2" and the tag 2, and the third button with the label "Picture 3" and the tag 3. The buttons use a **@State** property called **selectedLink** to store the current state. The initial value of this property is **nil**, which means that all the links are inactive, but when a button is pressed, the value of its tag is assigned to the property to allow the system to identify the active link and open the corresponding window.

All the buttons open the same view, called **DetailView**, but we send an integer to the view with the value of the button's tag to identify which button was pressed and select the picture we must show on the screen. The following is our implementation of this view.

```
import SwiftUI
struct DetailView: View {
   @EnvironmentObject var appData: AppData
   var selected: Int

   var body: some View {
      VStack {
         HStack {
            Text("Rating: ")
               .font(.subheadline)
            Slider(value: $appData.userData[selected].picture.rating, in:
0...5, step: 1.0)
               .frame(width: 150)
            Text("\(appData.userData[selected].rating)")
               .font(.title)
               .fontWeight(.bold)
               .foregroundColor(Color.orange)
            Spacer()
         }
         Image(appData.userData[selected].picture.image)
            .resizable()
            .aspectRatio(contentMode: .fill)
            .frame(minWidth: 0, maxWidth: .infinity, minHeight: 0,
maxHeight: .infinity)
            .clipped()
      }.padding(15)
      .background(Color(red: 0.95, green: 0.95, blue: 0.95))
      .navigationBarTitle("Picture", displayMode: .inline)
   }
}
```

```
struct DetailView_Previews: PreviewProvider {
    static var previews: some View {
        NavigationView {
            DetailView(selected: 0).environmentObject(AppData())
        }
    }
}
```

Listing 9-16: Showing the selected picture

In Listing 9-16, we organize the views in stacks and present a `Slider` view to let the user select the rating for the image. To manage the state of the slider, we use the `rating` property of the `Picture` structure, so the value is stored in our model. On the right side of the slider, we show a `Text` view with the value of the other `rating` property. This is the property defined by the view model that turns the value of type `Double` produced by the slider into an integer. Below this, we create the `Image` view to show the image with the string stored in the `image` property of the `Picture` structure.

The view opened by a `NavigationLink` button is closed when the value `nil` is assigned to the `Binding` property associated with the button. Although we could pass a reference of this property and modify its value manually, it is not necessary in our example. The Back button created by default by SwiftUI automatically assigns the value `nil` to the `selectedLink` property and therefore the view is closed when the button is pressed.

Every time a button is pressed in the initial view, a new `DetailView` view is initialized with the value of the button's tag. The view uses that value to get information about the selected picture and show it on the screen. For instance, if the button with the tag 1 is pressed, the value 1 is sent to the `DetailView` view, and the information at the index 1 of the array is used to load the image and show it along with a slider to select the rating.

Figure 9-10: Pictures selected by the navigation buttons

 Do It Yourself: Create a SwiftUI project. Download the nopicture.png, spot1.jpg, spot2.jpg and spot3.jpg images from our website and add them to the Assets Catalog. Create a new Swift file with the name AppData.swift and the code of Listing 9-14. Update the `AppDelegate` class with the code of Listing 7-14 and the `SceneDelegate` class with the code of Listing 7-20. Update the `ContentView` structure with the code of Listing 9-15. Create a new SwiftUI file called DetailView.swift and update the `DetailView` structure with the code of Listing 9-16. Because the initial value of the `selectedLink` property is set to `nil`, you should see the nopicture.png image on the canvas when the DetailView.swift file is selected. Select the ContentView.swift file and activate the live preview. Click on the buttons. You should see the pictures appear on the screen according to the button you press. Move the slider to select a rating and go back to the menu. The rating should be stored in the model and appear again next time you select the same picture.

Basic TabView View

Another way to organize multiple views (screens), is with a `TabView` view. This view designates two areas on the screen, one for the views and a small one at the bottom for a tool bar with tabs the users can tap to select the view they want to see. Each tab is associated with only one view and therefore users can tap on them to move from one view to another.

Figure 9-11: `TabView`

The `TabView` structure includes the following initializers.

TabView(content: Closure)—This initializer creates a `TabView` view. The content attribute is a closure that returns the views the tab view is going to include and their tabs.

TabView(selection: Binding, **content:** Closure)—This initializer creates a `TabView` view. The **selection** attribute is a `Binding` property that returns a value that identifies the view currently open, and the **content** attribute is a closure that returns the views the tab view is going to include and their tabs.

The following are the modifiers provided by the `View` protocol to define and identify the tabs.

tabItem(Closure)—This modifier provides the views that make up the tab for the view. The attribute is a closure with the view or views that define the tab.

tag(Value)—This modifier assigns an identifier to the view. The attribute is a `Hashable` value, usually defined with an integer.

To define the content of a `TabView` view, we must list the views we want to present to the user one after another, like in a stack, and apply the `tabItem()` modifier to each one of them to define their tabs.

```
import SwiftUI
struct ContentView: View {
   var body: some View {
      TabView {
```

```
        WeatherView()
            .tabItem({
                Image(systemName: "sun.max")
                Text("Weather")
            })
        SettingsView()
            .tabItem({
                Image(systemName: "gear")
                Text("Settings")
            })
    }.edgesIgnoringSafeArea(.top)
    }
}
```

Listing 9-17: Defining a `TabView`

The `TabView` view of Listing 9-17 includes two views, `WeatherView` and `SettingsView`. For the `WeatherView` view, we define a tab with an SF Symbol called sun.max and the text "Weather", and for the `SettingsView` view's tab we include the SF Symbol called gear and the text "Settings".

Figure 9-12: Tabs

The `WeatherView` and `SettingsView` views represent two different screens and therefore they should be stored in separate files. For this first example, we are going to define two simple views with a text in the center. The following is the code for the `WeatherView`, stored in the WeatherView.swift file.

```
import SwiftUI

struct WeatherView: View {
    var body: some View {
        Text("Weather")
            .font(.largeTitle)
    }
}
```

Listing 9-18: Defining the `WeatherView`

And for the `SettingsView` view, we created a file called SettingsView.swift and the following code.

```
import SwiftUI

struct SettingsView: View {
    var body: some View {
        Text("Settings")
            .font(.largeTitle)
    }
}
```

Listing 9-19: Defining the `SettingsView`

These are simple views but illustrate how a `TabView` view works. When the app is launched, the first view on the list is shown on the screen and then the rest is opened by the user from the tabs at the bottom.

Figure 9-13: *Views in a* `TabView` *view*

 Do It Yourself: Create a SwiftUI project. Update the ContentView.swift file with the code of Listing 9-17. Create two SwiftUI files called WeatherView.swift and SettingsView.swift and replace their codes with the codes of Listing 9-18 and 9-19, respectively. Activate the live preview on the canvas. You should see the screen of Figure 9-13, left. Click on the tabs to switch the views.

We can include all the views we want in a `TabView` view. If there is no room in the tool bar to display all the tabs, the system adds a tab called *More* that allows the user to select the tabs that are not visible.

Figure 9-14: *More tab*

We can define the size of the icons by applying the `font()` modifier to the `TabView` view. This only defines the size of the icons, not the labels, but also sets the default font for the views, so if we don't want the views to be affected, we have to set the font back to the default `body` type for each one of them, as in the following example.

```
import SwiftUI

struct ContentView: View {
   var body: some View {
      TabView {
         WeatherView()
            .tabItem({
               Image(systemName: "sun.max")
               Text("Weather")
            }).font(.body)
         SettingsView()
            .tabItem({
               Image(systemName: "gear")
               Text("Settings")
```

Chapter 9 - Navigation

```
        }).font(.body)
    }.font(.title)
  }
}
```

Listing 9-20: Changing the size of the icons

Figure 9-15: Bigger icons

A `TabView` view can use a `Binding` property to store a value that determines which view is currently opened. By modifying the value of this property, we can open a view programmatically. For this to work, we must assign the `Binding` property to the **selection** attribute of the `TabView` initializer and apply the `tag()` modifier to each view with a unique value that helps the system identify the view.

```
import SwiftUI

struct ContentView: View {
    @State private var selectedView: Int = 0

    var body: some View {
        TabView(selection: $selectedView) {
            WeatherView()
                .tabItem({
                    Image(systemName: "sun.max")
                    Text("Weather")
                }).tag(0)
            SettingsView(selected: $selectedView)
                .tabItem({
                    Image(systemName: "gear")
                    Text("Settings")
                }).tag(1)
        }.edgesIgnoringSafeArea(.top)
    }
}
```

Listing 9-21: Identifying the views with a tag

Once the views are identified with a tag, we can pass the `Binding` property to other views and select the one we want to open by assigning the value of its tag to this property. In Listing 9-21, we pass the property to the `SettingsView`. In the following example we modify this view to allow the user to move back to the `WeatherView` view by pressing a button.

```
import SwiftUI

struct SettingsView: View {
    @Binding var selected: Int

    var body: some View {
        VStack(spacing: 15) {
            Text("Settings")
                .font(.largeTitle)
```

```
        Button("Open Weather") {
            self.selected = 0
        }
      }
    }
  }
}
struct SettingsView_Previews: PreviewProvider {
    static var previews: some View {
        SettingsView(selected: .constant(0))
    }
}
```

Listing 9-22: Opening a view from code

In the `SettingsView` view of Listing 9-22, we include a `@Binding` property called `selected` to establish the bidirectional connection with the `selectedView` property of the `ContentView` view and add a `Button` view that assigns the value 0 to this property when pressed, which opens the `WeatherView` view.

 Do It Yourself: Update the `ContentView` structure with the code of Listing 9-21 and the `SettingsView` structure with the code of Listing 9-22. Activate the live preview and click on the Settings tab. You should see the Open Weather button on the screen. Press this button to move back to the `WeatherView` view.

A `TabView` view is no different from a `NavigationView` view other than the way the views are presented to the user, so we can integrate it with a model and define each screen as we did before. The following example defines a model to store information about the weather and expands the `WeatherView` and `SettingsView` views to display this information on the screen.

```
import SwiftUI

struct WeatherData {
    var temperature: Double
    var precipitation: Double
    var humidity: Int
    var wind: Double
    var pressure: Double
    var visibility: Double
    var feels: Double
}
struct City {
    var name: String
    var weather: WeatherData
}
struct CityViewModel {
    var city: City

    var formatter: MeasurementFormatter {
        let format = MeasurementFormatter()
        format.unitStyle = .short
        format.unitOptions = .providedUnit
        return format
    }
    var name: String {
        return city.name.capitalized
    }
```

```
    var temperatureCelsius: String {
        let temperature = Measurement(value: city.weather.temperature,
unit: UnitTemperature.celsius)
        return formatter.string(from: temperature)
    }
    var temperatureFahrenheit: String {
        var temperature = Measurement(value: city.weather.temperature,
unit: UnitTemperature.celsius)
        temperature.convert(to: UnitTemperature.fahrenheit)
        return formatter.string(from: temperature)
    }
    var feelsCelsius: String {
        let temperature = Measurement(value: city.weather.feels, unit:
UnitTemperature.celsius)
        return formatter.string(from: temperature) + " degrees"
    }
    var feelsFahrenheit: String {
        var temperature = Measurement(value: city.weather.feels, unit:
UnitTemperature.celsius)
        temperature.convert(to: UnitTemperature.fahrenheit)
        return formatter.string(from: temperature) + " degrees"
    }
    var precipitation: String {
        let precipitation = Measurement(value: city.weather.precipitation,
unit: UnitLength.centimeters)
        return formatter.string(from: precipitation)
    }
    var humidity: String {
        return "\(city.weather.humidity) %"
    }
    var wind: String {
        let wind = Measurement(value: city.weather.wind, unit:
UnitSpeed.kilometersPerHour)
        return formatter.string(from: wind)
    }
    var pressure: String {
        let pressure = Measurement(value: city.weather.pressure, unit:
UnitPressure.millibars)
        return formatter.string(from: pressure)
    }
    var visibility: String {
        let visibility = Measurement(value: city.weather.visibility, unit:
UnitLength.kilometers)
        return formatter.string(from: visibility)
    }
}
class AppData: ObservableObject {
    @Published var userData: [CityViewModel]
    @Published var celsius: Bool = true
    @Published var selectedCity: Int = 0

    init() {
        userData = [
            CityViewModel(city: City(name: "Toronto", weather:
WeatherData(temperature: 21, precipitation: 0.0, humidity: 83, wind: 0.0,
pressure: 1.016, visibility: 14.5, feels: 24))),
            CityViewModel(city: City(name: "New York", weather:
WeatherData(temperature: 18, precipitation: 3.0, humidity: 95, wind:
12.4, pressure: 1.020, visibility: 8.5, feels: 15))),
```

```
            CityViewModel(city: City(name: "Paris", weather:
WeatherData(temperature: 24, precipitation: 8.7, humidity: 90, wind: 5.4,
pressure: 1.055, visibility: 10.5, feels: 25)))
      ]
   }
}
```

Listing 9-23: Defining a model to store data about the weather

This model is longer than usual, but the organization is the same as before. First, we have two structures to store the model's data, **WeatherData** and **City**. The **WeatherData** structure stores all the information about the weather for a city, like temperature and humidity, and the **City** structure stores the instance of the **WeatherData** structure for the city and the city's name. Next is the view model, the longest data type of them all. We call it **CityViewModel**. Here, we store an instance of the **City** structure with the data for a city, and then define computed properties to format every value in the **WeatherData** structure and prepare them for the views. We instantiate a **MeasurementFormatter** object to format the values and then create the **Measurement** structures required to define each unit of measurement (see Measurements in Chapter 4).

Finally, we create the observable object. There are three **@Published** properties in this object. The **userData** property, as always, stores the data for the model, the **celsius** property is a Boolean value that indicates whether the temperature is shown in Celsius (**true**) or Fahrenheit (**false**), and the **selectedCity** property is the one we use to store the index of the selected city. At the end, we define an initializer to provide the same data for the application.

The **ContentView** for this example is the same defined in Listing 9-21, but the **WeatherView** and **SettingsView** views now have to include all the views required to show the data on the screen. For reference, we are building the interfaces of Figure 9-11. The following is the new code for the WeatherView.swift file, which includes the **WeatherView** view to organize the interface and two more custom views to present the content.

```
import SwiftUI
struct WeatherView: View {
   @EnvironmentObject var appData: AppData

   var body: some View {
      let city = appData.userData[appData.selectedCity]

      return ZStack {
         Image("clouds")
            .resizable()
            .aspectRatio(contentMode: .fill)
            .frame(minWidth: 0, maxWidth: .infinity, minHeight: 0,
maxHeight: .infinity)
            .edgesIgnoringSafeArea(.all)
         VStack {
            Text(city.name)
               .font(Font.system(size: 30))
            Text(appData.celsius ? city.temperatureCelsius :
city.temperatureFahrenheit)
               .font(Font.system(size: 70))
            WeatherDataView(city: city)
            WeatherFeelsView(city: city, celsius: appData.celsius)
            Spacer()
         }.padding(.top, 80)
      }
   }
}
```

Chapter 9 - Navigation

```
struct WeatherDataView: View {
    var city: CityViewModel

    var body: some View {
        Group {
            HStack(alignment: .top, spacing: 0) {
                VStack(alignment: .leading, spacing: 10) {
                    Text("Precipitation:")
                    Text("Humidity:")
                    Text("Wind:")
                    Text("Pressure:")
                    Text("Visibility:")
                }.frame(width: 120, alignment: .leading)

                VStack(alignment: .leading, spacing: 10) {
                    Text(city.precipitation)
                    Text(city.humidity)
                    Text(city.wind)
                    Text(city.pressure)
                    Text(city.visibility)
                }.font(Font.body.weight(.semibold))
            }.padding()
        }
        .frame(minWidth: 0, maxWidth: .infinity, alignment: .leading)
        .background(Color(red: 0.9, green: 0.9, blue: 0.9, opacity: 0.8))
        .cornerRadius(15)
        .padding()
    }
}
struct WeatherFeelsView: View {
    var city: CityViewModel
    var celsius: Bool

    var body: some View {
        Group {
            HStack(alignment: .top, spacing: 0) {
                Text("Feels Like:")
                    .frame(width: 120, alignment: .leading)
                Text(celsius ? city.feelsCelsius : city.feelsFahrenheit)
                    .font(Font.body.weight(.semibold))
            }.padding()
        }
        .frame(minWidth: 0, maxWidth: .infinity, alignment: .leading)
        .background(Color(red: 0.9, green: 0.9, blue: 0.9, opacity: 0.8))
        .cornerRadius(15)
        .padding([.leading, .trailing])
    }
}
struct WeatherView_Previews: PreviewProvider {
    static var previews: some View {
        WeatherView().environmentObject(AppData())
    }
}
```

Listing 9-24: Showing the weather

The code for this view is extensive, but it is mainly structural views and modifiers for styling purposes. As always, we access the model through the environment, so we need the **AppDelegate** class of Listing 7-14 and the **SceneDelegate** class of Listing 7-20 for the application to work. Inside the body, we first get the **CityViewModel** structure of the selected city and assign it to a constant called **city**. Using this constant, we get all the values for the city and its weather. The main view is a **ZStack** that includes an **Image** view for the background and a VStack to organize the information. First, we show the city's name (`city.name`) and check the `celsius` property to select the unit of measurement and read the values of the `temperatureCelsius` or `temperatureFahrenheit` properties accordingly. After this, we create an instance of the `WeatherDataView` structure, which takes care of showing most of the values for the weather, and an instance of the `WeatherFeelsView` structure, which displays the feels-like value. In the `WeatherDataView` view, we create a list of `Text` views with labels to identify each weather value and another list with the values themselves. Because these values are already formatted by the `CityViewModel` structure, they are ready to be shown on the screen. And in the `WeatherFeelsView` view, we create another group to apply some styles and check the `celsius` property again to show the feels-like value in Celsius or Fahrenheit.

The following is the `SettingsView` view for this example. In this view, we provide buttons to set the unit of measurement for the temperature (Celsius or Fahrenheit) and to select the city. Notice that besides the `@EnvironmentObject` property necessary to connect with the model, we also include a `@Binding` property called `selected`. This is the same property defined in de example of Listing 9-22 and its purpose is to open the `WeatherView` view back when the user presses a button to select a city.

```
import SwiftUI

struct SettingsView: View {
    @EnvironmentObject var appData: AppData
    @Binding var selected: Int

    var body: some View {
        ZStack {
            Image("seaside")
                .resizable()
                .aspectRatio(contentMode: .fill)
                .frame(minWidth: 0, maxWidth: .infinity, minHeight: 0,
maxHeight: .infinity)
                .edgesIgnoringSafeArea(.all)
            VStack {
                SettingsMeasurementView(celsius: $appData.celsius)
                SettingsCitiesView(selected: $selected)
            }.foregroundColor(Color.black)
        }
    }
}
struct SettingsMeasurementView: View {
    @Binding var celsius: Bool

    var body: some View {
        Group {
            HStack(alignment: .top, spacing: 0) {
                Button("Celsius") {
                    self.celsius = true
                }.frame(maxWidth: .infinity)
                .padding()
                .background(celsius ? Color.yellow : Color.clear)
                .disabled(celsius)

                Button("Fahrenheit") {
                    self.celsius = false
                }.frame(maxWidth: .infinity)
                .padding()
                .background(!celsius ? Color.yellow : Color.clear)
                .disabled(!celsius)
            }.padding()
        }
```

```
            .frame(minWidth: 0, maxWidth: .infinity, alignment: .leading)
            .background(Color(red: 0.9, green: 0.9, blue: 0.9, opacity: 0.9))
            .cornerRadius(15)
            .padding()
   }
}
struct SettingsCitiesView: View {
   @EnvironmentObject var appData: AppData
   @Binding var selected: Int

   var body: some View {
      Group {
         VStack(alignment: .leading, spacing: 10) {
            Text("Select City")
               .font(.footnote)
            Button(appData.userData[0].name) {
               self.appData.selectedCity = 0
               self.selected = 0
            }
            Button(appData.userData[1].name) {
               self.appData.selectedCity = 1
               self.selected = 0
            }
            Button(appData.userData[2].name) {
               self.appData.selectedCity = 2
               self.selected = 0
            }
            Spacer()
         }.padding()
      }
      .frame(minWidth: 0, maxWidth: .infinity, maxHeight: .infinity,
alignment: .leading)
         .background(Color(red: 0.9, green: 0.9, blue: 0.9, opacity: 0.9))
         .cornerRadius(15)
         .padding()
   }
}
struct SettingsView_Previews: PreviewProvider {
   static var previews: some View {
      SettingsView(selected: .constant(1)).environmentObject(AppData())
   }
}
```

Listing 9-25: Configuring the app

Again, this view is organized in three custom views. The `SettingsView` takes care of organizing the interface, the `SettingsMeasurementView` view defines the buttons to set the unit of measurement, and the `SettingsCitiesView` view defines the buttons to select a city.

The `SettingsMeasurementView` view includes two buttons, one for Celsius and another for Fahrenheit. If the Celsius button is pressed, the value `true` is assigned to the `celsius` property, and if the Fahrenheit button is pressed, the value assigned is `false`. We use this property in two modifiers, one to change the background color and the other to disable the button, so when a button is pressed, that unit is selected and the button is disabled, and when the other button is pressed, the situation is reversed (only one button can be enabled at a time).

In the `SettingsCitiesView` view, we create a list of buttons with the names of the cities available in the model to let users choose the city for which they want to see the weather. Each button represents one of the cities stored in the observable object and therefore they are identified with the indexes 0, 1, and 2 (we stored a total of three cities in the `userData` array). If a button is pressed, the index of that button is assigned to the `selectedCity` property, so the `WeatherView` view knows which city has to show, and the value 0 is assigned to the `selected` property, so the `TabView` loads the `WeatherView` view, which is identified with the tag 0.

 Do It Yourself: This example implements the same `ContentView` view defined for the previous example (see Listing 9-21). Download the clouds.jpg and seaside.png images from our website and add them to the Assets Catalog. Create a new Swift file called AppData.swift for the model of Listing 9-23. Update the AppDelegate.swift file with the code of Listing 7-14 and the SceneDelegate.swift file with the code of Listing 7-20. Update the WeatherView.swift file with the code of Listing 9-24 and the SettingsView.swift file with the code of Listing 9-25. Run the application on the iPhone simulator or a device. You should see the interface in Figure 9-11. Click on the Settings tab, click on the Fahrenheit button and click on the name of a city. The app should open the Weather view and you should see the temperature expressed in Fahrenheit.

(Basic) ## 9.2 Modal Views

Besides navigation and tab views, we can expand the interface with modal views. Modal views are normal views, but they are not part of the interface's view hierarchy and are presented on top of the rest of the views on the screen.

(Basic) ### Sheets

Sheets are general-purpose modal views. In iPhones, they occupy the whole screen, and on iPads and Mac computers they are shown as a rectangular view at the center of the screen. The `View` protocol defines the following modifiers to present a sheet.

sheet(isPresented: Binding, **onDismiss:** Closure?, **content:** Closure)—This modifier displays a sheet. The **isPresented** attribute is a `Binding` property of type `Bool` that determines whether the sheet has to be presented (`true`) or removed (`false`). The **onDismiss** attribute is a closure that is executed when the sheet is removed. And the **content** attribute is a closure that defines the view to be shown on the screen.

sheet(item: Binding, **onDismiss:** Closure?, **content:** Closure)—This modifier displays a sheet. The **item** attribute is an optional `Binding` value taken from a collection that determines whether the sheet has to be presented or removed (`nil`). The **onDismiss** attribute is a closure that is executed when the sheet is removed. And the **content** attribute is a closure that defines the view to be shown on the screen. The closure receives the value stored in the `Binding` property.

Sheets are presented and removed by these modifiers, but we must determine when this happens by modifying the value of a `Binding` property. For instance, the first modifier uses a `Binding` property of type `Bool`. When we want to open the sheet, we assign the value `true` to this property, and if we want to close it, we assign the value `false`.

We can apply the modifier to the control that open the sheet or to any other view in the interface, as in the following example.

```
import SwiftUI
```

```
struct ContentView: View {
    @State private var showSheet: Bool = false

    var body: some View {
        VStack {
            Button("Open Sheet") {
                self.showSheet = true
            }.font(.title)
            Spacer()
        }.padding()
        .sheet(isPresented: $showSheet) {
            SettingsView()
        }
    }
}
```

Listing 9-26: Displaying a sheet

The view in Listing 9-26 defines a `@State` property to control the state of the sheet and then includes a `Button` view that assigns the value `true` to this property to open the sheet when pressed. The sheet is managed by the `sheet()` modifier applied to the `VStack` view. The modifier is connected to the `showSheet` property, so when the value of this property is `true` the `SettingsView` view is presented on the screen and when the value is `false` the view is removed.

Sheets are independent views, so we should declare them on a separate file. The following is the `SettingsView` view for this example, which was stored in the SettingsView.swift file.

```
import SwiftUI

struct SettingsView: View {
    var body: some View {
        VStack {
            Text("Sheet")
                .font(.largeTitle)
            Spacer()
        }.padding()
    }
}
```

Listing 9-27: Defining the view for the sheet

The only function of this view is to display the word "Sheet" on the screen. When the button on the interface is pressed, the sheet is presented on top of it. The result is shown in Figure 9-16.

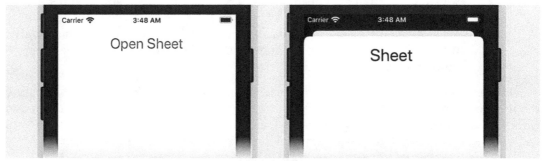

Figure 9-16: Sheet

In this example, we didn't include any option for the user to remove the view. This is because by default users can remove a sheet by dragging the view from top to bottom. This gesture is automatically enabled for every sheet, but we can provide our custom control as well. There are two ways to remove a sheet, one is to assign the value `false` to the `Binding` property that controls the sheet (the `showSheet` property in our example), and another is by modifying the state of the presentation from the environment with the `presentationMode` property, as we did before (see Listing 9-7).

```
import SwiftUI

struct SettingsView: View {
    @Environment(\.presentationMode) var presentation

    var body: some View {
        VStack {
            Button("X") {
                self.presentation.wrappedValue.dismiss()
            }.frame(minWidth: 0, maxWidth: .infinity, alignment: .trailing)
            Text("Sheet")
            Spacer()
        }.padding()
        .font(.title)
    }
}
```

Listing 9-28: *Removing the sheet programmatically*

The code of Listing 9-28 updates the `SettingsView` view to provide a button for the user to remove the sheet. We define an `@Environment` property called `presentation` and then call the `dismiss()` method when the button is pressed. We can still remove the view by dragging the sheet from top to bottom, but now we can also do it by pressing the X button.

Figure 9-17: *Button to remove the sheet*

 Do It Yourself: Create a SwiftUI project. Update the `ContentView` structure with the code of Listing 9-26. Create a SwiftUI file called SettingsView.swift. Update the `SettingsView` structure with the code of Listing 9-28. Run the application on the simulator and press the Open Sheet button. You should see the sheet scrolling up from the bottom. Close the view by dragging the sheet down or pressing the X button.

There is a second `sheet()` modifier designed to work with the values of a model and allow the user to open a sheet for each value. This version of the `sheet()` modifier was defined to work with `List` views. These are views that present rows of data, each with unique values from the model. For instance, if our model stores information about movies, each row created by the `List` view will contain information from one of those movies.

As we will see in the next chapter, `List` views require the model to provide a unique identifier for each row. Because the `sheet()` modifier was designed to work with these types of views, it presents the same requirement. For this purpose, Swift defines the following protocol.

Identifiable—This protocol defines a data type capable of uniquely identify each instance of itself. The protocol requires the data type to include a property called `id` to store the identifier for the instance.

The identifier can be any type of value, but it must be unique. Although we can provide a value ourselves, the Foundation framework defines the `UUID()` function to produce a random value that never repeats, and this is enough for most applications. The following is a model we have implemented before to store information about books but modified to get each value identified.

```
import SwiftUI

struct Book {
    var title: String
    var author: String
}
struct BookViewModel: Identifiable {
    var id = UUID()
    var book: Book
    var header: String {
        return book.title + " " + book.author
    }
}
class AppData: ObservableObject {
    @Published var userData: [BookViewModel]

    init() {
        userData = [
            BookViewModel(book: Book(title: "Misery", author: "Stephen King")),
            BookViewModel(book: Book(title: "IT", author: "Stephen King"))
        ]
    }
}
```

Listing 9-29: Identifying the data in the model

The first structure, called `Book`, represents the basic model. We use it to store the title and author of a book. The following structure, called `BookViewModel`, defines the view model, and is here where we must identify each instance of our data. For this purpose, we make the structure conform to the `Identifiable` protocol and implement the required `id` property. The property receives the value produced by the `UUID()` function, so every time an instance of the `BookViewModel` structure is created, it is automatically identified with a unique value. The rest of the properties are the same as before (see Listing 7-22), except this time we assign an array of `BookViewModel` structures to the `userData` property of the observable object to store multiple books.

Now that we have identified each item in the model, we can use them to create the sheets. The `sheet()` modifier needs an optional `Binding` property of the same data type of the items in our model. if the property contains a value, a sheet is opened with that value, and when the value `nil` is assigned to the property, the sheet is closed. The following example illustrates how to implement this version of the `sheet()` modifier and how the process works.

```
import SwiftUI

struct ContentView: View {
    @EnvironmentObject var appData: AppData
    @State private var openSheet: BookViewModel? = nil

    var body: some View {
        VStack(alignment: .leading, spacing: 10) {
            Button("Open Book 1") {
                self.openSheet = self.appData.userData[0]
            }
            Button("Open Book 2") {
                self.openSheet = self.appData.userData[1]
            }
            Spacer()
        }.padding()
        .font(.title)
        .frame(minWidth: 0, maxWidth: .infinity, alignment: .leading)
        .sheet(item: $openSheet) { value in
            ShowBookView(book: value)
        }
    }
}
```

Listing 9-30: Presenting a sheet for every value in the model

This view defines a `@State` property called `openSheet` to store the `BookViewModel` value for the sheet. Since we haven't learned yet how to work with a `List` view, we create a simple list of buttons to represent each item in the model. In this case, we stored only two movies, so we have two buttons. The first button assigns the `BookViewModel` structure at index 0 of the array to the `openSheet` property, and the second button does the same for the structure at index 1. At the end, we use the value of this property to determine whether the `sheet()` modifier should open a sheet with the `ShowBookView` view or not. If a value is assigned to the property, this value is sent to the closure, so we can process it or send it to the view, as in this example.

The view we use for the sheet is simple, it receives the value currently managed by the modifier and displays it on the screen.

```
import SwiftUI

struct ShowBookView: View {
    @Environment(\.presentationMode) var presentation
    let book: BookViewModel

    var body: some View {
        VStack {
            Button("X") {
                self.presentation.wrappedValue.dismiss()
            }.frame(minWidth: 0, maxWidth: .infinity, alignment: .trailing)
            Text(book.header)
            Spacer()
        }.padding()
        .font(.title)
    }
}
```

Chapter 9 - Navigation

```
struct ShowBookView_Previews: PreviewProvider {
    static var previews: some View {
        ShowBookView(book: BookViewModel(book: Book(title: "Test", author:
"Author")))
    }
}
```

Listing 9-31: Displaying the value selected by the user in a sheet

If a button is pressed, one of the `BookViewModel` structures with data about a book is assigned to the `openSheet` property, the `sheet()` modifier creates an instance of the `ShowBookView` view with this value, the instance receives the value with the `book` constant, and the content of the `header` property is displayed to the user.

Figure 9-18: Multiple sheets

Do It Yourself: Create a SwiftUI project. Create a Swift file called AppData.swift for the model of Listing 9-29. Update the AppDelegate.swift file with the code of Listing 7-14 and the SceneDelegate.swift file with the code of Listing 7-20. Update the `ContentView` structure with the code of Listing 9-30. Create a SwiftUI file called ShowBookView.swift and update the code with the code of Listing 9-31. Run the application in an iPhone simulator and press the buttons. You should see the interfaces in Figure 9-18.

(Basic) **Popovers**

Another types of views we can introduce to our interface are popovers. Popovers are presented like sheets on iPhones, and like small views on iPads and Mac computers. The `View` protocol defines the following modifiers to present them.

popover(isPresented: Binding, **attachmentAnchor:** PopoverAttachment-Anchor, **arrowEdge:** Edge, **content:** Closure)—This modifier displays a popover. The **isPresented** attribute is a `Binding` property of type `Bool` that determines whether the popover has to be presented (`true`) or removed (`false`). The **attachmentAnchor** attribute is an enumeration of type `PopoverAttachmentAnchor` that includes the method `rect()` to define a `CGRect` value that determines to which part of the view the popover should be anchored. The **arrowEdge** attribute is an enumeration of type `Edge` that determines the side in which the popover's arrow should be placed. The values available are `bottom`, `leading`, `top`, and `trailing`. And the **content** attribute is a closure that defines the view to be shown on the screen.

popover(item: Binding, **attachmentAnchor:** PopoverAttachmentAnchor, **arrowEdge:** Edge, **content:** Closure)—This modifier displays a popover. The **item** attribute is an optional `Binding` value taken from a collection that determines whether the popover has to be presented or removed (`nil`). The **attachmentAnchor** attribute is an enumeration of type `PopoverAttachmentAnchor` that includes the method `rect()` to define a `CGRect` value that determines to which part of the view the popover should be anchored. The **arrowEdge** attribute is an enumeration of type **Edge** that determines the side in which the popover's arrow should be placed. The values available are **bottom**, **leading**, **top**, and **trailing**. And the **content** attribute is a closure that defines the view to be shown on the screen. The closure receives the value in the **Binding** property.

At the time, we can't customize the size of the popover, so they are always presented as sheets on iPhones and as a small view with a Compact horizontal size class on iPad, but we can select where the popup is going to appear on the screen. The referential point used by the system to determine the popover's position is the view to which the modifier is applied. Then, depending on where we position the popover's arrow, the popover may be placed on top, left, right, or bottom of the view. For instance, the following example shows a popover anchored to a **Button** view with a **top** arrow.

```
import SwiftUI
struct ContentView: View {
    @State private var showPopover: Bool = false

    var body: some View {
        VStack {
            Button("Show Popover") {
                self.showPopover = true
            }.popover(isPresented: self.$showPopover, arrowEdge: .top) {
                MoreInfoView()
            }
            Spacer()
        }.font(.title)
    }
}
```

Listing 9-32: Showing a popover

The **popover()** modifier of Listing 9-32 has two attributes, the **isPresented** attribute to control when the popover is shown, and the **arrowEdge** attribute to determine the side where the arrow is placed and therefore the position of the view relative to the anchor. When the value of the **showPopover** property changes to **true**, the modifier creates an instance of the **MoreInfoView** view. This is the same view we defined for sheets. It can be dismissed by dragging it from top to bottom on iPhones, by clicking outside the view on iPads, or by calling the **dismiss()** method in the environment's **presentationMode** property, as we did before.

```
import SwiftUI
struct MoreInfoView: View {
    @Environment(\.presentationMode) var presentation

    var body: some View {
        VStack {
            Button("X") {
                self.presentation.wrappedValue.dismiss()
            }.frame(minWidth: 0, maxWidth: .infinity, alignment: .trailing)
            Text("More Information")
            Spacer()
        }.padding()
        .font(.title)
    }
}
```

Listing 9-33: Defining the content of the popover

Chapter 9 - Navigation

In this example, we apply the `popover()` modifier to the `Button` view and with a `top` arrow, so the popover view is anchored to the `Button` view and shown below the button when presented on iPads.

Show Popover

X

Popover Content

Figure 9-19: Popover on iPad

 Do It Yourself: Create a SwiftUI project. Update the `ContentView` structure with the code of Listing 9-32. Create a new file called MoreInfoView.swift and update the code with the code of Listing 9-33. Run the application on the iPad simulator and press the Show Popover button. You should see the popover of Figure 9-19. If you need to send some data to the view opened by the `popover()` modifier, you can specify the **item** attribute instead, like we did with the `sheet()` modifier before. See Listing 9-30.

(Basic) **Alert Views**

Alert views are predefined modal views that can display messages and receive input from the user. Their purpose is to deliver to the user important information that requires immediate attention. For example, an alert view may be used to ask confirmation from the user before deleting data from the model. They are defined by the `Alert` structure and may include a title, a message, and buttons. The structure includes the following initializers.

Alert(title: Text, **message:** Text, **dismissButton:** Button)—This initializer creates an alert view. The **title** attribute is a `Text` view with the text for the title, the **message** attribute is a `Text` view with the message to display below the title, and the **dismissButton** attribute is a structure of type `Alert.Button` that defines a button to dismiss the view.

Alert(title: Text, **message:** Text, **primaryButton:** Button, **secondaryButton:** Button)—This initializer creates an alert view. The **title** attribute is a `Text` view with the test for the title, the **message** attribute is a `Text` view with the message to display below the title, and the **primaryButton** and **secondaryButton** attributes are structures of type `Alert.Button` that define the primary and secondary button, respectively.

The `Button` structure used to create the buttons for an alert view is defined inside the `Alert` structure and includes the following type methods to create a button.

cancel(Text, **action:** Closure)—This type method creates a button that dismisses the view. The first attribute is a `Text` view that defines the button's label, and the **action** attribute is an optional closure to be executed when the button is pressed.

destructive(Text, **action:** Closure)—This type method creates a button that performs a destructive task, such as erasing data from the model. The first attribute is a `Text` view that defines the button's label (usually displayed in red to warn the user), and the **action** attribute is an optional closure to be executed when the button is pressed.

default(Text, **action:** Closure)—This type method creates a button with no predefined purpose. The first attribute is a `Text` view that defines the button's label, and the **action** attribute is an optional closure to be executed when the button is pressed.

The `Alert` initializers and these type methods define the view, but to show these views we must apply the following modifiers.

alert(isPresented: Binding, **content:** Closure)—This modifier presents an alert view. The **isPresented** attribute is a `Binding` value of type `Bool` that determines whether the alert view has to be presented (`true`) or removed (`false`). And the **content** attribute is the closure that defines the `Alert` view to be shown.

alert(item: Binding, **content:** Closure)—This modifier presents an alert view. The **item** attribute is an optional `Binding` value taken from a collection that determines whether the alert view has to be presented or removed (`nil`). The **content** attribute is a closure that defines the alert view to be shown. This closure receives the value stored in the `Binding` property.

The process is the same as with sheets. We have to define a `@State` property to manage the state of the view and then apply the `alert()` modifier.

```
import SwiftUI
struct ContentView: View {
    @State private var name: String = ""
    @State private var openAlert: Bool = false

    var body: some View {
        VStack(spacing: 10) {
            TextField("Insert your Name", text: $name)
                .textFieldStyle(RoundedBorderTextFieldStyle())
            HStack {
                Spacer()
                Button("Save") {
                    if self.name != "" {
                        self.name = ""
                    } else {
                        self.openAlert = true
                    }
                }
            }
            Spacer()
        }.padding()
        .font(.title)
        .alert(isPresented: $openAlert) {
            Alert(title: Text("Error"), message: Text("Insert your name"),
dismissButton: .cancel())
        }
    }
}
```

Listing 9-34: Displaying an alert view

The `@State` property for this view is called `openAlert`. The view includes a button to change the value of this property to `true` and open the alert view. The button checks the value of a `TextField` view before deciding what to do. If the input field contains a value, the button just clears the field, but if the value is empty, the alert view is opened. This view was defined with the title "Error", the message "Insert your name", and the `cancel()` button, to allow the user to dismiss the view.

Figure 9-20: Alert view

 Do It Yourself: Create a SwiftUI project. Update the `ContentView` structure with the code of Listing 9-34. Activate the live preview and press the Save button. If you didn't insert anything in the text field, you should see the alert window of Figure 9-20.

The second `Alert` view initializer introduced above includes a primary and a secondary button. These types of alert views are usually created to allow the user to perform an action. For instance, we can define a primary button that saves the data inserted by the user in the model and another button to dismiss the view. The following code initializes an `Alert` view with two buttons. The primary button assigns a string to the `name` property, and the secondary button dismisses the view.

```
Alert(title: Text("Error"), message: Text("Insert your name"),
   primaryButton: .default(Text("Assign Default")) {
      self.name = "Default Name"
   }, secondaryButton: .cancel())
```

Listing 9-35: Defining an alert view with two buttons

If we replace the `Alert` view initializer in Listing 9-34 by the initializer in Listing 9-35, the `alert()` modifier will produce an alert view with a button labeled Assign Default that when pressed assigns the text "Default Name" to the `TextField` view.

Figure 9-21: Alert view with two buttons

Basic Action Sheets

SwiftUI includes another type of alert views called *Action Sheets*. These views are usually presented when our application needs the user to make a decision and there is more than one option available. They are created with the `ActionSheet` structure, which includes the following initializer.

ActionSheet(title: Text, **message:** Text, **buttons:** [Button])—This initializer creates an action sheet. The **title** attribute is a `Text` view with the text for the title, the **message** attribute is a `Text` view with the message to display below the title, and the **buttons** attribute is an array with `Alert.Button` structures that define the buttons to include in the view.

The structure and the type methods used to create the buttons for the action sheet are the same as those used for alert views, but the modifiers are specific to the action sheets.

actionSheet(isPresented: Binding, **content:** Closure)—This modifier presents an action sheet. The **isPresented** attribute is a `Binding` value of type `Bool` that determines whether the action sheet has to be presented (`true`) or removed (`false`). And the **content** attribute is the closure that defines the `ActionSheet` view to be shown.

actionSheet(item: Binding, **content:** Closure)—This modifier presents an action sheet. The **item** attribute is an optional `Binding` value taken from a collection that determines whether the action sheet has to be presented or removed (`nil`). The **content** attribute is a closure that defines the action sheet to be shown. This closure receives the value stored in the `Binding` property.

There is no much difference between action sheets and alert views, but with action sheets we can specify multiple buttons. The following example creates an action sheet with three buttons. The buttons don't perform any action but illustrate how to implement and work with these kinds of views.

```
import SwiftUI

struct ContentView: View {
    @State private var openSheet: Bool = false

    var body: some View {
        VStack(spacing: 10) {
            Button("Open Action Sheet") {
                self.openSheet = true
            }
            Spacer()
        }.padding()
        .font(.title)
        .actionSheet(isPresented: $openSheet) {
            ActionSheet(title: Text("Email"), message: Text("What do you
want to do with the message?"), buttons: [
                .default(Text("Move to Inbox")),
                .destructive(Text("Delete")),
                .cancel()
            ])
        }
    }
}
```

Listing 9-36: Defining an action sheet

As always, the view includes a `@State` property to manage the view. When the value `true` is assigned to this property by the button, the `actionSheet()` modifier opens the `ActionSheet` view. The view includes three buttons, a button of type `default` to perform a normal operation, a button of type `destructive` to delete data, and a `cancel` button to allow the user to dismiss the view.

Figure 9-22: Action sheet

At the time, action sheets do not work on iPads. Action sheets require an anchor point when they are presented in a Regular size class and SwiftUI does not provide the tools to define this anchor. But we can replace the action sheet by an Alert view or a popover when the application is running on this type of device. All we have to do is to provide two `@State` properties, one to open an Action sheet and another to open an Alert view, a popover, or a normal sheet, and then read the `userInterfaceIdiom` property of the `UIDevice` object to detect the device and decide which view to open (see Listing 4-53).

```
import SwiftUI

struct ContentView: View {
    @State private var openSheet: Bool = false
    @State private var openAlert: Bool = false
    @State private var message: String = "No Message"

    var body: some View {
        VStack(spacing: 10) {
            Text(message)
            Button("Open View") {
                if UIDevice.current.userInterfaceIdiom == .pad {
                    self.openAlert = true
                } else {
                    self.openSheet = true
                }
            }
            Spacer()
        }.padding()
        .font(.title)
        .actionSheet(isPresented: $openSheet) {
            ActionSheet(title: Text("Email"),
                message: Text("What do you want to do with the message?"),
                buttons: [
                    .default(Text("Move to Inbox")) {
                        self.message = "Message Moved"
                    }, .cancel() ])
        }
        .alert(isPresented: $openAlert) {
            Alert(title: Text("Email"),
                message: Text("What do you want to do with the message?"),
                primaryButton: .default(Text("Move to Inbox")) {
                    self.message = "Message Moved"
                },
                secondaryButton: .cancel())
        }
    }
}
```

Listing 9-37: Showing different views for iPhones and iPads

The example of Listing 9-37 defines three `@State` properties, one to open an Action sheet (`openSheet`), another to open an Alert view (`openAlert`), and another to store a string and test the buttons (`message`). The view includes a `Text` view to show the value of the `message` property and a `Button` view to let the user open the additional views. In the closure assigned to the button, we read the `userInterfaceIdiom` property of the `UIDevice` object. If the value is equal to `pad`, which means that the application is running on an iPad, we show an `Alert` view, otherwise, we show an `ActionSheet` view. Both views include a button with the label Move to Inbox. If the button is pressed, the message "Message Moved" is assigned to the `message` property and we see it on the screen.

 Do It Yourself: Create a SwiftUI project and update the ContentView.swift file with the code of Listing 9-37. Run the application in the simulator and press the Open View button. If the simulator is an iPhone, you should see an action sheet, otherwise you should see an alert view. Press the Move to Inbox button. You should see the message "Message Moved" on the screen.

Basic 9.3 Split Views

Working with one view per screen, as we have done so far, is enough for small devices, such as iPhones and iPods, but the space available in iPads, modern iPhones in landscape mode, and computers demand a more elaborated design. SwiftUI offers a standard solution that allows the interface to present two views at the same time, one called Master view, and another called Detail view. The Master view is a small view on the left-hand side of the screen used to present control views that let the user select options and content, while the Detail view is a larger view on the right-hand side of the screen which purpose is to show the selected content.

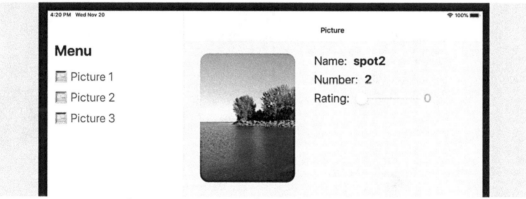

Figure 9-23: Two views sharing the screen on an iPad

This layout is easy to achieve. All we have to do is to declare the Master and Detail views within a `NavigationView` view, and the system takes care of presenting the views side by side.

```
import SwiftUI

struct ContentView: View {
    var body: some View {
        NavigationView {
            MenuView()
            PlaceholderView()
        }
    }
}
```

Listing 9-38: Defining a split view

These views are usually called *Split Views*. The first view on the list is shown on the left and the second view is shown on the right. Although they are both embedded in the same `NavigationView` view, they do not behave like normal navigation views. Both views include a navigation bar, but the `NavigationLink` buttons in the Master view (`MenuView` in our example) open the view in the space occupied by the Detail view. For instance, if we click on the buttons in the interface of Figure 9-23, above, the view on the right is replaced by another view with the selected picture, but the view on the left remains the same.

Both views in a split-view layout include a navigation bar, but in SwiftUI the first Detail view works as a placeholder and it does not include this bar. Therefore, we must provide an additional view that is going to be shown as the Detail view until it is replaced by content selected by the user from the Master view. In the example of Listing 9-38, we called this view `PlaceholderView`. The following is our implementation of this view.

```
import SwiftUI
struct PlaceholderView: View {
    var body: some View {
        VStack {
            Text("Select a Picture")
                .font(.title)
            Spacer()
        }.padding(50)
        .frame(minWidth: 0, maxWidth: .infinity, minHeight: 0, maxHeight:
.infinity)
        .background(Color(red: 0.95, green: 0.95, blue: 0.95))
    }
}
```

Listing 9-39: Defining the placeholder

There is no functionality required in this view, so we just include a flexible `Text` view with a gray background. The views that are going to replace this view with real content are opened from the Master view. The following is our implementation of this view.

```
import SwiftUI
struct MenuView: View {
    @State private var selectedLink: Int? = nil

    var body: some View {
        VStack(alignment: .leading, spacing: 15) {
            NavigationLink("🖼 Picture 1", destination: DetailView(selected:
1), tag: 1, selection: $selectedLink)
            NavigationLink("🖼 Picture 2", destination: DetailView(selected:
2), tag: 2, selection: $selectedLink)
            NavigationLink("🖼 Picture 3", destination: DetailView(selected:
3), tag: 3, selection: $selectedLink)
            Spacer()
        }.font(.title)
        .padding()
        .frame(minWidth: 0, maxWidth: .infinity, alignment: .leading)
        .navigationBarTitle("Menu")
    }
}
```

Listing 9-40: Defining the Master view

The `MenuView` view of Listing 9-40 includes three `NavigationLink` buttons, as a previous example, but because we are working with a split-view layout, the `DetailView` view is going to be opened on the right. The following is the code for this view.

```
import SwiftUI

struct DetailView: View {
   @EnvironmentObject var appData: AppData
   var selected: Int = 0

   var body: some View {
      VStack {
         HStack {
            Text("Rating: ")
               .font(.subheadline)
            Slider(value: $appData.userData[selected].picture.rating, in:
0...5, step: 1.0)
               .frame(width: 150)
            Text("\(appData.userData[selected].rating)")
               .font(.title)
               .fontWeight(.bold)
               .foregroundColor(Color.orange)
            Spacer()
         }.padding(5)

         Image(appData.userData[selected].picture.image)
            .resizable()
            .aspectRatio(contentMode: .fill)
            .frame(minWidth: 0, maxWidth: .infinity, minHeight: 0,
maxHeight: .infinity)
            .clipped()
            .zIndex(-1)
         Spacer()
      }.padding(15)
      .background(Color(red: 0.95, green: 0.95, blue: 0.95))
      .navigationBarTitle("Picture", displayMode: .inline)
   }
}
```

Listing 9-41: *Defining the Detail view*

This application works like the one created for single views before (see Listings 9-15 and 9-16), but now the views are shown side by side on devices with large screens. If we click on a button in the view on the left, the picture that corresponds to that button is displayed in the view on the right.

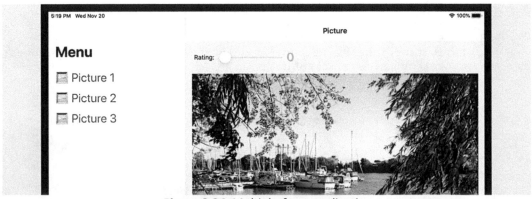

Figure 9-24: *Multiplatform application*

Chapter 9 - Navigation

Do It Yourself: Create a SwiftUI project. Download the files nopicture.png, spot1.jpg, spot2.jpg, and spot3.jpg from our website and add them to the Assets Catalog. Create a Swift file called AppData.swift with the model of Listing 9-14. Update the AppDelegate.swift file with the code of Listing 7-14 and the SceneDelegate.swift file with the code of Listing 7-20. Update the `ContentView` structure with the code of Listing 9-38. Create a SwiftUI file called PlaceholderView.swift for the code of Listing 9-39, another called MenuView.swift for the code of Listing 9-40, and another called DetailView.swift for the code of Listing 9-41. Run the application on the iPad simulator in landscape mode. You should see the interface of Figure 9-23. Click on the buttons on the left to select a picture.

This interface works on iPhones, iPads and Mac computers. On iPads and Mac computers the two views are presented on the screen at the same time, and on iPhones they are presented in a navigation stack (in iPads in portrait mode and iPhones with large screens in landscape mode, the Master view is hidden, but the user can bring it back by dragging a finger from the left side of the screen). This is the perfect design when we want our application to work on all devices, but we still must solve a problem. The space available on the screen is different for each type of device. A picture that looks the right size on an iPhone may look too small on an iPad. A vertical stack of views may look fine on iPhones but unnecessary on iPads or Mac computers. Although redesigning the interface for each device may seem like a lot of work, it is not difficult when the app follows the MVVM pattern, as the examples in this book do. In this pattern, the model takes care of storing the data, the view model prepares the data to be shown by the views, and the sole purpose of the views is to show that data to the user, so changing the interface is as easy as reading the `userInterfaceIdiom` property of the `UIDevice` object to identify the device and then selecting the views to display according to that value, as we did in previous examples (for Mac computers there are other options available, as we will see later).

There are different ways to adapt the content. For instance, we can create separate `NavigationView` views for each device.

```
import SwiftUI

struct ContentView: View {
    let device = UIDevice.current.userInterfaceIdiom

    var body: some View {
        Group {
            if device == .phone {
                NavigationView {
                    MenuView()
                    PlaceholderView()
                }
            } else {
                NavigationView {
                    iPadMenuView()
                    iPadPlaceholderView()
                }
            }
        }
    }
}
```

Listing 9-42: Selecting the navigation path depending on the device

The `ContentView` view of Listing 9-42 reads the `userInterfaceIdiom` property and then presents a `NavigationView` view depending on its value. If the value is equal to `phone`, which means the application is running on an iPhone or an iPod, the `NavigationView` view presents the `MenuView` and `PlaceholderView` views introduced before. But if the value is different than `phone`, then we use different Master and Details views to present a design specific for iPads.

Another alternative is to use the same Master view (`MenuView`) but load the Detail views depending on the device. In this case, we must select the view to open from the Master view. The following example shows a possible implementation.

```
import SwiftUI

struct MenuView: View {
    @State private var selectedLink: Int? = nil

    var body: some View {
        VStack(alignment: .leading, spacing: 15) {
            NavigationLink(" Picture 1", destination:
getDetailView(selected: 1), tag: 1, selection: $selectedLink)
            NavigationLink(" Picture 2", destination:
getDetailView(selected: 2), tag: 2, selection: $selectedLink)
            NavigationLink(" Picture 3", destination:
getDetailView(selected: 3), tag: 3, selection: $selectedLink)
            Spacer()
        }.padding()
        .frame(minWidth: 0, maxWidth: .infinity, alignment: .leading)
        .navigationBarTitle("Menu")
    }
    func getDetailView(selected: Int) -> AnyView {
        let device = UIDevice.current.userInterfaceIdiom
        if device == .phone {
            return AnyView(DetailView(selected: selected))
        } else {
            return AnyView(iPadDetailView(selected: selected))
        }
    }
}
```

Listing 9-43: Initializing a different Detail view depending on the device

Instead of initializing a view and assign it directly to the `NavigationLink` attribute, the code of Listing 9-43 gets the view from a method called `getDetailView()`. This method detects the device and returns an instance of the `DetailView` view if it is an iPhone or an instance of the `iPadDetailView` view otherwise. Notice that we wrapped these views in an `AnyView` view to be able to return them from the method (see Listing 6-70).

Although these are valid alternatives, they generate different navigation paths that require us to design a set of views for each device. Another possibility is to use the same views and navigation path for all devices but select different content for the views. For our example, we have decided to take this approach and only modify the content of the `DetailView` view.

```
import SwiftUI

struct DetailView: View {
    @EnvironmentObject var appData: AppData
    var selected: Int = 0
    let device = UIDevice.current.userInterfaceIdiom

    var body: some View {
        VStack(spacing: 0) {
            if device == .phone {
```

Chapter 9 - Navigation

```
            VStack(spacing: 0) {
               DescriptionView(selected: selected)
               PictureView(selected: selected)
            }.padding(20)
         } else {
            HStack(alignment: .top) {
               iPadPictureView(selected: selected)
               iPadDescriptionView(selected: selected)
            }.padding(.top, 30)
            .padding([.leading, .trailing], 10)
         }
         Spacer()
      }
      .background(Color(red: 0.95, green: 0.95, blue: 0.95))
      .navigationBarTitle("Picture", displayMode: .inline)
   }
}
struct DescriptionView: View {
   @EnvironmentObject var appData: AppData
   var selected: Int

   var body: some View {
      HStack {
         Text("Rating: ")
            .font(.subheadline)
         Slider(value: $appData.userData[selected].picture.rating, in:
0...5, step: 1.0)
            .frame(width: 150)
         Text("\(appData.userData[selected].rating)")
            .font(.title)
            .fontWeight(.bold)
            .foregroundColor(Color.orange)
         Spacer()
      }.padding(.bottom, 15)
   }
}
struct PictureView: View {
   @EnvironmentObject var appData: AppData
   var selected: Int

   var body: some View {
      Image(appData.userData[selected].picture.image)
         .resizable()
         .aspectRatio(contentMode: .fill)
         .frame(minWidth: 0, maxWidth: .infinity, minHeight: 0,
maxHeight: .infinity)
         .clipped()
   }
}
struct iPadDescriptionView: View {
   @EnvironmentObject var appData: AppData
   var selected: Int

   var body: some View {
      VStack(alignment: .leading, spacing: 10) {
         HStack {
            Text("Name: ")
            Text(appData.userData[selected].picture.image)
               .bold()
         }.font(.title)
         HStack {
            Text("Number: ")
```

```
                Text(String(selected))
                    .bold()
            }.font(.title)
            HStack {
                Text("Rating: ")
                Slider(value: $appData.userData[selected].picture.rating, in:
0...5, step: 1.0)
                    .frame(width: 150)
                Text("\(appData.userData[selected].rating)")
                    .font(.title)
                    .fontWeight(.bold)
                    .foregroundColor(Color.orange)
            }.font(.title)
        }.frame(minWidth: 0, maxWidth: .infinity, alignment: .leading)
    }
}
struct iPadPictureView: View {
    @EnvironmentObject var appData: AppData
    var selected: Int

    var body: some View {
        Image(appData.userData[selected].picture.image)
            .resizable()
            .scaledToFit()
            .cornerRadius(20)
            .frame(width: 300, height: 300)
            .clipped()
    }
}
```

Listing 9-44: Designing a different interface for iPads

In the **DetailView** view of Listing 9-44, we break apart the content in two smaller views, one
for the picture and another for the slider, but there are two versions of each, one for iPhones
and another for iPads. The views to show are selected in the **body** of the **DetailView** view. If
the value of the **userInterfaceIdiom** property is equal to **phone**, we create a **VStack** with
the views **DescriptionView** and **PictureView** to show the design for iPhones (see Figure 9-
10), otherwise, we create an **HStack** with the views **iPadPictureView** and
iPadDescriptionView to show the design for iPads.

The views for iPhones are the same as before, but iPads have more space, so we show the
picture and the slider side by side, give the picture a fixed size of 300 by 300 points, and add
more information along with the slider. The result is shown in Figure 9-24, above.

 Do It Yourself: Update the DetailView.swift file from the previous example with
the code of Listing 9-44. Run the application on the simulator. On iPads in
landscape mode, you should see the interface of Figure 9-24, and on iPhones in
portrait mode you should see the interface of Figure 9-10. Of course, the
design can also be adapted to the orientation, as we will see next.

By default, iPhones show the view in a navigation stack and devices with larger screens split
the interface in two to show the Master view on the left and the Details view on the right. These
styles are defined by SwiftUI and are assigned to the **NavigationView** view depending on the
device and the size of the screen, but the **View** protocol includes the following modifier in case
we need to change it.

navigationViewStyle(Style**)**—This modifier sets the style of the **NavigationView** view.
The attribute is a structure that conforms to the **NavigationViewStyle** protocol. The
structures defined by SwiftUI are **DefaultNavigationViewStyle**,
DoubleColumnNavigationViewStyle, and **StackNavigationViewStyle**.

There are different circumstances in which we may need to set a specific style. For example, iPhones with large screens allow the user to drag the Master view from the left. To avoid this behavior, we can set the `StackNavigationViewStyle` style for iPhones and leave the `DoubleColumnNavigationViewStyle` style for iPads.

```
import SwiftUI

struct ContentView: View {
    let device = UIDevice.current.userInterfaceIdiom

    var body: some View {
        Group {
            if device == .phone {
                NavigationView {
                    MenuView()
                    PlaceholderView()
                }.navigationViewStyle(StackNavigationViewStyle())
            } else {
                NavigationView {
                    MenuView()
                    PlaceholderView()
                }.navigationViewStyle(DoubleColumnNavigationViewStyle())
            }
        }
    }
}
```

Listing 9-45: Setting the style of the navigation view

If we update the `ContentView` view of the previous example with the one in Listing 9-45, we won't notice any difference, but in iPhones with large screens, like iPhones Plus in landscape mode, the views are always inside a navigation stack (the user cannot open the Master view by dragging a finger from the left side of the screen).

 IMPORTANT: At the time of writing, the navigation tools provided by SwiftUI to build multiplatform interfaces are broken. They present different behaviors depending on the device, and some functionality may cause the app to crash. If you come across these issues, we recommend you avoiding the use of the navigation bar and buttons provided by SwiftUI and implement custom navigation tools, as explained next.

(Basic) Custom Navigation

At the time, SwiftUI does not offer many options to customize the navigation bar, but we can hide the bar and create our own. The `View` protocol defines the `navigationBarHidden()` modifier for this purpose. To hide the bar, we have to assign the `navigationBarTitle()` modifier with an empty string and the `navigationBarHidden()` modifier with the value `true` to all the views in the hierarchy. Once the system bar is removed, creating a navigation bar is about combining the SwiftUI views and modifiers we already know. The following example illustrates how to define a custom navigation bar for our multiplatform application. Here are the modifications we must introduce to the Master view.

```
import SwiftUI

struct MenuView: View {
    @State private var selectedLink: Int? = nil
```

```
    var body: some View {
        VStack {
            BarMenuView()
            VStack(alignment: .leading, spacing: 15) {
                NavigationLink("🖼 Picture 1", destination:
DetailView(selected: 1), tag: 1, selection: $selectedLink)
                NavigationLink("🖼 Picture 2", destination:
DetailView(selected: 2), tag: 2, selection: $selectedLink)
                NavigationLink("🖼 Picture 3", destination:
DetailView(selected: 3), tag: 3, selection: $selectedLink)
                Spacer()
            }.font(.title)
            .padding()
            .frame(minWidth: 0, maxWidth: .infinity, alignment: .leading)
        }
        .edgesIgnoringSafeArea(.all)
        .navigationBarTitle("")
        .navigationBarHidden(true)
    }
}
struct BarMenuView: View {
    var body: some View {
        HStack {
            Text("Menu")
                .font(.title)
                .padding()
            Spacer()
        }.padding()
        .padding(.top, 35)
        .frame(height: 90)
        .frame(minWidth: 0, maxWidth: .infinity)
        .background(Color.white)
    }
}
```

Listing 9-46: Hiding the navigation bar

Besides the `navigationBarTitle()` and the `navigationBarHidden()` modifiers, we also apply the `edgeIgnoringSafeArea()` modifier to extend our custom navigation bar to the top of the screen. The bar is created in a custom view called `BarMenuView`. We embed the `NavigationLinks` in an additional `VStack` and initialize the `BarMenuView` view before defining the buttons, so the bar is displayed at the top and the buttons below. The `BarMenuView` view only includes a `Text` view for the title, but we include some padding, define a fixed height of 90 points for the bar and made it flexible with the `frame()` modifier.

Figure 9-25: Custom navigation bar

Chapter 9 - Navigation

This looks like the standard navigation bar provided by SwiftUI, but now we can customize every aspect of the view. For instance, we can assign a background color, or add buttons or images. The following are the changes we have introduced to the DetailView.swift file to provide a more customized navigation bar for the Detail view.

```swift
struct DetailView: View {
    @EnvironmentObject var appData: AppData
    var selected: Int = 0
    let device = UIDevice.current.userInterfaceIdiom

    var body: some View {
        VStack(spacing: 0) {
            BarDetailView()
            if device == .phone {
                VStack(spacing: 0) {
                    DescriptionView(selected: selected)
                    PictureView(selected: selected)
                }.padding(20)
            } else {
                HStack(alignment: .top) {
                    iPadPictureView(selected: selected)
                    iPadDescriptionView(selected: selected)
                }.padding(.top, 30)
                .padding([.leading, .trailing], 10)
            }
            Spacer()
        }
        .background(Color(red: 0.95, green: 0.95, blue: 0.95))
        .edgesIgnoringSafeArea(.all)
        .navigationBarTitle("")
        .navigationBarHidden(true)
    }
}
struct BarDetailView: View {
    let device = UIDevice.current.userInterfaceIdiom
    @Environment(\.presentationMode) var presentation
    @State private var openAlert: Bool = false

    var body: some View {
        HStack {
            if device == .phone {
                Button(action: {
                    self.presentation.wrappedValue.dismiss()
                }, label: {
                    Image(systemName: "arrow.left.circle")
                        .font(Font.system(size: 30))
                        .foregroundColor(.black)
                }).padding(.trailing, 8)
            }
            Text("Picture")
                .font(.title)
            Spacer()
            Button(action: {
                self.openAlert = true
            }, label: {
                Image(systemName: "trash.circle")
                    .font(Font.system(size: 30))
                    .foregroundColor(.black)
            }).padding(.trailing, 8)
            NavigationLink(destination: AddPictureView(), label: {
                Image(systemName: "plus.circle")
```

```
            .font(Font.system(size: 30))
            .foregroundColor(.black)
        })
    }.padding()
    .padding(.top, 35)
    .frame(height: 95)
    .frame(minWidth: 0, maxWidth: .infinity)
    .background(Color(red: 250/255, green: 255/255, blue: 178/255))
    .alert(isPresented: $openAlert, content: {
        Alert(title: Text("Delete Picture"), message: Text("Are you
sure?"), primaryButton: .cancel(), secondaryButton:
.destructive(Text("Delete")))
    })
    }
}
```

Listing 9-47: *Defining a custom navigation bar*

The view for the bar is called **BarDetailView**, but the way we included to the interface is the same as before. The view is embedded in a **VStack** along with the rest of the views, the default navigation bar is hidden, and the **edgesIgnoringSafeArea()** modifier is applied again to move the bar to the top. But this navigation bar includes more buttons and features. First, we include a button to dismiss the view. This is necessary only in iPhones, so we check the value of the **userInterfaceIdiom** property and if it is equal to **phone**, we create a button that calls the **dismiss()** method to remove the view (see Listing 9-7). And finally, we include a **Text** view for the title and two more buttons, one to open an alert view that allows the user to erase the picture, and another to navigate to a view for the user to be able to add a picture (we will learn how to erase and add data to the model in further chapters).

Figure 9-26: *Custom navigation bar for the Detail view*

And of course, this also works on iPads.

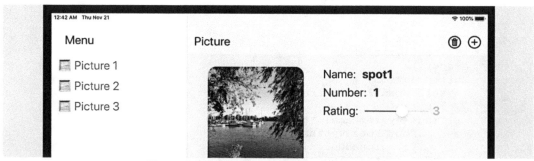

Figure 9-27: *Custom navigation bar for iPads*

Do It Yourself: Update the MenuView.swift file with the code of Listing 9-46 and the DetailView.swift file with the code of Listing 9-47. Create a SwiftUI file called AddPictureView.swift for the + button included in the navigation bar of the Detail view. Run the application in the iPhone and iPad simulators. You should see the interfaces of Figures 9-26 and 9-27.

IMPORTANT: Although some features from the UIKit framework are not available in SwiftUI yet, most SwiftUI views are created with UIKit views in the background, so we can modify the default appearance of UIKit views to change how they look in a SwiftUI application. For instance, the appearance of the navigation bar in SwiftUI can be changed by modifying the appearance of the `UINavigationBar` class. For more information, see Chapter 16.

(Basic) # 9.4 Orientation

SwiftUI views can adapt to the space available. We can implement flexible views to expand the interface or align the views using alignment values, but in practice this is only useful when the proportions of the window are always the same. For example, the screen of an iPhone 11 in portrait mode is slightly taller than the screen of an older iPhone in the same orientation, but the proportions between width and height are similar. Adapting the interface to these variations only requires simple transformations, such as extending or contracting the views. Things change when we compare devices with very different screens, such as iPhones and iPads, or the same device in different orientations. The interface must be drastically modified to adapt to these disparate conditions. To know when to perform these changes, the system defines values that represent the relative size of the space in which the interface is being presented. The classification is based on the magnitude of the space's horizontal and vertical dimensions. The value is called *Regular* if it is big enough to fit a regular interface or *Compact* otherwise. These values conform a unit of measurement called *Size Classes*.

(Basic) ## Size Classes

Because of the rectangular shape of the screen, the interface is defined by two size classes, one for the horizontal and another for the vertical space. Every device is assigned different size classes, depending on the size of their screens and orientations, as illustrated in Figure 9-28.

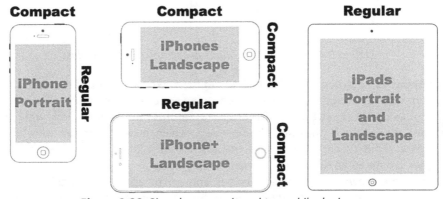

Figure 9-28: Size classes assigned to mobile devices

The examples in Figure 9-28 represent the only four possible combinations of size classes, but of course, they change according to the current layout. For instance, if the screen is split in two on an iPad, one of the windows may be too small to be considered Regular anymore and it may change to Compact. Another situation in which the size classes may change is when the device is rotated.

No matter what caused the change, we can detect it and adapt the interface accordingly. For this purpose, the environment includes the following properties.

horizontalSizeClass—This property returns the horizontal size class of the space occupied by the view. It is an enumeration of type `UserInterfaceSizeClass` with the values `compact` and `regular`.

verticalSizeClass—This property returns the vertical size class of the space occupied by the view. It is an enumeration of type `UserInterfaceSizeClass` with the values `compact` and `regular`.

As always, these environment properties are accessed with the `@Environment` property wrapper (see Listing 7-12). Once we create this binding to the properties, adapting the interface is a matter of organizing the views depending on the property's value (`compact` or `regular`). For instance, in the following example we define the interface's content in two custom views, `HeaderView` and `BodyView`, and then display them in a vertical or horizontal stack depending on the current horizontal size class.

```
import SwiftUI

struct ContentView: View {
    @Environment(\.horizontalSizeClass) var horizontal

    var body: some View {
        Group {
            if horizontal == .compact {
                VStack(spacing: 0) {
                    HeaderView(isCompact: true)
                    BodyView()
                }
            } else {
                HStack(spacing: 0) {
                    HeaderView(isCompact: false)
                    BodyView()
                }
            }
        }.edgesIgnoringSafeArea(.all)
    }
}
```

Listing 9-48: Detecting changes in the horizontal size class

The `ContentView` structure of Listing 9-48 defines the basic layout of our app. We begin by declaring an `@Environment` property called `horizontal` to monitor the environment's property `horizontalSizeClass`. This property returns an enumeration with the values `compact` and `regular`. If the value is `compact`, which means that the interface is being presented in a small space, we create a `VStack` to show the views on top of each other, otherwise, we create an `HStack` to show them side by side.

Organizing the views on the screen is not enough to adapt the interface to the space available, sometimes we also must adapt their content. To illustrate how to do it, we pass a value to the `HeaderView` to indicate whether the interface is been shown in a compact or a regular space, and then use this value inside the view to select the appropriate height. The following is the implementation of our `HeaderView` and `BodyView` views.

Chapter 9 - Navigation

```
struct HeaderView: View {
   var isCompact: Bool

   var body: some View {
      Text("Food Menu")
         .frame(minWidth: 0, maxWidth: .infinity, minHeight: 0,
maxHeight: isCompact ? 150: .infinity)
         .background(Color.yellow)
   }
}
struct BodyView: View {
   var body: some View {
      Text("Content Title")
         .frame(minWidth: 0, maxWidth: .infinity, minHeight: 0,
maxHeight: .infinity)
         .background(Color.gray)
   }
}
```

Listing 9-49: Defining the content views

Both views are flexible and therefore the space available is distributed between the two, but we limit the height of the **HeaderView** when they are presented in a vertical layout. To this end, we check the value received by the view in the **frame()** modifier. if the value is **true**, which means that the interface is being shown in a Compact size class and therefore the **HeaderView** is displayed on top of the **BodyView**, we give it a maximum height of 150 points, otherwise, we give it a flexible height with the **infinity** value to extend it from top to bottom.

Notice that **isCompact** is a normal property. We didn't have to use a **@Binding** property in this case because every time the value of the **horizontal** property changes, the views are redrawn and the **isCompact** property is updated with the current value. As a result, every time the device is rotated, the interface goes from a vertical to a horizontal layout, and vice versa.

Figure 9-29: Different layouts for Compact and Regular size classes

 Do It Yourself: Create a SwiftUI project. Update the **ContentView** structure with the code of Listing 9-48. Add the structures of Listing 9-49 below. Run the application in an iPhone simulator. Press the Command + Left arrow keys to rotate the screen. If the simulator is of a new iPhone model with a large screen, like the iPhone 11, you should see the interfaces of Figure 9-29.

The values of the `horizontalSizeClass` and `verticalSizeClass` properties only change when the interface's size classes are different, so the views are refreshed only when the size classes go from Compact to Regular or Regular to Compact. But in some devices the horizontal and vertical size classes are the same and therefore the state of the properties never changes. For instance, iPads are always Regular and Regular. But no matter the orientation, the difference in width and height is still significant. In cases like this, we must adapt the interface according to the device's orientation. To report changes in the orientation, the `UIWindowSceneDelegate` protocol defines the following method.

windowScene(UIWindowScene, **didUpdate:** UICoordinateSpace, **interfaceOrientation:** UIInterfaceOrientation, **traitCollection:** UITraitCollection)— This method is called when the orientation of the device changes.

When the device, and therefore the scene, is rotated, the system calls this protocol method on the `SceneDelegate` (see Listing 5-3). The method receives some information regarding the condition of the interface, such as the size of the scene and its orientation, but the values only reflect the previous state. To get the current state, we must read the properties provided by the `UIWIndowScene` object. The following are the most frequently used.

interfaceOrientation—This property returns an enumeration of type `UIInterfaceOrientation` with a value representing the current orientation of the scene. The possible values are `portrait`, `portraitUpsideDown`, `landscapeLeft`, `landscapeRight`, and `unknown`.

coordinateSpace—This property returns a protocol of type `UICoordinateSpace` that provides its own implementations of a property called `bounds` that returns a `CGRect` value with the size of the scene, and some methods to convert coordinate values in the scene to the corresponding coordinate values of the screen.

Because the state is reported by a protocol method inside the `SceneDelegate` class, we must work with an observable object and update a property in that object to report the changes in the state to the views. The following is a simple model we are going to use to detect changes in the orientation.

```
import SwiftUI

class AppData: ObservableObject {
    @Published var isPortrait: Bool = true
}
```

Listing 9-50: Storing the current orientation in the model

In this object, we only define one property called `isPortrait`. If the interface is in portrait mode, we assign the value `true` to this property, otherwise the value is `false`. The instance of this object must be created from the `AppDelegate` class, as we did before in the example of Listing 7-14. Once we have this instance, we must modify the value of the `isPortrait` property from the `SceneDelegate` class every time the state changes. Because this happens in two different circumstances, one when the app is launched and again when the device is rotated, we define a method to detect the current orientation and then call this method every time we need it. The following is the implementation of the `SceneDelegate` class for this example.

Chapter 9 - Navigation

```
import UIKit
import SwiftUI

class SceneDelegate: UIResponder, UIWindowSceneDelegate {
    var window: UIWindow?

    func scene(_ scene: UIScene, willConnectTo session: UISceneSession,
options connectionOptions: UIScene.ConnectionOptions) {
        let app = UIApplication.shared
        let delegate = app.delegate as! AppDelegate
        let contentView = ContentView(appData: delegate.myData)

        if let windowScene = scene as? UIWindowScene {
            delegate.myData?.isPortrait = getOrientation(scene: windowScene)

            let window = UIWindow(windowScene: windowScene)
            window.rootViewController = UIHostingController(rootView:
contentView)
            self.window = window
            window.makeKeyAndVisible()
        }
    }
    func windowScene(_ windowScene: UIWindowScene, didUpdate
previousCoordinateSpace: UICoordinateSpace, interfaceOrientation
previousInterfaceOrientation: UIInterfaceOrientation, traitCollection
previousTraitCollection: UITraitCollection) {
        let app = UIApplication.shared
        let delegate = app.delegate as! AppDelegate
        delegate.myData?.isPortrait = getOrientation(scene: windowScene)
    }
    func getOrientation(scene: UIWindowScene) -> Bool {
        let interfaceOrientation = scene.interfaceOrientation
        if interfaceOrientation == .portrait || interfaceOrientation ==
.portraitUpsideDown {
            return true
        }
        return false
    }
}
```

Listing 9-51: Reporting a change in orientation to the views

In Listing 9-51, we call our method `getOrientation()`. The method receives a reference to the scene and returns a Boolean value that determines whether the interface is in portrait mode or not. To get this value, we read the value of the `interfaceOrientation` property of the `UIWindowScene` object and return `true` if it is equal to `portrait` or `portraitUpsideDown`.

We first call this method before creating the window to set the value of the `isPortrait` property according to the initial orientation. Then, we implement the method from the `UIWindowSceneDelegate` protocol mentioned above, and call the `getOrientation()` method again every time the protocol method is called. The procedure is the same in both cases, we call the `getOrientation()` method and then assign the value returned by the method to the `isPortrait` property to update the state.

Now that we have a model with a `@Published` property that is updated every time the orientation changes, is time to refresh our views. The interface is the same as before, but instead of reading a value from the environment, we get it from our model. The following is the new implementation of the `ContentView` structure.

```
import SwiftUI
struct ContentView: View {
   @ObservedObject var appData: AppData

   var body: some View {
      Group {
         if appData.isPortrait {
            VStack(spacing: 0) {
               HeaderView(isCompact: true)
               BodyView()
            }
         } else {
            HStack(spacing: 0) {
               HeaderView(isCompact: false)
               BodyView()
            }
         }
      }.edgesIgnoringSafeArea(.all)
   }
}
struct ContentView_Previews: PreviewProvider {
   static var previews: some View {
      ContentView(appData: AppData())
   }
}
```

Listing 9-52: Updating the views when the orientation changes

This time, the views are included in a horizontal or a vertical stack depending on the orientation, not the size class. When the device is rotated, the protocol method is called in the **SceneDelegate** object, the value of the **isPortrait** property in our observable object is changed, the **@ObservedObject** property in our view detects the change, and finally the view is refreshed, as illustrated in Figure 9-29, above.

 Do It Yourself: This example updates the project created in the previous section. Create a new Swift file with the name AppData.swift for the model of Listing 9-50. Update the AppDelegate.swift file with the code of Listing 7-14. Update the SceneDelegate.swift file with the code of Listing 9-51. Finally, update the **ContentView** structure with the code of Listing 9-52. Run the application in the simulator and rotate the screen. You should see the interfaces of Figure 9-29, no matter the device.

(Medium) GeometryReader View

When we adapt the interface to the device or the orientation, the size and position of the views change. Applications usually need to modify aspects of the interface according to these new values. SwiftUI views don't provide this information, but the framework includes a view called **GeometryReader** to generate these values. The **GeometryReader** view takes the size of its container and then sends this information to its children, so they can adapt to those values. The following is the view's initializer.

GeometryReader(content: Closure)—This initializer creates a **GeometryReader** view. The **content** attribute is the closure that defines the content of the view. This closure receives a **GeometryProxy** value with the view's position and dimensions.

The **GeometryReader** view calculates its position and size and sends this information to the closure that defines its content. The values are stored in an instance of the **GeometryProxy** structure. This structure provides the following properties and method to get the values.

size—This property returns a **CGSize** value with the width and height of the **GeometryReader** view.

safeAreaInsets—This property returns an **EdgeInsets** value with the safe area's insets.

frame(in: CoordinateSpace)—This method returns a **CGRect** value with the position and size of the **GeometryReader** view. The values are returned according to the coordinate space specified by the **in** attribute. The attribute is an enumeration with the values **global**, **local**, and **named(String)**.

The **GeometryReader** view works like a flexible view. It stretches to occupy all the space available in its container and then sends a **GeometryProxy** value with its position and size to the closure. Using these values, we can adapt the views inside the closure or perform any change in style we want. For instance, we can determine the size of an image relative to the size of its container by including the **Image** view inside a **GeometryReader** view.

```
import SwiftUI
struct ContentView: View {
    var body: some View {
        GeometryReader { geometry in
            Image("spot1")
                .resizable()
                .scaledToFit()
                .frame(width: geometry.size.width / 2, height:
geometry.size.height / 4)
                .background(Color.gray)
        }
    }
}
```

Listing 9-53: Adapting an Image *view to the size of its container*

The code in Listing 9-53 creates a normal **Image** view, but the view is embedded in a **GeometryReader** view, so we know the space available for it. This information is provided by the value received by the closure. In this example, we call this value **geometry**, but we can use any name we want. From this value, we calculate the size of the image. In this example, we decided to give it a width that is half of the width of the container (**geometry.size.width / 2**) and a height that is a quarter of its height (**geometry.size.height / 4**). This determines the size of the **Image** view, but the aspect ratio of the image was set to **fit**, so the image is reduced even more to fit within the view's frame. The view's background was set to **gray** to be able to see the space remaining on the sides and how the view adapts to the space available when the orientation is in portrait or landscape mode, as shown in Figure 9-30.

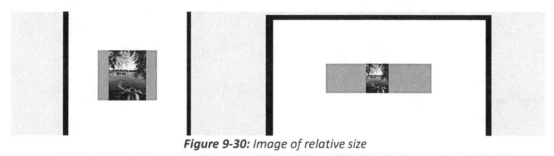

Figure 9-30: Image of relative size

Chapter 9 - Navigation

Do It Yourself: Create a SwiftUI project. Download the spot1.jpg image from our website and add it to the Assets Catalog. Update the `ContentView` structure with the code of Listing 9-53. Run the application on the iPhone simulator. Rotate the screen. You should see the size of the `Image` view adapt to the space available.

Besides the size, we can also obtain the position of the `GeometryReader` view. This information is returned by the `frame()` method of the `GeometryProxy` structure and the values depend on the selected coordinate space. A SwiftUI interface defines two types of coordinates spaces, one that represents the coordinates of the screen called `global`, and another that represents the coordinates of the view called `local` (every view has its own coordinate space). If we read the values considering the `local` coordinate space, the position is 0,0, because the coordinate space of the `GeometryReader` view always starts at the position 0,0, but if we select the `global` coordinate space, the values returned by the method represent the position of the view relative to the screen. The following example implements this method to show the difference between both values.

```
import SwiftUI

struct ContentView: View {
    var body: some View {
        GeometryReader { geometry in
            VStack {
                Image("spot1")
                    .resizable()
                    .scaledToFit()
                    .frame(width: geometry.size.width / 2, height:
geometry.size.height / 2)
                Text("Global: \(geometry.frame(in: .global).origin.x,
specifier: "%.f") / \(geometry.frame(in: .global).origin.y, specifier:
"%.f")")
                Text("Local: \(geometry.frame(in: .local).origin.x,
specifier: "%.f") / \(geometry.frame(in: .local).origin.y, specifier:
"%.f")")
            }
        }.frame(height: 200)
    }
}
```

Listing 9-54: Reading the position of the `GeometryReader` *view*

The view in Listing 9-54 includes the `Image` view from the previous example and two `Text` views to show the values in each coordinate space. To make sure that the values returned are not the same, we assign a height of 200 points to the `GeometryReader` view, so it is aligned at the center of the screen and therefore the position changes depending on the space available and the orientation. As shown in Figure 9-31, below, the local coordinate space always returns the coordinates 0, 0, but the global coordinate space returns values that reflect the position of the view on the screen.

Figure 9-31: Two coordinate spaces

Do It Yourself: Update the `ContentView` structure with the code of Listing 9-54. Run the application on the iPhone simulator. Rotate the screen. You should see the value of the y coordinate change because of the change of the `GeometryReader` view's position relative to the screen.

The `GeometryReader` view is a flexible view and therefore it takes all the space available in its container, independently of the size of its children. If instead of the space available we need to calculate the size and position of a view, we can use the `GeometryReader` view to present a secondary view. Secondary views are those assigned to other views, like the ones assigned to the view's background or overlay. For instance, we can add a background to an image and embed the background view in a `GeometryReader` view to get the position and size of the image.

```
import SwiftUI

struct ContentView: View {
    @State private var size: CGSize = CGSize.zero

    var body: some View {
        VStack {
            Image("spot1")
                .resizable()
                .scaledToFit()
                .background(
                    GeometryReader { geometry in
                        Color.clear
                            .onAppear(perform: {
                                self.size = geometry.size
                            })
                    })
            Text("\(size.width, specifier: "%.2f") x \(size.height,
specifier: "%.2f")")
        }.padding([.leading, .trailing], 100)
    }
}
```

Listing 9-55: Reading the position and size of a view

The example in Listing 9-55 includes an `Image` view inside a `VStack`. The `VStack` view has a padding of 100 points on the sides, so the image is centered on the screen. The `GeometryReader` view in this case is used to embed the `Color` view assigned as the image's background. Views assigned to the background adopt the size of the original view. In this case, the `GeometryReader` view expands to occupy the same space than the `Image` view and therefore its values reflect the image's position and size.

120.00 x 161.00

Figure 9-32: View measured by a `GeometryReader` *view*

Do It Yourself: Update the `ContentView` structure with the code of Listing 9-55. Run the application on the iPhone simulator. You should see the size of the `Image` view at the bottom, as shown in Figure 9-32.

(Medium) **Preferences**

The `GeometryReader` view sends the information down the hierarchy. Only the views that are within the `GeometryReader` view can read and use these values. If we need to send the values up the hierarchy, we must use Preferences.

Despite what the name suggests, Preferences are just values with a name that we can generate from one view and read from the views up in the hierarchy. For instance, if we have a `Text` view inside a `VStack` view, the preference values generated by the `Text` view are accessible from the `VStack` view. The values are stored in what is called a Preference Key. This is a structure that conforms to the `PreferenceKey` protocol. The protocol has the following requirements.

Value—This property is an associated type that defines the data type of the values we are going to work with.

defaultValue—This property defines the value the Preference Key is going to have by default.

reduce(value: Value, **nextValue:** Closure)—This method adds a new value to the structure. The **value** attribute is a reference to the values stored in the structure from previous calls, and the **nextValue** attribute is a closure that returns the new value.

We must define a structure that conforms to this protocol and then use it to pass the values from one view to another. For this purpose, the `View` protocol defines the following modifiers.

preference(key: Type, **value:** Value)—This modifier sets a value for a specific preference key. The **key** attribute is a reference to the key's data type, and the **value** attribute is the value we want to assign to that key.

onPreferenceChange(Type, **perform:** Closure)—This modifier executes a closure when the value of a preference key changes. The first attribute is a reference to the key's data type, and the **perform** attribute is the closure to be executed when the value changes.

The process to pass a value from one view to another up the hierarchy is simple. First, we must define a structure that conforms to the `PreferenceKey` protocol. Then, we must apply the `preference()` modifier to a view with the value we want to send. And finally, we must apply the `onPreferenceChange()` modifier to a view up the hierarchy (a parent view or a container of the previous view) to process the value. The following is a simple example that illustrates how this works. The code modifies the background color of a container view when the size of a view within this container is greater than 500 points.

```
import SwiftUI

struct BoxPreference: PreferenceKey {
    typealias Value = CGSize
    static var defaultValue: CGSize = CGSize.zero

    static func reduce(value: inout CGSize, nextValue: () -> CGSize) {
        value = nextValue()
    }
}
struct ContentView: View {
    @State private var setColor: Bool = false

    var body: some View {
        VStack {
            GeometryReader { geometry in
                Image("spot1")
                    .resizable()
                    .scaledToFit()
                    .frame(width: geometry.size.width, height:
geometry.size.height / 2)
                    .preference(key: BoxPreference.self, value: geometry.size)
            }
        }.frame(height: 200)
        .background(setColor ? Color.yellow : Color.clear)
        .onPreferenceChange(BoxPreference.self, perform: { value in
            self.setColor = value.width > 500
        })
    }
}
```

Listing 9-56: Setting and reading preferences

The first thing we do in Listing 9-56 is to define the structure to store the values. To conform to the **PreferenceKey** protocol, this structure must comply with a few requirements. Firstly, we must define a typealias called **Value**. Because we are going to store the **CGSize** value returned by the **size** property of the **GeometryProxy** structure produced by the **GeometryReader** view, we define **Value** as a typealias of **CGSize**. Next comes a type property called **defaultValue**. This property defines the value of the structure by default. Since we are working with a **CGSize** structure, we define it as a **CGSize** structure with its values set to 0 (**CGSize.zero**). Finally, we implement the **reduce()** method. This method receives a reference to the values already stored in the structure and a closure that returns the new value. To store this new value, we must execute the closure and add the value returned to the values already stored in the structure. In this case, we are working only with one value (a **CGSize** structure), so we assign it directly to the property (**value = nextValue()**).

Within the view, we use a **VStack** view as the main container. Inside, we include a **GeometryReader** view with an **Image** view, as we did in previous examples. What we want to do is to send the size of the **Image** view to the **VStack** view. For this purpose, we apply the **preference()** modifier to the **Image** view. The value of the **key** attribute is a reference to the definition of our **PreferenceKey** structure (**BoxPreference.self**), and for the **value** attribute we specify the **CGSize** structure returned by the **size** property of the **GeometryProxy** structure (**geometry.size**). Now, this value is defined as a Preference, and therefore we can read it from the views up the hierarchy with the **onPreferenceChange()** modifier. In this example, we apply this modifier to the **VStack** view. Again, we must provide a reference to the definition of the structure (**BoxPreference.self**), and then the closure to execute when a new value is received. In this closure, we check the size of the **Image** view. If it is greater than 500, the value `true` is assigned to a `@State` property called `setColor`, and because we use this property to set the background color of the `VStack` view, the color changes. As a result, the view is shown with a clear color in portrait mode, but in landscape mode the size of the `Image` view is greater than 500, and therefore the background color changes to yellow.

Figure 9-33: Interface modified with preferences

 Do It Yourself: Create a SwiftUI project. Download the spot1.jpg image from our website and add it to the Assets Catalog. Update the ContentView.swift file with the code of Listing 9-56. Run the application on the iPhone simulator. Rotate the screen. You should see the background of the `VStack` view turn yellow when the interface is in landscape mode.

 IMPORTANT: In this example, we store a single `CGSize` value, but the `PreferenceKey` protocol was designed to store values from multiple views and therefore these values are usually stored in arrays. For more information on Preferences, visit our website and follow the links for this chapter.

(Medium) 9.5 Mac Catalyst

SwiftUI is available in every platform. With SwiftUI we can program applications for iPhones, iPads, Mac computers, the Apple Watch, and Apple TV. But this doesn't mean we can use the same code. The system for iPhones and iPads is the same, but Mac computers, the Apple Watch and Apple TV require a separate set of frameworks. For instance, Mac computers work with a framework called AppKit to create the app's interface, the Apple Watch includes a framework called WatchKit to provide the tools required to program applications for such a distinctive device, and Apple TV is no exception, with multiple frameworks that are unique to the platform. This means that we can define the interface with SwiftUI, but the code must be adapted to the unique characteristics of each device. The good news is that, due to the similarities between modern iPads and Mac computers, Apple decided to introduce a new system, called *Mac Catalyst*, to allow us to run apps designed for iPads in Mac computers. With Mac Catalyst, we can use the same project and source code we programmed for iPhones and iPads in Mac computers.

(Medium) IPad Apps on the Mac

The process to port an iPad app into Mac is very simple. All we have to do is to tell Xcode that we want to make our app available in Mac computers and the system takes care of everything. The option is available in the project settings, in the General panel, as shown in Figure 9-34.

Target	Device
iOS 13.2 ◇	☑ iPhone
	☑ iPad
①	☑ Mac (requires macOS 10.15)

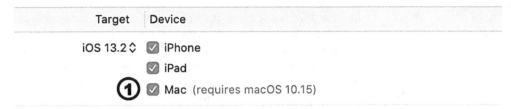

Figure 9-34: Mac option

Once this option is selected and we accept to enable Mac support, a new scheme appears on the list to select the Mac and run the application.

Figure 9-35: Mac scheme

In principle, this is all we have to do. Pressing the play button opens the app on the Mac. Catalyst adapts the interface to work in a window on the computer. But this means that the interface won't look the same. To adapt the interface to the Mac, we need to define some conditional code.

(Medium) **Conditional Code**

The Swift compiler supports conditionals. These are not the normal `if else` statements that are executed at run time, these are conditionals the are checked when the code is compiled and, therefore, we can use them to select the code we want to compile according to the target device.

The conditionals are built using the keywords `#if`, `#else`, and `#endif`. The `#if` and `#else` keywords work like the Swift conditionals `if else`, but because the code is not within a block, the `#endif` keyword is required to indicate the end of the conditional.

There are several parameters we can use to set the condition, but to detect whether the application is being compiled for the Mac, we have to define it with the `targetEnvironment()` instruction and the value `macCatalyst`, as in the following example.

```
import SwiftUI

struct ContentView: View {
    var body: some View {
        VStack {
            #if targetEnvironment(macCatalyst)
                Text("Mac Application")
            #else
                Text("Mobile Application")
            #endif
        }
    }
}
```

Listing 9-57: Programming conditional code

This is a very simple example, because the way we use this tool depends on the characteristics of our application, but it illustrates how to generate different code for each platform. If we run this project on the Mac, the message "Mac Application" is shown on the screen, otherwise the message "Mobile Application" is shown instead.

Menu

Mac applications include a menu bar that is displayed at the top of the screen for easy access to the application's key features. A Mac app compiled with Catalyst provides a standard menu bar with basic menus like File, Edit, Format, View, Window, and Help, but we can customize it from code. The option is provided by the `UIResponder` class. This class defines a method that we can override from the `AppDelegate` class. When the app is launched on the Mac, the following method is executed, and this is our chance to modify the menu bar.

> **buildMenu(with:** UIMenuBuilder)—This method is executed by the application before the menu bar is created. The method receives a value of type `UIMenuBuilder` to provide access to the menu and options for configuration.

The method receives a value of type `UIMenuBuilder`. This is a protocol that defines properties and methods to modify the menu bar. The following are the most frequently used.

> **system**—This property returns an object of type `UIMenuSystem` with information about the menu system.
>
> **insertChild(**UIMenu, **atStartOfMenu:** Identifier)—This method inserts an element or a group of elements at the beginning of the menu indicated by the **atStartOfMenu** attribute.
>
> **insertChild(**UIMenu, **atEndOfMenu:** Identifier)—This method inserts an element or a group of elements at the end of the menu indicated by the **atEndOfMenu** attribute.
>
> **insertSibling(**UIMenu, **beforeMenu:** Identifier)—This method inserts an element or a group of elements before the element indicated by the **beforeMenu** attribute.
>
> **insertSibling(**UIMenu, **afterMenu:** Identifier)—This method inserts an element or a group of elements after the element indicated by the **afterMenu** attribute.
>
> **remove(menu:** Identifier)—This method removes the element or group of elements indicated by the **menu** attribute.

There are two types of menus, the main menu at the top of the screen, and contextual menus that open when the user interacts with a view. To identify the system we are working with, the `UIMenuBuilder` protocol includes the `system` property. This property returns a `UIMenuSystem` object with information about the system. The class includes two type properties to represent the menu system and two methods to process the menu.

> **main**—This type property returns a reference to the main menu system (the menu bar).
>
> **context**—This type property returns a reference to the context menu system.
>
> **setNeedsRebuild()**—This method tells the menu system to rebuild all the menus.
>
> **setNeedsRevalidate()**—This method tells the menu system that the menus need to be revalidated. It is used to update the menus when the state of the app changes.

There are two types of elements we can add to a bar menu: a menu (or submenu) and a menu's option, but they are all added as `UIMenu` objects. These objects act as containers for menus or menu options. The class includes the following initializer.

> **UIMenu(title:** String, **image:** UIImage?, **identifier:** Identifier?, **options:** Options, **children:** [UIMenuElement])—This initializer creates a `UIMenu` object to represent a menu or an option. The **title** attribute is the title of the element. The **image**

attribute is the image associated with the element. The **identifier** attribute is the value we want to use to identify the element. The **options** attribute is a structure with type properties that determine the type of element we are adding. The properties available are `displayInline`, to indicate that the element is not a submenu but an option of a menu, and `destructive` to represent a destructive action. Finally, the **children** attribute is an array with the elements we want to add to the menu bar.

There are also two types of objects we can use to create the elements for the menu bar. They are created from the `UICommand` and `UIKeyCommand` classes. The `UICommand` class defines a simple element, while the `UIKeyCommand` class defines an element that can be selected with a combination of keys. The following are their initializers.

UICommand(title: String, **image:** UIImage?, **action:** Selector, **propertyList:** Any?, **alternates:** [UICommandAlternate], **discoverabilityTitle:** String?, **attributes:** Attributes, **state:** State)—This initializer creates a simple menu element. The **title** attribute is the option's title. The **image** attribute is the image associated with the option. The **action** attribute is a selector with the action we want to perform when the option is selected. The **propertyList** attribute is the data we want to associate with the option. The **alternates** attribute is an array of alternative options (options that are replaced by a different option when a key is press and hold). The **discoverabilityTitle** attribute is a string that describes the purpose of the option. The **attributes** attribute is a property of a structure of type `Attributes` that specifies the option's style. There are three properties available: `destructive`, `disabled`, and `hidden`. And finally, the **state** attribute is an enumeration of type `State` that specifies the option's initial state. The values available are `off`, `on`, and `mixed`.

UIKeyCommand(title: String, **image:** UIImage?, **action:** Selector, **input:** String, **modifierFlags:** UIKeyModifierFlags, **propertyList:** Any?, **alternates:** [UICommandAlternate], **discoverabilityTitle:** String?, **attributes:** Attributes, **state:** State)—This initializer creates an option with a shortcut key. The **title** attribute is the option's title. The **image** attribute is the image associated with the option. The **action** attribute is a selector with the action we want to perform when the option is selected. The **input** attribute is the textual representation of the key the user has to press to perform the action. The **modifierFlags** attribute is a property of a structure of type `UIKeyModifierFlags` that determines the modifier key the user has to press to perform the action. The properties available are `alphaShift`, `shift`, `control`, `alternate`, `command`, and `numericPad`. The **propertyList** attribute is the data we want to associate with the option. The **alternates** attribute is an array of alternative options (options that are replaced by a different option when a key is pressed and hold). The **discoverabilityTitle** attribute is a string that describes the purpose of the option. The **attributes** attribute is a property of a structure of type `Attributes` that specifies the option's style. There are three properties available: `destructive`, `disabled`, and `hidden`. And finally, the **state** attribute is an enumeration of type `State` that specifies the option's initial state. The values available are `off`, `on`, and `mixed`.

There is one more thing we need to be able to modify the menu bar and that is the identifier. Every option is identified with a structure of type `Identifier` defined by the `UIMenu` class. The structure provides the following initializer to create a custom identifier.

UIMenu.Identifier(String)—This initializer creates an identifier for a menu option. The attribute must be unique and therefore Apple recommends declaring it with a reverse domain, such as com.formasterminds-myapp.MyMenuBar.myOption.

The `Identifier` structure also includes type properties we can use to identify standard options. The properties available are `application`, `file`, `edit`, `view`, `window`, `help`, `about`, `preferences`, `services`, `hide`, `quit`, `newScene`, `close`, `print`, `undoRedo`, `standardEdit`, `find`, `replace`, `share`, `textStyle`, `spelling`, `spellingPanel`, `spellingOptions`, `substitutions`, `substitutionsPanel`, `substitutionOptions`, `transformations`, `speech`, `lookup`, `learn`, `format`, `font`, `textSize`, `textColor`, `textStylePasteboard`, `text`, `writingDirection`, `alignment`, `toolbar`, `fullscreen`, `minimizeAndZoom`, `bringAllToFront`, `root`.

To customize the menu bar, we must override the `buildMenu(builder: UIMenuBuilder)` method in the `AppDelegate` class. This method is called in the `AppDelegate` class when the application is about to create the menu bar, so we can customize it before it is shown to the user. The following example implements the method to add a new menu called *Selection* before the Format menu.

```
import UIKit

@UIApplicationMain
class AppDelegate: UIResponder, UIApplicationDelegate {
    func application(_ application: UIApplication,
didFinishLaunchingWithOptions launchOptions:
[UIApplication.LaunchOptionsKey: Any]?) -> Bool {
        return true
    }
    func application(_ application: UIApplication,
configurationForConnecting connectingSceneSession: UISceneSession,
options: UIScene.ConnectionOptions) -> UISceneConfiguration {
        return UISceneConfiguration(name: "Default Configuration",
sessionRole: connectingSceneSession.role)
    }
    override func buildMenu(with builder: UIMenuBuilder) {
        if builder.system == .main {
            let mymenu = UIMenu(title: "Selection", image: nil, identifier:
UIMenu.Identifier("com.formasterminds.test.selection"), children: [])
            builder.insertSibling(mymenu, beforeMenu: .format)
        } else {
            return
        }
    }
}
```

Listing 9-58: *Adding a menu to the menu bar*

Because the `buildMenu(builder: UIMenuBuilder)` method is defined by the `UIResponder` class and the `AppDelegate` class inherits from this class, we have to override it. In the method, we read the `system` property of the `UIMenuBuilder` object to check if the object contains a reference to the main menu and then proceed to modify it. In this example, we create a new `UIMenu` object to represent a menu in the bar with the title Selection. We give it a custom identifier and do not specify any options yet (`children: []`). Next, we insert the menu in the bar before the Format menu with the `insertSibling()` method. The result is shown in Figure 9-36.

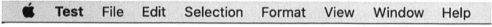

Figure 9-36: *Custom menu bar*

If we click on the Selection menu, nothing happens because we haven't added any options to the menu yet. The options are added with `UICommand` or `UIKeyCommand` objects. These objects define a menu option and specify the action to perform when the option is selected by the user. The actions are methods that the object calls in our code. In SwiftUI, these methods usually modify values in our model (the observable object) to update the app's data and the views. To demonstrate how this works, we are going to expand the previous example with a model and a view. The following is the model we need to update the values in the view.

```
import SwiftUI

class AppData: ObservableObject {
    @Published var selectedCity: Bool = false
    @Published var selectedCountry: Bool = false
}
```

Listing 9-59: Model to test the menu options

This model includes two `@Published` properties of type `Bool`. Now, we can use these properties to select the values to show in the view.

```
import SwiftUI

struct ContentView: View {
    @EnvironmentObject var appData: AppData

    var body: some View {
        VStack {
            HStack {
                Text(appData.selectedCity ? "♥" : "♡")
                    .font(.largeTitle)
                Text("City")
                Spacer()
            }
            HStack {
                Text(appData.selectedCountry ? "♥" : "♡")
                    .font(.largeTitle)
                Text("Country")
                Spacer()
            }
            Spacer()
        }.padding()
    }
}
```

Listing 9-60: Responding to the user's selection

The view in Listing 9-60 displays a full heart or an empty heart depending on the values of the `@Published` properties in the model. If the property is `true`, the `Text` view displays a full heart, otherwise, the empty heart is shown. Now, it is time to change the values of these properties from the menu.

```
import UIKit

@UIApplicationMain
class AppDelegate: UIResponder, UIApplicationDelegate {
    var myData: AppData!

    func application(_ application: UIApplication,
didFinishLaunchingWithOptions launchOptions:
[UIApplication.LaunchOptionsKey: Any]?) -> Bool {
        myData = AppData()
```

```
        return true
    }
    func application(_ application: UIApplication,
configurationForConnecting connectingSceneSession: UISceneSession,
options: UIScene.ConnectionOptions) -> UISceneConfiguration {
        return UISceneConfiguration(name: "Default Configuration",
sessionRole: connectingSceneSession.role)
    }
    override func buildMenu(with builder: UIMenuBuilder) {
        if builder.system == .main {
            let option1 = UICommand(title: "Select City", action:
#selector(processOption1))
            let option2 = UICommand(title: "Select Country", action:
#selector(processOption2))
            let mymenu = UIMenu(title: "Selection", image: nil, identifier:
UIMenu.Identifier("com.formasterminds.test.selection"), children:
[option1, option2])
            builder.insertSibling(mymenu, afterMenu: .format)
        } else {
            return
        }
    }
    @objc func processOption1() {
        myData.selectedCity.toggle()
    }
    @objc func processOption2() {
        myData.selectedCountry.toggle()
    }
}
```

Listing 9-61: Adding options to the menu

The `UICommand` object requires at least two values: a title and the method that is going to be executed when the option is selected. The method is specified with a selector. Selectors are a feature that Swift takes from Objective-C. They are declared with the instruction `#selector(method)` and the methods must be preceded with the `@objc` keyword, as we did in Listing 9-61. The first option, stored in the `option1` constant, executes a method called `processOption1()`, and the second option, called `option2`, executes a method called `processOption2()`. Once these options are defined, we assign them to the `UIMenu` object to show them on the screen.

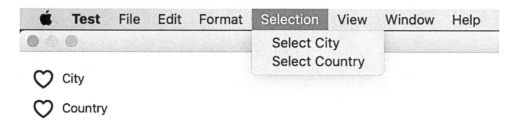

Figure 9-37: Custom options

The `processOption1()` and `processOption2()` methods in Listing 9-61 toggle the values of the `@Published` properties in our model, so every time the options are selected the values of these properties change and the view shows a different heart (full or empty).

Chapter 9 - Navigation

Test File Edit Format Selection View Window Help

Test

 City

Country

Figure 9-38: *Option selected*

Do It Yourself: Create a SwiftUI project. Create a Swift file called AppData.swift for the model in Listing 9-59. Update the `ContentView` structure with the code in Listing 9-60 and the `AppDelegate` class with the code in Listing 9-61. You also need to update the SceneDelegate.swift file with the code in Listing 7-20 to inject the model into the environment. Select the My Mac scheme and run the application. Click on the Selection menu and select any option. You should see the hearts change on the view.

The `UICommand` class includes a state value that we can set to show a checkmark next to the option's title. This is useful when the option is a two-state option, as in this case. We can show the checkmark when the option is selected and remove it when it is not. There are different ways to modify the options. In this example, we are going to set the states every time the menu is built, and then ask the system to update it with the `setNeedsRebuild()` method when a state changes.

```
override func buildMenu(with builder: UIMenuBuilder) {
   if builder.system == .main {
      let state1: UIMenu.State = myData.selectedCity ? .on : .off
      let state2: UIMenu.State = myData.selectedCountry ? .on : .off

      let option1 = UICommand(title: "Select City", action:
#selector(processOption1), state: state1)
      let option2 = UICommand(title: "Select Country", action:
#selector(processOption2), state: state2)

      let mymenu = UIMenu(title: "Selection", image: nil, identifier:
UIMenu.Identifier("com.formasterminds.test.selection"), children:
[option1, option2])
      builder.insertSibling(mymenu, afterMenu: .format)
   } else {
      return
   }
}
@objc func processOption1() {
   myData.selectedCity.toggle()

   let main = UIMenuSystem.main
   main.setNeedsRebuild()
}
@objc func processOption2() {
   myData.selectedCountry.toggle()

   let main = UIMenuSystem.main
   main.setNeedsRebuild()
}
```

Listing 9-62: *Updating the options*

Chapter 9 - Navigation

The `buildMenu()` method in Listing 9-62 includes two new constants called `state1` and `state2` to store the state of each option. Their values are set to `on` or `off` depending on the values of the `@Published` properties in our model, so every time the menu is created, their values change according to the values of those properties. In the `processOption1()` and `processOption2()` methods, we get access to the main menu and call the `setNeedsRebuild()` method on it to rebuild the menu after the values of the `@Published` properties are toggled. In consequence, every time the user clicks on an option, the corresponding `@Published` property's value is changed, the `setNeedsRebuild()` method is called, and a new state is assigned to the option, showing or removing the checkmark.

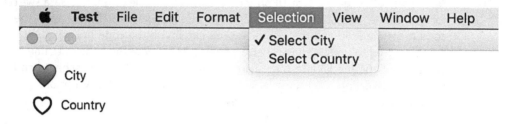

City

Country

Figure 9-39: Checkmark for options

 Do It Yourself: Update the `AppDelegate` class with the code in Listing 9-62. Run the application on the Mac again. Click on an option on the menu. You should see the checkmark on that option, as in Figure 9-39.

Besides creating our own menus, we can also remove or edit the standard menus provided by the system. In the following example, we add a new option to the standard View menu called Show Cities and remove the menus Edit and Format.

```
override func buildMenu(with builder: UIMenuBuilder) {
   if builder.system == .main {
      let state1: UIMenu.State = myData.selectedCity ? .on : .off
      let state2: UIMenu.State = myData.selectedCountry ? .on : .off
      let option1 = UICommand(title: "Select City", action:
#selector(processOption1), state: state1)
      let option2 = UICommand(title: "Select Country", action:
#selector(processOption2), state: state2)

      let mymenu = UIMenu(title: "Selection", image: nil, identifier:
UIMenu.Identifier("com.formasterminds.test.selection"), children:
[option1, option2])
      builder.insertSibling(mymenu, afterMenu: .format)

      let option3 = UIKeyCommand(title: "Show Cities", action:
#selector(showCities), input: "D", modifierFlags: [.command])
      let menuview = UIMenu(title: "", image: nil, identifier:
UIMenu.Identifier("com.formasterminds.test.showCities"), options:
.displayInline, children: [option3])
      builder.insertChild(menuview, atEndOfMenu: .view)

      builder.remove(menu: .edit)
      builder.remove(menu: .format)
   } else {
      return
   }
}
@objc func showCities() {
   print("Show City Message")
}
```

```
@objc func processOption1() {
    myData.selectedCity.toggle()
    let main = UIMenuSystem.main
    main.setNeedsRebuild()
}
@objc func processOption2() {
    myData.selectedCountry.toggle()
    let main = UIMenuSystem.main
    main.setNeedsRebuild()
}
```

Listing 9-63: Adding and removing options

The code in Listing 9-63 adds an option to the View menu and removes the Edit and Format menus. This time, the option is created with the **UIKeyCommand** class to provide the user the alternative to activate it by pressing a combination of keys on the keyboard. The main key is defined by the **input** attribute and the modifier key is defined by the **modifierFlags** attribute. In this example, we use the letter D and the Command key, so the user has to press Command-D to activate the option. The option is embedded in a **UIMenu** object with no title and the **displayInline** option to show the element along with the rest of the elements in the menu. Finally, we insert the option at the end of the View menu with the **insertChild()** method.

When the user clicks on the Show Cities option or presses the Command-D keys, the **showCities()** method is executed and a message is printed on the console. In this example, we just print a message, but the method can be used to modified properties in the model or the app's data, as we did with the other methods.

Figure 9-40: Option added to the View menu

 Do It Yourself: Update the **AppDelegate** class with the code in Listing 9-63. Run the application on the Mac again. Click on the Show Cities option in the View menu or press the Command + D keys on your keyboard. You should see a message printed on the console.

(Medium) Multiple Windows Support

iPads and Mac computers can open multiple instances of an application in separate windows (scenes), but this feature is not enabled by default. The option to support multiple windows is available from the General panel in the project's settings, as illustrate in Figure 9-41.

Status Bar Style	Default	⬍

☐ Hide status bar
☐ Requires full screen
☑ Supports multiple windows Configure ➡

Figure 9-41: Support Multiple Windows option

Activating this option allows the application to work from multiple windows. iPads and Mac computers provide built-in functionality for this purpose. For instance, if we compile the app to work on the Mac, an option appears on the standard File menu to create a new window.

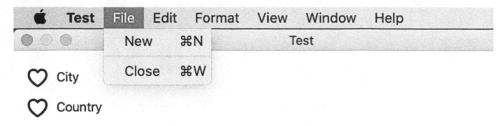

Figure 9-42: *Option to create new window*

 IMPORTANT: At the moment of writing, there is a bug that randomly crashes the app when the New option is selected. Later, we explain how to generate new windows programmatically to avoid this issue.

iPads offer multiple alternatives to open the app in a new window. The easiest way is to long-press and drag the app's icon from the dock to the center of the screen. The system shows a rectangle representing the window and when we drop it, a floating window with the app appears on the screen. Another alternative is to long-press the icon until a popup menu shows up with an option to show all the windows opened for the app (see Figure 9-43, below). After the option is selected, a collage with all the windows appear on the screen and a + button is displayed at the top-right corner to add a new one.

Figure 9-43: *Option to see all the windows available for the app*

In addition to the options provided by the system, we can open the app in a new window by creating a scene. The `UIApplication` class offers the following methods to manage scenes.

requestSceneSessionActivation(UISceneSession?,   userActivity: NSUser-Activity?, options: ActivationRequestOptions?, **errorHandler:** Closure?**)**— This method activates an existing session or creates a new one. The first attribute is a reference to the session we want to activate or the value `nil` if we want to create a new one. The **userActivity** attribute is a reference to an object of type `NSUserActivity` that stores the state we want to set when the scene is opened. The **options** attribute is an object with information for the session associated with the scene. And the **errorHandler** attribute is the closure to be executed if there is an error creating the session.

requestSceneSessionDestruction(UISceneSession,   options: UIScene-DestructionRequestOptions?, errorHandler: Closure?**)**—This method dismisses an existing session. The first attribute is a reference to the session we want to destroy. The **options** attribute is an object that provides information on how to remove the scene. And the **errorHandler** attribute is the closure to be execute if an error is found in the process.

Chapter 9 - Navigation

requestSceneSessionRefresh(UISceneSession**)**—This method requests the system to update the views in the scene specified by the attribute.

If all we want is to open a new window, we can just call the `requestSceneSession-Activation()` method with `nil` values, as in the following example.

```
import SwiftUI
struct ContentView: View {
    var body: some View {
        VStack {
            #if targetEnvironment(macCatalyst)
                Text("Mac Application")
                Button("Open New Window") {
                    let app = UIApplication.shared
                    app.requestSceneSessionActivation(nil, userActivity: nil,
options: nil)
                }
                Spacer()
            #else
                Text("Mobile Application")
            #endif
        }.padding()
    }
}
```

Listing 9-64: Opening a new window on Mac

The view in Listing 9-64 reproduces a previous example that shows a different message on the screen depending on where the app is running, but this time we include a Button view if the app is running on a Mac to open a new window. When the button is pressed, we get a reference to the `UIApplication` object assigned to the app and call the `requestSceneSession-Activation()` method on it to open a new window.

 Do It Yourself: Create a SwiftUI project. Go to the app's settings, open the General panel, and check the options Mac, to be able to compile the application for Mac computers, and Support multiple windows, to be able to open the app in multiple windows. Update the `ContentView` structure with the code in Listing 9-64 and run the application on your Mac. Click on the button to open the app in a new window.

The window opened by the example in Listing 9-64 launches the app with the configuration by default. This means that the app will display the initial screen as if it had been launched for the first time by clicking on the icon. But this is not always appropriate. Often, users expect to see something they have selected before, or the window to be in the state it was the last time they were working on it. To set the initial state of the session or recover an old state, the Foundation framework defines the `NSUserActivity` class. From this class, we can create objects that contain the information required to set the state of the session or restore a previous one. The following is the class' initializer.

NSUserActivity(activityType: String**)**—This initializer creates a new `NSUserActivity` object with the name specified by the attribute. The **activityType** attribute is a string that identifies the state. It is recommendable to declare it with an inverted domain, as in com.formasterminds.mystate.

The following are some of the properties and methods provided by the class to configure the state.

title—This property sets or returns the activity's title.

userInfo—This property sets or returns a dictionary with the values required to set or restore the state represented by the object.

becomeCurrent()—This method marks the activity as the one that is currently in use.

resignCurrent()—This method deactivates the activity.

invalidate()—This method invalidates the activity.

How the state is restored depends on the characteristics of our application, but the process to store the information that represents the state is always the same. We must create an `NSUserActivity` object, store the information we are going to need to set the session in the `userInfo` property, and then use that information to configure the state of the session when a previous session or a new one is opened. To illustrate how this works, we can use the project developed before in this chapter that provides links for the user to select a picture. The idea is to include a button in the detail view for the user to open a new window with that picture already selected. For this, we are going to need the model of Listing 9-14, and all the views defined in Listings 9-38, 9-39, and 9-40 to recreate the interface of Figure 9-24. First, let's see how to add the button and store the state in the `DetailView` view.

```
import SwiftUI
struct DetailView: View {
    @EnvironmentObject var appData: AppData
    var selected: Int = 0

    var body: some View {
        VStack {
            HStack {
                Text("Rating: ")
                    .font(.subheadline)
                Slider(value: $appData.userData[selected].picture.rating, in:
0...5, step: 1.0)
                    .frame(width: 150)
                Text("\(appData.userData[selected].rating)")
                    .font(.title)
                    .fontWeight(.bold)
                    .foregroundColor(Color.orange)
                Spacer()
                Button("Open in New Window") {
                    let activity = NSUserActivity(activityType:
"com.formasterminds.images")
                    activity.userInfo?["image"] =
self.appData.userData[self.selected].picture.image

                    let app = UIApplication.shared
                    app.requestSceneSessionActivation(nil, userActivity:
activity, options: nil)
                }
            }.padding(5)

            Image(appData.userData[selected].picture.image)
                .resizable()
                .aspectRatio(contentMode: .fill)
                .frame(minWidth: 0, maxWidth: .infinity, minHeight: 0,
maxHeight: .infinity)
                .clipped()
                .zIndex(-1)
            Spacer()
```

```
        }.padding(15)
        .background(Color(red: 0.95, green: 0.95, blue: 0.95))
        .navigationBarTitle("Picture", displayMode: .inline)
    }
}
struct DetailView_Previews: PreviewProvider {
    static var previews: some View {
        DetailView()
            .environmentObject(AppData())
    }
}
```

Listing 9-65: *Storing the state in an* `NSUserActivity` *object*

As in the previous example, the view shows a slider at the top to rate the image and the picture below, but now we also include a button to open a new window, as shown next.

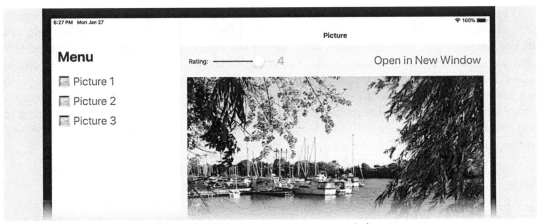

Figure 9-44: *Button to open a new window*

The button creates an **NSUserActivity** object and then sets a value in the **userInfo** dictionary with the key "image" and the value of the **image** property of the selected picture (the name of the picture's file). Finally, we execute the **requestSceneSessionActivation()** method on the **UIApplication** object with this value and the window is opened.

To set the state of the scene and get the new window to show the right image, we must read back the value stored in the **userInfo** property when the scene is created by the **SceneDelegate** object, as shown next.

```
import UIKit
import SwiftUI

class SceneDelegate: UIResponder, UIWindowSceneDelegate {
    var window: UIWindow?

    func scene(_ scene: UIScene, willConnectTo session: UISceneSession,
options connectionOptions: UIScene.ConnectionOptions) {
        let app = UIApplication.shared
        let delegate = app.delegate as! AppDelegate
        let contentView = ContentView()
            .environmentObject(delegate.myData)

        if let windowScene = scene as? UIWindowScene {
            if let activity = connectionOptions.userActivities.first(where:
{ $0.activityType == "com.formasterminds.images" }) {
                if let image = activity.userInfo?["image"] as? String {
```

```
                if let index = delegate.myData.userData.firstIndex(where:
{ $0.picture.image == image }) {
                    delegate.myData.selectedState = index
                }
            }
        }
        let window = UIWindow(windowScene: windowScene)
        window.rootViewController = UIHostingController(rootView:
contentView)
        self.window = window
        window.makeKeyAndVisible()
        }
    }
}
```

Listing 9-66: Reading the state from the NSUserActivity *object*

There are different ways to read the current activities set by the application. In this example, we get them from the **userActivities** property of the **ConnectionOptions** object received by the method. This property returns an array of **NSUserActivity** objects, so we get the first one that matches the type used in the **DetailView** view and then read the value from its **userInfo** property with the image key. The key returns a string with the name of the image, so we search for the **Picture** structure in the **userData** property in our model to get the picture's index and assign it to another property in the model called **selectedState**. We are going to use this property to tell the view which picture to show when the window is opened. The next step is to define the property in the model, as shown next.

```
import SwiftUI

struct Picture {
    var image: String
    var rating: Double
}
struct PictureViewModel {
    var picture: Picture

    var rating: Int {
        return Int(picture.rating)
    }
}
class AppData: ObservableObject {
    @Published var userData: [PictureViewModel]
    var selectedState: Int? = nil

    init() {
        userData = [
            PictureViewModel(picture: Picture(image: "nopicture", rating:
0)),
            PictureViewModel(picture: Picture(image: "spot1", rating: 0)),
            PictureViewModel(picture: Picture(image: "spot2", rating: 0)),
            PictureViewModel(picture: Picture(image: "spot3", rating: 0))
        ]
    }
}
```

Listing 9-67: Updating the model to restore a state

This is the same model defined in Listing 9-14, but now it includes the **selectedState** property we need to store the index of the picture selected by the user and activate the corresponding `NavigationLink` button to show the picture on the screen. This process is performed in the `MenuView` view of our example.

```
import SwiftUI

struct MenuView: View {
    @EnvironmentObject var appData: AppData
    @State private var selectedLink: Int? = nil

    var body: some View {
        VStack(alignment: .leading, spacing: 15) {
            NavigationLink("🖼 Picture 1", destination: DetailView(selected:
1), tag: 1, selection: $selectedLink)
            NavigationLink("🖼 Picture 2", destination: DetailView(selected:
2), tag: 2, selection: $selectedLink)
            NavigationLink("🖼 Picture 3", destination: DetailView(selected:
3), tag: 3, selection: $selectedLink)
            Spacer()
        }.font(.title)
        .padding()
        .frame(minWidth: 0, maxWidth: .infinity, alignment: .leading)
        .navigationBarTitle("Menu")
        .onAppear(perform: {
            if let index = self.appData.selectedState {
                self.selectedLink = index
                self.appData.selectedState = nil
            }
        })
    }
}
```

Listing 9-68: Activating the `NavigationLink` *button with the index of the selected image*

Again, this is the same view defined for the original example (see Listing 9-40), but now we apply the `onAppear()` modifier to assign the value of the `selectedState` property to the `selectedLink` property and activate the link.

The new project is ready. When the user presses the Open in New Window button from the `DetailView` view, the `NSUserActivity` object is created with the name of the current image, and a new window is opened. The `SceneDelegate` object of this new scene reads the `NSUserActivity` object, gets the name of the image, finds the image in the `userData` array, and assigns its index to the `selectedState` property in the model. When the `MenuView` view is opened, the `onAppear()` modifier reads the value of this property and assigns it to the `selectedLink` property, activating the corresponding `NavigationLink` button, which opens the `DetailView` view with the image selected by the user.

 Do It Yourself: Create a SwiftUI project. Go to the app's settings, open the General panel, and check the options Mac and Support multiple windows, as we did for previous examples. Download the images spot1.jpg, spot2.jpg, spot3.jpg, and nopicture.png from our website and add them to the Assets Catalog. Update the AppDelegate.swift file with the code in Listing 7-14 and the SceneDelegate.swift file with the code in Listing 9-66. Create a file called AppData.swift for the model in Listing 9-67. Update the `ContentView` structure with the code in Listing 9-38. Create a SwiftUI file called MenuView.swift for the view in Listing 9-68, a file called DetailView.swift for the view in Listing 9-65, and a file called PlaceholderView.swift for the view in

Listing 9-36. Run the application on the Mac, select a picture, and click on the Open in New Window button. Another window should open with the same picture selected in the previous window.

 IMPORTANT: In this example, we barely scratched the surface of what is possible to do when working with `NSUserActivity` objects and multiple windows. The topic is extensive and goes beyond the scope of this book. For more information, visit our website and follow the links for this chapter.

(Basic) ## 10.1 Lists of Views

One of the main characteristics of computers is their ability to process sequential data. Due to their elementary structure, consisting of sequences of switches on and off, computers are experts at organizing information as lists of values, and this is perfect for storing large amounts of data and presenting it to the user. We have implemented this type or organization before. A sequence of values is stored in the model and displayed to the user in a list of views, like the buttons used to select the pictures in the last example of Chapter 9. Until now, all these views were created manually, one by one, but SwiftUI provides tools to create dynamic and static lists of views and edit their content.

(Basic) ### ForEach View

The simplest tool provided by SwiftUI to create a list of views is the `ForEach` view. This view generates a loop that iterates through the values of a collection and creates a new view for each one of them. The structure includes the following initializers.

ForEach(Data, **id:** KeyPath, **content:** Closure)—This initializer creates a `ForEach` view. The first attribute is the collection of values the loop is going to iterate through. The **id** attribute is the key path to the unique identifier for each value. And the **content** attribute is the closure that creates the views in each cycle.

ForEach(Data, **content:** Closure)—This initializer creates a `ForEach` view. The first attribute is the collection of values the loop is going to iterate through. The values must conform to the **identifiable** protocol and implement the **id** property to provide a unique identifier (see Listing 9-29). And the **content** attribute is the closure that creates the views in each cycle.

A `ForEach` view needs two values: the collection that the view is going to iterate through, and a key path that determines how the view is going to identify each value. This is important because the view needs to recognize the values to be able to remove them or add new ones to the list when the collection is updated. If the collection is made of standard Swift values like `Int` and `String`, assigning an identifier is easy. These data types conform to the `Hashable` protocol and therefore they have a hash value that identifies each instance (see Listing 3-181). To use this hash value as the identifier, we must specify the `\.self` key path, as in the following example.

```
import SwiftUI

struct ContentView: View {
   var body: some View {
      VStack {
         ForEach(1...5, id: \.self) { value in
            Text("Value: \(value)")
         }
```

```
            Spacer()
        }
      }
}
```

The **ForEach** view adds the content to its container, so we must declare it inside a container view like a **VStack** or an **HStack**, as we did in the example of Listing 10-1. In this example, the loop is defined by a range of integers from 1 to 5, and the values are identified by the hash value of each structure (**\.self**). The **ForEach** view loops through the values in the range and sends them to the closure one by one. In the closure, we create a **Text** view that includes this value and shows it on the screen. The result is illustrated in Figure 10-1.

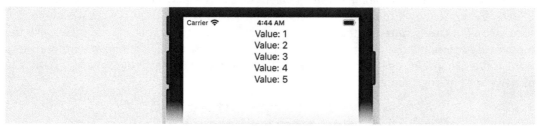

Figure 10-1: List of views generated by a ForEach *loop*

In this example, the values are presented on the screen with a **VStack** and the configuration by default (center alignment and a width determined by the widest view). Although we can use all the views at our disposal to present each value and apply any styles we want, there is a standard design that users immediately recognize in which the values are separated by a line. SwiftUI includes the following view for this purpose.

Divider()—This initializer creates a **Divider** view. The view creates a line used to separate content.

The **Divider** view is like any other view. If we want to position the line generated by this view below the value, we must embed the **Text** view and the **Divider** view in a **VStack**.

```
import SwiftUI

struct ContentView: View {
    let listCities: [String] = ["Paris", "Toronto", "Dublin"]

    var body: some View {
        VStack {
            ForEach(listCities, id: \.self) { value in
                VStack {
                    Text(value)
                    Divider()
                }
            }
            Spacer()
        }
    }
}
```

The **ForEach** view of Listing 10-2 creates a list of views from an array of strings. The structure defines the array with the name of three cities and then implements the **ForEach** view to create the list. Notice that the **string** values are also identified by their hash value (**\.self**).

Chapter 10 - Lists

Figure 10-2: List of views with a standard design

Values of primitive data types like integers and strings conform to the **Hashable** protocol and therefore we can use their hash value as the identifier, as we did in these examples. Although we could also make our custom data types, like the structures in our model, to conform to this protocol, a different hash value may be generated every time the app is launched. When working with data stored by the user in our model, it is better to provide a unique identifier that is stored along with the data and therefore is always the same. For this purpose, SwiftUI offers the **identifiable** protocol. We have worked with this protocol before to present multiple sheets (see Listings 9-29 and 9-30). The protocol requires the structure to define a property called **id** to store a unique identifier for each instance, and this is how we prepare the values in our model to work with list of views. Next is the model we are going to use for the following examples.

```swift
import SwiftUI

struct Book {
    var title: String
    var author: String
    var cover: String
    var year: Int
}
struct BookViewModel: Identifiable {
    var id = UUID()
    var book: Book

    var title: String {
        return book.title.capitalized
    }
    var author: String {
        return book.author.capitalized
    }
    var cover: String {
        return book.cover
    }
    var year: String {
        return String(book.year)
    }
}
class AppData: ObservableObject {
    @Published var userData: [BookViewModel]

    init() {
        userData = [
            BookViewModel(book: Book(title: "Steve Jobs", author: "Walter
Isaacson", cover: "book1", year: 2011)),
            BookViewModel(book: Book(title: "HTML5 for Masterminds", author:
"J.D Gauchat", cover: "book2", year: 2017)),
            BookViewModel(book: Book(title: "The Road Ahead", author: "Bill
Gates", cover: "book3", year: 1995))
        ]
```

```
        }
    }
```

Listing 10-3: Defining a model to work with lists of views

The `Book` structure defined first is our model. This structure includes properties to store the title of the book, the author, the name of the image for the cover, and the year the book was published. Next, the `BookViewModel` defines the view model. This structure includes the `id` property to store a UUID value to uniquely identify the book, a property to store all the information about the book, and computed properties to format the information for the views. Finally, the observable object is defined with our familiar `userData` property to store the user's data.

When the data conforms to the `identifiable` protocol, the system knows how to identify the items, so all we have to do is to declare the collection, and the list of views is automatically created from its values.

```
import SwiftUI
struct ContentView: View {
    @EnvironmentObject var appData: AppData

    var body: some View {
        NavigationView {
            VStack {
                ForEach(appData.userData) { book in
                    VStack {
                        HStack(alignment: .top) {
                            Image(book.cover)
                                .resizable()
                                .scaledToFit()
                                .frame(width: 80, height: 100)
                            VStack(alignment: .leading, spacing: 2) {
                                Text(book.title).bold()
                                Text(book.author)
                                Text(book.year).font(.caption)
                            }.padding(.top, 5)
                            Spacer()
                        }
                        Divider()
                    }
                }
                Spacer()
            }.navigationBarTitle("Books")
        }
    }
}
struct ContentView_Previews: PreviewProvider {
    static var previews: some View {
        ContentView().environmentObject(AppData())
    }
}
```

Listing 10-4: Creating a list of views with data from the model

This example assumes that we have connected the instance of our model to the environment, as we did in Listings 7-14 and 7-20. The `ForEach` view reads the array with all the books from the `userData` property of our observable object and sends the items one by one to the closure. This item is an instance of the `BookViewModel` structure with the information of a book, so we read its properties to show the information on the screen.

Chapter 10 - Lists

Figure 10-3: List of views created from the data in the model

Do It Yourself: Create a SwiftUI project. Download the book1.jpg, book2.jpg and book3.jpg images from our website and add them to the Assets Catalog. Create a Swift file called AppData.swift for the model of Listing 10-3. Update the AppDelegate.swift file with the code of Listing 7-14 and the SceneDelegate.swift file with the code of Listing 7-20. Update the ContentView.swift file with the code of Listing 10-4. Run the application in an iPhone simulator. You should see the interface of Figure 10-3.

Of course, apps would be useless if users could only work with predefined data. The data stored in the model of Listing 10-3 was included for testing purposes. Our application should never be published in the App Store with predefined information like this. Unless some common values are required, the data stored in the model, should be only the one inserted by the user. There are different ways to allow the user to add or remove data from the model. The MVVM pattern suggests that the views provide the tools for the user to perform the changes, and the model (the observable object) takes care of modifying the data. In the next example, we are going to allow the user to insert and remove books from our application. The following are the modifications we must introduce to the observable object.

```
class AppData: ObservableObject {
    @Published var userData: [BookViewModel] = []

    func addBook(book: Book) {
        userData.append(BookViewModel(book: book))
    }
    func removeBook(removeID: UUID) {
        if let index = userData.firstIndex(where: { $0.id == removeID}) {
            userData.remove(at: index)
        }
    }
}
```

Listing 10-5: Adding and removing data form the model

The **userData** property is initialized with an empty array this time. Now, the model will only contain information inserted by the user. To insert and remove this information, the observable object includes two methods. The **addBook()** method receives an instance of the **Book** structure, creates an instance of the **BookViewModel** structure with it, and adds it to the array.

On the other hand, the `removeBook()` method receives an `UUID` value, use it to find a book in the array with the `firstIndex()` method, and if a book is found, it is removed from the array with the `remove()` method.

Now, our views can use these methods to allow the user to insert and remove books. For this purpose, the following `ContentView` view includes a button to open a sheet to allow the user to insert a new book and a button for each book to remove it.

```
import SwiftUI

struct ContentView: View {
    @EnvironmentObject var appData: AppData
    @State private var openSheet: Bool = false

    var body: some View {
        VStack {
            HStack {
                Spacer()
                Button("Add Book") {
                    self.openSheet = true
                }
            }.padding()
            ForEach(appData.userData) { book in
                VStack {
                    HStack(alignment: .top) {
                        Image(book.cover)
                            .resizable()
                            .scaledToFit()
                            .frame(width: 80, height: 100)
                        VStack(alignment: .leading, spacing: 2) {
                            Text(book.title).bold()
                            Text(book.author)
                            Text(book.year).font(.caption)
                        }.padding(.top, 5)
                        Spacer()
                        Button(action: {
                            self.appData.removeBook(removeID: book.id)
                        }, label: {
                            Image(systemName: "trash.circle")
                                .font(.title)
                        })
                    }.padding([.leading, .trailing], 10)
                    .padding([.top, .bottom], 5)
                    Divider()
                }
            }
            Spacer()
        }.sheet(isPresented: $openSheet) {
            AddBookView().environmentObject(self.appData)
        }
    }
}
```

Listing 10-6: Providing tools to edit the data

Something important to notice in this example is that the `sheet()` modifier attaches the instance of the model to the environment again. This is because the views opened with this modifier do not belong to the same hierarchy than the view opened by the sheet. Therefore, every time we need to access the model from modal views, like sheets and popups, we must connect it to their environment as we did here for the `AddBookView` view.

Chapter 10 - Lists

The actions performed by the buttons in Listing 10-6 are simple. There is a button at the top of the list that assigns the value **true** to the **openSheet** property to open the sheet, and one button for each book that calls the **removeBook()** method on the observable object with the value of the book's **id** property to remove it from the model. Let's see how to prepare the form to add new books.

```
import SwiftUI

struct AddBookView: View {
    @EnvironmentObject var appData: AppData
    @Environment(\.presentationMode) var presentation

    @State private var newTitle: String = ""
    @State private var newAuthor: String = ""
    @State private var newYear: String = ""

    var body: some View {
        VStack(spacing: 15) {
            Text("Add Book")
                .font(.largeTitle)
            TextField("Insert the Title", text: $newTitle)
                .textFieldStyle(RoundedBorderTextFieldStyle())
            TextField("Insert the Author", text: $newAuthor)
                .textFieldStyle(RoundedBorderTextFieldStyle())
            TextField("Insert the Year", text: $newYear)
                .textFieldStyle(RoundedBorderTextFieldStyle())
            HStack {
                Spacer()
                Button("Save Book") {
                    let title = self.newTitle.trimmingCharacters(in:
.whitespaces)
                    let author = self.newAuthor.trimmingCharacters(in:
.whitespaces)
                    if let year = Int(self.newYear), !title.isEmpty,
!author.isEmpty {
                        let newBook = Book(title: title, author: author, cover:
"nopicture", year: year)
                        self.appData.addBook(book: newBook)
                        self.presentation.wrappedValue.dismiss()
                    }
                }
            }
            Spacer()
        }.padding(20)
    }
}
```

Listing 10-7: Adding data to the model

There is nothing new in the view of Listing 10-7. We access the model with an **@EnvironmentObject** property, then access the environment's **presentationMode** property to be able to close the sheet later, and define three **@State** properties to store the values inserted by the user for the title, the author, and the year (in this example, the cover is always assigned the image nopicture.png). The view itself contains three **TextField** views to insert the data, and a **Button** view to store it. Before storing the data, we trim the strings to make sure no spaces are left at the beginning or the end, check that the values are not empty and that the year is an integer, and then create an instance of the **Book** structure and call the **addBook()** method with it to add it to the model.

This, of course, it is just for didactic purposes. In a real application we would also check that only numbers are inserted in the field for the year and that the value contains no more than four digits, as we did in the examples of Listings 8-10 and 8-11. We will also check that the year is inside a reasonable range of values and the rest of the values are according to what our model is expecting.

Figure 10-4, below, shows what we see when we run this application. At first, there are no books in the model and therefore we see an empty list with a button at the top. Pressing that button opens the form to add a new book. After the information is inserted, the book is added to the model and shown on the list.

Figure 10-4: Adding data to the model

 Do It Yourself: Download the nopicture.png image from our website and add it to the Assets Catalog. Update the observable object in the AppData.swift file with the code of Listing 10-5. Update the `ContentView` structure with the code of Listing 10-6. Create a new SwiftUI file called `AddBookView` and update it with the code of Listing 10-7. Run the application. Press the Add Book button, insert the information of a book, and press the Save Book button. The sheet should be closed, and the book added to the list, as shown in Figure 10-4.

If we want to test the interface on the canvas, we can add testing data to the model from the `PreviewProvider` structure. There are different ways to initialize a model with some data, but if we do it inside the `PreviewProvider` structure, the data will only be available during development. For example, we can add a type computed property to the structure to create an instance of our model with some data in it and then assign it to the view's environment.

```
struct ContentView_Previews: PreviewProvider {
    static var previews: some View {
        ContentView().environmentObject(self.testingModel)
    }
    static var testingModel: AppData {
        let model = AppData()
        model.userData = [
            BookViewModel(book: Book(title: "Steve Jobs", author: "Walter
Isaacson", cover: "book1", year: 2011)),
            BookViewModel(book: Book(title: "HTML5 for Masterminds", author:
"J.D Gauchat", cover: "book2", year: 2017)),
            BookViewModel(book: Book(title: "The Road Ahead", author: "Bill
Gates", cover: "book3", year: 1995))
        ]
        return model
    }
}
```

Listing 10-8: Adding testing data to the model used by the preview

The structure of Listing 10-8 defines a type computed property that creates an instance of the model and fill it with three books. The books use the book1, book2, and book3 covers incorporated before into our project, but since this is testing data, we should include the images in the Preview Assets Catalog instead of the Assets Catalog so the files are not shipped to the App Store with our application.

 Do It Yourself: Update the `ContentView_Previews` structure in the ContentView.swift file with the code of Listing 10-8. Download the nopicture.png, book1.jpg, book2.jpg and book3.jpg images from our website and add them to the Preview Assets Catalog inside the Preview Content group (see Figure 5-15). Remove the images from the Assets Catalog, so they are not shipped with the app to the App Store. Press the Resume button to see the preview on the canvas. You should see a list with three books.

(Basic) ScrollView View

If we continue adding books to the model, the list will extend beyond the edge of the screen and the user won't be able to see it. For a list to effectively show all the content available in the model, it must be able to scroll. To convert a static list of views into a scrollable one, SwiftUI includes the `ScrollView` view. The following is the structure's initializer.

ScrollView(Axis, showsIndicators: Bool, **content:** Closure)—This initializer creates a `ScrollView` view. The first attribute is an enumeration of type `Axis` that indicates the axis in which the views are going to scroll. The values available are `horizontal` and `vertical` (default). The **showsIndicators** attribute is a Boolean value that determines if the view is going to display the scroll indicators or not. And the **content** attribute is the closure that defines the scrollable content.

By default, the axis is set to vertical, the indicators are shown, and the content adapts to the size of the view, so all we have to do to make the list of books of our previous example scrollable, is to embed the `ForEach` view in a `ScrollView` view, as shown next.

```
import SwiftUI
struct ContentView: View {
   @EnvironmentObject var appData: AppData
   @State private var openSheet: Bool = false

   var body: some View {
      VStack {
         HStack {
            Spacer()
            Button("Add Book") {
               self.openSheet = true
            }
         }.padding()

         ScrollView {
            ForEach(appData.userData) { book in
               VStack {
                  HStack(alignment: .top) {
                     Image(book.cover)
                        .resizable()
                        .scaledToFit()
                        .frame(width: 80, height: 100)
                     VStack(alignment: .leading, spacing: 2) {
                        Text(book.title).bold()
                        Text(book.author)
```

```
                    Text(book.year).font(.caption)
                }.padding(.top, 5)
                Spacer()
                Button(action: {
                    self.appData.removeBook(removeID: book.id)
                }, label: {
                    Image(systemName: "trash.circle")
                        .font(.title)
                })
            }.padding([.leading, .trailing], 10)
            .padding([.top, .bottom], 5)
            Divider()
        }
    }
}
        Spacer()
    }.sheet(isPresented: $openSheet) {
        AddBookView().environmentObject(self.appData)
    }
    }
    }
}
```

Listing 10-9: *Making a list of views scrollable*

This example presents the same views as before but now we can scroll the list vertically. If there are enough books to scroll the entire screen, the system shows a vertical indicator on the right to help the user navigate the list.

The content of a `ScrollView` view has to be inside a vertical or a horizontal stack, depending on its axis. In the example of Listing 10-9, the content was already part of a `VStack` and therefore we didn't have to specify it, but if we want to scroll the list of books horizontally, we must embed the `ForEach` view of our example in an `HStack`, as shown next.

```
import SwiftUI

struct ContentView: View {
    @EnvironmentObject var appData: AppData
    @State private var openSheet: Bool = false

    var body: some View {
        VStack {
            HStack {
                Spacer()
                Button("Add Book") {
                    self.openSheet = true
                }
            }.padding()

            ScrollView(.horizontal, showsIndicators: false) {
                HStack(spacing: 0) {
                    ForEach(appData.userData) { book in
                        VStack {
                            Image(book.cover)
                                .resizable()
                                .scaledToFit()
                                .frame(width: 80, height: 100)
                            Text(book.title)
                                .font(.caption)
                        }.padding(10)
                        .frame(width: 100, height: 150)
                    }
                }
```

```
    }.frame(height: 150)
    Spacer()
}.sheet(isPresented: $openSheet) {
    AddBookView().environmentObject(self.appData)
    }
}
}
```

Listing 10-10: Scrolling the list of views horizontally

A vertical list of views usually takes the width of the screen and the height of the space available, but a horizontal list must be of a specific height and all the items should be the same size. In Listing 10-10, we specify a size of 100 by 150 points for the items, and a height of 150 for the scroll view. The result is shown in Figure 10-5.

Figure 10-5: Horizontal scroll view

Basic 10.2 List View

Presenting information in a scrollable list of rows is the most common task of any mobile application. For short lists of values, a `ForEach` view embedded in a `ScrollView` view may suffice, but these types of views load all the values at once, which can introduce performance issues. To solve these problems and provide a standard solution for the creation of lists of views, SwiftUI defines the `List` view. The `List` view creates a vertical list of rows, separated by a line, scrollable, and with all the functionality built in to select, add or remove content. The following are some of the structure's initializers.

List(Data, id: KeyPath, **rowContent:** Closure)—This initializer creates a `List` view. The first attribute is the collection of values for the rows, the **id** attribute is the key path to the unique identifier for each value, and the **rowContent** attribute is a closure that defines the views used to create the rows.

List(Data, rowContent: Closure)—This initializer creates a `List` view. The first attribute is the collection of values for the rows. These values must conform to the **identifiable** protocol and implement the **id** property to provide a unique identifier. And the **rowContent** attribute is a closure that defines the views used to create the rows.

List(Data, selection: Binding, **rowContent:** Closure)—This initializer creates a `List` view. The first attribute is the collection of values for the rows (optional if we use a `ForEach` view). The **selection** attribute is a `Binding` property that stores one or a set of identifiers to indicate the selected rows. And the **rowContent** attribute is a closure that defines the views used to create the rows.

A `List` view works the same way as a `ForEach` view, but it is optimized to present a large set of data. The syntax is also the same. The view requires a reference to the collection of data to be shown and a closure with the views that define each row.

```
import SwiftUI

struct ContentView: View {
   @EnvironmentObject var appData: AppData

   var body: some View {
      List(appData.userData) { book in
         HStack(alignment: .top) {
            Image(book.cover)
               .resizable()
               .scaledToFit()
               .frame(width: 80, height: 100)
            VStack(alignment: .leading, spacing: 2) {
               Text(book.title).bold()
               Text(book.author)
               Text(book.year).font(.caption)
               Spacer()
            }.padding(.top, 5)
            Spacer()
         }
      }
   }
}
```

Listing 10-11: Creating a list of views

Like the `ForEach` view, the `List` view in Listing 10-11 reads the values in the model and creates the rows with the views defined by the closure. If we load testing data into the model, as we did in Listing 10-8, we will see the interface of Figure 10-6 on the canvas.

Figure 10-6: List of rows created by a `List` view

 Do It Yourself: Create a SwiftUI project. Download the nopicture.png, book1.jpg, book2.jpg and book3.jpg images from our website and add them to the Preview Assets Catalog. Create a Swift file called AppData.swift for the model of Listing 10-3 and 10-5. Update the AppDelegate.swift file with the code of Listing 7-14 and the SceneDelegate.swift file with the code of Listing 7-20. Update the ContentView.swift file with the code of Listing 10-11. To see the preview on the canvas, update the `PreviewProvider` structure with the code of Listing 10-8. You should see the interface of Figure 10-6.

Working with `List` views is very common in mobile development. To improve the workflow is good practice to separate the code for the view from the code for the rows. The following example moves the views for the rows to a custom view called `RowBook`.

```
import SwiftUI

struct ContentView: View {
    @EnvironmentObject var appData: AppData

    var body: some View {
        List(appData.userData) { book in
            RowBook(book: book)
        }
    }
}
struct RowBook: View {
    let book: BookViewModel

    var body: some View {
        HStack(alignment: .top) {
            Image(book.cover)
                .resizable()
                .scaledToFit()
                .frame(width: 80, height: 100)
            VStack(alignment: .leading, spacing: 2) {
                Text(book.title).bold()
                Text(book.author)
                Text(book.year).font(.caption)
                Spacer()
            }.padding(.top, 5)
            Spacer()
        }
    }
}
```

Listing 10-12: Breaking down the list into custom views

The code of Listing 10-12 defines a custom view to create the rows and creates an instance of that view in every cycle. Notice that the **RowBook** view needs access to the current value, so it defines a property called **book** to receive it. The rest of the code is the same as before.

 Do It Yourself: Update the ContentView.swift file with the code of Listing 10-12. Remember to include the **PreviewProvider** structure with the code of Listing 10-8 to see the preview on the canvas. You should see the same interface of Figure 10-6.

The **List** view was designed to work along with the **ForEach** view to mix static and dynamic content. The advantage is that we can create a list of rows with the data from the model and at the same time include other rows with static content to incorporate additional information or for styling purposes, as in the following example.

```
struct ContentView: View {
    @EnvironmentObject var appData: AppData

    var body: some View {
        List {
            HStack {
                Text("☰")
                    .font(.headline)
                Spacer()
                Text("My Favorite Books")
                    .font(.headline)
            }
```

```
            ForEach(appData.userData) { book in
                RowBook(book: book)
            }
        }
    }
}
```

A `List` view takes a list of views, one or more `ForEach` loops, or a combination of both, and includes every view in a row. In Listing 10-13, we create one static view with some text and then a `ForEach` view to list the data in the model. The static content is shown along with the dynamic content and even scrolls with the rest of the rows, as illustrated in Figure 10-7.

Figure 10-7: Static and dynamic content

 Do It Yourself: Update the `ContentView` structure with the code of Listing 10-13. Activate the live preview on the canvas and scroll up the interface. You should see something similar to Figure 10-7.

Embedding a `ForEach` loop inside a `List` view is so common that most of the functionality for the list is implemented by the `ForEach` view. For instance, if we use a `ForEach` view to create dynamic rows, we can apply the following modifiers to the rows.

listRowInsets(EdgeInsets)—This modifier defines the insets for the rows. The attribute is an `EdgeInsets` structure. The structure provides an initializer to define the top, leading, bottom, and trailing insets.

listRowBackground(View)—This modifier defines the background view for the row. The attribute is a SwiftUI view, such as `Color`.

By default, a standard inset is assigned to the row. This is the reason why we didn't have to apply padding to the rows in previews examples. But we can change or remove this padding with the `listRowInsets()` modifier.

```
struct ContentView: View {
    @EnvironmentObject var appData: AppData

    var body: some View {
        List {
            ForEach(appData.userData) { book in
                RowBook(book: book)
                    .listRowInsets(EdgeInsets(top: 0, leading: 0, bottom: 0,
trailing: 0))
                    .listRowBackground(Color(red: 0.95, green: 0.95, blue:
0.95))
        }
```

```
        }
      }
}
```

Listing 10-14: Customizing the rows

The `ContentView` view of Listing 10-14 assigns an inset of 0 and a gray background to the rows. The result is shown in Figure 10-8.

Figure 10-8: Custom rows

(Basic) **Sections**

A list may be organized in sections. Sections help the user identify groups of values that share common features. SwiftUI includes the `Section` view to create these sections.

Section(content: Closure)—This initializer creates a `Section` view to group related content. The **content** attribute is the closure that defines the rows for the section.

Section(header: View, **footer:** View, **content:** Closure)—This initializer creates a `Section` view to group related content. The **header** attribute is a view or a group of views that define the section's header, the **footer** attribute is a view or a group of views that define the section's footer, and the **content** attribute is the closure that defines the rows for the section.

Although a section may contain no header or footer, for most situations it is better to provide a visual cue of where a section begins and ends. The following example creates two sections with a header defined by a `Text` view.

```
struct ContentView: View {
   @EnvironmentObject var appData: AppData

   var body: some View {
      List {
         Section(header: Text("Statistics")) {
            HStack {
               Text("Total Books:")
               Spacer()
               Text(String(appData.userData.count))
            }
         }
         Section(header: Text("My Books")) {
            ForEach(appData.userData) { book in
               RowBook(book: book)
            }
         }
```

```
            }
        }
}
```

Listing 10-15: Dividing the content into sections

The example of Listing 10-15 creates two sections, one to show the total number of books in the model and another to list the books. The system automatically assigns a gray background to the header views to help the user identify the header and the beginning of each section.

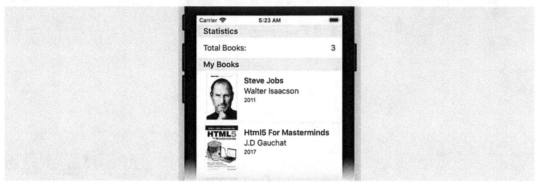

Figure 10-9: Sections with headers

Of course, the headers and footers can be customized. We can embed the **Text** view of our example in an **HStack**, apply modifiers to change the background color, or add more views. But the **List** view implements the following modifier to apply a standard style to the list.

listStyle(Style**)**—This modifier assigns a style to the **List** view. The attribute is a structure that conforms to the **ListStyle** protocol. SwiftUI defines three structures for iPhones and iPads: **DefaultListStyle**, **GroupedListStyle**, and **PlainListStyle**.

The **PlainListStyle** structure allows full customization of the header and footer views, but the **GroupedListStyle** structure provides some styles by default that generate a design that users are familiar with. The following code applies the **GroupedListStyle** design to the previous example.

```
struct ContentView: View {
    @EnvironmentObject var appData: AppData

    var body: some View {
        List {
            Section(header: Text("Statistics")) {
                HStack {
                    Text("Total Books:")
                    Spacer()
                    Text(String(appData.userData.count))
                }
            }
            Section(header: Text("My Books")) {
                ForEach(appData.userData) { book in
                    RowBook(book: book)
                }
            }
        }.listStyle(GroupedListStyle())
    }
}
```

Listing 10-16: Applying a standard design to the list

Chapter 10 - Lists

Figure 10-10: Standard design

Do It Yourself: Update the `ContentView` structure with the code of the example you want to try (Listings 10-15 or 10-16). Press Resume on the canvas to see the preview. Try to expand the views in the headers with stacks and modifiers to see how they work.

By default, the height of headers and rows is determined by their content, but the environment includes two properties to modify those values.

defaultMinListHeaderHeight—This property defines the minimum height for the headers. It is a value of type `CGFloat`.

defaultMinListRowHeight—This property defines the minimum height for the rows. It is a value of type `CGFloat`.

To change the values of these properties, we have to apply the `environment()` modifier to the `List` view (see Listing 6-79). These properties are useful when the content of the headers or the rows is variable. For instance, we can assign a minimum size to the rows of our previous example so the row in the first section is of the same height as the rows with the books.

```
struct ContentView: View {
   @EnvironmentObject var appData: AppData

   var body: some View {
      List {
         Section(header: Text("Statistics")) {
            HStack {
               Text("Total Books:")
               Spacer()
               Text(String(appData.userData.count))
            }
         }
         Section(header: Text("My Books")) {
            ForEach(appData.userData) { book in
               RowBook(book: book)
            }
         }
      }.listStyle(GroupedListStyle())
      .environment(\.defaultMinListRowHeight, 100)
   }
}
```

Listing 10-17: Configuring the list from the environment

Chapter 10 - Lists

Figure 10-11: Same height for all the rows

So far, we have used sections to group different types of content. The first section of our example contains information about the model and the second section contains the list of values. But sections become useful when they help the user identify groups of values with different characteristics, like the categories of movies, or when they separate content alphabetically. For this purpose, we must prepare the model to deliver the data in the order and with the organization the views require to show it on the screen. In the following example, we create a computed property that returns the list of books in alphabetical order.

```
class AppData: ObservableObject {
    @Published var userData: [BookViewModel] = []

    var orderList: [(key: String, value: [BookViewModel])] {
        let listGroup: [String: [BookViewModel]] = Dictionary(grouping:
userData, by: { value in
            let index = value.title.startIndex
            let initial = value.title[index]
            return String(initial)
        })
        return listGroup.sorted(by: { $0.key < $1.key })
    }
}
```

Listing 10-18: Providing an order list of values

The code in Listing 10-18 updates our model's observable object to provide an array of tuples with the books organized by the first letter of their titles. First, the closure applies the `Dictionary(grouping:, by:)` initializer to create a dictionary from the values of the `userData` array (the list of books). The way this initializer works is that for every value in the array, it executes a closure and then groups the results by the values returned by the closure (see Listing 3-124). In this example, we get the index of the first character in the book's title with the `startIndex` property. Then, we use that index to extract the first character. And finally, we turn it into a string and return it. This creates an array with tuples which first value is a letter of the alphabet and the second value is an array with all the books which titles begin with that letter (`[(key: String, value: [BookViewModel])]`). After this array is created, we sort the values alphabetically with the `sorted()` method and return it, so every time the views read the `orderList` property, they get an array of tuples with the books sorted alphabetically.

The values of the tuples were identified with the labels `key` and `value`, so we can use these labels to read them and create our list.

```
struct ContentView: View {
    @EnvironmentObject var appData: AppData
    var body: some View {
```

Chapter 10 - Lists

```
    List {
        ForEach(appData.orderList, id: \.key) { sections in
            Section(header: Text(sections.key)) {
                ForEach(sections.value) { book in
                    RowBook(book: book)
                }
            }
        }
    }
}
```

Listing 10-19: Listing the values in alphabetical sections

The `ContentView` in Listing 10-19 defines a `List` view with two `ForEach` loops inside, one to create the sections for each letter and another to list the books in that section. The first `ForEach` loop reads the content of the `orderList` property and creates a section with the value identified by the `key` label (the letter). Inside the section, another `ForEach` loop iterates through the array identified with the `value` label to create the list of books. As a result, we get three sections, H, S and T, for the three books inserted in the model by the preview.

Figure 10-12: Alphabetical sections

 Do It Yourself: Update the observable object in the AppData.swift file with the code of Listing 10-18. Update the `ContentView` structure with the code of Listing 10-19. The ContentView.swift file should also contain the `RowBook` view defined in Listing 10-12 and the `PreviewProvider` structure defined in Listing 10-8 for the application and the preview to work. You should see the interface of Figure 10-12 on the canvas.

(Basic) **Edition Mode**

`List` views also provide tools to work with the values on the list. The following are the modifiers available to remove and order views.

onDelete(perform: Closure)—This modifier executes a closure when the user tries to remove a row. The **perform** attribute is the closure to execute when the action is performed. The closure receives a value of type `IndexSet` with integers representing the indexes of the rows the user wants to delete.

deleteDisabled(Bool)—This modifier enables or disables the possibility for the user to delete a row.

onMove(perform: Closure)—This modifier executes a closure when the user tries to move a row to a different position on the list. The **perform** attribute is the closure to execute when the action is performed. The closure receives a value of type `IndexSet` with integers representing the indexes of the rows the user is moving, and an integer representing the index where the rows should be moved.

moveDisabled(Bool)—This modifier enables or disables the possibility for the user to move a row.

These modifiers produce a value of type `IndexSet` that contains a set of integers representing the indexes of the values to be modified in the collection. To modify an array from these values, the Swift Standard Library defines the following methods.

remove(atOffsets: IndexSet)—This method removes the items in the array with the indexes provided by the **atOffsets** attribute.

move(fromOffsets: IndexSet, **toOffset:** Int)—This method moves the items of the array in the indexes specified by the **fromOffsets** attribute to the index determined by the **toOffset** attribute.

Due to the values returned by the `onDelete()` and `onMove()` modifiers, removing and organizing the values in the model is a little bit different than what we did before. Instead of identifying the items by their `id` property, we have to do it by their indexes in the array. The following are the methods required by our observable object to work with these modifiers.

```
class AppData: ObservableObject {
    @Published var userData: [BookViewModel] = []

    func addBook(book: Book) {
        userData.append(BookViewModel(book: book))
    }
    func removeBook(removeSet: IndexSet) {
        userData.remove(atOffsets: removeSet)
    }
    func moveBook(from: IndexSet, to: Int) {
        userData.move(fromOffsets: from, toOffset: to)
    }
}
```

Listing 10-20: Adding, removing, and moving values in the model

Adding a book to the model didn't change. We have to create the `BookViewModel` instance with the information for the book and add it to the array with the `append()` method, but the `removeBook()` method is different. Now, instead of searching for the item in the array that matches a specific id value, as we did in Listing 10-5, we just call the `remove()` method with the `IndexSet` value received from the view and all the items are removed at once. The `moveBook()` method is similar. All we have to do to move the items to the position selected by the user is to call the `move()` method in the array with the values received from the view.

There are different ways to allow the user to modify the list. For instance, if we apply the `onDelete()` modifier to the list, the system automatically activates a feature that lets the user drag a row to the left to expose a Delete button. There is no need to add anything else.

```
struct ContentView: View {
    @EnvironmentObject var appData: AppData
```

```
var body: some View {
    NavigationView {
        List {
            ForEach(appData.userData) { book in
                RowBook(book: book)
            }
            .onDelete(perform: { indexes in
                self.appData.removeBook(removeSet: indexes)
            })
        }.navigationBarTitle("Books")
    }
}
}
```

Listing 10-21: Deleting rows

Notice that the modifiers are implemented by the **ForEach** view and therefore can only be applied to this view. In the example of Listing 10-21, we use the **onDelete()** modifier, so when a row is dragged to the left and the Delete button is pressed, the closure provided to the modifier is executed. This closure receives an **IndexSet** value with the index of the row to be deleted and calls the **removeBook()** method on the observable object to remove the item from the model.

Figure 10-13: Automatic delete feature

 Do It Yourself: Update the observable object in the model with the code of Listing 10-20. Update the **ContentView** structure with the code of Listing 10-21. Activate the live preview. Drag a row to the left and press the Delete button, as shown in Figure 10-13. The row should be removed from the list.

Besides this feature, **List** views also have a set of tools built-in that let the user select, remove, and move rows. The tools are displayed to the user when the list is in editing mode. The easiest way to active this mode is with the **EditButton** view. This view creates a button that activates and deactivates the editing mode when pressed, as shown next.

```
struct ContentView: View {
    @EnvironmentObject var appData: AppData

    var body: some View {
        NavigationView {
            List {
                ForEach(appData.userData) { book in
                    RowBook(book: book)
                }
                .onDelete(perform: { indexes in
                    self.appData.removeBook(removeSet: indexes)
```

```
            })
        }.navigationBarTitle("Books")
        .navigationBarItems(leading: EditButton())
        }
    }
}
```

The code of Listing 10-22 adds an `EditButton` to the navigation bar. When the button is pressed, the system activates the list's editing mode and the tools are shown according to the modifiers added to the view. For instance, in our example, we included the `onDelete()` modifier, so the view exposes buttons to let the user delete the row.

Figure 10-14: Edit button

The tool to move rows is included when the `onMove()` modifier is applied to the `ForEach` view, as in the following example.

```
struct ContentView: View {
    @EnvironmentObject var appData: AppData

    var body: some View {
        NavigationView {
            List {
                ForEach(appData.userData) { book in
                    RowBook(book: book)
                }
                .onDelete(perform: { indexes in
                    self.appData.removeBook(removeSet: indexes)
                })
                .onMove(perform: { source, destination in
                    self.appData.moveBook(from: source, to: destination)
                })
            }.navigationBarTitle("Books")
            .navigationBarItems(leading: EditButton())
        }
    }
}
```

Listing 10-23: Moving rows

The system detects that we have implemented the `onMove()` modifier and automatically provides the tools for the user to move the rows and reorganize the list. After the user drops a row in a new position, the modifier sends the indexes of the rows and the new location to the closure, and here is where we have the chance to call the `moveBook()` method in the model to also perform the change in the array, so the next time the list is redrawn, the rows remain in the position selected by the user.

Chapter 10 - Lists

Figure 10-15: Move buttons

Do It Yourself: Update the `ContentView` structure with the code of Listing 10-23 and activate the live preview on the canvas. Press the Edit button. Use the tools to remove a row or move it to a different position. You should see the interfaces in Figures 10-14 and 10-15.

The edition mode also provides the option to select one or more rows. The tool is presented when the `List` view is initialized with the **selection** attribute. The attribute takes a `Binding` property to store the ids of the selected rows, so we can use this property to modify multiple values at a time. To process the values, we can use the ids (in our case, `UUID` values) or turn those ids into an `IndexSet` structure to use the methods in the model to move or remove rows. This structure provides the following method to add values to the set.

insert(Int**)**—This method adds the integer specified by the attribute to the `IndexSet` set.

In the following example, we provide a `Binding` property to the `List` view to let the user select rows, and then create an `IndexSet` structure with the indexes of the selected rows to remove the values from the model.

```
struct ContentView: View {
   @EnvironmentObject var appData: AppData
   @State private var selectedRows: Set<UUID> = []

   var body: some View {
      NavigationView {
         List(selection: $selectedRows) {
            ForEach(appData.userData) { book in
               RowBook(book: book)
            }
         }
         .navigationBarTitle("Books")
         .navigationBarItems(leading: EditButton(),
            trailing: Button("Remove") {
               var indexes = IndexSet()
               for item in self.selectedRows {
                  if let index = self.appData.userData.firstIndex(where:
{ $0.id == item }) {
                     indexes.insert(index)
                  }
               }
               self.appData.removeBook(removeSet: indexes)
               self.selectedRows = []
            }.disabled(selectedRows.count == 0 ? true : false)
         )
      }
   }
```

```
        }
}
```

Listing 10-24: Selecting rows

The view in Listing 10-24 defines a `@State` property of type `Set<UUID>` (a set of `UUID` values) and then creates a `List` view with this property to allow the user to select rows. When the user activates the edition mode, checkboxes appear on the left to select the rows. If the user selects a row, the `List` view stores the `id` of that value in the `selectedRows` property, so we can use these values to modify the model. For instance, in the example of Listing 10-24, we add a button to the navigation bar, called Remove, and apply the `disabled()` modifier to this button to only enable it when the `selectedRows` property contains at least one value (at least one row was selected). When the user presses this button, we create an empty `IndexSet` structure and then iterate through the values of the `selectedRows` property to find the index of each book and add it to the set. Once all the indexes are found, we call the `removeBook()` method on the model to erase the books and clean the `selectedRows` property to let the user start the process again.

Figure 10-16: Selected rows

 Do It Yourself: Update the `ContentView` structure with the code of Listing 10-24 and activate the live preview. Press the Edit button. Select a row and click the Remove button. The row should be removed, as shown in Figure 10-16.

If we want to deactivate the editing mode after the books are removed, or any other action is performed, we must manage the mode manually. The environment offers the following property for this purpose.

editMode—This property defines the state of the editing mode for the view. It is `Binding` property of type `EditMode`, an enumeration with the values `active`, `inactive`, and `transient`.

To manage the mode ourselves, we need a `@State` property with a Boolean value that stores the state of the editing mode (active or inactive), we must set the mode according to the value of this property with the `environment()` modifier, as we did before for other environment properties, and we must create a button to toggle this value and change the mode.

```
struct ContentView: View {
    @EnvironmentObject var appData: AppData
    @State private var selectedRows: Set<UUID> = []
    @State private var editActive: Bool = false
```

```
var body: some View {
    NavigationView {
        List(selection: $selectedRows) {
            ForEach(appData.userData) { book in
                RowBook(book: book)
            }
        }
        .environment(\.editMode, .constant(self.editActive ?
EditMode.active : EditMode.inactive))
            .navigationBarTitle("Books")
            .navigationBarItems(leading:
                Button(self.editActive ? "Done" : "Edit") {
                    self.editActive.toggle()
                },
                trailing: Button("Remove") {
                    var indexes = IndexSet()
                    for item in self.selectedRows {
                        if let index = self.appData.userData.firstIndex(where:
{ $0.id == item }) {
                            indexes.insert(index)
                        }
                    }
                    self.appData.removeBook(removeSet: indexes)
                    self.editActive = false
                    self.selectedRows = []
                }.disabled(selectedRows.count == 0 ? true : false)
            )
        }
    }
}
```

Listing 10-25: Customizing the editing mode

In Listing 10-25, we define a `@State` property called `editActive` to keep track of the editing mode. If the value is `true`, it means that the mode is active, otherwise it means that the mode is inactive. Then, we use this property to select the label for the button ("Done" if `true`, "Edit" if `false`), and to deactivate the editing mode after the user removes a book. Notice that the environment's `editMode` property is a `Binding` property and therefore we use the `constant()` method to provide a `Binding` value of type `EditMode` (see Listing 7-11).

The result is the same as before, but the process is now customized and therefore we can change the editing mode from code anytime by assigning the value `true` or `false` to the `editActive` property.

 Do It Yourself: Update the `ContentView` structure with the code of Listing 10-25 and activate the live preview. Press the Edit button. Select a row and click the Remove button. The row should be removed, and the editing mode should be deactivated.

The selection process can also be customized, but it requires us to keep track of the selected rows ourselves and detect the selection with the `onTapGesture()` modifier. We have implemented this modifier before to detect when an image was tapped by the user (see Listing 8-17). We will study event modifiers in further chapters, but for our purpose all we need to know is that the modifier executes a closure when the user taps the view and, therefore, we can use this closure to respond to the event. In our case, we need to apply the modifier to every `RowBook` view and assign the id of the selected row to the `@State` property, as in the following example.

```
struct ContentView: View {
    @EnvironmentObject var appData: AppData
    @State private var selectedRow: UUID? = nil

    var body: some View {
        NavigationView {
            List {
                ForEach(appData.userData) { book in
                    RowBook(selected: self.$selectedRow, book: book)
                        .onTapGesture(perform: {
                            if self.selectedRow == book.id {
                                self.selectedRow = nil
                            } else {
                                self.selectedRow = book.id
                            }
                        })
                }
            }.navigationBarTitle("Books")
        }
    }
}
struct RowBook: View {
    @Binding var selected: UUID?
    let book: BookViewModel

    var body: some View {
        HStack(alignment: .top) {
            Image(book.cover)
                .resizable()
                .scaledToFit()
                .frame(width: 80, height: 100)
            VStack(alignment: .leading, spacing: 2) {
                Text(book.title).bold()
                Text(book.author)
                Text(book.year).font(.caption)
                Spacer()
            }.padding(.top, 5)
            Spacer()
            Image(systemName: self.selected == book.id ? "checkmark" : "")
                .font(.title)
                .foregroundColor(Color.green)
                .padding(5)
        }.background(Color.white)
    }
}
```

Listing 10-26: Customizing the selection

In this example we allow the selection of one row at a time. If the user taps on a row, the onTapGesture() modifier checks whether the book's id was already stored in the @State property. If it was, it deselects the row by assigning the value nil to the property, otherwise, the book's id is assigned to the property to indicate that the row was selected. To show the selection to the user, we connect the @State property with a @Binding property in the RowBook view and then show an image if the value of this property is equal to the book's id. As a result, a checkmark will be shown on the row if it is selected, or no image otherwise.

Chapter 10 - Lists

Figure 10-17: Custom selection

 Do It Yourself: Update the `ContentView` structure and the `RowBook` structure in your ContentView.swift file with the code of Listing 10-26. Activate the live preview on the canvas. Click on a row. You should see the checkmark shown in Figure 10-17. Of course, you can add a button to perform a task on the selected item, like removing the book from the model, as we did in Listing 10-24.

 The Basics: Notice that we have applied the `background()` modifier to the `HStack` in the `RowBook` view. The modifier generates a `Color` view that occupies the whole area, providing a surface for the `onTapGesture()` to respond to the taps and allowing the user to select the row by tapping anywhere, not only on its content. SwiftUI also provides the `contentShape()` modifier for this purpose. We will learn more about this modifier and gestures in Chapter 12.

(Basic) **Custom Buttons**

Besides the buttons generated by the system, we can include our own buttons. Of course, when we use custom buttons to perform the tasks, there is no need to implement the methods defined for the edit mode. The following example illustrates how to include a remove button.

```
struct ContentView: View {
   @EnvironmentObject var appData: AppData

   var body: some View {
      NavigationView {
         List {
            ForEach(appData.userData) { book in
               RowBook(book: book)
            }
         }.navigationBarTitle("Books")
      }
   }
}
struct RowBook: View {
   @EnvironmentObject var appData: AppData
   let book: BookViewModel

   var body: some View {
      HStack(alignment: .top) {
         Image(book.cover)
            .resizable()
            .scaledToFit()
            .frame(width: 80, height: 100)
```

```
        VStack(alignment: .leading, spacing: 2) {
            Text(book.title).bold()
            Text(book.author)
            Text(book.year).font(.caption)
            Spacer()
        }.padding(.top, 5)
        Spacer()

        Button(action: {
            var indexes = IndexSet()
            if let index = self.appData.userData.firstIndex(where: {
$0.id == self.book.id }) {
                indexes.insert(index)
            }
            self.appData.removeBook(removeSet: indexes)
        }, label: {
            Image(systemName: "trash")
                .font(.body)
                .foregroundColor(Color.red)
        }).padding(.top, 5)
        .buttonStyle(PlainButtonStyle())
    }
  }
}
```

Listing 10-27: Implementing a custom button to delete the rows

The buttons created by default by the `Button` view pass to the row the responsibility of responding to the user tapping the screen. To get the button to respond when it is tapped, we must define it as a plain button with the `PlainButtonStyle` style (see Button View in Chapter 8). The action and the label are defined as always. In this example, we create a button on the right-hand side of each row to delete it. The label is an SF Symbol of a trash can, and the action implements the `IndexSet` structure introduced before to add the book's index to a set and be able to call the `removeBook()` method on the model to remove it.

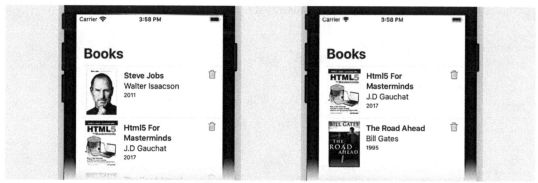

Figure 10-18: Custom button to remove a row

 Do It Yourself: Update the ContentView.swift file with the code of Listing 10-27. Activate the live preview on the canvas. Click on the trash bin icon. The row should be removed.

(Basic) ## Search

SwiftUI doesn't provide any built-in functionality to search for values in the model yet, but we can create our own search bar with the tools already available. How the search is performed depends on the characteristics of our model. In a model that stores values in an array, as the one we are using in this chapter, the search is performed by filtering the values in the array with the `filter()` method, but databases provide their own search tools, as we will see in Chapter 14.

To allow the user to perform a search, we must add a `TextField` view to the interface and define a few `@Published` properties to manage the values produced by this view. The following is the observable object we need for this example (this object works with the model introduced in Listing 10-3).

```
class AppData: ObservableObject {
    @Published var userData: [BookViewModel] = []

    @Published var search: String? = nil
    @Published var searchInput: String = "" {
        didSet {
            setSearch(term: searchInput)
        }
    }
    var filteredList: [BookViewModel] {
        if let searchText = search {
            return userData.filter({ $0.title.contains(searchText) })
        } else {
            return userData
        }
    }
    func setSearch(term: String) {
        let toSearch = term.trimmingCharacters(in: .whitespaces)
        search = toSearch == "" ? nil : toSearch
    }
}
```

Listing 10-28: Searching data in the model

Other than the `userData` property, the rest of the code in this observable object is required for the user to be able to search a value in the model. The `search` property is used to store the term searched by the user and the `searchInput` property is used by the `TextField` view to store the values typed by the user. This last property includes a `didSet` method to modify the value of the `search` property every time its value changes (every time the user inserts or removes a character in the text field, the current string is assigned to the `search` property). Next, we define a computed property called `filteredList` to filter the values in the model. This property checks if there is a value in the `search` property and searches for that value inside the `title` property of every book with the `contains()` method. If the value searched by the user is inside the string of characters in the `title` property, that `BookViewModel` instance is returned, otherwise it is ignored, so the `filteredList` property only contain the books which titles match the search. Finally, we define a method called `setSearch()` to assign new values to the `search` property. This is necessary because there are at least three actions the user can perform to initiate the search. One is the automatic search performed by the `searchInput` property, another is by pressing the search button in the interface, and another is by pressing the Done button in the keyboard. The method trims the value inserted by the user to remove spaces at the beginning and the end, and then checks if there is a value to work with. If the value is empty (`toSearch == ""`), we assign `nil` to the `search` property, otherwise the value inserted by the user is assigned instead.

The interface doesn't change much from previous examples. We must include a `TextField` view to let the user insert a string to search and show the filtered values below in a `List` view. To simplify the code, we are going to move the search bar to a custom view called `SearchBar`.

```
import SwiftUI
struct ContentView: View {
   @EnvironmentObject var appData: AppData

   var body: some View {
      VStack {
         SearchBar()
         List {
            ForEach(appData.filteredList) { book in
               RowBook(book: book)
            }
         }
      }
   }
}
struct SearchBar: View {
   @EnvironmentObject var appData: AppData

   var body: some View {
      HStack {
         TextField("", text: $appData.searchInput, onCommit: {
            self.appData.setSearch(term: self.appData.searchInput)
         }).textFieldStyle(RoundedBorderTextFieldStyle())
         Button("🔍") {
            self.appData.setSearch(term: self.appData.searchInput)
         }
      }.padding()
   }
}
struct RowBook: View {
   let book: BookViewModel

   var body: some View {
      HStack(alignment: .top) {
         Image(book.cover)
            .resizable()
            .scaledToFit()
            .frame(width: 80, height: 100)
         VStack(alignment: .leading, spacing: 2) {
            Text(book.title).bold()
            Text(book.author)
            Text(book.year).font(.caption)
            Spacer()
         }.padding(.top, 5)
         Spacer()
      }
   }
}
```

Listing 10-29: Adding a search bar to the interface

The **ForEach** loop creates a list of rows from the values provided by the **filteredList** property. At first, the value of the **search** property in the observable object is **nil** and therefore the **filteredList** property returns all the books in the model, but the user can change that from the search bar. To this end, we create a **TextField** view and a button. If the content of the **TextField** changes, the closure assigned to the **onCommit** attribute is executed and the **setSearch()** method is called with the value inserted by the user. The same happens if the button is pressed. The **setSearch()** method changes the value of the **search** property, the views are refreshed, and the **filteredList** property now only returns the books which titles match the search.

Chapter 10 - Lists

Figure 10-19: Search bar

 Do It Yourself: Update the observable object in the AppData.swift file with the code in Listing 10-28. Update the ContentView.swift file with the code of Listing 10-29. Remember to add the three books to the model to have something to work with, as we did in Listing 10-8. Activate the live preview on the canvas and perform a search. You should see something similar to Figure 10-19.

Basic **Navigation**

Navigation with `List` views works in the same way as with other views, but we have to identify the navigation links with a tag and provide a `Binding` property for the view to know which link is currently active, as we did in the example of Listing 9-40 and others.

The following example shows how to turn the rows of our previous examples into buttons to open a detail view with information about the selected book.

```
struct ContentView: View {
    @EnvironmentObject var appData: AppData
    @State private var selectedLink: UUID? = nil

    var body: some View {
        NavigationView {
            List {
                ForEach(appData.userData) { book in
                    NavigationLink(destination: DetailView(book: book), tag:
book.id, selection: self.$selectedLink) {
                        RowBook(book: book)
                    }
                }
            }
            .navigationBarTitle("Books")
        }
    }
}
```

Listing 10-30: Turning the rows into navigation buttons

The view of Listing 10-30 assigns the book's id to the navigation link's tag, so every button is identified by a `UUID` value. When a button is tapped, the system stores the id in the `selectedLink` property and therefore it knows which link is active at any time.

As we did before, the `NavigationLink` buttons always open the same view (`DetailView`), but they send the information about the selected book, so the view knows which one to show.

```
import SwiftUI

struct DetailView: View {
    let book: BookViewModel

    var body: some View {
        VStack {
            Image(book.cover)
                .resizable()
                .scaledToFit()
            Text(book.title)
            Text(book.author)
        }.padding()
        .navigationBarTitle("Book")
    }
}
struct DetailView_Previews: PreviewProvider {
    static var previews: some View {
        NavigationView {
            DetailView(book: BookViewModel(book: Book(title: "Steve Jobs",
author: "Walter Isaacson", cover: "book1", year: 2011)))
        }
    }
}
```

Listing 10-31: *Showing the details of the book*

The `DetailView` view defines a property called `book` to receive the information about the book and displays the values. The result is shown in Figure 10-20.

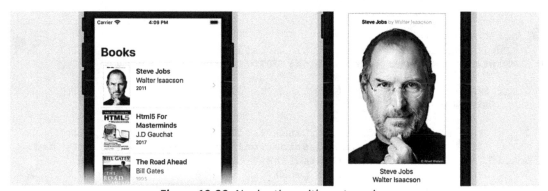

Figure 10-20: *Navigation with a* `List` *view*

Do It Yourself: Update the `ContentView` structure with the code of Listing 10-30. Create a new file called DetailView.swift and update the code with the code of Listing 10-31. Select the ContentView.swift file and activate the live preview. You should be able to click on a row and navigate to the detail view, as shown in Figure 10-20.

(Basic) **10.3 Pickers**

Other controls provided by SwiftUI to present lists of values are pickers. A picker can show the values in a graphic that simulates a wheel, on a list, or as a row of buttons, depending on the platform and the configuration. The framework includes two types of pickers, one to create a general-purpose list, and another to generate a list of dates and times.

The **Picker** view creates a general-purpose picker to show a list of values. The structure includes the following initializers.

> **Picker(String, selection:** Binding, **content:** Closure)—This initializer creates a `Picker` view with the label defined by the first attribute. The **selection** attribute is a `Binding` property that stores the value selected by the user, and the closure assigned to the **content** attribute provides the list of views that present the available values.

> **Picker(selection:** Binding, **label:** View, **content:** Closure)—This initializer creates a `Picker` view. The **selection** attribute is a `Binding` property that stores the value selected by the user, the **label** attribute is a view that defines the picker's label, and the closure assigned to the **content** attribute provides the list of views that present the available values.

A `Picker` view requires a `Binding` property to store the value currently selected by the user and a list of views to present the values available. The list of views can be created manually, one view per line, or dynamically with a `ForEach` view, as in the following example.

```
import SwiftUI

struct ContentView: View {
    @State private var selectedValue: String = "No Value"
    let listCities: [String] = ["Paris", "Toronto", "Dublin"]

    var body: some View {
        VStack {
            Text(selectedValue)
                .font(.largeTitle)
                .padding()
            Picker("Cities:", selection: $selectedValue) {
                ForEach(listCities, id: \.self) { value in
                    Text(value)
                }
            }
            Spacer()
        }.padding()
    }
}
```

Listing 10-32: Defining a picker

In the view of Listing 10-32, we define an array with the names of three cities and then use it to provide the values for a picker. A `ForEach` view within the `Picker` view presents the list of values using `Text` views. When one of these values is selected, the picker stores it in a `@State` property, so we can perform custom tasks with it. In this case, we just show it on the screen with another `Text` view.

A `Picker` view can take many forms. By default, in mobile devices, it is shown as a wheel that the user can rotate to select a value. If there is enough space, the label is shown on the picker's left-hand side, otherwise it is hidden, as illustrated in Figure 10-21.

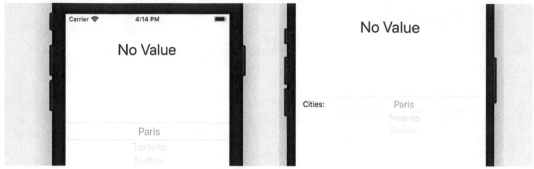

Figure 10-21: Pickers with and without a label

The value of the **Binding** property is used by the picker to select a value, so we can initialize this property with the value we want the picker to show first or change it later.

```swift
import SwiftUI

struct ContentView: View {
    @State private var selectedValue: String = "Toronto"
    let listCities: [String] = ["Paris", "Toronto", "Dublin"]

    var body: some View {
        VStack {
            Text(selectedValue)
                .font(.largeTitle)
                .padding()
            Picker("", selection: $selectedValue) {
                ForEach(listCities, id: \.self) { value in
                    Text(value)
                }
            }.labelsHidden()
            Spacer()
        }.padding()
    }
}
```

Listing 10-33: Selecting an initial value

In this example, we initialize the **selectedValue** property with the string "Toronto", and therefore this is the initial value selected by the **Picker** view. Notice that we also applied the **labelsHidden()** modifier to hide the label and make the picker look the same on every device.

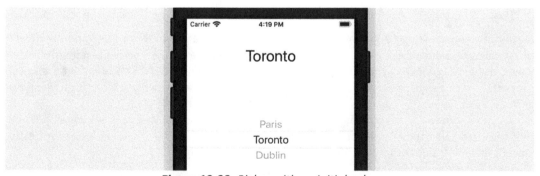

Figure 10-22: Picker with an initial value

Chapter 10 - Lists

Do It Yourself: Create a SwiftUI project. Update the `ContentView` structure with the code of Listing 10-33 and activate the live preview. You should see a wheel like in Figure 10-22, with the value Toronto already selected. Move the wheel. You should see the name of the selected city at the top of the screen.

When no value is provided, the picker identifies the items by their ids, and therefore the items on the list are identified with the same value shown to the user. If this is not what we want, we can provide a unique identifier for each item with the `tag()` modifier introduced before to work with `TabView` views in Chapter 9 (see Listing 9-21). For instance, we can provide the values for the list with an enumeration. The values of the enumeration are the tags and the raw values assigned to each case are the titles we are going to show to the user.

```
import SwiftUI

enum LengthType: String, CaseIterable, Hashable {
    case mm = "Millimeters"
    case cm = "Centimeters"
    case m = "Meters"
    case km = "Kilometers"
    case inch = "Inches"
    case ft = "Feet"
    case yd = "Yards"
    case mi = "Miles"
    case nmi = "Nautical Miles"
    case none = "Unknown"
}
struct ContentView: View {
    @State private var selectedValue: LengthType = .none

    var body: some View {
        VStack {
            Text(selectedValue.rawValue)
                .font(.largeTitle)
                .padding()
            Picker("", selection: $selectedValue) {
                ForEach(LengthType.allCases, id: \.self) { value in
                    Text(value.rawValue)
                        .tag(value)
                }
            }.labelsHidden()
            Spacer()
        }.padding()
    }
}
```

Listing 10-34: Listing values of an enumeration

To work with the `ForEach` view and the `tag()` modifier, the enumeration must conform to the `CaseIterable` and the `Hashable` protocols (see Swift Protocols in Chapter 3). Conforming to the `CaseIterable` protocol provides the enumeration with the type property `allCases` that we can use to create the list of values for the `ForEach` view, and conforming to the `Hashable` protocol allows us to use the enumeration values as identifiers with the `tag()` operator.

Notice that the `selectedValue` property is now of type `LengthType`. This is because the values assigned to the property are those provided by the `tag()` modifier and this modifier is working with enumeration values. When a value is selected by the user, the corresponding enumeration value is assigned to the property, and its raw value is show on the screen by the `Text` view (`Text(selectedValue.rawValue)`).

Figure 10-23: Picker created with values from an enumeration

As we will see later, the `Picker` view adopts a design according to the device and the conditions in which it is presented, but we can force the picker to adopt the design of a wheel or activate a style that turns the values into buttons with the following modifier.

pickerStyle(Style**)**—This modifier sets the picker's style. The attribute is a structure that conforms to the `PickerStyle` protocol. The system defines the structures `DefaultPickerStyle`, `WheelPickerStyle`, and `SegmentedPickerStyle` to provide standard styles.

The `DefaultPickerStyle` style allows the picker to adapt the design to the device and conditions, the `WheelPickerStyle` style forces the picker to display the values in a wheel, and the `SegmentedPickerStyle` style defines a unique picker where the values are turned into buttons. The latter is frequently used to allow the user to select a value from a limited set of options, as illustrated by the following example.

```
import SwiftUI

struct ContentView: View {
    @State private var selectedValue: String = "Toronto"
    let listCities: [String] = ["Paris", "Toronto", "Dublin"]

    var body: some View {
        VStack {
            Text(selectedValue)
                .font(.largeTitle)
                .padding()
            Picker("", selection: $selectedValue) {
                ForEach(listCities, id: \.self) { value in
                    Text(value)
                }
            }.labelsHidden()
            .pickerStyle(SegmentedPickerStyle())
            Spacer()
        }.padding()
    }
}
```

Listing 10-35: Selecting an initial value

The implementation is the same, but by applying the `SegmentedPickerStyle` style the picker is forced to show the values as buttons in a horizontal bar.

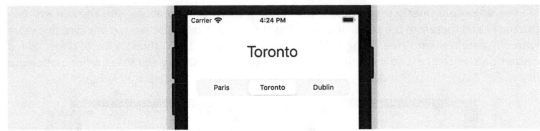

Figure 10-24: Segmented picker

 Do It Yourself: Update the `ContentView` structure with the code of Listing 10-35. Activate the live preview. You should be able to click on the buttons to select a different city.

Basic DatePicker View

The **DatePicker** view is designed to simplify the creation of pickers for dates and times. With this view, we can create pickers to select a date or a time. The following are some of the structure's initializer.

DatePicker(String, **selection:** Binding, **displayedComponents:** Components**)**— This initializer creates a `DatePicker` view with the label defined by the first attribute. The **selection** attribute is a `Binding` property of type `Date` that stores the date selected by the user. And the **displayComponents** attribute is a structure of type `DatePickerComponents` that defines the type of values managed by the picker. The structure includes two type properties for this purpose: `date` and `hourAndMinute`.

DatePicker(String, **selection:** Binding, **in:** Range, **displayedComponents:** Components**)**—This initializer creates a `DatePicker` view with the label defined by the first attribute. The **selection** attribute is a `Binding` property of type `Date` that stores the date selected by the user. The **in** attribute defines the range of dates the user can choose from. And the **displayComponents** attribute is a structure of type `DatePickerComponents` that defines the type of values managed by the picker. The structure includes two type properties for this purpose: `date` and `hourAndMinute`.

To define a `DatePicker` control, we must provide a `@State` property to store the value selected by the user and tell the picker the type of values we want to show. For instance, the following view includes a `DatePicker` control to select a date.

```
import SwiftUI
struct ContentView: View {
   @State private var selectedDate: Date = Date()

   var body: some View {
      VStack {
         DatePicker("", selection: $selectedDate, displayedComponents:
.date)
            .labelsHidden()
         Spacer()
      }.padding()
   }
}
```

Listing 10-36: Defining a `DatePicker` to select a date

The `@State` property used to store the selected value was initialized with the current date (`Date()`) and therefore the picker shows this as the selected date, but we can initialize this value with any date we want (see Listing 4-20). The picker in Listing 10-36 shows a list of dates from a distant date in the past to a distant date in the future. If we specify the value `hourAndMinute` instead of `date`, the picker displays a list of hours and minutes, as illustrated in Figure 10-25.

Figure 10-25: *Picker for dates and times*

Do It Yourself: Update the `ContentView` structure with the code of Listing 10-36. Activate the live preview on the canvas. You should see the interface in Figure 10-25, left. Replace the value `date` by the value `hourandminute`. You should see the interface in Figure 10-25, right.

Most of the time, we cannot let the user select any possible date but only a date between a range. For instance, an application that allows users to program an event, should let them only select a date in the future. To limit the list of dates the user can select from, we must provide a range of dates. The range can be closed (from one date to another), or open. The following example shows a list of dates from the current date to a distant date in the future using an open range.

```
import SwiftUI

struct ContentView: View {
    @State private var selectedDate: Date = Date()

    var body: some View {
        VStack {
            DatePicker("", selection: $selectedDate, in: Date()...,
displayedComponents: .date)
                .labelsHidden()
            Spacer()
        }.padding()
    }
}
```

Listing 10-37: *Limiting the* `DatePicker` *to a range of values*

In the example of Listing 10-37, we limit the picker with the range `Date()...` and therefore the user is not allowed to select a date before the current date. A range `...Date()` does the opposite, it only lets the user select a date from the past. But we can also provide specific dates by creating custom `Date` structures, as we did in Chapter 4 (see Listing 4-20).

The `DatePicker` view works with values of type `Date`. We can store these values, modify them, or combine them, but if we want to show them to the user, we must turn them into strings with the `DateFormatter` class (see Listing 4-25). When the date comes from our model, we should format the value in the view model, as we did with `Measurement` values in Listing 9-23, but we can also do it in the view if we are working with independent values. The following example formats the selected date and shows it on the screen when a button is pressed.

Chapter 10 - Lists

```
import SwiftUI

struct ContentView: View {
    @State private var selectedDate: Date = Date()
    @State private var message: String = ""

    var body: some View {
        VStack(spacing: 10) {
            DatePicker("", selection: $selectedDate, displayedComponents:
.date)
                .labelsHidden()
            Text("Date: \(message)")

            Button("Select Date") {
                let format = DateFormatter()
                format.dateStyle = DateFormatter.Style.medium
                self.message = format.string(from: self.selectedDate)
            }
            Spacer()
        }.font(.title)
        .padding()
    }
}
```

Listing 10-38: Showing the selected date to the user

The view in Listing 10-38 incorporates two new views: a **Text** view to show the value of a **@State** property and a **Button** view to let the user format and display the selected date. When the button is pressed, the code creates a **DateFormatter** object, configures the formatter with the style **medium**, formats the date, and assigns the result to the **message** property to display the value on the screen. The result is shown in Figure 10-26.

Figure 10-26: Selected date

 Do It Yourself: Update the **ContentView** structure with the code of Listing 10-38. Activate the live preview. Select a date and press the Select Date button. You should see the selected date printed on the screen.

A **DatePicker** view also adopts a design according to the device and the conditions in which it is presented, but it includes the following modifier to select the style we want.

datePickerStyle(Style**)**—This modifier sets the picker's style. The attribute is a structure that conforms to the **DatePickerStyle** protocol. The system defines the structures **DefaultDatePickerStyle** and **WheelDatePickerStyle** to provide standard styles.

Although there are no options like the `SegmentedPickerStyle` style available for `Picker` views, the `datePickerStyle()` modifier can be used to force the wheel style picker when working with forms, as we will see next.

(Basic) 10.4 Forms

Most applications require a screen with a list of options to set the app's configuration, the style, or to allow users to select the type of information they want to see. We can create a list of controls in a `VStack` or a `List` view, as we have done before, but SwiftUI includes a view specifically designed for this purpose called `Form`.

(Basic) Form View

The **Form** view is a container that organizes the views in a list, like the `List` view, but modifies the styles of the controls to look like a form and adapts them to the platform and device in which the app is running. Creating a form in SwiftUI is easy, we just have to include the controls one after another inside the `Form` view, as in the following example.

```
import SwiftUI

struct ContentView: View {
   @State private var setActive: Bool = false
   @State private var setShowPictures: Bool = false
   @State private var setTotal: Int = 10

   var body: some View {
      Form {
         Toggle("Active", isOn: $setActive)
         Toggle("Show Pictures", isOn: $setShowPictures)
         HStack {
            Text("Total")
            Spacer()
            Text(String(setTotal))
            Stepper("", value: $setTotal, in: 0...10)
               .labelsHidden()
         }
      }
   }
}
```

Listing 10-39: Defining a form

The `Form` view adds padding on the sides of the controls and present the list with a `GroupedListStyle` style (see Listing 10-16).

Figure 10-27: Simple form

Chapter 10 - Lists

A **Form** view works like a **List** view, so we can split the content in sections and embed it in a **NavigationView** view to provide a more standard design.

```
import SwiftUI
struct ContentView: View {
    @State private var setActive: Bool = false
    @State private var setShowPictures: Bool = false
    @State private var setTotal: Int = 10

    var body: some View {
        NavigationView {
            Form {
                Section {
                    Toggle("Active", isOn: $setActive)
                    Toggle("Show Pictures", isOn: $setShowPictures)
                }
                Section {
                    HStack {
                        Text("Total")
                        Spacer()
                        Text(String(setTotal))
                        Stepper("", value: $setTotal, in: 0...10)
                            .labelsHidden()
                    }
                }
            }.navigationBarTitle("Settings")
        }
    }
}
```

Listing 10-40: Styling a form

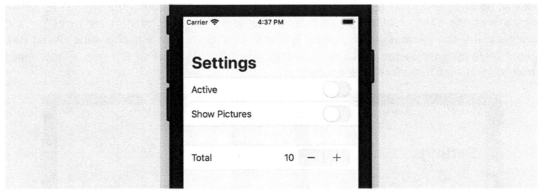

Figure 10-28: Form with a standard design

 Do It Yourself: Create a SwiftUI project. Update the **ContentView** structure with the code of Listing 10-40. You should see the interface in Figure 10-28 on the canvas. Try to add more controls to the **Form** view and create more sections to see how they look like. You can also add headers and footers to the sections, as we did in Listing 10-15.

Something different with forms is how they present pickers. When a picker is included in a **Form** view, it is compacted into a single row that displays the selected value. If the user taps on it, the **NavigationView** opens a **List** view with all the values for the user to choose from. The following example includes two types of pickers, a segmented picker and a general-purpose picker to illustrate this difference.

```
import SwiftUI

struct ContentView: View {
    @State private var setTemperature: Int = 0
    @State private var setCity: String = "Paris"
    let listCities: [String] = ["Paris", "Toronto", "Dublin"]

    var body: some View {
        NavigationView {
            Form {
                Section {
                    Picker("", selection: $setTemperature) {
                        Text("Celsius").tag(0)
                        Text("Fahrenheit").tag(1)
                    }.labelsHidden()
                    .pickerStyle(SegmentedPickerStyle())
                }
                Section {
                    Picker("", selection: $setCity) {
                        ForEach(listCities, id: \.self) { city in
                            Text(city)
                        }
                    }.labelsHidden()
                }
            }.navigationBarTitle("Settings")
        }
    }
}
```

Listing 10-41: *Including pickers in a form*

The view of Listing 10-41 defines two `@State` properties to store the values for the pickers and an array to provide a list of strings for the general-purpose picker. The segmented picker reproduces the same tool we created before to select the unit of measurements for the temperature. The general-purpose picker is shown as a single row with the value "Paris" (the initial value assigned to the `setCity` property). When the user taps on this row, all the values are shown in a list to perform a new selection.

Figure 10-29: *Pickers in forms*

When a form with a picker is presented in a Regular size class, which is usually the space provided by iPads and Mac computers, the view is split in two parts; on one side is the form and on the other is an empty space reserved to display the list of values when the user taps on the row that represents the picker. For instance, if we present a form with a picker in a sheet on an iPad, we get the interface of Figure 10-30 below.

Figure 10-30: Picker presented in a Regular size class

If we want to display this form in a single view, we must define the style for the **NavigationView** as **StackNavigationViewStyle**, as we did in Listing 9-45. The following example reproduces the interface of Figure 10-30, but it shows the form in a single view. First, we define a view with a button to open the sheet.

```
import SwiftUI

struct ContentView: View {
   @State private var openSettings: Bool = false
   @State private var setCity: String = "Paris"

   var body: some View {
      NavigationView {
         VStack(spacing: 20) {
            Text("City: \(setCity)")
               .font(.title)
            Button("Open Settings") {
               self.openSettings = true
            }
            Spacer()
         }.padding()
         .navigationBarTitle("Main Screen")
      }
      .sheet(isPresented: $openSettings) {
         SettingsView(setCity: self.$setCity)
      }
   }
}
```

Listing 10-42: Testing forms in a sheet

There is nothing new in the code of Listing 10-42. We define a **@State** property of type **Bool** to keep track of the state of the sheet, and then apply the **sheet()** modifier to open the view when the value of this property is **true**. The **SettingsView** view, opened by the modifier is where we present the form with the picker.

```
import SwiftUI

struct SettingsView: View {
   @Binding var setCity: String
   @Environment(\.presentationMode) var presentation
   let listCities: [String] = ["Paris", "Toronto", "Dublin"]
```

```
    var body: some View {
        NavigationView {
            Form {
                Picker("", selection: $setCity) {
                    ForEach(listCities, id: \.self) { city in
                        Text(city)
                    }
                }.labelsHidden()
            }
            .navigationBarTitle("Settings")
            .navigationBarItems(trailing: Button("Save") {
                self.presentation.wrappedValue.dismiss()
            })
        }
        .navigationViewStyle(StackNavigationViewStyle())
    }
}
struct SettingsView_Previews: PreviewProvider {
    static var previews: some View {
        SettingsView(setCity: .constant("Undefined"))
    }
}
```

Listing 10-43: Presenting the form in a single view

The `SettingsView` structure includes a `@Binding` property to send the value selected by the user back to the `ContentView` view, an `@Environment` property to access the `presentationMode` value from the environment to be able to remove the sheet, and an array with the names of the cities. The `Form` view includes a single row with a general-purpose picker, but it is presented in a single view, no matter the space available, because we force this style by applying the `StackNavigationViewStyle` style to the `NavigationView` view.

Figure 10-31: Picker presented in a single view

 Do It Yourself: Update the `ContentView` structure with the code of Listing 10-42. Create a new SwiftUI file called SettingsView.swift for the code of Listing 10-43. Run the application on the iPad simulator and tap the Open Settings button. You should see the interface of Figure 10-31 (the form in a single view).

There is one more option if we don't like the way pickers are presented in a form and that is to force the `WheelPickerStyle` style on the picker with the `pickerStyle()` modifier, as we did in previous examples to define a segmented picker.

```
import SwiftUI

struct ContentView: View {
    @State private var setCity: String = "Paris"
    let listCities: [String] = ["Paris", "Toronto", "Dublin"]

    var body: some View {
        NavigationView {
            Form {
                Section(header: Text(setCity).font(.headline)) {
                    Picker("", selection: $setCity) {
                        ForEach(listCities, id: \.self) { city in
                            Text(city)
                        }
                    }.labelsHidden()
                    .pickerStyle(WheelPickerStyle())
                }.frame(minWidth: 0, maxWidth: .infinity)
            }.navigationBarTitle("Settings")
        }
    }
}
```

Listing 10-44: Showing a wheel picker in a form

This example defines the same general-purpose picker we used before to select a city, but now it is shown as a wheel. Notice that we are responsible of aligning the picker. The `Section` view takes the size of the picker, therefore, if the picker's ideal size is smaller than the size of its container, it will not be aligned to the center. To center the picker on the screen or provide a custom alignment, we must remove the label with the `labelsHidden()` modifier and make the `Section` view flexible with the `frame()` modifier.

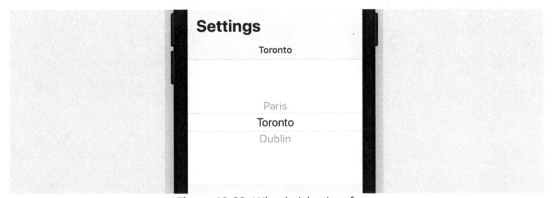

Figure 10-32: Wheel picker in a form

 The Basics: Embedding the `Form` view in a `NavigationView` view is required when you let the form decide how the picker is going to be displayed because the system needs to create an additional view to let the user select the values, but it is not necessary if we force the picker to be shown with the `WheelPickerStyle` style, as in this last example.

Chapter 10 - Lists

Chapter 11
Graphics and Animations

Basic **11.1 Shapes**

All the views we have used so far work as containers or present predefined content on the screen, but SwiftUI also includes graphic views to create custom controls or to use for decoration. These views work the same way than those introduced before and can take advantage of most of the modifiers we have seen so far but are specifically designed to draw custom graphics.

Basic **Common Shapes**

SwiftUI allow us to create predefined or custom shapes. The following are the views available to create common shapes.

Rectangle()—This initializer creates a `Rectangle` view. The size of the rectangle is determined by the view's frame.

RoundedRectangle(cornerRadius: CGFloat, **style:** RoundedCornerStyle)—This initializer creates a `RoundedRectangle` view. The **cornerRadius** attribute determines the radius of the curvature of the corners, and the **style** attribute is an enumeration of type `RoundedCornerStyle` that determines the type of curvature. The values available are `circular` and `continuous`. The view also includes the following initializer to define the radius with a `CGSize` value `RoundedRectangle(cornerSize: CGSize, style: RoundedCornerStyle)`.

Circle()—This initializer creates a `Circle` view. The diameter of the circle is determined by the view's frame.

Ellipse()—This initializer creates an `Ellipse` view. The size of the ellipse is determined by the width and height of the view's frame.

Capsule(style: RoundedCornerStyle)—This initializer creates a `Capsule` view. The style attribute is an enumeration of type `RoundedCornerStyle` that determines the type of curvature for the corners. The values available are `circular` and `continuous`.

If no size is specified, the views take the size of their container, but we can declare a specific size with the **frame()** modifier. The following view provides an example of all the standard shapes available. We included the views in a horizontal `ScrollView` to allow the list to scroll.

```
import SwiftUI

struct ContentView: View {
    var body: some View {
        VStack {
            ScrollView(.horizontal, showsIndicators: true) {
                HStack {
                    Rectangle()
                        .frame(width: 100, height: 100)
                    RoundedRectangle(cornerRadius: 25, style: .continuous)
                        .frame(width: 100, height: 100)
```

```
            Circle()
                .frame(width: 100, height: 100)
            Ellipse()
                .frame(width: 100, height: 50)
            Capsule()
                .frame(width: 100, height: 50)
        }.padding()
      }
      Spacer()
    }
  }
}
```

Listing 11-1: Drawing standard shapes

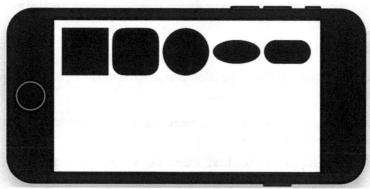

Figure 11-1: Standard shapes

 Do It Yourself: Create a SwiftUI project. Update the `ContentView` structure with the code of Listing 11-1. Run the application in the simulator. If you don't see all the shapes on the screen, scroll the views to the left. Use this project to test the rest of the examples in this chapter.

By default, the views are rendered with a color depending on the appearance mode (black for light and white for dark), but we can change the filling and stroke of the shapes with the following modifiers.

fill(View**)**—This modifier fills the shape with the view specified by the attribute. The attribute is a view that represents a color, a gradient or an image.

stroke(View, **lineWidth:** CGFloat**)**—This modifier defines the shape's border. The first attribute is a view that represents a color, a gradient, or an image, and the **lineWidth** attribute defines the border's width.

stroke(View, **style:** StrokeStyle**)**—This modifier defines the shape's border. The first attribute is a view that represents a color, a gradient or an image, and the **style** attribute is a structure of type `StrokeStyle` that defines the border's width, cap, join, miter limit, dash, and dash phase.

strokeBorder(View, **lineWidth:** CGFloat**)**—This modifier defines the shape's inner border. The first attribute is a view that represents a color, a gradient, or an image, and the **lineWidth** attribute defines the border's width.

strokeBorder(View, **style:** StrokeStyle**)**—This modifier defines the shape's inner border. The first attribute is a view that represents a color, a gradient or an image, and the **style** attribute is a structure of type `StrokeStyle` that defines the border's width, cap, join, miter limit, dash, and dash phase.

Chapter 11 - Graphics and Animations

There are two aspects we can change with these modifiers, the filling of the shape and its border. The filling is simple, we must apply the `fill()` modifier with a view that defines the content, like a `Color` view.

```
import SwiftUI

struct ContentView: View {
    var body: some View {
        RoundedRectangle(cornerRadius: 25)
            .fill(Color.red)
            .frame(width: 100, height: 100)
    }
}
```

Listing 11-2: Filling a shape with a color

Notice that the `fill()` modifier is implemented by the `RoundedRectangle` view and the `frame()` modifier returns a different view, therefore all the modifiers defined for shapes, like `fill()`, must be applied before common modifiers like `frame()`. The result is shown below.

Figure 11-2: Rectangle

Adding a border is similar, but there are two types of modifiers and they produce a slightly different result. For instance, the `stroke()` modifier expands the border outward and inward.

```
import SwiftUI

struct ContentView: View {
    var body: some View {
        RoundedRectangle(cornerRadius: 25)
            .stroke(Color.red, lineWidth: 20)
            .frame(width: 100, height: 100)
    }
}
```

Listing 11-3: Defining a border

The view of Listing 11-3 creates a `RoundedRectangle` view with a border of 20 points, but because we use the `stroke()` modifier to create it, half of the border is drawn outside and the other half is drawn within the view's frame.

Figure 11-3: Rectangle with a border

Chapter 11 - Graphics and Animations

On the other hand, the `strokeBorder()` modifier draws an inner border. The following example creates the same shape and border than before, but the whole border is drawn within the view.

```
import SwiftUI
struct ContentView: View {
    var body: some View {
        RoundedRectangle(cornerRadius: 25)
            .strokeBorder(Color.red, lineWidth: 20)
            .frame(width: 100, height: 100)
    }
}
```

Listing 11-4: Defining an inner border

Figure 11-4: Rectangle with an inner border

These two modifiers can also take a `StrokeStyle` structure to fine-tune the border. The structure provides the following initializer.

StrokeStyle(lineWidth: CGFloat, **lineCap:** CGLineCap, **lineJoin:** CGLineJoin, **miterLimit:** CGFloat, **dash:** [CGFloat], **dashPhase:** CGFloat)—This initializer creates a `StrokeStyle` structure to configure a stroke. The **lineWidth** attribute determines the width of the stroke, the **lineCap** attribute determines the style of the end of the lines. It is an enumeration with the values **butt** (squared end), **round** (rounded end), and **square** (squared end). The **lineJoin** attribute sets the style of the joint of two connected lines. It is an enumeration with the values **miter** (sharp end), **round** (rounded end), and **bevel** (squared end). The **miterLimit** attribute determines how long the lines extend when the **lineJoin** attribute is set to **miter**. The **dash** attribute determines the length of the segments for a dashed stroke. And the **dashPhase** attribute determines where the dashed line begins.

The following example creates a `RoundedRectangle` view with the stroke configured as a dashed line with a width of 15 points and rounded endings.

```
import SwiftUI
struct ContentView: View {
    let lineStyle = StrokeStyle(lineWidth: 15, lineCap: .round, lineJoin:
.round, miterLimit: 0, dash: [20], dashPhase: 0)

    var body: some View {
        RoundedRectangle(cornerRadius: 25)
            .stroke(Color.red, style: lineStyle)
            .frame(width: 100, height: 100)
    }
}
```

Listing 11-5: Defining a custom border

Chapter 11 - Graphics and Animations

Figure 11-5: Rectangle with a custom border

Shapes are views and therefore they can be combined with other SwiftUI views and controls. For instance, the following example assigns a `Capsule` shape as the background of a button.

```swift
import SwiftUI

struct ContentView: View {
   @State private var setActive: Bool = true

   var body: some View {
      VStack {
         Button(action: {
            self.setActive.toggle()
         }, label: {
            Text(setActive ? "Active" : "Inactive")
               .font(.title)
               .foregroundColor(Color.white)
               .padding(.horizontal, 30)
               .padding(.vertical, 10)
         })
         .background(
            Capsule()
               .fill(setActive ? Color.green : Color.red)
         )
         Spacer()
      }.padding()
   }
}
```

Listing 11-6: Combining shapes with other views

The button in Listing 11-6 toggles the value of a `@State` property. If the value is `true`, we show the label "Active" and fill the capsule with a green color, otherwise, we display the "Inactive" label and paint the capsule red.

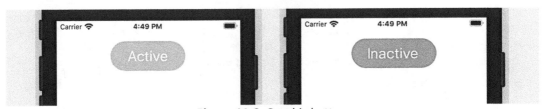

Figure 11-6: Graphic button

(Basic) Gradients

The filling and border of a shape can also be defined with gradients. SwiftUI includes three structures designed to present gradients. The following are their initializers.

LinearGradient(gradient: Gradient, **startPoint:** UnitPoint, **endPoint:** UnitPoint)—This initializer creates a linear gradient. The **gradient** attribute is the gradient of colors to be used, and the **startPoint** and **endPoint** attributes determine the points inside the shape where the gradient starts and ends.

RadialGradient(gradient: Gradient, **center:** UnitPoint, **startRadius:** CGFloat, **endRadius:** CGFloat)—This initializer creates a circular gradient. The **gradient** attribute is the gradient of colors to be used. The **center** attribute determines the position of the center of the circle, and the **startRadius** and **endRadius** attributes determine where the gradient starts and ends in points.

AngularGradient(gradient: Gradient, **center:** UnitPoint, **angle:** Angle)—This initializer creates a conic gradient. The **gradient** attribute is the gradient of colors to be used. The **center** attribute determines the position of the tip of the cone, and the **angle** attribute determines the angle where the gradient begins. The structure also provides an additional initializer to specify the angles where the gradient starts and ends: `AngularGradient(gradient: Gradient, center: UnitPoint, startAngle: Angle, endAngle: Angle)`.

These structures present a gradient, but the gradient is defined by the `Gradient` structure. The following are the structure's initializers.

Gradient(colors: [Color])—This initializer creates a gradient with the colors specified by the attribute. The **colors** attribute is an array of `Color` views.

Gradient(stops: [Gradient.Stop])—This initializer creates a gradient with the colors specified by the attribute. The **stops** attribute is an array of `Stop` structures that determine the colors and when they stop.

Another value required to present a gradient is the `UnitPoint` structures. These are like `CGPoint` structures but specifically designed to work with SwiftUI structures.

UnitPoint(x: CGFloat, **y:** CGFloat)—This initializer creates a `UnitPoint` structure. The **x** and **y** attributes determine the x and y coordinates of the point. For gradients, these attributes are defined with values from 0.0 to 1.0.

The `UnitPoint` structure also includes the type properties `bottom`, `bottomLeading`, `bottomTrailing`, `center`, `leading`, `top`, `topLeading`, `topTrailing`, `trailing`, and `zero` to define common points. For example, we can apply a linear gradient with the values `bottom` and `top` to draw the gradient from the bottom to the top of the shape.

```
import SwiftUI

struct ContentView: View {
   let gradient = Gradient(colors: [Color.red, Color.green])

   var body: some View {
      RoundedRectangle(cornerRadius: 25)
         .fill(LinearGradient(gradient: gradient, startPoint: .bottom,
endPoint: .top))
         .frame(width: 100, height: 100)
   }
}
```

Listing 11-7: Defining a linear gradient

Chapter 11 - Graphics and Animations

The code of Listing 11-7 defines a gradient with two colors, red and green, and then applies the gradient to a `RoundedRectangle` view with the `LinearGradient` structure. Because we declare the value `bottom` as the starting point and the value `top` as the ending point, the colors are shown from bottom to top in the order declared by the `Gradient` structure.

Figure 11-7: Linear gradient

When a gradient is created without specifying color stops, the colors are evenly distributed throughout the area occupied by the gradient. If we want to customize the distribution, we must define the colors for the gradient with `Stop` structures. The `Stop` structure is defined inside the `Gradient` structure and includes the following initializer.

Stop(color: Color, **location:** CGFloat)—This initializer creates a color with a stop value. The **color** attribute determines the color, and the **location** attribute determines the position of the gradient where the color begins. The location must be specified in values between 0.0 and 1.0.

The following example reproduces the previous gradient, but this time the green color begins at the position 0.4 (40% of the area occupied by the gradient).

```
import SwiftUI
struct ContentView: View {
   let gradient = Gradient(stops: [
      Gradient.Stop(color: Color.red, location: 0.0),
      Gradient.Stop(color: Color.green, location: 0.4)
   ])
   var body: some View {
      RoundedRectangle(cornerRadius: 25)
         .fill(LinearGradient(gradient: gradient, startPoint: .bottom,
endPoint: .top))
         .frame(width: 100, height: 100)
   }
}
```

Listing 11-8: Defining a linear gradient with custom stop locations

Figure 11-8: Linear gradient with custom stops

Besides the linear gradient, we can also create a circular gradient with the `RadialGradient` structure. The gradient is created with circular layers drawn from the center of a circle outwards, so we must specify the gradient, the position of the center of the circle, and the location within the shape where the gradient begins and ends.

```
import SwiftUI

struct ContentView: View {
   let gradient = Gradient(colors: [Color.red, Color.white])

   var body: some View {
      RoundedRectangle(cornerRadius: 25)
         .fill(RadialGradient(gradient: gradient, center: .center,
startRadius: 0, endRadius: 120))
         .frame(width: 100, height: 100)
   }
}
```

Listing 11-9: Defining a circular gradient

The starting and ending values are defined in points. They determine where the gradient begins and ends, but only the part of the gradient that falls within the shape is drawn. In the example of Listing 11-9, the **endRadius** attribute was declared as 120, but because the size of the shape is 100 by 100, only part of the gradient is visible.

Figure 11-9: Circular gradient

Another type of gradient we can use for our shapes is the angular gradient defined by the `AngularGradient` structure. This gradient is usually called conic gradient because it draws the colors around a circle and therefore the result looks like a cone seen from the top. The structure needs a gradient, the position of the center of the circle, and the angle where the gradient begins (by default this value is set to 0 degrees).

```
import SwiftUI

struct ContentView: View {
   let gradient = Gradient(colors: [Color.red, Color.white])

   var body: some View {
      RoundedRectangle(cornerRadius: 25)
         .fill(AngularGradient(gradient: gradient, center: .center,
angle: .degrees(180)))
         .frame(width: 100, height: 100)
   }
}
```

Listing 11-10: Defining a conic gradient

The angles for the gradient are declared with an instance of the `Angle` structure. The structure includes two type methods to defined the value in degrees or radians:

Chapter 11 - Graphics and Animations

`degrees(Double)` and `radians(Double)`. In the example of Listing 11-10, we declare the beginning of the gradient at an angle of 180 degrees, which is the opposite side of the default starting point.

Figure 11-10: Conic gradient

Images

Besides colors and gradients, we can also use images to fill a shape. SwiftUI includes the `ImagePaint` structure for this purpose. The following is the structure's initializer.

ImagePaint(image: Image, **sourceRect:** CGRect, **scale:** CGFloat)**—This initializer creates an `ImagePaint` structure with the image and configuration specified by the attributes. The **image** attribute provides the `Image` view, the **sourceRect** attribute determines the part of the image to be drawn (by default, the entire image is used), and the **scale** attribute defines the scale of the image (by default, the original scale is used).

By default, the `ImagePaint` structure uses the whole image in the original scale, so most of the time specifying the image is enough for the system to create the pattern, as in the following example.

```
import SwiftUI
struct ContentView: View {
   var body: some View {
      Rectangle()
         .fill(ImagePaint(image: Image("pattern")))
         .frame(width: 100, height: 100)
   }
}
```

Listing 11-11: Filling a shape with an image

The image provided by the `ImagePaint` structure repeats indefinitely to fill the whole are occupied by the shape. In the example of Listing 11-11, we define a square of 100 by 100 points and then paint it with an image of a size of 25 by 25 points. Because the image is smaller than the shape, it is drawn multiple times to cover the shape's area.

Figure 11-11: Pattern

11.2 Paths

The shapes we have implemented so far are defined by paths. A path is a set of instructions that determine the outline of a 2D shape. Besides the paths defined by common shapes, we can create our own. For this purpose, SwiftUI includes the `Path` view.

Path View

The `Path` view is designed to create a view that contains a custom path. The following are some of the structure's initializers.

Path()—This initializer creates an empty `Path` view. The path is created by applying modifiers to this instance.

Path(Closure)—This initializer creates an empty `Path` view. The attribute is the closure that defines the path. The closure receives a reference to the `Path` structure that we can use to create the path.

The path is created with a combination of lines and curves. The strokes move from one point to another in the view's coordinates, as if following the movement of a pencil. The `Path` structure defines a set of modifiers to define the position of the pencil and generate the path. The following are the most frequently used.

move(to: CGPoint)—This modifier moves the pencil to the coordinates determined by the **to** attribute.

addLine(to: CGPoint)—This modifier adds a straight line to the path, from the pencil's current position to the coordinates indicated by the **to** attribute.

addLines([CGPoint])—This modifier adds multiple straight lines to the path. The lines are added in sequence according to the order the points are declared in the array.

addArc(center: CGPoint, radius: CGFloat, startAngle: Angle, endAngle: Angle, clockwise: Bool)—This modifier adds an arc to the path. The **center** attribute specifies the coordinates of the center of the circle formed by the arc, the **radius** attribute is the length of the circle's radius, the **startAngle** and **endAngle** attributes are the angles in which the arc starts and ends, and the **clockwise** attribute determines the orientation in which the arc is calculated (`true` for clockwise and `false` for counterclockwise).

addArc(tangent1End: CGPoint, tangent2End: CGPoint, radius: CGFloat)—This modifier adds an arc to the path using tangent points. The **tangent1End** attribute defines the coordinates of the end of the first tangent line, the **tangent2End** attribute defines the coordinates of the end of the second tangent line, and the **radius** attribute determines the length of the circle's radius.

addCurve(to: CGPoint, control1: CGPoint, control2: CGPoint)—This modifier adds a cubic Bezier curve to the path with two control points. The **to** attribute defines the coordinates of the ending point, and the **control1** and **control2** attributes define the coordinates of the first and second control points, respectively.

addQuadCurve(to: CGPoint, control: CGPoint)—This modifier adds a quadratic Bezier curve to the path with one control point. The **to** attribute defines the coordinates of the ending point, and the **control** attribute defines the coordinates of the control point.

addEllipse(in: CGRect)—This modifier adds an ellipse to the path. The **in** attribute determines the area of the ellipse. If the rectangle is a square, the ellipse becomes a circle.

addRect(CGRect)—This modifier adds the rectangle defined by the attribute to the path. There is a version of this modifier that takes an array of `CGRect` values to add multiple rectangles at a time (`addRects([CGRect])`).

addRoundedRect(in: CGRect, cornerSize: CGSize, style: RoundedCorner-Style)—This modifier adds a rounded rectangle to the path. The in attribute determines the dimensions of the rectangle, the **cornerRadius** attribute determines the radius of the curvature of the corners, and the **style** attribute is an enumeration of type `RoundedCornerStyle` that determines the type of curvature. The values available are `circular` and `continuous`.

A custom path works the same way as a predefined path. If we don't specify the filling or the stroke, the path is drawn with a color that depends on the appearance mode (black for light and white for dark), but we can change that with the `fill()` and `stroke()` modifiers, as we did before for common shapes (see Listing 11-2). If we paint the path with the `fill()` modifier the path is automatically closed, but if we do it with the `stroke()` modifier, the path remains open. To close the path and make sure all the lines are joined, the `Path` structure includes the following modifier.

closeSubpath()—This modifier closes the current path. If the path is not a closed path, the modifier adds a line between the end of the path and the beginning to close it.

To create a path, we must apply the modifiers in order, following the line of an imaginary pencil. The following example creates a path with the shape of a triangle.

```
import SwiftUI

struct ContentView: View {
    var body: some View {
        Path { path in
            path.move(to: CGPoint(x: 100, y: 150))
            path.addLine(to: CGPoint(x: 200, y: 150))
            path.addLine(to: CGPoint(x: 100, y: 250))
            path.closeSubpath()
        }.stroke(Color.blue, lineWidth: 5)
    }
}
```

Listing 11-12: Defining a custom path

By default, the pencil's initial position is at the coordinates 0, 0 (top-left corner of the view). If we want our graphic to start from a different position, we must apply the `move()` modifier first. In Listing 11-12, we move the pencil to the coordinates 100, 150 before adding the first line. Subsequent lines are generated from the current position of the pencil to the coordinates indicated by the modifier. For instance, after setting the initial point in our example, we create a line from that point to the point 200, 150, therefore, the next line starts at that point and ends at 100, 250.

Notice that we only created two lines. The line that goes from the point 100, 250 to the point 100, 150 is generated automatically by the `closeSubpath()` modifier to close the path. If we want to create an open path, we can ignore this modifier.

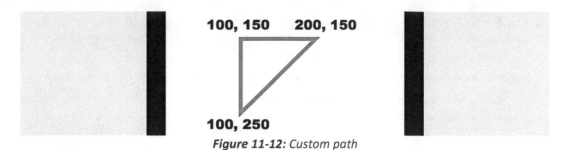

100, 150   **200, 150**

100, 250

Figure 11-12: Custom path

Combining different modifiers, we can create complex paths. The following path is defined with two lines and an arc.

```
import SwiftUI

struct ContentView: View {
   var body: some View {
      Path { path in
         path.move(to: CGPoint(x: 100, y: 150))
         path.addLine(to: CGPoint(x: 200, y: 150))
         path.addArc(center: CGPoint(x: 200, y: 170), radius: 20,
startAngle: .degrees(270), endAngle: .degrees(90), clockwise: false)
         path.addLine(to: CGPoint(x: 100, y: 190))
      }.stroke(Color.blue, lineWidth: 5)
   }
}
```

Listing 11-13: Combining lines and arcs

Because arcs are calculated from the coordinates of the center of the circle and its radius, we must consider these two values to connect the arc with the previous line. If the initial coordinates of the arc do not coincide with the current position of the pencil, a line is created between these two points to connect the path. Figure 11-13 shows the path we get with the example of Listing 11-13 and what we see if we move up the center of the arc by 10 points.

Figure 11-13: Lines and arcs

The **addRect()** and **addEllipse()** modifiers allow us to add rectangles and circles to the path. The modifiers add the shapes to the current path, but they move the pencil to the position indicated by the **CGRect** value, so they can be considered independent shapes.

```
import SwiftUI

struct ContentView: View {
   var body: some View {
      Path { path in
         path.move(to: CGPoint(x: 100, y: 150))
         path.addLine(to: CGPoint(x: 200, y: 150))
         path.addEllipse(in: CGRect(x: 200, y: 140, width: 20, height:
20))
      }.stroke(Color.blue, lineWidth: 5)
```

Chapter 11 - Graphics and Animations

```
        }
}
```

Listing 11-14: Combining lines and ellipses

In this case, no line is generated between the current position of the pencil and the ellipse if they are not connected. Figure 11-14 shows the path we get with the example of Listing 11-14 and what we will see if we move the area of the circle 10 points to the right.

Figure 11-14: Lines and ellipses

Beside `addArc()` and `addEllipse()`, we have two more modifiers to draw curves. The `addQuadCurve()` modifier generates a quadratic Bezier curve, and the `addCurve()` modifier generates a cubic Bezier curve. The difference between these modifiers is that the first one has only one point of control and the second has two, thus creating different types of curves.

```
import SwiftUI
struct ContentView: View {
   var body: some View {
      Path { path in
         path.move(to: CGPoint(x: 50, y: 50))
         path.addQuadCurve(to: CGPoint(x: 50, y: 200), control:
CGPoint(x: 100, y: 125))
         path.move(to: CGPoint(x: 250, y: 50))
         path.addCurve(to: CGPoint(x: 250, y: 200), control1: CGPoint(x:
200, y: 125), control2: CGPoint(x: 300, y: 125))
      }.stroke(Color.blue, lineWidth: 5)
   }
}
```

Listing 11-15: Creating complex curves

To create a quadratic curve in this example, we move the pencil to the point 50, 50, finish the curve at the point 50, 200, and set the control point at the position 100, 125.

The cubic curve generated by the `addCurve()` modifier is more complicated. There are two control points for this curve, the first one at the position 200, 125, and the second one at the position 300, 125. These points shape the curve, as shown in Figure 11-15.

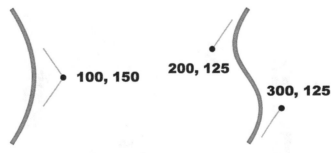

Figure 11-15: Complex curves

The paths we have created so far use fixed values. This means that the shape is always going to be of the same size, no matter the size of the view. To adapt the path to the size of the view, we must calculate how much space is available with the **GeometryReader** view (see Listing 9-53).

```
import SwiftUI

struct ContentView: View {
    var body: some View {
        GeometryReader { geometry in
            Path { path in
                let width = geometry.size.width / 2
                let height = width
                let posX = (geometry.size.width - width) / 2
                let posY = (geometry.size.height - height) / 2

                path.move(to: CGPoint(x: posX, y: posY))
                path.addLine(to: CGPoint(x: posX + width, y: posY))
                path.addLine(to: CGPoint(x: posX, y: posY + height))
                path.closeSubpath()
            }.stroke(Color.blue, lineWidth: 5)
        }
    }
}
```

Listing 11-16: *Adapting a path to the size of its container*

The code of Listing 11-16 draws a triangle that is always half the width of its container. For this purpose, we first calculate the triangle's width dividing the width of the geometry by 2. Then, we assign this value to the **height** constant to set the height equal to the width. After the dimensions are calculated, we determine the position of the initial point. Because we want to center the triangle in the container, we get the remaining space by subtracting the triangle's width from the width of the geometry and then divide the result by 2 to get the initial point. We do the same for the vertical position and store the values in the **posX** and **posY** constants. With these values, we can finally draw the path. The **move()** modifier moves the pencil to the initial position determined by **posX** and **posY**. Next, the **addLine()** modifier draws a line from this point to the point located at the right end of the triangle (**posX + width**). The next **addLine()** modifier draws a line from this point to the point at the bottom left of the triangle (**posY + height**). And finally, the **closeSubpath()** modifier draws the vertical line to close the path.

Because we calculate all the coordinates of the path from the values of the geometry, the triangle adapts to the size of its container and is always half the container's size and centered in the view, no matter the device or the size of the screen.

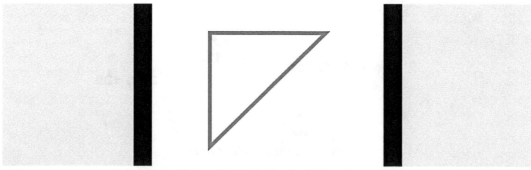

Figure 11-16: *Path of relative size*

Chapter 11 - Graphics and Animations

Custom Shapes

The common shapes introduced at the beginning of this chapter are structures that conform to the **Shape** protocol. A structure that conforms to this protocol defines its own path, which is created the same way as the path for a **Path** view, but the advantage of working with **Shape** structures instead of **Path** views is that a **Shape** structure receives a **CGRect** value with the dimensions of the view in which the shape is going to be drawn, so we can use this value to adapt the shape to the size of the view without having to embed it in a **GeometryReader** view.

The protocol requires the structure to implement the following method to define the path of the shape.

path(in: CGRect)—This method receives a **CGRect** value with the dimensions of the view and must return a **Path** view with the path we want to assign to the shape.

Creating a custom shape is easy. We must define a structure that conforms to the **Shape** protocol, implement the **path()** method, and create and return a **Path** view. The following example defines a shape structure called **Triangle** that draws a triangle.

```
import SwiftUI

struct Triangle: Shape {
    func path(in rect: CGRect) -> Path {
        var path = Path()
        let width = rect.width
        let height = rect.height
        let posX = rect.origin.x
        let posY = rect.origin.y

        path.move(to: CGPoint(x: posX, y: posY))
        path.addLine(to: CGPoint(x: posX + width, y: posY))
        path.addLine(to: CGPoint(x: posX, y: posY + height))
        path.closeSubpath()

        return path
    }
}
```

Listing 11-17: Creating a custom shape view

The path is the same as previous examples, but now we take the values from the **CGRect** structure received by the method from the view. The size of a shape view is supposed to be controlled by the interface and therefore we should use all the space available in the view to draw the path. In this case, we extend the triangle from left to right and top to bottom to cover the whole view (the size and shape of the triangle depends on the view's width and height).

Once the shape view is defined, we can implement it in our interface as any other view. To illustrate how this works, we are going to instantiate multiple **Triangle** views of different sizes within a horizontal **ScrollView**.

```
import SwiftUI

struct ContentView: View {
    var body: some View {
        VStack {
            ScrollView(.horizontal, showsIndicators: true) {
                HStack {
                    Triangle()
                        .fill(Color.blue)
                        .frame(width: 120, height: 50)
```

```
            Triangle()
                .fill(Color.green)
                .frame(width: 120, height: 100)
            Triangle()
                .fill(Color.yellow)
                .frame(width: 120, height: 80)
            Triangle()
                .fill(Color.red)
                .frame(width: 50, height: 50)
        }
    }.padding()
    Spacer()
    }
  }
}
```

Listing 11-18: Implementing custom shape views

When a `Triangle` view is created, the `path()` method is called with the dimensions of the view and the triangle is drawn according to those values. Therefore, if we define `Triangle` views of different sizes, we get triangles of different sizes and shapes.

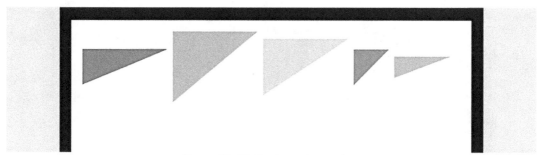

Figure 11-17: Custom shape views

 Do It Yourself: Create a Swift file called Triangle.swift for the code of Listing 11-17. Update the `ContentView` structure with the code of Listing 11-18. Run the application on the simulator. If you don't see all the triangles, scroll the view or rotate the device.

Medium **11.3 Transformations**

There are multiple tools provided by SwiftUI to change physical aspects of a view or a shape view, like its orientation, perspective or the position of its content. The following are some of the modifiers defined for common views.

offset(CGSize**)**—This modifier displaces the content of the view to the horizontal and vertical distances defined by the attribute.

rotationEffect(Angle**)**—This modifier rotates the content of the view to the angle determined by the attribute.

rotation3DEffect(Angle, Tuple**)**—This modifier rotates the content of the view in 3D. The first attribute declares the angle in degrees or radians, and the second attribute is a tuple with three values to represent the axes, as in (x: Double, y: Double, z: Double). Values different than 0 rotate the image in that axis.

clipShape(Shape**)**—This modifier clips the view with the shape specified by the attribute.

Chapter 11 - Graphics and Animations

These modifiers affect the content of the view. For instance, if we apply an offset to an `Image` view, the image inside the view is displaced the distance determined by the modifier, but the view's frame is not affected.

```
import SwiftUI

struct ContentView: View {
   var body: some View {
      Image("book1")
         .resizable()
         .scaledToFit()
         .frame(width: 100, height: 180)
         .offset(CGSize(width: 50, height: 0))
   }
}
```

Listing 11-19: Displacing an image

The example of Listing 11-19 displaces the image 50 points to the right side of the `Image` view.

Figure 11-18: Image displaced to the right

The rotation modifiers work in a similar way. They rotate the content of the view in 2D or 3D. The most interesting is the `rotation3DEffect()` that can rotate the content in each of the three axes.

```
import SwiftUI

struct ContentView: View {
   var body: some View {
      Image("book1")
         .resizable()
         .scaledToFit()
         .frame(width: 100, height: 180)
         .scaleEffect(CGSize(width: 0.9, height: 0.9))
         .rotation3DEffect(.degrees(30), axis: (x: 0, y: 1, z: 0))
   }
}
```

Listing 11-20: Rotating the image

The `rotation3DEffect()` modifier requires a tuple with values that determine the axes in which the content will be rotated. A value of 0 indicates no rotation and a value different than 0 indicates the direction of the rotation, negative to one side and positive to the other.

Figure 11-19: Image rotated in the y axis

Another transformation we can perform is clipping the view with the `clipShape()` modifier. This modifier superposes the view with a shape and only preserves the parts of the view covered by the shape. This is particularly useful with images. For instance, we can clip the cover of the book with a `Circle` shape to create a nice thumbnail.

```
import SwiftUI
struct ContentView: View {
    var body: some View {
        Image("book1")
            .resizable()
            .scaledToFit()
            .frame(width: 100, height: 180)
            .clipShape(Circle())
    }
}
```

Listing 11-21: Clipping the image

Figure 11-20: Image clipped with a `Circle` *shape*

SwiftUI also includes modifiers specifically designed to work and transform shape views. The following are the most frequently used.

rotation(Angle, **anchor:** UnitPoint**)**—This modifier rotates the shape by the angle specified by the first attribute. The **anchor** attribute determines the anchor point the shape will be rotated around. The point is defined with values between 0.0 and 1.0.

scale(CGFloat, **anchor:** UnitPoint**)**—This modifier changes the scale of the shape. The first attribute determines the new scale (1.0 by default), and the **anchor** attribute determines the point from which the shape is scaled. There is an additional modifier to change the scale independently for the x and y axis: `scale(x: CGFloat, y: CGFloat, anchor: UnitPoint)`.

trim(from: CGFloat, **to:** CGFloat**)**—This modifier trims the shape from the point determined by the **from** attribute to the point determined by the **to** attribute.

Chapter 11 - Graphics and Animations

These modifiers are implemented by shape views and therefore they must be applied before other modifiers, as in the following example.

```
import SwiftUI
struct ContentView: View {
    var body: some View {
        RoundedRectangle(cornerRadius: 20)
            .rotation(.degrees(45))
            .fill(Color.blue)
            .frame(width: 100, height: 100)
    }
}
```

Listing 11-22: Rotating a shape

Again, the transformation modifiers affect the content of the view, in this case the shape, but the view itself remains the same. In the example of Listing 11-22, we create a **RoundedRectangle** view and rotate it 45 degrees, as shown in Figure 11-21.

Figure 11-21: Rotation

The **scale()** modifier is not only used to resize the shape but also to achieve cool effects. For instance, we can squeeze or expand shapes by declaring different values for the horizontal and vertical scales or create a mirror image by declaring a negative value. The following example implements this trick to invert the coordinate system and draw an inverted shape.

```
import SwiftUI
struct ContentView: View {
    var body: some View {
        HStack {
            Triangle()
                .fill(Color.blue)
                .frame(width: 100, height: 100)
            Triangle()
                .scale(x: -1, y: 1)
                .fill(Color.blue)
                .frame(width: 100, height: 100)
        }
    }
}
```

Listing 11-23: Inverting a shape with the scale() *modifier*

This example implements the **Triangle** view defined in Listing 11-17. The first instance is displayed with a regular scale, but the second instance is transformed with the **scale()** modifier and a horizontal scale of -1, which inverts the coordinate system, creating a mirror image, as shown in Figure 11-22.

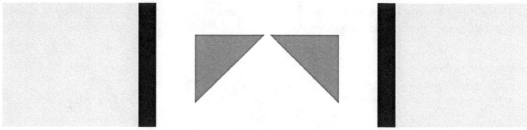

Figure 11-22: Scaling shapes

 Do It Yourself: Update the `ContentView` with the code of Listing 11-23. To test this example, you also need the Triangle.swift file we created before with the `Triangle` view defined in Listing 11-17. You should see the shapes in Figure 11-22 on the canvas.

As we already mentioned, paths are drawn from one point to another, as if they were following the movement of a pencil. We can remove a part of the process with the `trim()` modifier. This modifier determines what part of the path is drawn with values from 0.0 to 1.0, where 0.0 means the beginning of the path and 1.0 the end.

```
import SwiftUI
struct ContentView: View {
    var body: some View {
        HStack {
            Triangle()
                .trim(from: 0, to: 0.70)
                .stroke(Color.blue, lineWidth: 10)
                .frame(width: 100, height: 100)
        }
    }
}
```

Listing 11-24: Trimming a path

The example of Listing 11-24 creates a `Triangle` view, but trims the path at the point 0.70, which represent the 70% of the drawing. This allows the system to draw the first and second lines in full, but the process is interrupted, and therefore the triangle is never finished.

Figure 11-23: Incomplete shape

(Basic) **11.4 Animations**

SwiftUI views can be animated. The process is easy to implement. We set the new values for the view, declare the type of animation we want, and SwiftUI takes care of creating it. For instance, if we set a new opacity for the view, SwiftUI calculates the values in between the initial opacity and the new one, and then recreates the view for each of those values to produce every frame of the animation. To apply an animation to a view, the `View` protocol defines the following modifiers.

animation(Animation)—This modifier animates the view with the animation defined by the attribute.

animation(Animation, value: Value)—This modifier animates the view with the animation defined by the first attribute, but only when the value referenced by the **value** attribute changes.

These modifiers apply the animation to the view, but the animation is determined by an instance of the **Animation** structure. The structure provides properties and methods to create and configure the animation, including the following type properties that returned different types of standard animations.

default—This type property returns the animation defined by the system by default.

easeIn—This type property returns an animation that is slow at the beginning and faster at the end.

easeInOut—This type property returns an animation that is slow at the beginning and the end.

easeOut—This type property returns an animation that is fast at the beginning and slow at the end.

linear—This type property returns an animation that is always performed at the same speed.

The **animation()** modifiers must be applied after the modifiers we want to animate. For instance, in the following example, we change the scale of a **Rectangle** view from 1 to 2 when a button is pressed, but because the **animation()** modifier is declared after the **scaleEffect()** modifier, the change is animated.

```
import SwiftUI
struct ContentView: View {
    @State private var boxScale: CGFloat = 1

    var body: some View {
        VStack {
            HStack {
                Rectangle()
                    .fill(Color.blue)
                    .frame(width: 50, height: 50)
                    .scaleEffect(boxScale)
                    .animation(.default)
            }
            .frame(width: 250, height: 120)
            Button("Animate") {
                self.boxScale = 2
            }
        }.padding()
    }
}
```

Listing 11-25: Animating a view

The structure of Listing 11-25 defines a **@State** property of type **CGFloat** with the value 1 and then assigns the value 2 to this property when the button is pressed. The **animation()** modifier detects the change and generates the animation, from a scale of 1 to a scale of 2.

Figure 11-24: Animation by default

The animation in this example is of type `default`, which in most systems is set as an `easeInOut` animation, but we can specify a different type if we think it looks better for our interface. The following example applies a `linear` animation instead.

```
Rectangle()
   .fill(Color.blue)
   .frame(width: 50, height: 50)
   .scaleEffect(boxScale)
   .animation(.linear)
```

Listing 11-26: Applying a linear animation

 Do It Yourself: Create a SwiftUI project. Update the `ContentView` structure with the code of Listing 11-25. Activate the live preview on the canvas and press the Animate button. You should see the animated square grow, as shown in Figure 11-24. Specify another type of animation, as we did in Listing 11-26, to see the difference between one type and another.

The animations created by the type properties used so far are configured with values by default, but the `Animation` structure offers the following methods to configure the animation.

delay(Double**)**—This method sets the seconds the animator waits before starting the animation.

repeatCount(Int, **autoreverses:** Bool**)**—This method sets the number of times the animator performs an animation. The first attribute determines the number of animations to be performed, and the **autoreverses** attribute determines if the process of going back to the initial state is going to be animated as well (**true** by default).

repeatForever(autoreverses: Bool**)**—This method determines if the animator is going to perform the animation indefinitely. The **autoreverses** attribute determines if the process of going back to the initial state is going to be animated as well (**true** by default).

speed(Double**)**—This method sets the speed of the animation (1 by default).

These methods are applied to the `Animation` structure like view modifiers. The only requirement is to declare the `Animation` structure explicitly, as in the following example.

```
Rectangle()
   .fill(Color.blue)
   .frame(width: 50, height: 50)
   .scaleEffect(boxScale)
   .animation(
      Animation.easeInOut
         .delay(1)
         .speed(2)
         .repeatCount(3)
   )
```

Listing 11-27: Configuring the animation

Chapter 11 - Graphics and Animations

The `Rectangle` view of Listing 11-27 is animated with an `easeInOut` animation. The animation is delayed 1 second, reproduced at twice the normal speed, and repeated 3 times. Notice that by default, the `repeatCount()` method defines the auto reverse option as `true`. This means that the view is going to animate back to its initial state. But because we specified 3 cycles, the animation is going forward and backward a total of 3 times (forward, backward, and forward again).

 Do It Yourself: Update the `Rectangle` view in your project with the view of Listing 11-27. Activate the live preview and press the Animate button. You should see the square animate two times forward and one time backward.

Up to now, we have applied standard animations, but the Animation structure also includes type methods to create custom animations.

easeIn(duration: Double)—This type method creates an `easeIn` animation with the duration determined by the attribute.

easeInOut(duration: Double)—This type method creates an `easeInOut` animation with the duration determined by the attribute.

easeOut(duration: Double)—This type method creates an `easeOut` animation with the duration determined by the attribute.

linear(duration: Double)—This type method creates a `linear` animation with the duration determined by the attribute.

spring(response: Double, dampingFraction: Double, blendDuration: Double)—This type method creates a spring animation. The **response** attribute determines the duration of one animation period, the **dampingFraction** attribute determines the amount of oscillation, and the **blendDuration** attribute determines the time it takes for the animation to stop and the next animation to begin.

interactiveSpring(response: Double, dampingFraction: Double, blendDuration: Double)—This type method creates a spring animation that can interact with the user. The **response** attribute determines the duration of one animation period, the **dampingFraction** attribute determines the amount of oscillation, and the **blendDuration** attribute determines the time it takes for the animation to stop and the next animation to begin.

interpolatingSpring(mass: Double, stiffness: Double, damping: initialVelocity: Double)—This type method creates a spring animation that combines the values with previous animations. The **mass** attribute determines the mass we want to assign to the view, the **stiffness** attribute determines the stiffness of the spring, the **damping** attribute determines the amount of oscillation, and the **initialVelocity** determines the animation's initial velocity.

timingCurve(Double, Double, Double, Double, duration: Double)—This type method creates an animation with a custom timing curve. The four initial attributes determine the coordinates of the control points of a cubic Bezier curve, and the **duration** attribute determines the duration of the animation.

These custom animations are created like the standard animations, and they can even take the same methods for configuration. For instance, we can create a customized spring animation (an animation that bounces the view back and forth) and set its speed and cycle.

```
Rectangle()
   .fill(Color.blue)
   .frame(width: 50, height: 50)
   .scaleEffect(boxScale)
   .animation(
      Animation.interpolatingSpring(mass: 0.2, stiffness: 0.5, damping:
0.5, initialVelocity: 5)
         .speed(5)
         .repeatForever()
   )
```

Listing 11-28: Defining a custom animation

 Do It Yourself: Update the `Rectangle` view in your project with the view of Listing 11-28. Activate the live preview and press the Animate button. You should see the square bounce indefinitely. Try different values for the `interpolatingSpring()` animation and implement other types of animations to see how they work.

The `animation()` modifier can animate multiple changes at a time. Every modification performed before the modifier is applied will be animated, as in the following example.

```
import SwiftUI

struct ContentView: View {
   @State private var boxScale: CGFloat = 1
   @State private var roundCorners: Bool = false

   var body: some View {
      VStack {
         HStack {
            Rectangle()
               .fill(Color.blue)
               .frame(width: 50, height: 50)
               .cornerRadius(roundCorners ? 10 : 0)
               .scaleEffect(boxScale)
               .animation(
                  Animation.easeInOut(duration: 2)
               )
         }
         .frame(width: 250, height: 120)
         Button("Animate") {
            self.boxScale = 2
            self.roundCorners = true
         }
      }.padding()
   }
}
```

Listing 11-29: Animating multiple values at a time

The example of Listing 11-29 defines two `@State` properties to control the scale of the box and the radius of the corners. When the button is pressed, we change the values of these two properties, and because the `animation()` modifier is applied after the `cornerRadius()` and `scaleEffect()` modifiers, both changes are animated.

Chapter 11 - Graphics and Animations

Do It Yourself: Update the `ContentView` structure with the code of Listing 11-29. Activate the live preview and press the Animate button. You should see the square grow and the corners become round.

In the last example, we applied the same animation to both values, but SwiftUI allows us to perform as many animations as we need. All we have to do is to apply an `animation()` modifier after each value we want to animate. The `animation()` modifier animates all the changes that are performed after the previous animation, so we can animate multiple values with the same animation and perform multiple animations on the same view.

```
Rectangle()
    .fill(Color.blue)
    .frame(width: 50, height: 50)
    .cornerRadius(roundCorners ? 10 : 0)
    .animation(Animation.easeOut.delay(1))
    .scaleEffect(boxScale)
    .animation(.linear)
```

Listing 11-30: Applying a different animation to each value

The `Rectangle` view of Listing 11-30 performs two animations. The first one is an `easeOut` animation with a delay of 1 second. This animation animates the changes performed by the `cornerRadius()` modifier, but it doesn't affect the `scaleEffect()` modifier because it was applied before it. Instead, the scale is animated with a `linear` animation by the last modifier. As a result, the box is scaled up first with a linear animation, and 1 second later the corners of the box are animated with the `easeOut` animation.

Figure 11-25: Two animations

 Do It Yourself: Update the `Rectangle` view of the previous example with the view of Listing 11-30. Activate the live preview and press the Animate button. You should see the square grow and 1 second later the corners being rounded.

There is a second `animation()` modifier that includes an additional value. This value is a reference to a state. What it does is to tell the modifier when to perform the animation. Therefore, the changes are animated only when the value changes. In the following example, we use this modifier to update the view with and without an animation.

```
import SwiftUI

struct ContentView: View {
    @State private var boxScale: CGFloat = 1
    @State private var animate: Bool = false

    var body: some View {
        VStack {
            HStack {
                Rectangle()
                    .fill(Color.blue)
                    .frame(width: 50, height: 50)
                    .scaleEffect(boxScale)
```

```
            .animation(Animation.easeOut, value: animate)
      }
      .frame(width: 250, height: 120)
      Button("With Animation") {
         self.boxScale = 2
         self.animate.toggle()
      }.padding()
      Button("Without Animation") {
         self.boxScale = 2
      }
      Button("Reset") {
         self.boxScale = 1
      }.padding()
   }.padding()
   }
}
```

Listing 11-31: Defining a selective animation

The structure of Listing 11-31 defines the same `@State` property we used before to store the scale of the box and a second `@State` property to determine whether a change on the scale is going to be animated. We use this second property in the `animation()` modifier and then define three buttons. The first button modifies the `boxScale` and `animate` properties. This modifies the scale of the box and also tells the `animation()` modifier to animate the change. The next button only modifies the `boxScale` property. This means that the scale is going to change, but the process is not going to be animated. And the third button moves back the value of the `boxScale` property to its initial value of 1, so the user can perform the process again. When the user presses the With Animation button, the size of the box is incremented and the change is animated, and when the user presses the Without Animation button, the same change occurs but without an animation.

 Do It Yourself: Update the `ContentView` structure with the code of Listing 11-31. Activate the live preview. Press the With Animation button. You should see the box growing with an animation. Press the Reset button to move the box back to the initial state. Now press the Without Animation button. You should see the box change size but without an animation.

In the previous examples we have used the `animation()` modifiers to animate changes applied by other modifiers, but there are situations in which the change of a state must be animated, independently of where the state is used. To define an explicit animation, SwiftUI includes the following global method.

withAnimation(Animation, Closure**)**—This method performs an animation and returns the result. The first attribute defines the type of animation to use. If ignored, the animation is defined as `default`. The second attribute defines the closure that performs the changes we want to animate.

The `withAnimation()` method is used when we want to tell the system to perform an animation if a state changes, no matter where that state is used. It is useful when we need to animate multiple views that work with the same state, as in the following example.

```
import SwiftUI

struct ContentView: View {
   @State private var roundCorners: Bool = false
```

Chapter 11 - Graphics and Animations

```
    var body: some View {
        VStack {
            HStack {
                Rectangle()
                    .fill(Color.blue)
                    .frame(width: 100, height: 100)
                    .cornerRadius(roundCorners ? 20 : 0)
                Rectangle()
                    .fill(Color.blue)
                    .frame(width: 100, height: 100)
                    .cornerRadius(roundCorners ? 20 : 0)
            }.frame(width: 250, height: 120)
            Button("Animate") {
                withAnimation(Animation.easeOut) {
                    self.roundCorners.toggle()
                }
            }
        }.padding()
    }
}
```

Listing 11-32: Defining an explicit animation

The example of Listing 11-32 creates two `Rectangle` views. Both views use the `cornerRadius()` modifier and the `roundCorners` property to determine the radius of their corners. There is no `animation()` modifier attached to these views, but below the views we define a button that implements the `withAnimation()` method with an `easeOut` animation. When the button is pressed, this method is executed and the value of the `roundCorners` property is toggled. This changes the state and therefore modifies both views, but because the change was performed within the `withAnimation()` method, the process is animated.

Animate   Animate

Figure 11-26: Multiple views animated at the same time

 Do It Yourself: Update the `ContentView` structure with the code of Listing 11-32. You should see two boxes on the canvas. Activate the live preview and press the Animate button. You should see the animation performed in both boxes.

Another way to animate a state explicitly is to apply the `animation()` modifier directly to the `@State` property. This technique usually applies to controls. For instance, we can animate the change produced by a `Toggle` view.

```
import SwiftUI

struct ContentView: View {
    @State private var roundCorners: Bool = false

    var body: some View {
        VStack {
            HStack {
```

```
          Rectangle()
              .fill(Color.blue)
              .frame(width: 100, height: 100)
              .cornerRadius(roundCorners ? 20 : 0)
          Rectangle()
              .fill(Color.blue)
              .frame(width: 100, height: 100)
              .cornerRadius(roundCorners ? 20 : 0)
        }.frame(width: 250, height: 120)
        Toggle("", isOn: $roundCorners.animation(.default))
            .labelsHidden()
      }.padding()
   }
}
```

Listing 11-33: Animating the state

This view is the same as the previous one, but we have replaced the `Button` view with a `Toggle` view and animate the state with the `animation()` modifier. The effect is the same as before. Every time the `Toggle` view changes the value of the `roundCorners` property, the boxes are animated.

 Do It Yourself: Update the `ContentView` structure with the code of Listing 11-33. You should see two boxes on the canvas. Activate the live preview and turn the switch on and off. You should see the animation performed in both boxes, as before.

The value assigned to the `animation()` modifier is an optional. This means that we can provide to the modifier an `Animation` structure or the value `nil` if we don't want to perform any animation. This can be used to interrupt the animation. For instance, the following example uses a Boolean property to determine whether the modifier should contain an animation or not. If the value of this property is changed to `false`, the value `nil` is assigned to the modifier and the current animation is interrupted.

```
import SwiftUI

struct ContentView: View {
   @State private var roundCorners: Bool = false
   @State private var active: Bool = false

   var body: some View {
      VStack {
         HStack {
            Rectangle()
               .fill(Color.blue)
               .frame(width: 100, height: 100)
               .cornerRadius(roundCorners ? 50 : 0)
               .animation(active ? Animation.default.speed(0.1) : nil)
         }.frame(width: 250, height: 120)
         Button("Animate") {
            self.roundCorners.toggle()
            self.active.toggle()
         }
      }.padding()
   }
}
```

Listing 11-34: Interrupting an animation

Chapter 11 - Graphics and Animations

Do It Yourself: Update the `ContentView` structure with the code of Listing 11-34. Activate the live preview. Press the Animate button and press it again while the animation is running. You should see the animation being interrupted and the box going back to its initial state.

The system knows how to animate the views because they conform to a protocol included in SwiftUI called `Animatable`. The protocol defines a computed property called `animatableData` that provides to the system the data required to create the frames for the animation. Every time we animate a view, the system gets the value from this property, increases or decreases it by a small amount, redraws the view, and repeats the process until the value matches the new one. For instance, the view returned by the `opacity()` modifier includes an `animatableData` property that provides the view's opacity value, so the system can gradually increase or decrease this value and redraw the view each time with a different opacity to make it look like it's being animated. Most SwiftUI views include this property and therefore the system knows how to animate them, but sometimes we must provide these values ourselves. For instance, if we want to animate a path in a `Shape` view, we have to make the structure conform to the `Animatable` protocol and implement the `animatableData` property to tell the system what's the value it has to modify to get all the frames for the animation.

The `Shape` protocol inherits from the `Animatable` protocol, so in this case all we have to do is to implement the `animatableData` property to provide the value to animate. This value has to be something we can use to draw the path. For instance, if we want to animate a circle, we can provide its radius. If the animation goes from a radius of 0 to a radius of 10, the view will be able to draw the intermediate values (1, 2, 3, etc.) required to create the animation. If the value we use to create the path is not animatable, we must turn it into something that can be animated. For instance, in the following example, we have a Boolean `@State` property used to determine whether the graphic of a mouth should be smiling or not, but we turn this value into a number 0 or a number 1, so the system can generate values in between to animate the path (0.1, 0.2, 0.3, etc.).

```
import SwiftUI

struct ContentView: View {
    @State private var smiling: Bool = true

    var body: some View {
        VStack {
            Face(smile: smiling ? 1 : 0)
                .stroke(Color.blue, lineWidth: 5)
                .frame(width: 100, height: 100)
                .animation(.default)
            Button("Change") {
                self.smiling.toggle()
            }
        }
    }
}
```

Listing 11-35: Instantiating a view with a value that can be animated

If the `smiling` property is `true`, we send the value 1 to the view, otherwise, we send the value 0. This means that the system can create an animation by instantiating this view with values from 0 to 1. The view takes this value and draws a mouth with the curve defined by an `addCurve()` method.

```
import SwiftUI

struct Face: Shape {
    var smile: CGFloat
    var animatableData: CGFloat {
        get {
            return smile
        }
        set {
            self.smile = newValue
        }
    }
    func path(in rect: CGRect) -> Path {
        var path = Path()
        let width = rect.width
        let smileClamp = min(max(smile, 0), 1)
        let section = rect.height / 5
        let smilePos = section + (section * 3 * smileClamp)

        path.move(to: CGPoint(x: width / 10, y: rect.midY))
        path.addCurve(to: CGPoint(x: width - (width / 10), y: rect.midY),
control1: CGPoint(x: width / 4, y: smilePos), control2: CGPoint(x: width
/ 4 * 3, y: smilePos))

        return path
    }
}
```

Listing 11-36: Defining an animatable path

The only difference with previous **Shape** structures is that now we have an **animatableData** property that provides the system with the value to animate. The system accesses this property, gets the value of the **smile** property from it, increases or decreases this value by a small amount, sends the result back to the **animatableData** property, and the path is redrawn with this new value.

Because the values received by the **Face** view are between 0 and 1, we must convert them to a range we can use to draw the mouth. First, we make sure that the value is between 0 and 1 with the **min()** and **max()** functions. After that, we calculate the position of the bottom of the mouth according to this value. If the value is close to 0, the bottom of the mouth will be close to the top of the view, and if the value is close to 1, it will be close to the bottom of the view, so we can get a mouth that is smiling or not.

Figure 11-27: Animated path

Do It Yourself: Update the **ContentView** structure with the code of Listing 11-35. Create a new Swift file called Face.swift for the structure of Listing 11-36. Activate the live preview and press the Change button. You should see the curves of Figure 11-27.

Chapter 11 - Graphics and Animations

(Medium) Transitions

As we have seen in Chapter 8, we can add or remove views from the interface depending on a state (see Listing 8-2). The process by which the view appears or disappears from the screen is called *transition*. By default, the system doesn't use any transition, it just displays or removes the view, but we can assign a specific transition for a view with the following modifier.

transition(AnyTransition)—This modifier assigns the transition specified by the attribute to the view.

As with animations, SwiftUI defines standard transitions. The following are the type properties provided by the `AnyTransition` structure to create these transitions.

opacity—This type property returns a transition that inserts or removes a view by modifying its opacity.

scale—This type property returns a transition that inserts or removes a view by modifying its scale.

slide—This type property returns a transition that inserts or removes a view by sliding it from the sides.

identity—This type property returns a transition that inserts or removes a view without any effect. This is the transition by default.

The `AnyTransition` structure defines the type of transition, but for the transition to be applied, we also must define the type of animation used to produce it. In the following example, we animate a state explicitly with the `withAnimation()` method and apply a transition of type `scale` to the view.

```
import SwiftUI

struct ContentView: View {
    @State private var showInfo = false

    var body: some View {
        VStack {
            Button("Show Information") {
                withAnimation {
                    self.showInfo.toggle()
                }
            }.padding()
            if showInfo {
                Text("This is the information")
                    .transition(.scale)
            }
            Spacer()
        }
    }
}
```

Listing 11-37: Adding and removing a view with a transition

The button in the view of Listing 11-37 toggles the value of the `showInfo` property. When the value is `true`, a `Text` view is added to the interface with a `scale` transition, otherwise, the view is removed. The view expands until it reaches its natural size when the value of the property is `true`, and shrinks until it disappears from the screen when it is `false`.

Do It Yourself: Create a SwiftUI project. Update the `ContentView` structure with the code of Listing 11-37. Run the application in the simulator and press the Show Information button. You should see the `Text` view appear or disappear from the screen every time the button is pressed. Replace the `scale` transition by the `opacity` and `slide` types to see how they work.

The `AnyTransition` structure also includes the following type methods to create custom transitions.

move(edge: Edge)—This type method defines a transition that moves the view in and out of the interface from the side defined by the attribute. The **edge** attribute is an enumeration of type `Edge` with the values `bottom`, `leading`, `top`, and `trailing`.

offset(x: CGFloat, **y:** CGFloat)—This type method defines a transition that moves the view in and out of the interface by the space determined by the attributes. The **x** and **y** attributes specify the offset of the view from the center of its frame.

scale(scale: CGFloat, **anchor:** UnitPoint)—This type method defines a transition that scales the view. The **scale** attribute determines the initial scale for the transition, and the **anchor** attribute determines the point from which the view is going to be scaled.

For instance, the following example creates a transition that moves the view in and out of the interface from the left side of the screen. Notice that this is like the `slide` transition, but in this case the view always uses the same side of the screen.

```
import SwiftUI

struct ContentView: View {
    @State private var showInfo = false

    var body: some View {
        VStack {
            Button("Show Information") {
                withAnimation {
                    self.showInfo.toggle()
                }
            }.padding()
            if showInfo {
                Text("This is the information")
                    .transition(.move(edge: .leading))
            }
            Spacer()
        }
    }
}
```

Listing 11-38: Customizing the transition

Do It Yourself: Update the `ContentView` structure with the code of Listing 11-38. Run the application in the simulator and press the Show Information button. You should see the text slide from the left side of the screen and then slide back to the same side when the button is pressed again. Replace the `move()` method by the `offset()` or `scale()` methods to see how they work.

The transitions we have implemented so far are symmetric; they are the same when the view is added to the interface than when the view is removed. To create an asymmetric transition, the `AnyTransition` structure includes the following type method.

asymmetric(insertion: AnyTransition, **removal:** AnyTransition)—This type method defines an asymmetric transition. The **insertion** attribute specifies the transition to use when the view is inserted, and the **removal** attribute specifies the transition to use when the view is removed.

For example, we can fade-in the view by modifying the opacity when it is added to the interface, and then remove it by reducing its scale.

```
Text("This is the information")
    .transition(.asymmetric(insertion: .opacity, removal: .scale))
```

Listing 11-39: Defining an asymmetric transition

In this example, we use the standard transitions `opacity` and `scale`, but the `asymmetric()` method can take any type of transition we want.

 Do It Yourself: Update the `transition()` modifier of the previous example with the code of Listing 11-39. Run the application in the simulator and press the Show Information button. You should see the text fade-in and then shrink when the button is pressed again. Replace the `opacity` and `scale` transitions by the transitions created by the `move()`, `offset()` or `scale()` methods.

Besides defining one transition for the insertion and another for the removal, we can combine two transitions with the following method.

combined(with: AnyTransition)—This method combines the transition with the transition specified by the **with** attribute.

The method is applied to an instance of the `AnyTransition` structure, so we must create a transition first and then call this method to combine that transition with another one. The following example combines a transition of type `scale` with a transition of type `slide`. Notice that to be able to call the `combined()` method on the `scale` transition, we must specify the `AnyTransition` type explicitly, otherwise Xcode shows an error.

```
Text("This is the information")
    .transition(AnyTransition.scale.combined(with: .slide))
```

Listing 11-40: Combining transitions

Combined transitions are performed at the same time, so we will see the text expanding and moving from one side of the screen when inserted and shrinking and moving to the other side of the screen when removed.

 Do It Yourself: Update the `transition()` modifier of the previous example with the code of Listing 11-40. Run the application in the simulator and press the Show Information button. You should see the text slide from the left while growing until it reaches the final size and position.

So far, we have used an explicit animation, but there are three ways to declare the animation for a transition. We can declare an explicit animation with the `withAnimation()` method, as we did for these examples (see Listing 11-37), we can declare an implicit animation with the `animation()` modifier (in this case the modifier has to be declared before the `transition()` modifier), or we can use the following method provided by the `AnyTransition` structure.

animation(Animation)—This method applies the animation defined by the attribute to the transition.

Like the `combined()` method, the `animation()` method is called on the instance of the `AnyTransition` structure, so we have to define the transition and then call this method to determine the animation we are going to apply to that transition, as in the following example.

```
import SwiftUI

struct ContentView: View {
    @State private var showInfo = false

    var body: some View {
        VStack {
            Button("Show Information") {
                self.showInfo.toggle()
            }.padding()
            if showInfo {
                Text("This is the information")
                    .transition(AnyTransition.scale.animation(.easeInOut))
            }
            Spacer()
        }
    }
}
```

Listing 11-41: Declaring the animation for the transition

The view of Listing 11-41 produces a `scale` transition with an `easeInOut` animation, similar to what we have achieved before, but now the animation is defined by the transition itself. Because of this, we don't have to declare the explicit animation with the `withAnimation()` method anymore.

In this example, we use a standard animation and the code is still readable, but it can get cumbersome if we apply our own animations or combine custom transitions with custom animations. In cases like this, it is better to define the transition externally. There are different ways to do it, but what is considered best practice is to declare an extension of the `AnyTransition` structure and declare our custom transition as if it belonged to the structure itself. In the following example, we define a custom transition called `mytransition`.

```
import SwiftUI

struct ContentView: View {
    @State private var showInfo = false

    var body: some View {
        VStack {
            Button("Show Information") {
                self.showInfo.toggle()
            }.padding()
            if showInfo {
                Text("This is the information")
                    .transition(.mytransition)
            }
            Spacer()
        }
    }
}
```

```
extension AnyTransition {
    static var mytransition: AnyTransition {
        let animation = Animation.easeInOut(duration: 2)
        let transition = AnyTransition.scale.animation(animation)
        return transition
    }
}
```

Listing 11-42: Extending the AnyTransition *structure*

The code of Listing 11-42 defines an extension of the **AnyTransition** structure with a type property called **mytransition**. This is a computed property that creates and returns a custom transition. Of course, we can define any transition with any animation we want, the only requirement is that the property returns a structure of type **AnyTransition**, so we can use it to specify the transition for a view. In this example, we create a custom **easeInOut** animation with a duration of 2 seconds and apply it to a standard transition of type **scale**.

Because we declare our custom transition as an extension of the **AnyTransition** structure, we can assign it to the view as we do with any standard transition defined by the structure (**transition(.mytransition)**).

 Do It Yourself: Update the ContentView.swift file with the code of Listing 11-42. Run the application in the simulator and press the Show Information button. You should see the **Text** view appear with a **scale** transition, but the animation should last 2 seconds.

 IMPORTANT: SwiftUI offers ways to customize transitions even further. The topic is beyond the scope of this book. For more information and tutorials, visit our website and follow the links for this chapter.

Chapter 11 - Graphics and Animations

(Basic) **12.1 Gestures**

Gestures are actions performed by the user on the screen, such as tapping, swiping, or pinching. These gestures are difficult to detect because the only thing the screen returns is the position of the fingers. That is why Apple provides gesture recognizers. A gesture recognizer performs all the necessary calculations to recognize a gesture, so instead of processing multiple events and values, we just wait for the notifications sent by the system when complex gestures are detected and respond accordingly.

(Basic) **Gesture Modifiers**

The most common gesture used in a mobile device is a tap gesture, detected when the user touches the screen with a finger. Because of how common it is to work with this gesture, SwiftUI defines two convenient modifiers to process it.

onTapGesture(count: Int, **perform:** Closure)—This modifier recognizes a single or multiple taps gesture. The **count** attribute determines how many taps are required for the gesture to be recognized (1 by default), and the **perform** attribute is the closure to be executed when the gesture is detected.

onLongPressGesture(minimumDuration: Double, **maximumDistance:** CGFloat, **pressing:** Closure, **perform:** Closure)—This modifier recognizes a long press gesture (the user keeps pressing the screen with a finger). The **minimumDuration** attribute is the time in seconds the user must press the screen with the finger until the gesture is recognized. The **maximumDistance** attribute is the distance in points the user can move the finger from the original position before the gesture is no longer recognized. The **pressing** attribute is the closure to be executed when the user begins and ends pressing the view. The closure receives a Boolean value to indicate whether the user is pressing or not. And finally, the **perform** attribute is the closure to be executed when the gesture is confirmed.

We worked with the `onTapGesture()` modifier before to recognize a tap (see Listings 8-17 and 10-26). When the modifier is applied to a view, if the system detects a tap on that view it executes the closure. The view can be any SwiftUI view available. For instance, we can recognize a tap on an image.

```
import SwiftUI

struct ContentView: View {
   @State private var expand: Bool = false

   var body: some View {
      Image("spot1")
         .resizable()
         .scaledToFit()
         .frame(width: 160, height: 200)
```

```
        .onTapGesture {
            self.expand = true
        }
        .sheet(isPresented: $expand) {
            ShowImage()
        }
    }
}
```

Listing 12-1: Detecting a tap gesture on an image

The code in Listing 12-1 defines an `Image` view of a size of 80 by 100 points. The `onTapGesture()` modifier is applied to the view to detect the tap, and the `sheet()` modifier to present a sheet. When the image is tapped by the user, a sheet with the `ShowImage` view is opened. The following is our implementation of this view.

```
import SwiftUI

struct ShowImage: View {
    var body: some View {
        Image("spot1")
            .resizable()
            .scaledToFill()
            .edgesIgnoringSafeArea(.all)
    }
}
```

Listing 12-2: Expanding the image

There is nothing new in the code of Listing 12-2. The view creates an `Image` view and expands it to occupy the whole sheet, including the safe area. As a result, the interface presents a small image on the screen and when the user taps on it, it opens a sheet to show it in full size.

Figure 12-1: Image responding to the tap gesture

 Do It Yourself: Create a SwiftUI project. Download the spot1.jpg image from our website and add it to the Assets Catalog. Update the `ContentView` structure with the code of Listing 12-1. Create a Swift file called ShowImage.swift for the code of Listing 12-2. Run the application. You should see the image in Figure 12-1 (left). Tap on it. A sheet should open with the image in full size (right).

Chapter 12 - Gesture Recognizers

The long press gesture is very similar to the tap gesture, but the system waits a moment before confirming the gesture and performing the task. With the **onLongPressGesture()** modifier, we can set the waiting time and also perform a task while the user is pressing and waiting for the gesture to complete, as in the following example.

```
import SwiftUI

struct ContentView: View {
    @State private var expand: Bool = false
    @State private var pressing: Bool = false

    var body: some View {
        Image("spot1")
            .resizable()
            .scaledToFit()
            .frame(width: 160, height: 200)
            .opacity(pressing ? 0 : 1)
            .animation(.easeInOut(duration: 1.5))

            .onLongPressGesture(minimumDuration: 1, maximumDistance: 10,
                pressing: { value in
                    self.pressing = value
                }, perform: {
                    self.expand = true
            })
            .sheet(isPresented: $expand) {
                ShowImage()
            }
    }
}
```

Listing 12-3: Detecting a long press gesture

This is the same example as before but now we apply a long press gesture to the **Image** view, so the user must hold the finger in position for a moment to open the sheet. In this case, we set the waiting time to 1 second and the maximum distance to 10 points, so the user can't move the finger more than 10 points away from the initial position or the gesture is invalidated. The closure performed while the view is being pressed modifies a **@State** property called **pressing** that we use to set the view's opacity. When the user puts the finger on the view, the value received by the closure is **true**, so the value 0 is assigned to the **opacity()** modifier, and when the user moves the finger away, lifts it, or the gesture ends, the closure receives the value **false** and therefore the value 1 is assigned to the view's opacity. The process is animated with an **easeInOut** animation that lasts 1.5 seconds. Because the animation is longer than the waiting time for the gesture, the sheet is opened before the image completely disappears, which provides the necessary feedback for the user to know that it must wait for the process to be finished.

 Do It Yourself: For this example, you need the same **ShowImage** view of Listing 12-2. Update the **ContentView** structure with the code of Listing 12-3. Run the application. Press and hold the finger on the image. You should see the image fading-out and the sheet opening after 1 second.

(Basic) Hit Testing

Because views may sometimes overlap each other and some even implement their own gestures, the system must decide whether a view should process a gesture or pass it to other views. The process of finding the view the user is interacting with and decide whether it should respond to the gesture or not is called *hit testing*. The `View` protocol defines the following modifiers to control this process.

allowsHitTesting(Bool)—This modifier determines whether the detection of hits is enabled on the view or not.

contentShape(Shape, eoFill: Bool)—This modifier defines the shape of the hitting area. The first attribute is a shape view that determines the area the user can interact with, and the **eoFill** attribute determines the algorithm to use to detect the hit.

The `allowsHitTesting()` modifier can be used to disable a gesture. The modifier must be applied to the view that can recognize the gesture and its value set to `false` when we don't want to allow the user to perform it. For instance, we can disable the tap gesture on the `Image` view of the previous example.

```
import SwiftUI

struct ContentView: View {
    @State private var expand: Bool = false
    @State private var allowExpansion: Bool = false

    var body: some View {
        VStack(spacing: 20) {
            Image("spot1")
                .resizable()
                .scaledToFit()
                .frame(width: 160, height: 200)
                .onTapGesture {
                    self.expand = true
                }
                .allowsHitTesting(allowExpansion)
                .sheet(isPresented: $expand) {
                    ShowImage()
                }
            Toggle("", isOn: $allowExpansion)
                .labelsHidden()
        }
    }
}
```

Listing 12-4: Disabling the tap gesture

The view in Listing 12-4 adds a `Toggle` view below the image to control the value of a `@State` property. We use this property to determine if hit testing is allowed on the `Image` view. The initial value of the property is set to `false`, so the user is not able to tap on the image to open the sheet, but when the toggle is turned on, the value of the property changes to `true` and therefore the gesture is recognized by the `Image` view.

 Do It Yourself: Update the `ContentView` structure with the code of Listing 12-4. Run the application on the simulator. Tap on the image. Nothing should happen. Turn on the switch below the image. Now, the image should open the sheet when you tap on it.

The `contentShape()` modifier also plays an important role on the process of recognizing a gesture. If we apply a gesture recognizer to an `Image` view or a `Text` view, the gesture is recognized when the user's finger touches any part of the area occupied by the view. But this is

Chapter 12 - Gesture Recognizers

not always the case. Container views, like `VStack` and `HStack`, only recognize the gesture when it is performed on the area occupied by their content. To make sure that any part of the view can recognize a gesture, we must force the content to occupy the entire area. We came across this issue before. In Listing 10-26, we had to define a background with a `Color` view to provide a surface for the tap gesture to be recognized. This was enough for our purpose, but it generates content that may not be required by the interface. A better solution is to apply the `contentShape()` modifier. This modifier allows us to define the hit surface for the gesture without adding any real content to the view.

In the following example, we recreate the view we used to present the rows in the projects of Chapter 10, but this time, instead of using a `Color` view to respond to the tap gesture, we define the row's content with a `Rectangle` view and the `contentShape()` modifier. This allows the user to tap anywhere in the row to select it.

```
import SwiftUI

struct ContentView: View {
    @State private var selected: Bool = false

    var body: some View {
        VStack {
            HStack(alignment: .top) {
                Image("book1")
                    .resizable()
                    .scaledToFit()
                    .frame(width: 80, height: 100)
                    .border(selected ? Color.yellow : Color.clear, width: 2)

                VStack(alignment: .leading, spacing: 2) {
                    Text("Steve Jobs").bold()
                    Text("Walter Isaacson")
                    Text("2011").font(.caption)
                    Spacer()
                }.padding(.top, 5)
                Spacer()
            }.padding(5)
            .frame(maxWidth: .infinity, maxHeight: 110)
            .contentShape(Rectangle())
            .onTapGesture {
                self.selected.toggle()
            }
            Spacer()
        }
    }
}
```

Listing 12-5: Defining the shape of the content

The view in Listing 12-5 displays information about a book (only one row). If the user taps the row, the gesture recognizer toggles the value of a `@State` property called `selected`, which we use to define the color for the border of the cover. The value `true` makes the border yellow (selected) and the value `false` makes it transparent (deselected). Because of the `contentShape()` modifier, the tap works on any part of the area occupied by the row.

Figure 12-2: Responsive row

Do It Yourself: Download the book1.jpg image from our website and add it to the Assets Catalog. Update the `ContentView` structure with the code of Listing 12-5. Run the application. You should be able to tap on any part of the row to select it.

(Basic) ## Gesture Structures

The `onTapGesture()` and `onLongPressGesture()` modifiers are a convenient way to process a tap on the screen, but these gestures are defined by structures that conform to the `Gesture` protocol. SwiftUI includes a total of five structures to create gesture recognizers. The following are their initializers.

TapGesture(count: Int)—This initializer creates a gesture recognizer to detect a tap gesture. The **count** attribute determines the number of taps required for the gesture to be recognized.

LongPressGesture(minimumDuration: Double, **maximumDistance:** CGFloat)—This initializer creates a gesture recognizer to detect a long press gesture. The **minimumDuration** attribute is the time in seconds the user must press the screen with the finger until the gesture is recognized. The **maximumDistance** attribute is the distance in points the user can move the finger from the original position before the gesture is no longer recognized.

DragGesture(minimumDistance: CGFloat, **coordinateSpace:** Coordinate-Space)—This initializer creates a gesture recognizer to detect a drag gesture. The **minimumDistance** attribute is the distance in points the user must move the finger before the system starts recognizing the gesture, and the **coordinateSpace** attribute determines the coordinate space from which the location values are going to be calculated. This attribute is an enumeration with the values `global` (the coordinates of the screen), `local` (the coordinates of the view), and `named(AnyHashable)` (a coordinate space identified by a name).

MagnificationGesture(minimumScaleDelta: CGFloat)—This initializer creates a gesture recognizer to detect a magnification gesture. The **minimumScaleDelta** attribute is the minimum increment or decrement on the scale required for the gesture to be recognized.

RotationGesture(minimumAngleDelta: Angle)—This initializer creates a gesture recognizer to detect a rotation gesture. The **minimumAngleDelta** attribute is the minimum increment or decrement on the angle of the view required for the gesture to be recognized.

These initializers configure the gestures recognizers, but to respond to the different states of the gestures, the structures implement the following methods.

onChanged(Closure)—This method executes a closure when the state of the gesture changes. The closure receives a value with information about the gesture's state.

onEnded(Closure)—This method executes a closure when the gesture ends. The closure receives a value with information about the gesture's state.

updating(GestureState, **body:** Closure)—This method executes a closure when the state of the gesture is updated, either because its value changed or the gesture was cancelled. The first attribute is a `Binding` property that stores the gesture's state values, and the **body** attribute is the closure to be executed every time the state is updated. The closure receives a value with information about the gesture's state, a reference to the `Binding` property, and a value of type `Transaction` that contains information about the animation.

Because of the frequency at which the `updating()` method is called, we can't use a normal `@State` property to keep track of the state of the gesture. Any attempt to modify a state from inside the updating closure will return an error. Therefore, SwiftUI defines a specific property wrapper to work with this method.

@GestureState—This property wrapper stores the state of a gesture and resets its value to its initial value when the gesture ends.

Once we have the gesture recognizer instance properly configured, we must apply it to the view. The `View` protocol defines the following modifiers for this purpose.

gesture(Gesture)—This modifier assigns a gesture recognizer to the view with a lower priority than the gesture recognizers already defined by the view.

highPriorityGesture(Gesture)—This modifier assigns a gesture recognizer to the view with a higher priority than the gesture recognizers already defined by the view.

simultaneousGesture(Gesture)—This modifier assigns a gesture recognizer to the view that is processed along with the gesture recognizers already defined by the view.

The process is simple. We must instantiate a gesture structure to define the gesture recognizer, apply the `onChanged()`, `onEnded()` or `updating()` methods to the structure depending on what we want to do during the process, and assign that instance to the view with a modifier like `gesture()`. What methods to apply depends on the gesture and what we want to achieve, and the values received by these methods also depend on the type of gesture recognizer we are using, so there are multiple options available, as we will see next.

(Basic) **Tap Gesture**

Due to the simplicity of the tap gesture, there is no much difference on applying the `onTapGesture()` modifier or implementing the `TapGesture` structure. The structure can define the number of taps required for the gesture to be recognized, and since there are no changes to report over time, it only uses the `onEnded()` method to perform a task when the gesture is detected. The following example reproduces the previous project, but this time we define the gesture recognizer with a `TapGesture` structure.

```
import SwiftUI

struct ContentView: View {
   @State private var expand: Bool = false
```

```
var body: some View {
    Image("spot1")
        .resizable()
        .scaledToFit()
        .frame(width: 160, height: 200)
        .gesture(
            TapGesture(count: 1)
                .onEnded {
                    self.expand = true
                }
        )
        .sheet(isPresented: $expand) {
            ShowImage()
        }
    }
}
```

Listing 12-6: Defining a TapGesture *recognizer*

The **TapGesture** structure defines the gesture recognizer, but to attach it to a view we must apply the **gesture()** modifier. The result is the same as before. When the image is tapped, the closure assigned to the **onEnded()** method is executed, the value **true** is assigned to the **expand** property, and the sheet is opened. Notice that the **onEnded()** method is a method of the **TapGesture** structure and therefore it is called on the instance of this structure, not on the view.

 Do It Yourself: Update the **ContentView** structure from the previous project with the code of Listing 12-6. Remember that you still need the ShowImage.swift file with the code of Listing 12-2 for this example to work. Run the application on the simulator. You should see a small image on the screen. Tap the image to open the sheet.

(Basic) Long Press Gesture

Like the **TapGesture** structure, the **LongPressGesture** structure creates a simple gesture recognizer, but in this case there is some activity while the gesture is performed, so besides the **onEnded()** method, we also must implement the **updating()** method if we want to perform a task while the view is being pressed.

There are two things we must considered before implementing the **updating()** method. First, as mentioned before, this method requires a **@GestureState** property instead of a **@State** property. A **@GestureState** property stores the current state but it also resets itself to its initial value when the gesture ends, so the initial value assigned to this property is the value we want the property to always have as default. And second, we have to take care of updating the value of this property ourselves from the closure assigned to the method, but we can't modify the property directly, we must do it from the reference received by the method (usually called **state**), as in the following example.

```
import SwiftUI

struct ContentView: View {
    @GestureState private var pressing: Bool = false
    @State private var expand: Bool = false
```

```
var body: some View {
    Image("spot1")
        .resizable()
        .scaledToFit()
        .frame(width: 160, height: 200)
        .opacity(pressing ? 0 : 1)
        .animation(.easeInOut(duration: 1.5))

        .gesture(LongPressGesture(minimumDuration: 1)
            .updating($pressing) { value, state, transition in
                state = value
            }
            .onEnded { value in
                self.expand = true
            }
        )
        .sheet(isPresented: $expand) {
            ShowImage()
        }
    }
}
```

Listing 12-7: Defining a LongPressGesture *recognizer*

This is the same example used for the **onLongPressGesture()** modifier (see Listing 12-3). When the user touches the image, its opacity changes and after one second the sheet is opened. The values are also processed the same way but notice how the Boolean values received by the updating closure are assigned to the **pressing** property. Instead of working with the property directly, we assign the new value received by the closure to a reference of the **pressing** property. We called the value and the reference **value** and **state**, but the names are arbitrary. Once the new value is assigned to **state**, the value of the **pressing** property changes and the opacity is changed accordingly. After a second, the **onEnded()** method is executed, the value of the **expand** property is changed to **true**, and the sheet is opened.

 Do It Yourself: Update the **ContentView** structure with the code of Listing 12-7 and run the application on the simulator. Press the image for more than a second. The sheet should open.

Although we can work with the values produced by the **updating()** method directly, as we did in Listing 12-7, this method was designed to process the state through an enumeration. Instead of assigning the value received by the method directly to the **@GestureState** property, we assign an enumeration value to this property and then get the state from the enumeration, as in the following example.

```
import SwiftUI

enum PressingState {
    case active
    case inactive

    var isActive: Bool {
        switch self {
        case .active:
            return true
        case .inactive:
            return false
        }
    }
}
```

```
struct ContentView: View {
    @GestureState private var pressingState = PressingState.inactive
    @State private var expand: Bool = false

    var body: some View {
        Image("spot1")
            .resizable()
            .scaledToFit()
            .frame(width: 160, height: 200)
            .opacity(pressingState.isActive ? 0 : 1)
            .animation(.easeInOut(duration: 1.5))

            .gesture(LongPressGesture(minimumDuration: 1)
                .updating($pressingState) { value, state, transition in
                    state = value ? .active : .inactive
                }
                .onEnded { value in
                    self.expand = true
                }
            )
            .sheet(isPresented: $expand) {
                ShowImage()
            }
    }
}
```

Listing 12-8: Controlling the states of a gesture with an enumeration

This is the same example as before but now we use an enumeration to keep track of the state of the gesture. The enumeration is called `PressingState` and it includes two cases, `active` and `inactive`, and a computed property that returns a Boolean value according to the current value of the instance (`true` for `active` and `false` for `inactive`). Now, instead of defining a `@GestureState` property of type `Bool` to store the value received by the `updating()` method, we can define a property of type `PressingState` and store an enumeration value. We call this property `pressingState` and assign it to the `updating()` method. When the method is called, we assign the value `active` or `inactive` to this property depending on the value received by the method. When is time to read the state in the `opacity()` modifier, instead of reading the `@GestureState` property directly, we get the Boolean value from the `isActive` computed property defined by the enumeration. If the current value of the `pressingState` property is `active`, the `isActive` property returns `true` and the opacity is set to 0, otherwise the value returned is `false` and the opacity is set to 1. The result is the same as before but using enumerations can be necessary when working with more complex gestures or when we must combine multiple gestures, as we will see at the end of this chapter.

 Do It Yourself: Update the ContentView.swift file with the code of Listing 12-8 and run the application on the simulator. Press the image for more than a second. The sheet should open.

Basic **Drag Gesture**

The drag gesture is detected when the user touches the screen and then moves the finger to a different position. The gesture is used to move a view around according to the position of the finger (drag the view). To achieve this effect, we need multiple values, such as the location of the view and how much it moved. These values are provided by a structure of type `Value` defined by the `DragGesture` structure, which includes the following properties.

location—This property returns the current location of the finger. It is a value of type `CGPoint` with the coordinates of the location.

translation—This property returns the distance between the last location and the current one. It is a value of type `CGSize` with the difference between the coordinates.

startLocation—This property returns the initial location from where the gesture started. It is a value of type `CGPoint` with the coordinates of the location.

predictedEndLocation—This property returns the location where the dragging would stop if the gesture ends immediately. It is a value of type `CGPoint` with the coordinates of the location.

predictedEndTranslation—This property returns the distance between the last location and the location where the dragging would stop if the gesture ends immediately. It is a value of type `CGSize` with the difference between coordinates.

The coordinates returned by these properties depend on the coordinate space used by the gesture recognizer. There are two coordinate spaces: `local` and `global`. By default, the coordinate space used by the gesture recognizer is `local`, which means that the values are based on the coordinate system of the view that is being dragged, but we can set it to `global` if we need the values to be calculated according to the screen's coordinate system. For a simple drag, the `local` space is enough. For instance, the value used to estimate the position of the view is `translation`. This property returns a `CGSize` value with the difference between the location where the drag started and the new one. If we apply this offset to the view with the `offset()` modifier, the view moves to the new position, independently of the coordinate space we are working with.

```
import SwiftUI

struct ContentView: View {
    @State private var offset = CGSize.zero

    var body: some View {
        Image("spot1")
            .resizable()
            .scaledToFit()
            .frame(width: 160, height: 200)
            .offset(offset)
            .animation(.linear)

            .gesture(DragGesture(minimumDistance: 10)
                .onChanged { value in
                    self.offset = value.translation
                }
                .onEnded { value in
                    self.offset = CGSize.zero
                }
            )
    }
}
```

Listing 12-9: Defining a `DragGesture` *recognizer*

In the gesture recognizer of Listing 12-9 we use the `onChanged()` method to update the position of the view. When the user moves the finger, this method is called. The method receives a structure with all the current values, so we read the value of the `translation` property and assign it to a `@State` property called `offset`. Because we use this property to set the offset of the view, the view automatically moves to the new position, following the finger. When the user lifts the finger or the drag gesture is cancelled, the `onEnded()` method is called. In this method, we assign a `CGSize` structure with the values set to 0 to the `offset` property to return the image to its initial position.

 Do It Yourself: Create a SwiftUI project. Download the spot1.jpg image from our website and add it to the Assets Catalog. Update the `ContentView` structure with the code of Listing 12-9. Run the application on the simulator. Touch the image with your finger and move the finger around. The image should follow you. Lift the finger to terminate the gesture. The image should go back to its initial position with a linear animation.

In the last example, we used the `onChanged()` method to update the position of the view. This method is called every time the value of the state changes, but it doesn't do anything when the gesture ends. For this reason, we had to set the `offset` property to its initial value ourselves in the `onEnded()` method to move the image back to its initial position. This technique applies in some situations but most of the time it is better to let the `@GestureState` property wrapper and the `updating()` method take care of the process, as in the following example.

```
import SwiftUI

struct ContentView: View {
    @GestureState private var offset = CGSize.zero

    var body: some View {
        Image("spot1")
            .resizable()
            .scaledToFit()
            .frame(width: 160, height: 200)
            .offset(offset)
            .animation(.linear)

            .gesture(DragGesture(minimumDistance: 10)
                .updating($offset) { value, state, transition in
                    state = value.translation
                }
            )
    }
}
```

Listing 12-10: Updating the position of the view with the `updating()` *method*

The `ContentView` structure in Listing 12-10 defines the `offset` property as a `@GestureState` property, so we can use it with the `updating()` method to update the position of the view. Every time the position changes, the `updating()` method is executed and the property is updated with the value of the `translation` property. The result is the same as before, the image moves along with the finger, and when the finger is lifted or the gesture is cancelled (the finger goes outside the boundaries of the screen), the `offset` property is reset to its initial value and the image moves back to its initial position, although this time the initial value is assigned to the property by the property wrapper itself.

 Do It Yourself: Update the `ContentView` structure with the code of Listing 12-10. Run the application on the simulator and drag the image. It should work as in the previous example.

Chapter 12 - Gesture Recognizers

All the examples so far move the view back to its initial position when the drag gesture ends, but sometimes the application must let the user drag the view in successive steps, so the user can move the view to one location, leave it there, then drag it again to another location, leave it there, and so on. In cases like this, we can't use the value of the **translation** property to set the offset of the view anymore. This property returns the difference between the position where the gesture started and the current position, so its initial values are always 0 (zero). If we use this property to set the offset, at the beginning of every stage the view will go back to its original position (the coordinates 0,0). To solve this problem, we must keep track of two states, one for the movement of the finger (the translation), and another for the final offset of the view.

```
import SwiftUI

struct ContentView: View {
    @GestureState private var translation = CGSize.zero
    @State private var offset = CGSize.zero

    var body: some View {
        Image("spot1")
            .resizable()
            .scaledToFit()
            .frame(width: 160, height: 200)
            .offset(addToOffset(translation: translation))

            .gesture(DragGesture(minimumDistance: 10)
                .updating($translation) { value, state, transaction in
                    state = value.translation
                }
                .onEnded { value in
                    self.offset = self.addToOffset(translation:
value.translation)
                }
            )
    }
    func addToOffset(translation: CGSize) -> CGSize {
        let newOffset = CGSize(width: offset.width + translation.width,
height: offset.height + translation.height)
        return newOffset
    }
}
```

Listing 12-11: Dragging the view multiple times

The example in Listing 12-11 begins by defining a **@GestureState** property to track the translation (the movement of the finger), and a **@State** property to store the last view offset. The **translation** property is updated from the **updating()** method, as we did before, but now the **offset** property must be updated only when the gesture ends to set the initial offset for the next drag gesture (the initial offset is 0,0, but the successive offsets depend on the location where the user left the view the last time).

There are two times when we must calculate the offset of the view. One is when the drag gesture is taking place, and another is when the gesture ends. For this purpose, we define a method called **addToOffset()** that receives a **CGSize** value, adds it to the value of the **offset** property, and returns the result. To get the value for the **offset()** modifier and move the view along with the finger, we call this method with the current value of the **translation** property, and to assign the final offset to the **offset** property when the gesture ends, we call this method with the **translation** value received by the **onEnded()** method. As a result, every time the user moves the finger, the translation is added to the view's offset to move the view along with the finger, and when the user lifts the finger, we set the current position as the initial offset for the next drag gesture.

 Do It Yourself: Update the `ContentView` structure with the code of Listing 12-11. Run the application on the simulator. Drag the image to a different location. The image should stay in place. Drag it again. You should be able to drag the image to any place on the screen and as many times as you want.

At the time, SwiftUI does not implement functionality to perform drag and drop on mobile devices (it is only available on macOS), but we can allow the user to drag and drop elements on the same interface with the tools currently at our disposal. For instance, we can create an interface like the one in Figure 12-3, with a list of images to drag and a view below where they can be dropped.

Figure 12-3: Drag and drop interface

In this application, when the pictures at the top are dragged and dropped on the view at the bottom, they are removed from the list and the image is shown in the drop area. To process this information, we are going to need a model, and this model not only has to store the information about the pictures but also the states required for the drag and drop gesture to work.

```
import SwiftUI

struct Picture: Identifiable {
   var id: UUID = UUID()
   var image: String
}
class AppData: ObservableObject {
   @Published var userData: [Picture]

   @Published var selected: String? = nil
   @Published var dropFrame: CGRect = CGRect.zero
   @Published var dropOver: Bool = false

   init() {
      userData = [
         Picture(image: "spot1"),
         Picture(image: "spot2"),
         Picture(image: "spot3")
      ]
   }
}
```

Chapter 12 - Gesture Recognizers

```
    func remove(id: UUID) {
        if let index = userData.firstIndex(where: { $0.id == id }) {
            userData.remove(at: index)
        }
    }
}
```

Listing 12-12: Defining a model to control drag and drop

The first structure, called `Picture`, is the identifiable structure needed to store the information about each picture. In this case, we only need the `id` property to identify the values on the list, and a `String` property to store the name of the image. Next, there is the observable object. In this object, we have our typical `userData` property to store an array of values, an initializer to add a few values to populate the model, a `remove()` method to remove values from the array, and three more `@Published` properties to control the drag and drop gesture. The `selected` property stores the name of the image dropped in the drop area, the `dropFrame` property stores a `CGRect` value with the position and size of the drop area, and the `dropOver` property stores a Boolean value that indicates whether the user's finger is on top of the drop area while dragging a picture.

Now that we have the model, the next step is to define the main view, which requires a few stacks to organize the interface.

```
import SwiftUI

struct ContentView: View {
    @EnvironmentObject var appData: AppData

    var body: some View {
        VStack {
            HStack(spacing: 10) {
                ForEach(self.appData.userData) { picture in
                    PictureView(picture: picture)
                }
            }
            .frame(minWidth: 0, maxWidth: .infinity)
            .frame(height: 100)

            GeometryReader { geometry in
                VStack {
                    Image(self.appData.selected ?? "nopicture")
                        .resizable()
                        .scaledToFill()
                        .frame(minWidth: 0, maxWidth: .infinity, minHeight: 0,
maxHeight: .infinity)
                        .clipped()
                        .overlay(self.appData.dropOver ?
Color.green.opacity(0.2) : Color.clear)
                }
                .onAppear(perform: {
                    self.appData.dropFrame = geometry.frame(in: .global)
                })
            }
            .padding()
            .zIndex(-1)
        }.padding(.top)
    }
}
```

```
struct ContentView_Previews: PreviewProvider {
    static var previews: some View {
        ContentView().environmentObject(AppData())
    }
}
```

Listing 12-13: Creating the interface to drag and drop images

The interface contains two main areas organized vertically by a **VStack** (see Figure 12-3) The top area contains an **HStack** with a **ForEach** loop to display the list of pictures, and the drop area is at the bottom, defined by a **VStack** embedded in a **GeometryReader** view. Although the views created by the **ForEach** loop take care of displaying the pictures and managing the drag gesture, there are still a few tasks we must performed in the **ContentView** view to prepare the drop area. One of these tasks is to check whether a picture was already dropped in this area and show it. To be able to do this, we include an **Image** view inside the **VStack** contained by the **GeometryReader** view, If the value of the **selected** property in the model is different than **nil**, which means that a picture was already dropped in the drop area, we show that image, otherwise we show the image nopicture.

Another task our code must perform is to determine if the picture being dragged by the user is inside the drop area. To get the information required to do it, we apply the **onAppear()** modifier to the **VStack** view. When the view appears, we get its position and size in the global coordinate space and store the values in the **dropFrame** property of our observable object, so we can use them later to determine if the finger is inside this area.

The information required for the user to drop a picture in the drop area is ready, but we still must solve a few issues with the interface. First, we must consider that the **GeometryReader** view is created after the container for the pictures, so it's going to appear in front of them. To move it to the back, we must assign a lower Z index to it with the **zIndex()** modifier (see Listing 6-54). In this example, we assign the value -1, which moves the view to the back in the Z axis and therefore the pictures dragged by the user will appear in front of it. Another issue with the interface is that there is no indication for the user to know where he or she is allowed to drop the picture. For this purpose, we create an overlay with the **overlay()** modifier and the value of the **dropOver** property. If the value of this property is **true**, which means that the picture is inside the drop area, we assign a translucent color to the overlay, otherwise the color is clear.

The drop area is ready. Now, we must set up the drag and drop process for each picture in the **PictureView** view. The following is our implementation of this view.

```
import SwiftUI

struct PictureView: View {
    @EnvironmentObject var appData: AppData

    @State private var offset = CGSize.zero
    var picture: Picture

    var body: some View {
        Image(picture.image)
            .resizable()
            .scaledToFit()
            .offset(offset)
            .gesture(DragGesture(coordinateSpace: .global)
                .onChanged { value in
                    self.appData.dropOver =
self.appData.dropFrame.contains(value.location)
                    self.offset = value.translation
                }
```

```
            .onEnded { value in
                if self.appData.dropOver {
                    self.appData.selected = self.picture.image
                    self.appData.remove(id: self.picture.id)
                    self.appData.dropOver = false
                } else {
                    self.offset = CGSize.zero
                }
            }
        )
    }
}
struct PictureView_Previews: PreviewProvider {
    static var previews: some View {
        PictureView(picture: Picture(image: "spot1"))
            .environmentObject(AppData())
    }
}
```

Listing 12-14: Managing the drag gesture

This is the view used by the **ForEach** loop to display each picture. The view contains a single **Image** view, but with all the modifiers necessary to allow the user to drag it. The code to configure the drag gesture is the same as before, but we must control a few more values to allow the user to drop the picture in the drop area. First, we determine if the picture is inside the drop area with the **contains()** method. This method checks whether the point in a **CGPoint** value is inside the rectangle determined by a **CGRect** value and returns **true** in case of success or **false** otherwise. In our example, we use it every time the state of the drag gesture changes to detect if the current location of the finger (**value.location**) is inside the rectangle occupied by the drop area (**self.appData.dropFrame**), and assign the result to the **dropOver** property.

When the gesture ends, either because the user lifted the finger or moved it outside the boundaries of the screen, the **onEnded()** method is executed. Here is where we must determine if the user was trying to drop the picture in the drop area or not. For this purpose, we check the value of the **dropOver** property. If the value is **true**, which means that the picture is inside the drop area, we assign the name of the image to the **selected** property. This tells the **ContentView** view that it must show this image in the drop area. Next, we call the **remove()** method on the model to remove the image. And finally, we set the **dropOver** property to **false** to let the user drag and drop another picture. Notice that if the value of the **dropOver** property is **false**, we just set the **offset** property to **zero**, as we did in a previous example, so the picture is moved back to the list. The result of this process is shown in Figure 12-4.

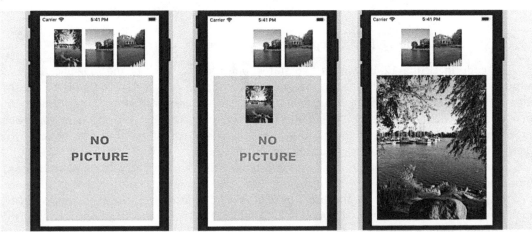

Figure 12-4: Pictures dragged and dropped in the drop area

Chapter 12 - Gesture Recognizers   473 | P a g e

Do It Yourself: Create a SwiftUI project. Download the nopicture.png, spot1.jpg, spot2.jpg, and spot3.jpg images from our website and add them to the Assets Catalog. Create a Swift file called AppData.swift for the model of Listing 12-12. Update the AppDelegate.swift file with the code of Listing 7-14 and the SceneDelegate.swift file with the code of Listing 7-20 to instantiate the model and insert it in the environment. Update the ContentView.swift file with the code of Listing 12-13. Create a Swift file called PictureView.swift for the view in Listing 12-14. Run the application. You should be able to drag and drop the pictures in the drop area, as shown in Figure 12-4.

Basic Magnification Gesture

The magnification gesture is usually called the pinch gesture, because it is the gesture detected when the user moves two fingers apart or bring them together as if he or she were pinching the screen. This gesture is mostly implemented to let the user zoom an image in and out.

The value sent to the **updating()**, **onChanged()** and **onEnded()** methods is a **CGFloat** that represents a multiple of the current scale, so we must multiply this value by the current scale to get the final scale of the picture, as in the following example.

```
import SwiftUI

struct ContentView: View {
    @GestureState private var magnification: CGFloat = 1
    @State private var zoom: CGFloat = 1

    var body: some View {
        Image("spot1")
            .resizable()
            .scaledToFit()
            .frame(width: 160, height: 200)
            .scaleEffect(zoom * magnification)

            .gesture(MagnificationGesture()
                .updating($magnification) { value, state, transition in
                    state = value
                }
                .onEnded { value in
                    self.zoom = self.zoom * value
                }
            )
    }
}
```

Listing 12-15: Defining a MagnificationGesture *recognizer*

The code in Listing 12-15 defines two states, one to keep track of the magnification and another to store the final value. This is the same we did for the drag gesture in Listing 12-11. The idea is to let the user zoom in and out multiple times. While the gesture is performed, the magnification value is stored in the **magnification** property, but the value of the **zoom** property is only modified when the gesture is over, so the next time the user tries to zoom the picture in or out, the new scale is calculated from the last one.

To set the scale of the image to the one selected by the user, we apply the **scaleEffect()** modifier to the **Image** view and calculate the new scale by multiplying the value of the **zoom** property (the last scale set by the user) by the value of the **magnification** property (the multiple generated by the gesture). As a result, the image is zoomed in and out following the movement of the fingers.

Do It Yourself: Create a SwiftUI project. Download the spot1.jpg image from our website and added to the Assets Catalog. Update the `ContentView` structure with the code of Listing 12-15 and run the application. Pinch the view with two fingers to zoom it in or out.

The example of Listing 12-15 lets the user zoom the image in and out as far as he or she wants, but most of the time we must limit the scale of the view to values that make sense for the interface and the purpose of the application. To establish these limits, the scale must be controlled in two places: when it is applied to the view with the `scaleEffect()` modifier and when the gesture ends and the final scale is assigned to the `zoom` property.

```
import SwiftUI
struct ContentView: View {
    @GestureState private var magnification: CGFloat = 1
    @State private var zoom: CGFloat = 1

    var body: some View {
        Image("spot1")
            .resizable()
            .scaledToFit()
            .frame(width: 160, height: 200)
            .scaleEffect(getCurrentZoom(magnification: self.magnification))

            .gesture(MagnificationGesture()
                .updating($magnification) { value, state, transition in
                    state = value
                }
                .onEnded { value in
                    self.zoom = self.getCurrentZoom(magnification: value)
                }
            )
    }
    func getCurrentZoom(magnification: CGFloat) -> CGFloat {
        let minZoom: CGFloat = 1
        let maxZoom: CGFloat = 2

        var current = self.zoom * magnification
        current = max(min(current, maxZoom), minZoom)
        return current
    }
}
```

Listing 12-16: Determining a minimum and a maximum scale

The example in Listing 12-16 limits the scale of the view to a minimum of 1 and a maximum of 2. Because there are a few operations we must perform to limit the scale to these values, we move the process to a method called `getCurrentZoom()` and call this method every time necessary. The method defines two constants with the minimum and maximum values for the scale, then calculates the current scale by multiplying the values of the `zoom` property by the magnification, and limits the result to a minimum of 1 and a maximum of 2 with the `max()` and `min()` functions (see Listing 3-16). The `min()` function compares the scale with the maximum scale allowed and returns the smallest value (if the value is greater than 2, it returns 2), and then the `max()` function compares the result with the minimum scale allowed and returns the largest value (if the value is less than 1, it returns 1). The method is called by the `scaleEffect()` modifier to set the scale for the view, and by the `onEnded()` method to set the final scale. Consequently, the user can zoom the image in and out, but up to a maximum of 2 and a minimum of 1.

Do It Yourself: Update the `ContentView` structure with the code of Listing 12-16 and run the application. You should be able to scale the view to the limits set by the `minZoom` and `maxZoom` constants.

(Basic) **Rotation Gesture**

The rotation gesture is recognized when the user touches the screen with two fingers and performs a circular motion. It is often used to rotate an image. As with previous gestures, if we want to let the user perform the gesture multiple times, we need to keep track of two states, one for the current rotation and another for the last rotation. The value produced by the gesture is a structure of type `Angle`. We work with this structure before. It includes two type methods, one to create an instance with a value in degrees (`degrees(Double)`) and another to do it with a value in radians (`radians(Double)`), but in our example we are going to rotate an image to follow the fingers, and for that we just need to add the current angle to the delta angle produced by the gesture.

```
import SwiftUI
struct ContentView: View {
   @GestureState private var rotationAngle: Angle = Angle.zero
   @State private var rotation: Angle = Angle.zero

   var body: some View {
      Image("spot1")
         .resizable()
         .scaledToFit()
         .frame(width: 160, height: 200)
         .rotationEffect(rotation + rotationAngle)

         .gesture(RotationGesture()
            .updating($rotationAngle) { value, state, transition in
               state = value
            }
            .onEnded { value in
               self.rotation = self.rotation + value
            }
         )
   }
}
```

Listing 12-17: Defining a RotationGesture *recognizer*

The example in Listing 12-17 applies the `rotationEffect()` modifier to the view to rotate it. The angle is calculated by adding the values of the two state properties. We also add the current rotation to the previous one when the gesture ends to preserve the current state in case the user wants to rotate the image again from that angle.

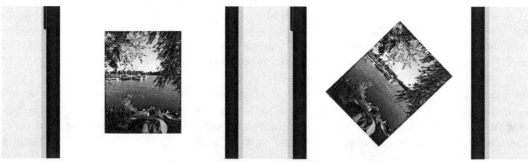

Figure 12-5: Image rotated by the user

Chapter 12 - Gesture Recognizers

Do It Yourself: Update the `ContentView` structure from the previous example with the code of Listing 12-17 and run the application. You should be able to rotate the view with your fingers, as shown in Figure 12-5.

Medium **Composing Gestures**

The gesture recognizers provided by SwiftUI recognize simple gestures, but they can be combined to detect complex interactions. The `Gesture` protocol defines the following methods for this purpose.

sequenced(before: Gesture)—This method creates a structure of type `SequenceGesture` that defines a sequence with the gesture and the gesture provided by the **before** attribute. The gesture from which the method is called is recognized first, and the gesture specified by the attribute is recognized second.

simultaneously(with: Gesture)—This method creates a structure of type `SimultaneousGesture` that recognizes the gesture and the one provided by the attribute simultaneously.

These methods are implemented like the rest of the methods defined by the `Gesture` protocol. We must call them on an instance of a gesture structure. After one of these methods is called, the gesture is contained in a `SequenceGesture` or `SimultaneousGesture` structure, and therefore the values passed to the `updating()`, `onChanged()` and `onEnded()` methods are different. To create these values, the `SequenceGesture` or `SimultaneousGesture` structures define an enumeration with the following cases.

first(First.Value)—This case is returned when the first gesture hasn't ended. It contains an associated value with the value produced by the first gesture.

second(First.Value, Second.Value)—This case is returned when the first gesture has ended. It contains two associated values. The first value is the last value produced by the first gesture, and the second value is the value produced by the second gesture.

The best way to understand how to work with these values is with an example. We are going to reproduce the project we have created before for the drag gesture, but combine that gesture with a long press gesture, so the user must press the image for a second before being able to drag it.

Because composing gestures requires tracking multiple states, it is better to define the `@GestureState` with an enumeration, as we did in the example of Listing 12-10. In our example, we call this enumeration `GesturesControl`.

```
import SwiftUI

enum GesturesControl {
   case inactive
   case active
   case dragging(translation: CGSize)

   var isActive: Bool {
     switch self {
       case .active:
          return true
       default:
          return false
     }
   }
}
```

```
    var isDragging: Bool {
        switch self {
        case .dragging:
            return true
        default:
            return false
        }
    }
    var translation: CGSize {
        switch self {
        case .dragging(let translation):
            return translation
        default:
            return .zero
        }
    }
}
struct ContentView: View {
    @GestureState private var control = GesturesControl.inactive
    @State private var offset = CGSize.zero

    var body: some View {
        Image("spot1")
            .resizable()
            .scaledToFit()
            .frame(width: 160, height: 200)

            .overlay(control.isActive ? Color.white.opacity(0.1) :
Color.clear)
            .animation(nil)
            .scaleEffect(control.isDragging ? 1.1 : 1.0)
            .shadow(color: control.isDragging ? Color.black : Color.clear,
radius: 5, x: 0, y: 0)
            .animation(.easeOut(duration: 0.2))
            .offset(addToOffset(translation: control.translation))

            .gesture(LongPressGesture(minimumDuration: 1)
                .sequenced(before: DragGesture())
                .updating($control) { value, state, transaction in
                    switch value {
                    case .first(true):
                        state = .active
                    case .second(true, let dragValues):
                        state = .dragging(translation:
dragValues?.translation ?? CGSize.zero)
                    default:
                        state = .inactive
                    }
                }
                .onEnded { value in
                    if case .second(true, let dragValues?) = value {
                        self.offset = self.addToOffset(translation:
dragValues.translation)
                    }
                }
            )
    }
    func addToOffset(translation: CGSize) -> CGSize {
        let newOffset = CGSize(
            width: offset.width + translation.width,
            height: offset.height + translation.height
        )
```

```
        return newOffset
    }
}
```

Listing 12-18: Composing gestures

The enumeration defines three values, `inactive` to indicate nothing is happening, `active` to indicate that the user is touching the image, and `dragging` to indicate that the long press gesture ended and the image is being dragged. The `dragging` value has an associated value to store the translation, so we don't need another state to store the displacement.

The enumeration also includes convenient computed properties to turn the enumeration values into values we can use to set the view. The `isActive` property returns `true` if the value of the enumeration is `active` or `false` otherwise. The `isDragging` property returns `true` if the value of the enumeration is `dragging` or `false` otherwise. And the `translation` property returns the associated value when the value of the enumeration is `dragging`, otherwise it returns a `CGSize` structure with the values set to zero (`zero`).

With these values in place, we can now recognize the gestures. We first initialize the `LongPressGesture` structure and then call the `sequenced()` method on it with an instance of the `DragGesture` structure. This method creates a `SequenceGesture` structure with the long press gesture as the first gesture and the drag gesture as the second. After that, we implement the `updating()` method with a `@GestureState` property called `control`. This property is initialized with the `inactive` value, which means that no gesture is being performed at the time. To determine if the state of the gestures changed, we must read the values produced by the `SequenceGesture` structure. If the value is `first`, it means that the long press gesture started, so we set the state as `active`. Notice that when the state is active, the `overlay()` modifier adds a translucent `Color` view on top of the `Image` view. This is to tell the user that the process started. On the other hand, if the value produced by the `SequenceGesture` structure is `second`, it means that the long press gesture ended or the drag gesture is taking place. In either situation, we set the state to `dragging`. The way to know why the `second` value was returned is by checking the second associated value. This value, that we called `dragValues` in our example, is `nil` if the `second` value is returned because the long press gesture ended, and not `nil` if the `second` value was returned because the user is dragging the image. Therefore, if the long press gesture ended but the drag gesture hasn't started yet, we provide the value `CGSize.zero` as the associated value of the `dragging` state, otherwise we assign the value of the `translation` property to keep track of the position of the view.

After this, we implement the `onEnded()` method to store the last position when the drag gesture ends. Because this method can also be called by the long press gesture, we check that the value returned by the `SequenceGesture` structure is `second` and then add the current translation to the `offset` property (see Listing 3-140).

As we already mentioned, there is an `overlay()` modifier that shows a translucent view on top of the image when the state is `active`, but there are also a `scaleEffect()` and a `shadow()` modifier that change the scale and the color of the shadow when the state is `dragging`. This helps the user identify the image that is being dragged from the rest of the interface. All these effects disappear when the value of the `control` property is set back to its `inactive` value by the `updating()` method after the gestures are over.

Figure 12-6: Composed gestures

 Do It Yourself: Create a SwiftUI project. Download the spot1.jpg image from our website and add it to the Assets Catalog. Update the ContentView.swift file with the code of Listing 12-18. Run the application on the simulator. After pressing the image for 1 second, you should see the effects applied to it (Figure 12-6, right) and should be able to drag it around.

Chapter 12 - Gesture Recognizers

⟨ Basic ⟩ 13.1 Notification Center

Besides the techniques we have seen so far to transfer data between different parts of an application, such as sending values from one view to another or providing a common model from which every view can get the information it needs, we can also send notifications to report changes across the application. Foundation includes the `NotificationCenter` class from which the system creates an object that serves as a Notification Center for the whole application. We can send notifications (messages) to this object and then listen to those notifications from anywhere in the code. The class includes the following property to get a reference to this object.

default—This type property returns the `NotificationCenter` object assigned to the application by default.

The `NotificationCenter` class includes the following method to post notifications.

post(Notification)—This method posts a notification to the Notification Center. The attribute is a structure of type `Notification` with the information to be sent.

post(name: Name, **object:** Any, **userInfo:** Dictionary)—This method creates a new notification and posts it to the Notification Center. The **name** attribute is the name of the notification, the **object** attribute is a reference to the object or a copy of the structure that sent the notification, and the **userInfo** attribute is a dictionary with additional information.

Notifications are created from the `Notification` class. The following is the class' initializer.

Notification(name: Name, **object:** Any, **userInfo:** Dictionary)—This initializer creates a `Notification` structure with the information defined by the attributes. The **name** attribute is the name of the notification, the **object** attribute is a reference to the object or a copy of the structure that is sending the notification, and the **userInfo** attribute is a dictionary with additional information.

The `Notification` class includes the following properties to read the notification's values.

name—This property returns the name of the notification.

object—This property returns the object or the structure that posted the notification.

userInfo—This property returns the dictionary attached to the notification.

The name of the notification is created from a structure included in the `Notification` structure called **Name**. The structure provides the following initializer to define new names.

Name(String)—This initializer creates a structure that represents the notification's name. The attribute is a string with the name we want to assign to the notification.

In SwiftUI, notifications are sent and received using Combine. A notification is published by the Notification Center and it is received by a subscriber. The `NotificationCenter` class includes the `Publisher` structure to create a publisher that emits a notification. The following is the structure's initializer.

Publisher(center: NotificationCenter, name: Name, object: AnyObject)—This initializer creates a `Publisher` structure that emits a notification. The **center** attribute is a reference to the Notification Center assigned to the application, the **name** attribute is the name of the notification we want to emit, and the **object** attribute is a reference to the object posting the notification. This last value determines which object is allowed to emit the notification. If the value is declared as `nil` or the attribute is ignored, the publisher emits all the notifications with the name specified by the **name** attribute, no matter who posted it.

The `NotificationCenter` class also implements a convenient method to create this publisher.

publisher(for: Name, object: Object)—This method publishes a notification. The **for** attribute is the name of the notification, and the **object** attribute is a reference to the object posting the notification. This last value determines which object is allowed to emit the notification. If the value is declared as `nil` or the attribute is ignored, the publisher emits all the notifications with the name specified by the **for** attribute, no matter who posted it.

Notifications are used for multiple purposes. We can post a notification after a long process is over to tell the system that it is time to update the interface, we can communicate views with each other, or we can keep a view up to date posting notifications from the model with information we receive from the Internet, to name a few. The following example includes a model that posts a notification every time a new value is inserted by the user. For didactic purposes, we are going to use a simple interface that includes a view to show the number of books stored in the model and another to insert new ones.

Figure 13-1: Interface to test notifications

In the model, we must create a publisher and then post a notification every time a new book is inserted by the user., so the initial view can update its interface.

```
import SwiftUI

struct Book {
   var title: String
}
struct BookViewModel: Identifiable {
   var id = UUID()
   var book: Book
}
class AppData: ObservableObject {
   @Published var userData: [BookViewModel] = []

   let publisher = NotificationCenter.Publisher(center: .default, name:
Notification.Name("Update Data"))
      .receive(on: RunLoop.main)
```

Chapter 13 - Notifications

```
func addBook(book: Book) {
    userData.append(BookViewModel(book: book))

    let center = NotificationCenter.default
    let notification = Notification(name: Notification.Name("Update
Data"), object: userData.count, userInfo: nil)
    center.post(notification)
    }
}
```

Listing 13-1: Sending notifications from the model

The model in Listing 13-1 includes the `Book` structure to store the title of each book, the `BookViewModel` structure to prepare the data to be shown by the views, and the observable object to store all the values. In this object, we define a `Publisher` structure that works with the Notification Center assigned to the application by default (`default`), and a notification called "Update Data". When a notification with this name is posted from anywhere in the code, the publisher emits the value and we can read it from the views. The observable object also includes a method called `addBook()` to store a book and post the notification. First, we get a reference to the Notification Center by default. Then, we create a notification with the name "Update Data" and the integer returned by the `count` property (the number of books in the model). And finally, we post the notification with the `post()` method. Notice that we apply the `receive()` operator to the publisher to make sure that the value is received in the main queue.

The initial view has to subscribe to the publisher to receive this notification. For this purpose, we use the `onReceive()` modifier. We have implemented this modifier before when we were publishing values from the `Timer` structure (see Listing 7-31). The modifier needs a reference to the publisher and a closure to receive and process the value, as shown next.

```
import SwiftUI

struct ContentView: View {
    @EnvironmentObject var appData: AppData
    @State private var total: Int = 0

    var body: some View {
        NavigationView {
            VStack {
                HStack {
                    Text("Total Books:")
                    Text("\(total)")
                        .font(.largeTitle)
                }
                Spacer()
            }.padding()
            .navigationBarTitle("Books")
            .navigationBarItems(trailing: NavigationLink("Add Book",
destination: AddBook()))
        }
        .onReceive(appData.publisher, perform: { notification in
            if let value = notification.object as? Int {
                self.total = value
            }
        })
    }
}
```

Listing 13-2: Receiving the value with a subscriber

The view in Listing 13-2 defines a @State property to store the total number of books. When the onReceive() modifier receives a value from the publisher, it assigns it to this property, so the interface is always up-to-date. But this value is not the integer assigned to the notification, it is a Notification structure. To get the integer that represents the total number of books in the model, we must read the notification's object property and convert it into an Int value. If the process is successful, we assign the integer to the total property and the value is shown on the screen.

The following is the AddBook view opened by the Add Book button to insert new books. The view includes a TextField view to insert a value and a Button view to save it.

```
import SwiftUI

struct AddBook: View {
    @EnvironmentObject var appData: AppData
    @Environment(\.presentationMode) var presentation
    @State private var titleInput: String = ""

    var body: some View {
        VStack {
            HStack {
                Text("Title")
                TextField("Insert title", text: $titleInput)
                    .textFieldStyle(RoundedBorderTextFieldStyle())
            }
            HStack {
                Spacer()
                Button("Save") {
                    let title = self.titleInput.trimmingCharacters(in:
.whitespaces)
                    if !title.isEmpty {
                        self.appData.addBook(book: Book(title: title))
                        self.titleInput = ""
                        self.presentation.wrappedValue.dismiss()
                    }
                }
            }
            Spacer()
        }.padding()
        .navigationBarTitle("Add Book")
    }
}
```

Listing 13-3: Inserting values in the model

When the button is pressed, we trim the string to remove spaces, check that the value is not an empty string, and call the addBook() method in the observable object to add the book to the model. Once the book is added, the method creates the notification, posts it, and the initial view receives the notification and updates the interface.

 Do It Yourself: Create a SwiftUI project. Create a Swift file called AppData.swift for the model of Listing 13-1. Update the AppDelegate.swift file with the code of Listing 7-14 and the SceneDelegate.swift file with the code of Listing 7-20 to instantiate the model and insert it in the environment. Update the ContentView structure with the code of Listing 13-2. Create a SwiftUI file called AddBook.swift for the view in Listing 13-3. Run the application on the simulator or a device (recommended). Press the Add Book button, insert a title, and press the Save button. You should see the number 1 on the initial screen indicating that there is one book in the model.

Chapter 13 - Notifications

As we mentioned in previous chapters, in SwiftUI, views should only be responsible for showing the interface. Tasks like converting or processing values, should be done by the model. In our example, we are extracting the integer value we need to update the view from the `Notification` structure received by the subscriber. This can become problematic when multiple views receive this same value. A solution is to filter the value produced by the publisher with operators. In this case, we can use a `map()` operator to extract the integer from the `Notification` value and emit that integer instead.

```
import SwiftUI

struct Book {
    var title: String
}
struct BookViewModel: Identifiable {
    var id = UUID()
    var book: Book
}
class AppData: ObservableObject {
    @Published var userData: [BookViewModel] = []

    let publisher = NotificationCenter.Publisher(center: .default, name:
Notification.Name("Update Data"))
        .map { notification -> Int in
            if let value = notification.object as? Int {
                return value
            } else {
                return 0
            }
        }
        .receive(on: RunLoop.main)

    func addBook(book: Book) {
        userData.append(BookViewModel(book: book))

        let center = NotificationCenter.default
        center.post(name: Notification.Name("Update Data"), object:
userData.count)
    }
}
```

Listing 13-4: Filtering the values emitted by the publisher

The publisher in Listing 13-4 is modified by the `map()` operator. The operator receives the `Notification` structure and returns another publisher that emits an integer value. Notice that in this example we also simplified the creation of the notification with the additional `post()` method offered by the `NotificationCenter` class. This method takes care of creating and posting the `Notification` structure, so we don't have to create the structure ourselves. When the method is executed, the notification is posted to the Notification Center, the publisher emits the value, the `map()` operator gets the integer and returns a new publisher that emits that number. On the view, the `onReceive()` modifier receives the integer, assign it to the `total` property, and the value is shown on the screen. But this time the value received by the view is of type `Int`, so we don't have to get it from the `object` property anymore, as shown next.

```
.onReceive(appData.publisher, perform: { value in
    self.total = value
})
```

Listing 13-5: Receiving integer values

Do It Yourself: Update the AppData.swift file with the code of Listing 13-4 and the `ContentView` structure with the code of Listing 13-5. Run the application on the simulator or a device (recommended). Press the Add Book button, insert a title, and press the Save button. You should see the number 1 again on the initial screen.

(Medium) **System Notifications**

Besides the notifications posted by our app, the system also posts notifications to the Notification Center all the time to report changes in the interface or the device. There are dozens of notifications available. They work exactly like the custom notifications studied before but are predefined as type properties of UIKit classes. We will probably never use most of the notifications available, but some are very useful. For example, the following are the properties available from the `UIWindow` class to get the notifications related to the keyboard.

keyboardWillShowNotification—This notification is posted before the keyboard is shown.

keyboardDidShowNotification—This notification is posted after the keyboard was shown.

keyboardWillHideNotification—This notification is posted before the keyboard is hidden.

keyboardDidHideNotification—This notification is posted after the keyboard was hidden.

keyboardWillChangeFrameNotification—This notification is posted before the keyboard's frame changes (due to a device rotation).

keyboardDidChangeFrameNotification—This notification is posted after the keyboard's frame changes (due to a device rotation).

These notifications not only report the state of the keyboard, but they also provide the values of the keyboard's frame through the `userInfo` property, so we can calculate the space available to reposition the views in the interface. The values in the `userInfo` dictionary are identified by strings stored in additional `UIWindow` properties. The most frequently used properties are `keyboardFrameBeginUserInfoKey` (returns a value with the frame occupied by the keyboard when closed) and `keyboardFrameEndUserInfoKey` (returns a value with the frame occupied by the keyboard when opened). What we do with these values depends on our application and what we want to achieve, but they are commonly used to move up the interface when the input field the user is typing in is covered by the keyboard, as shown in Figure 13-2.

Figure 13-2: Interface to test keyboard notifications

Chapter 13 - Notifications

To create this example, we need to define two publishers in our model, one to emit a value when the `keyboardWillShowNotification` notification is received (the keyboard is opened), and another to emit a value when the `keyboardDidShowNotification` notification is received (the keyboard is closed).

```
import SwiftUI
struct Book {
   var title: String
}
struct BookViewModel: Identifiable {
   var id = UUID()
   var book: Book
}
class AppData: ObservableObject {
   @Published var userData: [BookViewModel] = []

   let openPublisher = NotificationCenter.Publisher(center: .default,
name: UIWindow.keyboardWillShowNotification)
      .map({ notification -> CGFloat in
         if let info = notification.userInfo {
            let value = info[UIWindow.keyboardFrameEndUserInfoKey] as!
NSValue
            let height = value.cgRectValue.height
            return height
         } else {
            return 0
         }
      })
      .receive(on: RunLoop.main)

   let closePublisher = NotificationCenter.Publisher(center: .default,
name: UIWindow.keyboardDidHideNotification)
      .receive(on: RunLoop.main)
}
```

Listing 13-6: Publishing keyboard notifications

The `openPublisher` publisher emits a value when the keyboard is opened. The value attached to the notification is a dictionary with information about the keyboard, but all we need to calculate the new interface is the keyboard's height. To get this value, we apply the `map()` operator. The operator gets the value from the notification's `userInfo` property, then reads the value associated to the `keyboardFrameEndUserInfoKey` key in the dictionary, and finally gets the height of the keyboard from the frame returned by the key.

Notice that the value returned by the `keyboardFrameEndUserInfoKey` key is of type `NSValue`. This is a basic class in Foundation that can store values of different types, including all the structures from the Core Graphics framework. The only problem is that the class was designed to store objects, not structures, so it provides some properties that return the structure we need. The following are the most frequently used.

cgRectValue—This property returns a `CGRect` value.

cgSizeValue—This property returns a `CGSize` value.

cgPointValue—This property returns a `CGPoint` value.

The second publisher in our model, `closePublisher`, emits a value when the keyboard is closed. In this case, all we need to know for our example is that the keyboard is no longer visible, so we can ignore the value.

Now, it is time to subscribe to these publishers from the view and adapt the interface accordingly. For this purpose, we must calculate the position and size of the `TextField` view with a `GeometryReader` view and then estimate how much we must move the interface up to make this view visible again when the keyboard is opened.

```swift
import SwiftUI

struct ContentView: View {
    @EnvironmentObject var appData: AppData
    @State private var textInput: String = ""
    @State private var offsetContainer: CGSize = CGSize.zero

    var body: some View {
        VStack {
            Image("spot1")
                .resizable()
                .scaledToFit()
            TextField("Insert Caption", text: self.$textInput)
                .textFieldStyle(RoundedBorderTextFieldStyle())
                .background(BackgroundView(offset: $offsetContainer))
            Spacer()
        }.padding()
        .offset(self.offsetContainer)
        .animation(.linear)
        .onReceive(self.appData.closePublisher, perform: { value in
            self.offsetContainer.height = 0
        })
    }
}
struct BackgroundView: View {
    @EnvironmentObject var appData: AppData
    @Binding var offset: CGSize

    var body: some View {
        GeometryReader { geometry in
            Color.clear
                .onReceive(self.appData.openPublisher, perform: {
keyboardHeight in
                    let screenWidth = UIScreen.main.bounds.width
                    let screenHeight = UIScreen.main.bounds.height
                    let visibleFrame = CGRect(x: 0, y: 0, width: screenWidth,
height: screenHeight - keyboardHeight)

                    let textFrame = geometry.frame(in: .global)
                    if !visibleFrame.contains(textFrame) {
                        let newOffset = visibleFrame.height -
geometry.size.height - 20 - textFrame.origin.y
                        self.offset.height = newOffset
                    }
                })
        }
    }
}
```

Listing 13-7: Moving the interface up

As we have seen in Chapter 9 (see Listing 9-55), to measure the position and size of a view, we must declare the `GeometryReader` view as a secondary view with the `background()` or `overlay()` modifiers. In Listing 13-7, we use it as a background view, but we define it in a custom view called `BackgroundView` to have more room to process the values. In this view, we apply the `onReceive()` modifier to the `Color` view assigned as the background. When a value

Chapter 13 - Notifications

is received from the **openPublisher** publisher, we calculate the offset we must apply to the interface to uncover the text field. First, we get the width and height of the screen from the **UIScreen** object. Next, we determine the frame of the remaining area on top of the keyboard. The width of this area is the same as the screen, but the height is the space remaining on the screen after the keyboard is shown (**screenHeight - keyboardHeight**). Then, we get the position and size of the **TextField** view with the **frame(in:)** method, and check whether this frame is inside the visible area with the **contains()** method of the **CGRect** structure (see Listing 4-51). If the **TextField** view is not inside the visible area, it means that it is behind the keyboard, so we must move the interface up. For this purpose, we calculate the offset plus 20 points to move it a little bit over the keyboard and assign the result to the **offset** property. Back in the **ContentView** view, this value is assigned to the **VStack** view with the **offset()** modifier, and therefore the whole interface moves up and the text field becomes visible again.

Finally, we apply another **onReceive()** modifier, in this case to the **VStack** view, to subscribe to the **closePublisher** publisher and set the offset back to 0 when the keyboard is dismissed. The result is shown in Figure 13-2, above.

 Do It Yourself: Create a SwiftUI project. Download the spot1.jpg image from our website and add it to the Assets Catalog. Create a Swift file called AppData.swift for the model of Listing 13-6. Update the AppDelegate.swift file with the code of Listing 7-14 and the SceneDelegate.swift file with the code of Listing 7-20 to instantiate the model and insert it in the environment. Update the ContentView.swift file with the code of Listing 13-7. Run the application on a simulator or a device (recommended). When you tap on the text field, the interface should move up, and when you press the Return key on the keyboard, the interface should move back to its original position.

If the interface includes multiple text fields, we must embed it in a **ScrollView** view to allow the user to scroll it up and down when necessary. At the time of writing, SwiftUI does not include the tools to scroll the content of a **ScrollView** view programmatically, but we can still apply an offset to the content to move it up and uncover the text field selected by the user.

The process is the same as before, but because we are working with multiple **TextField** views, we need to make sure that the offset is set for the text field that is currently active. For this purpose, we are going to define a **@State** property to store an index that identifies the text field selected by the user and implement the **onEditingChanged** attribute to change this value (see Listing 8-8).

```
import SwiftUI

struct ContentView: View {
    @EnvironmentObject var appData: AppData
    @State private var offsetContainer: CGSize = CGSize.zero
    @State private var selectedField: Int? = nil

    @State private var textInput: [String] = Array.init(repeating: "",
count: 10)
    let listLabels = ["Name", "Last Name", "Nickname", "Street", "Suite",
"Postal Code", "City", "State", "Country", "Occupation"]

    var body: some View {
        ScrollView {
            VStack {
                Image("spot1")
                    .resizable()
                    .scaledToFit()
```

```
                    ForEach(0..<10, id: \.self) { index in
                        HStack {
                            Text("\(self.listLabels[index]):")
                            TextField("Insert \(self.listLabels[index])", text:
self.$textInput[index], onEditingChanged: { value in
                                self.selectedField = value ? index : nil
                            }).textFieldStyle(RoundedBorderTextFieldStyle())
                        }
                        .background(BackgroundView(offset: self.$offsetContainer,
selected: self.$selectedField, index: index))
                    }
                    Spacer()
                }.padding()
                .offset(self.offsetContainer)
            }
            .animation(.linear)
            .onReceive(self.appData.closePublisher, perform: { value in
                self.offsetContainer.height = 0
            })
        }
    }
}
struct BackgroundView: View {
    @EnvironmentObject var appData: AppData
    @Binding var offset: CGSize
    @Binding var selected: Int?
    let index: Int

    var body: some View {
        GeometryReader { geometry in
            Color.clear
                .onReceive(self.appData.openPublisher, perform: {
keyboardHeight in
                    if let selIndex = self.selected, selIndex == self.index {
                        let screenWidth = UIScreen.main.bounds.width
                        let screenHeight = UIScreen.main.bounds.height
                        let visibleFrame = CGRect(x: 0, y: 0, width:
screenWidth, height: screenHeight - keyboardHeight)

                        let textFrame = geometry.frame(in: .global)
                        if !visibleFrame.contains(textFrame) {
                            let newOffset = visibleFrame.height -
geometry.size.height - 20 - textFrame.origin.y
                            self.offset.height = newOffset
                        }
                    }
                })
        }
    }
}
```

Listing 13-8: Working with multiple text fields

For didactical purposes, the view in Listing 13-8 defines a `ForEach` loop that creates up to 10 `TextField` views below the image. Each row includes a label and a text field with values defined in an array called `listLabels`. To manage the values inserted in these text fields, we define a `@State` property with an array of `String` values and initialize it with 10 elements and empty strings. The index of the active text field is stored in another `@State` property called `selectedField`. When the state of a text field changes, either because the user taps on it or taps on another view, the closure assigned to the `onEditingChanged` attribute is executed. If the value received by this closure is `true`, we assign the index of that text field to the

selectedField property, otherwise, we assign the value **nil** to communicate to the rest of the code that the text field is not active anymore. The index assigned to this property is generated by the **ForEach** loop, and it is also passed to the **BackgroundView** view to let the view know which text field it belongs to.

Nothing changes in the **BackgroundView** view, but now we only modify the offset if the view is part of the active **TextField** view (**let selIndex = self.selected, selIndex == self.index**). The result is the same, but now the interface includes multiple text fields and the users can scroll it up or down the select the one they want to work with.

Figure 13-3: Scrolling interface with multiple text fields

 Do It Yourself: Update the ContentView.swift file with the code of Listing 13-8. Run the application on the simulator or a device (recommended). You should see the interface in Figure 13-3, left. Scroll the Interface and tap on a text field. If the text field is covered by the keyboard, the interface should move to make it visible.

 IMPORTANT: Changing the offset of the content of the **ScrollView** view is not the same as scrolling the view. When the content is displaced with the **offset()** modifier, parts of the interface become inaccessible. The solution implemented in this example is one of many tricks we can use to solve this issue until the right tools become available.

The keyboard appears when the user taps on a text field and disappears when the user presses the Return button on the keyboard. This functionality is provided by the system by default, we don't have to do anything to enable it, but sometimes is not enough. To dismiss the keyboard programmatically, we can use the following method.

endEditing(Bool**)**—This method forces the view to resign first responder, which means that the view will no longer accept input from the user.

This method is implemented by a UIKit class called **UIView**, but it is accessible from the **UIWindow** objects created by the application. Because the application can have multiple windows opened at the same time, we must find the window the user is currently working on. The list with all the windows available is provided by the **windows** property of the **UIApplication** object introduced before, and to know which window is the active one, the **UIWindow** class includes the following property.

isKeyWindow—This property returns a Boolean value that indicates whether this is the active window or not.

The most common requirement for users is to be able to tap anywhere on the screen to close the keyboard. To that effect, we can assign a background view to the entire interface, detect when the user taps on this view with a tap gesture recognizer, and call the `endEditing()` method on the window when the gesture is detected, as in the following example.

```
import SwiftUI

struct ContentView: View {
    @State private var textInput: String = ""

    var body: some View {
        VStack {
            TextField("Insert Caption", text: self.$textInput)
                .textFieldStyle(RoundedBorderTextFieldStyle())
            Spacer()
        }.padding()
        .background(Color.white
            .onTapGesture {
                self.dismissKeyboard()
            }
        )
    }
    func dismissKeyboard() {
        let windows = UIApplication.shared.windows
        let keyWindows = windows.filter({ $0.isKeyWindow })
        if !keyWindows.isEmpty {
            let window = keyWindows.first
            window?.endEditing(true)
        }
    }
}
```

Listing 13-9: Dismissing the keyboard

This is a simple example with just one `TextField` inside a `VStack`. To detect the tap gesture, we assign a background to the `VStack` view with a `Color` view and then apply the `onTapGesture()` modifier to it. When the user taps on this view, the `dismissKeyboard()` method is executed. In this method, we get the list of windows available from the `windows` property of the `UIApplication` object assigned to the app, filter this list to get only the windows that are active, and if the list is not empty, we get the first one, which is always the one the user is interacting with, and call the `endEditing()` method with the value `true` on it to force all the views in the window to resign first responder. In consequence, the views do not respond to user interaction anymore and therefore the keyboard is automatically closed.

 Do It Yourself: Create a SwiftUI project. Update the ContentView.swift file with the code in Listing 13-9. Run the application on the simulator or a device. Tap on the text field. Tap anywhere else to close the keyboard.

Basic 13.2 User Notifications

A different type of notification is the User Notification. These are notifications shown to the user by the system when the app has an event to report, such as the completion of a task or real-life events that the user wants to be reminded of. There are three different types of User Notifications: alert, badge, and sound. A badge-type notification displays a badge with a number over the app's icon, a sound-type notification plays a sound, and an alert-type notification may be displayed as a banner, an Alert View, or a message on the lock screen, depending on the current state of the device and the configuration set by the user. They can be scheduled all at once or independently. For instance, we can schedule a notification that displays an alert and plays a sound, another that displays an alert and shows a badge, or another that just plays a sound to warn the user that something happened.

 IMPORTANT: User Notifications are divided in Local Notifications and Remote Notifications (also known as Push Notifications). Local Notifications are notifications generated by the application running on the device, while Remote Notifications are generated by remote servers and pushed to devices through the network. In this chapter, we are going to study Local Notifications. For more information on Remote Notifications, visit our website and follow the links for this chapter.

(Basic) User Notifications Framework

User Notifications are created and managed by classes of the User Notifications framework. The framework includes multiple classes to control every step of the process. The most important is the `UNUserNotificationCenter` class, which creates a Notification Center to schedule and manage user notifications. This is like the Notification Center studied before but specific for User Notifications. The system automatically creates a `UNUserNotificationCenter` object to serve as the Notification Center for the application that we can retrieve with the following type method.

current()—This type method returns a reference to the `UNUserNotificationCenter` object assigned to the application.

From the `UNUserNotificationCenter` object, we can manage the notifications and ask the user permission to show them. For this purpose, the class includes the following methods.

requestAuthorization(options: UNAuthorizationOptions, **completionHandler:** Closure)—This method asks the user for authorization to show notifications. The **options** attribute is a set of properties that determine the type of notifications we want to show. The properties available are `badge`, `sound`, `alert`, `carPlay`, `criticalAlert`, and `provisional`. The **completionHandler** attribute is a closure that is executed after the response from the user is received. The closure includes two parameters, a Boolean value that determines if the permission was granted and an `Error` value to report errors.

getNotificationSettings(completionHandler: Closure)—This method gets the current configuration set on the device to deliver notifications and sends the values to the closure specified by the **completionHandler** attribute. The closure receives an object of type `UNNotificationSettings` that contains properties to report the current settings. The most useful property is `authorizationStatus`, which returns an enumeration value that reflects the current status of the authorization (the user may change the status of the authorization anytime from the Settings app). The possible values are `denied`, `authorized`, `notDetermined`, and `provisional`.

add(UNNotificationRequest, **withCompletionHandler:** Closure)—This method schedules a new notification in the Notification Center. The first attribute is an object with the request for the notification, and the `withCompletionHandler` attribute is a closure that is executed when the process is over. The closure receives a parameter of type `Error` to report errors.

removePendingNotificationRequests(withIdentifiers: [String])—This method removes the pending notifications with the identifiers specified by the attribute.

setNotificationCategories(Set)—This method configures the Notification Center to work with the types of notifications and actions we want to support. The settings are established by a set of objects of the `UNNotificationCategory` class called *Categories*.

The framework includes the `UNMutableNotificationContent` class to store the content of a notification. The following are the most frequently used properties included in this class.

title—This property sets or returns the notification's title.

subtitle—This property sets or returns the notification's subtitle.

body—This property sets or returns the notification's message or description.

badge—This property sets or returns a number to show over the app's icon.

sound—This property sets or returns the sound we want to play when the notification is delivered to the user. It is an object of type `UNNotificationSound`.

threadIdentifier—This property sets or returns a string used to identify each group of notifications. If no identifier is provided, the system groups the notifications by app.

summaryArgument—This property sets or returns the string that is added by the notification to the category's summary.

summaryArgumentCount—This property sets or returns the number of items the notification adds to the category's summary.

userInfo—This property sets or returns a dictionary with the additional information we want to associate to the notification.

categoryIdentifier—This property sets or returns the identifier of the category we want to use to configure the notification. Categories are objects that establish the type of notification and the actions allowed.

attachments—This property sets or returns an array of `UNNotificationAttachment` objects with the information about the media files we want to show with the notification.

Some of these properties define the information the notification is going to show to the user. Most of them, like the `title` and `body`, work with strings, except for the `badge` property, which takes a number, and the `sound` property which takes an object of the `UNNotificationSound` class. This class includes the following initializer and property.

UNNotificationSound(named: UNNotificationSoundName)—This initializer creates a `UNNotificationSound` object with the sound in the file specified by the **named** attribute.

default—This type property returns a `UNNotificationSound` object with the sound defined in the system by default.

The names of the sounds are defined by a structure of type `UNNotificationSoundName`. The structure includes the following initializer.

UNNotificationSoundName(rawValue: String)—This initializer creates a `UNNotificationSoundName` object with the name of the file that contains the sound we want to play with the notification.

User Notifications are posted to the User Notification Center and then presented by the system when a certain condition is met. These conditions are established by objects called *Triggers*. There are three types of triggers available for Local Notifications (the notifications posted by the app): Time Interval, (the notification is delivered after a certain period of time), Calendar (the notification is delivered on a specific date), and Location (the notification is delivered in a specific location). The framework defines three classes to create these triggers: `UNTimeIntervalNotificationTrigger`, `UNCalendarNotificationTrigger`, and `UNLocationNotificationTrigger`. The following are their initializers.

UNTimeIntervalNotificationTrigger(timeInterval: TimeInterval, **repeats: Bool)**—This initializer creates a Time Interval trigger that will deliver the notification after the period of time determined by the **timeInterval** attribute (in seconds). The **repeats** attribute determines if the notification will be delivered once or infinite times.

UNCalendarNotificationTrigger(dateMatching: DateComponents, **repeats: Bool)**—This initializer creates a Calendar trigger that delivers the notification at the date determined by the **dateMatching** attribute. The **repeats** attribute determines if the notification will be delivered once or infinite times.

UNLocationNotificationTrigger(region: CLRegion, **repeats:** Bool)—This initializer creates a Location trigger that delivers the notification when the device is inside a region in the real world determined by the **region** attribute (this value must be specified as an instance of a subclass of the `CLRegion` class called `CLCircularRegion`). The **repeats** attribute determines if the notification will be delivered once or infinite times.

To deliver a notification, we must create a request with the notification, an identifier, and a trigger. The framework defines the `UNNotificationRequest` class for this purpose.

UNNotificationRequest(identifier: String, **content:** UNNotificationContent, **trigger:** UNNotificationTrigger)—This initializer creates a request to deliver the notification specified by the **content** attribute and at the time or place specified by the **trigger** attribute. The **identifier** attribute is a string that we can use later to manage or remove the request.

To be able to work with the User Notifications framework, we must import it with the `import` instruction. Once we have access to the framework, we must request authorization from the user with the `requestAuthorization()` method. The application can ask for authorization at any time, but it is recommendable to do it when we are about to perform a task that requires it, so the user knows why is being asked. In the following example, we ask permission when the view appears to enable a button that will allow the user to post a notification.

```
import SwiftUI
import UserNotifications

struct ContentView: View {
    @State private var inputMessage: String = ""
    @State private var isButtonEnabled: Bool = false

    var body: some View {
        VStack(spacing: 13) {
            HStack {
                Text("Message:")
                TextField("Insert Message", text: $inputMessage)
                    .textFieldStyle(RoundedBorderTextFieldStyle())
            }
```

```
        HStack {
            Spacer()
            Button("Save Notification") {
                let message = self.inputMessage.trimmingCharacters(in:
.whitespaces)
                if !message.isEmpty {
                    self.postNotification()
                    self.inputMessage = ""
                }
            }.disabled(!isButtonEnabled)
        }
        Spacer()
    }.padding()
    .onAppear(perform: {
        self.getAuthorization()
    })
    }
}
```

Listing 13-10: Posting notifications

The view in Listing 13-10 includes a `TextField` view for the user to write a message and a button to send a notification with it, as show next.

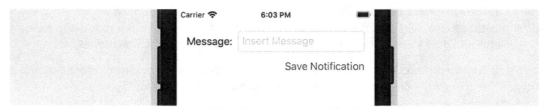

Figure 13-4: Form to post notifications

This view builds the interface, but the process is performed by two custom methods. The `getAuthorization()` method is called when the view appears to request authorization to send notifications, and the `postNotification()` method is called when the button is pressed to post a notification with the message inserted by the user. In the `getAuthorization()` method, we are going to check the current status and then ask permission if necessary.

```
func getAuthorization() {
    let center = UNUserNotificationCenter.current()
    center.getNotificationSettings(completionHandler: { settings in
        if settings.authorizationStatus == .authorized {
            self.isButtonEnabled = true
        } else {
            center.requestAuthorization(options: [.alert, .sound],
completionHandler: { granted, error in
                if granted && error == nil {
                    self.isButtonEnabled = true
                } else {
                    self.isButtonEnabled = false
                }
            })
        }
    })
}
```

Listing 13-11: Asking permission to the user to post notifications

Chapter 13 - Notifications

The first thing we have to do to work with the User Notification Center is to get a reference to the **UNUserNotificationCenter** object with the **current()** method. Once we get this reference, we can call the methods to process the notifications. In the example of Listing 13-11, we start by calling the **getNotificationSettings()** method to check the current status. This method reads the status from the system and executes a closure when the request is completed. The method sends an object of type **UNNotificationSettings** to the closure with this information. This object contains the property **authorizationStatus** with a value that represents the current status. If the status is **authorized**, it means that the user already authorized the application to post notifications, so we assign the value **true** to the **isButtonEnabled** property to enable the button in the interface. But if the value is different, we must request authorization from the user. In this example, we want to deliver notifications of type alert and sound, so we call the **requestAuthorization()** method with the value **[.alert, .sound]**. When this code is executed for the first time, the system shows an Alert View with two buttons for the user to decide what to do, as shown in Figure 13-5.

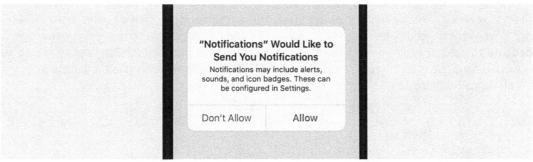

Figure 13-5: *Authorization to deliver notifications*

If permission is granted, we assign the value **true** to the **isButtonEnabled** property to enable the button and let the user post a notification, and when this button is pressed, we call the **postNotification()** method to post the notification. The following is our implementation of this method.

```
func postNotification() {
    let content = UNMutableNotificationContent()
    content.title = "Reminder"
    content.body = self.inputMessage
    content.sound = UNNotificationSound(named:
UNNotificationSoundName(rawValue: "alarm.mp3"))

    let trigger = UNTimeIntervalNotificationTrigger(timeInterval: 30,
repeats: false)
    let id = "reminder-\(UUID())"
    let request = UNNotificationRequest(identifier: id, content: content,
trigger: trigger)

    let center = UNUserNotificationCenter.current()
    center.add(request, withCompletionHandler: nil)
}
```

Listing 13-12: *Posting a notification*

The process to schedule a notification is simple. We have to create an instance of the **UNMutableNotificationContent** class with the values we want the notification to show to the user, create a trigger (in this case we use a Time Interval trigger), create an instance of the

`UNNotificationRequest` class with these values to request the delivery of the notification, and finally add the request to the User Notification Center with the `add()` method. Notice that the request identifier must be unique. To assign a unique value to each request, we created a string with the word "reminder" followed by a random value generated by the `UUID()` function.

 Do It Yourself: Create a SwiftUI project. Download the alarm.mp3 file from our website and drag it to your project. Update the `ContentView` structure with the code of Listing 13-10. Add the methods of Listings 13-11 and 13-12 to the `ContentView` structure, below the `body` property. Run the application on a simulator or a device (recommended). The first time the app runs, the system will ask you to allow the app to deliver notifications. Press the Allow button. Insert a text in the input field and press the Save Notification button. Press the Home button to close the app. After a few seconds, you should see the notification popping up at the top of the screen.

The `add()` method includes an attribute to execute a completion handler. This is a closure that is executed after the notification is posted. We can perform any task we want in this closure, but if we want to modify the interface, we must remember to do it from the main queue. This is because the closure can be executed in a secondary thread and the interface always has to be accessed from the main thread. The following example shows how to disable the button after the first notification is posted.

```
func postNotification() {
    let content = UNMutableNotificationContent()
    content.title = "Reminder"
    content.body = self.inputMessage
    content.sound = UNNotificationSound(named:
UNNotificationSoundName(rawValue: "alarm.mp3"))

    let trigger = UNTimeIntervalNotificationTrigger(timeInterval: 30,
repeats: false)
    let id = "reminder-\(UUID())"
    let request = UNNotificationRequest(identifier: id, content: content,
trigger: trigger)

    let center = UNUserNotificationCenter.current()
    center.add(request, withCompletionHandler: { error in
        let main = OperationQueue.main
        main.addOperation {
            self.isButtonEnabled = false
        }
    })
}
```

Listing 13-13: Modifying the interface after posting a notification

 Do It Yourself: Update the `postNotification()` method from the previous example with the code of Listing 13-13. Run the application on a device and schedule a notification. The button should be disabled.

Medium | ## Notification Groups

The system automatically groups notifications together by app. For instance, if our application sends multiple notifications to the Notification Center, they will all be grouped together and only the last one will be shown to the user. This is the automatic behavior. If notifications from multiple apps accumulate in the Notification Center, the system groups them by application. But we can separate them in custom groups by assigning a value to the `threadIdentifier` property of the `UNMutableNotificationContent` object. All the notifications with the same identifier will be grouped together. The following example separates notifications in two groups called Group One and Group Two.

```
func postNotification() {
    let center = UNUserNotificationCenter.current()

    for index in 1...5 {
        let content = UNMutableNotificationContent()
        content.title = "Reminder"
        content.body = self.inputMessage + " Attempt: \(index)"
        content.threadIdentifier = index < 3 ? "Group One" : "Group Two"

        let time = Double(5 * index)
        let trigger = UNTimeIntervalNotificationTrigger(timeInterval: time,
repeats: false)
        let id = "reminder-\(UUID())"
        let request = UNNotificationRequest(identifier: id, content:
content, trigger: trigger)
        center.add(request, withCompletionHandler: nil)
    }
}
```

Listing 13-14: *Organizing notifications into groups*

For didactic purposes, this example posts 5 notifications every time the user presses the button. To identify each message, we add a string with the index number to the text inserted by the user (" `Attempt:` `\(index)` ") and define the groups based on the number of notifications already posted. The first two notifications scheduled by the application go into Group One and the rest are assigned to Group Two (`index < 3 ? "Group One" : "Group Two"`). As a result, the notifications are separated into two groups.

Figure 13-6: *Notifications organized in groups*

 Do It Yourself: Update the `postNotification()` method from the previous example with the code of Listing 13-14. Run the application on a device and schedule one notification. Lock the device. You should see the notifications grouped by the value of their identifier, as shown in Figure 13-6.

Medium **Provisional Notifications**

Asking the user for permission can be a bit disruptive for some applications. If we consider that in our app the user's acceptance to receive notifications may be implicit, we can post provisional notifications. These are quiet notifications that only show in the Notification Center (they are not displayed in the Locked or Home screens) and include buttons for the user to decide whether to keep them or turn them off.

To get our app to post provisional notifications, we must add the `provisional` option to the `requestAuthorization()` method and also check the `provisional` status before enabling the button, as shown next.

```
func getAuthorization() {
    let center = UNUserNotificationCenter.current()
    center.getNotificationSettings(completionHandler: { settings in
        if settings.authorizationStatus == .authorized ||
settings.authorizationStatus == .provisional {
            self.isButtonEnabled = true
        } else {
            center.requestAuthorization(options: [.alert, .sound,
.provisional], completionHandler: { granted, error in
                if granted && error == nil {
                    self.isButtonEnabled = true
                } else {
                    self.isButtonEnabled = false
                }
            })
        }
    })
}
```

Listing 13-15: Scheduling provisional notifications

Because provisional notifications are only shown on the Notification Center, the user has to open the Notification Center to see them, and then decide whether to keep them or turn them off, as shown in Figure 13-7.

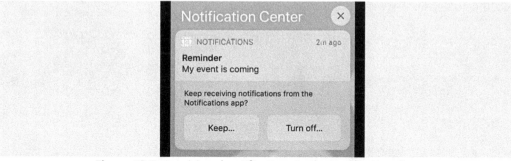

Figure 13-7: Provisional notifications in the Notification Center

 Do It Yourself: Update the `getAuthorization()` method from the previous example with the code of Listing 13-15. Uninstall the app and run it again on the device. Post a notification. Go to the Home screen and drag your finger from the top to open the Notification Center. You should see the provisional notification, as shown in Figure 13-7.

(Medium) **User Notifications Delegate**

If the user is working with the app when a notification is delivered, the notification is not displayed on the screen, but we can assign a delegate to the User Notification Center to change this behavior. We introduced delegates in Chapter 3. The idea is that we assign one object as the delegate of another, so when the second object needs to communicate with the first one, it can call methods on it. The User Notification Center uses this pattern to let us configure how the notifications are delivered and perform custom tasks when the user interacts with a notification. For this purpose, the framework includes the `UNUserNotificationCenterDelegate` protocol, which defines the following methods.

userNotificationCenter(UNUserNotificationCenter,   **willPresent:** UNNotification, **withCompletionHandler:** Closure**)**—This method is called by the User Notification Center on the delegate when the application is active and a notification has to be delivered. The **withCompletionHandler** attribute is a closure that we must execute to tell the system what to do with the notification. The closure receives an attribute of type `UNNotificationPresentationOptions` to define what type of notification to show. The possible values are **badge**, **sound**, and **alert**.

userNotificationCenter(UNUserNotificationCenter,   **didReceive:** UNNotificationResponse, **withCompletionHandler:** Closure**)**—This method is called on the delegate by the User Notification Center when the user interacts with the notification (performs an action). The **didReceive** attribute is an object with information about the notification and the action performed, and the **withCompletionHandler** attribute is a closure we must execute after we finish processing the user response.

The `UNUserNotificationCenterDelegate` protocol was designed for applications developed with the UIKit framework, but we can still implement it in SwiftUI by assigning our `SceneDelegate` object as the User Notification Center's delegate, as shown next.

```
import UIKit
import SwiftUI
import UserNotifications

class SceneDelegate: UIResponder, UIWindowSceneDelegate,
UNUserNotificationCenterDelegate {
    var window: UIWindow?

    func scene(_ scene: UIScene, willConnectTo session: UISceneSession,
options connectionOptions: UIScene.ConnectionOptions) {
        let contentView = ContentView()
        if let windowScene = scene as? UIWindowScene {
            let window = UIWindow(windowScene: windowScene)
            window.rootViewController = UIHostingController(rootView:
contentView)
            self.window = window
            window.makeKeyAndVisible()
        }
        let center = UNUserNotificationCenter.current()
        center.delegate = self
    }
    func userNotificationCenter(_ center: UNUserNotificationCenter,
willPresent notification: UNNotification, withCompletionHandler
completionHandler: @escaping (UNNotificationPresentationOptions) -> Void)
{
        completionHandler([.alert])
    }
}
```

Listing 13-16: Showing notifications when the app is being used

The example in Listing 13-16 modifies the application's `SceneDelegate` class to turn it into the User Notifications Center's delegate and implements a protocol method to tell the system what to do with the notifications. First, we make the class conform to the `UNUserNotificationCenterDelegate` protocol. Then, we declare the class as the delegate of the `UNUserNotificationCenter` object by assigning a reference of the `SceneDelegate` object to the `delegate` property of the `UNUserNotificationCenter` object (`center.delegate = self`). Now, when the User Notifications Center needs to communicate with our code, it can call the methods on this class. Finally, we implement the `userNotificationCenter(UNUserNotificationCenter, willPresent:, withCompletionHandler:)` method. This method is called when a notification is triggered to ask the application what to do. Here, we can perform any task we need and then we must execute the closure received by the method to specify what we want the system to do. If we do not want to show the notification, we must execute the closure with no parameters, otherwise we must provide a value that determines the type of notification we want to show. In this example, we tell the system to show an alert with the `alert` value. In consequence, notifications posted by the application are now shown while the app is running.

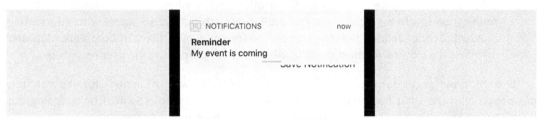

Figure 13-8: *Notifications shown while the app is running*

 Do It Yourself: Update your `SceneDelegate` class with the code of Listing 13-16. For the notifications to appear, they shouldn't be provisional. We recommend you to implement the `getAuthorization()` method of Listing 13-11 and remove the previous application from the device before trying this example. Run the application, insert a message, and press the Save Notification button. Wait 30 seconds. You should see the notification on the screen while the app is running, as shown in Figure 13-8.

Notifications can show custom actions in the form of buttons and input fields that the user can use to provide feedback without having to open our app. The actions are defined by two classes: `UNNotificationAction` and `UNTextInputNotificationAction`. The following are their initializers.

UNNotificationAction(identifier: String, **title:** String, **options:** UNNotification-ActionOptions)—This initializer creates an action represented by a custom button. The **identifier** attribute is a string that we can use to identify the action, the **title** attribute is the text shown on the button, and the **options** attribute is a set of properties that determine how the action should be performed. The properties available are `authenticationRequired` (the user is required to unlock the device), `destructive` (the button is highlighted), and `foreground` (the app is launched to perform the action).

UNTextInputNotificationAction(identifier: String, **title:** String, **options:** UNNotificationActionOptions, **textInputButtonTitle:** String, **textInput-Placeholder:** String)—This initializer creates an action represented by a custom button that when pressed prompts the system to display an input field. Besides the attributes included by a normal action, these types of actions also include the

Chapter 13 - Notifications

textInputButtonTitle and **textInputPlaceholder** attributes to define the button and the placeholder for the input field.

After defining the actions that we want to include in the notification, we must create a category to group them together. The framework offers the `UNNotificationCategory` class to create a category. The following is the class' initializer.

UNNotificationCategory(identifier: String, **actions:** [UNNotificationAction], **intentIdentifiers:** [String], **options:** UNNotificationCategoryOptions)—This initializer creates a category with the actions specified by the **actions** attribute. The **identifier** attribute is a string that allows us to identify the category, the **intentIdentifiers** attribute is an array of strings used to guide Siri to produce a better response, and the **options** attribute is a property that determines how the notifications associated to this category are going to be handled. The properties available are `customDismissAction` (processes the dismiss action) and `allowInCarPlay` (allows car play to show notifications).

The following example adds an action to the notification scheduled in previous examples. The action is represented by a button the user can press to perform a task.

```
func postNotification() {
    let center = UNUserNotificationCenter.current()

    let actionDelete = UNNotificationAction(identifier: "deleteButton",
title: "Delete", options: .destructive)
    let category = UNNotificationCategory(identifier: "listActions",
actions: [actionDelete], intentIdentifiers: [], options: [])
    center.setNotificationCategories([category])

    let content = UNMutableNotificationContent()
    content.title = "Reminder"
    content.body = self.inputMessage
    content.categoryIdentifier = "listActions"

    let trigger = UNTimeIntervalNotificationTrigger(timeInterval: 30,
repeats: false)
    let id = "reminder-\(UUID())"
    let request = UNNotificationRequest(identifier: id, content: content,
trigger: trigger)
    center.add(request)
}
```

Listing 13-17: Adding and processing actions for notifications

The `postNotification()` method of Listing 13-17 creates a destructive action with the title Delete and includes it in a category called "listActions". Categories have to be added to the User Notification Center first with the `setNotificationCategories()` method and then assigned to the notification's `categoryIdentifier` property to configure the notification.

When the action is performed, the User Notification Center calls the `userNotificationCenter(UNUserNotificationCenter,` `didReceive:,` `withCompletionHandler:)` method on its delegate to let the application perform a task. The method receives an object of type `UNNotificationResponse` with information about the notification and the action performed by the user that we can use to decide what to do. The `UNNotificationResponse` class includes the following properties to read those values.

actionIdentifier—This property returns a string with the action's identifier.

notification—This property returns a `UNNotification` object representing the notification. The object includes the `date` property to get the date the notification was delivered and the `request` property with a reference to the `UNNotificationRequest` object used to schedule the notification, which in turn offers the `content` property to access the values of the notification.

The following is our implementation of this method in the `SceneDelegate` class. In this example, we read the `actionIdentifier` property and compare it with the string "deleteButton" to confirm that the user pressed the Delete button.

```
import UIKit
import SwiftUI
import UserNotifications

class SceneDelegate: UIResponder, UIWindowSceneDelegate,
UNUserNotificationCenterDelegate {
   var window: UIWindow?

   func scene(_ scene: UIScene, willConnectTo session: UISceneSession,
options connectionOptions: UIScene.ConnectionOptions) {
      let contentView = ContentView()
      if let windowScene = scene as? UIWindowScene {
         let window = UIWindow(windowScene: windowScene)
         window.rootViewController = UIHostingController(rootView:
contentView)
         self.window = window
         window.makeKeyAndVisible()
      }
      let center = UNUserNotificationCenter.current()
      center.delegate = self
   }
   func userNotificationCenter(_ center: UNUserNotificationCenter,
didReceive response: UNNotificationResponse, withCompletionHandler
completionHandler: @escaping () -> Void) {
      let identifier = response.actionIdentifier
      if identifier == "deleteButton" {
         print("Delete Message")
      }
      completionHandler()
   }
}
```

Listing 13-18: Responding to actions performed by the user in a notification

In this example, we just print a message on the console when the user presses the Delete button on the notification, but we can perform more complex tasks, such as modifying a `@Published` property in the model, as we did in the example of Listing 9-51.

With these modifications, our notifications now include a Delete button and our application knows when the button is pressed. In devices with 3D Touch enabled, this button is displayed when the user presses over the notification, otherwise it is displayed when the user drags the notification down or selects the View option to see it.

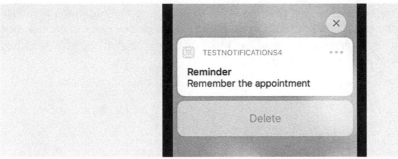

Figure 13-9: *Actions in a notification*

Do It Yourself: Update the `postNotification()` method with the code of Listing 13-17 and the `SceneDelegate` class with the code of Listing 13-18. Run the application on a device and post a notification. Press the Home button to close the application. When the notification appears on the screen, drag it to the bottom. You should see the Delete button. When you press this button, a message should be printed on the console. Remember to work with normal notifications. Provisional notifications has to be accepted before being shown on the Home screen.

This example implements a simple action for the notification that shows a button when the notification is expanded, but we can also include an action that shows an input field, so the user can provide feedback right from the notification. The following are the changes we must introduce to the notification to include an input field.

```
func postNotification() {
    let center = UNUserNotificationCenter.current()

    let actionDelete = UNNotificationAction(identifier: "deleteButton",
title: "Delete", options: .destructive)
    let actionInput = UNTextInputNotificationAction(identifier:
"inputField", title: "Message", options: [])
    let category = UNNotificationCategory(identifier: "listActions",
actions: [actionDelete, actionInput], intentIdentifiers: [], options: [])
    center.setNotificationCategories([category])

    let content = UNMutableNotificationContent()
    content.title = "Reminder"
    content.body = self.inputMessage
    content.categoryIdentifier = "listActions"

    let trigger = UNTimeIntervalNotificationTrigger(timeInterval: 10,
repeats: false)
    let id = "reminder-\(UUID())"
    let request = UNNotificationRequest(identifier: id, content: content,
trigger: trigger)
    center.add(request)
}
```

Listing 13-19: *Adding a text field to the notification*

The example in Listing 13-19 defines two actions: the `actionDelete` action creates the same Delete button as before, and the `actionInput` action initializes a `UNTextInputNotificationAction` object to create a button that opens a text field. Finally, both actions are included in the category and the notification is created as always.

The text inserted by the user in the text field is sent to the delegate method in the response object. The framework offers the `UNTextInputNotificationResponse` class to contain this response. To access the value inserted by the user, we must cast the response object to this class and then read its `userText` property, as we do next.

```
import UIKit
import SwiftUI
import UserNotifications

class SceneDelegate: UIResponder, UIWindowSceneDelegate,
UNUserNotificationCenterDelegate {
   var window: UIWindow?

   func scene(_ scene: UIScene, willConnectTo session: UISceneSession,
options connectionOptions: UIScene.ConnectionOptions) {
      let contentView = ContentView()
      if let windowScene = scene as? UIWindowScene {
         let window = UIWindow(windowScene: windowScene)
         window.rootViewController = UIHostingController(rootView:
contentView)
         self.window = window
         window.makeKeyAndVisible()
      }
      let center = UNUserNotificationCenter.current()
      center.delegate = self
   }
   func userNotificationCenter(_ center: UNUserNotificationCenter,
didReceive response: UNNotificationResponse, withCompletionHandler
completionHandler: @escaping () -> Void) {
      let identifier = response.actionIdentifier
      if identifier == "deleteButton" {
         print("Delete Message")
      } else if identifier == "inputField" {
         print("Send: \((response as!
UNTextInputNotificationResponse).userText)")
      }
      completionHandler()
   }
}
```

Listing 13-20: Processing the text received from the notification

We have two actions to respond to this time, the `deleteButton` action and the `inputField` action. If the action performed is the `deleteButton` action, we print a message on the console as we did before, but if the action is the `inputField` action, we cast the response as a `UNTextInputNotificationResponse` object, get the text inserted by the user from the object's `userText` property, and then print it on the console.

 Do It Yourself: Update the `postNotification()` method with the code of Listing 13-19 and the `SceneDelegate` class with the code of Listing 13-20. Run the application. Insert a message to schedule a notification. Go to the home screen and wait until the notification is displayed. Expand the notification to see the actions. Click the Message button. You should see an input field over the keyboard. Insert a value and press the Send button. You should see a message on the console with the text you have just inserted.

Chapter 14
Storage

Basic **14.1 User Preferences**

Up to this point, all the data was stored in arrays and dictionaries created in the model and the values were hard-coded, which means they are always the same every time the app is launched. If we add a new value to the model, it is only preserved for the time the app is running, but as soon as the app is closed, we lose that value, and everything is back to the initial state. This is useful when our application requires values that never change or when a long process generates partial results that we have to access later to complete a task, but most of the data generated by the user must be stored permanently on the device or a server. Apple includes several systems to store persistent data. The easiest to use is called *Users Defaults*. This system was designed to store user preferences, which may include values set by the user to determine how our app should work or values set by the app itself to restore a previous state. These values are stored in a database managed by the system and therefore they continue to exist after the app is closed and for as long as the user or the application decide to keep them.

Basic **User Defaults**

The Foundation framework defines a class called `UserDefaults` to manage the preferences of our application. Only one `UserDefaults` object is assigned per application, so we can reference this object anywhere in the code and always process the same values. The class offers the following type property to get a reference to the object created for the app.

standard—This type property returns a reference to the app's `UserDefaults` object.

The values are assigned to the `UserDefaults` object with an associated key that we can use to retrieve them later, like dictionaries. The types of values we can work with are restricted to Property List values. These are values of specific data types that include `NSNumber`, `NSString`, `NSDate`, `NSArray`, `NSDictionary`, `NSData`, and their equivalents in Swift. But we can also work with other types of values, including custom objects, by converting them into `NSData` objects. The `UserDefaults` class includes the following methods to store, retrieve, and delete values of any of these types.

set(Any, forKey: String)—This method stores the value specified by the first attribute with the key specified by the **forKey** attribute. If the value already exists, it is updated.

object(forKey: String)—This method retrieves the value associated with the key specified by the **forKey** attribute. If the value does not exist, it returns `nil`. The attribute is the same string used to store the value.

removeObject(forKey: String)—This method removes the value associated with the key specified by the **forKey** attribute. The attribute is the same string used to store the value.

Because the methods above process values of any type, they return them as objects of type `Any`. This means that we must cast the values to the right type before using them. To simplify our work, the class includes methods to retrieve the values for specific types.

bool(forKey: String)—This method retrieves a value of type `Bool`. If there is no value set for the key, the method returns the value `false`.

float(forKey: String)—This method retrieves a value of type `Float`. If there is no value set for the key, the method returns the value 0.0.

integer(forKey: String)—This method retrieves a value of type `Int`. If there is no value set for the key, the method returns the value 0.

double(forKey: String)—This method retrieves a value of type `Double`. If there is no value set for the key, the method returns the value 0.0.

string(forKey: String)—This method retrieves a value of type `String`.

array(forKey: String)—This method retrieves an array.

dictionary(forKey: String)—This method retrieves a dictionary.

data(forKey: String)—This method retrieves a value of type `Data`.

url(forKey: String)—This method retrieves a value of type `URL`.

The User Defaults system can store any amount of data we want, but it is recommendable to use it to store simple strings and values. Its main purpose is to serve as a storage system for the app's settings. For example, we may have an app that plays videos and we want to let the user set the volume by default. Using the User Defaults system, we can store this value and set the volume back to its last state every time the app is executed. The interface of Figure 14-1 includes a stepper and a label to illustrate how the process works.

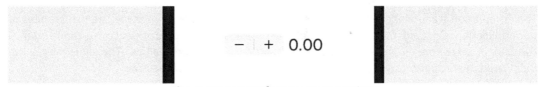

Figure 14-1: *Interface to store settings*

The `UserDefaults` object assigned to our application is accessible from anywhere in the code. All we have to do to read or store a value is to get a reference to this object from the `standard` property. This is convenient, but not the best practice. In SwiftUI, we must consider that when a value changes, all the views that access that value have to be notified. Therefore, it is better to report any change with a publisher, and the easiest way to implement this is with a `@Published` property. The process is simple. We read the current values stored in User Defaults and assign them to `@Published` properties when the app is launched, and then implement the `didSet` method on each property to update the User Defaults when new values are assigned to them. The following is a simple model to demonstrate how this works. The model only includes an observable object with a single `@Published` property to store the value produced by the stepper of the interface in Figure 14-1.

```
import SwiftUI

class AppData: ObservableObject {
    @Published var counter: Double = UserDefaults.standard.double(forKey:
"counter") {
        didSet {
            UserDefaults.standard.set(counter, forKey: "counter")
        }
    }
}
```

Listing 14-1: *Storing values in the User Defaults system*

Chapter 14 - Storage

To read the current value, we get a reference to the `UserDefaults` object assigned to the app with the `standard` property and call the `double(forKey:)` method. This method reads a value in User Defaults with the "counter" key and returns it. If no value is found, the value returned is 0 (zero). Then, we implement the `didSet()` method, so every time a new value is assigned to the `@Published` property, this method is executed. Here, we access the `UserDefaults` object again and store the new value in User Defaults with the `set()` method and the same key.

The view must include a `Stepper` view to let the user change the value and a `Text` view to show it, and these views must work with the `@Published` property to read and store the values.

```
import SwiftUI

struct ContentView: View {
    @EnvironmentObject var appData: AppData

    var body: some View {
        HStack {
            Stepper("", value: self.$appData.counter)
                .labelsHidden()
            Text("\(self.appData.counter, specifier: "%.2f")")
                .font(.title)
        }
    }
}
```

Listing 14-2: Using the values stored in User Defaults

There is nothing new in the view in Listing 14-2. We get access to the model through the environment and work with the `@Published` property as we did with any other property before. When the user presses the buttons on the stepper, the new value is assigned to the `counter` property, but because we defined the `didSet()` method on the property, the `set()` method is called and the value is permanently stored in User Defaults. In consequence, the `Text` view, and any view that access the `counter` property, always displays the current value. When the app is closed and opened again, the property gets the value from User Defaults, and therefore the latest value stored by the user is shown on the screen.

 Do It Yourself: Create a SwiftUI project. Create a Swift file called AppData.swift for the model of Listing 14-1. Update the AppDelegate.swift file with the code of Listing 7-14 and the SceneDelegate.swift file with the code of Listing 7-20 to instantiate the model and insert it in the environment. Update the `ContentView` structure with the code of Listing 14-2. Run the application on the simulator or a device. Press the buttons on the stepper to change the value. Stop the execution of the app from the Stop button in Xcode. Run the application again. The value displayed on the screen should be the last one you selected. Notice that the values are not stored in the database right away. Sometimes it may take a few seconds before the new values are available.

As we already mentioned, we can also store values generated by the app. For example, we may add a value to User Settings to keep track of the time the user has spent without using the app. The process to read and store the value is the same. We have to create a `@Published` property and implement the `didSet()` method, but User Defaults doesn't know how to work with `Date` values and therefore we have to read it as a generic object with the `object(forKey:)` method and cast it as a `Date` value with the `as?` operator. The following is the model for this example.

```
import SwiftUI

class AppData: ObservableObject {
    @Published var lastDate: Date {
        didSet {
            UserDefaults.standard.set(lastDate, forKey: "lastDate")
        }
    }
    var interval: String {
        let calendar = Calendar.current
        let components = calendar.dateComponents([.year, .month, .day,
.hour, .minute, .second], from: lastDate, to: Date())
        let message = "You haven't use this app in \(components.year!)
years, \(components.month!) months, \(components.day!) days,
\(components.hour!) hours, \(components.minute!) minutes,
\(components.second!) seconds"
        return message
    }
    init() {
        if let date = UserDefaults.standard.object(forKey: "lastDate") as?
Date {
            self.lastDate = date
        } else {
            self.lastDate = Date()
        }
    }
}
```

Listing 14-3: Storing object in User Defaults

The property we use to store the value in User Defaults is called `lastDate`. This property contains the `didSet()` method to store new values in User Defaults, but because we have to cast the value to a `Date`, we have decided to initialize the property from the initializer below. If there is a value and can be casted to a `Date` type, we assign it to the property, otherwise, it means that this is the first time the app is running so we assign the current date.

The model also includes a computed property called `interval` to prepare a string for the view. The code calculates the interval between the date in User Defaults and the current date and creates a string with the components.

Because we want to show the users how much time has passed since the last time they used the app, we must store the current date when the app is closed or removed from the screen. The `onAppear()` and `onDisappear()` modifiers introduced before are only used when the view appears or is removed from the hierarchy, but they are not executed when the app is closed or reappears on the screen. To keep track of this activity, the system assigns different states to every scene (window). The scene is in the foreground when is visible and it is responding to user events, or in the background, when it is not visible but still running (see Scene Delegate in Chapter 5). In our application, we need to set the date when the scene is no longer in the foreground state and read it again when it goes back to that state. For this purpose, the `SceneDelegate` class includes two methods. The `sceneWillResignActive()` method is called when the scene is moving to the background, and the `sceneDidBecomeActive()` method is called when the scene moves to the foreground again. And here is where we can update the date in our model. If the scene is being removed from the screen (going to the background state), we store the current date in User Defaults, and if the scene becomes visible (moves to the foreground), we read the current date to update the interface.

```
import UIKit
import SwiftUI

class SceneDelegate: UIResponder, UIWindowSceneDelegate {
   var window: UIWindow?

   func scene(_ scene: UIScene, willConnectTo session: UISceneSession,
options connectionOptions: UIScene.ConnectionOptions) {
      let app = UIApplication.shared
      let delegate = app.delegate as! AppDelegate
      let contentView = ContentView()
         .environmentObject(delegate.myData)

      if let windowScene = scene as? UIWindowScene {
         let window = UIWindow(windowScene: windowScene)
         window.rootViewController = UIHostingController(rootView:
contentView)
         self.window = window
         window.makeKeyAndVisible()
      }
   }
   func sceneWillResignActive(_ scene: UIScene) {
      let app = UIApplication.shared
      let delegate = app.delegate as! AppDelegate
      let appData = delegate.myData
      appData?.lastDate = Date()
   }
   func sceneDidBecomeActive(_ scene: UIScene) {
      let app = UIApplication.shared
      let delegate = app.delegate as! AppDelegate
      let appData = delegate.myData
      if let date = UserDefaults.standard.object(forKey: "lastDate") as?
Date {
         appData?.lastDate = date
      } else {
         appData?.lastDate = Date()
      }
   }
}
```

Listing 14-4: Responding to changes in the state of the app

When the user opens the app (the scene becomes active), the **sceneDidBecomeActive()** method gets a reference to the model from the **AppDelegate** object, reads the value stored in User Defaults, and assigns it to the **lastDate** property. And when the user removes the scene to go to the Home screen or open another app, the **sceneWillResignActive()** method gets a reference to the model again and assigns the current date to the **lastDate** property, so this property always have the date of the last time the app was visible and running.

Because all the work is done by the model and the **SceneDelegate** class, the view is very simple. We just have to show the value produced by the **interval** property on the screen.

```
import SwiftUI

struct ContentView: View {
   @EnvironmentObject var appData: AppData
```

```
    var body: some View {
        HStack {
            Text("\(self.appData.interval)")
                .lineLimit(nil)
                .padding()
        }
    }
}
```

Listing 14-5: Showing the values

You haven't use this app in 0 years, 0 months, 0 days, 0 hours, 2 minutes, 38 seconds

Figure 14-2: Interface with values from User Settings

 Do It Yourself: Update the `AppData` class with the code of Listing 14-3, the `SceneDelegate` class with the code of Listing 14-4, and the `ContentView` structure with the code of Listing 14-5. Run the application on the simulator or a device. The first time, you should see all the date components with the value 0. Press the Home button to close the app. Tap on the app's icon to open it again. You should see the time elapsed from the time the application was closed to when it was reopened.

The previous examples were designed for didactic purposes. The information stored in User Settings is frequently used to store the app's settings and users are provided a separate view where they can change these values and configure the app to their liking. In the following example, we are going to follow this approach to let the user configure the rows of a `List` view that presents a list of books. By modifying the values from the settings view, the user can set the corners of the book's cover and hide the cover and the year.

Figure 14-3: Settings view

The model for this project needs the usual `Book` and `BookViewModel` structures, and the observable object with the `@Published` property to store the books, but now we must add a few more properties for the settings.

```
import SwiftUI

struct Book {
    var title: String
    var author: String
```

Chapter 14 - Storage

```
        var cover: String
        var year: Int
}
struct BookViewModel: Identifiable {
    var id = UUID()
    var book: Book

    var title: String {
        return book.title.capitalized
    }
    var author: String {
        return book.author.capitalized
    }
    var cover: String {
        return book.cover
    }
    var year: String {
        return String(book.year)
    }
}
class AppData: ObservableObject {
    @Published var userData: [BookViewModel]

    @Published var cornerSize: CGFloat {
        didSet {
            UserDefaults.standard.set(Double(cornerSize), forKey:
"cornerSize")
        }
    }
    @Published var showYear: Bool {
        didSet {
            UserDefaults.standard.set(showYear, forKey: "showYear")
        }
    }
    @Published var showCover: Bool {
        didSet {
            UserDefaults.standard.set(showCover, forKey: "showCover")
        }
    }
    init() {
        userData = [
            BookViewModel(book: Book(title: "Steve Jobs", author: "Walter
Isaacson", cover: "book1", year: 2011)),
            BookViewModel(book: Book(title: "HTML5 for Masterminds", author:
"J.D Gauchat", cover: "book2", year: 2017)),
            BookViewModel(book: Book(title: "The Road Ahead", author: "Bill
Gates", cover: "book3", year: 1995))
        ]
        self.cornerSize = CGFloat(UserDefaults.standard.double(forKey:
"cornerSize"))
        self.showYear = UserDefaults.standard.bool(forKey: "showYear")
        self.showCover = UserDefaults.standard.bool(forKey: "showCover")
    }
}
```

Listing 14-6: *Managing the app's settings from the model*

This model defines three `@Published` properties to store the app's settings. The `cornerSize` property stores a `CGFloat` value (casted to a `Double` value) that determines the radius of the corner of the book's cover, and the `showYear` and `showCover` properties store a Boolean value to determine if the year and the cover should be shown or hidden.

Now, we can use the values of this properties to configure the list of books. The following view includes a `List` view to display the books embedded in a `NavigationView` view.

```
import SwiftUI

struct ContentView: View {
    @EnvironmentObject var appData: AppData

    var body: some View {
        NavigationView {
            List(appData.userData) { book in
                HStack(alignment: .top) {
                    if self.appData.showCover {
                        Image(book.cover)
                            .resizable()
                            .aspectRatio(contentMode: .fit)
                            .cornerRadius(self.appData.cornerSize)
                            .frame(width: 80, height: 100)
                    }
                    VStack(alignment: .leading, spacing: 2) {
                        Text(book.title).bold()
                        Text(book.author)
                        if self.appData.showYear {
                            Text(book.year).font(.caption)
                        }
                    }.padding(.top, 5)
                    Spacer()
                }
            }
            .navigationBarTitle("Books")
            .navigationBarItems(trailing: NavigationLink("⚒", destination:
SettingsView()))
        }
    }
}
```

Listing 14-7: *Adapting the interface to the app's settings*

Each row on the list is configured according to the values in User Settings. The `Image` view is only displayed when the value of the `showCover` property is `true`, the radius of the corner for the cover is determined by the value stored in the `cornerSize` property, and the year is shown depending on the value of the `showYear` property.

The navigation bar of the `ContentView` view includes a button on the right to open a view called `SettingsView`. This is the view where we are letting the user change the configuration.

```
import SwiftUI

struct SettingsView: View {
    @EnvironmentObject var appData: AppData

    var body: some View {
        Form {
            Section {
                HStack(alignment: .top) {
                    Text("Corner Radius")
                        .padding(.top, 6)
```

```
            VStack {
                Slider(value: self.$appData.cornerSize, in: 0...30)
                Image("book1")
                    .resizable()
                    .scaledToFit()
                    .cornerRadius(self.appData.cornerSize)
                    .frame(width: 80, height: 100)
            }
        }
    }
    Section {
        List {
            Toggle("Show Picture", isOn: self.$appData.showCover)
            Toggle("Show Year", isOn: self.$appData.showYear)
        }
    }
}
.navigationBarTitle("Settings")
    }
}
```

Listing 14-8: Modifying the app's settings

The settings view includes a `Slider` view to assign a value between 0 and 30 to the `cornerSize` property, and two `Toggle` views to toggle the values of the `showCover` and `showYear` properties. When the user modifies any of these values, the values in User Defaults are updated, and the views are redrawn, as shown in Figure 14-3, above.

 Do It Yourself: Download the book1.jpg, book2.jpg, and book3.jpg images from our website and add them to the Assets Catalog. Update the `AppData` class with the code of Listing 14-6 and the `ContentView` structure with the code of Listing 14-7. Create a SwiftUI file called SettingsView.swift for the view of Listing 14-8. Run the application on a device. You should see the interface in Figure 14-3, left. Press the settings button. In the settings view, change the corner radius and activate the switch for the picture (Figure 14-3, center). Press the Back button. You should see the interface in Figure 14-3, right.

When the observable object is initialized, the object tries to get the values from User Defaults to initialize the `@Published` properties. If no value is found with those keys, values by default are returned. For example, if there is no value with the key showYear in User Defaults, the system returns the value `false`. This is the reason why when the app is launched for the first time, the year and the cover of the books are not shown on the list. If this is not what we want for our app, we can set our own default values. The `UserDefaults` class includes the `register()` method to set these values. The method receives a dictionary of type `[String: Any]` with the keys and values we want to set by default and stores them in User Defaults. Because this information pertains to the entire application, not just a scene, the values by default should be declared in the `AppDelegate` class when the app is launched, as shown next.

```
import UIKit

@UIApplicationMain
class AppDelegate: UIResponder, UIApplicationDelegate {
    var myData: AppData!

    func application(_ application: UIApplication,
didFinishLaunchingWithOptions launchOptions:
[UIApplication.LaunchOptionsKey: Any]?) -> Bool {
```

```
        let listDefault: [String : Any] = ["cornerSize": 0, "showYear":
true, "showCover": true]
        UserDefaults.standard.register(defaults: listDefault)

        myData = AppData()
        return true
    }
    func application(_ application: UIApplication,
configurationForConnecting connectingSceneSession: UISceneSession,
options: UIScene.ConnectionOptions) -> UISceneConfiguration {
        return UISceneConfiguration(name: "Default Configuration",
sessionRole: connectingSceneSession.role)
    }
}
```

__Listing 14-9:__ Setting values by default

In Listing 14-9, we create a dictionary with the values we want to assign to all the properties when the app is launched for the first time, and then register these values in User Defaults with the **register()** method. From now on, the app will show the covers and the year unless the user changes these values from the settings view later.

 Do It Yourself: Update the **AppDelegate** class in your project with the code of Listing 14-9. Remove the application from the simulator or the device to start fresh. Run the application again. You should see the covers and the year of each book on the list.

 IMPORTANT: iOS allows you to include your app's settings in the Settings app. To add your app to the list of applications in Settings, you must create a Settings Bundle. The option is available in the Resource panel. The topic is beyond the scope of this book. For more information, visit our website and follow the links for this chapter.

(Basic) 14.2 Files

The User Defaults system is meant to be used to store single values with the purpose of customizing the application and preserving user's preferences. For large amounts of data, we need to create our own files. Mobile operative systems allow users to create and access files, but their file system is like no other. The system restricts applications to their own space and a handful of directories to ensure that they do not interfere with each other. This means that we can only access the files and directories that belong to our application.

(Basic) File Manager

Several frameworks and classes use files to store data in a variety of formats. For this reason, the Foundation framework defines a class called **FileManager** that has the sole purpose of managing files and directories. One object of this class is assigned to the app and from it we can create, delete, copy, and move files and directories in the storage space reserved for our app. The class offers the following type property to get a reference to this object.

default—This type property returns a reference to the app's **FileManager** object.

The **FileManager** class offers multiple properties and methods to manage files and directories. The following are the most frequently used.

urls(for: SearchPathDirectory, **in:** SearchPathDomainMask**)**—This method returns an array with the locations of a directory. The **for** attribute is an enumeration with values that represent common system directories, such as `documentDirectory` to represent the Documents directory. And the **in** attribute is another enumeration with values that determine the domain in which the files are located.

createDirectory(at: URL, **withIntermediateDirectories:** Bool, **attributes:** Dictionary?**)**—This method creates a new directory. The **at** attribute specifies the location of the directory, including its name, the **withIntermediateDirectories** attribute indicates whether intermediate directories will also be created or not, and the **attributes** attribute is a dictionary with values that determine the directory's attributes (e.g., ownership). The value `nil` sets the attributes by default, which are usually enough for mobile applications.

createFile(atPath: String, **contents:** Data?, **attributes:** Dictionary?**)**—This method creates a file. The **atPath** attribute specifies the location of the file, including its name and extension, the **contents** attribute represents the content of the file, and the **attributes** attribute is a dictionary with values that determine the file's attributes (e.g., ownership). The value `nil` sets the attributes by default, which are usually enough for mobile applications.

contents(atPath: String**)**—This method returns the content of the file at the path specified by the **atPath** attribute. The value returned is an optional of type `Data`.

contentsOfDirectory(atPath: String**)**—This method returns an array with the paths of the files and directories inside the directory indicated by the **atPath** attribute.

copyItem(atPath: String, **toPath:** String**)**—This method copies the file or directory at the path specified by the **at** attribute to the path specified by the **to** attribute.

moveItem(atPath: String, **toPath:** String**)**—This method moves the file or directory at the path specified by the **at** attribute to the path specified by the **to** attribute.

removeItem(atPath: String**)**—This method removes the file or directory at the path indicated by the **atPath** attribute.

fileExists(atPath: String**)**—This method returns a Boolean value that determines whether the file or the directory at the path specified by the **atPath** attribute exists or not.

attributesOfItem(atPath: String**)**—This method returns a dictionary with the attributes of the file or directory at the location indicated by the **atPath** attribute. The `FileManager` class includes constants to define the attributes, including `creationDate`, `modificationDate`, `size`, and `type`, among others.

(Basic) ## URLs and Paths

As in any other operative system, files are organized in directories (folders). There is a basic directory called *root*, which can contain other files and directories, creating a tree-like structure. To establish a route to reference a file, Apple systems adopt a conventional syntax that separates each part of the route with a forward slash (/), starting with a single slash to indicate the root directory (e.g., /Pictures/Travels/Hawaii.png). This is called *path*, and it is used to access any file in the system. Paths are a simple way to access files but are not enough for the system to identify the location of a file in the storage system. This is because in practice files are usually not stored in a single storage space, but in several units or even in remote servers. Following a long path to find a file also takes time and consumes resources. For these reasons, locations are always identified by URLs (Uniform Resource Locator). URLs are the most efficient way to identify the location of a resource (usually a file) in local or remote systems. They are just strings, like paths, but provide more information to the system and follow a convention that systems can use to manage and access files in a more efficient way. Foundation defines a structure to work with URLs called **URL**. The following are some of its initializers, properties and methods.

URL(fileURLWithPath: String)—This initializer returns a **URL** object referencing a local file or directory. The **fileURLWithPath** attribute is a string with the file's path.

URL(fileURLWithPath: String, **relativeTo:** URL)—This initializer returns a **URL** object referencing a local file or directory. The **fileURLWithPath** attribute is a string with the file's path, and the **relativeTo** attribute is a **URL** object referencing the base URL.

path—This property returns the path of a URL. It is a conditional of type **String**.

pathComponents—This property returns an array of **String** values that represent the components of a path extracted from a URL (the strings between forward slashes).

lastPathComponent—This property returns a string with the last component of a path extracted from a URL. It is usually used to get the file's name and extension.

pathExtension—This property returns a string with the extension of the path extracted from a URL. It is used to get the file's extension.

appendingPathComponent(String)—This method returns a new **URL** structure with the URL of the original object plus the component specified by the attribute.

 IMPORTANT: The **FileManager** class includes methods to work with both paths and URLs. For example, there are two versions of the **createDirectory()** method, one to create the directory from a path and another from a URL. The methods that work with paths take care of converting the path into a URL and are usually easier to implement, but you can use anyone you want. For a complete list, visit our website and follow the links for this chapter.

(Basic) **Files and Directories**

When the application is installed on the device, the system creates a group of standard directories that we can use to store our files. The most useful are the Documents directory, where we can store the user's files, and the Application Support directory, for files that our app needs to create during run time that are not directly generated by the user. The location of these directories is not guaranteed, so we always must ask the system for the current URL that points to the directory or file we want to access. To get the location of common directories like Documents, the **FileManager** class includes the **urls()** method. This method requires two attributes. The first attribute is an enumeration with values that represent different directories. There are several values available, including **documentDirectory** to reference the Documents directory and **applicationSupportDirectory** to reference the Application Support directory. The second attribute is another enumeration with values that indicate the domain where the directory is located. The system organizes directories and files in separate domains depending on their intended usage. The domain where our app's files are stored is the User Domain, identified with the constant **userDomainMask**. In consequence, to get the URL of any of the directories generated for our app and create files to store the user's data, we have to get a reference to the **FileManager** object and then call the **urls()** method with the values that represent the location we want to use.

Although we can read and create files from anywhere in the code, it is recommendable to manage all our files from the model. The following is a simple model with an observable object to illustrate how to access the directories available for the application and how to create a file.

```
import SwiftUI

class AppData: ObservableObject {
    func saveFile(name: String) {
        let manager = FileManager.default
        let documents = manager.urls(for: .documentDirectory, in:
.userDomainMask)
        let docURL = documents.first!

        let newFileURL = docURL.appendingPathComponent(name)
        let path = newFileURL.path
        manager.createFile(atPath: path, contents: nil, attributes: nil)
    }
}
```

Listing 14-10: Accessing directories and creating files

This model defines a method called **saveFile()** to create a file with the name in the attribute. The method gets a reference to the **FileManager** object assigned to the application and then calls the **urls()** method on the manager to get the URL for the Documents directory. The **urls()** method returns an array of optional **URL** structures with all the possible locations of the directory. In the case of the Documents directory, the right value is the first item of the array, that we get from the **first** property. Once we have this URL, we must add the name of our file to it to get the complete URL pointing to the file we want to create. For this purpose, the **URL** class includes the **appendingPathComponent()** method. This method adds a string to the end of the URL and takes care of including the necessary forward slashes to ensure its validity. Because we are going to work with paths, we get the URL's path from the **path** property and finally call the **createFile()** method to create the file (if the file already exists, the method updates its content).

The model is ready, now we must create the view. The idea is to create a simple project that later we can expand to add more functionality. Therefore, we are going to create a simple view to present the files and open a sheet to let the user add a new one, as shown in Figure 14-4.

Figure 14-4: Interface to create files

The following is the code for the initial view.

```
import SwiftUI

struct ContentView: View {
    @EnvironmentObject var appData: AppData
    @State private var openSheet: Bool = false

    var body: some View {
        NavigationView {
            VStack {
                Text("No Files")
                Spacer()
            }.padding()
```

```
            .navigationBarTitle("Files")
            .navigationBarItems(trailing: Button("Add File") {
                self.openSheet = true
            })
            .sheet(isPresented: $openSheet) {
                AddFileView(openSheet: self.$openSheet)
                    .environmentObject(self.appData)
            }
        }
    }
}
struct ContentView_Previews: PreviewProvider {
    static var previews: some View {
        ContentView().environmentObject(AppData())
    }
}
```

Listing 14-11: Opening a sheet to add files to the model

As always, we get access to the model from the environment. Because we are not showing the files yet, there is no much to do in this view. We provide a button in the navigation bar to open the sheet and define the sheet with a view called **AddFileView**. Notice that because we need access to the model from the sheet, we must pass a reference to its environment (see Listing 10-6). The following is the view for the sheet.

```
import SwiftUI

struct AddFileView: View {
    @EnvironmentObject var appData: AppData
    @Binding var openSheet: Bool
    @State private var nameInput: String = ""

    var body: some View {
        VStack {
            HStack {
                Text("Name:")
                TextField("Insert File Name", text: $nameInput)
                    .textFieldStyle(RoundedBorderTextFieldStyle())
                    .autocapitalization(.none)
                    .disableAutocorrection(true)
            }.padding(.top, 25)
            HStack {
                Spacer()
                Button("Create") {
                    var fileName = self.nameInput.trimmingCharacters(in:
.whitespaces)
                    if !fileName.isEmpty {
                        fileName += ".txt"
                        self.appData.saveFile(name: fileName)
                        self.openSheet = false
                    }
                }
            }
            Spacer()
        }.padding()
    }
}
struct AddFileView_Previews: PreviewProvider {
    static var previews: some View {
        AddFileView(openSheet: .constant(false))
```

```
        .environmentObject(AppData())
    }
}
```

Listing 14-12: Creating new files

In this view, we do a little more work, but nothing new. The view includes a **TextField** view for the user to insert the name of the file and a **Button** view to create it. When the button is pressed, we trim the string to remove white spaces, add the ".txt" string at the end of the name (adding an extension is not necessary), and then call the **saveFile()** method in the model to create the file. After this, the Documents directory designated to our app will contain an empty file with the name inserted by the user and the extension txt.

 Do It Yourself: Create a SwiftUI project. Create a Swift file called AppData.swift for the model in Listing 14-10. Update the AppDelegate.swift file with the code of Listing 7-14 and the SceneDelegate.swift file with the code of Listing 7-20 to instantiate the model and insert it in the environment. Update the **ContentView** structure with the code of Listing 14-11. Create a SwiftUI file called AddFileView.swift for the view in Listing 14-12. Run the application on the simulator or a device and press the Add File button. Insert the name of the file and press the Create button. The file is created, and the sheet is closed.

The initial view only shows the message "No Files" but the purpose of this application is to let the user create files and show them on the screen. The **FileManager** class offers methods to list the content of a directory. For instance, we can use the **contentsOfDirectory()** method to get an array of strings with the names of the files and directories in a specific path. This is useful, because we can store these values in an array and present the content of that array to the user with a **List** view. For this purpose, we need a model to store the names of the files along with an id, as we did for books in previous models, and a **@Published** property to contain the list. The following is the new model for this project.

```
import SwiftUI

struct File: Identifiable {
    let id: UUID = UUID()
    let name: String
}
class AppData: ObservableObject {
    @Published var listOfFiles: [File] = []

    var manager: FileManager
    var docURL: URL

    func saveFile(name: String) {
        let newFileURL = docURL.appendingPathComponent(name)
        let path = newFileURL.path
        manager.createFile(atPath: path, contents: nil, attributes: nil)
        if !listOfFiles.contains(where: { $0.name == name}) {
            listOfFiles.append(File(name: name))
        }
    }

    init() {
        manager = FileManager.default
        let documents = manager.urls(for: .documentDirectory, in:
.userDomainMask)
        docURL = documents.first!
```

```
        if let list = try? manager.contentsOfDirectory(atPath: docURL.path) {
            for name in list {
                let newFile = File(name: name)
                listOfFiles.append(newFile)
            }
        }
    }
}
```

Listing 14-13: Managing the app's files

The first structure, called `File`, provides the model. It conforms to the `Identifiable` protocol and includes the corresponding `id` property to identify each value and a property called `name` to store the name of the file. Next, we define a property to store a reference to the `FileManager` object assigned to the application and another to store the URL of the Documents directory. The `saveFile()` method is the same as before, but after creating a new file we now check if the name of the file already exists in the `listOfFiles` property and if not, we create an instance of the `File` structure with that name and add it to the array. Finally, we initialize the properties. First, we get a reference to the `FileManager` object with the `default` property and assign it to the `manager` property. Then, we get the URL of the Documents directory with the `urls()` method and assigns it to the `docURL` property. Finally we get the list of files in the directory with the `contentsOfDirectory()` method. This method returns an array of strings with the name of the files, so we create a loop, initialize an instance of the `File` structure with each name, and add them to the `listOfFiles` array. Notice that the method throws errors, so we use the `try?` keyword to handle them and only store the name of the files if the value returned is not `nil`.

After the `AppData` structure is initialized, the `listOfFiles` property contains the names of all the files in the directory, so we can show them to the user. The following is the new initial view designed for this purpose.

```
struct ContentView: View {
    @EnvironmentObject var appData: AppData
    @State private var openSheet: Bool = false

    var body: some View {
        NavigationView {
            VStack {
                List {
                    ForEach(self.appData.listOfFiles) { file in
                        Text(file.name)
                    }
                }
            }.padding()
            .navigationBarTitle("Files")
            .navigationBarItems(trailing: Button("Add File") {
                self.openSheet = true
            })
            .sheet(isPresented: $openSheet) {
                AddFileView(openSheet: self.$openSheet)
                    .environmentObject(self.appData)
            }
        }
    }
}
```

Listing 14-14: Listing the files created by the user

Again, there is nothing new in this view. All the work is done by the model. The `List` view includes a `ForEach` view that lists the values of the `listOfFiles` property. Each row includes the name of the file, as shown in Figure 14-5.

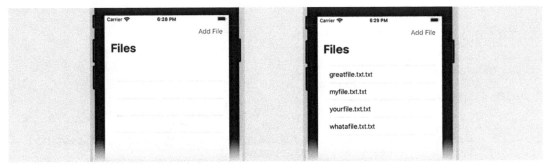

Figure 14-5: List of files

 Do It Yourself: Update the AppData.swift file with the code of Listing 14-13 and the `ContentView` structure with the code of Listing 14-14. Run the application on the simulator or a device. Press the Add File button to add a file. Insert the name of the file and press the Create button. You should see on the screen the list of all the files you have created.

The same way we create a file, we can create a directory. The method to create a directory is called `createDirectory()`. Again, the method takes three values: the path of the new directory (including its name), a Boolean value that indicates if we want to create all the directories included in the path that does not exist (in case the path includes directories we have not created yet), and the directory's attributes. This method throws an error if it cannot complete the task, so we must handle the error with the `try` keyword. Using this method, we are going to expand our project to store files in two directories called *original* and *archived*. The original folder will contain the files created by the user, and the archived folder will contain the files the user decides to archive. The following is the model we need for this purpose.

```
import SwiftUI

struct File: Identifiable {
    let id: UUID = UUID()
    let name: String
}
class AppData: ObservableObject {
    @Published var listOfFiles: [Int:[File]] = [:]
    @Published var currentDirectory: Int

    var manager: FileManager
    var docURL: URL
    let directories = ["original", "archived"]

    func saveFile(name: String) {
        let newFileURL =
docURL.appendingPathComponent("\(directories[0])/\(name)")
        let path = newFileURL.path
        manager.createFile(atPath: path, contents: nil, attributes: nil)

        if let exists = listOfFiles[0]?.contains(where: { $0.name == name
}) {
```

```
            if !exists {
                let newFile = File(name: name)
                listOfFiles[0]?.append(newFile)
            }
        }
    }
    init() {
        listOfFiles = [0: [], 1: []]
        currentDirectory = 0
        manager = FileManager.default
        docURL = manager.urls(for: .documentDirectory, in:
.userDomainMask).first!

        for (index, directory) in directories.enumerated() {
            let newDirectoryURL = docURL.appendingPathComponent(directory)
            let path = newDirectoryURL.path
            do {
                try manager.createDirectory(atPath: path,
withIntermediateDirectories: false, attributes: nil)
            } catch {
                print("The directory already exists")
            }
            if let list = try? manager.contentsOfDirectory(atPath: path) {
                for name in list {
                    let newFile = File(name: name)
                    listOfFiles[index]?.append(newFile)
                }
            }
        }
    }
}
```

Listing 14-15: Working with custom directories

The model must store two lists of files, one for the original directory and another for the archive directory. In this case, we have decided to turn the `listOfFiles` array from an array into a dictionary to store these lists. The items in the dictionary are identified with an integer and their values are array of strings. The item with the key 0 is going to contain an array with the names of the files in the original directory, and the item with the key 1 is going to contain an array with the names of the files in the archived directory. To know which directory the user is currently working on, we define a new `@Published` property called `currentDirectory`, and to easily get the name of the directories, we define an array called `directories` with two strings: "original" and "archived".

The `saveFile()` method stores the files as always, but the path now includes the name of the original directory, so the new files are always stored in that folder (notice the forward slash in between the name of the directory and the name of the file). We also have to contemplate the directory when we check whether the file already exists or not (`listOfFiles[0]?.contains(where: { $0.name == name })`).

In the structure's initializer, we initialize the `listOfFiles` dictionary with two items, 0 and 1, and empty arrays (no files were loaded yet). We also assign the value 0 to the `currentDirectory` property to select the original directory by default and prepare the rest of the properties as before. Finally, we load the files for each directory with a `for in` loop; first the original (0) and then the archived (1).

The view must provide a way for the user to switch between one directory and another (although at this time the application doesn't provide a way to assign files to the archived directory). For this example, we have decided to use a segmented picker with two buttons.

```
struct ContentView: View {
    @EnvironmentObject var appData: AppData
    @State private var openSheet: Bool = false

    var body: some View {
        NavigationView {
            VStack {
                Picker("", selection: self.$appData.currentDirectory) {
                    ForEach(0..<self.appData.directories.count) { index in
                        Text(self.appData.directories[index]).tag(index)
                    }
                }.padding([.leading, .trailing], 8)
                .labelsHidden()
                .pickerStyle(SegmentedPickerStyle())

                List {
ForEach(self.appData.listOfFiles[self.appData.currentDirectory] ?? []) {
file in
                        Text(file.name)
                    }
                }
            }
            .navigationBarTitle("Files")
            .navigationBarItems(trailing: Button("Add File") {
                self.openSheet = true
            }.disabled(self.appData.currentDirectory != 0 ? true : false))
            .sheet(isPresented: $openSheet) {
                AddFileView(openSheet: self.$openSheet)
                    .environmentObject(self.appData)
            }
        }
    }
}
```

Listing 14-16: Listing files from two directories

The `ContentView` view in Listing 14-16 includes a `Picker` view with the values in the `directories` property ("original" and "archived"). When the user selects one or the other, the value of the `currentDirectory` changes, and this tells our model which directory the user is currently working on. To create the list of files, we read again the value of this property. If the value is 0, we list the files of the original directory and if the value is 1, we list the files of the archived directory.

One thing we must contemplate when working with dictionaries, is that they return an optional. Therefore, the `ForEach` view won't work unless we provide an alternative value. In this case, we use the nil-coalescing operator (`??`) to create the list with an empty array if the value of the `currentDirectory` property does not exists in the dictionary (it is different than 0 or 1).

Because we want the user to be able to add new files only to the original directory, we applied the `disabled()` modifier to the Add File button in the navigation bar. If the user is working in the archived directory, the button is disabled and therefore only the original directory will contain files for now, as shown in Figure 14-6.

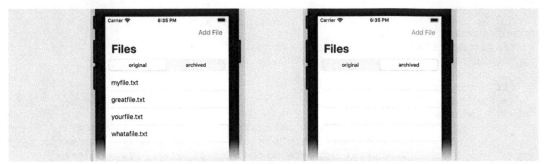

Figure 14-6: *Files from two directories*

It is time to let the user archive files and delete them. For this, we need to move files from the original directory to the archived directory and remove them from storage. The **FileManager** class includes the **moveItem()** and **removeItem()** methods for this purpose. The following are the methods we need to add to our model to be able to move and remove files from the view.

```
func deleteFile(name: String) {
   let fileURL =
docURL.appendingPathComponent("\(directories[currentDirectory])/\(name)")
   do {
      try manager.removeItem(atPath: fileURL.path)
      listOfFiles[currentDirectory]?.removeAll(where: {$0.name == name})
   } catch {
      print("File was not removed")
   }
}
func moveToArchived(name: String) {
   let origin =
docURL.appendingPathComponent("\(directories[0])/\(name)")
   let destination =
docURL.appendingPathComponent("\(directories[1])/\(name)")
   if !manager.fileExists(atPath: destination.path) {
      do {
         try manager.moveItem(atPath: origin.path, toPath:
destination.path)
         listOfFiles[0]?.removeAll(where: { $0.name == name} )
         listOfFiles[1]?.append(File(name: name))
      } catch {
         print("File was not moved")
      }
   }
}
```

Listing 14-17: *Moving and deleting files*

The first method is called **deleteFile()** and it receives the name of the file to remove. Because the user can only delete files from the directory in which is currently working, we use the value of the **currentDirectory** property to define the file's URL. With this URL, we call the **removeItem()** method on the **FileManager** object to delete the file. If the operation is successful, we also remove the name of the file from the array corresponding to the current directory with the **removeAll(where:)** method, so the file is removed from the screen.

The next method is called **moveToArchived()**. The purpose of this method is to move the file selected by the user from the original directory to the archived directory. For this purpose, we define two URLs, one to indicate the current location of the file

(\\(directories[0])/\\(name)) and another to indicate where the file is going to be created and with what name (\\(directories[1])/\\(name)). Before doing anything, we check if the file already exists at the destination with the `fileExists()` method. If the file doesn't exist, we use those two URLs to call the `moveItem()` method on the `FileManager` object and move it. If the operation is successful, we still must update the information in the model. First, we remove the file from the array of the original directory (0) with the `removeAll(where:)` method. This removes all the strings in the array that are equal to the name of the file we are moving. And second, we add the file to the array corresponding to the archived directory, so the name appears on the right folder.

The view now needs to provide the tools for the user to move and remove each file. For this example, we have decided to show the files in rows that include two buttons, one to move the file to the archived folder and another to delete it. We call the view for this row `RowFile`.

```
struct ContentView: View {
    @EnvironmentObject var appData: AppData
    @State private var openSheet: Bool = false

    var body: some View {
        NavigationView {
            VStack {
                Picker("", selection: self.$appData.currentDirectory) {
                    ForEach(0..<self.appData.directories.count) { index in
                        Text(self.appData.directories[index]).tag(index)
                    }
                }.labelsHidden()
                .pickerStyle(SegmentedPickerStyle())

                List {
                    ForEach(self.appData.listOfFiles[
self.appData.currentDirectory] ?? []) { file in
                        RowFile(file: file)
                    }
                }
            }
            .navigationBarTitle("Files")
            .navigationBarItems(trailing: Button("Add File") {
                self.openSheet = true
            }.disabled(self.appData.currentDirectory != 0 ? true : false))
            .sheet(isPresented: $openSheet) {
                AddFileView(openSheet: self.$openSheet)
                    .environmentObject(self.appData)
            }
        }
    }
}
struct RowFile: View {
    @EnvironmentObject var appData: AppData
    let file: File

    var body: some View {
        HStack {
            Text(file.name)
            Spacer()
            if self.appData.currentDirectory == 0 {
                Button(action: {
                    self.appData.moveToArchived(name: self.file.name)
                }, label: {
                    Image(systemName: "folder")
                        .font(.body)
```

```
                .foregroundColor(Color.green)
        }).buttonStyle(PlainButtonStyle())
    }
    Button(action: {
        self.appData.deleteFile(name: self.file.name)
    }, label: {
        Image(systemName: "trash")
            .font(.body)
            .foregroundColor(Color.red)
    }).buttonStyle(PlainButtonStyle())
    }
   }
}
```

Listing 14-18: Adding tools to move and delete files

Nothing changes in the view, except that instead of showing the name of the file with a `Text` view, we now create a `RowFile` view to include the buttons. The buttons are created with SF Symbols, one that represents a folder and another that represents a trash bin. The button with the image of a folder calls the `moveToArchived()` method in the model to move the file to the archived folder, but it is only displayed when the current directory is original (`currentDirectory == 0`). On the other hand, the button with the image of a trash bin is displayed in both directories, and calls the `deleteFile()` method in the model to delete the file. Notice that we declare the styles for the buttons as `PlainButtonStyle`. This makes the buttons responsive when they are inserted in a row (the buttons have precedence over the selection of the row). The result is shown in Figure 14-7.

Figure 14-7: Buttons to move and delete a file

 Do It Yourself: Add the methods in Listing 14-17 to the observable object in your model (the `AppData` class). Update the ContentView.swift file with the code of Listing 14-18. Run the application on a device. Press the Add File button to add some files and then press the folder icon on a file. You should see the file in the archived folder. Press the trash icon on a file to remove it.

(Medium) **Files Attributes**

Some applications need to know more than the name of the file. The `FileManager` class offers the `attributesOfItem()` method to get the file's attributes, such as the date of creation or the size. The method returns a dictionary with predefined keys to identify each value. There are several constants available we can use as keys. The most common are `creationDate` (the date the file was created), `modificationDate` (last time it was modified), `size`, and `type`. We are going to use these keys in the following method to get the attributes of the file selected by the user and return a tuple with those values.

```
func getDetails(file: UUID) -> (String, String, String) {
    var values = ("", "", "")
    if let fileIndex = listOfFiles[currentDirectory]?.firstIndex(where: {
$0.id == file }) {
        let fileName = listOfFiles[currentDirectory]![fileIndex].name
        let fileURL =
docURL.appendingPathComponent("\(directories[currentDirectory])/\(fileNam
e)")
        let filePath = fileURL.path

        if manager.fileExists(atPath: filePath) {
            if let attributes = try? manager.attributesOfItem(atPath:
filePath) {
                let type = attributes[.type] as! FileAttributeType
                let size = attributes[.size] as! Int
                let date = attributes[.creationDate] as! Date
                if type != FileAttributeType.typeDirectory {
                    values.0 = fileURL.pathExtension
                    values.1 = String(size)

                    let formatter = DateFormatter()
                    formatter.dateStyle = .medium
                    formatter.timeStyle = .none
                    values.2 = formatter.string(from: date)
                }
            }
        }
    }
    return values
}
```

Listing 14-19: Reading the file's attributes

In this example, we are working with the **UUID** value used to identify each file in the model. We could have used the file's name, but it is best practice to identify the data in the model by the identification values. The **getDetails()** method in Listing 14-19 follows this approach and therefore the first task performed by the method is to get the name of the file associated to the id and build the path. Once we get the path to the file, we are able to call the **attributesOfItem()** method to read its attributes. The method returns a dictionary with those values. Notice that besides using the predefined keys to read the values in this dictionary, such as **type**, **size**, and **creationDate**, the values are returned of type **Any**, so we must cast them to the right types. The **type** value must be converted into a **FileAttributeType** structure, the **size** into an **Int**, and the **creationDate** into a **Date** structure. The **FileAttributeType** structure determines the resource's type. The structure includes properties to represent different types of resources. The most frequently used are **typeRegular** to represent files and **typeDirectory** to represent directories. By reading these properties, we can determine if the item is a file or a directory. This is useful when in addition to files our application allows the user to create folders. If the item is a file, we assign the attributes to a tuple and return it.

To show the details of a file to the user, we have decided to create an additional view that is opened when the user taps on a file on the list. We call it **FileDetailsView**.

```
import SwiftUI
```

```
struct FileDetailsView: View {
    @EnvironmentObject var appData: AppData
    let file: UUID

    var body: some View {
        let values = appData.getDetails(file: file)
        return VStack {
            HStack {
                Text("Extension:")
                    .frame(width: 80, alignment: .trailing)
                Text(values.0)
                    .frame(minWidth: 0, maxWidth: .infinity, alignment:
.leading)
            }
            HStack {
                Text("Size:")
                    .frame(width: 80, alignment: .trailing)
                Text(values.1)
                    .frame(minWidth: 0, maxWidth: .infinity, alignment:
.leading)
            }
            HStack {
                Text("Date:")
                    .frame(width: 80, alignment: .trailing)
                Text(values.2)
                    .frame(minWidth: 0, maxWidth: .infinity, alignment:
.leading)
            }
            Spacer()
        }.padding()
        .navigationBarTitle("Details")
    }
}
struct FileDetailsView_Previews: PreviewProvider {
    static var previews: some View {
        FileDetailsView(file: UUID()).environmentObject(AppData())
    }
}
```

Listing 14-20: Showing the file's attributes

This view receives the file's id from the list and then calls the **getDetails()** method in the model with that value. The tuple returned is assigned to the **values** constant, and finally the constant is used to show the attributes to the user (**values.0** for the extension, **values.1** for the size, and **values.2** for the date).

Of course, to open this view we must embed each row in a **NavigationLink** view that creates an instance of the **FilesDetailsView** structure with the file's id. The following are the modifications we must introduce to the **List** view in the **ContentView** structure for this purpose.

```
List {
    ForEach(self.appData.listOfFiles[self.appData.currentDirectory] ?? [])
{ file in
        NavigationLink(destination: FileDetailsView(file: file.id), label:{
            RowFile(file: file)
        })
    }
}
```

Listing 14-21: Opening the details view

Notice that we send the value of the `id` property to the instance of the `FileDetailsView` structure to work with the file's id, not its name. The result is shown in Figure 14-8.

Figure 14-8: Details view with the file's attributes

 Do It Yourself: Add the method in Listing 14-19 to the observable object (the `AppData` class). Create a SwiftUI file called FileDetailsView.swift for the view in Listing 14-20. Update the `List` view in the `ContentView` structure with the code of Listing 14-21. Run the application on a device. Tap on a file. You should see the attributes of that file on the screen, as shown in Figure 14-8.

Basic   Files Content

Storage systems, like hard drives and solid-state drives, store information the only way a computer knows, as a series of ones and zeros. Therefore, the information we want to store in files has to be converted into a stream of bytes that can be later turned back into the original data. Foundation offers the `Data` structure for this purpose. The structure provides properties and methods to process raw data. Although we can work directly with a `Data` structure, most frameworks provided by Apple include tools to convert our data, including text and images, into `Data` structures that we can process or store on files. There are several alternatives available depending on the type of data we want to store. For instance, the UIKit framework includes the `UIImage` class to manage images. The class includes the following initializers to create an image from data.

UIImage(named: String)—This initializer creates an object that contains the image specified by the **named** attribute. The attribute is a string with the name of the file or the image in the Assets Catalog (the extension is not required).

UIImage(contentsOfFile: String)—This initializer creates an object that contains the image stored in the file indicated by the **contentsOfFile** attribute. The attribute is a string with a path that determines the location of the file.

UIImage(data: Data, **scale:** CGFloat)—This initializer creates an object that contains an image generated from the data provided by the **data** attribute and with an associated scale specified by the **scale** attribute.

Once we load an image with the `UIImage` class, we can process it or display it on the screen with an `Image` view. The `Image` structure includes the following initializer to create a view with the image contained by an `UIImage` object.

Image(uiImage: UIImage)—This initializer creates an `Image` view with the image provided by the `uiImage` attribute.

The opposite process, converting the image into data to store it in a file, is performed by the following methods defined in the `UIImage` class.

pngData()—This method converts the image into raw data in the PNG format and returns a `Data` structure with the result.

jpegData(compressionQuality: CGFloat)—This method converts the image into raw data in the JPEG format and returns a `Data` structure with the result. The **compressionQuality** attribute determines the level of compression (from 0.0 to 1.0).

As mentioned before, to load data from a file, the `FileManager` object includes the `contents()` method. Once we get the data, we can convert it into an image with the `UIImage(data:)` initializer. On the other hand, storing an image into a file requires a few steps. The image must be loaded with a `UIImage` object, then the object must be converted into a `Data` structure with the `pngData()` or `jpegData()` methods, and finally stored in a file with the `createFile()` method of the `FileManager` object implemented before. This method creates a file if it doesn't exist or updates its content otherwise, so we can use it to store different images. In the following example, we are going to use it to store the image selected by the user. If the user selects another image later, we just replace the old image in the file with the new one. Next is the model for this project.

```
import SwiftUI

class AppData: ObservableObject {
    @Published var imageInFile: UIImage?
    var manager: FileManager
    var docURL: URL
    let listPictures = ["spot1", "spot2", "spot3"]

    func saveFile(namePicture: String) {
        let image = UIImage(named: namePicture)
        if let imageData = image?.pngData() {
            let fileURL = docURL.appendingPathComponent("imagedata.dat")
            let filePath = fileURL.path
            if manager.createFile(atPath: filePath, contents: imageData,
attributes: nil) {
                imageInFile = image
            }
        }
    }
    init() {
        manager = FileManager.default
        docURL = manager.urls(for: .documentDirectory, in:
.userDomainMask).first!

        let fileURL = docURL.appendingPathComponent("imagedata.dat")
        let filePath = fileURL.path
        if manager.fileExists(atPath: filePath) {
            if let content = manager.contents(atPath: filePath) {
                imageInFile = UIImage(data: content)
            }
        }
    }
}
```

Listing 14-22: Loading and saving an image

This is a simple model with just an observable object. It includes a `@Published` property called `imageInFile` to store the image loaded from the file and a method to store a new one. The initializer defines the `manager` and `docURL` properties, as always, and then it checks if there is a file called imagedata.dat. If the file exists, we get its content with the `contents()` method of the `FileManager` object. This method returns a `Data` structure with the data to reconstruct the image, so we create a `UIImage` object with it and assign it to the `imageInFile` property to keep it in the model for later use.

The model also includes an array with the names of three images, spot1, spot2, and spot3. These are the images we are going to let the user select to store in the file. When the user selects one of these images, the `saveFile()` method in the model is called. In this method, we create a new `UIImage` object with the image selected by the user and then convert it into a `Data` structure with the `pngData()` method. If the method is successful, we use the `createFile()` method of the `FileManager` object to create the file or update it with the new image if already exists. Notice that the `Data` structure created from the image is assigned to the method's `contents` attribute to provide the content to store in the file. If the file is successfully created or updated, we assign the `UIImage` object to the `imageInFile` property to update the image in the model.

The views are simple. The initial view displays the image in the `imageInFile` property (the current image in the file), and it lets the user open a sheet to select another one.

```
import SwiftUI

struct ContentView: View {
    @EnvironmentObject var appData: AppData
    @State private var openSheet: Bool = false

    var body: some View {
        VStack {
            Image(uiImage: appData.imageInFile ?? UIImage(named:
"nopicture")!)
                .resizable()
                .scaledToFill()
                .frame(minWidth: 0, maxWidth: .infinity, minHeight: 0,
maxHeight: .infinity)
                .onTapGesture {
                    self.openSheet = true
                }
        }
        .edgesIgnoringSafeArea(.all)
        .sheet(isPresented: self.$openSheet) {
            SelectPictureView(openSheet: self.$openSheet)
                .environmentObject(self.appData)
        }
    }
}
struct ContentView_Previews: PreviewProvider {
    static var previews: some View {
        ContentView().environmentObject(AppData())
    }
}
```

Listing 14-23: Showing the image in the file

The `Image` view in Listing 14-23 is created from the `UIImage` value stored in the `imageInFile` property (the image stored in the file). Notice that the `UIImage` initializer always returns an optional, so we must provide an alternative image in case the file can't be loaded, or it doesn't exist yet. For this purpose, we use the nil-coalescing operator (??) to load the image nopicture from the Assets Catalog. The `Image` view includes the `onTapGesture()` modifier to open a sheet when the image is tapped by the user. In the view opened by the sheet, we are going to show to the user three images to select from. We call this view `SelectPictureView`.

```
import SwiftUI
struct SelectPictureView: View {
    @EnvironmentObject var appData: AppData
    @Binding var openSheet: Bool

    var body: some View {
        VStack {
            ScrollView(.horizontal, showsIndicators: true) {
                HStack(spacing: 15) {
                    ForEach(self.appData.listPictures, id: \.self) { name in
                        ZStack(alignment: .bottom) {
                            Image(name)
                                .resizable()
                                .scaledToFit()
                                .frame(width: 160)
                            Button(action: {
                                self.appData.saveFile(namePicture: name)
                                self.openSheet = false
                            }, label: {
                                Text("Select Picture")
                                    .foregroundColor(Color.white)
                            }).padding(8)
                            .background(Color.blue)
                            .cornerRadius(5)
                            .offset(x: 0, y: -15)
                        }
                    }
                }
            }.padding(.top, 25)
            Spacer()
        }.padding()
    }
}
struct SelectPictureView_Previews: PreviewProvider {
    static var previews: some View {
        SelectPictureView(openSheet: .constant(false))
            .environmentObject(AppData())
    }
}
```

Listing 14-24: *Displaying a list of images for the user to select*

The images are inside a horizontal `ScrollView` view and are embedded in a `ZStack` to be able to display a button on top that the user can tap to select the image. When the button is pressed, we call the `saveFile()` method in the model with the name of the selected image and that image is stored in the file. The result is shown in Figure 14-9.

Figure 14-9: *Interface to select and store an image*

Chapter 14 - Storage

Do It Yourself: Create a SwiftUI project. Download the nopicture.png, spot1.jpg, spot2.jpg, and spot3.jpg images from our website and add them to the Assets Catalog. Update the AppDelegate.swift file with the code of Listing 7-14 and the SceneDelegate.swift file with the code of Listing 7-20 to instantiate the model and insert it in the environment. Create the AppData.swift file for the model of Listing 14-22. Update the `ContentView` structure with the code in Listing 14-23. Create a Swift file called SelectPictureView.swift for the view in Listing 14-24. Run the application on the simulator or a device. You should see the image nopicture on the screen. Tap on the image and select a new image from the list. Stop the application from Xcode and run it again. You should see the selected image on the screen, as shown in Figure 14-9.

Besides the `UIImage` class, there are other classes and structures available in Apple's frameworks to turn values into `Data` structure for storage. For instance, the `String` structure includes a method that turns a string into data an also an initializer that can get back the string from a `Data` structure.

String(data: Data, **encoding:** Encoding)—This initializer creates a `String` value with the text in the `Data` structure provided by the **data** attribute. The **encoding** attribute is a value provided by properties of a structure called `Encoding` included in the `String` structure that determine the type of encoding used to generate the string. The encoding usually depends on the language the text was written in. The most frequently used are `utf8` and `ascii`.

data(using: Encoding, **allowLossyConversion:** Bool)—This method returns a `Data` structure containing the string in the original `String` value. The **using** attribute is a value provided by properties of the `Encoding` structure that determine the type of encoding used to generate the string. The encoding usually depends on the language the text was written in. The most frequently used are `utf8` and `ascii`. The **allowLossyConversion** attribute determines the precision of the conversion.

The `String` structure also includes a convenient method to turn a string into data and store it in a file, all at once.

write(to: URL, **atomically:** Bool, **encoding:** Encoding)—This method converts a string into a `Data` structure and stores it in the file located at the URL specified by the **to** attribute. The **atomically** attribute determines if we want the data to be stored in an auxiliary file first to ensure that the original file is not corrupted (recommended). The **encoding** attribute is a value provided by properties of the `Encoding` structure that determine the type of encoding used to generate the string. The most frequently used are `utf8` and `ascii`.

Storing text in a file is a very similar process. We must convert the string to data to store it in the file and the data to a string when we get it back. The following code shows the changes we must introduce to the model to work with text instead of images.

```
import SwiftUI

class AppData: ObservableObject {
    @Published var textInFile: String = "Undefined"
    var manager: FileManager
    var docURL: URL
```

```
       func saveFile(text: String) {
          if let textData = text.data(using: .utf8, allowLossyConversion:
true) {
             let fileURL = docURL.appendingPathComponent("textdata.dat")
             let filePath = fileURL.path
             if manager.createFile(atPath: filePath, contents: textData,
attributes: nil) {
                textInFile = text
             }
          }
       }
       init() {
          manager = FileManager.default
          docURL = manager.urls(for: .documentDirectory, in:
.userDomainMask).first!

          let fileURL = docURL.appendingPathComponent("textdata.dat")
          let filePath = fileURL.path
          if manager.fileExists(atPath: filePath) {
             if let content = manager.contents(atPath: filePath) {
                if let text = String(data: content, encoding: .utf8) {
                   textInFile = text
                }
             }
          }
       }
    }
}
```

Listing 14-25: Storing text in a file

In the model's initializer, we look for a file with the name textdata.dat. If the file exists, we get its content with the **contents()** method, as we did before for images, and then convert the data into a string with the **String(data:)** initializer and assign the result to the **textInFile** property to keep the value in the model. The process to store text in the file is also similar. We convert the string into a **Data** structure with the **data()** method and then store the data in the file with the **createFile()** method of the **FileManager** object.

The view for this example shows the text currently stored in the file, that we get from the **textInFile** property, and provides a **TextField** view to let the user insert a new message and a button to store it.

```
import SwiftUI

struct ContentView: View {
   @EnvironmentObject var appData: AppData
   @State private var inputText: String = ""

   var body: some View {
      VStack(spacing: 12) {
         Text(appData.textInFile)
            .lineLimit(nil)
            .padding(15)
            .frame(minWidth: 0, maxWidth: .infinity)
            .background(Color(white: 0.8))
         TextField("Insert New Message", text: $inputText)
            .textFieldStyle(RoundedBorderTextFieldStyle())
         HStack {
            Spacer()
            Button("Save Message") {
```

Chapter 14 - Storage

```
                let message = self.inputText.trimmingCharacters(in:
.whitespaces)
                if !message.isEmpty {
                    self.appData.saveFile(text: message)
                    self.inputText = ""
                }
            }
        }
        Spacer()
    }.padding()
}
}
struct ContentView_Previews: PreviewProvider {
    static var previews: some View {
        ContentView().environmentObject(AppData())
    }
}
```

Listing 14-26: Showing the string stored in a file

When the user presses the button, the `saveFile()` method is executed with the string inserted in the input field and the file is created or updated with this new message, so the last message inserted by the user is shown on the screen every time the app is launched.

Figure 14-10: Interface to insert and store a text

 Do It Yourself: Update the `AppData` class with the code in Listing 14-25 and the `ContentView` structure with the code in Listing 14-26. Run the application on the simulator or a device. Insert a message in the input field and press the Save Message button. Stop the application from Xcode and run it again. You should see your message on the screen.

(Medium) Bundle

In previous examples, we have worked with files created at run time, but sometimes we need to get access to files added to our project during development. This could be simple text files or even complex databases. But the app's files, code, and resources are not just stored in a single directory; they are encapsulated in a bundle. Bundles are directories assigned exclusively to each application. They create a hierarchical structure to organize all the app's files and resources. For this reason, to get access to the files in our project, we first must access our app's bundle.

To create and manage bundles, Foundation includes the `Bundle` class. The class offers properties and methods to work with bundles and get their location, including a type property that returns a reference to the bundle created by default for our application.

main—This type property returns a reference to the app's bundle.

bundleURL—This property returns a `URL` structure with the bundle's URL.

bundlePath—This property returns a string with the bundle's path.

Because we are not able to determine the location of our app's files and resources during development, every time we want to access these files from code, we must get their URLs from the `Bundle` object. The class provides the following methods for this purpose.

url(forResource: String?, **withExtension:** String?)—This method returns a `URL` structure with the URL of a file or directory inside the bundle. The first attribute specifies the name of the file or directory we are looking for, and the **withExtension** attribute specifies its extension.

path(forResource: String?, **ofType:** String?)—This method returns the path of a file or directory inside the bundle. The first attribute specifies the name of the file or directory we are looking for, and the **ofType** attribute specifies its extension.

We frequently have to use the `Bundle` object in professional applications to access files that are required for some services, like databases, for example, but we can also take advantage of this object to load files with initial data to populate the model when the app is launched for the first time or to restore an initial state. The following example loads a text file called quote.txt from the bundle as soon as the application is launched. The file must be added to the project during development by dragging it from Finder to the Navigator Area, as we did before for sounds and images.

```
import SwiftUI

class AppData: ObservableObject {
    @Published var textInFile: String = "Undefined"

    init() {
        let bundle = Bundle.main
        if let filePath = bundle.path(forResource: "quote", ofType: "txt")
{

            let manager = FileManager.default
            if let data = manager.contents(atPath: filePath) {
                if let message = String(data: data, encoding: .utf8) {
                    textInFile = message
                }
            }
        } else {
            print("File not found")
        }
    }
}
```

Listing 14-27: Loading a file from the bundle

The initializer of the model in Listing 14-27 gets a reference to the app's bundle and then finds the path for the quote.txt file with the `path()` method. After we get the path, we can read the file as we did before. As always, the value is stored in the `@Published` property, so we can read it from the view, as shown next.

```
import SwiftUI

struct ContentView: View {
    @EnvironmentObject var appData: AppData
```

```
var body: some View {
    VStack {
        Text(appData.textInFile)
            .lineLimit(nil)
            .padding(15)
            .frame(minWidth: 0, maxWidth: .infinity)
            .background(Color(white: 0.8))
        Spacer()
    }.padding()
}
}
```

Listing 14-28: Showing the text stored in a file in the bundle

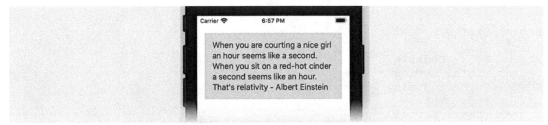

Figure 14-11: Content of a text file in the bundle

 Do It Yourself: Update the `AppData` class with the code in Listing 14-27 and the `ContentView` structure with the code in Listing 14-28. Download the quote.txt file from our website or create your own and add it to the project (Figures 5-19 and 5-20). Run the application. You should see the text in the file printed on the screen, as shown in Figure 14-11.

(Basic) # 14.3 Archiving

The methods we have introduced in the previous section to store data in files are enough for simple models but present some limitations. We can only work with single values, an image or a text, and with classes that already provide a way to turn their content into data. But as we have seen, professional applications rely on more elaborated models that include collection of values and custom structures. To give us more flexibility, Foundation offers the `NSCoder` class. This class can encode and decode single or multiple structures and objects to `Data` structures for storage purposes in a process called *Archiving* (`NSCoder` is also used for data distribution but archiving is its most important feature).

(Basic) **Encoding and Decoding**

The `NSCoder` class provides all the methods necessary to encode and decode the values of an object, but these methods only work with Property List values. We introduced them before. These are values that can be serialized for storage. Therefore, if we want to store our own data types, we must turn them into Property List values. Foundation offers two classes for this purpose, `PropertyListEncoder` and `PropertyListDecoder`, which include the following methods to encode and decode the values.

encode(Value**)**—This method of the `PropertyListEncoder` class encodes a value into a Property List value.

decode(Type, **from:** Data)—This method of the `PropertyListDecoder` class decodes a Property List value into a value of the type specified by the first attribute. The **from** attribute is a **Data** structure with the data to be decoded.

Another requirement for custom structures is that they implement the initializers and methods defined in a protocol called **NSCoding**. These initializers and methods tell the system how to encode and decode the data for storage or distribution. Fortunately, the Swift Standard Library defines a protocol called **Codable** that turns a structure into an encodable and decodable data type. All we have to do is to get our structure to conform to this protocol and the compiler takes care of adding all the methods required to encode and decode its values. The following example recreates a model used in previous examples to store information about a book, but now it implements these tools to store the data on file.

```
import SwiftUI

struct Book: Codable {
   var title: String
   var author: String
   var year: Int
   var cover: String?
}
struct BookViewModel: Identifiable {
   let id: UUID = UUID()
   var book: Book

   var title: String {
      return book.title.capitalized
   }
   var author: String {
      return book.author.capitalized
   }
   var year: String {
      return String(book.year)
   }
   var cover: UIImage {
      if let imageName = book.cover {
         let manager = FileManager.default
         let docURL = manager.urls(for: .documentDirectory, in:
.userDomainMask).first!
         let imageURL = docURL.appendingPathComponent(imageName)
         if let coverImage = UIImage(contentsOfFile: imageURL.path) {
            return coverImage
         }
      }
      return UIImage(named: "nopicture")!
   }
}
class AppData: ObservableObject {
   @Published var bookInFile: BookViewModel
   var manager: FileManager
   var docURL: URL

   func saveBook(book: Book) {
      let filePath = docURL.appendingPathComponent("userdata.dat").path
      let encoder = PropertyListEncoder()
      if let data = try? encoder.encode(book) {
         if manager.createFile(atPath: filePath, contents: data,
attributes: nil) {
```

```
            bookInFile = BookViewModel(book: book)
        }
    }
}
func storeCover() -> String? {
    let placeholder = UIImage(named: "bookcover")
    let imageName = "bookcover.dat"
    if let imageData = placeholder?.pngData() {
        let fileURL = docURL.appendingPathComponent(imageName)
        if manager.createFile(atPath: fileURL.path, contents: imageData,
attributes: nil) {
            return imageName
        }
    }
    return nil
}
init() {
    bookInFile = BookViewModel(book: Book(title: "", author: "", year:
0, cover: nil))
    manager = FileManager.default
    docURL = manager.urls(for: .documentDirectory, in:
.userDomainMask).first!

    let filePath = docURL.appendingPathComponent("userdata.dat").path
    if manager.fileExists(atPath: filePath) {
        if let content = manager.contents(atPath: filePath) {
            let decoder = PropertyListDecoder()
            if let book = try? decoder.decode(Book.self, from: content) {
                bookInFile.book = book
            }
        }
    }
}
}
```

Listing 14-29: Encoding and decoding a custom structure

The **Book** structure is our data model, as always, but now it conforms to the **Codable** protocol, so we can encode it into a **Data** structure and store it in a file. The structure includes properties to store the title, the author, the cover and the publication year of a book.

The observable object includes a **@Published** property to store the book, a method to store new values in the file, a method to store the cover of the book, and an initializer that reads the values from the file. The **saveFiles()** method takes care of creating or updating the file. The process to save the data into the file is the same, but first we must convert the **Book** structure into a **Data** structure. For this purpose, the method creates an instance of the **PropertyListEncoder** class and calls the **encode()** method on it with the instance of the **Book** structure created by the user. Finally, we store the data in the file with the **createFile()** method, as always.

The initializer performs the opposite process. It gets the content of the file, creates an instance of the **PropertyListDecoder** class, and calls the **decode()** method on it to decode the data into a **Book** structure (**Book.self**). If successful, the structure is assigned to the **book** property of the **BookViewModel** structure stored in the **bookInFile** property to make the values available for the view.

When storing data in files or databases, it is recommended to store the images in separate files. This is the job of the **storeCover()** method. This method is called before the **saveFile()** method to store the book's cover in a file and return the file's name to include it in the data model with the rest of the values. In this example we always use the same image and the same file for the book's cover, but in a real application the image is usually taken from the device's Photo library or the camera and each image is stored in different files (we will see how to name these files in the next project and how to access the Photo library and the camera in Chapter 16).

As always, all the work is done by the model. The view just have to read the values from the view model, show them on the screen, and provide the user the possibility to open a sheet to modify them.

```
import SwiftUI

struct ContentView: View {
   @EnvironmentObject var appData: AppData
   @State private var openSheet: Bool = false

   var body: some View {
      NavigationView {
         VStack(alignment: .leading) {
            Text("Title: \(appData.bookInFile.title)")
            Text("Author: \(appData.bookInFile.author)")
            Text("Year: \(appData.bookInFile.year)")
            Image(uiImage: appData.bookInFile.cover)
               .resizable()
               .scaledToFit()
         }.padding()
         .frame(minWidth: 0, maxWidth: .infinity)
         .navigationBarTitle("Book")
         .navigationBarItems(trailing: Button("Change") {
            self.openSheet = true
         })
         .sheet(isPresented: $openSheet) {
            InsertBookView(openSheet: self.$openSheet)
               .environmentObject(self.appData)
         }
      }
   }
}
struct ContentView_Previews: PreviewProvider {
   static var previews: some View {
      ContentView().environmentObject(AppData())
   }
}
```

Listing 14-30: *Showing the values stored in the file*

This view opens a sheet with an instance of the **InsertBookView** view when a button in the navigation bar is pressed. The following is the definition of this view.

```
import SwiftUI

struct InsertBookView: View {
   @EnvironmentObject var appData: AppData
   @Binding var openSheet: Bool
   @State private var inputTitle: String = ""
   @State private var inputAuthor: String = ""
   @State private var inputYear: String = ""
```

```
        var body: some View {
            VStack {
                HStack {
                    Text("Title:")
                    TextField("Insert Title", text: $inputTitle)
                        .textFieldStyle(RoundedBorderTextFieldStyle())
                }
                HStack {
                    Text("Author:")
                    TextField("Insert Author", text: $inputAuthor)
                        .textFieldStyle(RoundedBorderTextFieldStyle())
                }
                HStack {
                    Text("Year:")
                    TextField("Insert Year", text: $inputYear)
                        .textFieldStyle(RoundedBorderTextFieldStyle())
                }
                HStack {
                    Spacer()
                    Button("Save") {
                        let newTitle = self.inputTitle.trimmingCharacters(in:
.whitespaces)
                        let newAuthor = self.inputAuthor.trimmingCharacters(in:
.whitespaces)
                        let newYear = Int(self.inputYear)
                        if !newTitle.isEmpty && !newAuthor.isEmpty && newYear !=
nil {
                            let coverName = self.appData.storeCover()
                            self.appData.saveBook(book: Book(title: newTitle,
author: newAuthor, year: newYear!, cover: coverName))
                            self.openSheet = false
                        }
                    }
                }
                Spacer()
            }.padding()
        }
    }
}
struct InsertBookView_Previews: PreviewProvider {
    static var previews: some View {
        InsertBookView(openSheet: .constant(false))
            .environmentObject(AppData())
    }
}
```

Listing 14-31: *Allowing the user to insert new values*

The **InsertBookView** view includes three **TextField** views to let the user insert the book's title, author, and year (the cover is always the same). The view stores the values inserted by the user in **@State** properties. When the user presses the Save button to save the book, we check the values in these properties. If they are all valid, we call the **storeCover()** method in the model to create a file with the cover, create a new instance of the **Book** structure with all these values, and call the **saveFile()** method to store this structure in the file.

Figure 14-12: *Interface to store a custom value in a file*

 Do It Yourself: Create a SwiftUI project. Download the nopicture.png and the bookcover.png images from our website and add them to the Assets Catalog. Update the AppDelegate.swift file with the code of Listing 7-14 and the SceneDelegate.swift file with the code of Listing 7-20 to instantiate the model and insert it in the environment. Create the AppData.swift file for the model of Listing 14-29. Update the `ContentView` structure with the code in Listing 14-30. Create a Swift file called InsertBookView.swift for the view in Listing 14-31. Run the application on the simulator or a device. Press the Change button and insert new values. Stop the application and run it again. You should see the same values on the screen.

The previous model stores the values of one book. If new values are inserted, a new `Book` structure is instantiated with those values and stored in the same file, replacing the previous one. This example illustrates how custom data types, like the `Book` structure, are encoded and stored in files, but normally we need to work with collections of values. The process to go from storing one instance of the `Book` structure to store an array of instances is very simple. All we have to do is to encode an array of structures instead of a single one. The following are the modifications required by our observable object to store multiple books.

```
class AppData: ObservableObject {
    @Published var userData: [BookViewModel] = []
    var manager: FileManager
    var docURL: URL

    func saveBook(book: Book) {
        userData.append(BookViewModel(book: book))
        saveModel()
    }
    func saveModel() {
        let list = userData.map({ value in
            return value.book
        })
        let filePath = docURL.appendingPathComponent("userdata.dat").path
        let encoder = PropertyListEncoder()
        if let data = try? encoder.encode(list) {
            manager.createFile(atPath: filePath, contents: data, attributes:
nil)
        }
    }
    func storeCover() -> String? {
        let placeholder = UIImage(named: "bookcover")
        let imageName = "image-\(UUID()).dat"
```

```
        if let imageData = placeholder?.pngData() {
            let fileURL = docURL.appendingPathComponent(imageName)
            if manager.createFile(atPath: fileURL.path, contents: imageData,
attributes: nil) {
                return imageName
            }
        }
        return nil
    }
    init() {
        manager = FileManager.default
        docURL = manager.urls(for: .documentDirectory, in:
.userDomainMask).first!

        let filePath = docURL.appendingPathComponent("userdata.dat").path
        if manager.fileExists(atPath: filePath) {
            if let content = manager.contents(atPath: filePath) {
                let decoder = PropertyListDecoder()
                if let list = try? decoder.decode([Book].self, from: content) {
                    userData = list.map({ value in
                        return BookViewModel(book: value)
                    })
                }
            }
        }
    }
}
```

Listing 14-32: Storing multiple books

Every time the values in the model are modified, either because a book is added or removed, or the information of a book is updated, we must update the data in the file. For this purpose, we define a method called **saveModel()**. This method prepares the data and stores it in a file called userdata.dat. In this example, we store in the file instances of the data model (the **Book** structure), but the observable object stores an array of **BookViewModel** structures. These are instances of the view model used to prepare the values for the view. To convert this array into an array of **Book** structures, the method extracts the values with the **map()** method. This method processes the items in the array and returns the instance of the **Book** structure inside each **BookViewModel** structure, creating the list of **Book** structures we need to store in the file.

In this example, we only let the user add books. The books can't be erased or modified. This is why there is only one method to edit the information called **addBook()**. This method receives an instance of the **Book** structure with the values inserted by the user, adds it to the array in the **userData** property, and calls the **saveModel()** method to store all the values in the file again, so the file always contains the latest information.

The initializer performs the opposite process of the **saveModel()** method. It reads the content of the file, decodes the data with the **decode()** method into an array of **Book** structures (**[Book].self**), and then converts the **Book** structures into **BookViewModel** structures with the **map()** method before assigning them to the **userData** property to make them available for the views.

Another change introduced in this observable object is the name assigned to the files for the covers in the **storeCover()** method. We are still using the same image for every book (bookcover), but because the user can now store multiple books, we define the file's name with a **UUID** value to make every name unique.

The view must create a list with all the books in the **userData** property and provide the user a button to open a sheet to insert new ones.

```
struct ContentView: View {
    @EnvironmentObject var appData: AppData
    @State private var openSheet: Bool = false

    var body: some View {
        NavigationView {
            List {
                ForEach(appData.userData) { book in
                    RowBook(book: book)
                }
            }
            .navigationBarTitle("Books")
            .navigationBarItems(trailing: Button("Add Book") {
                self.openSheet = true
            })
            .sheet(isPresented: $openSheet) {
                InsertBookView(openSheet: self.$openSheet)
                    .environmentObject(self.appData)
            }
        }
    }
}
struct RowBook: View {
    let book: BookViewModel

    var body: some View {
        HStack(alignment: .top) {
            Image(uiImage: book.cover)
                .resizable()
                .scaledToFit()
                .frame(width: 80, height: 100)
                .cornerRadius(10)
            VStack(alignment: .leading, spacing: 2) {
                Text(book.title).bold()
                Text(book.author)
                Text(book.year).font(.caption)
                Spacer()
            }.padding(.top, 5)
            Spacer()
        }
    }
}
```

Listing 14-33: Showing multiple values stored in a file

The view in Listing 14-33 includes a List view that shows the list of the books stored in the file. To present the information of each book, we use the RowBook view introduced in previous examples. The navigation bar includes a button to open the InsertBookView view defined before to let the user add new books. Therefore, the application works like before, but now instead of one the user can insert multiple books.

Figure 14-13: Interface to store multiple values in a file

 Do It Yourself: Update the observable object in your model (the **AppData** class) with the code of Listing 14-32 and the ContentView.swift file with the code of Listing 14-33. Run the application on the simulator. Press the Add Book button to add a book and press the Save button to save it. Stop and run the application again. You should see the book on the screen.

(Medium) JSON

Another way to encode and decode custom data types is with JSON (JavaScript Object Notation). This format was created to transmit information on the web, but this and the fact that it is a very simple format to read and process, made it suitable to store data for applications. Apple systems adopted JSON long time ago to store and retrieve information. Foundation includes the **JSONDecoder** class to decode JSON data into Swift structures and the **JSONEncoder** class to encode Swift structures into JSON data. The classes include their respective methods to decode and encode the values.

decode(Type, **from:** Data**)**—This method returns a value of the type specified by the first attribute with the information contained by the **from** attribute. The **from** attribute is a **Data** structure that contains the JSON data we want to decode.

encode(Value**)**—This method returns a JSON representation of the data provided by the attribute.

A JSON file is just a text file that stores the data in a specific format. The format includes the values of an object or a structure as key/value pairs separated by a colon, like dictionaries. The name of the property is turned into a string and included as the key for the value, and each object or structure is enclosed in curly brackets. The following example shows how the JSON file looks like if we store one instance of our **Book** structure.

```
{
    "author": "Stephen King",
    "title": "The Shining",
    "year": 1977,
    "cover": "bookcover.dat"
}
```

Listing 14-34: JSON file

As always, the objects or structures we want to encode must conform to the **Codable** protocol and the data must be encoded and decoded before it is stored or read. Therefore, adapting our app to work with JSON is very simple. We just have to replace the Property List encoders and decoders with JSON's, as in the following example.

```
class AppData: ObservableObject {
    @Published var userData: [BookViewModel] = []
    var manager: FileManager
    var docURL: URL

    func saveBook(book: Book) {
        userData.append(BookViewModel(book: book))
        saveModel()
    }
    func saveModel() {
        let list = userData.map({ value in
            return value.book
        })
        let filePath = docURL.appendingPathComponent("userdata.dat").path
        let encoder = JSONEncoder()
        if let data = try? encoder.encode(list) {
            manager.createFile(atPath: filePath, contents: data, attributes:
nil)
        }
    }
    func storeCover() -> String? {
        let placeholder = UIImage(named: "bookcover")
        let imageName = "image-\(UUID()).dat"
        if let imageData = placeholder?.pngData() {
            let fileURL = docURL.appendingPathComponent(imageName)
            if manager.createFile(atPath: fileURL.path, contents: imageData,
attributes: nil) {
                return imageName
            }
        }
        return nil
    }
    init() {
        manager = FileManager.default
        docURL = manager.urls(for: .documentDirectory, in:
.userDomainMask).first!

        let filePath = docURL.appendingPathComponent("userdata.dat").path
        if manager.fileExists(atPath: filePath) {
            if let content = manager.contents(atPath: filePath) {
                let decoder = JSONDecoder()
                if let list = try? decoder.decode([Book].self, from: content){
                    userData = list.map({ value in
                        return BookViewModel(book: value)
                    })
                }
            }
        }
    }
}
```

Listing 14-35: Encoding and decoding the data with JSON

This example works exactly like the one before, but now the data is stored in JSON format.

 Do It Yourself: Update the observable object in your model (the **AppData** class) with the code of Listing 14-35. Remove the application on the simulator to erase the previous files and run it again. The list should be empty. Press the Add Book button to add a book and press the Save button to save it. Stop and run the application again. You should see the book on the screen.

Chapter 14 - Storage

Of course, JSON can format nested structures and objects. For instance, we may have a `Book` structure with a property that stores another structure with information about the publisher.

```
struct Publisher: Codable {
    let name: String
    let date: Date
}
struct Book: Codable {
    let title: String
    let author: String
    let publisher: Publisher
}
```

Listing 14-36: Defining nested structures

If we store an instance of this `Book` structure in JSON format, it may look like the following.

```
{
    "title": "The Shining",
    "author": "Stephen King",
    "publisher": {
        "name": "Random House",
        "date": 598999514.87258303
    }
}
```

Listing 14-37: Nested data in JSON

Notice that the date in JSON doesn't look like a date. This is because `Date` values contain the difference in seconds from a specific date in the past to the date they represent. To convert these values into values of type `Date`, we must declare what kind of format the decoder has to use. For this purpose, the `JSONDecoder` class includes the following property.

dateDecodingStrategy—This property defines a strategy the decoder has to follow to decode a date. It is an enumeration of type `DateDecodingStrategy` with the values `millisecondsSince1970`, `secondsSince1970`, `deferredToDate`, and `iso8601`. The enumeration also includes the methods `formatted()` and `custom()` to define custom formats.

Dates in JSON are shared in different formats, but when we are working with `Date` values, we just have to declare the `deferredToDate` formatting and the decoder will have enough information to decode the value back into a `Date` structure.

The following is a simple model that illustrates how to read and process these values. The observable object in this model loads a JSON file from the bundle with the code introduced in Listing 14-37 and decodes it into the structures introduced in Listing 14-36.

```
import SwiftUI

struct Publisher: Codable {
    let name: String
    let date: Date
}
struct Book: Codable {
    let title: String?
    let author: String?
    let publisher: Publisher?
}
```

```
struct BookViewModel {
    var book: Book

    var title: String {
        return book.title?.capitalized ?? "Undefined"
    }
    var author: String {
        return book.author?.capitalized ?? "Undefined"
    }
    var publisher: String {
        return book.publisher?.name.capitalized ?? "Undefined"
    }
    var date: String {
        if let date = book.publisher?.date {
            let formatter = DateFormatter()
            formatter.dateStyle = .medium
            return formatter.string(from: date)
        } else {
            return "Undefined"
        }
    }
}
class AppData: ObservableObject {
    @Published var bookInFile: BookViewModel

    init() {
        bookInFile = BookViewModel(book: Book(title: nil, author: nil,
publisher: nil))

        let bundle = Bundle.main
        if let filePath = bundle.path(forResource: "template", ofType:
"json") {
            let manager = FileManager.default
            if let data = manager.contents(atPath: filePath) {
                let decoder = JSONDecoder()
                decoder.dateDecodingStrategy = .deferredToDate
                if let book = try? decoder.decode(Book.self, from: data) {
                    bookInFile.book = book
                }
            }
        }
    }
}
```

Listing 14-38: Reading values in a nested structure

Besides the **Publisher** and **Book** structures introduced before, the model in Listing 14-38 also includes the **BookViewModel** structure to prepare the values for the view, and the observable object to load the data. The initializer of this object looks for a file called template.json. The code assumes that the file has a structure like the example in Listing 14-37. If found, the content of the file is loaded with the **contents()** method of the **FileManager** object, decoded with a **JSONDecoder** object, and the **Book** structure resulting from this process is assigned to the **bookInFile** property to make it available for the view. The following is the view we need to show these values on the screen.

```
import SwiftUI

struct ContentView: View {
    @EnvironmentObject var appData: AppData
```

```
    var body: some View {
        VStack(alignment: .leading) {
            Text(appData.bookInFile.title)
            Text(appData.bookInFile.author)
            Text(appData.bookInFile.publisher)
            Text(appData.bookInFile.date)
            Spacer()
        }.padding()
    }
}
struct ContentView_Previews: PreviewProvider {
    static var previews: some View {
        ContentView().environmentObject(AppData())
    }
}
```

Listing 14-39: *Showing the values of a nested structure*

Figure 14-14, below, shows what we see if the project includes a file called template.json in the bundle with the JSON code of Listing 14-37.

Figure 14-14: *Values from a JSON file*

 Do It Yourself: Create a SwiftUI project. Download the template.json file form our website or create your own text file with this name and the code in Listing 14-37 and drag it into the Navigation Area with the rest of the files. Update the AppDelegate.swift file with the code of Listing 7-14 and the SceneDelegate.swift file with the code of Listing 7-20 to instantiate the model and insert it in the environment. Create the AppData.swift file for the model in Listing 14-38. Update the **ContentView** structure with the code in Listing 14-39. Run the application. You should see all the values in the file printed on the screen.

Basic | 14.4 Core Data

With archiving, we can store not only objects but also the objects they are connected to, as shown in the last example. This structure of objects and the connections between them is called *Object Graph*. Archiving is a good tool to store an Object Graph on file but presents some limitations. The Object Graph we can store is difficult to expand and usually inflexible. The entire graph must be stored in the file again after the smallest change, and it is hard to control the connections between objects and determine exactly which objects are going to be stored. The solution is called *Core Data*. Core Data is an Object Graph manager that defines and manages its own objects and connections and stores them in a database. We can establish the composition of those objects and how they are going to relate to each other, and store as many objects as we need. The system takes care of encoding and decoding the objects, preserving consistency, and storing the Object Graph on file in an efficient way, allowing us to search for a specific object or get only the objects we need.

The structure of the Core Data's Object Graph is defined with a data model. This has nothing to do with the data model of the MVVM pattern created in previous chapters. A Core Data model is a definition of the type of objects the graph is going to contain (called *Entities*) and their connections (called *Relationships*).

A model can be created from code, but Xcode offers a practical editor that we can use to define the structure of the graph. The model is stored in a file and then the file is compiled and included in the Core Data system created for our app. Xcode offers a template to create this file.

Figure 14-15: Option to create a Core Data model in the iOS panel

The file may be created with any name we want but it has to have the extension xcdatamodel. Once created, it is included in our project along with the rest of the files. Clicking on it reveals the Xcode editor, illustrated in Figure 14-16, below.

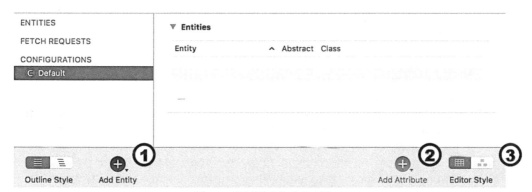

Figure 14-16: Model editor

The model contains three main components: Entities, Attributes, and Relationships. Entities are the objects, Attributes are the objects' properties, and Relationships are the connections that can be established between objects. The first step is to add Entities to the model. Entities are created from the Add Entity button at the bottom of the editor (Figure 14-16, number 1). When we press this button, Xcode creates an entity with the generic name "Entity".

Figure 14-17: New Entities

We can change the name of the newly created entity by double-clicking the name (Figure 14-17, number 1) or editing the field in the Data Model Inspector panel (Figure 14-17, number 2).

An entity defines the objects that are going to be part of the Object Graph, so the next step is to declare the type of values those objects are going to manage. For this purpose, entities include Attributes. To add an attribute, we must select the entity and press the + button under the Attributes area (Figure 14-17, number 3) or press the Add Attribute button at the bottom of the editor (Figure 14-16, number 2). The attribute is added with the generic name "attribute" and the data type Undefined. Again, we can change the name of the attribute by double-clicking on it or editing the Name field in the Data Model Inspector panel. For our example, we called the entity *Books* and the first attribute *title* (Figure 14-18, number 1).

Figure 14-18: *New Attributes*

 IMPORTANT: The name of entities has to start with an upper-case letter and the names of attributes and relationships have to start with a lower-case letter.

Every attribute must be associated with a data type for the objects to know what kind of values they can manage (Figure 14-18, number 2). Clicking on the attribute's type, we can open a menu to select the right data type. The most frequently used are Integer 16, Integer 32, Integer 64, Decimal, Double, Float, String, Boolean, Date, and Binary Data. The Integer 16, 32, or 64 options are for `Int16`, `Int32`, and `Int64` values, Decimal is for `NSDecimalNumber` values, Double and Float are for `Double` and `Float` values, String is for `String` values, Boolean is for `Bool` values, Date is for `Date` values, and Binary Data is for `Data` values, such as images.

An entity may contain as many attributes as our objects need. For example, we may add a few more attributes to complement the book's information.

Figure 14-19: *Multiple Attributes*

In the example of Figure 14-19, we added an attribute called year to store the year in which the book was published, and two attributes of type Binary Data to store images (the cover and a thumbnail). The data types used by these attributes are analog to the Swift data types we have being working so far. The title attribute takes a `String` value, the year attribute stores a value of type `Int32`, and the images are `Data` structures, like the ones we created to store images in file in previous examples. But before storing images in the Core Data database, there is something we must considered. Storing large amounts of data in a persistent store can affect the system's performance and slow down essential processes like searching for values or migrating the model. One alternative is to store the images in separate files, as we did when we were archiving data before, but it can get cumbersome to coordinate hundreds or even thousands of files with the data in the database. Fortunately, Core Data can perform the process for us. All we have to do is to store the image as Binary Data and select the option Allows External Storage, available in the Data Model inspector panel inside the Utilities Area, as shown in Figure 14-20, below. After the option is selected, the images assigned to that attribute are going to be stored in separate files managed by the system.

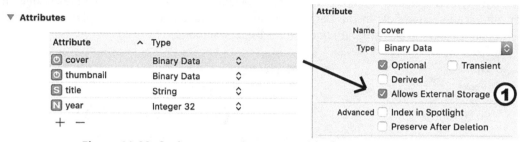

Figure 14-20: Option to store images outside the persistent store

We could have also included another attribute for the author's name in the Books entity, but here is when we have to start thinking about the structure of the Object Graph and how we need the information to be stored. If we include a String type attribute for the author's name inside the Books entity, every time the user inserts a new book it will have to type the name of the author. This is error prone, time consuming, and when several books of the same author are available, it is impossible to make sure that all share the same exact name (one book could have the author's middle name and others just the first one, for example). Without the certainty of having the exact same name, we can never incorporate features in our app such as ordering the books by author or getting the list of books written by a particular author. Things get worse when, along with the name, we also decide to store other information about the author, like his or her date of birth. A proper organization of this information demands the creation of separate objects and therefore we must create new entities to represent them. Additional entities are added to the model the same way we did with the first one. Figure 14-21, next, shows our example with a new entity called *Authors* containing an attribute called *name*.

Figure 14-21: Multiple Entities

Entities are blueprints for objects, so we use them to define the characteristics of the objects we want to store. For instance, when we want to store a new book, we create a new object based on the Books entity. That object will have four properties corresponding to the values of its title, year, cover, and thumbnail. The same happens when we want to store the information of an author. We create a new object based on the Authors entity and assign the name of the author to its name property. At the end, we will have two objects in the storage space, one for the book and another for the author. But if we want to retrieve these objects later, we need a way to know what Books object is related to what Authors object. We must connect these objects, so when we look for the Books object, we can also get the corresponding Authors object representing its author, otherwise we will not be able to show the name of the author along with the information of the book. To create this connection, the Core Data model includes Relationships.

Chapter 14 - Storage

Relationships are like properties in an object containing references to another object. They could have a reference to one object or a set of objects. For example, in the Books entity, we can create a relationship that contains a reference to only one object of the Authors entity, because there could only be one author per book (for this example we are assuming that our app is storing books written only by one author). On the contrary, in the Authors entity, we need to establish a relationship that contains references to multiple Books objects, because an author may have written several books, not just one. Core Data calls these relationships according to the number of objects they may reference. The names are To-One and To-Many and they are created pressing the + button in the Relationships area below the Attributes area. Figure 14-22 shows a relationship called *author* we have created for the Books entity of our example (we called it *author* because it is going to be used to retrieve the author of the book).

Figure 14-22: *Relationship for the Books entity*

A relationship only needs two values: its name (the name of the property) and the destination (the type of objects it is referencing), but it requires some parameters to be set. We must tell the model if the relationship is going to be optional, define its type (To-One or To-Many), and determine what should happen to the destination object if the source object is deleted (the Delete Rule). All these options are available in the Data Model Inspector panel when the relationship is selected, as shown in Figure 14-23.

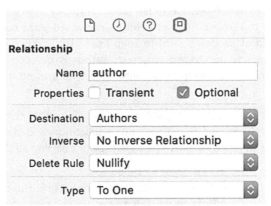

Figure 14-23: *Relationship settings*

By default, the relationship is set as Optional, which means that the source may be connected to a destination object or not (a book can have an author or not), the Type of the relationship is set to To-One (a book can only have one author), and the Delete Rule is set to Nullify. The following are all the values available for this rule.

- **Deny:** If there is at least one object at the destination, the source is not deleted (if there is an Authors object assigned to the Books object, the book is not deleted).
- **Nullify:** The connection between objects are removed, but the objects at the destination are not deleted (if a Books object is deleted, the Authors object associated with that book loses the connection but is not deleted).
- **Cascade:** The objects at the destination are deleted when the source is deleted (the Authors object is deleted if one of its books is deleted).

- **No Action:** The objects at the destination are not deleted or modified (the connections are preserved, even when the source object does not exist anymore).

To find the right rule for a relationship, we must think in terms of the information we are manipulating. Is it right to delete the author if one of its books is deleted? In our case, the answer is simple. An author can have more than one book, so we cannot delete the author when we delete a book because there could be other books that are connected to that same author. Therefore, the Nullify rule set by default is the right one for this relationship. But this could change when we create the opposite relationship, connecting the Authors entity to the Books entity. We need this second relationship to search for books that belong to an author. Figure 14-24 shows a relationship called *books* that we have created for the Authors entity.

▼ **Relationships**

Relationship	^	Destination		Inverse
🔘 books		Books	↕	No Inverse ↕

Figure 14-24: *Relationship for the Authors entity*

 IMPORTANT: Relationships must always be bidirectional. If we set a relationship from entity A to entity B, we must set the opposite relationship from entity B to A. Core Data offers another type of relationship called *Fetched Properties* to connect entities in only one direction. You can add a Fetched Property from the area below the Relationships area in the model's editor.

The new relationship added in Figure 14-24 is in the Authors entity, so every Authors object will have a property called **book** that we can use to retrieve the Books objects the author is connected to. Because one author can have many books, the setting of this relationship is going to differ from the previous one. Now, we must set the Type of the relationship as To-Many (to many books) and modify the Delete Rule according to how we want our application to respond when an author is deleted. If we don't want to keep books that do not have an author assigned, we should select the Cascade option, so when an author is deleted all his or her books are deleted too. But if we don't mind having books with no author around, then the option should be kept as Nullify.

 The Basics: The Delete Rules are a way to ensure that the objects remaining in the Object Graph are those that our application and the user need. We can always set the rule as Nullify and take care of deleting all the objects ourselves.

There is a third value for the relationship called *Inverse*. Once we set the relationships on both sides, it is highly recommended to set this value. It just tells the model what the name of the opposite relationship is. Core Data needs this to ensure the consistency of the Object Graph. Figure 14-25 shows the final setup for both relationships.

Relationship for the Books entity

Relationship	^	Destination		Inverse
🔘 author		Authors	↕	books ↕

Relationship for the Authors entity

Relationship	^	Destination		Inverse
🔘 books		Books	↕	author ↕

Figure 14-25: *Inverse Relationships*

Chapter 14 - Storage

Two relationships are simple to follow, but multiple relationships connecting several entities together can turn the model into an indecipherable mess. To help us identify every component of the model, Xcode offers an additional visualization style that displays the entities as boxes and the relationships as arrows connecting the boxes. The option, called *Editor Style*, is at the bottom of the screen (Figure 14-16, number 3). Figure 14-26, next, shows what our model looks like when we switch to this style (Notice that the To-Many relationship is represented by double arrows).

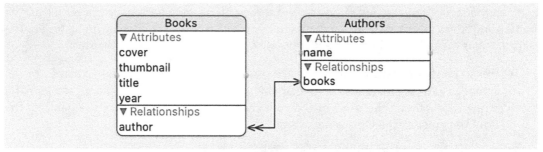

Figure 14-26: Graphic Style

 Do It Yourself: Create a SwiftUI project. Open the File menu and select the File... option to create a new file. Move to the Core Data section and select the option Data Model from the iOS panel (Figure 14-15). Save the file with the name "books". Click on the file to open the editor (Figure 14-16). Press the Add Entity button to create two entities with the names Authors and Books. Create the attributes for these entities as illustrated in Figures 14-19 and 14-20. Create the relationships for both entities as shown in Figure 14-25. Set the books relationship as To-Many and keep the rest of the values by default. Click on the Editor Style button to see a graphic representation of the model (Figure 14-26).

Basic Core Data Stack

The creation of the model is just the first step in the definition of the Core Data system. Once we have all the entities along with their attributes and relationships set up, we must initialize Core Data for our application. Core Data is created from a group of objects that manage all the processes, from the organization of the Object Graph to the storage of the graph on file. There is an object that manages the model, an object that stores the data on file, and an object that intermediates between this persistent store and our own code. The scheme is called *stack*. Figure 14-27 illustrates a common Core Data stack.

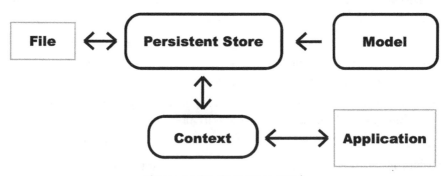

Figure 14-27: Core Data stack

The code in our application interacts with the Context to manage the objects it needs to access and their values, the Context asks the persistent store to read or add new objects to the graph, and the persistent store processes the Object Graph and saves it in a file.

The Core Data framework offers classes to create objects that represent every part of the stack. The `NSManagedObjectModel` class manages the model, the `NSPersistentStore` class manages a persistent store, the `NSPersistentStoreCoordinator` class is used to manage all the persistent stores available (a Core Data stack may have multiple persistent stores), and the `NSManagedObjectContext` creates and manages the context that intermediates between our app and the store. Although we can instantiate these objects and create the stack ourselves, the framework offers the `NSPersistentContainer` class that takes care of everything for us. The class includes the following initializer and properties to access each object of the stack.

NSPersistentContainer(name: String)—This initializer creates an `NSPersistentContainer` object that defines a Core Data stack. The **name** attribute is a string representing the name of the container. This value must match the name of the Core Data model (the file's name, without the extension).

managedObjectModel—This property sets or returns an `NSManagedObjectModel` object that represents the Core Data model.

persistentStoreCoordinator—This property sets or returns the `NSPersistentStoreCoordinator` object that manages all the persistent stores available.

viewContext—This property sets or returns the `NSManagedObjectContext` object in charge of the stack's context that we have to use to access and modify the Object Graph.

To create the Core Data stack from our app, we must initialize a new `NSPersistentContainer` object and then load the persistent stores (one by default). Because the stores may take time to load, the class offers a specific method for this purpose.

loadPersistentStores(completionHandler: Closure)—This method loads the persistent stores and executes a closure when the process is over. The closure receives two attributes, an `NSPersistentStoreDescription` object with the configuration of the stack, and an optional `Error` value to report errors.

All the communication between our app and the data in the persistent store is done through the context. The context is created by the container from the `NSManagedObjectContext` class. This class includes properties and methods to manage the context and the objects in the persistent store. The following are the most frequently used.

hasChanges—This property returns a Boolean value that indicates if the context has changes that must be saved to the persistent store.

save()—This method saves the changes in the context to the persistent store.

reset()—This method resets the context to a basic state. All the objects and modifications our app introduced to the context are ignored.

fetch(NSFetchRequest)—This method returns an array with the objects requested by the `NSFetchRequest` object assigned to the attribute.

delete(NSManagedObject)—This method deletes an object from the persistent store.

count(for: NSFetchRequest)—This method returns the number of objects found in the persistent store for the request. The **for** attribute is an object that allows us to configure a request.

Chapter 14 - Storage

When working with Core Data, the Core Data's persistent store becomes our app's data model. Therefore, Apple recommends initializing the Core Data stack in the app's delegate, as we did with our models so far. The following example creates a computed property that initializes the stack and returns a reference to the Persistent Container object.

```swift
import UIKit
import CoreData

@UIApplicationMain
class AppDelegate: UIResponder, UIApplicationDelegate {

    func application(_ application: UIApplication,
didFinishLaunchingWithOptions launchOptions:
[UIApplication.LaunchOptionsKey: Any]?) -> Bool {
        return true
    }
    func application(_ application: UIApplication,
configurationForConnecting connectingSceneSession: UISceneSession,
options: UIScene.ConnectionOptions) -> UISceneConfiguration {
        return UISceneConfiguration(name: "Default Configuration",
sessionRole: connectingSceneSession.role)
    }
    lazy var persistentContainer: NSPersistentContainer = {
        let container = NSPersistentContainer(name: "books")
        container.loadPersistentStores(completionHandler: {
(storeDescription, error) in
            if let error = error as NSError? {
                fatalError("Unresolved error \(error), \(error.userInfo)")
            }
        })
        return container
    }()
}
```

Listing 14-40: Initializing the Core Data stack in the app's delegate

The **AppDelegate** class in Listing 14-40 defines a computed property called **persistentContainer** to create the persistent store. Apple recommends declaring this property as **lazy**, so the Core Data stack is only initialized when required. The property creates an instance of the **NSPersistentContainer** class with the name of the Core Data model (in our example, we called it "books"). The object creates the stack but does not load the persistent stores, we have to do it ourselves by calling the **loadPersistentStores()** method. After completion, this method executes a closure with two values, a reference to the persistent store just created, and an **Error** value to report errors. Errors are infrequent, but if an error occurs, we should warn the user. In this example, we just call the **fatalError()** function to stop the execution of the app.

Once we have the Persistent Container, we must get the context from it and share it with the views, so they can add, fetch, or remove objects from the persistent store. The environment offers the **managedObjectContext** property for this purpose. The following are the modifications we must introduced to the **SceneDelegate** class to inject a reference to the context into the environment for the views in the scene.

```swift
import UIKit
import SwiftUI
```

```
class SceneDelegate: UIResponder, UIWindowSceneDelegate {
    var window: UIWindow?

    func scene(_ scene: UIScene, willConnectTo session: UISceneSession,
options connectionOptions: UIScene.ConnectionOptions) {
        let app = UIApplication.shared
        let delegate = app.delegate as! AppDelegate
        let context = delegate.persistentContainer.viewContext
        let contentView = ContentView().environment(\.managedObjectContext,
context)

        if let windowScene = scene as? UIWindowScene {
            let window = UIWindow(windowScene: windowScene)
            window.rootViewController = UIHostingController(rootView:
contentView)
            self.window = window
            window.makeKeyAndVisible()
        }
    }
}
```

Listing 14-41: Injecting the context into the environment

The process is the same we followed before to inject our `AppData` model. We get a reference to the `AppDelegate` object from the app's `UIApplication` object, and then access its properties. In this case, we get a reference to the Core Data context from the `viewContext` property of the `NSPersistentContainer` object and then assign it to the environment's `managedObjectContext` property with the `environment()` modifier. From now on, the views can access the Core Data context from the environment and add, modify or remove objects in the persistent store.

 Do It Yourself: Update the `AppDelegate` class of the project created before for the model with the code in Listing 14-40 and the `SceneDelegate` class with the code in Listing 14-41. Replace the value of the `name` attribute in the `NSPersistentContainer` initializer with the name of your model's file. At this moment, the app doesn't do anything other than creating the stack. We will see how to read and store data next.

(Basic) **Managed Objects**

Core Data does not store our custom objects; it defines a class called `NSManagedObject` to provide the basic functionality for the objects stored in the persistent store. The class includes the following initializer and methods to create and manage the instances.

init(context: NSManagedObjectContext)—This initializer creates a new instance of the `NSManagedObject` class, or a subclass of it, and adds it to the context specified by the **context** attribute.

fetchRequest()—This type method generates a fetch request for an entity. A fetch request is a request we use to fetch objects of a particular entity from the persistent store.

entity()—This type method returns a reference to the entity from which the managed object was created. It is an object of type `NSEntityDescription` with a description of the entity.

Every time we want to store information in the persistent store, we must create an `NSManagedObject` object, associate that object to an entity, and store the data the entity allows. For example, if we create an object associated to the Books entity, we are only allowed to store five values that corresponds to the entity's attributes (title, year, cover, thumbnail, and author). To simplify our work, the system lets us define subclasses of this class that correspond to the entities of our model (Instead of creating instances of the `NSManagedObject` class, we create instances of the `Books` or `Authors` classes). Because this is a common task for any developer, Xcode does it automatically for us. All we have to do is associate each entity with a subclass from the Data Model Inspector panel. The option is available in a section called *Class*, as shown in Figure 14-28.

Figure 14-28: Entity's subclass

By default, Xcode creates a subclass for every entity defined in the model. The option to get the subclasses created for us is called Codegen. The value must be set to Class Definition (Figure 14-28, number 2), and the name of the subclass is defined by the Name option (Figure 14-28, number 1). Once the options are set, the classes are automatically created. For example, when we set these options for the entities incorporated to our model before, Xcode creates a subclass of `NSManagedObject` called `Books` with the properties `title`, `year`, `cover`, `thumbnail`, and `author`, and another subclass called `Authors` with the properties `name` and `books`. From now on, all we have to do to store a book in the persistent store is to create an instance of the `Books` class with the `NSManagedObject` initializer.

 Do It Yourself: Click on the Core Data model file to open the model. Select the Books and the Authors entity, open the Data Model Inspector panel, and make sure that the value of the Codegen option is set to Class Definition and the name of the class is assigned to the Name field, as shown in Figure 14-28.

 The Basics: The subclasses of the `NSManagedObject` class created to represent each entity in our model are not visible in Xcode. They are created internally when the project is built and automatically modified every time entities or attributes are added or removed from the model. If you decide not to use these subclasses, you can select the value Manual/None from the Codegen option and work directly with `NSManagedObject` objects or define your own subclasses.

(Basic) Fetch Request

As we already mentioned, to store an object in the persistent store, we must create an `NSManagedObject` (or an instance of our subclasses), add it to the context, and then save the context. The process to get the objects back from the persistent store is the opposite. Instead of moving the changes in the context to the persistent store, we must get the objects from the persistent store and move them into the context. Once the objects are in the context, we can read their properties, modify their values, or delete them. Core Data includes the `NSFetchRequest` class to request objects from the persistent store. The class includes the following properties for configuration.

predicate—This property sets or returns the predicate used to filter the objects fetched by the request. It is a value of type `NSPredicate`, a Foundation class used to establish logical conditions that describe objects in the persistent store.

sortDescriptors—This property sets or returns an array of sort descriptors that determine how the objects obtained by the request should be ordered. It is an array of values of type `NSSortDescriptor`, a Foundation class used to sort the objects according to the value of a property in ascending or descending order.

fetchLimit—This property sets or returns the maximum number of objects that the request should return. It takes a value of type `Int`.

propertiesToFetch—This property sets or returns an array of values that determine the properties we want to get (by default, all the properties of the `NSManagedObject` objects are returned). The properties of an entity (attributes) are represented by objects of the `NSPropertyDescription` class, or subclasses of it.

Every time we want to read objects from the persistent store, we must create an `NSFetchRequest` object to determine what type of objects we want. Although we can create this request manually, as we will see later, SwiftUI includes the `@FetchRequest` property wrapper that takes care of creating the `NSFetchRequest` object for us and keep the views synchronized with the values returned by the request. The property wrapper is created from a structure of type `FetchRequest`. The following are some of the structure's initializers.

FetchRequest(entity: NSEntityDescription, **sortDescriptors:** [NSSortDescriptor], **predicate:** NSPredicate?)—This initializer creates a fetch request with the configuration determined by the attributes and produces a `FetchedResults` structure that manages and delivers the objects to the view. The **entity** attribute determines the type of objects the request is going to fetch from the persistent store, the **sortDescriptors** attribute is an array of `NSSortDescriptor` objects that determine the order of the objects, and the **predicate** attribute is an `NSPredicate` object that filters the objects the request is going to fetch.

FetchRequest(fetchRequest: NSFetchRequest)—This initializer creates a fetch request with the `NSFetchRequest` provided by the attribute and produces a `FetchedResults` structure that manages and delivers the objects to the view.

A fetch request loads all the objects available in the persistent store. This is not a problem when the number of objects is not significant. But a persistent store can manage thousands of objects, which can occupy too much memory and consume resources the app and the system need to run. Therefore, instead of the fetch request, the `@FetchRequest` property wrapper produces a value of type `FetchedResults`. This is a structure that takes care of loading into the context only the objects that are required by the view at any given moment.

(Basic) **Working with Core Data**

It is time to see how all these tools work together to store and retrieve data from a persistent store. We are going to use a project like the one we used for archiving. The purpose of this application is to show the list of objects already stored in the persistent store and create new ones, as shown in Figure 14-29.

Figure 14-29: Interface to work with Core Data

The initial view is going to list all the books available in the persistent store and include a button to open a second view to create new objects with the values provided by the user.

```
import SwiftUI
import CoreData
struct ContentView: View {
    @FetchRequest(entity: Books.entity(), sortDescriptors: []) var
listOfBooks: FetchedResults<Books>

    var body: some View {
        NavigationView {
            List {
                ForEach(listOfBooks, id: \.self) { book in
                    RowBook(book: book)
                }
            }
            .navigationBarTitle("Books")
            .navigationBarItems(trailing: NavigationLink(destination:
InsertBookView(), label: {
                Text("Add Book")
            }))
        }
    }
}
struct RowBook: View {
    let book: Books

    var imageCover: UIImage {
        if let data = book.thumbnail, let image = UIImage(data: data) {
            return image
        } else {
            return UIImage(named: "nopicture")!
        }
    }
    var body: some View {
        HStack(alignment: .top) {
            Image(uiImage: imageCover)
                .resizable()
                .scaledToFit()
                .frame(width: 80, height: 100)
                .cornerRadius(10)
            VStack(alignment: .leading, spacing: 2) {
                Text(book.title ?? "Undefined").bold()
                Text(book.author?.name ?? "Undefined")
                Text(String(book.year)).font(.caption)
```

```
                Spacer()
            }.padding(.top, 5)
            Spacer()
        }
    }
}
struct ContentView_Previews: PreviewProvider {
    static var previews: some View {
        let app = UIApplication.shared
        let delegate = app.delegate as! AppDelegate
        let dbContext = delegate.persistentContainer.viewContext
        return ContentView()
            .environment(\.managedObjectContext, dbContext)
    }
}
```

Listing 14-42: Fetching objects from the persistent store

To have access to Core Data from the view, we must import the framework with the `import` keyword, as we did in Listing 14-42. After that, we are ready to fetch and store objects from the persistent store, and the first step is to get the list of objects already inserted by the user. To this end, the `ContentView` view defines a `@FetchRequest` property. This property creates a fetch request to fetch objects of the `Books` entity in no specific order (the `sortDescriptor` attribute was declared with an empty array). Notice that this property wrapper produces a structure of type `FetchedResults` and this structure is generic, so we must specify the data type is going to work with (`FetchedResults<Books>`).

Once the `@FetchRequest` property is ready, we can provide it to a `List` view to show the objects on the screen. The `ForEach` view in our example goes through this list and creates a `RowBook` view for each object to show its values. Reading these values is easy. The attributes of an entity are turned into properties of the `NSManagedObject` (the `Books` object in our example), and they are available as any other property. The only thing we must considered is that some of these properties return optional values. For instance, the `title` property returns an optional string. To show this value, we use a nil-coalescing operator (`??`). If there is a value in the property, we display it, otherwise, we show the string "Undefined". The `author` property is a little bit different. This property doesn't represent an attribute but a relationship. The value we need is actually the name of the author, which is returned by the `name` property inside the `Authors` object (`book.author?.name`). If this property contains a value, we show it, otherwise, we show the text "Undefined" again. With the image is more complicated. The value returned by the `thumbnail` property is a `Data` structure that we must convert to an `UIImage` object before creating the `Image` view with it. There are different ways to perform this process. In this example, we have decided to do it with a computed property called `imageCover`. When the property is read by the view, it checks if there is a value in the object's `thumbnail` property, creates an `UIImage` object with it, and returns that object. On the other hand, if the `thumbnail` property is empty, or there was a problem converting the data into an image, it returns a `UIImage` object with the image nopicture from the Assets Catalog.

Now, it is time to let the user create new `Books` objects. The `ContentView` view includes a `NavigationLink` in the navigation bar that opens the `InsertBookView` view for this purpose.

```
import SwiftUI
import CoreData

struct InsertBookView: View {
    @Environment(\.managedObjectContext) var dbContext
    @Environment(\.presentationMode) var presentation
    @State private var inputTitle: String = ""
```

```
    @State private var inputYear: String = ""

    var body: some View {
        VStack(spacing: 12) {
            HStack {
                Text("Title:")
                TextField("Insert Title", text: $inputTitle)
                    .textFieldStyle(RoundedBorderTextFieldStyle())
            }
            HStack {
                Text("Year:")
                TextField("Insert Year", text: $inputYear)
                    .textFieldStyle(RoundedBorderTextFieldStyle())
            }
            HStack {
                Text("Author:")
                Text("Undefined")
            }.frame(minWidth: 0, maxWidth: .infinity, alignment: .leading)
            Spacer()
        }.padding()
        .navigationBarTitle("Add Book")
        .navigationBarItems(trailing: Button("Save") {
            let newTitle = self.inputTitle.trimmingCharacters(in:
.whitespaces)
            let newYear = Int32(self.inputYear)
            if !newTitle.isEmpty && newYear != nil {
                let newBook = Books(context: self.dbContext)
                newBook.title = newTitle
                newBook.year = newYear!
                newBook.author = nil
                newBook.cover = UIImage(named: "bookcover")?.pngData()
                newBook.thumbnail = UIImage(named:
"bookthumbnail")?.pngData()
                do {
                    try self.dbContext.save()
                    self.presentation.wrappedValue.dismiss()
                } catch {
                    print("Error saving record")
                }
            }
        })
    }
}
```

Listing 14-43: Adding new objects to the persistent store

All the interaction between our code and the persistent store is done through the context. When we want to access the objects already stored, add new ones, remove them, or modify any of their values, we have to do it in the context and then move those changes from the context to the persistent store. The **@FetchRequest** property wrapper automatically gets a reference of the context from the environment (this is the reference we injected into the context in the **SceneDelegate** class in Listing 14-41), but when working directly with Core Data, we must get this reference ourselves. We have seen how to access values from the environment with the **@Environment** property wrapper before (see Listing 7-12). In this case, all we have to do is to define an **@Environment** property that accesses the **managedObjectContext** property in the environment. In the **InsertBookView** of Listing 14-43, we called this property **dbContext**.

The view includes two **TextField** views to let the user insert the title of the book and the year it was published, and a button in the navigation bar to save the values. When the button is pressed, the code checks if the values are valid and then creates and stores a new object in the persistent store. The process begins with the creation of the new object with the `Books()` initializer. This not only creates a new object of type `Books` but it also adds it to the context specified by the attribute (`self.dbContext`). The next step is to assign the values to the object's properties. We assign the value of the first input field to the `title` property, the value of the second input field to the `year` property (casted as an `Int32` type), the images bookcover and bookthumbnail to the `cover` and `thumbnail` properties, respectively (we assign standard images to every book for now), and the `nil` value to the `author` property (we still don't have an `Authors` object to associate with this book).

The `Books()` initializer inserts the new object into the context, but this change is not permanent. If we close the app after the values are assigned to the properties, the object is lost. To persist the changes, we must save the context with the `save()` method. This should be done every time we finish a process that changes the context. The method takes the information in the context and modifies the persistent store with it, so everything is stored permanently on file.

Do It Yourself: This example assumes that you have followed the previous steps to create a project, define a model with the Books and Authors entities, define the Core Data stack in the `AppDelegate` class, and inject the context into the environment in the `SceneDelegate` class. Download the bookcover.png, bookthumbnail.png, and nopicture.png images from our website and add them to the Assets Catalog. Update the ContentView.swift file with the code in Listing 14-42. Create a Swift file called InsertBookView.swift and update its content with the code in Listing 14-43. Run the application on a device and press the Add Book button. Insert a book and press Save. You should see something similar to Figure 14-29, above.

IMPORTANT: Core Data classes are created when the app is built. Until the app is built for the first time, Xcode can't recognize the classes created from the entities and returns an error. One way to remove the errors is to build the application by pressing the Command + B keys. If this doesn't solve the issues, you can try running the application on the simulator. It doesn't always work right away; it may take some time until the classes are built and recognized.

There are no view models in Core Data. The objects stored in the persistent store (`Books` and `Authors` in our example), represent the application's data model (the `Book` structure in previous examples). They store the values and return them as they are. But the views need the values to be formatted or casted before showing them on the screen. For instance, in the `RowBook` view in Listing 14-42, we had to process the value of the `thumbnail` property with a computed property to turn it into an `UIImage` view. We also had to use the nil-coalescing operator to show a string if there was no value in the `title` and `author` properties. And we even had to cast the value of the `year` property to a string with the `String()` initializer. All this work shouldn't be done by the view, it should be done by a view model. To create a view model for the Core Data objects, we can extend the classes defined by the system (see Extensions in Chapter 3). For example, we can create an extension of the `Books` class to provide computed properties that always return `String` values the views can show on the screen, and process the image in the `thumbnail` and `cover` properties, so we don't have to do it inside the view.

```
import SwiftUI

extension Books {
    var showTitle: String {
        return title ?? "Undefined"
    }
```

```
        var showYear: String {
            return String(year)
        }
        var showAuthor: String {
            return author?.name ?? "Undefined"
        }
        var showCover: UIImage {
            if let data = cover, let image = UIImage(data: data) {
                return image
            } else {
                return UIImage(named: "nopicture")!
            }
        }
        var showThumbnail: UIImage {
            if let data = thumbnail, let image = UIImage(data: data) {
                return image
            } else {
                return UIImage(named: "nopicture")!
            }
        }
    }
}
extension Authors {
    var showName: String {
        return name ?? "Undefined"
    }
}
```

Listing 14-44: Defining a view model for the Core Data objects

Extensions have access to the properties defined by the data type. This means that we can access those properties, process their values, and return something else. The example in Listing 14-44 defines an extension for the **Books** class and an extension for the **Authors** class (we stored these extensions in a separate file called Extensions.swift). The extensions include computed properties that format the values in the original properties and return a value the views can show on the screen. In the extension for the **Books** class, we also include a property that returns a string with the name of the author, so the views don't have to read this value from the **Authors** object anymore, they can do it directly from the **Books** object, as shown next.

```
struct RowBook: View {
    let book: Books

    var body: some View {
        HStack(alignment: .top) {
            Image(uiImage: book.showThumbnail)
                .resizable()
                .scaledToFit()
                .frame(width: 80, height: 100)
                .cornerRadius(10)
            VStack(alignment: .leading, spacing: 2) {
                Text(book.showTitle).bold()
                Text(book.showAuthor)
                Text(book.showYear).font(.caption)
                Spacer()
            }.padding(.top, 5)
            Spacer()
        }
    }
}
```

Listing 14-45: Using the values from the view model

The view has been greatly simplified. There is no formatting or processing. All it has to do is to read the values from the view model and show them to the user.

 Do It Yourself: Create a Swift file called Extensions.swift for the code in Listing 14-44. Update the `RowBook` view in the ContentView.swift file with the code in Listing 14-45. Run the application on a device. You should see the same interface shown in Figure 14-29.

The `Authors` objects are generated and stored the same way as the `Books` objects. This demands our application to provide new views where the user can select and add new objects. For our example, we have decided to expand our interface with a view that lists the authors already inserted by the user and another view to insert new ones.

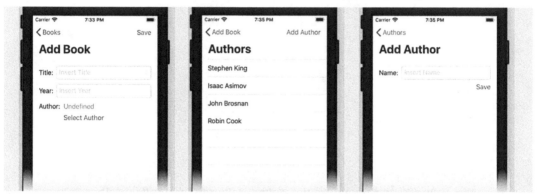

Figure 14-30: Interface to list and add authors

the view on the left is the one opened from the initial view when the user presses the Add Book button. This view now shows three input options, an input field to insert the title of the book, an input field to insert the year, and the Select Author button to select the author (Figure 14-30, left). This button is generated by a `NavigationLink` view that opens a view that lists all the authors available (Figure 14-30, center). In addition, this view includes a button in the navigation bar called Add Author to open a view that includes an input field to insert the name of a new author (Figure 14-30, right). The first step we must take to create this interface is to add the Select Author button to the `InsertBookView` view.

```
struct InsertBookView: View {
    @Environment(\.managedObjectContext) var dbContext
    @Environment(\.presentationMode) var presentation

    @State private var selectedAuthor: Authors? = nil
    @State private var inputTitle: String = ""
    @State private var inputYear: String = ""

    var body: some View {
        VStack(spacing: 12) {
            HStack {
                Text("Title:")
                TextField("Insert Title", text: $inputTitle)
                    .textFieldStyle(RoundedBorderTextFieldStyle())
            }
            HStack {
                Text("Year:")
                TextField("Insert Year", text: $inputYear)
                    .textFieldStyle(RoundedBorderTextFieldStyle())
            }
```

```
              HStack(alignment: .top) {
                  Text("Author:")
                  VStack(alignment: .leading, spacing: 8) {
                      Text(self.selectedAuthor?.name ?? "Undefined")
                          .foregroundColor(self.selectedAuthor != nil ?
Color.black : Color.gray)
                      NavigationLink(destination: AuthorsView(selected:
self.$selectedAuthor), label: {
                          Text("Select Author")
                      })
                  }
              }.frame(minWidth: 0, maxWidth: .infinity, alignment: .leading)
              Spacer()
          }.padding()
          .navigationBarTitle("Add Book")
          .navigationBarItems(trailing: Button("Save") {
              let newTitle = self.inputTitle.trimmingCharacters(in:
.whitespaces)
              let newYear = Int32(self.inputYear)
              if !newTitle.isEmpty && newYear != nil {
                  let newBook = Books(context: self.dbContext)
                  newBook.title = newTitle
                  newBook.year = newYear!
                  newBook.author = self.selectedAuthor
                  newBook.cover = UIImage(named: "bookcover")?.pngData()
                  newBook.thumbnail = UIImage(named:
"bookthumbnail")?.pngData()
                  do {
                      try self.dbContext.save()
                      self.presentation.wrappedValue.dismiss()
                  } catch {
                      print("Error saving record")
                  }
              }
          })
      }
  }
}
```

Listing 14-46: Selecting the author

Every time an author is selected or created, we must get its `Authors` object and send it back to the `InsertBookView` view to assign it to the book. To store this value, the view includes a `@State` property called `selectedAuthor`. If the property contains an `Authors` object, we show the value of its `name` property to the user, otherwise, we show the text "Undefined" (Notice that in this case we don't use the properties from the view models created before because the `selectedAuthor` property is an optional, so we have to check its value anyway). Below the name, we include a `NavigationLink` button to open a view called `AuthorsView` to let the user select an author.

```
import SwiftUI

struct AuthorsView: View {
   @Environment(\.presentationMode) var presentation
   @FetchRequest(entity: Authors.entity(), sortDescriptors: []) var
listOfAuthors: FetchedResults<Authors>
   @Binding var selected: Authors?
```

```
    var body: some View {
        List {
            ForEach(listOfAuthors, id: \.self) { author in
                HStack {
                    Text(author.showName)
                }
                .frame(minWidth: 0, maxWidth: .infinity, minHeight: 0,
maxHeight: .infinity, alignment: .leading)
                .contentShape(Rectangle())
                .onTapGesture {
                    self.selected = author
                    self.presentation.wrappedValue.dismiss()
                }
            }
        }
        .navigationBarTitle("Authors")
        .navigationBarItems(trailing: NavigationLink(destination:
InsertAuthorView(), label: {
            Text("Add Author")
        }))
    }
}
struct AuthorsView_Previews: PreviewProvider {
    static var previews: some View {
        let app = UIApplication.shared
        let delegate = app.delegate as! AppDelegate
        let dbContext = delegate.persistentContainer.viewContext
        return AuthorsView(selected: .constant(nil))
            .environment(\.managedObjectContext, dbContext)
    }
}
```

Listing 14-47: *Listing the authors available*

The view in Listing 14-47 lists the authors already inserted by the user. The **@FetchRequest** property is called **listOfAuthors** and it is defined to work with **Authors** objects, but other than that, the rest of the code is the same we used to list books. The only significant difference is that the rows now include the **onTapGesture()** modifier to let the user select an author. When the user taps on the name of an author, we assign the **Authors** object to a **@Binding** property called **selected** and close the view. Because the **selected** property is connected to the **selectedAuthor** property defined in the **InsertBookView** view, the name of the author selected by the user is now shown on the screen.

If there are no authors in the persistent store yet, or the author the user is looking for is not on the list, the user can press a button in the navigation bar that opens the **InsertAuthorView** view to insert a new author.

```
import SwiftUI

struct InsertAuthorView: View {
    @Environment(\.managedObjectContext) var dbContext
    @Environment(\.presentationMode) var presentation
    @State private var inputName: String = ""

    var body: some View {
        VStack {
            HStack {
                Text("Name:")
```

```
                TextField("Insert Name", text: $inputName)
                    .textFieldStyle(RoundedBorderTextFieldStyle())
            }
            HStack {
                Spacer()
                Button("Save") {
                    let newName = self.inputName.trimmingCharacters(in:
.whitespaces)
                    if !newName.isEmpty {
                        let newAuthor = Authors(context: self.dbContext)
                        newAuthor.name = newName
                        do {
                            try self.dbContext.save()
                            self.presentation.wrappedValue.dismiss()
                        } catch {
                            print("Error saving record")
                        }
                    }
                }
                Spacer()
            }.padding()
            .navigationBarTitle("Add Author")
        }
    }
}
struct InsertAuthorView_Previews: PreviewProvider {
    static var previews: some View {
        let app = UIApplication.shared
        let delegate = app.delegate as! AppDelegate
        let dbContext = delegate.persistentContainer.viewContext
        return InsertAuthorView()
            .environment(\.managedObjectContext, dbContext)
    }
}
```

Listing 14-48: Inserting new authors

This is a simple view. It includes one **TextField** view to insert the name of the author and a button to save it. When the button is pressed, we follow the same process as before. The **Authors** object is initialized and stored in the context, the name inserted by the user is assigned to the object's **name** property, and the context is saved to make the changes permanent.

With these additions, our basic app is complete. Now authors can be assigned to new books. When we pressed the Select Author button, the app opens a view with all the authors available (Figure 14-30, center). If there are no authors yet or the author we want is not on the list, we can press the Add Author button and insert a new one (Figure 14-30, right). Every time we select an author from the list, the app goes back to the view with the book's information and shows the name of the selected author on the screen (Figure 14-30, left). The **Authors** object that represents the author is assigned to the book's **author** property and therefore the name of the author is now shown on the list of books.

Do It Yourself: Update the **InsertBookView** view with the code in Listing 14-46. Create a SwiftUI file called AuthorsView.swift for the code in Listing 14-47 and a SwiftUI file called InsertAuthorView.swift for the code in Listing 14-48. Run the application on a device. Press the Add Book button. Press the Select Author button. Press the Add Author button to add an author. After adding the author, click on it to select it. You should see the name of the author below the input fields.

Sort Descriptors

Objects returned from a request are usually in the order they were created, but this is not guaranteed. To sort the objects in a specific order, Core Data lets us associate the request with objects of type `NSSortDescriptor`. From this class, we can create objects that specify an order according to the values of a property. The sorting criteria is determined by methods provided by the values themselves. For example, data types like `Date` implement only the `compare()` methods to compare their values, but the `NSString` class implements other methods that allow us to do things like order strings without differentiating between lowercase and uppercase letters (see `NSString` in Chapter 4). By default, an `NSSortDescriptor` object uses the `compare()` method to compare any type of value, but we can specify others from the initializers.

NSSortDescriptor(key: String?, ascending: Bool)—This initializer creates an `NSSortDescriptor` object that orders the objects according to the value of the property specified by the **key** attribute. The **key** attribute is a string with the name of the property, and the **ascending** attribute determines if the objects will be sort in ascending or descending order. The object created by this initializer sorts the values with the `compare()` method.

NSSortDescriptor(key: String?, ascending: Bool, selector: Selector?)—This initializer creates an `NSSortDescriptor` object that orders the objects according to the value of the property specified by the **key** attribute. The **key** attribute is a string with the name of the property, the **ascending** attribute determines if the objects will be sorted in ascending or descending order, and the **selector** attribute is the comparison method that determines the sorting criteria.

The `@FetchRequest` property wrapper includes the `sortDescriptors` attribute to define the order of the objects in the request. All we have to do to define the order is to create at least one `NSSortDescriptor` object and assign it to this attribute. The following example sorts the `Books` objects by title in ascending order.

```
struct ContentView: View {
   @FetchRequest(entity: Books.entity(), sortDescriptors:
[NSSortDescriptor(key: "title", ascending: true)]) var listOfBooks:
FetchedResults<Books>

   var body: some View {
      NavigationView {
         List {
            ForEach(listOfBooks, id: \.self) { book in
               RowBook(book: book)
            }
         }
         .navigationBarTitle("Books")
         .navigationBarItems(trailing: NavigationLink(destination:
InsertBookView(), label: {
            Text("Add Book")
         }))
      }
   }
}
```

Listing 14-49: Sorting the books by title

The **sortDescriptors** attribute takes an array of **NSSortDescriptor** objects, so we can specify different conditions to sort the list. The final order is established according to the location of the **NSSortDescriptor** objects in the array. For example, we can sort the books by author first and then by year.

```
struct ContentView: View {
    @FetchRequest(entity: Books.entity(), sortDescriptors:
[NSSortDescriptor(key: "author.name", ascending: true),
NSSortDescriptor(key: "year", ascending: true)]) var listOfBooks:
FetchedResults<Books>

    var body: some View {
        NavigationView {
            List {
                ForEach(listOfBooks, id: \.self) { book in
                    RowBook(book: book)
                }
            }
            .navigationBarTitle("Books")
            .navigationBarItems(trailing: NavigationLink(destination:
InsertBookView(), label: {
                Text("Add Book")
            }))
        }
    }
}
```

Listing 14-50: Sorting books by author and year

When we compare string values, we can use other comparison methods than **compare()**. The method must be assigned to the **selector** attribute of the **NSSortDescriptor** initializer. The most frequently used method is **caseInsensitiveCompare()** because it compares values without differentiating between lowercase and uppercase letters. The following example implements this method to sort the books by title.

```
struct ContentView: View {
    @FetchRequest(entity: Books.entity(), sortDescriptors:
[NSSortDescriptor(key: "title", ascending: true, selector:
#selector(NSString.caseInsensitiveCompare(_:)))]) var listOfBooks:
FetchedResults<Books>

    var body: some View {
        NavigationView {
            List {
                ForEach(listOfBooks, id: \.self) { book in
                    RowBook(book: book)
                }
            }
            .navigationBarTitle("Books")
            .navigationBarItems(trailing: NavigationLink(destination:
InsertBookView(), label: {
                Text("Add Book")
            }))
        }
    }
}
```

Listing 14-51: Sorting by title without differentiating between lowercase and uppercase letters

To declare the method to sort the objects, we must use a selector, as we did in Chapter 9, Listing 9-61. In this example, the `NSSortDescriptor` object executes the `caseInsensitiveCompare()` method to sort the values. When the method is called, it receives the objects from the request and returns them in alphabetical order, without considering lowercase and uppercase letters.

 Do It Yourself: Update the `ContentView` view in your project with any of the examples presented above to see how sort descriptors work. Change the value of the **ascending** attribute to see how the order changes in each case.

(Basic) Predicates

The requests performed in previous examples are getting all the objects associated to a particular entity and the values of all their properties. The Core Data framework defines a class called `NSPredicate` to set filters that allow us to fetch only the objects that comply to certain rules. For example, we could get only the books that were published in the year 1983 or the authors which names begin with "Stephen". The class defines the following initializer to create a predicate with all the conditions we need.

NSPredicate(format: String, **argumentArray:** [Any]?**)**—This initializer creates a `NSPredicate` object with the conditions set by the **format** attribute. The **argumentArray** attribute is an optional array of values that replace placeholders in the string assigned to the **format** attribute. The **argumentArray** attribute may be ignored or replaced by a list of values separated by commas.

To filter values in a request, we must create the `NSPredicate` object and assign it to the predicate attribute of the `@FetchRequest` property wrapper. The following example assigns an `NSPredicate` object to the request in the `ContentView` view to search for the books that has the value 1983 assigned to their **year** property.

```
struct ContentView: View {
   @FetchRequest(entity: Books.entity(), sortDescriptors: [], predicate:
NSPredicate(format: "year = 1983")) var listOfBooks:
FetchedResults<Books>

   var body: some View {
      NavigationView {
         List {
            ForEach(listOfBooks, id: \.self) { book in
               RowBook(book: book)
            }
         }
         .navigationBarTitle("Books")
         .navigationBarItems(trailing: NavigationLink(destination:
InsertBookView(), label: {
            Text("Add Book")
         }))
      }
   }
}
```

Listing 14-52: Filtering books by year

If we are trying to search for a value in a relationship, we can concatenate the properties with dot notation, as we did before to read the **name** property in the **Authors** object. For example, the following request searches for books written by Stephen King.

Chapter 14 - Storage

```
struct ContentView: View {
    @FetchRequest(entity: Books.entity(), sortDescriptors: [], predicate:
NSPredicate(format: "author.name = 'Stephen King'")) var listOfBooks:
FetchedResults<Books>

    var body: some View {
        NavigationView {
            List {
                ForEach(listOfBooks, id: \.self) { book in
                    RowBook(book: book)
                }
            }
            .navigationBarTitle("Books")
            .navigationBarItems(trailing: NavigationLink(destination:
InsertBookView(), label: {
                Text("Add Book")
            }))
        }
    }
}
```

Listing 14-53: *Filtering books by author*

 Do It Yourself: Update the `ContentView` view in your project with any of the examples presented above to see how predicates work. Add books with different authors and years to test the filters.

Of course, these are predefined conditions, but we can let the user introduce the value and use predicates to perform a search. There are a few things we must change in the view to let the user search for objects. First, the view must include a search bar, with an input field and a button, like the one introduced in Listing 10-29. This also requires an observable object with `@Published` properties to manage the values inserted by the user. And finally, we must create the `FetchRequest` and the `FetchedResults` structures manually from a separate view, so they are recreated with the new values every time a search is performed. The following code includes the observable object required for this example and the `ContentView` view with the search bar necessary for the user to perform a search.

```
class ContentData: ObservableObject {
    @Published var search: String? = nil
    @Published var searchInput: String = "" {
        didSet {
            setSearch(term: searchInput)
        }
    }
    func setSearch(term: String) {
        let toSearch = term.trimmingCharacters(in: .whitespaces)
        search = toSearch == "" ? nil : toSearch
    }
}
struct ContentView: View {
    @ObservedObject var contentData = ContentData()

    var body: some View {
        NavigationView {
            VStack {
                HStack {
```

```
                 TextField("Insert Search", text: $contentData.searchInput,
onCommit: {
                      self.contentData.setSearch(term:
self.contentData.searchInput)
                 }).textFieldStyle(RoundedBorderTextFieldStyle())
                 Button("🔍") {
                      self.contentData.setSearch(term:
self.contentData.searchInput)
                 }
            }.padding()
            ListBooksView(search: contentData.search)
        }
        .navigationBarTitle("Books")
        .navigationBarItems(trailing: NavigationLink(destination:
InsertBookView(), label: {
            Text("Add Book")
        }))
    }
   }
}
```

Listing 14-54: Creating a search bar to search values in the persistent store

The observable object in Listing 14-54 is almost the same used in the example in Listing 10-28 to search for values in a model, and the search bar is also the same implemented in that example. The bar includes a `TextField` view to insert a term and a button to perform the search. When a value is introduced in this input field, the `didSet()` method of the `searchInput` property is executed and the new value is assigned to the `search` property by the `setSearch()` method. This change forces the `ContentView` view to update its content and that recreates the `ListBooksView` view, which takes care of defining the predicate and present the list, as shown next.

```
struct ListBooksView: View {
  @FetchRequest(entity: Books.entity(), sortDescriptors:
[NSSortDescriptor(key: "title", ascending: true)]) var listOfBooks:
FetchedResults<Books>

  init(search: String?) {
    if let term = search {
      self._listOfBooks = FetchRequest(entity: Books.entity(),
sortDescriptors: [NSSortDescriptor(key: "title", ascending: true)],
predicate: NSPredicate(format: "year = %@", term))
    }
  }
  var body: some View {
    List {
      ForEach(listOfBooks, id: \.self) { book in
        RowBook(book: book)
      }
    }
  }
}
```

Listing 14-55: Defining the fetch request according to the search

The `ListBooksView` structure defines a `@FetchRequest` property with standard values, and then checks the value received from the `ContentView` view in the initializer. If the user inserted a value in the search bar, it replaces the `FetchRequest` structure inside the `@FetchRequest` property with a new one (`self._listOfBooks`). The new `FetchRequest` structure is defined with a predicate that compares the value inserted by the user with the value of the **year** property of each **Books** object. In consequence, this request returns only the books that were published the year indicated by the user.

Notice that the string searched by the user is incorporated into the string that defines the format of the predicate with placeholders. In this case, we used the **%@** placeholder, which indicates to the initializer that the value is going to be an object or a structure. The initializer takes the **String** value stored in the **term** constant and replace the placeholder with it (e.g., "year = 1983"). The result is shown in Figure 14-31. Only the books that were published the year inserted in the input field are displayed.

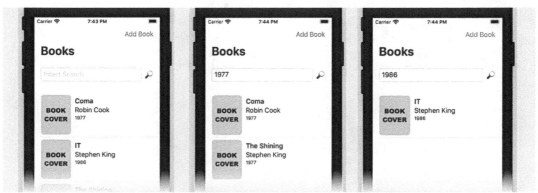

Figure 14-31: Search

 Do It Yourself: Update the ContentView.swift file with the codes in Listings 14-54 and 14-55. Remember that you still need the **RowBook** view introduced in Listing 14-45. Run the application on a device. Insert some books and then insert a year in the input field. Only the books published that year should be shown on the list, as illustrated in Figure 14-31.

 IMPORTANT: The placeholder **%@** is replaced by the value specified in the attributes between quotes. If you need to add the value to the predicate without the quotes, you must use the placeholder **%K** instead (usually called *Dynamic Key*). This is also useful to insert key paths into the format string.

Predicates use comparison and logical operators like those offered by Swift. For example, we can compare values with the operators =, !=, >, <, >= and <=, and also concatenate conditions with the characters && (or the word **AND**), || (or the word **OR**) and ! (or the word **NOT**). Predicates also include keywords for a more precise search. The following are the most frequently used.

BEGINSWITH—The condition determined by this keyword is true when the expression on the left begins with the expression on the right.

CONTAINS—The condition determined by this keyword is true when the expression on the left contains the expression on the right.

ENDSWITH—The condition determined by this keyword is true when the expression on the left ends with the expression on the right.

LIKE—The condition determined by this keyword is true when the expression on the left is equal to the expression on the right.

IN—The condition determined by this keyword is true when the expression on the left is equal to any of the values included in the expression on the right. The values are provided as an array between parentheses.

These keywords may be accompanied by the characters **c** or **d** between square brackets to specify a case and diacritic insensitive search. For example, we may search for books which authors' names begin with the characters inserted by the user, but without considering uppercase or lowercase letters ([c]).

```
struct ListBooksView: View {
    @FetchRequest(entity: Books.entity(), sortDescriptors:
[NSSortDescriptor(key: "title", ascending: true)]) var listOfBooks:
FetchedResults<Books>

    init(search: String?) {
        if let term = search {
            self._listOfBooks = FetchRequest(entity: Books.entity(),
sortDescriptors: [NSSortDescriptor(key: "title", ascending: true)],
predicate: NSPredicate(format: "author.name BEGINSWITH[c] %@", term))
        }
    }
    var body: some View {
        List {
            ForEach(listOfBooks, id: \.self) { book in
                RowBook(book: book)
            }
        }
    }
}
```

Listing 14-56: Filtering values with predicate keywords

Another useful keyword is CONTAINS, used to search for a value within a string. For instance, we can check if the characters inserted by the user can be found in the title of a book.

```
struct ListBooksView: View {
    @FetchRequest(entity: Books.entity(), sortDescriptors:
[NSSortDescriptor(key: "title", ascending: true)]) var listOfBooks:
FetchedResults<Books>

    init(search: String?) {
        if let term = search {
            self._listOfBooks = FetchRequest(entity: Books.entity(),
sortDescriptors: [NSSortDescriptor(key: "title", ascending: true)],
predicate: NSPredicate(format: "title CONTAINS[dc] %@", term))
        }
    }
    var body: some View {
        List {
            ForEach(listOfBooks, id: \.self) { book in
                RowBook(book: book)
            }
        }
    }
}
```

Listing 14-57: Searching for characters in a string

The predicate in Listing 14-57 implements the dc modifiers to make the search case insensitive and ignore diacritic characters. For example, we can search for the term "éry" (with a stress in the letter e) and the request will return books which title contains the characters "ery" (e.g., "Misery").

Chapter 14 - Storage

Do It Yourself: Update the `ListBooksView` view in your project with the example you want to try. Run the application on a device and perform a search to see how the predicate keywords work.

The Basics: Diacritics are the small marks used in some languages to change the pronunciation of a letter, like the visible stress over Spanish vowels. When we specify the character **d** between square brackets, the search ignores these marks and looks for the letter in its basic form. The **c** and **d** characters are usually implemented together, as we did in the example in Listing 14-57.

Basic Delete Objects

Deleting objects in the persistent store is no different than any other values in the model. As we did in the example in Listing 10-21, we must apply the `onDelete()` modifier to the `ForEach` view and remove from the model the objects in the indexes received by the closure.

```
struct ListBooksView: View {
    @Environment(\.managedObjectContext) var dbContext
    @FetchRequest(entity: Books.entity(), sortDescriptors:
[NSSortDescriptor(key: "title", ascending: true)]) var listOfBooks:
FetchedResults<Books>

    init(search: String?) {
        if let term = search {
            self._listOfBooks = FetchRequest(entity: Books.entity(),
sortDescriptors: [NSSortDescriptor(key: "title", ascending: true)],
predicate: NSPredicate(format: "title CONTAINS[dc] %@", term))
        }
    }
    var body: some View {
        List {
            ForEach(listOfBooks, id: \.self) { book in
                RowBook(book: book)
            }
            .onDelete(perform: { indexes in
                for index in indexes {
                    self.dbContext.delete(self.listOfBooks[index])
                }
                do {
                    try self.dbContext.save()
                } catch {
                    print("Error deleting objects")
                }
            })
        }
    }
}
```

Listing 14-58: Deleting objects

In our example, the objects retrieved from the persistent store are stored in the `listOfBooks` property. The indexes received by the closure in the `onDelete()` modifier are the indexes of the objects the user wants to delete from this collection. Therefore, to remove the objects selected by the user, we iterate through the indexes of all the objects to be removed with a `for in` loop, get the object from the `listOfBooks` collection using each index, and remove it with the context's `delete()` method. Once the object is removed from the context, the listOfBooks property is automatically updated and the changes are reflected on the screen. The last step is to save the context with the **save()** method to modify the persistent store with the changes in the context, as we did before.

 Do It Yourself: Update the **ListBooksView** structure with the code in Listing 14-58. Run the application on a device. Drag one of the books to the left. You should see the Delete button. Press the button to remove the book. In this example, we implemented the code to remove the object in the view, but you can move it to a method or an observable object, as we did in the example in Listing 10-21, and also implement the **EditButton()** view or some of the tools introduced in Chapter 10 to provide more options to the user.

(Basic) Modify Objects

Modifying an object in the persistent store is easy. The interface must let the user select an object, pass it to a view that provides input fields to change its values, assign the values inserted by the user back to the object, and save the context to make the changes permanent. First, we must add the navigation link in the **ListBooksView** view to let the user select a book.

```
struct ListBooksView: View {
   @Environment(\.managedObjectContext) var dbContext
   @FetchRequest(entity: Books.entity(), sortDescriptors:
[NSSortDescriptor(key: "title", ascending: true)]) var listOfBooks:
FetchedResults<Books>

   init(search: String?) {
      if let term = search {
         self._listOfBooks = FetchRequest(entity: Books.entity(),
sortDescriptors: [NSSortDescriptor(key: "title", ascending: true)],
predicate: NSPredicate(format: "title CONTAINS[dc] %@", term))
      }
   }
   var body: some View {
      List {
         ForEach(listOfBooks, id: \.self) { book in
            NavigationLink(destination: ModifyBookView(book: book),
label: {
               RowBook(book: book)
                  .id(UUID())
            })
         }
         .onDelete(perform: { indexes in
            for index in indexes {
               self.dbContext.delete(self.listOfBooks[index])
            }
            do {
               try self.dbContext.save()
            } catch {
               print("Error deleting objects")
            }
         })
      }
   }
}
```

Listing 14-59: Selecting the book to modify

Chapter 14 - Storage

IMPORTANT: Notice that in this example we apply a modifier called `id()` to the `RowBook` view. This modifier assigns a unique identifier to the view every time the content of the `body` property is processed. It is useful when we need to force SwiftUI to recreate the view. In this case, we apply it to generate a new `RowBook` view every time a value is updated. This is because SwiftUI considers the view to be the same as before when it is generated from an external view and therefore it does not update its content. By assigning a unique identifier to it, we tell SwiftUI that this is a different view and it should draw it again. The modifier is also useful to regenerate `List` views when the system takes too much time to update them. For more information, visit our website and follow the links for this chapter.

The `NavigationLink` view opens a view called `ModifyBookView` to let the user modify the values of the selected book. The following is our implementation of this view.

```
import SwiftUI
import CoreData

class ModifyData: ObservableObject {
    @Published var selectedAuthor: Authors? = nil
    @Published var inputTitle: String = ""
    @Published var inputYear: String = ""
}
struct ModifyBookView: View {
    @Environment(\.managedObjectContext) var dbContext
    @Environment(\.presentationMode) var presentation
    @ObservedObject var modifyData = ModifyData()

    let book: Books
    init(book: Books) {
        self.book = book
        self.modifyData.selectedAuthor = book.author
        self.modifyData.inputTitle = book.title ?? "Undefined"
        self.modifyData.inputYear = book.showYear
    }
    var body: some View {
        VStack(spacing: 12) {
            HStack {
                Text("Title:")
                TextField("Insert Title", text: $modifyData.inputTitle)
                    .textFieldStyle(RoundedBorderTextFieldStyle())
            }
            HStack {
                Text("Year:")
                TextField("Insert Year", text: $modifyData.inputYear)
                    .textFieldStyle(RoundedBorderTextFieldStyle())
            }
            HStack(alignment: .top) {
                Text("Author:")
                VStack(alignment: .leading, spacing: 8) {
                    Text(self.modifyData.selectedAuthor?.name ?? "Undefined")
                        .foregroundColor(self.modifyData.selectedAuthor != nil
? Color.black : Color.gray)
                    NavigationLink(destination: AuthorsView(selected:
self.$modifyData.selectedAuthor), label: {
                        Text("Select Author")
                    })
                }
            }.frame(minWidth: 0, maxWidth: .infinity, alignment: .leading)
```

```
                Spacer()
        }.padding()
        .navigationBarTitle("Modify Book")
        .navigationBarItems(trailing: Button("Save") {
            let newTitle = self.modifyData.inputTitle.trimmingCharacters(in:
.whitespaces)
            let newYear = Int32(self.modifyData.inputYear)
            if !newTitle.isEmpty && newYear != nil {
                self.book.title = newTitle
                self.book.year = newYear!
                self.book.author = self.modifyData.selectedAuthor
                do {
                    try self.dbContext.save()
                    self.presentation.wrappedValue.dismiss()
                } catch {
                    print("Error saving record")
                }
            }
        })
    }
}
struct ModifyBookView_Previews: PreviewProvider {
    static var previews: some View {
        let app = UIApplication.shared
        let delegate = app.delegate as! AppDelegate
        let dbContext = delegate.persistentContainer.viewContext
        let book = Books(context: dbContext)
        book.title = "Test"
        book.year = 1990
        return ModifyBookView(book: book)
            .environment(\.managedObjectContext, dbContext)
    }
}
```

Listing 14-60: Modifying the values of a managed object

The structure in Listing 14-60 defines a constant called **book** to receive the **Books** object that represents the book selected by the user. Because the user needs to see the book to be able to modify it, we use an observable object and **@Published** properties to manage the user input and initialize them with the values in the **book** property. The view includes two **TextField** views for the title and the year, and the same Select Author button included before to open the **AuthorsView** view and let the user select an author. When the Save button is pressed, the values inserted by the user are assigned to the object's properties and the context is saved. Notice that in this opportunity we do not create a new **Books** object, we just modify the properties of the **Books** object received by the view.

Figure 14-32: Interface to modify managed objects

Do It Yourself: Update the `ListBooksView` view with the code in Listing 14-59. Create a SwiftUI file called ModifyBookView.swift for the view in Listing 14-60. Run the application on a device. Tap on a book to select it. Change the title and press Save. You should see the changes on the list.

Medium | **Custom Fetch Requests**

So far, we have let the `@FetchRequest` property wrapper create the requests for us, but there are situations in which we must create our own fetch requests to process the values in the persistent store. Because a request has to be associated to an entity, the subclasses of the `NSManagedObject` class, like `Books` and `Authors`, include the `fetchRequest()` method. This method returns an `NSFetchRequest` object with a fetch request associated to the entity. To perform this request, the context includes the `fetch()` method. The following example creates a fetch request when the view appears on the screen and when an object is removed to count the number of books in the persistent store and show the value at the top of the list.

```
struct ListBooksView: View {
    @Environment(\.managedObjectContext) var dbContext
    @FetchRequest(entity: Books.entity(), sortDescriptors:
[NSSortDescriptor(key: "title", ascending: true)]) var listOfBooks:
FetchedResults<Books>
    @State private var totalBooks: Int = 0

    init(search: String?) {
        if let term = search {
            self._listOfBooks = FetchRequest(entity: Books.entity(),
sortDescriptors: [NSSortDescriptor(key: "title", ascending: true)],
predicate: NSPredicate(format: "title CONTAINS[dc] %@", term))
        }
    }
    var body: some View {
        List {
            HStack {
                Text("Total Books")
                Spacer()
                Text(String(totalBooks)).bold()
            }.foregroundColor(Color.green)

            ForEach(listOfBooks, id: \.self) { book in
                NavigationLink(destination: ModifyBookView(book: book),
label: {
                    RowBook(book: book)
                        .id(UUID())
                })
            }
            .onDelete(perform: { indexes in
                for index in indexes {
                    self.dbContext.delete(self.listOfBooks[index])
                    self.countBooks()
                }
                do {
                    try self.dbContext.save()
                } catch {
                    print("Error deleting objects")
                }
            })
        }
```

```
        .onAppear(perform: {
            self.countBooks()
        })
    }
    func countBooks() {
        let request: NSFetchRequest<Books> = Books.fetchRequest()
        if let list = try? self.dbContext.fetch(request) {
            let count = list.count
            self.totalBooks = count
        }
    }
}
```

Listing 14-61: Counting the books available

To store the number of books, the structure defines a `@State` property called `totalBooks`, and to show the value, the view includes a `HStack` with a `Text` view on top of the list. The request is created by a method called `countBooks()`. The method is called when the view appears and when an object is removed. It creates a fetch request for the `Books` entity, and then executes the request in the context with the `fetch()` method. If there are no errors, this method returns an array with all the objects that match the request. In this case, we didn't define any predicate, so the array contains all the `Books` objects in the persistent store. Finally, we count the objects with the `count` property and assign the value to the `totalBooks` property to show it to the user.

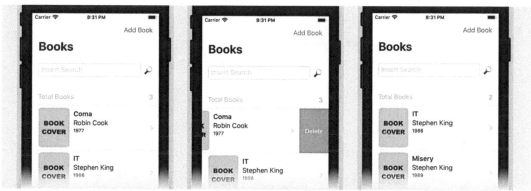

Figure 14-33: Total number of books in the persistent store

 Do It Yourself: Update the `ListBooksView` structure with the code in Listing 14-61. Run the application on a device. You should see the total number of books on the screen. Slide a row to the left and press the Delete button. You should see the number on the screen go down by one unit.

Although this is a legitimate way to count objects in the persistent store, it loads all the objects into memory and consumes too many resources. To avoid any issues, the `NSManagedObjectContext` class includes the `count()` method. This method returns an integer with the number of objects we would get if we call the `fetch()` method with the same request. The method does not fetch the objects, so we can call it without being afraid of consuming too much memory. The following example improves the `countBooks()` method using the `count()` method.

```
func countBooks() {
    let request: NSFetchRequest<Books> = Books.fetchRequest()
```

```
    if let count = try? self.dbContext.count(for: request) {
        self.totalBooks = count
    }
}
```

Listing 14-62: Counting the books with the count() *method*

Do It Yourself: Update the `countBooks()` method from the previous example with the code of Listing 14-62. The method counts the `Books` objects as before, but without consuming resources.

If what we want is to get the number of objects associated to a To-Many relationship, we just have to count the number of items returned by the property that represents the relationship. For example, we can count the number of books of every author and show it along with the name.

```
struct AuthorsView: View {
    @Environment(\.presentationMode) var presentation
    @FetchRequest(entity: Authors.entity(), sortDescriptors: []) var
listOfAuthors: FetchedResults<Authors>
    @Binding var selected: Authors?

    var body: some View {
        List {
            ForEach(listOfAuthors, id: \.self) { author in
                HStack {
                    Text(author.showName)
                    Spacer()
                    Text(String(author.books?.count ?? 0))
                }
                .frame(minWidth: 0, maxWidth: .infinity, minHeight: 0,
maxHeight: .infinity, alignment: .leading)
                .contentShape(Rectangle())
                .onTapGesture {
                    self.selected = author
                    self.presentation.wrappedValue.dismiss()
                }
            }
        }
        .navigationBarTitle("Authors")
        .navigationBarItems(trailing: NavigationLink(destination:
InsertAuthorView(), label: {
            Text("Add Author")
        }))
    }
}
```

Listing 14-63: Counting the books of each author

The `AuthorsView` view in Listing 14-63 includes a `Text` view that shows the total number of books next to the author's name. To get this value, we count the number of items in the `books` property or show the value 0 if the property is equal to `nil`.

Do It Yourself: Update the `AuthorsView` view with the code in Listing 14-63. Run the application on a device. Select a book and press the Select Author button. You should see the list of authors available and the number of books assigned to each author on the right.

Another practical application of custom fetch requests and the `count()` method is checking for duplicates. The inclusion of duplicated values is something that every application must be prepared to prevent. For example, if in the application we have created so far, we insert an author that already exists, two `Authors` objects with the same name are stored in the persistent store. To avoid this situation, we can use a request with a predicate that searches for authors of the same name before creating a new object. The following example modifies the `InsertAuthorView` view to check if the author inserted by the user already exists in the persistent store.

```
import SwiftUI
import CoreData
struct InsertAuthorView: View {
    @Environment(\.managedObjectContext) var dbContext
    @Environment(\.presentationMode) var presentation
    @State private var inputName: String = ""

    var body: some View {
        VStack {
            HStack {
                Text("Name:")
                TextField("Insert Name", text: $inputName)
                    .textFieldStyle(RoundedBorderTextFieldStyle())
            }
            HStack {
                Spacer()
                Button("Save") {
                    let newName = self.inputName.trimmingCharacters(in:
.whitespaces)
                    if !newName.isEmpty {
                        let request: NSFetchRequest<Authors> =
Authors.fetchRequest()
                        request.predicate = NSPredicate(format: "name = %@",
newName)
                        if let total = try? self.dbContext.count(for: request),
total == 0 {
                            let newAuthor = Authors(context: self.dbContext)
                            newAuthor.name = newName
                            do {
                                try self.dbContext.save()
                            } catch {
                                print("Error saving record")
                            }
                        }
                    }
                    self.presentation.wrappedValue.dismiss()
                }
            }
            Spacer()
        }.padding()
        .navigationBarTitle("Add Author")
    }
}
```

Listing 14-64: Checking for duplicates

The code in Listing 14-64 creates a request for the Authors entity and uses the value inserted in the **TextField** view to create a predicate. The predicate searches for objects with the name equal to the value of the **newName** constant. Using this request, we call the **count()** method in the context to get the total amount of objects that match the conditions in the predicate. If the value returned is 0, we know that there are no authors in the persistent store with that name and we can create and add the new **Authors** object.

Do It Yourself: Update the `InsertAuthorView` view in your project with the code in Listing 14-64. Run the application on a device. Select a book, press the Select Author button, and press the Add Author button. You should only be able to insert a new author if there is no other author in the persistent store with the same name.

 IMPORTANT: There is an option provided by Core Data called *Constraints* that you can use to configure an Entity to not allow the insertion of objects with duplicated values, but it doesn't work with CloudKit and therefore we don't implement it in the examples of this book. For more information, visit our website and follow the links for this chapter.

(Medium) **Sections**

The information in the persistent store may be presented in sections. SwiftUI does not offer the tools to create the sections at the time, but the Core Data model can be structured to provide this kind of organization. The first step is to create an additional entity that represents the sections available. For instance, if we want to create alphabetical sections, we must add an entity to store the letters corresponding to each section. In the following example, we will organize the books alphabetically. For this purpose, we are going to add an entity called *SortLetters* with an attribute of type String called *letter*.

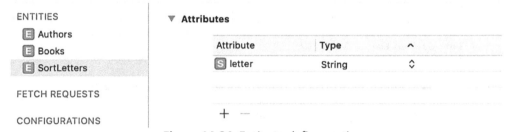

Figure 14-34: Entity to define sections

The purpose of the SortLetters entity is to store the initials of the titles of the books. If the title of a book begins with the letter M, we must create an object of this entity with the value M. At the time of creating the sections, we read all the objects of this type in the persistent store and generate `Section` views with their values. To list the books for each section, we need to connect the `SortLetters` objects with the `Books` objects. This requires two relationships. A To-Many relationship for the SortLetters entity to point to all the books that begin with a letter, and a To-One relationship for the Books entity to point to the letter the book belongs to.

Relationship for the SortLetters entity

Relationship	^ Destination	Inverse
M books	Books	◊ sortletter ◊

Relationships for the Books entity

Relationship	^ Destination	Inverse
O author	Authors	◊ books ◊
O sortletter	SortLetters	◊ books ◊

Figure 14-35: Relationships for the SortLetters and Books entities

The books relationship in the SortLetters entity is going to reference all the `Books` objects which `title` properties begin with a letter. For instance, the `SortLetters` object that stores the letter A will have a `books` property with references to all the books which titles begin with the letter A. Therefore, when we define the section for the letter A, we can read the `books` property and display all the books which titles begin with that letter. This means that every time we create a new book, we must create a new `SortLetters` object with its initial or add it to the `SortLetters` object with that letter that already exists in the persistent store. The following are the modifications we must introduce to our `InsertBookView` view for this purpose.

```
.navigationBarItems(trailing: Button("Save") {
    let newTitle = self.inputTitle.trimmingCharacters(in: .whitespaces)
    let newYear = Int32(self.inputYear)
    if !newTitle.isEmpty && newYear != nil {
        let newBook = Books(context: self.dbContext)
        newBook.title = newTitle
        newBook.year = newYear!
        newBook.author = self.selectedAuthor
        newBook.cover = UIImage(named: "bookcover")?.pngData()
        newBook.thumbnail = UIImage(named: "bookthumbnail")?.pngData()

        let firstLetter =
String(newTitle[newTitle.startIndex]).uppercased()
        let request: NSFetchRequest<SortLetters> =
SortLetters.fetchRequest()
        request.predicate = NSPredicate(format: "letter = %@", firstLetter)
        if let list = try? self.dbContext.fetch(request), list.count > 0 {
            let oldLetter = list[0]
            newBook.sortletter = oldLetter
        } else {
            let newLetter = SortLetters(context: self.dbContext)
            newLetter.letter = firstLetter
            newBook.sortletter = newLetter
        }
        do {
            try self.dbContext.save()
            self.presentation.wrappedValue.dismiss()
        } catch {
            print("Error saving record")
        }
    }
})
```

Listing 14-65: Assigning the new book to a letter

The code in Listing 14-65 replaces the Save button in the navigation bar of the interface created by the `InsertBookView` view. This is the button that creates and stores a new `Books` object defined with the values inserted by the user. After this object is created, we get the first letter of the book's title and define a request with a predicate to search for a `SortLetters` object with that letter. If the object exists (the value returned by `count` is greater than 0), we assign the `SortLetters` object to the `sortletter` property of the new `Books` structure. This creates the connection from the book to the letter and vice versa, adding the book to the list of books the letter is associated with. But if a `SortLetters` object with that letter doesn't exist, we create one and then assign it to the book. Notice that this time we don't use the `count()` method from the context to count the number of `SortLetters` objects in the persistent store, we get the object if it exists because we need it to be able to add the book to it.

Now, every new book inserted by the user is associated with a letter, and every `SortLetters` object knows which books begin with its letter, so we can organize the books alphabetically in sections. But before doing this, there is one issue we must solved. Relationships return a collection of type `NSSet`. This is an old Objective-C type that we must cast to an array to be able to use it in SwiftUI. The solution is to extend the `SortLetters` class created by the system with a computed property that generates an array from this `NSSet` value and returns it. The following extension should be added to the Extensions.swift file created in Listing 14-44.

```
extension SortLetters {
    var listBooks: [Books] {
        if let list = books as? Set<Books> {
            return list.sorted(by: { $0.showTitle < $1.showTitle })
        } else {
            return []
        }
    }
}
```

Listing 14-66: Extending the SortLetters *class*

The computed property in the extension casts the `NSSet` value into a Swift set (`Set<Books>`) and then executes the `sorted()` method on it to sort the `Books` objects by their title in ascending order. This method returns an array of `Books` objects, which is what we need to create the `ForEach` loop for each section.

It is time to show the books in the `ContentView` view. The main difference in the view's code is that instead of fetching `Books` objects, we must create a fetch request to get the `SortLetters` objects in alphabetical order, and then include two nested `ForEach` views, one to list the `SortLetters` objects and create the sections, and another inside the sections to list the books that belong to it.

```
import SwiftUI
import CoreData

struct ContentView: View {
    @Environment(\.managedObjectContext) var dbContext
    @FetchRequest(entity: SortLetters.entity(), sortDescriptors:
[NSSortDescriptor(key: "letter", ascending: true)]) var listOfLetters:
FetchedResults<SortLetters>

    var body: some View {
        NavigationView {
            List {
                ForEach(listOfLetters, id: \.self) { sort in
                    Section(header: Text(sort.letter ?? "")) {
                        ForEach(sort.listBooks, id: \.self) { book in
                            RowBook(book: book)
                        }
                        .onDelete(perform: { indexes in
                            self.deleteBook(indexes: indexes, letter: sort)
                        })
                    }
                }
            }
            .navigationBarTitle("Books")
            .navigationBarItems(trailing: NavigationLink(destination:
InsertBookView(), label: {
```

```
                Text("Add Book")
            }))
        }
    }
    func deleteBook(indexes: IndexSet, letter: SortLetters) {
        let listBooks = letter.listBooks
        for index in indexes {
            let book = listBooks[index]
            self.dbContext.delete(book)
        }
        do {
            try self.dbContext.save()
            if letter.listBooks.count <= 0 {
                self.dbContext.delete(letter)
                try self.dbContext.save()
            }
        } catch {
            print("Error deleting objects")
        }
    }
}
struct RowBook: View {
    let book: Books

    var body: some View {
        HStack(alignment: .top) {
            Image(uiImage: book.showThumbnail)
                .resizable()
                .scaledToFit()
                .frame(width: 80, height: 100)
                .cornerRadius(10)
            VStack(alignment: .leading, spacing: 2) {
                Text(book.showTitle).bold()
                Text(book.showAuthor)
                Text(book.showYear).font(.caption)
                Spacer()
            }.padding(.top, 5)
            Spacer()
        }
    }
}
```

Listing 14-67: Organizing the Books *objects in sections*

The sections are created from the listOfLetters property, which contains all the SortLetters objects available in the persistent store. For each object, we create a Section view with a header that shows the section's letter. Within each Section view, we create another ForEach loop from the values of the listBooks property of the SortLetters object. In consequence, we get a list of sections with all the letters available at the moment, and in each section a list of books which titles begin with the section's letter.

The process to delete a book is also different. Because they are presented with two nested ForEach loops, the indexes associated to the books start from 0 in each section. This means that a book in the section for the letter A may have the same index than a book in the section for the letter B. Therefore, we need to know what section the book belongs to before being able to erase it. That is why we apply the onDelete() modifier to the ForEach view that lists the books instead of the one that lists the sections. When the user slides a row and presses the Delete button, we execute a method called deleteBook() that receives the indexes of the books to delete and a reference to the SortLetters object corresponding to the section of the book. From this reference, we get the list of books in that section and then remove them with the

Chapter 14 - Storage

`delete()` method as we did before. At the end, we save the context and then check if there are more books associated to that letter. If not, we also delete the `SortLetters` object, which removes the empty section from the screen. Notice that if we delete this object, the context has to be saved again. The result is shown in Figure 14-36.

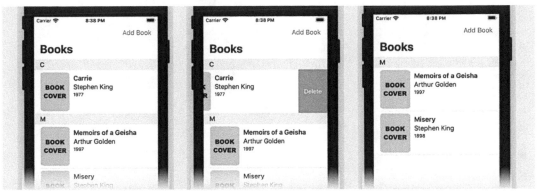

Figure 14-36: Books in sections

 Do It Yourself: Open the Core Data model and create a new entity called SortLetters with an attribute of type String called letter (Figure 14-34). Add a relationship to the SortLetters entity called books with the Books entity as the destination (Figure 14-35). Select this relationship and open the Data Model Inspector in the Attribute Inspector panel. Set the Type of relationship as To-Many (to many books) and the Delete Rule as Cascade. This is to make sure that when a `SortLetters` object is deleted, there are no books left associated with it. Click on the Books entity and add a relationship of type String to it called sortletter. Set the SortLetters entity as the destination and the Inverse relationship as books (Figure 14-35). Replace the `navigationBarItems()` modifier in the `InsertBookView` view with the code in Listing 14-65. Add the extension in Listing 14-66 to the rest of the extensions in the Extensions.swift file. Update the ContentView.swift file with the code in Listing 14-67. Uninstall the application from your device to remove previous books and authors (books inserted before won't be associated to any letter). Insert books with titles that start with a different letter. You should see the interface in Figure 14-36.

(Basic) 15.1 Data in the Cloud

These days, users own more than one device. If we create an application that works on multiple devices, we must provide a way for the users to share their data, otherwise they will have to insert the same information on every device they own. But the only way to do it effectively is through a server. The data from one device has to be stored in a server and then retrieved from other devices. Setting up a server to run this kind of system is complicated and costly. To provide a standard solution that every developer can easily implement without any prior investment, Apple created a system called *iCloud*. iCloud allows applications to synchronize data across devices using Apple servers. It provides three basic services: Key-Value Storage, to store single values, Document Storage, to store files, and CloudKit Storage, to store structured data in public and private databases.

(Basic) Enabling iCloud

iCloud must be enabled for each application we create. The system requires entitlements to authorize our app to use the service and a container where our app's data will be stored. Fortunately, Xcode can set up everything for us by just selecting an option. The option is available in the Signing & Capabilities panel inside the app's settings window (Figure 5-14). The panel includes a + button at the top-left corner to add a new capability to the application. The button opens a view with all the capabilities available, as shown in Figure 15-1, below. The capability is added by clicking on it and pressing Return.

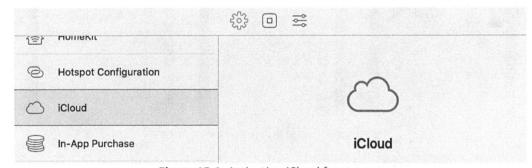

Figure 15-1: Activating iCloud for our app

 IMPORTANT: iCloud services are only available for developers that are members of the Apple Developer Program. At the time of this writing, the membership costs $99 US Dollars per year. You also must register your account with Xcode, as explained in Chapter 5 (see Figure 5-3).

After iCloud is added to the app, it is shown on the panel, below the signing section. From here, we can select the services we want to activate for our app and Xcode takes care of creating the entitlements and the container if necessary. Figure 15-2 shows the panel with the Key-Value storage service activated.

▼ ☁ **iCloud**

Services ☑ Key-value storage
⬜ iCloud Documents
⬜ CloudKit

Figure 15-2: Activating iCloud services

 Do It Yourself: Create a SwiftUI project. Click on the app's settings option at the top of the Navigator Area (Figure 5-4, number 10) and open the Signing & Capabilities panel (Figures 5-11 and 5-14). Click on the + button at the top-left corner of the panel to add a capability. Select the iCloud option, press return, and check the option Key-value storage. This iCloud service is now available in your application.

(Basic) ## Testing Devices

The best way to test an iCloud application is running the app in two different devices, but Apple has made iCloud services available in the simulator as well. Thanks to this feature, we can synchronize data between a device and the simulator to test our app.

For the devices and the simulators to be able to access iCloud services, we must register our iCloud account in the Settings app. We have to go to the Home screen, access the Settings app, tap on the option Sign in to your iPhone/iPad (Figure 15-3, center), and sign in to Apple's services with our Apple ID (Figure 15-3, right). The process must be repeated for every device or simulator we want to use.

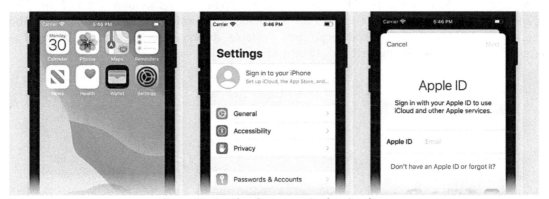

Figure 15-3: iCloud account in the simulator

(Basic) ## 15.2 Key-Value Storage

The Key-Value storage system is the `UserDefaults` system for iCloud. It works exactly like the User Defaults system studied in Chapter 14, and even has similar methods to assign and retrieve values, but all the data is stored in iCloud servers instead of the device. We can use it to store the app's preferences, the current state, or any other value that we need to be set automatically in every device.

Foundation defines the `NSUbiquitousKeyValueStore` class to provide access to this system. The class includes the following methods to store and retrieve values.

set(Value, **forKey:** String**)**—This method stores the value specified by the first attribute with the key specified by the **forKey** attribute. The class provides versions of this method for every data type we are allowed to store in the system, such as `String`, `Bool`, `Data`, `Double`, `Int64`, dictionaries, arrays, and also Property List values (`NSNumber`, `NSString`, `NSDate`, `NSArray`, `NSDictionary`, `NSData`, and their equivalents in Swift).

bool(forKey: String**)**—This method retrieves a value of type `Bool`.

double(forKey: String**)**—This method retrieves a value of type `Double`.

longLong(forKey: String**)**—This method retrieves a value of type `Int64`.

string(forKey: String**)**—This method retrieves a value of type `String`.

array(forKey: String**)**—This method retrieves an array.

dictionary(forKey: String**)**—This method retrieves a dictionary.

data(forKey: String**)**—This method retrieves a value of type `Data`.

object(forKey: String**)**—This method retrieves an object.

To store or access a value, we must initialize an `NSUbiquitousKeyValueStore` object and then call its methods. The object takes care of establishing the connection with iCloud and downloading or uploading the values, but it can't keep the values up to date. If a value is modified in one device, the change must be reflected on the others in real time. For this purpose, the `NSUbiquitousKeyValueStore` class defines the following notification.

didChangeExternallyNotification—This notification is posted by the system when a change in the values on the Key-Value storage is detected.

As we already mentioned, the system is used to storing discrete values that represent the user's preferences or the app's status. For example, we may have a stepper that lets the user set a limit to the number of items the application can manage.

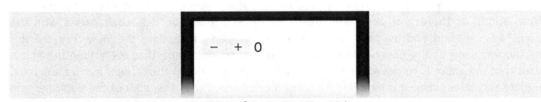

Figure 15-4: Interface to test Key-Value storage

The application must be initialized with the current value stored in iCloud, but it also has to send it back when the user sets a new one and update it when it is changed from another device. The best way to manage this information is from an observable object. In the following example, we are going to implement our familiar `AppData` model to manage this information.

```
import SwiftUI
import Combine

class AppData: ObservableObject {
    @Published var control: Double = 0 {
        didSet {
            let kvStorage = NSUbiquitousKeyValueStore()
            kvStorage.set(control, forKey: "control")
            kvStorage.synchronize()
        }
    }
    init() {
        self.readControl()
```

```
        let publisher = NotificationCenter.Publisher(center: .default,
name: NSUbiquitousKeyValueStore.didChangeExternallyNotification)
            .receive(on: RunLoop.main)
        let subscriber = Subscribers.Sink<Notification,
Never>(receiveCompletion: {_ in }, receiveValue: {_ in
            self.readControl()
        })
        publisher.subscribe(subscriber)
    }
    func readControl() {
        let kvStorage = NSUbiquitousKeyValueStore()
        let sharedControl = kvStorage.double(forKey: "control")
        control = sharedControl
    }
}
```

Listing 15-1: Storing a value in iCloud

The observable object in Listing 15-1 contains a `@Published` property called `control` with a `didSet()` method. This is the property we are going to use to keep track of the value set by the stepper. When the value of the property is updated (the user presses a button on the stepper), a new `NSUbiquitousKeyValueStore` object is created, and the `set()` method is called on it to save the value of the property in the Key/Value storage with the "control" key. After this, the code executes the `synchronize()` method. This is a method provided by the `NSUbiquitousKeyValueStore` class to force the system to send the new value to iCloud right away. It is not always necessary, only when we want to make sure that the value is there as soon as possible.

The observable object must read the value stored in the Key/Value storage twice. Once when the object is initialized and another when the `didChangeExternallyNotification` notification is received. For this purpose, we define a method called `readControl()`. The method creates an `NSUbiquitousKeyValueStore` object again, but this time to read the value from iCloud. If there is a value with the "control" key available, it is downloaded with the `double()` method and assigned to the `control` property to update the view. We call this method as soon as the observable object is initialized to make sure that every time the app is executed the value is retrieved from iCloud servers and shown on the screen, but we still must update the value when it is modified from another device. This is the work of the publisher and subscriber defined next. The publisher is associated to the Notification Center, so every time a `didChangeExternallyNotification` notification is posted, the subscriber is notified, and the `readControl()` method is called again to read the current value and update the view.

Once more, all the job is done by the model, so all we have to do in the view is to show the value and let the user select a new one.

```
import SwiftUI

struct ContentView: View {
    @EnvironmentObject var appData: AppData

    var body: some View {
        VStack {
            HStack {
                Stepper("", value: $appData.control)
                    .labelsHidden()
                Text("\(appData.control, specifier: "%.f")")
                    .font(.title)
                Spacer()
            }
            Spacer()
```

Chapter 15 - iCloud

```
        }.padding()
    }
}
struct ContentView_Previews: PreviewProvider {
    static var previews: some View {
        ContentView().environmentObject(AppData())
    }
}
```

Listing 15-2: Defining the interface to change values in iCloud

 Do It Yourself: Update the AppDelegate.swift file with the code of Listing 7-14 and the SceneDelegate.swift file with the code of Listing 7-20 to instantiate the model and insert it in the environment. Create a Swift file called AppData.swift for the model in Listing 15-1. Update the ContentView.swift file with the code in Listing 15-2. Remember to enable the Key/Value storage service for the app. Run the application on a simulator or a device. Press the stepper's buttons to change the value to 5. Stop the application from Xcode and run it again. You should see the value 5 on the screen. If you run the app on a device or a different simulator, you should see the value 5 again (remember to activate the same iCloud account in any of the simulators or devices you try).

 IMPORTANT: The simulator does not update the information automatically. Most of the time, you must force the update. If you modify the value on your device and do not see it changing on the simulator, open the Debug menu at the top of the screen and select the option Trigger iCloud Sync. This will synchronize the application with iCloud and update the values right away.

The same way we can store one value we can store several. The Key/Value storage service can manage multiple values using different keys, but if we want to simplify our work, we can use a structure to store all the values, encode that structure into data with JSON, and then store only one value in iCloud with that data. The following example follows this approach. We define a structure to store the user's name, address and city, and then encode and decode an instance of that structure to store the values in iCloud.

```
import SwiftUI
import Combine

struct PersonalInfo: Codable {
    var name: String
    var address: String
    var city: String
}
class AppData: ObservableObject {
    @Published var userInfo: PersonalInfo

    init() {
        self.userInfo = PersonalInfo(name: "", address: "", city: "")
        self.readInfo()

        let publisher = NotificationCenter.Publisher(center: .default,
name: NSUbiquitousKeyValueStore.didChangeExternallyNotification)
            .receive(on: RunLoop.main)
        let subscriber = Subscribers.Sink<Notification,
Never>(receiveCompletion: {_ in }, receiveValue: {_ in
            self.readInfo()
        })
```

```
        publisher.subscribe(subscriber)
    }
    func readInfo() {
        let kvStorage = NSUbiquitousKeyValueStore()
        if let dataInfo = kvStorage.data(forKey: "info") {
            let decoder = JSONDecoder()
            if let info = try? decoder.decode(PersonalInfo.self, from:
dataInfo) {
                userInfo = info
            }
        }
    }
    func setInfo() {
        let kvStorage = NSUbiquitousKeyValueStore()
        let encoder = JSONEncoder()
        if let data = try? encoder.encode(userInfo) {
            kvStorage.set(data, forKey: "info")
        }
    }
}
```

Listing 15-3: Storing multiple values in iCloud

This time, we define two methods to interact with iCloud, one to read the values, called **readInfo()**, and another to set the values, called **setInfo()**. The **readInfo()** method reads the value in iCloud with the "info" key and then decodes the data with a **JSONDecoder** object. If the operation is successful, the decoded **PersonalInfo** structure is assigned to the **@Published** property to update the values in the view. On the other hand, the **setInfo()** method encodes the value in the **@Published** property with a **JSONEncoder** object and sends the data to iCloud. The **readInfo()** method is called when the observable object is initialized to get the current value from iCloud and also when a notification is received to update the view with the value inserted in another device, but the **setInfo()** method is only called when the user presses a button in the view to store new values, as we will see next. Notice that we didn't use the **synchronize()** method this time. The values are not generated dynamically, only when the user decides to do it, so we can wait for the system to synchronize itself.

We need two views for this example, one to show the current values and another to let the user insert new ones. The initial view is simple, we just have to read the **@Published** property and display its values on the screen.

```
import SwiftUI

struct ContentView: View {
    @EnvironmentObject var appData: AppData
    @State private var openSheet: Bool = false

    var body: some View {
        NavigationView {
            VStack {
                HStack {
                    Text("Name:")
                    Text(appData.userInfo.name)
                    Spacer()
                }
                HStack {
                    Text("Address:")
                    Text(appData.userInfo.address)
                    Spacer()
                }
```

Chapter 15 - iCloud

```
                HStack {
                    Text("City:")
                    Text(appData.userInfo.city)
                    Spacer()
                }
                Spacer()
            }.padding()
            .navigationBarTitle("Personal Info")
            .navigationBarItems(trailing: Button("Change") {
                self.openSheet = true
            })
            .sheet(isPresented: $openSheet) {
                InsertInfoView(openSheet: self.$openSheet)
                    .environmentObject(self.appData)
            }
        }
    }
}
struct ContentView_Previews: PreviewProvider {
    static var previews: some View {
        ContentView().environmentObject(AppData())
    }
}
```

Listing 15-4: Reading multiple values from iCloud

This view includes a button in the navigation bar to open a view called `InsertInfoView` in a sheet. The following is our implementation of this view.

```
import SwiftUI

struct InsertInfoView: View {
    @EnvironmentObject var appData: AppData
    @Binding var openSheet: Bool

    @State private var inputName: String = ""
    @State private var inputAddress: String = ""
    @State private var inputCity: String = ""

    var body: some View {
        VStack(spacing: 10) {
            TextField("Insert Name", text: $inputName)
                .textFieldStyle(RoundedBorderTextFieldStyle())
            TextField("Insert Address", text: $inputAddress)
                .textFieldStyle(RoundedBorderTextFieldStyle())
            TextField("Insert City", text: $inputCity)
                .textFieldStyle(RoundedBorderTextFieldStyle())
            HStack {
                Spacer()
                Button("Save") {
                    self.appData.userInfo = PersonalInfo(name: self.inputName,
address: self.inputAddress, city: self.inputCity)
                    self.appData.setInfo()
                    self.openSheet = false
                }
            }
            Spacer()
        }.padding()
```

```
        .onAppear(perform: {
            self.inputName = self.appData.userInfo.name
            self.inputAddress = self.appData.userInfo.address
            self.inputCity = self.appData.userInfo.city
        })
    }
}
struct InsertInfoView_Previews: PreviewProvider {
    static var previews: some View {
        InsertInfoView(openSheet: .constant(false))
            .environmentObject(AppData())
    }
}
```

Listing 15-5: Saving multiple values in iCloud

This is a normal view with three `TextField` views to let the user insert and modify the values. Because there might be values already stored in iCloud, we assign the values in the `userInfo` property to the `@State` properties to show them to the user when the view appears. If the user presses the button to save the values, we create a new `PersonalInfo` structure and call the `setInfo()` method in the model to encode it and send it to iCloud.

The application is ready. When the user inserts new values, they are sent to iCloud, and when the app is launched or a notification is received, the values in iCloud are downloaded and shown on the screen.

Figure 15-5: Interface to store multiple values in Key/Value storage

 Do It Yourself: Update the AppData.swift file with the code in Listing 15-3. Update the ContentView.swift file with the code in Listing 15-4. Create a SwiftUI file called InsertInfoView.swift for the code in Listing 15-5. Run the application on a simulator or a device. Press the Change button. Insert new values and press Save. Wait a few seconds (the system can take up to 15 seconds to send the values to iCloud). Stop the application from Xcode and run it again. The values inserted in the input fields should appear on the screen.

(Basic) **15.3 iCloud Documents**

The Key-Value storage system was developed to store small values. The purpose is to allow users to set preferences or configuration parameters across devices. Although very useful, it presents some limitations, especially on the amount of data we can store (currently no more than 1 megabyte). If what we need is to store large amounts of data, we can activate the iCloud Documents option in the Capabilities panel and upload files instead.

Chapter 15 - iCloud

Figure 15-6: iCloud Documents service

The operative system uses a container to store iCloud files. This container is a folder in the app's storage space where iCloud files are created. Once a file is added, modified or removed from this container, the system automatically reports the changes to iCloud, so the copies of the app running in other devices can modify their own container to stay synchronized. If the container is not created by Xcode, we have to do it ourselves by pressing the + button (Figure 15-6, number 1). This opens a window to insert the container's name.

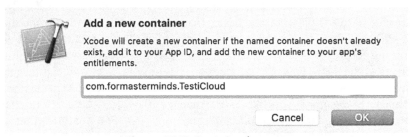

Add a new container

Xcode will create a new container if the named container doesn't already exist, add it to your App ID, and add the new container to your app's entitlements.

com.formasterminds.TestiCloud

Cancel   OK

Figure 15-7: Container's name

The name must be unique, and the best way to guaranty it is to use the app's bundle identifier. In our example, we use the bundle identifier to create the container for an app called TestiCloud. Once the container is created, we should press the Refresh button to make sure the information is uploaded to Apple servers right away (Figure 15-6, number 2). After this, the container is added and selected as the active container for the application.

Services ☐ Key-value storage
☑ iCloud Documents
☐ CloudKit

Containers ☑ iCloud.com.formasterminds.TestiCloud
☐ 48S7G5U7J3.ca.invid.MicroTasks
☐ iCloud.ca.invid.AnotherTest

+ ↺

Figure 15-8: Selected container

 Do It Yourself: Create a SwiftUI project. Click on the app's settings option at the top of the Navigator Area (Figure 5-4, number 10) and open the Signing & Capabilities panel (Figures 5-11 and 5-14). Click on the + button at the top-left corner of the panel to add a capability. Select the iCloud option, press return, and check the option iCloud Documents. Press the + button to add a container

(Figure 15-6, number 1). Insert the app's bundle identifier for the container's name and press the OK button (you can find the bundle identifier on top of the iCloud section). If the name of the container appears in red, press the Refresh button to upload the information to Apple servers (Figure 15-6, number 2).

An iCloud container is called *ubiquitous container* because its content is shared with other devices and therefore available everywhere. The `FileManager` class includes properties and methods to work with a ubiquitous container. The following are the most frequently used.

url(forUbiquityContainerIdentifier: String?)—This method returns the URL of the app's iCloud container. The **forUbiquityContainerIdentifier** attribute is the name of the container we want to access. The value `nil` returns the container assigned by default.

evictUbiquitousItem(at: URL)—This method removes the local copy of the document at the URL specified by the **at** attribute.

Although the files are stored in a container in the device and synchronized by the system automatically, working with iCloud introduces some challenges that the `FileManager` class cannot overcome. The most important is coordination. Because of the unreliability of network connections, at any moment iCloud may find different versions of the same file. Modifications that were introduced to the file from one device may not have reached iCloud and therefore may later conflict with updates introduced from another device. The application must decide which version of the file to preserve or what data is more valuable when the file is edited from two different devices at the same time. These issues are not easy to solve and can turn development into a nightmare. Considering all the problems a developer has to face, Apple introduced a class called `UIDocument` designed specifically to manage files for iCloud. The class includes capabilities to coordinate and synchronize files of any size and features that simplify the manipulation of documents in mobile devices, like progression reports, automatic thumbnail generation, undo manager, and others.

The `UIDocument` class was not designed to be implemented directly in our code; it is like an interface between the app's data and the files we use to store it. To take advantage of this class, we must create a subclass and overwrite some of its methods. Once we define the subclass, we can create the object with the following initializer.

init(fileURL: URL)—This initializer creates a new `UIDocument` object. The **fileURL** attribute is a `URL` structure with the location of the file in iCloud's container.

The following are the methods we need to overwrite in the subclass of `UIDocument` to provide the data for the file and to retrieve it later.

contents(forType: String)—This method is called when the `UIDocument` object needs to store the content of the document on file. The method must return an object with the document's data (usually a `Data` structure). The **forType** attribute identifies the type of the file (by default, it is determined from the file's extension).

load(fromContents: Any, **ofType:** String?)—This method is called when the `UIDocument` object loads the content of the document from the file. The **fromContents** attribute is an object with the content of the file (usually a `Data` structure), and the **ofType** attribute is a string that identifies the file's type (by default, it is determined from the file's extension).

The `UIDocument` class also offers methods to manage the file, including the following.

open(completionHandler: Block)—This method asks the `UIDocument` object to open the file and load its content. The **completionHandler** attribute is a closure with the statements to execute after the process is over.

save(to: URL, **for:** SaveOperation, **completionHandler:** Block)—This method asks the `UIDocument` object to save the content of the document on file. The **for** attribute is an enumeration called `SaveOperation` included in the `UIDocument` class that indicates the type of operation to perform. The values available are `forCreating` (to save the file for the first time) and `forOverwriting` (to overwrite the file). The **completionHandler** attribute is a closure with the statements to execute after the process is over.

close(completionHandler: Closure?)—This method saves any pending changes and closes the document.

The first thing we have to do to work with documents in iCloud is to define a subclass of `UIDocument`. The following is the one we are going to use for the examples in this chapter.

```swift
import SwiftUI

class MyDocument: UIDocument {
    var fileContent: Data?

    override func contents(forType typeName: String) throws -> Any {
        return fileContent ?? Data()
    }
    override func load(fromContents contents: Any, ofType typeName:
String?) throws {
        if let data = contents as? Data, !data.isEmpty {
            fileContent = data
        }
    }
}
```

Listing 15-6: Creating the document

The subclass needs at least three elements. A property to store the file's content, the `contents()` method to provide the data to store on file, and the `load()` method to get the data from the file. When the `UIDocument` object is asked to store or load the data in file, it calls these methods and use the property as a proxy to move the data around. Therefore, every time we want to access the file's content, we must open the document and read this property. In our example, we called it `fileContent`.

(Basic) **Metadata Query**

Accessing the files is also complicated in iCloud. We cannot just get a list of files with methods like `contentsOfDirectory()` from the `FileManager` class because there could be some files that have not been downloaded yet to the device. What we can do instead is to get the information pertaining to the files. This information is called *metadata*, and involves the file's attributes, such as its name, the date it was created, etc. To get the metadata, Foundation defines the `NSMetadataQuery` class. This class provides the properties and methods necessary to retrieve the information and keep watching for updates.

predicate—This property sets or returns the predicate for the query. It is an optional of type `NSPredicate`.

sortDescriptors—This property sets or returns the sort descriptors for the query. It is an array of `NSSortDescriptor` objects.

searchScopes—This property sets or returns a value that indicates the scope of the query. It is an array with constants that represent a predefined scope. The constants available for mobile devices are `NSMetadataQueryUbiquitousDocumentsScope` (searches for all files in the Documents directory of the iCloud's container) and `NSMetadataQuery-UbiquitousDataScope` (searches for all the files that are not in the Documents directory of the iCloud's container).

results—This property returns an array with the query's results. By default, the array contains `NSMetadataItem` objects with the metadata of every file found.

resultCount—This property returns an `Int` with the number of results produced by the query.

result(at: Int)—This method returns the `NSMetadataItem` object from the query's results array at the index specified by the **at** attribute.

start()—This method initiates the query.

stop()—This method stops the query.

enableUpdates()—This method enables query updates.

disableUpdates()—This method disables query updates.

The `NSMetadataQuery` class also includes some notifications to report when new data is available. The following are the most frequently used.

NSMetadataQueryDidUpdate—This notification is posted when the results of the query change.

NSMetadataQueryDidFinishGathering—This notification is posted when the query finishes getting all the information.

The results of a query are communicated through the `results` property in the form of an array of `NSMetadataItem` objects. This is a simple class created to contain the attributes of a file. The class provides the following method to retrieve the values.

value(forAttribute: String)—This method returns the value of the file's attribute determined by the **forAtttribute** attribute. The `NSMetadataItem` class defines a list of constants to represent the attributes. The constants available are `NSMetadataItemFSNameKey` (file's name), `NSMetadataItemDisplayNameKey` (document's name), `NSMetadataItemURLKey` (file's URL), `NSMetadataItemPathKey` (file's path), `NSMetadataItemFSSizeKey` (file's size), `NSMetadataItemFSCreationDateKey` (date of creation), and `NSMetadataItemFSContentChangeDateKey` (date the file was last modified).

(Basic)   **Single Document**

iCloud Documents is a service designed to manage multiple documents, but we can also work with one document at a time. No matter the number of documents the user is allowed to create, the process is always the same; we must check the files available, get the one we are interested in, and create the `MyDocument` object to represent it. To learn how to work with this service, we are going to develop the same application used before to work with the Key/Value storage service, but this time we are going to store the data in a document called myfile.dat.

Figure 15-9: *Interface to read and save a document*

The following is the model required for this example. It includes the `PersonalInfo` structure we need to store the values inserted by the user and an observable object to process the values and provide them to the views.

```
import SwiftUI
import Combine

struct PersonalInfo: Codable {
    var name: String
    var address: String
    var city: String
}
class AppData: ObservableObject {
    @Published var userInfo: PersonalInfo

    var document: MyDocument!
    var metaData: NSMetadataQuery!

    init() {
        self.userInfo = PersonalInfo(name: "", address: "", city: "")

        let publisherFinish = NotificationCenter.Publisher(center:
.default, name: NSNotification.Name.NSMetadataQueryDidFinishGathering)
            .receive(on: RunLoop.main)
        let subscriberFinish = Subscribers.Sink<Notification,
Never>(receiveCompletion: { _ in }, receiveValue: { _ in
            self.createFile()
        })
        publisherFinish.subscribe(subscriberFinish)

        let publisherUpdate = NotificationCenter.Publisher(center:
.default, name: NSNotification.Name.NSMetadataQueryDidUpdate)
            .receive(on: RunLoop.main)
        let subscriberUpdate = Subscribers.Sink<Notification,
Never>(receiveCompletion: { _ in }, receiveValue: { _ in
            self.updateFile()
        })
        publisherUpdate.subscribe(subscriberUpdate)

        self.getMetadata()
    }
}
```

Listing 15-7: *Initializing the model required to store a document in iCloud*

The observable object in Listing 15-7 defines a `@Published` property called `userInfo` to store an instance of the `PersonalInfo` structure. Because of the logic of our application, we also need a property to store the reference to the `MyDocument` object we are going to use to access the file and a property to reference the `NSMetadataQuery` object that we will use to search for the files available in the ubiquitous container. In this example, we call these properties `document` and `metaData`.

The results of the query produced by the **NSMetadataQuery** object is reported through notifications. Because these notifications can be posted right after the process begins, we must define the publishers and subscribers before initializing the query. In this example, we listen to two notifications. The **NSMetadataQueryDidFinishGathering** notification is posted after the query gets the list of files available in the container, and the **NSMetadataQueryDidUpdate** notification is posted every time the container is updated (files are added, removed, or modified).

After the publishers and subscribers are ready, we must configure the **NSMetadataQuery** object and start the query. For this purpose, the initializer calls the **getMetadata()** method.

```
func getMetadata() {
    self.metaData = NSMetadataQuery()
    self.metaData.predicate = NSPredicate(format: "%K == %@",
NSMetadataItemFSNameKey, "myfile.dat")
    self.metaData.searchScopes = [NSMetadataQueryUbiquitousDocumentsScope]
    self.metaData.start()
}
```

Listing 15-8: Configuring the query

The method of Listing 15-8 initializes the **NSMetadataQuery** object, configures the query to search for documents inside the iCloud's container (**NSMetadataQueryUbiquitous-DocumentsScope**), and starts the process with the **start()** method. Because in this example we are working with only one document, we make sure that the query returns the right file with a predicate. The format of the predicate for a query requires comparing the value of a file's attribute with the string we are looking for. The attribute is represented by the constants defined in the **NSMetadataItem** class. In this case, we use the **NSMetadataItemFSNameKey** constant to filter the files by name (Notice that the value of the constant has to be introduced to the string with the **%K** placeholder).

The query gets the document if available, and then posts a **NSMetadataQuery-DidFinishGathering** notification. Here is when we can get the list of documents in the container and process them or show them to the user. In our example, this work is done in the **createFile()** method.

```
func createFile() {
    if self.metaData.resultCount > 0 {
        let file = metaData.result(at: 0) as! NSMetadataItem
        let fileURL = file.value(forAttribute: NSMetadataItemURLKey) as! URL
        self.document = MyDocument(fileURL: fileURL)
        self.document.open(completionHandler: { (success) in
            if success {
                let decoder = JSONDecoder()
                if let data = self.document.fileContent {
                    if let info = try? decoder.decode(PersonalInfo.self, from:
data) {
                        self.userInfo = info
                    }
                }
            }
            self.document.close(completionHandler: nil)
        })
    } else {
        let manager = FileManager.default
        if let fileURL = manager.url(forUbiquityContainerIdentifier: nil) {
            let iCloudURL =
fileURL.appendingPathComponent("Documents/myfile.dat")
```

```
            let encoder = JSONEncoder()
            if let data = try? encoder.encode(self.userInfo) {
                document = MyDocument(fileURL: iCloudURL)
                document.fileContent = data
                if manager.fileExists(atPath: iCloudURL.path) {
                    document.save(to: iCloudURL, for: .forOverwriting,
completionHandler: nil)
                } else {
                    document.save(to: iCloudURL, for: .forCreating,
completionHandler: nil)
                }
                document.close(completionHandler: nil)
            }
        }
    }
}
```

Listing 15-9: Processing query results

Because in this application we are only working with one document, the `createFile()` method has to perform two tasks. If a document is found, we must open it and get its content to show it to the user, but if there is no document available yet, we must create one. To know if the query has found a document, we check the value of the `resultCount` property of the `NSMetadataQuery` object. This property returns the number of documents (files) available. If the number is greater than 0, we get the metadata of the first document on the list with the `result(at:)` method, get its URL with the `value(forAttribute:)` method, and create a `MyDocument` instance with it. The `MyDocument` object allows us to access and modify the document's content, so next, we open the document with the `open()` method, decode the data in the object's `fileContent` property, and assign the value to the `userInfo` property in the observable object to update the views.

On the other hand, if no document was created yet, the `createFile()` method has to generate the URL and create a new one. To build our document's URL, we get the URL of the app's iCloud container with the `url(forUbiquityContainerIdentifier:)` method provided by the `FileManager` object. The URL returned by this method is the container's root directory, to which we must append the Documents directory and the document's name (Documents/myfile.dat). With the URL ready, we create a `MyDocument` object and call its `save()` method. If a document in the URL already exists, we call this method with the `forOverwriting` attribute to modify it, otherwise, we call it with the `forCreating` attribute to create a new document. Internally, the `MyDocument` instance calls its `contents()` method to get the content and creates the file inside the container.

The `createFile()` method responds to the `NSMetadataQueryDidFinishGathering` notification, posted when the query gets the list of documents and returns it. To report for updates, the `NSMetadataQuery` object posts the `NSMetadataQueryDidUpdate` notification. The following is the method we need to respond to this notification.

```
func updateFile() {
    if self.metaData.resultCount > 0 {
        document.open(completionHandler: { (success) in
            if success {
                let decoder = JSONDecoder()
                if let data = self.document.fileContent {
                    if let info = try? decoder.decode(PersonalInfo.self, from:
data) {
                        self.userInfo = info
                    }
                }
```

```
        }
    })
  }
}
```

Listing 15-10: Updating the document

The **updateFile()** method is executed every time the query finds an update (a file was added, removed, or modified). As we did before, we check the value of the **resultCount** property to make sure a document was changed, and then proceed to open the file, decode the value of the document's **fileContent** property, and assign the result to the **userInfo** property to show the new values to the user.

The **createFile()** method downloads or creates a new document if it doesn't exists, and the **updateFile()** method processes any changes introduced to the document. The last thing we have to do in our model is to provide a method to save the new values introduced by the user in the document. We call this method **saveFile()**.

```
func saveFile() {
    let manager = FileManager.default
    if let fileURL = manager.url(forUbiquityContainerIdentifier: nil) {
        let iCloudURL =
fileURL.appendingPathComponent("Documents/myfile.dat")

        let encoder = JSONEncoder()
        if let data = try? encoder.encode(self.userInfo) {
            document.fileContent = data
            document.save(to: iCloudURL, for: .forOverwriting,
completionHandler: nil)
            document.close(completionHandler: nil)
        }
    }
}
```

Listing 15-11: Saving changes in the document

The **saveFile()** method constructs the document's URL again, encodes the values currently stored in the **userInfo** property, and saves the data with the **save()** method.

With this last method, the model is ready. The next step is to provide the views. And as always, they are very simple. The initial view has to display the current values on the screen and provide a button for the user to open a sheet to modify them.

```
import SwiftUI

struct ContentView: View {
    @EnvironmentObject var appData: AppData
    @State private var openSheet: Bool = false

    var body: some View {
        NavigationView {
            VStack {
                HStack {
                    Text("Name:")
                    Text(appData.userInfo.name)
                    Spacer()
                }
                HStack {
                    Text("Address:")
                    Text(appData.userInfo.address)
```

Chapter 15 - iCloud

```
                Spacer()
            }
            HStack {
                Text("City:")
                Text(appData.userInfo.city)
                Spacer()
            }
            Spacer()
        }.padding()
        .navigationBarTitle("Personal Info")
        .navigationBarItems(trailing: Button("Change") {
            self.openSheet = true
        })
        .sheet(isPresented: $openSheet) {
            InsertInfoView(openSheet: self.$openSheet)
                .environmentObject(self.appData)
        }
    }
  }
 }
}
struct ContentView_Previews: PreviewProvider {
    static var previews: some View {
        ContentView().environmentObject(AppData())
    }
}
```

Listing 15-12: *Displaying the values stored in the document*

The view reads the values in the **PersonalInfo** structure stored in the model's **userInfo** property and shows them to the user. To let the user modify these values, the **sheet()** modifier opens a view called **InsertInfoView**.

```
import SwiftUI

struct InsertInfoView: View {
    @EnvironmentObject var appData: AppData
    @Binding var openSheet: Bool

    @State private var inputName: String = ""
    @State private var inputAddress: String = ""
    @State private var inputCity: String = ""

    var body: some View {
        VStack(spacing: 10) {
            TextField("Insert Name", text: $inputName)
                .textFieldStyle(RoundedBorderTextFieldStyle())
            TextField("Insert Address", text: $inputAddress)
                .textFieldStyle(RoundedBorderTextFieldStyle())
            TextField("Insert City", text: $inputCity)
                .textFieldStyle(RoundedBorderTextFieldStyle())
            HStack {
                Spacer()
                Button("Save") {
                    self.appData.userInfo = PersonalInfo(name: self.inputName,
address: self.inputAddress, city: self.inputCity)
                    self.appData.saveFile()
                    self.openSheet = false
                }
            }
            Spacer()
        }.padding()
```

```
        .onAppear(perform: {
            self.inputName = self.appData.userInfo.name
            self.inputAddress = self.appData.userInfo.address
            self.inputCity = self.appData.userInfo.city
        })
    }
}
struct InsertInfoView_Previews: PreviewProvider {
    static var previews: some View {
        InsertInfoView(openSheet: .constant(false))
            .environmentObject(AppData())
    }
}
```

Listing 15-13: Modifying the values in the document

This view includes three **TextField** views to insert the user's name, address and city, and a button to save the values. When the button is pressed, we instantiate a new **PersonalInfo** structure with the new values, assign it to the **userInfo** property, and finally call the **saveFile()** method to update the document.

 Do It Yourself: In the project initiated before to work with iCloud Documents, create a Swift file called MyDocument.swift for the **UIDocument** subclass defined in Listing 15-6. Create another Swift file called AppData.swift for the model in Listing 15-7. Add to the **AppData** class, the methods in Listings 15-8, 15-9, 15-10, and 15-11 (you can place them before or after the class' initializer). Update the AppDelegate.swift file with the code of Listing 7-14 and the SceneDelegate.swift file with the code of Listing 7-20 to instantiate the model and insert it in the environment. Update the ContentView.swift file with the code in Listing 15-12. Create a SwiftUI file called InsertInfoView.swift and update the code with the one in Listing 15-13. Run the application simultaneously in two devices (if you use the simulator, remember to register an iCloud account and to select the option Trigger iCloud Sync from the Debug menu when necessary to force the synchronization). Press the Change button on one device. Insert new values. After a few seconds, you should see the values appear on the screen of the second device (Notice that sometimes may take up to a minute for the other device to update).

(Basic) **Multiple Documents**

In the previous example, we have been working with only one document, but most applications allow users to create and manage all the documents they need. As we already mentioned, working with a single document or many presents the same requirements. We must define a query and listen to the notifications to update the data in our model and the interface. But this time we also need to include a structure to store information about each document in the container, so the views can show the list of documents available and the users can select the one they want to see. The following model includes a structure called **FileInfo** for this purpose.

```
import SwiftUI
import Combine

struct PersonalInfo: Codable {
    let name: String
    let address: String
    let city: String
}
```

```
struct FileInfo: Identifiable {
    let id: UUID = UUID()
    let name: String
    let document: MyDocument
}
class AppData: ObservableObject {
    @Published var listOfFiles: [FileInfo] = []
    var metaData: NSMetadataQuery!

    init() {
        let publisherFinish = NotificationCenter.Publisher(center:
.default, name: NSNotification.Name.NSMetadataQueryDidFinishGathering)
            .receive(on: RunLoop.main)
        let subscriberFinish = Subscribers.Sink<Notification,
Never>(receiveCompletion: {_ in }, receiveValue: { value in
            self.getFiles()
        })
        publisherFinish.subscribe(subscriberFinish)

        let publisherUpdate = NotificationCenter.Publisher(center:
.default, name: NSNotification.Name.NSMetadataQueryDidUpdate)
            .receive(on: RunLoop.main)
        let subscriberUpdate = Subscribers.Sink<Notification,
Never>(receiveCompletion: {_ in }, receiveValue: { value in
            self.updateFiles(notification: value)
        })
        publisherUpdate.subscribe(subscriberUpdate)

        self.getMetadata()
    }
    func getMetadata() {
        self.metaData = NSMetadataQuery()
        self.metaData.searchScopes =
[NSMetadataQueryUbiquitousDocumentsScope]
        self.metaData.start()
    }
}
```

Listing 15-14: Working with multiple documents

The model in Listing 15-14 includes a new structure called `FileInfo` and a `@Published` property called `listOfFiles` to store the instances of this structure that represent the documents in the container. The rest of the code in the observable object is the same as before, only the methods change. For instance, when the `NSMetadataQueryDidFinishGathering` notification is posted by the `NSMetadataQuery` object, the subscriber executes a method called `getFiles()` to process the list of files available in the container.

```
func getFiles() {
    if self.metaData.resultCount > 0 {
        let files = metaData.results as! [NSMetadataItem]
        for item in files {
            let fileName = item.value(forAttribute: NSMetadataItemFSNameKey)
as! String
            if !listOfFiles.contains(where: { $0.name == fileName }) {
                let fileURL = item.value(forAttribute: NSMetadataItemURLKey)
as! URL
                let document = MyDocument(fileURL: fileURL)
                document.open(completionHandler: nil)
                self.listOfFiles.append(FileInfo(name: fileName, document:
document))
```

```
            }
         }
         self.listOfFiles.sort(by: { $0.name < $1.name })
      }
   }
}
```

Listing 15-15: Processing the list of files in the container

The `getFiles()` method goes through the list of documents retrieved by the query, implements the same tools used before to create a `MyDocument` instance for each one of them, and adds a `FileInfo` instance with the document and its name to the `listOfFiles` array. Notice that to simplify our code, we open the documents after they are created and keep them open, but the documents should be opened only when it is requested by the user, as we did in the previous example.

Another method that must be adapted to work with multiple files is the one executed after a `NSMetadataQueryDidUpdate` notification is posted. This method is executed when the `NSMetadataQuery` object detects an update in the container. The difference is that now we not only have to consider changes in the document, but also respond to a document being added or removed. To detect the type of change, the `NSMetadataQuery` class defines the following constants.

NSMetadataQueryUpdateAddedItemsKey—This constant retrieves an array of `NSMetadataItem` objects that represent the documents added to the container.

NSMetadataQueryUpdateChangedItemsKey—This constant retrieves an array of `NSMetadataItem` objects that represent the documents that were modified.

NSMetadataQueryUpdateRemovedItemsKey—This constant retrieves an array of `NSMetadataItem` objects that represent the documents that were removed from the container.

This information is shared through the `userInfo` property of the `Notification` object produced by the `NSMetadataQueryDidUpdate` notification. The value is received by the subscriber and we pass it to the `updateFiles()` method to access it from our code, as shown in the following example.

```
func updateFiles(notification: Notification) {
   metaData.disableUpdates()

   let manager = FileManager.default
   if let modifications = notification.userInfo {
      if let removed =
modifications[NSMetadataQueryUpdateRemovedItemsKey] as? [NSMetadataItem] {
         for item in removed {
            let name = item.value(forAttribute: NSMetadataItemFSNameKey)
as! String
            if let index = listOfFiles.firstIndex(where: { $0.name ==
name }) {
               self.listOfFiles.remove(at: index)
            }
         }
      }
      if let added = modifications[NSMetadataQueryUpdateAddedItemsKey]
as? [NSMetadataItem] {
         for item in added {
            let name = item.value(forAttribute: NSMetadataItemFSNameKey)
as! String
```

```
            if !listOfFiles.contains(where: { $0.name == name }) {
                if let fileURL =
manager.url(forUbiquityContainerIdentifier: nil) {
                    let iCloudURL =
fileURL.appendingPathComponent("Documents/\(name)")
                        let document = MyDocument(fileURL: iCloudURL)
                        document.open(completionHandler: nil)
                        self.listOfFiles.append(FileInfo(name: name, document:
document))
                }
            }
        }
        self.listOfFiles.sort(by: { $0.name < $1.name })
    }
}
    metaData.enableUpdates()
}
```

Listing 15-16: Updating the container

The **updateFiles()** method in Listing 15-16 receives the **Notification** object from the subscriber, so we can read its **userInfo** property and determine the type of update performed by the user. If the value is of type **NSMetadataQueryUpdateRemovedItemsKey**, we remove the deleted documents from the **listOfFiles** array, but if the value is of type **NSMetadataQueryUpdateAddedItemsKey**, we create the **MyDocument** objects to represent each document and add them to the **listOfFiles** array as we did before.

Notice that to avoid simultaneous updates, we disable the **NSMetadataQuery** object momentarily with the **disableUpdates()** method and enable it again with the **enableUpdates()** method when the updates are over.

There are two more files we need to add to the model to respond to the user interaction. One to create new documents and another to remove them. As we did before, we called the method to create new documents **createFile()**.

```
func createFile(name: String, info: PersonalInfo) {
    let manager = FileManager.default
    if let fileURL = manager.url(forUbiquityContainerIdentifier: nil) {
        let iCloudURL = fileURL.appendingPathComponent("Documents/\(name)")

        let encoder = JSONEncoder()
        if let data = try? encoder.encode(info) {
            let document = MyDocument(fileURL: iCloudURL)
            document.fileContent = data
            document.save(to: iCloudURL, for: .forCreating,
completionHandler: nil)
            self.listOfFiles.append(FileInfo(name: name, document:
document))
            self.listOfFiles.sort(by: { $0.name < $1.name })
        }
    }
}
```

Listing 15-17: Adding a new document to the container

There is nothing new in this method other than the name of the file being defined by the user. We create the **MyDocument** object, assign the data with the values inserted by the user to its **fileContent** property, and then save it with the **save()** method.

Deleting a document from the container is the only process that doesn't present any special requirements. We just have to use the **removeItem()** method of the **FileManager** object and the file is removed from the device and iCloud. There is only one condition, and that is that the task must be performed asynchronously from a background thread. For this purpose, we can use a `DispatchQueue` object, as shown next.

```
func removeFiles(indexes: IndexSet) {
    let queue = DispatchQueue(label: "delete")
    queue.async {
        for index in indexes {
            let document = self.listOfFiles[index].document
            do {
                let manager = FileManager.default
                try manager.removeItem(atPath: document.fileURL.path)
                let main = OperationQueue.main
                main.addOperation {
                    self.listOfFiles.remove(at: index)
                }
            } catch {
                print("Error deleting file")
            }
        }
    }
}
```

Listing 15-18: Removing documents from the container

The `removeFiles()` method in Listing 15-18 receives an `IndexSet` value with the indexes of the documents to be removed. This is the value generated by the `onDelete()` modifier applied to the `ForEach` view (see Listing 10-21). The method iterates through these values with a `for in` loop, gets the URL of each file from a property provided by the `UIDocument` class called `fileURL`, and removes them with the `removeItem()` method. Notice that besides the file, we also have to remove the `FileInfo` structure in the `listOfFiles` array that was representing the document, but because `listOfFiles` is a `@Published` property we can only modify its value from the main queue (changes to the interface must always be performed from the main queue), so we get a reference to the main queue from the `main` property of the `OperationQueue` class and add an operation to it.

The model is ready, now we must define the views. We need three views for this example, one to list the documents available, one to let the user add new documents, and another to show the content of the selected document. The following are the changes we need to introduce to the `ContentView` view.

```
import SwiftUI

struct ContentView: View {
    @EnvironmentObject var appData: AppData
    @State private var openSheet: Bool = false

    var body: some View {
        NavigationView {
            List {
                ForEach(appData.listOfFiles) { file in
                    NavigationLink(destination: ShowFileView(info: file)) {
                        Text(file.name)
                    }
                }.onDelete(perform: { indexes in
                    self.appData.removeFiles(indexes: indexes)
                })
            }
```

```
            .navigationBarTitle("List of Files")
            .navigationBarItems(trailing: Button("Create File") {
                self.openSheet = true
            })
            .sheet(isPresented: $openSheet) {
                CreateFileView(openSheet: self.$openSheet)
                    .environmentObject(self.appData)
            }
        }
    }
}
struct ContentView_Previews: PreviewProvider {
    static var previews: some View {
        ContentView().environmentObject(AppData())
    }
}
```

Listing 15-19: Listing the documents available in the container

The view in Listing 15-19 creates a list with the values in the **listOfFiles** property, applies the **onDelete()** modifier to the **ForEach** view to let the user delete a document, and includes a button in the navigation bar to open a sheet to add new documents. The view opened by the **sheet()** modifier is called **CreateFileView**.

```
import SwiftUI

struct CreateFileView: View {
    @EnvironmentObject var appData: AppData
    @Binding var openSheet: Bool

    @State private var inputFileName: String = ""
    @State private var inputName: String = ""
    @State private var inputAddress: String = ""
    @State private var inputCity: String = ""

    var body: some View {
        Form {
            Section(header: Text("File Name")) {
                TextField("Insert name and extension", text: $inputFileName)
                    .textFieldStyle(RoundedBorderTextFieldStyle())
                    .autocapitalization(.none)
            }
            Section(header: Text("User Info")) {
                TextField("Insert Name", text: $inputName)
                    .textFieldStyle(RoundedBorderTextFieldStyle())
                TextField("Insert Address", text: $inputAddress)
                    .textFieldStyle(RoundedBorderTextFieldStyle())
                TextField("Insert City", text: $inputCity)
                    .textFieldStyle(RoundedBorderTextFieldStyle())
            }
            Section {
                HStack {
                    Spacer()
                    Button("Save") {
                        let fileName =
self.inputFileName.trimmingCharacters(in: .whitespaces)
                        if !fileName.isEmpty &&
!self.appData.listOfFiles.contains(where: { $0.name == fileName }) {
                            let info = PersonalInfo(name: self.inputName,
address: self.inputAddress, city: self.inputCity)
                            self.appData.createFile(name: fileName, info: info)
```

Chapter 15 - iCloud

```
                self.openSheet = false
             }
          }.buttonStyle(BorderlessButtonStyle())
       }
    }
  }
 }
}
struct CreateFileView_Previews: PreviewProvider {
   static var previews: some View {
      CreateFileView(openSheet: .constant(false))
         .environmentObject(AppData())
   }
}
```

Listing 15-20: Creating new documents

The view in Listing 15-20 includes an additional **TextField** to let the user insert the name of the document, but the rest of the information is the same as before (name, address and city). When the user presses the Save button, the code checks whether a file with that name already exists in the **listOfFiles** array, and if it doesn't, it creates an instance of the **PersonalInfo** structure with the information inserted by the user and calls the **createFile()** method in the model to create the document.

The **ForEach** loop in the **ContentView** view defined in Listing 15-19 also includes a **NavigationLink** view in each row to open an additional view to show the content of the selected document. We call this view **ShowFileView**.

```
import SwiftUI
struct ShowFileView: View {
    let fileInfo: FileInfo
    var personalInfo: PersonalInfo

    init(info: FileInfo) {
       self.fileInfo = info
       self.personalInfo = PersonalInfo(name: "", address: "", city: "")

       let decoder = JSONDecoder()
       if let data = info.document.fileContent {
          if let documentInfo = try? decoder.decode(PersonalInfo.self,
from: data) {
             self.personalInfo = documentInfo
          }
       }
    }
    var body: some View {
       VStack {
          HStack {
             Text(fileInfo.name)
             Spacer()
          }
          HStack {
             Text("Name:")
             Text(personalInfo.name)
             Spacer()
          }
          HStack {
             Text("Address:")
             Text(personalInfo.address)
```

```
            Spacer()
        }
        HStack {
            Text("City:")
            Text(personalInfo.city)
            Spacer()
        }
        Spacer()
    }.padding()
    .navigationBarTitle("File")
    }
}
struct ShowFileView_Previews: PreviewProvider {
    static var previews: some View {
        let manager = FileManager.default
        var tempURL = manager.urls(for: .documentDirectory, in:
.userDomainMask).first!
        tempURL = tempURL.appendingPathComponent("temp.dat")
        return ShowFileView(info: FileInfo(name: "Test", document:
MyDocument(fileURL: tempURL)))
    }
}
```

Listing 15-21: Displaying the document's content

The view receives a value of type **FileInfo**. Therefore, to display the information on the screen, we must decode it. This is the task of the structure's initializer. The initializer receives the value from the **NavigationLink** view, decodes the data in the document's **fileContent** property into a **PersonalInfo** structure, and assigns the structure to the **personalInfo** property to make the values available for the view. All the view has to do is to read the values from these properties and display them to the user.

Figure 15-10: Interface to read and save multiple documents

 Do It Yourself: Remove the code in the AppData.swift file and replace it with the code in Listing 15-14. Add the methods in Listings 15-15, 15-16, 15-17, and 15-19 to the **AppData** class. Update the ContentView.swift file with the code in Listing 15-19. Create a SwiftUI file called CreateFileView.swift for the code in Listing 15-20, and a SwiftUI file called ShowFileView.swift for the code in Listing 15-21. Remove the previous application from every simulator and device to clean the container. Run the application simultaneously in two devices. Press the Create File button to add a document. You should see the document listed on both devices. Slide the row to the left and press the Delete button. The document should be removed in both devices.

Basic 15.4 CloudKit

CloudKit is a database system in iCloud. Using this system, we can store structured data online with different levels of accessibility. The system offers three types of databases to determine who has access to the information.

- **Private Database** to store data that is accessible only to the user.
- **Public Database** to store data that is accessible to every user running the app.
- **Shared Database** to store data the user wants to share with other users.

As we did with the rest of the iCloud services, the first step to use CloudKit is to activate it from the Signing & Capabilities panel.

Figure 15-11: *CloudKit service*

CloudKit requires a container to manage the databases. If the container is not automatically generated by Xcode when we activate the CloudKit service, we must create it ourselves, as we did before for the iCloud Documents service (see Figures 15-6 and 15-7).

Because CloudKit uses Remote Notifications to report changes in the databases, when we activate CloudKit, Xcode automatically activates an additional service called *Push Notifications*, as shown in Figure 15-12.

Figure 15-12: *Push Notifications*

Remote Notifications are like the Local Notifications introduced in Chapter 13, but instead of being posted by the app they are sent from a server to inform our app or the user that something changed or needs attention. The Remote Notifications posted by CloudKit are sent from Apple servers when something changes in the databases. Because this may happen not only when the user is working with the app but also when the app is in the background, to get these notifications, we must add the Background Mode capability (see Figure 15-1) and activate two services called *Background Fetch* and *Remote Notifications*.

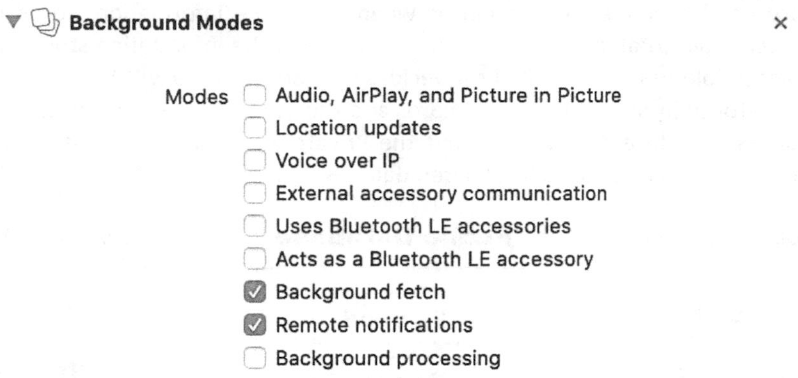

Modes ⬜ Audio, AirPlay, and Picture in Picture
⬜ Location updates
⬜ Voice over IP
⬜ External accessory communication
⬜ Uses Bluetooth LE accessories
⬜ Acts as a Bluetooth LE accessory
☑ Background fetch
☑ Remote notifications
⬜ Background processing

Figure 15-13: Background Mode

Do It Yourself: Create a SwiftUI project. Click on the app's settings option at the top of the Navigator Area (Figure 5-4, number 10) and open the Signing & Capabilities panel (Figures 5-11 and 5-14). Click on the + button at the top-left corner of the panel to add a capability. Select the iCloud option and press return. Repeat the process to add the Background Modes capability. In the Background Modes section, check the options Background fetch and Remote Notifications (Figure 15-13). In the iCloud section, check the option CloudKit. Press the + button to add a container (see Figure 15-6, number 1). Insert the app's bundle identifier for the container's name and press the OK button (you can find the bundle identifier at the top of the panel). If the name of the container appears in red, press the Refresh button to upload the information to Apple servers (see Figure 15-6, number 2).

(Basic) ## Container

The CloudKit container is like a space in Apple's servers designated to our app. The framework provides a class called `CKContainer` to access this container and the databases it contains. Because an app may have more than one container, the class includes an initializer to get a reference to a specific container and a type method to get a reference to the container by default.

CKContainer(identifier: String)—This initializer creates the `CKContainer` object that references the container identified with the name specified by the **identifier** attribute.

default()—This type method returns the `CKContainer` object that references the container by default.

Container objects provide the following properties to get access to each database.

privateCloudDatabase—This property returns a `CKDatabase` object with a reference to the user's Private database.

publicCloudDatabase—This property returns a `CKDatabase` object with a reference to the app's Public database.

sharedCloudDatabase—This property returns a `CKDatabase` object with a reference to the user's Shared database.

CloudKit databases have specific purposes and functionalities. The Private database is used when we want the user to be able to share private information among his or her own devices (only the user can access the information stored in this database), and the Public and Shared databases are used to share information between users (the information stored in the Public database is accessible to all the users running our app and the information stored in the Shared database is accessible to the users the user decides to share the data with).

The data is stored in the database as records and records are stored in zones. The Private and Public databases include a default zone, but the Private and Shared databases also work with custom zones (called Shared Zones in a Shared database), as illustrated in Figure 15-14.

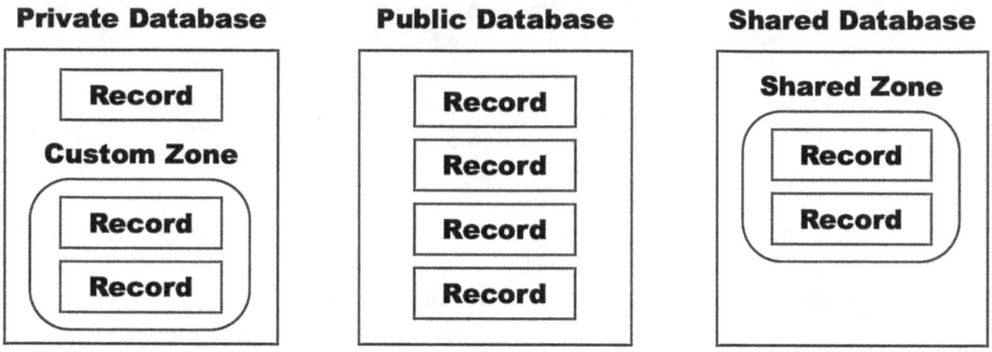

Figure 15-14: Databases configuration

Basic   Records

Once we have decided which database we are going to use, we must generate records to store the user's data. Records are objects that store information as key/value pairs, like dictionaries. These objects are classified by types to determine the characteristics of the record. For example, if we want to store records that contain information about books, we can use the type "Books", and if later we want to store records with information about authors, we can use the type "Authors" (a type is analog to the Entities in Core Data). The framework provides the CKRecord class to create and manage records. The class includes the following initializer.

CKRecord(recordType: String, **recordID:** CKRecord.ID)—This initializer creates a CKRecord object of the type and with the ID specified by the attributes. The **recordType** attribute is a custom identifier for the type, and the **recordID** attribute is the record's identifier.

Records are identified with an ID that includes a name and a reference to the zone the record belongs to (if a custom ID is not specified, the record is stored with an ID generated by CloudKit). To create and access the ID and its values, the CKRecord class defines the ID class with the following initializers and properties.

CKRecord.ID(recordName: String)—This initializer creates a CKRecord.ID object to identify a record. The **recordName** attribute is the name we want to give to the record (it must be unique).

CKRecord.ID(recordName: String, **zoneID:** CKRecordZone.ID)—This initializer creates a CKRecord.ID object to identify a record stored with the name and in the zone specified by the attributes. The **recordName** attribute is the name we want to give to the record, and the **zoneID** attribute is the identifier of the custom zone where we want to store the record.

recordName—This property returns a string with the name of the record.

zoneID—This property returns a CKRecordZone.ID object with the ID of the zone the record belongs to.

The `CKRecord` class offers properties to set or get the record's ID and other attributes. The following are the most frequently used.

recordID—This property returns the `CKRecord.ID` object that identifies the record.

recordType—This property returns a string that determines the record's type.

recordChangeTag—This property returns a string with the tag assigned to the record (each record is assigned a tag by the server).

creationDate—This property returns a `Date` value with the date in which the record was created.

modificationDate—This property returns a `Date` value that indicates the last time the record was modified.

Because the values of a record are stored as key/value pairs, we can use square brackets to read and modify them (as we do with dictionaries), but the class also includes the following methods.

setObject(Value?, **forKey:** String**)**—This method sets or updates a value in the record. The fist attribute is the value we want to store, and the **forKey** attribute is the key we want to use to identify the value. The value must be of any of the following types: `NSString`, `NSNumber`, `NSData`, `NSDate`, `NSArray`, `CLLocation`, `CKAsset`, and `Reference`.

object(forKey: String**)**—This method returns the value associated with the key specified by the **forKey** attribute. The value is returned as a generic `CKRecordValue` type that we must cast to the right data type.

(Basic) **Zones**

As illustrated in Figure 15-14, the Public database can only store records in a default zone, but the Private and Shared databases can include custom zones. In the case of the Private database, the custom zones are optional (although they are required for synchronization, as we will see later). Zones are like divisions inside a database to separate records that are not directly related. For example, we may have an app that stores locations, like the names of cities and countries, but also lets the user store a list of Christmas gifts. In cases like this, we can create a zone to store the records that include information about cities and countries and another zone to store the records that include information about the gifts. The CloudKit framework provides the `CKRecordZone` class to represent these zones. The class includes an initializer to create new custom zones and a type method to get a reference to the zone by default.

CKRecordZone(zoneName: String**)**—This initializer creates a `CKRecordZone` object to represent a zone with the name specified by the **zoneName** attribute.

default()—This type method returns the `CKRecordZone` object that represents the zone by default in the database.

(Basic) **Query**

When we want to access data stored in CloudKit, we must download the records from the database and read their values. Records may be fetched from a database one by one using their ID or in a batch using a query. To define a query, the framework provides the `CKQuery` class. The class includes the following initializer and properties.

CKQuery(recordType: String, **predicate:** NSPredicate)—This initializer creates a CKQuery object to fetch multiple records from a database. The **recordType** attribute specifies the type of records we want to fetch, and the **predicate** attribute determines the matching criteria we want to use to select the records.

recordType—This property sets or returns a string that determines the type of records we want to fetch.

predicate—This property sets or returns an NSPredicate object that defines the matching criteria for the query.

sortDescriptors—This property sets or returns an array of NSSortDescriptor objects that determine the order of the records returned by the query.

Basic Operations

CloudKit is an online service and therefore any task may take some time to process. For this reason, the CloudKit framework uses asynchronous operations to access the information on the servers. An operation has to be created for every process we want to perform in a database, including storing, reading, and organizing records. These are the same operations we have studied in Chapter 3, but they are created from subclasses of a base class called CKDatabaseOperation. Once the operation is defined, it must be added to the CKDatabase object that represents the database we want to modify. The CKDatabase class offers the following method for this purpose.

add(CKDatabaseOperation)—This method executes the operation specified by the attribute on the database. The attribute is an object of a subclass of the CKDatabaseOperation class.

Besides this method, the CKDatabase class also offers convenient methods to generate and execute the most common operations. The following are the methods available to process records.

fetch(withRecordID: CKRecord.ID, **completionHandler:** Block)—This method fetches the record with the ID specified by the **withRecordID** attribute. The **completionHandler** attribute is a closure that is executed when the process is over. The closure receives two values, a CKRecord object representing the record fetched, and a CKError object to report errors.

save(CKRecord, **completionHandler:** Block)—This method stores a record in the database (if the record already exists, it updates its values). The first attribute is a reference to the record we want to store, and the **completionHandler** attribute is a closure that is executed when the process is over. The closure receives two values, a reference to the CKRecord object we tried to save, and a CKError object to report errors.

delete(withRecordID: CKRecord.ID, **completionHandler:** Block)—This method deletes from the database the record with the ID specified by the **withRecordID** attribute. The **completionHandler** attribute is a closure that is executed when the process is over. The closure receives two values, a CKRecord.ID object with the ID of the record we tried to delete, and a CKError object to report errors.

The following are the methods provided by the CKDatabase class to process zones.

fetch(withRecordZoneID: CKRecordZone.ID, **completionHandler:** Block)—This method fetches the zone with the ID specified by the **withRecordZoneID** attribute. The **completionHandler** attribute is a closure that is executed when the process is over. The closure receives two values, a `CKRecordZone` object representing the zone that was fetched, and a `CKError` object to report errors.

fetchAllRecordZones(completionHandler: Block)—This method fetches all the zones available in the database. The **completionHandler** attribute is a closure that is executed when the process is over. The closure receives two values, an array with `CKRecordZone` objects representing the zones that were fetched, and a `CKError` object to report errors.

save(CKRecordZone, **completionHandler:** Block)—This method creates a zone in the database. The first attribute is the object representing the zone we want to create, and the **completionHandler** attribute is a closure that is executed when the process is over. The closure receives two values, a reference to the `CKRecordZone` object we tried to save, and a `CKError` object to report errors.

delete(withRecordZoneID: CKRecordZone.ID, **completionHandler:** Block)— This method deletes from the database the zone with the ID specified by the **withRecordZoneID** attribute. The **completionHandler** attribute is a closure that is executed when the process is over. The closure receives two values, a `CKRecordZone.ID` object with the ID of the zone we tried to delete, and a `CKError` object to report errors.

To perform a query, the `CKDatabase` class includes the following method.

perform(CKQuery, **inZoneWith:** CKRecordZone.ID?, **completionHandler:** Block)—This method performs the query specified by the first attribute in the zone specified by the `inZoneWith` attribute. The **completionHandler** attribute is a closure that is executed when the process is over. The closure receives two values, an array of `CKRecord` objects representing the records that were fetched, and a `CKError` object to report errors.

(Medium) **Batch Operations**

Although the methods provided by the `CKDatabase` class are very convenient and easy to implement, they only perform one request at a time. The problem is that CloudKit servers have a limit on the number of operations we can perform per second (currently 40 requests per second are allowed), so if our application relies heavily on CloudKit, at one point some of the requests might be rejected if we send them one by one. The solution is to create operations that allow us to perform multiple requests at once. The CloudKit framework defines three subclasses of the `CKDatabaseOperation` class for this purpose. The `CKModifySubscriptionsOperation` class creates an operation to add or modify subscriptions, the `CKModifyRecordZonesOperation` class is used to add or modify record zones, and the `CKModifyRecordsOperation` class is for adding and modifying records. The following are their initializers.

CKModifySubscriptionsOperation(subscriptionsToSave: [CKSubscription], **subscriptionIDsToDelete:** [CKSubscription.ID])—This initializer returns an operation that adds or modifies one or more subscriptions. The **subscriptionsToSave** attribute is an array with the subscriptions we want to add or modify, and the **subscriptionIDsToDelete** is an array with the IDs of the subscriptions we want to delete from the server.

CKModifyRecordZonesOperation(recordZonesToSave: [CKRecordZone], **recordZoneIDsToDelete:** [CKRecordZone.ID])—This initializer returns an operation that adds or modifies one or more record zones. The **recordZonesToSave** attribute is an array with the record zones we want to add or modify, and the **recordZoneIDsToDelete** is an array with the IDs of the record zones we want to delete from the server.

CKModifyRecordsOperation(recordsToSave: [CKRecord], **recordIDsToDelete:** [CKRecord.ID])—This operation adds or modifies one or more records. The **recordsToSave** attribute is an array with the records we want to add or modify, and the **recordIDsToDelete** attribute is an array with the IDs of the records we want to delete from the server.

The operations must be initialized first and then added to the database with the `add()` method of the `CKDatabase` class. Each initializer offers the options to modify elements and remove them. If we only need to perform one task, the other can be declared as `nil`.

(Basic)   # References

Records of different types are usually related. For example, along with records of type Countries we may have records of type Cities to store information about the cities of each country. To create these relationships, records may include references. References are objects that store information about a connection between one record and another. They are created from the `Reference` class defined inside the `CKRecord` class. The following are its initializers.

CKRecord.Reference(recordID: CKRecord.ID, **action:** CKRecord_Reference-_Action)—This initializer creates a `Reference` object pointing to the record identified with the ID specified by the `recordID` attribute. The **action** attribute is an enumeration that determines what the database should do with the record when the record that is referencing is deleted. The possible values are `none` (nothing is done) and `deleteSelf` (when the record referenced by the reference is deleted, the record with the reference is deleted as well).

CKRecord.Reference(record: CKRecord, **action:** CKRecord_Reference-_Action)—This initializer creates a `Reference` object pointing to the record specified by the `record` attribute. The **action** attribute is an enumeration that determines what the database should do with the record when the record that is referencing is deleted. The possible values are `none` (nothing is done) and `deleteSelf` (when the record referenced by the reference is deleted, the record with the reference is deleted as well).

References in CloudKit are called *Back References* because they are assigned to the record that is the children of another record. Following our example, the reference should be assigned to the city and not the country, as illustrated next.

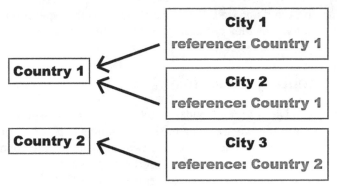

Figure 15-15: *Back references*

Basic **CloudKit Dashboard**

CloudKit creates a model of our app's database on its servers as the records are added to the database. For example, if our app stores records of type "Books", the first time a record is created CloudKit adds the type "Books" to the list of record types available for our app and creates fields to represent each of the record's values. This way, the system establishes the database's structure from the data we store during development, saving us the trouble of configuring the database beforehand (we do not have to create a model as we do with Core Data). But there are some configuration parameters that the system cannot determine by itself and we must set up ourselves. For this purpose and to help us develop a CloudKit application, Apple provides the CloudKit dashboard. This is an online control panel that we can use to manage the CloudKit databases, add, update, or remove records, and configure the model.

The panel is available at icloud.developer.apple.com/dashboard/ or by clicking on the CloudKit Dashboard button at the bottom of the iCloud section in the Signing & Capabilities panel. The first thing we see when we access this dashboard is a list of containers on the left, and two sections on the right called Development and Production. The Development section is where our records and all the configuration of our CloudKit database is stored during development. Once the app is ready for distribution, we deploy the database to production and the database's structure defined in Development is copied to the Production section.

To manage our CloudKit container, we must select it from the list on the left and then click on the tool we want to work with in the Development section, as illustrated in Figure 15-16.

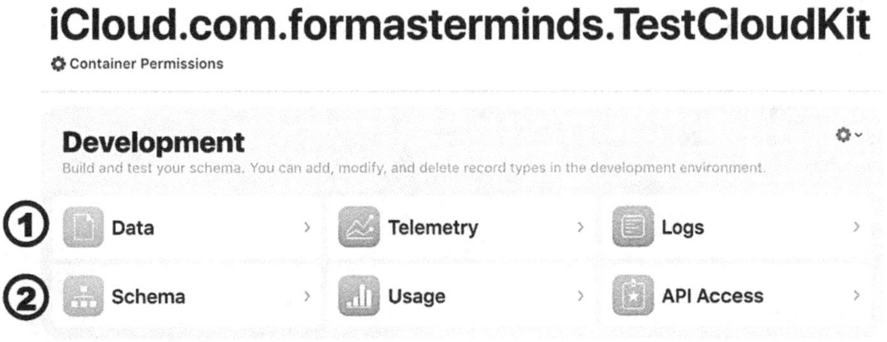

iCloud.com.formasterminds.TestCloudKit

⚙ Container Permissions

Development
Build and test your schema. You can add, modify, and delete record types in the development environment.

① 📄 Data　　　＞　　📈 Telemetry　　＞　　📋 Logs　　＞

② ⊞ Schema　　＞　　📊 Usage　　　＞　　⭐ API Access　＞

Figure 15-16: *Container in CloudKit's dashboard*

There are two tools we always need during development: Data and Schema (Figure 15-16, number 1 and 2). The Data is a panel where we can list the records, zones, and subscriptions created by the app, delete them, or even create new ones. On the other hand, the Schema is a panel where we can edit the database schema, which includes the type of records the database can manage, the type of values they can store, and the indexes required to query, search, and sort them.

Basic Implementing CloudKit

Sharing values between devices with a CloudKit database is easy but requires some work on our part. For the following example, we are going to create a simple application that allows the user to save a list of locations. The interface consists of two lists, one for the countries and another for the cities, and the usual sheets to let the user insert new values.

Figure 15-17: *Interface to work with CloudKit*

There are several ways to implement CloudKit. It all depends on the characteristics of our application and how it is organized. For this example, we are going to centralize all the logic of our program in the model. The following is a possible implementation for the application in Figure 15-17.

```
import SwiftUI
import CloudKit

struct Country {
   let name: String?
   let record: CKRecord
}
struct City {
   let name: String?
   let record: CKRecord
}
struct CountryViewModel: Identifiable {
   let id: CKRecord.ID
   let country: Country

   var countryName: String {
      return country.name ?? "Undefined"
   }
}
struct CityViewModel: Identifiable {
   let id: CKRecord.ID
   let city: City

   var cityName: String {
      return city.name ?? "Undefined"
   }
}
```

Chapter 15 - iCloud

```
class AppData: ObservableObject {
    @Published var listCountries: [CountryViewModel] = []
    @Published var listCities: [CityViewModel] = []
    var database: CKDatabase!

    init() {
        let container = CKContainer.default()
        database = container.privateCloudDatabase

        self.readCountries()
    }
    func insertCountry(name: String) {
        let id = CKRecord.ID(recordName: "idcountry-\(UUID())")
        let record = CKRecord(recordType: "Countries", recordID: id)
        record.setObject(name as NSString, forKey: "name")

        database.save(record, completionHandler: { (recordSaved, error) in
            if error == nil {
                let main = OperationQueue.main
                main.addOperation {
                    let newCountry = Country(name: record["name"], record:
record)
                    let newItem = CountryViewModel(id: record.recordID,
country: newCountry)
                    self.listCountries.append(newItem)
                    self.listCountries.sort(by: { $0.countryName <
$1.countryName })
                }
            } else {
                print("Error: record not saved \(error!)")
            }
        })
    }
    func insertCity(name: String, country: CKRecord.ID) {
        let id = CKRecord.ID(recordName: "idcity-\(UUID())")
        let record = CKRecord(recordType: "Cities", recordID: id)
        record.setObject(name as NSString, forKey: "name")

        let reference = CKRecord.Reference(recordID: country, action:
.deleteSelf)
        record.setObject(reference, forKey: "country")

        database.save(record, completionHandler: { (recordSaved, error) in
            if error == nil {
                let main = OperationQueue.main
                main.addOperation {
                    let newCity = City(name: record["name"], record: record)
                    let newItem = CityViewModel(id: record.recordID, city:
newCity)
                    self.listCities.append(newItem)
                    self.listCities.sort(by: { $0.cityName < $1.cityName })
                }
            } else {
                print("Error: record not saved \(error!)")
            }
        })
    }
    func readCountries() {
        let predicate = NSPredicate(format: "TRUEPREDICATE")
        let query = CKQuery(recordType: "Countries", predicate: predicate)
        database.perform(query, inZoneWith: nil, completionHandler: {
(records, error) in
```

```
                if let list = records, error == nil {
                    let main = OperationQueue.main
                    main.addOperation {
                        self.listCountries = []
                        for record in list {
                            let newCountry = Country(name: record["name"], record:
record)
                            let newItem = CountryViewModel(id: record.recordID,
country: newCountry)
                            self.listCountries.append(newItem)
                        }
                        self.listCountries.sort(by: { $0.countryName <
$1.countryName })
                    }
                } else {
                    print("Error: records not found \(error!)")
                }
            })
        }
    func readCities(country: CKRecord.ID) {
        let predicate = NSPredicate(format: "country = %@", country)
        let query = CKQuery(recordType: "Cities", predicate: predicate)
        database.perform(query, inZoneWith: nil, completionHandler: {
(records, error) in
            if let list = records, error == nil {
                let main = OperationQueue.main
                main.addOperation {
                    self.listCities = []
                    for record in list {
                        let newCity = City(name: record["name"], record:
record)
                        let newItem = CityViewModel(id: record.recordID, city:
newCity)
                        self.listCities.append(newItem)
                    }
                    self.listCities.sort(by: { $0.cityName < $1.cityName })
                }
            } else {
                print("Error: records not found \(error!)")
            }
        })
    }
}
```

Listing 15-22: *Creating the model*

We begin by defining our models and view models. There are two data models in the code in Listing 15-22, Country and City. These structures store the name of the country and city and a reference to the record downloaded from the CloudKit database. The view models identify each value by the record ID (**CKRecord.ID**) and include a computed property to return a string with the name.

Next is the observable object. The first thing we do in this object is to define the **@Published** properties we need to store the data locally and show it to the user. The **listCountries** property is an array with the list of the countries already inserted in the database, and the **listCities** property is another array with the list of cities available for a specific country. Another property included in this class is **database**. This property stores a reference to the CloudKit's database, so we can have access to it from anywhere in the code. The property is initialized in the **init()** method with a reference to the Private Database (we use the private database because we only want the user to be able to share the data between his own devices).

Chapter 15 - iCloud

After the object's initialization, we define two methods: `insertCountry()` and `insertCity()`. These methods are going to be called from the views when the user inserts a new country or city. Their task is to create the records and upload them to CloudKit. The process begins by defining a record ID, which is a unique value that identifies each record. For the countries, we use the string "idcountry" followed by a random value generated by the `UUID()` function. With this ID, we create a `CKRecord` object of type Countries (this is like the entities in Core Data), then add a property called "name" with the value received by the method, and finally save it in CloudKit servers with the `save()` method of the `CKDatabase` object. This method generates an operation that communicates with the servers asynchronously and reports back the result to the closure assigned to the `completionHandler` attribute when the process is over. The closure receives two values, the first value is a reference to the record we tried to save, and the second value contains the errors produced by the operation. If there are no errors (the `error` parameter is equal to `nil`), we create a new `CountryViewModel` structure with the record and add it to the `listCountries` property.

The method to add a city is the same, with the exceptions that we must define the type of records as Cities and add an extra attribute to the record with a reference to the country the city belongs to. For this purpose, we create a `Reference` object with the country's record ID received by the method and an action of type `deleteSelf`, so when the record of the country is deleted, this record is deleted as well.

Next are the methods we need to get the countries and cities already stored in the database. In the `readCountries()` method, we define a predicate with the TRUEPREDICATE keyword and a query for records of type Countries. The record type asks the server to only look for records of type Countries, and the TRUEPREDICATE keyword determines that the predicate will always return the value `true`, so we get back all the records available. If the query doesn't return any errors, we create a `CountryViewModel` structure for each record and add them to the `listCountries` array.

The `readCities()` method is very similar, except that this time we are getting the list of cities that belong to the country selected by the user (the view that shows the cities only opens when the user taps on a row to select a country). The rest of the code is the same. We get the records that represent the cities, create the `CityViewModel` structures with them, and store them in the `listCities` array.

For the interface, we need a total of four views. A view to show the list of countries, a view to let the user insert a new country, a view to show the list of the cities that belong to the selected country, and another view to let the user insert a new city. The following is the initial view.

```
import SwiftUI

struct ContentView: View {
    @EnvironmentObject var appData: AppData
    @State private var openSheet: Bool = false

    var body: some View {
        NavigationView {
            List {
                ForEach(appData.listCountries) { country in
                    NavigationLink(destination:
ShowCitiesView(selectedCountry: country)) {
                        Text(country.countryName)
                    }
                }
            }
            .navigationBarTitle("Countries")
            .navigationBarItems(trailing: Button("Add Country") {
                self.openSheet = true
            })
```

```
            .sheet(isPresented: $openSheet) {
                InsertCountryView(openSheet: self.$openSheet)
                    .environmentObject(self.appData)
            }
        }
    }
}
struct ContentView_Previews: PreviewProvider {
    static var previews: some View {
        ContentView().environmentObject(AppData())
    }
}
```

Listing 15-23: Listing the countries in the Private Database

The countries stored in the CloudKit database are retrieved by the **readCountries()** method in our model. This method is called when the observable object is initialized, so all the view has to do is to list the countries stored in the **listCountries** property.

To let the user add a new country, the view includes a **sheet()** modifier that opens the **InsertCountryView** view. The following is our implementation of this view.

```
import SwiftUI

struct InsertCountryView: View {
    @EnvironmentObject var appData: AppData
    @Binding var openSheet: Bool
    @State private var inputName: String = ""

    var body: some View {
        VStack {
            HStack {
                Text("Country:")
                TextField("Insert Country", text: $inputName)
                    .textFieldStyle(RoundedBorderTextFieldStyle())
            }
            HStack {
                Spacer()
                Button("Save") {
                    let text = self.inputName.trimmingCharacters(in:
.whitespaces)
                    if !text.isEmpty {
                        self.appData.insertCountry(name: text)
                        self.openSheet = false
                    }
                }
            }
            Spacer()
        }.padding()
    }
}
struct InsertCountryView_Previews: PreviewProvider {
    static var previews: some View {
        InsertCountryView(openSheet: .constant(false))
            .environmentObject(AppData())
    }
}
```

Listing 15-24: Storing countries in the Private database

Chapter 15 - iCloud

The view includes a `TextField` view to insert the name of the country and a button to save it in the database. When the button is pressed, we call the `insertCountry()` method in the model, the method creates the record with the value inserted by the user and calls the `save()` method on the database to store it in CloudKit servers.

Next is the view necessary to show the list of cities available for each country. The view is called `ShowCitiesView` and it is opened when the user taps on a row in the initial view to select a country.

```
import SwiftUI
import CloudKit

struct ShowCitiesView: View {
    @EnvironmentObject var appData: AppData
    @State private var openSheet: Bool = false
    let selectedCountry: CountryViewModel

    var body: some View {
        VStack {
            List {
                ForEach(appData.listCities) { city in
                    Text(city.cityName)
                }
            }
        }
        .navigationBarTitle(self.selectedCountry.countryName)
        .navigationBarItems(trailing: Button("Add City") {
            self.openSheet = true
        })
        .sheet(isPresented: $openSheet) {
            InsertCityView(openSheet: self.$openSheet, country:
self.selectedCountry.id)
                .environmentObject(self.appData)
        }
        .onAppear(perform: {
            self.appData.readCities(country: self.selectedCountry.id)
        })
    }
}
struct ShowCitiesView_Previews: PreviewProvider {
    static var previews: some View {
        ShowCitiesView(selectedCountry: CountryViewModel(id:
CKRecord.ID(recordName: "Test"), country: Country(name: "Test", record:
CKRecord(recordType: "Cities", recordID: CKRecord.ID(recordName:
"Test")))))
            .environmentObject(AppData())
    }
}
```

Listing 15-25: Listing the cities of a country

The view includes a property of type `CountryViewModel` called `selectedCountry` to receive the information about the selected country. Form this property, we get the country's record ID and call the `readCities()` method in the model when the view appears to retrieve the cities available for that country. The view creates a list with these values and then includes a `sheet()` modifier to let the user add more. The modifier opens a view called `InsertCityView` for this purpose.

```
import SwiftUI
import CloudKit

struct InsertCityView: View {
    @EnvironmentObject var appData: AppData
    @Binding var openSheet: Bool
    @State private var inputName: String = ""
    let country: CKRecord.ID

    var body: some View {
        VStack {
            HStack {
                Text("City:")
                TextField("Insert City", text: $inputName)
                    .textFieldStyle(RoundedBorderTextFieldStyle())
            }
            HStack {
                Spacer()
                Button("Save") {
                    let text = self.inputName.trimmingCharacters(in:
.whitespaces)
                    if !text.isEmpty {
                        self.appData.insertCity(name: text, country:
self.country)
                        self.openSheet = false
                    }
                }
            }
            Spacer()
        }.padding()
    }
}
struct InsertCityView_Previews: PreviewProvider {
    static var previews: some View {
        InsertCityView(openSheet: .constant(false), country:
CKRecord.ID(recordName: "Test"))
            .environmentObject(AppData())
    }
}
```

Listing 15-26: Storing cities in the Private Database

The view receives the country's record ID to know which country the city belongs to, and then calls the **insertCity()** method in the model with the name inserted by the user and this ID to create a Cities record connected to that Countries record in the CloudKit database.

 Do It Yourself: In the project initiated before to activate CloudKit, create a Swift file called AppData.swift for the model in Listing 15-22. Update the AppDelegate.swift file with the code in Listing 7-14 and the SceneDelegate.swift file with the code in Listing 7-20 to instantiate the model and insert it in the environment. Update the ContentView.swift file with the code in Listing 15-23. Create SwiftUI files with the names InsertCountryView.swift, ShowCitiesView.swift, and InsertCityView.swift for the codes in Listings 15-24, 15-25, and 15-26, respectively. Run the application in a device and press the Add Country button to insert a country.

The application is ready. When the user inserts a new value, the code creates a record and uploads it to CloudKit's servers, but the values are not shown on the screen. This is because we haven't defined the required indexes. CloudKit automatically creates indexes for every value we include in the records, except for the record's ID. Therefore, when we query the Cities records by their country attribute to get the cities that belong to the selected country, CloudKit knows how to find and return those records, but when we try to retrieve the countries records without a predicate, CloudKit tries to fetch them by their record ID and fails because there is no index associate with that attribute. To create an index for this attribute, we must open the Schema tool in CloudKit's dashboard (Figure 15-16, number 2). Figure 15-18 shows what we see when we open this panel.

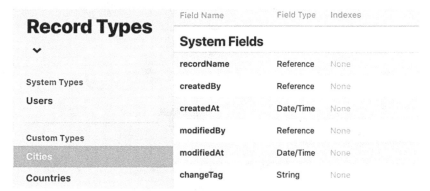

Figure 15-18: Schema tool

By default, the panel shows the record types created by our application on the left, and the attributes of each type on the right. In this case, we see the Cities and Countries record types. If we select any of these types, the panel shows a list with the attributes created by the system at the top and the attributes our application assigns to the records at the bottom (name and country).

The Record Types title is a menu. If we click on it, we can select the Indexes option to modify the indexes for each record type, as shown next.

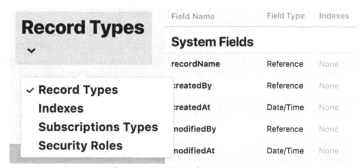

Figure 15-19: Schema menu

If we select the Indexes option, the panel lists the record types on the left, as before, but now the list of attributes on the right include a button to add a new index.

Figure 15-20: Add Index button

There are three types of indexes: Queryable (it can be included in a query), Searchable (it can be searched), and Sortable (it can be sorted). By default, all these indexes are associated to custom attributes but not to the record's ID (Figure 15-20 shows the three types of indexes associated to the name attribute of the Countries record type). When we query the database from the `readCountries()` method in the model, we do not specify any field in the predicate and therefore the system fetches the records from their identifier, which is described in the database as recordName. For this reason, to retrieve the countries in our example, we must add a Queryable index to the recordName field for the Countries record type, as shown next.

name	QUERYABLE	⊖
name	SEARCHABLE	⊖
name	SORTABLE	⊖
recordName ⇕	QUERYABLE ⇕	⊖

⊕ Add Index

Figure 15-21: New Index

Once we select the field recordName and the index Queryable, we can press the Save Changes button at the bottom-right corner of the window to save the changes. Now, if we run the application again from Xcode, the records added to the database are shown on the table.

 Do It Yourself: Open the CloudKit dashboard (icloud.developer.apple.com-/dashboard/), click on you app's container, click on the Schema button to open this tool, click on the Record Types title and select the Indexes option, click on the record type Countries, click on the Add Index button, and add the index for the recordName field, as shown in Figure 15-21. Press the Save Changes button to save the changes and run the application again. You should see on the screen the countries you have inserted before. Select a country and add a city to generate the Cities record type. Open the CloudKit dashboard and repeat the process to add the index to the cities as well, just in case you need it later.

(Basic) **Assets**

Records may also include files, and the files may contain anything from pictures to sound or even videos. To add a file to a record, we must create an asset with the `CKAsset` class. The class includes the following initializer.

CKAsset(fileURL: URL)—This initializer creates a `CKAsset` object with the content of the file in the location determined by the **fileURL** attribute.

The assets are added to a record with a key, as any other value. For our example, we are going to store a picture in the record of every city and add a view to show the picture when the city is selected.

Figure 15-22: Interface to work with assets

The following are the changes we have to introduce to the `insertCity()` method in the model to get the URL of the image and assign the asset to the record.

```
func insertCity(name: String, country: CKRecord.ID) {
    let id = CKRecord.ID(recordName: "idcity-\(UUID())")
    let record = CKRecord(recordType: "Cities", recordID: id)
    record.setObject(name as NSString, forKey: "name")
    let reference = CKRecord.Reference(recordID: country, action:
.deleteSelf)
    record.setObject(reference, forKey: "country")

    let bundle = Bundle.main
    if let fileURL = bundle.url(forResource: "Toronto", withExtension:
"jpg") {
        let asset = CKAsset(fileURL: fileURL)
        record.setObject(asset, forKey: "picture")
    }
    database.save(record, completionHandler: { (recordSaved, error) in
        if error == nil {
            let main = OperationQueue.main
            main.addOperation {
                let newCity = City(name: record["name"], record: record)
                let newItem = CityViewModel(id: record.recordID, city:
newCity)
                self.listCities.append(newItem)
                self.listCities.sort(by: { $0.cityName < $1.cityName })
            }
        } else {
            print("Error: record not saved \(error!)")
        }
    })
}
```

Listing 15-27: Storing assets

In the new `insertCity()` method introduced in Listing 15-27, we get the URL of an image included in the project called Toronto.jpg, create a `CKAsset` object with it, and assign the object to the record of every city with the key "picture" (see Listing 14-27). Now, besides the name, a file with this image will be stored for every city inserted by the user. To get the asset back, we must provide a computed property in the view model, as shown next.

```
struct CityViewModel: Identifiable {
    let id: CKRecord.ID
    let city: City

    var cityName: String {
        return city.name ?? "Undefined"
    }
    var cityPicture: UIImage {
        if let asset = city.record["picture"] as? CKAsset, let fileURL =
asset.fileURL {
            if let picture = UIImage(contentsOfFile: fileURL.path) {
                return picture
            }
        }
        return UIImage(named: "nopicture")!
    }
}
```

Listing 15-28: *Preparing the image for the view*

How to read the assets stored in the record depends on the type of content managed by the asset. In this example, we must use the asset's URL to create a `UIImage` object to show the image to the user. For this purpose, the `cityPicture` property in Listing 15-28 reads the value in the record with the picture key, casts it as a `CKAsset` object, and gets the asset's URL from the `fileURL` property. If the process is successful, it creates a `UIImage` object with the image in this URL and returns it, otherwise, it creates a `UIImage` object with the image nopicture.

The following are the modifications we must introduce to the `ShowCitiesView` view to provide the `NavigationLink` view required for the user to be able to select a city and open a view to see the city's picture.

```
List {
    ForEach(appData.listCities) { city in
        NavigationLink(destination: ShowPictureView(selectedCity: city)) {
            Text(city.cityName)
        }
    }
}
```

Listing 15-29: *Opening a view to show the asset*

The `NavigationLink` view in Listing 15-29 opens a view called `ShowPictureView` to show the city's picture. The following is our implementation of that view.

```
import SwiftUI
import CloudKit

struct ShowPictureView: View {
    @EnvironmentObject var appData: AppData
    let selectedCity: CityViewModel

    var body: some View {
        Image(uiImage: self.selectedCity.cityPicture)
            .resizable()
            .scaledToFit()
            .navigationBarTitle(selectedCity.cityName)
    }
}
```

Chapter 15 - iCloud

```
struct ShowPictureView_Previews: PreviewProvider {
    static var previews: some View {
        ShowPictureView(selectedCity: CityViewModel(id:
CKRecord.ID(recordName: "Test"), city: City(name: "Test", record:
CKRecord(recordType: "Cities", recordID: CKRecord.ID(recordName:
"Test")))))
    }
}
```

Listing 15-30: *Showing the asset*

The view in Listing 15-30 receives the information about the selected city through the `selectedCity` property. From this property, the view gets the city's picture and name and shows them to the user. As a result, every time the user selects a city, the asset is turned into an image and shown on the screen.

In this example, we always load the same image from the bundle. We will study how to get images from the Photo Library and take photos from the camera in Chapter 16.

 Do It Yourself: Update the `insertCity()` method in the `AppData` class with the code in Listing 15-27, the `CityViewModel` structure in the model with the code in Listing 15-28, and the `ShowCitiesView` view with the code in Listing 15-29. Download the nopicture.png and the Toronto.jpg images from our website. Add the nopicture.png image to the Assets Catalog and the Toronto.jpg file to the project (we read this file from the bundle). Create a SwiftUI file with the name ShowPictureView.swift for the code in Listing 15-30. Run the application, select a country and add a new city. Select the city. You should see the Toronto.jpg image on the screen.

 IMPORTANT: Uploading and downloading images takes time. Therefore, it is better to keep a local cache, so the users don't have to wait for the images to download every time they want to see them. We will learn how to store the information locally later in this chapter.

(Basic) **Subscriptions**

The previous examples fetch the records available and show them on the screen every time the app is launched. This means that records added to the database from another device will not be visible until the app is launched again. This is not the behavior expected by the user. When working with applications that store information online, users expects the information to be updated as soon as it becomes available. To provide this feature, CloudKit uses subscriptions. Subscriptions are queries stored by our application in the CloudKit servers. When a change occurs in the database, the query detects the modification and triggers the delivery of a Remote Notification from the iCloud servers to the copy of the app that registered the subscription.

Database subscriptions are created from the `CKDatabaseSubscription` class (a subclass of a more generic class called `CKSubscription`). The class includes the following initializer and property to create and configure the subscription.

CKDatabaseSubscription(subscriptionID: String)—This initializer creates a `CKDatabaseSubscription` object that represents a subscription with the ID specified by the **subscriptionID** attribute.

notificationInfo—This property is a value of type `NotificationInfo`, a class included in the `CKSubscription` class, that contains a configuration of the Remote Notification the server is going to send to the application when the subscription detects changes in the database.

As always, a subscription must be added to CloudKit servers with an operation, but the `CKDatabase` class offers convenient methods to create these operations as well.

save(CKSubscription, **completionHandler:** Block)**—This method stores in the servers the subscription specified by the first attribute. The **completionHandler** attribute is a closure that is executed when the process is over. The closure receives two values, a `CKSubscription` object representing the subscription we tried to save, and a `CKError` object to report errors.

delete(withSubscriptionID: String, **completionHandler:** Block)**—This method removes from the server the subscription with the ID specified by the **withSubscriptionID** attribute. The **completionHandler** attribute is a closure that is executed when the process is over. The closure receives two values, a string with the subscription ID that we tried to delete and a `CKError` object to report errors.

After our app registers a subscription in the servers, we must listen to Remote Notifications and download the changes. The first step our application has to take to be able to receive these notifications is to register with the iCloud servers. The `UIApplication` class offers the following method for this purpose.

registerForRemoteNotifications()—This method registers the app in the iCloud servers to receive Remote Notifications. A token is generated to identify each copy of our app, so the notifications are delivered to the right user.

To report to our application that a Remote Notification was received, the `UIApplication` object calls a method in the app's delegate. The following is the method defined by the `UIApplicationDelegate` class for this purpose.

application(UIApplication, **didReceiveRemoteNotification:** Dictionary, **fetch-CompletionHandler:** Block)**—This method is called by the application on its delegate when a Remote Notification is received. The **didReceiveRemoteNotification** attribute is a dictionary with information about the notification, and the **fetchCompletionHandler** attribute is a closure that we must execute after all the custom tasks are performed. The closure must be called with a value that describes the result of the operation. For this purpose, UIKit offers the `UIBackgroundFetchResult` enumeration with the values `newData` (new data was downloaded), `noData` (no data was downloaded), and `failed` (the app failed to download the data).

Setting up a subscription on CloudKit servers is easy, but because subscriptions report the changes through Remote Notifications, there are several steps we must take to prepare our application. We will begin with the changes we have to introduce in the `AppDelegate` class of our example. Here, we need to call the `registerForRemoteNotifications()` method of the `UIApplication` object as soon as the application is launched to tell the system that we want to register the application to receive Remote Notifications from iCloud servers (the Apple Push Notification service). If the registration is successful, the system calls the delegate method every time a notification is received, so we must implement this method as well.

```
import UIKit
import CloudKit

@UIApplicationMain
class AppDelegate: UIResponder, UIApplicationDelegate {
   var myData: AppData!
```

```
func application(_ application: UIApplication,
didFinishLaunchingWithOptions launchOptions:
[UIApplication.LaunchOptionsKey: Any]?) -> Bool {
    let listDefault = ["subscriptionSaved": false, "zoneCreated":
false]
    UserDefaults.standard.register(defaults: listDefault)
    application.registerForRemoteNotifications()

    myData = AppData()
    myData.configureDatabase(executeClosure: {})

    return true
}
func application(_ application: UIApplication,
configurationForConnecting connectingSceneSession: UISceneSession,
options: UIScene.ConnectionOptions) -> UISceneConfiguration {
    return UISceneConfiguration(name: "Default Configuration",
sessionRole: connectingSceneSession.role)
}
func application(_ application: UIApplication,
didReceiveRemoteNotification userInfo: [AnyHashable : Any],
fetchCompletionHandler completionHandler: @escaping
(UIBackgroundFetchResult) -> Void) {
    let notification = CKNotification(fromRemoteNotificationDictionary:
userInfo) as? CKDatabaseNotification
    if notification != nil {
        myData.checkUpdates(finishClosure: { (result) in
            let main = OperationQueue.main
            main.addOperation({
                completionHandler(result)
            })
        })
    }
}
}
```

Listing 15-31: Processing Remote Notifications

Subscriptions only report changes in customs zones. Therefore, if we want to receive notifications, besides creating the subscription we also have to create a record zone and store all our records in it. Therefore, the first thing we do when the application is launched, is to store two Boolean values in the User Defaults database called "subscriptionSaved" and "zoneCreated". These values will be used later to know whether we already have created the subscription and the custom zone.

Next, we call the `registerForRemoteNotifications()` method on the `UIApplication` object to register the application with iCloud servers and a method called `configureDatabase()` that we are going to define later in our `AppData` class to create the subscription and the custom zone for the first time.

The `registerForRemoteNotifications()` method prepares the application to receive notifications, but the notifications are processed by the delegate method. The first thing we have to do in this method is to check whether the notification received is a notification sent by a CloudKit server. For this purpose, the CloudKit framework includes the `CKNotification` class with properties we can use to process the dictionary and read its values. The class includes the following initializer.

CKNotification(fromRemoteNotificationDictionary: Dictionary)—This initializer creates a `CKNotification` object from the information included in the notification (the value of the `userInfo` parameter in the delegate method).

Because CloudKit servers can send other types of notifications, after we get the `CKNotification` object with this initializer, we check whether the notification received is of type `CKDatabaseNotification` with the `as?` operator. In case of success, we proceed to download the new data from the application.

Before going to the process of downloading the new information from CloudKit servers, we must consider that the system requires us to report the result of the operation. Notifications may be received when the application is closed or in the background. If this happens, the system launches our application and puts it in the background to allow it to connect to the servers and process the information. But because this process consumes resources, the system needs to know when the operation is over and therefore it requires us to report it by calling the closure received by the `completionHandler` parameter with a `UIBackgroundFetchResult` enumeration value that determines what happened (`newData` if we downloaded new data, `noData` if there was nothing to download, and `failed` if the process failed). By calling the closure, we tell the system that the process is over, but because the operations are performed asynchronously, we can't do it until they are finished. That is why, in the example of Listing 15-31, we send a closure to the method we use to download the new information which sole purpose is to execute the `completionHandler` closure with the value returned by the operation.

All the code we need to prepare our application is ready. Now we must implement the methods that are going to contact the CloudKit servers and process the information. In the application's delegate, we call two methods of our `AppData` class: the `configureDatabase()` method to create the subscription and the zone, and the `checkUpdates()` method to download and process the information. The following is our implementation of the `configureDatabase()` method.

```
func configureDatabase(executeClosure: @escaping () -> Void) {
    let userSettings = UserDefaults.standard
    if !userSettings.bool(forKey: "subscriptionSaved") {
        let newSubscription = CKDatabaseSubscription(subscriptionID:
"updatesDatabase")
        let info = CKSubscription.NotificationInfo()
        info.shouldSendContentAvailable = true
        newSubscription.notificationInfo = info

        database.save(newSubscription, completionHandler: { (subscription,
error) in
            if error == nil {
                userSettings.set(true, forKey: "subscriptionSaved")
            } else {
                print("Error Creating Subscription")
            }
        })
    }
    if !userSettings.bool(forKey: "zoneCreated") {
        let newZone = CKRecordZone(zoneName: "listPlaces")
        database.save(newZone, completionHandler: { (zone, error) in
            if error == nil {
                userSettings.set(true, forKey: "zoneCreated")
                executeClosure()
            } else {
                print("Error Creating Zone")
            }
        })
    } else {
```

Chapter 15 - iCloud

```
          executeClosure()
      }
  }
}
```

Listing 15-32: Configuring the database

Every process executed in CloudKit servers has to be performed through asynchronous operations. This means that we must consider the order in which the operations are executed. For some operations, the order doesn't matter, but for others it is crucial. For instance, we cannot store records in a zone before the zone is created. As we have seen in Chapter 4, we can use Dependencies or even Dispatch Groups to control the order in which operations are performed, but we can also use closures to execute code only after an operation is over, and this is the approach we take in this example. The procedure is as follows. Every time we call the `configureDatabase()` method to create the subscription and the zone, we send a closure to the method with the code we want to be executed once the operation is over. This way, we make sure that the operations are over before doing anything else.

 The Basics: There are two types of closures, escaping and non-escaping. An escaping closure lives outside the function in which it is declared, and a non-escaping closure is destroyed (removed from memory) when the execution of the function is over. By default, all closures are non-escaping, this is why in the `configureDatabase()` method of Listing 15-32 we use the `@escaping` keyword to declare the closure as escaping and being able to execute it outside the method (see Listing 3-26).

The first thing we do in the `configureDatabase()` method is to check the subscriptionSaved value in the User Defaults to know if the subscription was already created. If not, we use the `CKDatabaseSubscription` initializer to create the subscription and then define the `notificationInfo` property to configure the notifications that are going to be sent by the server. For this purpose, the framework defines the `CKNotificationInfo` class. This class includes multiple properties to configure Remote Notifications for CloudKit, but database subscriptions only require us to set the `shouldSendContentAvailable` property to `true`. Next, the subscription is saved in the server with the `save()` method of the `CKDatabase` object and the subscriptionSaved value is changed to `true` if the operation is successful.

Next, we create the custom zone. Again, we check the Boolean value stored in User Defaults to know if the zone was already created, and if not, we create a zone called listPlaces to store our records. In this case, if the operation is successful, besides assigning the value `true` to the zoneCreated value, we also must execute the closure. This is because we don't care whether the subscription was saved or not, but we have to be sure that the zone was created before trying to store any records in it. Notice that the closure is also called if the zone was already created to make sure that its code is always executed.

Finally, we have to create the `checkUpdates()` method to download and process the changes in the database. As we already mentioned, this method has to receive a closure to be able to report to the system the result of the operation, but we also have to consider that there could have being an error when we tried to create the subscription and the zone, so we have to call the `configureDatabase()` method again just in case.

```
func checkUpdates(finishClosure: @escaping (UIBackgroundFetchResult) ->
Void) {
   self.configureDatabase(executeClosure: {
      let main = OperationQueue.main
      main.addOperation({
         self.downloadUpdates(finishClosure: finishClosure)
```

```
            })
        })
}
```

Listing 15-33: Initiating the process to get the updates from the server

The `checkUpdates()` method receives the closure we have to execute to report the result of the operation and then calls the `configureDatabase()` method to make sure that the database is configured properly. The value we send to this method is another closure that contains the code we want to execute after we make sure that the zone was created.

To simplify the code, we moved the statements to an additional method called `downloadUpdates()`, so after confirming that the zone was created, we call this method with a reference to the closure received by the `configureDatabase()` method.

 The Basics: Passing closures from one function to another is a way to control the order in which the code is executed when we use asynchronous operations. We chose this programming pattern for the examples in this chapter because it simplifies the code, but as mentioned before, you can use Dependencies or Dispatch Groups. For more information, see Chapter 4.

Before implementing the `downloadUpdates()` method and process the changes in the database, we have to study the operations provided by the CloudKit framework for this purpose. The operation to fetch the list of changes available in the database is created from a subclass of the `CKDatabaseOperation` class called `CKFetchDatabaseChangesOperation`. This class includes the following initializer.

CKFetchDatabaseChangesOperation(previousServerChangeToken: CKServerChangeToken?)—This initializer creates a `CKFetchDatabaseChangesOperation` object to fetch changes from a database. The attribute is a token that determines which changes were already fetched. If we specify a token, only the changes that occurred after the token was created are fetched.

The class also includes properties to define completion handlers for every step of the process.

recordZoneWithIDChangedBlock—This property sets a closure that is executed to report which zones present changes. The closure receives a value of type `CKRecordZone.ID` with the ID of the zone that changed.

changeTokenUpdatedBlock—This property sets a closure that is executed to report the last database token. The closure receives an object of type `CKServerChangeToken` with the current token that we can store to send to subsequent operations.

fetchDatabaseChangesCompletionBlock—This property sets a closure that is executed when the operation is over. The closure receives three values, a `CKServerChangeToken` object with the last token, a Boolean value that indicates if there are more changes available, and a `CKError` value to report errors.

After this operation is completed, we must perform another operation to download the changes. For this purpose, the framework includes the `CKFetchRecordZoneChangesOperation` class with the following initializer.

CKFetchRecordZoneChangesOperation(recordZoneIDs: [CKRecordZone.ID], **configurationsByRecordZoneID:** Dictionary)—This initializer creates a `CKFetchRecordZoneChangesOperation` object to download changes from a database. The **recordZoneIDs** attribute is an array with the IDs of all the zones that present changes, and the **configurationsByRecordZoneID** attribute is a dictionary with configuration values for each zone. The dictionary takes `CKRecordZone.ID` objects as keys and options determined by an object of the `ZoneConfiguration` class. The class includes three properties to define the options: `desiredKeys` (array of strings with the keys we want to retrieve), `previousServerChangeToken` (`CKServerChangeToken` object with the current token), and `resultsLimit` (integer that determines the maximum number of records to retrieve).

The `CKFetchRecordZoneChangesOperation` class also includes properties to define completion handlers for every step of the process.

recordChangedBlock—This property sets a closure that is executed when a new or updated record is downloaded. The closure receives a `CKRecord` object representing the record that changed.

recordWithIDWasDeletedBlock—This property sets a closure that is executed when the operation finds a deleted record. The closure receives two values, a `CKRecord.ID` object with the ID of the record that was deleted, and a string with the record's type.

recordZoneChangeTokensUpdatedBlock—This property sets a closure that is executed when the change token for the zone is updated. The closure receives three values, a `CKRecordZone.ID` with the ID of the zone associated to the token, a `CKServerChangeToken` object with the current token, and a `Data` structure with the last token sent by the app to the server.

recordZoneFetchCompletionBlock—This property sets a closure that is executed when the operation finishes downloading the changes of a zone. The closure receives five values, a `CKRecordZone.ID` with the zone's ID, a `CKServerChangeToken` object with the current token, a `Data` structure with the last token sent by the app to the server, a Boolean value that indicates if there are more changes available, and a `CKError` value to report errors.

fetchRecordZoneChangesCompletionBlock—This property sets a closure that is executed after the operation is over. The closure receives a `CKError` value to report errors.

CloudKit servers use tokens to know which changes were already sent to every copy of the app, so the information is not downloaded twice from the same device. If a device stores or modifies a record, the server generates a new token, so next time a device accesses the servers only the changes introduced after the last token will be downloaded, as shown in Figure 15-23.

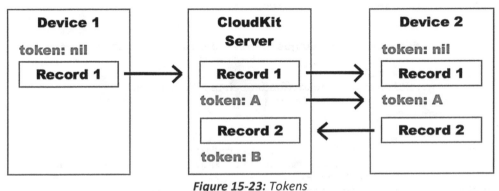

Figure 15-23: Tokens

In the process depicted in Figure 15-23, the app in Device 1 stores a new record in the server (Record 1). To report the changes, the server generates a new token (A). When the app in Device 2 connects to the server, the server detects that this device does not have the latest token, so it returns Record 1 and the current token (A) to update the state in this device. If later the user decides to create a new record from Device 2 (Record 2), a new token will be created (B). The next time Device 1 connects with the server, it will find that its token is different than the server's token, so it will download the modifications inserted after its token (in this case, every change on the server, including Record 1).

Tokens are great because they allow us to only get the latest changes, but this process is not automatic, we are responsible of storing the current tokens and preserve the state for our app. The server creates a token for the database and a token for each of the custom zones. For our example, we need two tokens, one to keep track of the changes in the database and another for the custom zone created by the `configureDatabase()` method. To work with these values, we are going to use two variables `changeToken` for the database token and `fetchChangeToken` for the token of our custom zone, and we are going to store them permanently in User Settings for future reference. All this process is performed by the `downloadUpdates()` method, as shown next.

```
func downloadUpdates(finishClosure: @escaping (UIBackgroundFetchResult) -
> Void) {
    var changeToken: CKServerChangeToken!
    var changeZoneToken: CKServerChangeToken!

    let userSettings = UserDefaults.standard
    if let data = userSettings.value(forKey: "changeToken") as? Data {
        if let token = try? NSKeyedUnarchiver.unarchivedObject(ofClass:
CKServerChangeToken.self, from: data) {
            changeToken = token
        }
    }
    if let data = userSettings.value(forKey: "changeZoneToken") as? Data {
        if let token = try? NSKeyedUnarchiver.unarchivedObject(ofClass:
CKServerChangeToken.self, from: data) {
            changeZoneToken = token
        }
    }
    var zonesIDs: [CKRecordZone.ID] = []
    let operation =
CKFetchDatabaseChangesOperation(previousServerChangeToken: changeToken)
    operation.recordZoneWithIDChangedBlock = { (zoneID) in
        zonesIDs.append(zoneID)
    }
    operation.changeTokenUpdatedBlock = { (token) in
        changeToken = token
    }
    operation.fetchDatabaseChangesCompletionBlock = { (token, more, error)
in
        if error != nil {
            finishClosure(UIBackgroundFetchResult.failed)
        } else if !zonesIDs.isEmpty {
            changeToken = token

            let configuration =
CKFetchRecordZoneChangesOperation.ZoneConfiguration()
            configuration.previousServerChangeToken = changeZoneToken
            let fetchOperation =
CKFetchRecordZoneChangesOperation(recordZoneIDs: zonesIDs,
configurationsByRecordZoneID: [zonesIDs[0]: configuration])
```

```swift
        fetchOperation.recordChangedBlock = { (record) in
            let main = OperationQueue.main
            main.addOperation {
                if record.recordType == "Countries" {
                    let index = self.listCountries.firstIndex(where: {
(item) in
                        return item.id == record.recordID
                    })
                    let newCountry = Country(name: record["name"], record:
record)
                    let newItem = CountryViewModel(id: record.recordID,
country: newCountry)
                    if index != nil {
                        self.listCountries[index!] = newItem
                    } else {
                        self.listCountries.append(newItem)
                    }
                    self.listCountries.sort(by: { $0.countryName <
$1.countryName })
                }
            }
        }
        fetchOperation.recordWithIDWasDeletedBlock = { (recordID,
recordType) in
            let main = OperationQueue.main
            main.addOperation {
                if recordType == "Countries" {
                    let index = self.listCountries.firstIndex(where:
{ (item) in
                        return item.id == recordID
                    })
                    if index != nil {
                        self.listCountries.remove(at: index!)
                    }
                    self.listCountries.sort(by: { $0.countryName <
$1.countryName })
                }
            }
        }
        fetchOperation.recordZoneChangeTokensUpdatedBlock = { (zoneID,
token, data) in
            changeZoneToken = token
        }
        fetchOperation.recordZoneFetchCompletionBlock = { (zoneID,
token, data, more, error) in
            if error != nil {
                print("Error")
            } else {
                changeZoneToken = token
            }
        }
        fetchOperation.fetchRecordZoneChangesCompletionBlock = { (error)
in
            if error != nil {
                finishClosure(UIBackgroundFetchResult.failed)
            } else {

                if changeToken != nil {
                    if let data = try?
NSKeyedArchiver.archivedData(withRootObject: changeToken!,
requiringSecureCoding: false) {
```

```
                        userSettings.set(data, forKey: "changeToken")
                    }
                }
                if changeZoneToken != nil {
                    if let data = try?
NSKeyedArchiver.archivedData(withRootObject: changeZoneToken!,
requiringSecureCoding: false) {
                        userSettings.set(data, forKey: "changeZoneToken")
                    }
                }
                finishClosure(UIBackgroundFetchResult.newData)
            }
        }
        self.database.add(fetchOperation)
    } else {
        finishClosure(UIBackgroundFetchResult.noData)
    }
}
database.add(operation)
}
```

Listing 15-34: Downloading the updates from the server

This is a very long method that we need to study piece by piece. As mentioned before, we start by defining the variables we are going to use to store the tokens (one for the database and another for the custom zone). Next, we check if there are tokens already stored in the User Defaults database. Because the tokens are instances of the CKServerChangeToken class, we can't store their values directly in User Defaults, we first must convert them into Data structures. That is why, when we read the values in the User defaults, we cast them as Data with the as? operator and then unarchive them with the unarchivedObject() method of the NSKeyedUnarchiver class (see Chapter 14).The first time we do this, there won't be any values stored in User Defaults and therefore the values of the variables will be nil and all the changes will be downloaded from the database.

Next, we configure the operations necessary to get the updates from the server. We must perform two operations on the database, one to download the list of changes available and another to download the actual changes and show them to the user. The operations are performed and then the results are reported to the closures assigned to their properties.

The first operation we need to perform is the CKFetchDatabaseChangesOperation operation. Its initializer requires the previous database token to get only the changes that are not available on the device, so we pass the value of the changeToken property. Next, we define the closures for each of its properties. The first property defined in our example is recordZoneWithIDChangedBlock. The closure assigned to this property is executed every time the system finds a zone whose content has changed. In this closure, we add the zone ID to an array to keep a reference of each zone that changed. Something similar happens with the closure assigned next to the changeTokenUpdatedBlock property. This closure is executed every time the system decides to perform the operation again to download the changes in separate processes. To make sure that we only receive the changes that we did not process yet, we update the changeToken property with the current token. The last property we have defined for this operation is fetchDatabaseChangesCompletionBlock. The closure assigned to this property is executed to let the app know that the operation is over, and this is the signal that indicates that we have all the information we need to begin downloading the changes with the second operation. This last closure receives three values: the latest database token, a Boolean value that indicates whether there are more changes available (by default, the system takes care of fetching all the changes, so we don't need to consider this value), and a CKError structure to report errors. If there are errors (error != nil), we execute the finishClosure

closure with the value `failed` and the operation is over. If there are no errors, we check if the `zoneIDs` array contains any zone ID. If it is empty, it means that there are no changes available and therefore we execute the `finishClosure` closure with the value `noData` (see the `else` at the end of the method), but if the array is not empty, we configure the `CKFetchRecordZoneChangesOperation` operation to get the changes.

The `CKFetchRecordZoneChangesOperation` operation is performed over the zones that changed, so we must initialize it with the array of zone IDs generated by the previous operation. The initializer also requires a dictionary with the zone IDs as keys and `ZoneConfiguration` objects that include the previous token for each zone as values. Because in this example we only work with one zone, we read the first element of the `zonesIDs` array to get the ID of our custom zone and provide a `ZoneConfiguration` object with the current token stored in the `changeZoneToken` property.

This operation works like the previous one. The changes are fetched, and the results are reported to the closures assigned to its properties. The first property declared in Listing 15-34 is `recordChangedBlock`. This closure is called every time a new or updated record is received. Here, we check if the record is of type Countries and store it in the corresponding array (in this application we only need to update the countries because the cities are always updated when a country is selected). We use the `firstIndex()` method to look for duplicates. If the record already exists, we update its values, otherwise, we add the record to the list.

The closure of the `recordWithIDWasDeletedBlock` property defined next is executed every time the app receives the ID of a deleted record (a record that was deleted from the CloudKit database). In this case, we do the same as before but instead of updating or adding the record we remove it from the list with the `remove()` method.

The closures of the next two properties, `recordZoneChangeTokensUpdatedBlock` and `recordZoneFetchCompletionBlock`, are executed when the process completes a cycle, either because the system decides to download the data in multiple processes, or the operation finished fetching the changes in a zone. Depending on the characteristics of our application, we may need to perform some tasks in these closures, but in our example, we just have to store the current token in the `fetchChangeToken` variable so the next time the operation is performed we only get the changes we have not downloaded yet.

Finally, the closure assigned to the `fetchRecordZoneChangesCompletionBlock` property is executed to report that the operation is over. This closure receives a value to report errors. If there is an error (`error != nil`), we execute the `finishClosure` closure with the value `failed`, to tell the system that the operation failed, but if no error is found, we store the current tokens in the User Defaults database and execute the `finishClosure` closure with the value `newData` to tell the system that new data has been downloaded. Notice that to store the tokens we have to turn them into `Data` structures and encode them with the `archivedData()` method of the `NSKeyedArchiver` class, as we mentioned before.

Lastly, after the definition of each operation and their properties, we call the `add()` method of the `CKDatabase` object to add them to the database.

There is one more change we must introduce to our model for subscriptions to work. So far, we have stored the records in the zone by default, but as we already mentioned, subscriptions require the records to be stored in a custom zone. The following are the changes we have to introduce to the `insertCountry()` and `insertCity()` methods to store the records inside the listPlaces zone created before.

```
func insertCountry(name: String) {
    configureDatabase(executeClosure: {
        let zone = CKRecordZone(zoneName: "listPlaces")
        let id = CKRecord.ID(recordName: "idcountry-\(UUID())", zoneID:
zone.zoneID)
        let record = CKRecord(recordType: "Countries", recordID: id)
        record.setObject(name as NSString, forKey: "name")

        self.database.save(record, completionHandler: { (recordSaved,
error) in
            if error == nil {
                let main = OperationQueue.main
                main.addOperation {
                    let newCountry = Country(name: record["name"], record:
record)
                    let newItem = CountryViewModel(id: record.recordID,
country: newCountry)
                    self.listCountries.append(newItem)
                    self.listCountries.sort(by: { $0.countryName <
$1.countryName })
                }
            } else {
                print("Error: record not saved \(error!)")
            }
        })
    })
}
func insertCity(name: String, country: CKRecord.ID) {
    configureDatabase(executeClosure: {
        let zone = CKRecordZone(zoneName: "listPlaces")
        let id = CKRecord.ID(recordName: "idcity-\(UUID())", zoneID:
zone.zoneID)
        let record = CKRecord(recordType: "Cities", recordID: id)
        record.setObject(name as NSString, forKey: "name")

        let reference = CKRecord.Reference(recordID: country, action:
.deleteSelf)
        record.setObject(reference, forKey: "country")

        let bundle = Bundle.main
        if let fileURL = bundle.url(forResource: "Toronto", withExtension:
"jpg") {
            let asset = CKAsset(fileURL: fileURL)
            record.setObject(asset, forKey: "picture")
        }
        self.database.save(record, completionHandler: { (recordSaved,
error) in
            if error == nil {
                let main = OperationQueue.main
                main.addOperation {
                    let newCity = City(name: record["name"], record: record)
                    let newItem = CityViewModel(id: record.recordID, city:
newCity)
                    self.listCities.append(newItem)
                    self.listCities.sort(by: { $0.cityName < $1.cityName })
                }
            } else {
                print("Error: record not saved \(error!)")
            }
```

```
        })
    })
}
```

Listing 15-35: Storing the records in a custom zone

All we have to do to store a record in a custom zone is to create the `CKRecordZone` object and assign its ID to the record ID by including it in the initializer of the `CKRecord.ID` object.

Notice that the code for both methods was inserted in a closure assigned to the `configureDatabase()` method. We call this method again, so every time a record is inserted, we check that the subscription and the zone were already added to the database. The `configureDatabase()` method checks that the database is configured properly and then calls the closure to execute the code.

 Do It Yourself: Update the `AppDelegate` class with the code of Listing 15-32. Add the methods of Listings 15-32, 15-33, and 15-34 to the `AppData` class. Update the `insertCountry()` and `insertCity()` methods of the `AppData` class with the code in Listing 15-35. Run the application in two different devices and insert a new country. You should see the country appear on the screen of the second device.

 IMPORTANT: Remote Notifications can only be tested on a real device (they do not work on the simulator). If you only have one device, you can test your applications with the CloudKit dashboard. Open the Data panel, select the Countries type from the Type option, click on the New Record button at the bottom-left corner, insert the name of the country in the panel on the right, and press the Save button to save the record. The new record should appear on the screen of your device.

Basic Errors

Errors are an important part of CloudKit. The service is highly dependable on the network connection and how reliable it is. If the device is disconnected or the connection is not good enough, the operations are not performed or may be lost. CloudKit does not provide a standard solution for these situations, it just returns an error and expects our app to solve the problem. If the user creates a new record but at that moment the device is disconnected from the Internet, our app is responsible of registering the incident and trying again later.

The most common error is related to the user's iCloud account. Every user must have an iCloud account to access CloudKit servers. If an iCloud account is not set on the device or has restrictions due to Parental Control or Device Management, the app will not be able to connect to the CloudKit servers. The `CKContainer` class offers the following method to check the status of the user's account.

accountStatus(completionHandler: Block)—This method attempts to access the user's iCloud account and calls the closure specified by the **completionHandler** attribute with a value that determines the current state. The closure receives two values, a `CKAccountStatus` enumeration to report the current state and a `CKError` value to report errors. The enumeration includes the values `couldNotDetermine`, `available`, `restricted`, and `noAccount`.

If the status of the iCloud account changes during execution, the system posts a notification that we can use to perform updates and synchronization tasks.

CKAccountChanged—This notification is posted by the system when the status of the user's iCloud account registered on the device changes.

If our app receives an error because the iCloud account is not available or CloudKit servers failed to perform a task, we cannot just ignore it, we have to program our app to try to perform the operation again later and make it transparent enough to still offer a good user experience. There are different ways we can organize these background tasks. An alternative is to store information about every change performed over the data in a local storage and check the list later to perform pending operations. For instance, we can modify the `insertCountry()` method in our model to keep track of changes and perform pending operations every time the user inserts a new country.

```
var listChanges: Set<String> = []
func insertCountry(name: String) {
   self.listChanges.insert(name)

   configureDatabase(executeClosure: {
      let container = CKContainer.default()
      container.accountStatus(completionHandler: { (status, error) in
         if status == CKAccountStatus.available &&
!self.listChanges.isEmpty {
            for itemName in self.listChanges {
               let zone = CKRecordZone(zoneName: "listPlaces")
               let id = CKRecord.ID(recordName: "idcountry-\(UUID())",
zoneID: zone.zoneID)
               let record = CKRecord(recordType: "Countries", recordID:
id)
               record.setObject(itemName as NSString, forKey: "name")

               self.database.save(record, completionHandler: {
(recordSaved, error) in
                  if error == nil {
                     let main = OperationQueue.main
                     main.addOperation {
                        let newCountry = Country(name: record["name"],
record: record)
                        let newItem = CountryViewModel(id:
record.recordID, country: newCountry)
                        self.listCountries.append(newItem)
                        self.listCountries.sort(by: { $0.countryName <
$1.countryName })
                        self.listChanges.remove(itemName)
                     }
                  } else {
                     print("Error: record not saved \(error!)")
                  }
               })
            }
         }
      })
   })
}
```

Listing 15-36: Checking CloudKit availability

The code in Listing 15-36 adds a property called `listChanges` to the observable object to store a set of `String` values. When the `insertCountry()` method is called to add a new country to the CloudKit database, the first thing the method does is to add the name inserted by the user to this Set. This way, we keep a list of the countries that must be saved in CloudKit servers. In the next step, we check whether the app can access the user's iCloud account or not with the `accountStatus()` method and then go through the list of names in the `listChanges` property to upload all the countries on the list. Because we are keeping a list of the countries that must be uploaded to CloudKit, those that are not stored due to temporary failure will be stored the next time this code is executed.

Do It Yourself: Add the `listChanges` property to the `AppData` class. Update the `insertCountry()` method with the code in Listing 15-36. Run the application in a device and activate Airplane Mode from Settings. Add new countries. The names will be stored in the `listChanges` property, but they will not be saved to CloudKit. Deactivate Airplane Mode and insert another country. Now all the countries should be uploaded to CloudKit servers. You can query records from the Data panel in your CloudKit Dashboard to check the state of the database at any time.

IMPORTANT: This example was provided for didactic purposes. We only keep track of the records that have to be saved (we do nothing for those that have to be modified or deleted) and we only process the values on the list when the user inserts a new book, but the app should perform these tasks for every type of operation and check whether the operations were completed or not multiple times during execution. Also, this example stores the list in a property, which means that when the user closes the app, the information is lost. We will learn how to store the information permanently with Core Data next.

In the last example, we just checked whether an error occurred or not and proceeded accordingly, but we can also identify the type of error returned by the operation reading the value received by the closure. Errors are sent to the closures as objects that conform to the `Error` protocol. Every time we want to read an error, we must cast it to the right type. In CloudKit, the errors are of type `CKError`, which is a structure initialized from an object of type `NSError` and therefore it inherits the following property to return the error code.

code—This property returns a value that identifies the error found. The property is of type `CKError.Code`, an enumeration inside the `CKError` structure with values that correspond to each type of error produced by CloudKit. The list of values available is extensive. The most frequently used are `partialFailure`, `networkUnavailable`, `networkFailure`, `serviceUnavailable`, `unknownItem`, `operationCancelled`, `changeTokenExpired`, `quotaExceeded`, `zoneNotFound`, and `limitExceeded`.

The following example uses the `fetch()` method of the `CKDatabase` object to check whether a zone exists in the database. In the completion handler, we cast the value of the `error` parameter as a `CKError` structure and then compare the value of its `code` property against the value `zoneNotFound` of the `Code` enumeration. If the values match, it means that the zone we tried to access does not exist.

```
func checkZones() {
    let newZone = CKRecordZone(zoneName: "myNewZone")
    database.fetch(withRecordZoneID: newZone.zoneID, completionHandler: {
(zone, error) in
        if let error = error as? CKError {
            if error.code == CKError.Code.zoneNotFound {
                print("Not found")
            } else {
```

```
            print ("Zone Found")
         }
      }
   })
}
```

 Do It Yourself: Add the `checkZones()` method in Listing 15-37 to the `AppData` class. Call this method from the `AppData` class' initializer (`self.checkZones()`). Run the application again. You should see the message "Not Found" on the console because we are trying to access a zone with a different name than the one we have created before.

 IMPORTANT: As we already mentioned, how to handle errors depends on the error itself and the characteristics of your application, but you cannot ignore them, you always have to perform a task that solves the problem or tells the user what to do or otherwise your app sooner or later will become useless. To learn more about the errors returned by CloudKit operations, you can read the descriptions of all the values included in the `CKError.Code` enumeration. The link is available on our website.

(Basic) CloudKit and Core Data

Loading the information from CloudKit every time the app is launched is not practical or even reliable. The device may get disconnected, the servers may not be always available, or the response may take too long to arrive. For these reasons, Subscriptions are usually implemented to keep data updated in a local storage. The application stores the information in a local storage, like a Core Data persistent store, and uses CloudKit to share that data with other devices and keep them synchronized. Using Cloudkit in this manner, we can create an application that automatically uploads and downloads the data to the servers, so we always display the same information to the user no matter where the app is running.

Synchronizing a Core Data persistent store with a CloudKit database requires multiple methods to control the information that is uploaded and downloaded from the servers, to check for errors, to resolve conflicts, and to make sure that no value gets duplicated or lost, which can take thousands of lines of code. Fortunately, along with SwiftUI, Apple introduced a new API that performs all this work for us. All we have to do is to create the Core Data stack with the `NSPersistentCloudKitContainer` class instead of the `NSPersistentContainer` class and the persistent store is automatically synchronized. This class is a subclass of the `NSPersistentContainer` class and therefore it includes the following initializer.

NSPersistentCloudKitContainer(name: String)—This initializer creates a persistent store with the name specified by the attribute.

Besides the common properties, like the `viewContext` property that returns a reference to the context, this subclass also includes the following methods in case our application needs to retrieve records manually.

record(for: NSManagedObjectID)—This method returns a `CKRecord` object with the record that corresponds to the Core Data object specified by the attribute. The attribute is the object's id (returned by the `objectID` property). If no record is found, the method returns `nil`.

records(for: [NSManagedObjectID])—This method returns an array of `CKRecord` objects with the records that correspond to the Core Data objects specified by the attribute. The attribute is an array of objects ids (returned by the `objectID` property).

recordID(for: NSManagedObjectID)—This method returns a `CKRecord.ID` value with the id of the record that corresponds to the Core Data object specified by the attribute. The attribute is the object's id (returned by the `objectID` property).

recordIDs(for: [NSManagedObjectID])—This method returns an array of `CKRecord.ID` values with the ids of the records that correspond to the Core Data objects specified by the attribute. The attribute is an array of object ids (returned by the `objectID` property).

The `NSPersistentCloudKitContainer` object automatically resolves conflicts for us, but we must configure the context to determine how those conflicts are going to be solved. The `NSManagedObjectContext` class includes the following properties for this purpose.

automaticallyMergesChangesFromParent—This property sets or returns a Boolean value that determines whether the context automatically merges the changes in the persistent store and the context.

mergePolicy—This property sets or returns an object that decides the policy that the context is going to use to merge the changes in the persistent store and the context. The Core Data framework defines global variables to set standard policies. The `NSErrorMergePolicy` variable returns an error if the objects are different, the `NSMergeByPropertyStoreTrumpMergePolicy` variable replaces changes in memory by the external changes, the `NSMergeByPropertyObjectTrumpMergePolicy` replaces the external changes by the changes in memory, the `NSOverwriteMergePolicy` variable replaces the values in the persistent stored by the current changes, and the `NSRollbackMergePolicy` uses the version of the objects in the persistent store.

Because of this amazing API, creating an application that stores information locally in a Core Data persistent store and synchronizes that data with a CloudKit database is extremely simple. All we have to do is to define the Core Data stack with the `NSPersistentCloudKitContainer` class and then create the Core Data application as we always do. For instance, we can reproduce the previous example to store countries and cities. The following is the Core Data model we need for this application.

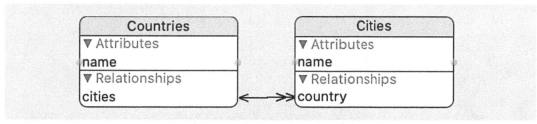

Figure 15-24: Core Data Model

For this example, we only need two entities, Countries and Cities, with only one attribute each of type String called name, and a relationship from one entity to the other (the relationship in the Countries entity has to be set to To-Many because a country can have many cities).

There is one more requirement for the model to be ready to work with CloudKit. We must select the Configuration (Figure 15-25, number 1) and check the option Used with CloudKit in the Data Model Inspector panel (Figure 15-25, number 2).

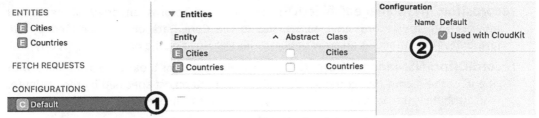

ENTITIES
Cities
Countries

FETCH REQUESTS

CONFIGURATIONS
Default

Figure 15-25: Used with CloudKit option

Do It Yourself: Create a SwiftUI project. Open the Signing & Capabilities panel, add the iCloud capability, and check the CloudKit option (see Figure 15-11). If Xcode doesn't include a container, add a container with the app's bundle as the name, and press the Refresh button. Add the Background Modes capability and check the options Background fetch and Remote Notifications. Create a Core Data model from the File menu (see Figure 14-15). Add two entities to the model called Countries and Cities. Add an attribute of type String to both entities and call it name. Add a To-Many relationship to the Countries entity called cities and a To-One relationship to the Cities entity called country. Select the Inverse value in the relationship (countries for the Cities entity and cities for the Countries entity). Select the Default configuration (Figure 15-25, number 1), open the Data Model Inspector panel on the right, and check the Used with CloudKit option (Figure 15-25, number 2).

Once the application is configured to work with CloudKit and the Core Data model is ready, we can work on our code. First, we must initialize the Core Data stack in the `AppDelegate` class, as we did before (see Listing 14-40).

```
import UIKit
import CoreData

@UIApplicationMain
class AppDelegate: UIResponder, UIApplicationDelegate {
   func application(_ application: UIApplication,
didFinishLaunchingWithOptions launchOptions:
[UIApplication.LaunchOptionsKey: Any]?) -> Bool {
      return true
   }
   func application(_ application: UIApplication,
configurationForConnecting connectingSceneSession: UISceneSession,
options: UIScene.ConnectionOptions) -> UISceneConfiguration {
      return UISceneConfiguration(name: "Default Configuration",
sessionRole: connectingSceneSession.role)
   }
   lazy var persistentContainer: NSPersistentCloudKitContainer = {
      let container = NSPersistentCloudKitContainer(name: "TestCloudKit")
      container.loadPersistentStores(completionHandler: {
(storeDescription, error) in
         if let error = error as NSError? {
            fatalError("Unresolved error \(error), \(error.userInfo)")
         }
      })
      container.viewContext.automaticallyMergesChangesFromParent = true
      container.viewContext.mergePolicy =
NSMergeByPropertyObjectTrumpMergePolicy
```

Chapter 15 - iCloud

```
        return container
    }()
}
```

Listing 15-38: Preparing Core Data to work with CloudKit

The **persistentContainer** property is set as before, but instead of returning an **NSPersistentContainer** value it returns an **NSPersistentCloudKitContainer** value to synchronize the persistent store with CloudKit servers. Another difference with previous examples is that now we must tell the context that we need to merge the changes and how to do it. For this purpose, we assign the value **true** to the **automaticallyMergesChanges-FromParent** property and the value **NSMergeByPropertyObjectTrumpMergePolicy** to the **mergePolicy** property.

And that's all it takes. From now on, all the changes introduced in the persistent store are going to be uploaded to CloudKit and every device running the application is going to be automatically synchronized. All that is left is to design the views to display the objects or add new ones. Here is the initial view for our example.

```
import SwiftUI
import CoreData

struct ContentView: View {
   @Environment(\.managedObjectContext) var dbContext
   @FetchRequest(entity: Countries.entity(), sortDescriptors:
[NSSortDescriptor(key: "name", ascending: true)]) var listCountries:
FetchedResults<Countries>
   @State private var openSheet: Bool = false

   var body: some View {
      NavigationView {
         List {
            ForEach(listCountries, id: \.self) { country in
               NavigationLink(destination:
ShowCitiesView(selectedCountry: country)) {
                  Text(country.name ?? "Undefined")
               }
            }
         }
         .navigationBarTitle("Countries")
         .navigationBarItems(trailing: Button("Add Country") {
            self.openSheet = true
         })
         .sheet(isPresented: $openSheet) {
            InsertCountryView(openSheet: self.$openSheet)
               .environment(\.managedObjectContext, self.dbContext)
         }
      }
   }
}
struct ContentView_Previews: PreviewProvider {
   static var previews: some View {
      let app = UIApplication.shared
      let delegate = app.delegate as! AppDelegate
      let dbContext = delegate.persistentContainer.viewContext
      return ContentView().environment(\.managedObjectContext, dbContext)
   }
}
```

Listing 15-39: Listing the countries stored in the persistent store

This view defines the `@FetchRequest` property to load the objects of type Countries from the persistent store and then lists those values with a `List` view. As previous examples, the view opens the `InsertCountryView` view to let the user insert a new country.

```swift
import SwiftUI
import CoreData

struct InsertCountryView: View {
    @Environment(\.managedObjectContext) var dbContext
    @Binding var openSheet: Bool
    @State private var inputName: String = ""

    var body: some View {
        VStack {
            HStack {
                Text("Country:")
                TextField("Insert Country", text: $inputName)
                    .textFieldStyle(RoundedBorderTextFieldStyle())
            }
            HStack {
                Spacer()
                Button("Save") {
                    let text = self.inputName.trimmingCharacters(in:
.whitespaces)
                    if !text.isEmpty {
                        let newCountry = Countries(context: self.dbContext)
                        newCountry.name = text
                        do {
                            try self.dbContext.save()
                        } catch {
                            print("Error saving country")
                        }
                        self.openSheet = false
                    }
                }
            }
            Spacer()
        }.padding()
    }
}
struct InsertCountryView_Previews: PreviewProvider {
    static var previews: some View {
        let app = UIApplication.shared
        let delegate = app.delegate as! AppDelegate
        let dbContext = delegate.persistentContainer.viewContext
        return InsertCountryView(openSheet: .constant(false))
            .environment(\.managedObjectContext, dbContext)
    }
}
```

Listing 15-40: Inserting new countries in the persistent store

There is also nothing new in this view. We create a new `Countries` object with the value inserted by the user when the Save button is pressed and save the context with the `save()` method, but because the application is connected to CloudKit the system automatically creates a record from the `Countries` object and uploads it to CloudKit servers.

The following is the `ShowsCitiesView` view opened when a country is selected by the user.

```
import SwiftUI
import CoreData

struct ShowCitiesView: View {
    @Environment(\.managedObjectContext) var dbContext
    @State private var openSheet: Bool = false
    let selectedCountry: Countries

    var body: some View {
        VStack {
            ListCitiesView(country: self.selectedCountry)
        }
        .navigationBarTitle(self.selectedCountry.name ?? "Undefined")
        .navigationBarItems(trailing: Button("Add City") {
            self.openSheet = true
        })
        .sheet(isPresented: $openSheet) {
            InsertCityView(openSheet: self.$openSheet, country:
self.selectedCountry)
                .environment(\.managedObjectContext, self.dbContext)
        }
    }
}
struct ListCitiesView: View {
    @FetchRequest(entity: Cities.entity(), sortDescriptors: []) var
listCities: FetchedResults<Cities>

    init(country: Countries) {
        self._listCities = FetchRequest(entity: Cities.entity(),
sortDescriptors: [NSSortDescriptor(key: "name", ascending: true)],
predicate: NSPredicate(format: "country = %@", country))
    }
    var body: some View {
        List {
            ForEach(listCities, id: \.self) { city in
                Text(city.name ?? "Undefined")
            }
        }
    }
}
struct ShowCitiesView_Previews: PreviewProvider {
    static var previews: some View {
        let app = UIApplication.shared
        let delegate = app.delegate as! AppDelegate
        let dbContext = delegate.persistentContainer.viewContext

        let country = Countries(context: dbContext)
        country.name = "Test"
        return ShowCitiesView(selectedCountry: country)
            .environment(\.managedObjectContext, dbContext)
    }
}
```

Listing 15-41: Listing the cities stored in the persistent store

This view lists the cities with a `List` view, as we did before for the countries, but because only the cities that belong to the selected country must be displayed, we define the `@FetchRequest` property in a separate view (see Listing 14-55). When this view is initialized, we use the `Countries` object to create a predicate, so only the cities that are related to that country are fetched.

The view also includes a button to let the user insert new cities. The following is the view opened by the `sheet()` modifier when the button is pressed.

```
import SwiftUI
import CoreData
struct InsertCityView: View {
    @Environment(\.managedObjectContext) var dbContext
    @Binding var openSheet: Bool
    @State private var inputName: String = ""
    let country: Countries

    var body: some View {
        VStack {
            HStack {
                Text("City:")
                TextField("Insert City", text: $inputName)
                    .textFieldStyle(RoundedBorderTextFieldStyle())
            }
            HStack {
                Spacer()
                Button("Save") {
                    let text = self.inputName.trimmingCharacters(in:
.whitespaces)
                    if !text.isEmpty {
                        let newCity = Cities(context: self.dbContext)
                        newCity.name = text
                        newCity.country = self.country
                        do {
                            try self.dbContext.save()
                        } catch {
                            print("Error saving city")
                        }
                        self.openSheet = false
                    }
                }
            }
            Spacer()
        }.padding()
    }
}
struct InsertCityView_Previews: PreviewProvider {
    static var previews: some View {
        let app = UIApplication.shared
        let delegate = app.delegate as! AppDelegate
        let dbContext = delegate.persistentContainer.viewContext

        let country = Countries(context: dbContext)
        country.name = "Test"
        return InsertCityView(openSheet: .constant(false), country:
country).environment(\.managedObjectContext, dbContext)
    }
}
```

Listing 15-42: Inserting new cities in the persistent store

Again, we just create a new `Cities` object with the value inserted by the user when the Save button is pressed and the system takes care of creating the record an uploading it to CloudKit.

The application works like in previous examples. It shows a list of the countries and cities in the persistent store, and lets the user insert new values, but now all the information is uploaded to CloudKit servers automatically and shared with other devices.

Chapter 15 - iCloud

Do It Yourself: Update the AppDelegate.swift file with the code in Listing 15-38. Replace the name in the `NSPersistentCloudKitContainer` initializer with the name of your Core Data model (the file's name). Update the SceneDelegate.swift file with the code in Listing 14-41. Update the ContentView.swift file with the code in Listing 15-39. Create SwiftUI files called InsertCountryView.swift, ShowCitiesView.swift, and InsertCityView.swift for the codes in Listings 15-40, 15-41, and 15-42. Run the application in two devices. Press the Add Country button and insert a new country. After a few seconds, you should see the same value appear on the second device. Repeat the process for the cities. Notice that it may take up to a minute for the information to be updated on the other device.

 IMPORTANT: When you create a new SwiftUI project, there is an option at the bottom called Use Core Data, and when that option is activated, another one becomes available called Use CloudKit. If you check these two options, Xcode creates a project with a Core Data model and all the code required for the `AppDelegate` class and the `SceneDelegate` class, so you don't have to type it yourself. The only thing left to do is to activate iCloud and the Background Modes and then design the interface.

Basic Deploy to Production

Once our app is ready and the definition of the schema in the CloudKit dashboard is complete, we must deploy it to production. The option to start the process is called Deploy Schema to Production and it is available in a popup menu that opens when we click the button on the left-hand side of the Development section, as shown in Figure 15-26.

Figure 15-26: Development options

The Deploy Schema to Production button opens a popup window where we can see the features that are going to be transferred to the Production environment. This includes record types and indexes, but it does not include records. If we agree, we must press the Deploy button to finish the process, and our database in CloudKit will be ready for distribution.

 IMPORTANT: The Production environment is used by apps that were submitted to Apple or built for testing. To learn how to publish your app, read Chapter 17. For more information on how to build your app for testing, visit our website and follow the links for this chapter.

Chapter 15 - iCloud

Chapter 16
Framework Integration

(Basic) ## 16.1 Integration with UIKit

SwiftUI is a new framework and, therefore, is still in development. At the time of writing, the framework does not provide all the tools required to develop a professional application and, in consequence, we still depend on older frameworks to finish our projects. For mobile applications, this means we must implement the tools provided by the UIKit framework. We have introduced UIKit before. Some of its classes are used to run the application (`UIApplication`), to load images (`UIImage`), to manage the device (`UIDevice`), the window (`UIWindow`), and some to define the delegates we use to set up the application and the scenes (`UIApplicationDelegate` and `UIWindowSceneDelegate`), but the framework also defines two basic classes to create and manage views, `UIView` and `UIViewController`. Subclasses of the `UIView` class are designed to present information on the screen, such as labels or images, or controls, such as buttons, sliders or switches. Subclasses of the `UIViewController` class are designed to manage the entire interface for a screen. They present the views to display the information and include the functionality necessary to process their values and interact with the user. To integrate these tools into a SwiftUI interface, the SwiftUI framework defines two protocols, `UIViewRepresentable` and `UIViewControllerRepresentable`.

(Basic) ### Representable View

The `UIViewRepresentable` protocol defines a structure that acts as a wrapper for objects created from the `UIView` class or its subclasses. A structure that conforms to this protocol can present a UIKit view within a SwiftUI interface. To create and manage the UIKit view, the structure must implement the following methods.

makeUIView(context: Context)—This method creates the UIKit view and returns it. The **context** attribute is a reference to a structure of type `UIViewRepresentableContext` that provides information about the state of the view.

updateUIView(UIViewType, **context:** Context)—This method updates the UIKit view with information provided by the SwiftUI interface. The first attribute is a reference to the UIKit view, and the **context** attribute is a reference to a structure of type `UIViewRepresentableContext` that provides information about the state of the view.

dismantleUIView(UIViewType, **coordinator:** Coordinator)—This type method prepares the view to be dismissed. The first attribute is a reference to the UIKit view, and the **coordinator** attribute is the object that sends values back to the SwiftUI interface.

makeCoordinator()—This method creates the object that communicates information from the UIKit view back to the SwiftUI interface.

To include a `UIView` object, or an object created from any of its subclasses, in a SwiftUI interface, we must define a structure that conforms to the `UIViewRepresentable` protocol and implement these methods. The `makeUIView()` and `updateUIView()` methods are mandatory. In the `makeUIView()` method, we must create the instance of the UIKit view and return it, and we can use the `updateUIView()` method to update the view with values coming from the SwiftUI interface, such as values inserted by the user in a text field, for example. This method is also called when there are changes in the representable view, so we can use it to update the view when the orientation of the screen changes.

If we want to send values from the UIKit view to the SwiftUI interface, we must implement the `makeCoordinator()` method. From this method, we must create an instance of a coordinator object and return it, as we will see next.

(Basic) ## Representable View Controller

The `UIViewControllerRepresentable` protocol defines a structure that acts as a wrapper for objects created from the `UIViewController` class or its subclasses. A structure that conforms to this protocol can present a UIKit view controller within a SwiftUI interface. To create and manage the view controller, the structure must implement the following methods.

makeUIViewController(context: Context)—This method creates the UIKit view controller and returns it. The **context** attribute is a reference to a structure of type `UIViewControllerRepresentableContext` that provides information about the state of the view controller.

updateUIViewController(UIViewControllerType, **context:** Context)—This method updates the UIKit view controller with information provided by the SwiftUI interface. The first attribute is a reference to the UIKit view controller, and the **context** attribute is a reference to a structure of type `UIViewControllerRepresentable-Context` that provides information about the state of the view controller.

dismantleUIViewController(UIViewControllerType, **coordinator:** Coordinator)—This type method prepares the view controller to be dismissed. The first attribute is a reference to the UIKit view controller, and the **coordinator** attribute is the object that sends values back to the SwiftUI interface.

makeCoordinator()—This method creates the object that communicates information from the UIKit view controller back to the SwiftUI interface.

This protocol works like the `UIViewControllerRepresentable` protocol. We define a structure that conforms to it and then include the methods we need to create and update the view. We will see some practical examples later in this chapter.

(Basic) ## Styles

Representable view structures can be integrated into a SwiftUI interface and their size and position can be set with SwiftUI modifiers like `frame()` or `offset()`, but the UIKit views they contain are not affected by modifiers like `foregroundColor()` or `font()`. They provide their own properties to set these values. And those values can't be defined with SwiftUI views like `Color`, either, they require UIKit classes. For instance, the foreground and background colors are defined by objects of type `UIColor`. The following are some of the class' initializers.

UIColor(red: CGFloat, **green:** CGFloat, **blue:** CGFloat, **alpha:** CGFloat)—This initializer creates a `UIColor` object with a color set by the values of its attributes. It takes values from 0.0 to 1.0. The **red** attribute defines the level of red, **green** the level of green, **blue** the level of blue, and **alpha** defines the alpha level (transparency).

UIColor(patternImage: UIImage)—This initializer creates a `UIColor` object with a color defined as the image provided by the **patternImage** attribute. The image will be replicated as many times as necessary to cover the area.

Like the `Color` view, the `UIColor` class also offers an extensive list of type properties that return a `UIColor` object with a predefined color. Some of these properties are `black`, `gray`, darkGray, lightGray, white, red, green, blue, cyan, yellow, magenta, orange, purple, and brown.

Another useful UIKit class is UIFont. This class defines a font type and therefore it is used to configure views that present text on the screen. The class includes properties and methods to store and manage fonts. The following are the class' initializer and some of its methods.

UIFont(name: String, size: CGFloat)—This initializer creates a UIFont object with the font referenced by the **name** attribute and a size determined by the **size** attribute. The **name** attribute is a string with the font's PostScript name.

preferredFont(forTextStyle: TextStyle)—This type method returns a UIFont object with the dynamic font specified by the **forTextStyle** attribute and a size specified by the user in Settings. The attribute is a property of a structure called TextStyle included in the UIFont class. The properties available are body, callout, caption1, caption2, footnote, headline, subheadline, largeTitle, title1, title2, title3.

systemFont(ofSize: CGFloat)—This type method returns a UIFont object with the font set by default on the system and a size determined by the **ofSize** attribute.

boldSystemFont(ofSize: CGFloat)—This type method returns a UIFont object with the font of type bold set by the system and a size determined by the **ofSize** attribute.

italicSystemFont(ofSize: CGFloat)—This type method returns a UIFont object with the font of type italic set by the system and a size determined by the **ofSize** attribute.

IMPORTANT: The UIColor and UIFont classes are the most useful but not the only classes available in UIKit to define the styles for the views. For more information, you can read the documentation provided by Apple or get a copy of our book iOS Apps for Masterminds, where we explain how to create applications for mobile devices using the UIKit framework.

(Medium) **Appearance**

Besides views and view controllers, SwiftUI also lacks tools to assign styles to some of its views and controls. One of the notable shortcomings are the few options available to configure the navigation bar (see Chapter 9). Fortunately, we can exploit UIKit for this purpose. Most SwiftUI views are created in the background with UIKit views, so by modifying the UIKit views we are able to modify the SwiftUI views. The problem is that SwiftUI does not provide access to the UIKit classes, all the work is done in the background by the compiler. But there is a solution. Instead of modifying the UIKit views directly, we can modify their appearance.

The UIKit framework includes several classes to define the appearance of an object. For instance, to modify the appearance of a navigation bar, we must create an instance of the UINavigationBarAppearance class. The following are some of the properties included in this class to define the styles.

backgroundColor—This property sets the bar's background color. It is a value of type UIColor.

backgroundImage—This property assigns an image to the bar's background. It is a value of type UIImage.

shadowColor—This property sets the color for the bar's shadow. It is a value of type UIColor.

titleTextAttributes—This property sets the attributes applied to the bar's title.

largeTitleTextAttributes—This property sets the attributes applied to large titles.

The values of the `titleTextAttributes` and `largeTitleTextAttributes` properties are dictionaries with keys that identify the attributes and their values. The keys are defined by a structure called `Key` included in the `NSAttributedString` class. The list of properties is extensive, with the most frequently used being `font` (`UIFont`), `foregroundColor` (`UIColor`), `strokeColor` (`UIColor`), `strokeWidth` (`NSNumber`), and `shadow` (`NSShadow`).

The navigation bar is defined by the `UINavigationBar` class. To modify the appearance of the objects created from this class, we must access the class' appearance proxy. For this purpose, the `UINavigationBar` class implements the following method.

appearance()—This type method returns the appearance proxy for the class.

Once we have access to the appearance proxy, we can modify its values. The `UINavigationBar` class defines the following properties to change the bar's appearance.

standardAppearance—This property sets the appearance of the navigation bar when it is displayed with a standard height.

compactAppearance—This property sets the appearance of the navigation bar when it is displayed with a compact height.

scrollEdgeAppearance—This property sets the appearance of the navigation bar when the content is scrolled.

The appearance of a UIKit view can be set anywhere in the code, such as when the app is launched or when the model is loaded. For instance, the following is a simple example that changes the bar's background color as soon as the view appears on the screen.

```
import SwiftUI

struct ContentView: View {
    var body: some View {
        NavigationView {
            List {
                Text("Hello World")
            }
            .navigationBarTitle("Test Bar")
        }
        .onAppear(perform: {
            let appearance = UINavigationBarAppearance()
            appearance.backgroundColor = UIColor.green

            let barAppearance = UINavigationBar.appearance()
            barAppearance.standardAppearance = appearance
            barAppearance.compactAppearance = appearance
            barAppearance.scrollEdgeAppearance = appearance
        })
    }
}
```

Listing 16-1: Modifying the appearance of the navigation bar

The closure assigned to the `onAppear()` modifier in Listing 16-1 creates an instance of the `UINavigationBarAppearance` class, assigns the color green to the `backgroundColor` property, and then assigns this object to the three properties to set the style for the bar in every possible mode. The result is shown in Figure 16-1.

Chapter 16 - Framework Integration

Figure 16-1: Navigation bar with custom appearance

In the example of Listing 16-1, we only change the background color to green, but we can modify other aspects of the bar and the title. For instance, we can change the font for large titles using the `largeTitleTextAttributes` property.

```swift
import SwiftUI

struct ContentView: View {
    var body: some View {
        NavigationView {
            List {
                Text("Hello World")
            }
            .navigationBarTitle("Test Bar")
        }
        .onAppear(perform: {
            let appearance = UINavigationBarAppearance()
            if let myfont = UIFont(name: "Horsepower-Regular", size: 50) {
                appearance.largeTitleTextAttributes = [
                    NSAttributedString.Key.font: myfont
                ]
            }
            let barAppearance = UINavigationBar.appearance()
            barAppearance.standardAppearance = appearance
            barAppearance.compactAppearance = appearance
            barAppearance.scrollEdgeAppearance = appearance
        })
    }
}
```

Listing 16-2: Changing the font for the title

This example creates a `UIFont` object with a custom font called HorsePower and assign it to the `font` attribute to change the font for large titles. The process to incorporate the font into our project is the same we used in Chapter 6 for the `Font` view. We have to drag the font's file to the Navigator Area and set the "Fonts provided by the application" option in the info.plist file (see Figure 6-13). If we do it right, we will see the large title with the custom font and the normal title with the standard font.

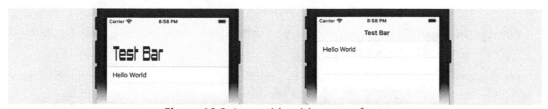

Figure 16-2: Large title with custom font

  Do It Yourself: Create a SwiftUI project. Replace the code in the ContentView.swift file with the code you want to try. If you are using a custom font, remember to drag the font's file to the Navigator Area and add it to the info.plist as we did in Chapter 6 (see Figure 6-13).

Chapter 16 - Framework Integration

16.2 Text View

At the moment of writing, SwiftUI does not include a view to insert multiple lines of text, but we can take advantage of the `UITextView` class defined by the UIKit framework to include this feature. The class provides properties and methods to create a scrollable view that can be used to present long texts. This view can display text and receive input from the user. If the size of the text surpasses the size of the view, the view allows the user to scroll it. The following is the class' initializer.

UITextView()—This initializer creates an object of the `UITextView` class with the configuration by default.

The following are the most frequently used properties included in this class.

text—This property sets or returns the text in the view. It is an optional of type `String`.

font—This property sets or returns the font used by the text view to display the text. It is an optional of type `UIFont`.

textColor—This property sets or returns the color of the text. It is an optional of type `UIColor`.

backgroundColor—This property sets or returns the view's background color. It is an optional of type `UIColor`.

textAlignment—This property sets or returns the text's alignment. It is an enumeration of type `NSTextAlignment` with the values `left`, `center`, `right`, `justified`, and `natural`.

textStorage—This property returns an object that represents the attributed text in the text view. The object is of a subclass of `NSMutableAttributedString` called `NSTextStorage`. The code provided by the `NSMutableAttributedString` class allows us to edit the text's attributes, and the code provided by the `NSTextStorage` class notifies the changes to the text view as soon as they are made.

textContainerInset—This property sets or returns a `UIEdgeInsets` value that determines the internal margins of the view. This is a structure used to define the distance between the content and the view on each side (e.g., `UIEdgeInsets(top: 20, left: 20, bottom: 20, right: 20)`).

isEditable—This property sets or returns a Boolean value that determines whether the user can edit the text inside the text view or not.

isSelectable—This property sets or returns a Boolean value that determines whether the user can select text inside the text view or not.

selectedRange—This property sets or returns the range of the text selected inside the text view. It is of type `NSRange`.

scrollRangeToVisible(NSRange)—This method scrolls the view to show on the screen the text that corresponds to the range specified by the attribute.

The `UITextView` class can also designate a delegate to call methods to report the state of the process. The object assigned as the text view's delegate must conform to the `UITextViewDelegate` protocol, which includes the following methods.

Chapter 16 - Framework Integration

textViewShouldBeginEditing(UITextView)—This method is called by the text view on the delegate object to know if edition should be allowed. The method must return a Boolean value that indicates if edition is allowed (`true`) or not (`false`).

textViewDidBeginEditing(UITextView)—This method is called by the text view on the delegate object when the user begins editing its content.

textViewShouldEndEditing(UITextView)—This method is called by the text view on the delegate object when the user tries to switch focus to another element. The method must return a Boolean value that indicates if edition should stop or not.

textViewDidEndEditing(UITextView)—This method is called by the text view on the delegate object when the element loses focus.

textView(UITextView, shouldChangeTextIn: NSRange, replacementText: String)—This method is called by the text view on the delegate object every time the user inserts or deletes a character or a string of characters. The **shouldChangeTextIn** attribute determines the range of characters on the view affected by the operation, and the **replacementText** attribute is the new character or string inserted by the user. The method returns a Boolean value that indicates whether the text should be replaced or not.

textViewDidChange(UITextView)—This method is called by the text view on the delegate object when the user changes the text or any of its attributes.

textViewDidChangeSelection(UITextView)—This method is called by the text view on the delegate object when the user selects text.

The `UITextView` class offers two properties to access the object's content: `text` and `attributedText`. With the `text` property, we can set plain text with general attributes, and with the `attributedText` property we can assign attributed text to the view. These properties store different types of texts but are connected with each other. If a value is assigned to one property, the text on the other property is automatically modified. This allows us to use the text view to display any type of text we want at any moment. If we want to display plain text, we assign a `String` value to the `text` property, but if we want to display text that presents ranges of characters with different attributes, we assign an `NSAttributedString` object to the `attributedText` property.

(Basic) **Text View in SwiftUI**

The first thing we have to do to incorporate a `UITextView` view into our SwiftUI interface is to create a structure that conforms to the `UIViewRepresentable` protocol and implement its methods. In this example, we call it `TextView`.

```
import SwiftUI
struct TextView: UIViewRepresentable {
   func makeUIView(context: Context) -> UITextView {
      let view = UITextView()
      return view
   }
   func updateUIView(_ uiView: UITextView, context: Context) {
   }
}
```

Listing 16-3: Creating a representable view

Although in this example we only use the `makeUIView()` method to create the UIKit view, we also had to implement the `updateUIView()` method because it is required by the protocol. The `makeUIView()` method is called every time a new instance of the `TextView` structure is created. In this method, we create the `UITextView` view and return it. Therefore, all we have to do to incorporate this `UITextView` view in our interface is to create an instance of the `TextView` structure, as in the following example.

```
import SwiftUI

struct ContentView: View {
    var body: some View {
        VStack {
            TextView()
        }.padding()
    }
}
```

Listing 16-4: Including a UIKit view in a SwfitUI interface

A representable view has a flexible size by default, and the `UITextView` view is shown with a white background. Therefore, the view created in Listing 16-4 is not distinguishable on the screen, but if we tap on it, we can write a text, as shown in Figure 16-3.

Figure 16-3: `UITextView` *in a SwiftUI interface*

 Do It Yourself: Create a SwiftUI project. Create a Swift file with the name TextView.swift and the code of Listing 16-3. Update the `ContentView` structure with the code in Listing 16-4. Run the application, tap the screen, and type a text. You should see the interface in Figure 16-3. Use this project to test the rest of the examples in this section.

The size of the font is determined by the `UITextView` view and therefore is not the same as the size used by SwiftUI (usually 17 points). If we try to apply modifiers to the representable view, they won't work. The only way to modify the characteristics of the `UITextView` view is from its own properties. The following example shows how to change the view's font, background and margins.

```
import SwiftUI

struct TextView: UIViewRepresentable {
    func makeUIView(context: Context) -> UITextView {
        let view = UITextView()
        view.backgroundColor = UIColor.yellow
        view.font = UIFont.systemFont(ofSize: 17)
        view.textContainerInset = UIEdgeInsets(top: 20, left: 20, bottom:
20, right: 20)
        return view
    }
    func updateUIView(_ uiView: UITextView, context: Context) {}
}
```

Listing 16-5: Configuring the UIKit view

Chapter 16 - Framework Integration

The representable view in Listing 16-5 creates the `UITextView` view and assigns new values to its properties to give the view a yellow background, a margin of 20 points (between the view and its content), and a font size of the same size as the standard font in SwiftUI (17 points). The result is shown in Figure 16-4, below.

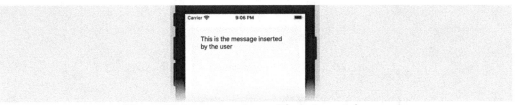

Figure 16-4: `UITextView` *with custom styles*

If we need to manage the text in the `UITextView` view from the SwiftUI interface, we can pass it with a `Binding` property. For instance, the following view defines a `@State` property with a message and pass it to the `TextView` structure.

```
import SwiftUI

struct ContentView: View {
    @State private var inputText: String = "There is a wide, yawning black
infinity. In every direction, the extension is endless; the sensation of
depth is overwhelming. And the darkness is immortal. Where light exists,
it is pure, blazing, fierce; but light exists almost nowhere, and the
blackness itself is also pure and blazing and fierce. Carl Sagan"

    var body: some View {
        VStack {
            TextView(input: $inputText)
        }.padding()
    }
}
```

Listing 16-6: Sending a value to the representable view

In the `TextView` structure we must define a `@Binding` property to receive the value and assign it to the `text` property of the `UITextView` view, as shown next.

```
import SwiftUI

struct TextView: UIViewRepresentable {
    @Binding var input: String

    func makeUIView(context: Context) -> UITextView {
        let view = UITextView()
        view.backgroundColor = UIColor.yellow
        view.font = UIFont.systemFont(ofSize: 17)
        view.textContainerInset = UIEdgeInsets(top: 20, left: 20, bottom:
20, right: 20)
        view.text = input
        return view
    }
    func updateUIView(_ uiView: UITextView, context: Context) {}
}
```

Listing 16-7: Initializing the UIKit view

Figure 16-5: `UITextView` *view with an initial value*

(Basic) ## Updating the View

If we expect the user or the application to assign new values to the text view after the `UITextView` view was created, we must assign the value of the `Binding` property to the `text` property in the `updateUIView()` method. This method is executed every time the value of a `Binding` property changes, so we can update the UIKit view from the SwiftUI interface. For instance, the following view includes a `Picker` view with three buttons. When a button is pressed, a text is assigned to a `@Published` property and because that property is connected to a `@Binding` property in the representable view, the text is assigned to the `UITextView` view.

```
import SwiftUI

class ContentData: ObservableObject {
    @Published var inputText: String = ""
    @Published var selectedText: Int = 0 {
        didSet {
            self.inputText = listTexts[self.selectedText]
        }
    }
    let listTexts: [String] = [
        "This is the first text",
        "This is the second text",
        "This is the third text"
    ]
    init() {
        self.inputText = listTexts[self.selectedText]
    }
}
struct ContentView: View {
    @ObservedObject var contentData = ContentData()

    var body: some View {
        VStack {
            Picker("", selection: $contentData.selectedText) {
                Text("First").tag(0)
                Text("Second").tag(1)
                Text("Third").tag(2)
            }.pickerStyle(SegmentedPickerStyle())

            TextView(input: $contentData.inputText)
        }.padding()
    }
}
```

Listing 16-8: *Sending new values to the UIKit view*

Chapter 16 - Framework Integration

In this example, we use an observable object and two `@Published` properties to store the values. The `inputText` property stores the value we want to send to the `UITextView` view, and the `selectedText` property stores the integer we use to select the text from an array. If the user presses a button on the picker, the tag of that option is assigned to the `selectedText` property, this property's `didSet()` method looks for the text in the `listTexts` array with that index, and assigns it to the `inputText` property. To modify the value of the `UITextView` view every time the `inputText` property changes, we must assign the `Binding` property to the `text` property in the `updateUIView()` method, as shown next.

```
import SwiftUI

struct TextView: UIViewRepresentable {
   @Binding var input: String

   func makeUIView(context: Context) -> UITextView {
      let view = UITextView()
      view.backgroundColor = UIColor.yellow
      view.font = UIFont.systemFont(ofSize: 17)
      view.textContainerInset = UIEdgeInsets(top: 20, left: 20, bottom:
20, right: 20)
      return view
   }
   func updateUIView(_ uiView: UITextView, context: Context) {
      uiView.text = self.input
   }
}
```

Listing 16-9: Sending new values to the UIKit view

Now, every time the value of the `inputText` property in the SwiftUI interface changes, it is assigned to the `UITextView` view and shown on the screen.

Figure 16-6: Multiple values assigned to the `UITextView` *view*

(Basic) **Coordinator**

Our text view works, and users can type whatever they want in it, but the text view and the `Binding` property are not connected, so there is no way to process the input. For that, we need to define a coordinator. A coordinator is an object that can send information back from the view to the SwiftUI interface, usually by modifying `Binding` properties. How to process these values depends on the type of UIKit view we are working with. A `UITextView` view reports changes on its value by calling delegate methods. Therefore, to get the text inserted by the user in a `UITextView` view and process it in SwiftUI, we must create a coordinator class that conforms to the `UITextViewDelegate` protocol and implements its methods. The following example illustrates how to define and instantiate this class.

```
import SwiftUI

struct TextView: UIViewRepresentable {
   @Binding var input: String

   func makeUIView(context: Context) -> UITextView {
      let view = UITextView()
      view.backgroundColor = UIColor.yellow
      view.font = UIFont.systemFont(ofSize: 17)
      view.textContainerInset = UIEdgeInsets(top: 20, left: 20, bottom:
20, right: 20)
      view.text = input
      view.delegate = context.coordinator
      return view
   }
   func updateUIView(_ uiView: UITextView, context: Context) {}

   func makeCoordinator() -> CoordinatorTextView {
      return CoordinatorTextView(input: $input)
   }
}
class CoordinatorTextView: NSObject, UITextViewDelegate {
   var input: Binding<String>

   init(input: Binding<String>) {
      self.input = input
   }
   func textViewDidChange(_ textView: UITextView) {
      if let text = textView.text {
         self.input.wrappedValue = text
      }
   }
}
```

Listing 16-10: *Sending values to the SwiftUI interface*

In addition to conforming to the **UITextViewDelegate** protocol, the coordinator class must inherit from the **NSObject** class; a class that provides the basic functionality that all UIKit classes need to work properly. In the example of Listing 16-10, we call the coordinator class **CoordinatorTextView**. Once it is ready, we must create an instance of it and return it from the **makeCoordinator()** method.

The coordinator conforms to the delegate protocol, but that is not enough to designate it as the delegate of the **UITextView** view. This is done in the **makeUIView()** method. The method receives a reference to the context and this context provides the **coordinator** property with a reference to our coordinator. Assigning this value to the **delegate** property of the **UITextView** class, we turn the coordinator into the view's delegate. Now, the **UITextView** view knows where to call the delegate methods and we can implement them.

Because all we want to do this time is to report changes in the content of the **UITextView** view to the SwiftUI interface, we only implement the **textViewDidChange()** method. This method is called by the **UITextView** view on the delegate every time its content changes (every time the user types or removes characters in the text view). This means that every time the content of the **UITextView** view is modified, the value is assigned to the **input** property.

The function of the coordinator in this example is to modify the value of the **input** property with the text inserted by the user, so the SwiftUI interface can access the value. In the example of Listing 16-10, we pass the property to the coordinator and the coordinator receives the value with a generic data type (**Binding<String>**), but we can also pass a reference to the representable view and access the **@Binding** properties from it, as in the following example.

Chapter 16 - Framework Integration

```
import SwiftUI

struct TextView: UIViewRepresentable {
   @Binding var input: String

   func makeUIView(context: Context) -> UITextView {
      let view = UITextView()
      view.backgroundColor = UIColor.yellow
      view.font = UIFont.systemFont(ofSize: 17)
      view.textContainerInset = UIEdgeInsets(top: 20, left: 20, bottom:
20, right: 20)
      view.text = input
      view.delegate = context.coordinator
      return view
   }
   func updateUIView(_ uiView: UITextView, context: Context) {}

   func makeCoordinator() -> CoordinatorTextView {
      CoordinatorTextView(representable: self)
   }
}
class CoordinatorTextView: NSObject, UITextViewDelegate {
   var representable: TextView

   init(representable: TextView) {
      self.representable = representable
   }
   func textViewDidChange(_ textView: UITextView) {
      if let text = textView.text {
         self.representable.input = text
      }
   }
}
```

Listing 16-11: Referencing values from the coordinator

This example is the same as before, but instead of passing the `@Binding` property, we pass a reference to the `TextView` structure and then access the `@Binding` property from it.

 The Basics: When only one `Binding` property is required, you can pass the property directly, as we did in Listing 16-10, but when the coordinator modifies multiple properties, passing a reference to the representable view can simplify your code.

Continuing with our example, it is time to process the value received from the coordinator. What we do with this value depends on our application. In this example, we are going to store the text inserted by the user in a file. To this end, we need the following model.

```
import SwiftUI

struct FileContent: Codable {
   var text: String
}
class AppData: ObservableObject {
   @Published var fileContent = FileContent(text: "") {
      didSet {
         self.saveFile()
      }
   }
}
```

```
    let manager: FileManager
    let fileURL: URL

    init() {
        manager = FileManager.default
        let documents = manager.urls(for: .documentDirectory, in:
.userDomainMask).first!
        fileURL = documents.appendingPathComponent("userdata.dat")

        if manager.fileExists(atPath: fileURL.path) {
            if let data = manager.contents(atPath: fileURL.path) {
                let decoder = JSONDecoder()
                if let content = try? decoder.decode(FileContent.self, from:
data) {
                    self.fileContent = content
                }
            }
        }
    }
    func saveFile() {
        let encoder = JSONEncoder()
        if let data = try? encoder.encode(self.fileContent) {
            manager.createFile(atPath: fileURL.path, contents: data,
attributes: nil)
        }
    }
}
```

Listing 16-12: Saving the content of a UITextView *view on file*

The model in Listing 16-12 defines a structure called **FileContent** to store the content of the file, and a property called **fileContent** to provide this value to the view. When the model is initialized, we open a file called userdata.dat and assign its content to the **fileContent** property, and when the value of this property changes (the user adds or removes characters in the text view), the **didSet()** method applied to this property calls the **saveFile()** method in the model to update the file. In consequence, the text typed by the user is constantly stored in the file, and it is going to be available every time the app is launched.

In the view, we just have to access the model through the environment and send a reference of the **text** property in the **FileContent** structure to the representable view.

```
import SwiftUI

struct ContentView: View {
    @EnvironmentObject var appData: AppData

    var body: some View {
        VStack {
            TextView(input: $appData.fileContent.text)
        }.padding(10)
    }
}
```

Listing 16-13: Connecting the TextView *structure with the value in the model*

 Do It Yourself: Update the AppDelegate.swift file in the previous project with the code in Listing 7-14 and the SceneDelegate.swift file with the code of Listing 7-20 to instantiate the model and insert it in the environment. Create a Swift file called AppData.swift for the model in Listing 16-12. Update the TextView.swift file with the code in Listing 16-10 and the **ContentView**

Chapter 16 - Framework Integration

structure with the code in Listing 16-13. Run the application and insert a text. Stop the application and run it again. You should see on the screen the text you inserted before.

<u>Medium</u> ## Selection

In addition to working with the full text, **UITextView** views also allow us to process the text selected by the user. The **UITextViewDelegate** protocol defines the **textViewDidChange-Selection()** method for this purpose. Every time the user selects text in the text view, this method is called on the delegate, and the location of the selected characters is reported through the **selectedRange** property. In the following example, we use this property to get the selected characters and return the string to the SwiftUI interface.

```
import SwiftUI

struct TextView: UIViewRepresentable {
    @Binding var selected: String

    func makeUIView(context: Context) -> UITextView {
        let view = UITextView()
        view.backgroundColor = UIColor.yellow
        view.font = UIFont.systemFont(ofSize: 17)
        view.textContainerInset = UIEdgeInsets(top: 20, left: 20, bottom:
20, right: 20)
        view.delegate = context.coordinator
        return view
    }
    func updateUIView(_ uiView: UITextView, context: Context) {}

    func makeCoordinator() -> CoordinatorTextView {
        CoordinatorTextView(selected: $selected)
    }
}
class CoordinatorTextView: NSObject, UITextViewDelegate {
    var selected: Binding<String>

    init(selected: Binding<String>) {
        self.selected = selected
    }
    func textViewDidChangeSelection(_ textView: UITextView) {
        if let text = textView.text {
            if let range = Range(textView.selectedRange, in: text) {
                self.selected.wrappedValue = String(text[range])
            }
        }
    }
}
```

Listing 16-14: Selecting text

The range returned by the **selectedRange** property is of type **NSRange**. To be able to get the selected characters from the text, we transform this range into a **Range** type with the **Range(in:)** initializer (see Ranges in Chapter 4) and assign the string to the **selected** property. In the view, we show the value of this property on the screen.

```
import SwiftUI

struct ContentView: View {
   @State private var selectedText: String = ""

   var body: some View {
      VStack {
         Text("Selection: \(selectedText)")
            .lineLimit(1)
         TextView(selected: $selectedText)
      }.padding()
   }
}
```

Listing 16-15: Showing the selected text

The view in Listing 16-15 defines a `@State` property called `selectedText`. This is the property we send to the `TextView` structure and therefore it contains the text selected by the user. Every time the user performs a selection in the `UITextView` view, the text is assigned to this property and shown on the screen with a `Text` view.

 Do It Yourself: Create a SwiftUI project. Create a Swift file called TextView.swift for the representable view in Listing 16-14. Update the `ContentView` structure with the code in Listing 16-15. Run the application. Write a few lines of text and double tap a word to select it. You should see the selected word at the top of the screen.

(Medium) ## Attributed Text

Besides plain text, we can also work with attributed text. Attributed text is text with attributes (styles) that are assigned to an individual character or a range of characters, such as color, font size, etc. The `UITextView` class includes the `textStorage` property to work with this type of text. This property is of type `NSTextStorage`, a class that inherits from the `NSMutableAttributedString` class, which includes the following methods to modify the attributes of the text.

setAttributes(Dictionary, range: NSRange)—This method assigns attributes to a range of characters (previous attributes are removed). The first attribute is a dictionary containing properties that describe the attributes and the values for the corresponding styles (font, color, etc.), and the **range** attribute defines the range of characters to be affected.

addAttributes(Dictionary, range: NSRange)—This method adds attributes to a range of characters. The new attributes are added to the attributes already assigned to the characters in the range. The first attribute is a dictionary containing properties that describe the attributes and values for the corresponding styles (font, color, etc.), and the **range** attribute defines the range of characters to be affected.

addAttribute(NSAttributedString.Key, value: Any, **range:** NSRange)—This method adds a single attribute to a range of characters. The new attribute is added to the attributes already assigned to the characters in the range. The first attribute is the property that describes the attribute, the **value** attribute is the value of the corresponding style (font, color, etc.), and the **range** attribute defines the range of characters to be affected.

removeAttribute(NSAttributedString.Key, range: NSRange)—This method removes an attribute previously assigned to a range of characters. The first attribute is the property that describes the attribute, and the **range** attribute is an `NSRange` object defining the range of characters to be affected.

The attributes are defined by the same `NSAttributedString` class we used before to change the appearance of the navigation bar. The list of properties provided by this class is extensive, with the most frequently used being `font` (`UIFont`), `foregroundColor` (`UIColor`), `strokeColor` (`UIColor`), `strokeWidth` (`NSNumber`), and `shadow` (`NSShadow`). The following `TextView` structure includes a method that modifies the `foregroundColor` attribute to assign a red color to the text selected by the user.

```
import SwiftUI

struct TextView: UIViewRepresentable {
    let view = UITextView()

    func makeUIView(context: Context) -> UITextView {
        view.backgroundColor = UIColor.yellow
        view.font = UIFont.systemFont(ofSize: 17)
        view.textContainerInset = UIEdgeInsets(top: 20, left: 20, bottom:
20, right: 20)
        return view
    }
    func updateUIView(_ uiView: UITextView, context: Context) {}

    func changeAttributes() {
        let attributedText = view.textStorage
        attributedText.addAttribute(.foregroundColor, value: UIColor.red,
range: view.selectedRange)
    }
}
```

Listing 16-16: Adding attributes to the attributed text of a text view

Notice that this time we create the `UITextView` object outside the `makeUIView()` method. This is to be able to access this object from the `changeAttributes()` method defined below and modify the content of the `textStorage` property.

The `changeAttributes()` method gets the value of the `textStorage` property and executes the `addAttribute()` method on it to assign the red color to the range of characters currently selected by the user. As a result, every time the method is executed, the selected text turns red.

The easiest way to execute methods on a representable view is to assign the instance to a constant and then call the methods on it, as in the following example.

```
import SwiftUI

struct ContentView: View {
    let textView = TextView()

    var body: some View {
        VStack {
            Button("Modify") {
                self.textView.changeAttributes()
            }
            textView
```

```
      }.padding()
   }
}
```

Listing 16-17: Assigning attributes to the text from the SwiftUI interface

The code in Listing 16-17 assigns the `TextView` structure to a constant and then uses that constant to display the view and to call the `changeAttributes()` method when the button is pressed. Notice that we instantiate the `TextView` structure outside the body. This is to prevent the view from being recreated every time a state in the interface changes.

 Do It Yourself: Update the TextView.swift file with the code in Listing 16-16 and the `ContentView` structure with the code in Listing 16-17. Run the application. Double tap on a word to select it and press the Modify button. The word should turn red.

(Medium) **Keyboard**

If we try the previous examples in the live preview or the simulator, the keyboard is not shown or may be hidden, but in a real device, the `UITextView` has to adapt to the space available or otherwise it will get covered by the keyboard and the user won't be able to see what he or she is typing. Fortunately, the `UITextView` view is flexible and therefore we only need to modify the size of the representable view to adjust the interface when the keyboard is opened or closed. We explain how to do this in Chapter 13 (see Listing 13-6). We must set up two publishers, one for the `keyboardWillShowNotification` notification, posted when the keyboard is going to be opened, and another for the `keyboardDidHideNotification` notification, posted when the keyboard is closed.

```
import SwiftUI

class ContentData: ObservableObject {
   @Published var textViewHeight: CGFloat = .infinity

   let openPublisher = NotificationCenter.Publisher(center: .default,
name: UIWindow.keyboardWillShowNotification)
      .map({ notification -> CGFloat in
         if let info = notification.userInfo {
            let value = info[UIWindow.keyboardFrameEndUserInfoKey] as!
NSValue
            let height = value.cgRectValue.height
            return height
         } else {
            return .infinity
         }
      })
      .receive(on: RunLoop.main)
   let closePublisher = NotificationCenter.Publisher(center: .default,
name: UIWindow.keyboardDidHideNotification)
      .receive(on: RunLoop.main)
}
struct ContentView: View {
   @ObservedObject var contentData = ContentData()

   var body: some View {
      VStack {
         TextView()
            .frame(minWidth: 0, maxWidth: .infinity, minHeight: 0,
maxHeight: self.contentData.textViewHeight)
```

Chapter 16 - Framework Integration

```
            .animation(.easeInOut)
          Spacer()
       }.padding(10)
       .onReceive(contentData.openPublisher, perform: { keyboardHeight in
          let screenHeight = UIScreen.main.bounds.height
          self.contentData.textViewHeight = screenHeight - keyboardHeight
- 50
       })
       .onReceive(contentData.closePublisher, perform: { _ in
          self.contentData.textViewHeight = .infinity
       })
    }
}
```

Listing 16-18: Adapting the `TextView` *view's height to the space available*

To simplify the example, we define the publishers in an observable object, but they could be declared in the model if necessary, as we did in Listing 13-6.

The view includes two `onReceive()` modifiers to subscribe to these publishers. When the `keyboardWillShowNotification` notification is posted, we calculate the height of the representable view from the height of the screen and the keyboard, and when the `keyboardDidHideNotification` notification is posted, we return the view to its natural height (`infinity`).

Figure 16-7: `UITextView` *adapts to the space available*

 Do It Yourself: Update the ContentView.swift file with the code in Listing 16-18. Run the application and tap on the text view to open the keyboard. You should see the view adapt to the space available, as shown in Figure 16-7.

(Basic) **16.3 Web**

Another feature that has not yet been incorporated into SwiftUI is the tools for browsing the web. But as with the `UITextView` view, we can use representable views and view controllers to incorporate them into our interface. Multiple frameworks provide different services to access the web. We can define links to open a document in an external browser, open a browser within our application, create a custom browser, or load and process web content.

(Basic) **Links**

The most important aspect of the web is the ease with which we can access documents with a simple link. A link is a text or an image associated with a URL that indicates the location of a document. When the user clicks the link, the document is opened. Links were designed for the web, but we can add them to our applications and let the system decide where to open the document. If the link contains a web address, the system opens the default browser and asks the browser to load the document.

Web addresses are created from `URL` structures. We have used these types of structures before to determine the location of files, but we can also use them to access remote documents. The class includes the following initializer to create a URL.

URL(string: String)—This initializer creates a `URL` structure with the URL specified by the **string** attribute.

URL(string: String, **relativeTo:** URL?)—This initializer creates a `URL` structure with the URL specified by the attributes. The URL is created by adding the value of the **string** attribute to the value of the **relativeTo** attribute. For example, if the value of the **string** attribute is the string "http://www.formasterminds.com" and the value of the **relativeTo** attribute is the string "index.php", the `URL` structure will contain the URL "http://www.formasterminds.com/index.php".

URL(dataRepresentation: Data, **relativeTo:** URL?, **isAbsolute:** Bool)—This initializer creates a `URL` structure with the URL specified by the attributes. The URL is created by adding the value of the **dataRepresentation** attribute to the value of the **relativeTo** attribute. The `isAbsolute` attribute is a Boolean value that determines if the URL is absolute or not (it includes all the information required to access the resource).

The `URL` structure is just a container for the location of the document we want to open, but the document is opened from the scene. The `UIScene` class offers the following method for this purpose.

open(URL, **options:** OpenExternalURLOptions?, **completionHandler:** Closure?)—This method opens the URL specified by the first attribute. The **options** attribute is an object that configures the operation (defined as `nil` for standard options), and the **completionHandler** attribute is the closure to be executed when the process is over. The closure receives a Boolean value that determines whether the document was opened or not.

The following example opens the website www.formasterminds.com when a button is pressed. The code defines a `@state` property of type `URL` and initializes it with the URL we want to open. The button gets a reference to the `UIScene` object that is managing the scene from the `connectedScenes` property of the `UIApplication` object and then opens the URL with the `open()` method. The system reads the URL, detects that it is a web address and opens the browser to load the website.

```
import SwiftUI

struct ContentView: View {
    @State private var searchURL: URL = URL(string:
"http://www.formasterminds.com")!

    var body: some View {
        VStack {
            Button("Open Web") {
                let app = UIApplication.shared
                if let scene = app.connectedScenes.first {
                    scene.open(self.searchURL, options: nil,
completionHandler: nil)
```

Chapter 16 - Framework Integration

```
            }
        }
        Spacer()
    }.padding()
    }
}
```

Listing 16-19: Opening a website

 Do It Yourself: Create a SwiftUI project. Update the `ContentView` structure with the code in Listing 16-19. Run the application and press the button. The system should open an external browser and load the website www.formasterminds.com. Use this project to test the following example.

In this example, we have defined the URL in code, but sometimes the URL is provided by the user or taken from another document. In cases like this, the URL may contain characters that are not allowed and can cause the location to be impossible to identify. To make sure that the URL is valid, we must turn unsafe characters into percent-encoding characters. These are characters represented by the % sign followed by a hexadecimal number. Fortunately, we already know a method that can easily correct unsafe characters in a string for us (see Chapter 14). It is called `data(using: Encoding, allowLossyConversion: Bool)` and it turns a string into a `Data` structure using a type of encoding that corrects those characters.

```
import SwiftUI

struct ContentView: View {
    @State private var searchURL: String = ""

    var body: some View {
        VStack {
            HStack {
                TextField("Insert URL", text: $searchURL)
                    .textFieldStyle(RoundedBorderTextFieldStyle())
                    .autocapitalization(.none)
                    .disableAutocorrection(true)
                Button("Open Web") {
                    let app = UIApplication.shared
                    if let scene = app.connectedScenes.first {
                        let dataURL = self.searchURL.data(using:
String.Encoding.utf8, allowLossyConversion: false)
                        if let webURL = URL(dataRepresentation: dataURL!,
relativeTo: nil, isAbsolute: true) {
                            scene.open(webURL, options: nil, completionHandler:
nil)
                        }
                    }
                }
            }
            Spacer()
        }.padding()
    }
}
```

Listing 16-20: Encoding URLs

The `utf8` format used in Listing 16-20 works with ASCII characters and therefore it is suitable for the creation of URLs. The method returns a `Data` structure containing the URL, so we must use the appropriate `URL` initializer for this type of value. Once the `URL` structure is created, the process to open the URL is the same.

Basic Safari View Controller

Links provide access to the web from our app, but they open the document in an external application. Considering how important it is for our application to capture the user's attention, Apple includes a framework called SafariServices. This framework allows us to incorporate the Safari browser into our app to offer a better experience to our users. The framework includes the `SFSafariViewController` class to create a view controller that incorporates its own view to display web pages and tools for navigation. The following are its initializers.

SFSafariViewController(url: URL)—This initializer creates a new Safari view controller that automatically loads the website indicated by the **url** attribute.

SFSafariViewController(url: URL, **configuration:** Configuration)—This initializer creates a new Safari view controller with the configuration specified by the **configuration** attribute that automatically loads the website indicated by the **url** attribute. The **configuration** attribute is a property of an object of the `Configuration` class included in the `SFSafariViewController` class. The properties available are `entersReaderIfAvailable` and `barCollapsingEnabled`.

The `SFSafariViewController` class creates a view controller. This object defines the interface for the entire screen an manages all the views in it. Therefore, instead of a representable view, we must create a representable view controller with the `UIViewControllerRepresentable` protocol, as in the following example.

```
import SwiftUI
import SafariServices

struct SafariBrowser: UIViewControllerRepresentable {
   @Binding var searchURL: URL

   func makeUIViewController(context: Context) -> SFSafariViewController
{
       let safari = SFSafariViewController(url: searchURL)
       return safari
   }
   func updateUIViewController(_ uiViewController:
SFSafariViewController, context: Context) {}
}
```

Listing 16-21: Creating a Safari Browser

The `UIViewControllerRepresentable` protocol has the same requirements than the `UIViewRepresentable` protocol. We must implement the `makeUIViewController()` method to create the view controller and the `updateUIViewController()` method to update the view controller with the values received from the SwiftUI interface. In the example in Listing 16-21, we create the `SFSafariViewController` object with the URL in the `Binding` property and return it.

This view creates a view controller that contains a functional Safari browser that we can incorporate into our SwiftUI interface. But there is one condition. The view must be opened inside a sheet, as in the following example.

```
import SwiftUI

struct ContentView: View {
    @State private var searchURL: URL = URL(string:
"http://www.formasterminds.com")!
    @State private var openSheet: Bool = false

    var body: some View {
        VStack {
            Button("Open Browser") {
                self.openSheet = true
            }
            Spacer()
        }.padding()
        .sheet(isPresented: $openSheet) {
            SafariBrowser(searchURL: self.$searchURL)
        }
    }
}
```

Listing 16-22: Opening a Safari Browser

The view in Listing 16-22 defines a `@State` property of type `URL` that is initialized with the URL http://www.formasterminds.com. When the button is pressed, a `SafariBrowser` view is initialized with this value, the browser is opened in a sheet, and the website is loaded.

Figure 16-8: Safari browser

 Do It Yourself: Create a SwiftUI project. Create a Swift file called SafariBrowser.swift for the code in Listing 16-21. Update the `ContentView` structure with the code in Listing 16-22. Run the application and press the button. You should see the Safari browser in a sheet with the www.formasterminds.com website.

The `SFSafariViewController` class also offers the following properties for configuration.

dismissButtonStyle—This property sets or returns a value that determines the type of button the view controller is going to show to dismiss the view. It is an enumeration of type `DismissButtonStyle` with the values `done` (default), `close`, and `cancel`.

preferredBarTintColor—This property sets or returns a `UIColor` value that determines the color of the bars.

preferredControlTintColor—This property sets or returns a `UIColor` value that determines the color of the controls.

The following example takes advantage of these properties to match the colors of the browser with the colors of the www.formasterminds.com website.

```
import SwiftUI
import SafariServices

struct SafariBrowser: UIViewControllerRepresentable {
    @Binding var searchURL: URL

    func makeUIViewController(context: Context) -> SFSafariViewController {
        let safari = SFSafariViewController(url: searchURL)
        safari.dismissButtonStyle = .close
        safari.preferredBarTintColor = UIColor(red: 81/255, green: 91/255,
blue: 119/255, alpha: 1.0)
        safari.preferredControlTintColor = UIColor.white
        return safari
    }
    func updateUIViewController(_ uiViewController:
SFSafariViewController, context: Context) {}
}
```

Listing 16-23: Configuring the view controller

The code of Listing 16-23 also modifies the `dismissButtonStyle` property to change the type of button shown by the browser. Instead of saying Done, the button now has the label Close. The result is shown in Figure 16-9.

Figure 16-9: Custom Safari view controller

When the user scrolls the page, the controller collapses the bars to make more room for the content. This makes difficult for the user to dismiss the view or use its tools. If we think that is more appropriate for our app to always keep the bars at their original size, we can initialize the controller with a configuration object and assign the value `false` to the `barCollapsingEnabled` property. The `Configuration` class is defined inside the `SFSafariViewController` class and provides a simple initializer with no parameters. Once the object is created, we can configure its properties, and finally assign it to the Safari View Controller from the controller's initializer.

```
import SwiftUI
import SafariServices

struct SafariBrowser: UIViewControllerRepresentable {
    @Binding var searchURL: URL

    func makeUIViewController(context: Context) -> SFSafariViewController {
        let config = SFSafariViewController.Configuration()
        config.barCollapsingEnabled = false
        let safari = SFSafariViewController(url: searchURL, configuration:
config)
        return safari
    }
```

Chapter 16 - Framework Integration

```
    func updateUIViewController(_ uiViewController:
SFSafariViewController, context: Context) {}
}
```

Listing 16-24: Preserving the size of the bars

 Do It Yourself: Update the `SafariBrowser` structure with the code in Listing 16-24. Run the application and scroll the page. The bars should stay at the same size and the buttons should always be visible.

Basic WebKit Framework

For some applications, the options for customization offered by the Safari view controller are not enough. To provide more alternatives, Apple offers the WebKit framework. With this framework we can display web content within a view. The view is defined by a subclass of `UIView` called `WKWebView`. The class provides the following properties and methods to manage the content.

title—This property returns a string with the current page's title.

url—This property returns a URL structure with the current page's URL.

isLoading—This property returns a Boolean value that determines if the view is in the process of loading a URL or not.

canGoBack—This property returns a Boolean value that determines if the view can navigate to the previews page.

canGoForward—This property returns a Boolean value that determines if the view can navigate to the next page.

estimatedProgress—This property returns a value of type `Double` between 0.0 and 1.0 that determines the fraction of the content that has been already loaded.

load(URLRequest**)**—This method loads the content of a URL. The attribute is an object with the request for the URL we want to open.

goBack()—This method navigates to the previous web page on the list.

goForward()—This method navigates to the next web page on the list.

go(to: WKBackForwardListItem**)**—This method navigates to the web page indicated by the attribute. The **to** attribute is an object that represents a web page in a navigation list.

reload()—This method reloads the current page (it refreshes the web page).

stopLoading()—This method stops the loading of the content.

To load a website, we must create a request. The UIKit framework offers the `URLRequest` structure for this purpose. The structure includes the following initializers.

URLRequest(url: URL, **cachePolicy:** CachePolicy, **timeoutInterval:** TimeInterval**)**—This initializer creates a `URLRequest` structure for the URL and protocol specified by the **url** attribute. The **cachePolicy** attribute is an enumeration that determines how the request will work with the cache. The possible values are: `useProtocolCachePolicy` (default), `reloadIgnoringLocalCacheData`, `reloadIgnoringLocalAndRemoteCacheData`, `returnCacheDataElseLoad`, `returnCacheDataDontLoad`, and `reloadRevalidatingCacheData`. The **timeoutInterval** attribute is the maximum time allowed to the system to process the request (60.0 by default).

URLRequest(url: URL)—This initializer creates a `URLRequest` structure for the URL and protocol specified by the **url** attribute (the rest of the parameters required by the request are defined with values by default).

A WebKit view can report the state of the content through a delegate. For this purpose, the framework defines the `WKNavigationDelegate` protocol. The following are some of its methods.

webView(WKWebView, decidePolicyFor: WKNavigationAction, **decision-Handler:** Closure)—This method is called on the delegate to determine if the view should process a request. The **decidePolicyFor** attribute is an object with information about the request, and the **decisionHandler** attribute is a closure that we must execute to report our decision. The closure takes a value of type `WKNavigationActionPolicy`, an enumeration with the properties `cancel` and `allow`.

webView(WKWebView, didStartProvisionalNavigation: WKNavigation!)—This method is called on the delegate when the view begins loading new content.

webView(WKWebView, didFinish: WKNavigation!)—This method is called on the delegate when the view finishes loading the content.

webView(WKWebView, didFailProvisionalNavigation: WKNavigation!, **withError:** Error)—This method is called on the delegate when an error occurs loading the content.

webView(WKWebView, didReceiveServerRedirectForProvisionalNavigation: WKNavigation!)—This method is called on the delegate when the server redirects the navigator to a different destination.

The WebKit view is a UIKit view and therefore we must use the `UIViewRepresentable` protocol to create it. Once we define the representable view, the process to load a website in a WebKit View is simple. We define the URL, create a request, and ask the view to load it.

```
import SwiftUI
import WebKit

struct WebView: UIViewRepresentable {
   let searchURL: URL

   func makeUIView(context: Context) -> WKWebView {
      let view = WKWebView()
      let request = URLRequest(url: searchURL)
      view.load(request)
      return view
   }
   func updateUIView(_ uiView: WKWebView, context: Context) {}
}
```

Listing 16-25: Loading a website with a WebKit View

The example of Listing 16-25 prepares the request with the URL received from the SwiftUI interface and loads the website with the `load()` method. Because we always load the same website, the view just has to define the URL and pass it to the `WebView` instance.

```
import SwiftUI

struct ContentView: View {
    var body: some View {
        WebView(searchURL: URL(string: "https://www.google.com")!)
    }
}
```

Listing 16-26: Showing the WebKit view

 Do It Yourself: Create a SwiftUI project. Create a Swift file called WebView.swift for the code in Listing 16-25. Update the `ContentView` structure with the code in Listing 16-26 and run the application. You should see Google's website on the screen.

 IMPORTANT: In the example of Listing 16-26, we open a secure URL (a URL that begins with the prefix https://), because these are the URLs allowed by default. Apple implements a system called App Transport Security (ATS) to block insecure URLs. If you want to let your users load insecure URLs with a `WKWebView` view, such as http://www.formasterminds.com, you must configure the app from the info.plist file to circumvent this security measure for every website or specific domains. For more information, visit our website and follow the links for this chapter.

With a `WKWebView` view, we can load any website we want, including those specified by the user. We just need to provide a way for the user to insert a URL and then execute the `load()` method again to load it. For this purpose, the following view includes a `TextField` view and a button. When the button is pressed, we call a method in the `WebView` structure to update the view with the URL inserted by the user.

```
import SwiftUI

class ContentData: ObservableObject {
    @Published var inputURL: String = "https://"
}
struct ContentView: View {
    @ObservedObject var contentData = ContentData()
    var webView: WebView!

    init() {
        self.webView = WebView(inputURL: $contentData.inputURL)
    }
    var body: some View {
        VStack {
            HStack {
                TextField("Insert URL", text: $contentData.inputURL)
                Button("Load") {
                    let text =
self.contentData.inputURL.trimmingCharacters(in: .whitespaces)
                    if !text.isEmpty {
                        self.webView.loadWeb(loadWeb: text)
                    }
                }
            }.padding(5)
```

```
                webView
            }
        }
    }
}
```

Listing 16-27: Allowing the user the insert a URL

As we did with the `UITextView` view, we assign an instance of the `WebView` structure to a property and then use that property to call methods on it and present the view. The URL inserted by the user is stored in a property called `inputURL`, which is passed to the `WebView` structure. This is to be able to update the value of the text field every time the user navigates to a new page. Notice that to be able to pass the `inputURL` property to the view, we had to declare it as a `@Published` property inside an observable object and initialize the view in the structure's initializer.

The `WebView` structure for this example has to create the `WKWebView` view and implement the methods to load new URLs and keep the views updated.

```swift
import SwiftUI
import WebKit

struct WebView : UIViewRepresentable {
    @Binding var inputURL: String
    let view: WKWebView = WKWebView()

    func makeUIView(context: Context) -> WKWebView {
        view.navigationDelegate = context.coordinator
        let request = URLRequest(url: URL(string:
"https://www.google.com")!)
        self.view.load(request)
        return view
    }
    func updateUIView(_ uiView: WKWebView, context: Context) {}

    func loadWeb(loadWeb: String) {
        let dataURL = loadWeb.data(using: String.Encoding.utf8,
allowLossyConversion: false)
        if let webURL = URL(dataRepresentation: dataURL!, relativeTo: nil,
isAbsolute: true) {
            let request = URLRequest(url: webURL)
            view.load(request)
        }
    }
    func makeCoordinator() -> CoordinatorWebView {
        return CoordinatorWebView(input: $inputURL)
    }
}
class CoordinatorWebView: NSObject, WKNavigationDelegate {
    var inputURL: Binding<String>

    init(input: Binding<String>) {
        self.inputURL = input
    }
    func webView(_ webView: WKWebView, didCommit navigation:
WKNavigation!) {
        if let webURL = webView.url {
            self.inputURL.wrappedValue = webURL.absoluteString
        }
    }
}
```

Listing 16-28: Updating the `WKWebView` *with the URLs inserted by the user*

Chapter 16 - Framework Integration

We introduced several modifications in this `WebView` structure to be able to load multiple URLs. First, we instantiate the `WKWebView` view outside the `makeUIView()` method to access the view from our custom methods. In the `makeUIView()` method, we declare the coordinator as the delegate of the view by assigning a reference of the coordinator to the view's `navigationDelegate` property, and then the request is created and load it. The view is now initialized, and it will call methods on the coordinator to report changes. But before implementing the coordinator, we define the `loadWeb()` method to load the URL inserted by the user. This is the method executed when the user taps the Load button next to the text field. The method receives a string, prepares the URL with the `data()` method, as we did before when working with links, and loads it with the `load()` method.

The URLs inserted by the user are loaded and their content is shown on the screen. Now we must do the opposite, we need to update the URL in the text field when the content of the view changes. This happens when the user taps on the links in the website to navigate to another. For this purpose, we make the coordinator conform to the `WKNavigationDelegate` protocol and implement the `webView(WKWebView, didCommit:)` method. This method is called by the `WKWebView` view when it is loading new content. In this method, we get the current URL from the view's `url` property and assign it to the `inputURL` property, which modifies the value in the `TextField` view, matching the URL in this field with the website being displayed on the screen.

 Do It Yourself: Update the `ContentView` structure with the code in Listing 16-27 and the WebView.swift file with the code in Listing 16-28. Run the application. Insert a URL and press the Load button. The view should load the URL and show the website. Click on a link to navigate to another page. The URL in the text field should change to reflect the address of the page on the screen. Remember that only secure URLs are allowed by default (https://). If you want to change this, you must add the required keys to the info.plist file to deactivate the App Transport Security system. For more information, visit our website and follow the links for this chapter.

The user can visit any URL and navigate by clicking on the links, but our interface doesn't offer the possibility to move back or forward in the navigation history. WebKit views offer several methods to manipulate their content. For instance, there is the `goBack()` method to go back to the previous page, the `goForward()` method to go to the page we came back from, and the `reload()` method to refresh the page. To execute these methods, we are going to add three buttons below the navigation bar.

```
import SwiftUI

class ContentData: ObservableObject {
   @Published var inputURL: String = "https://"
   @Published var backDisabled: Bool = true
   @Published var forwardDisabled: Bool = true
}
struct ContentView: View {
   @ObservedObject var contentData = ContentData()
   var webView: WebView!

   init() {
      webView = WebView(inputURL: $contentData.inputURL, backDisabled:
$contentData.backDisabled, forwardDisabled: $contentData.forwardDisabled)
   }
   var body: some View {
      VStack {
         HStack {
            TextField("Insert URL", text: $contentData.inputURL)
```

```
            Button("Load") {
                let text =
self.contentData.inputURL.trimmingCharacters(in: .whitespaces)
                if !text.isEmpty {
                    self.webView.loadWeb(loadWeb: text)
                }
            }
        }.padding(5)

        HStack {
            Button(action: {
                self.webView.goBack()
            }, label: {
                Image(systemName: "arrow.left.circle")
                    .font(.title)
            }).disabled(self.contentData.backDisabled)
            Button(action: {
                self.webView.goForward()
            }, label: {
                Image(systemName: "arrow.right.circle")
                    .font(.title)
            }).disabled(self.contentData.forwardDisabled)
            Spacer()
            Button(action: {
                self.webView.refresh()
            }, label: {
                Image(systemName: "arrow.clockwise.circle")
                    .font(.title)
            })
        }.padding(5)
        webView
    }
  }
}
```

Listing 16-29: *Providing buttons for navigation*

The view in Listing 16-29 also defines two more `@Published` properties in the observable object to determine whether the back and forward buttons should be enabled or not. When the view is displayed for the first time, the buttons are disabled because only one document was loaded into the view, but after a new document is loaded, we have to enable the buttons to let the user go back and forward in the navigation history. For this purpose, we must pass the properties to the `WebView` structure and modify their values from the coordinator every time a document is loaded.

```
import SwiftUI
import WebKit

struct WebView : UIViewRepresentable {
    @Binding var inputURL: String
    @Binding var backDisabled: Bool
    @Binding var forwardDisabled: Bool

    let view: WKWebView = WKWebView()

    func makeUIView(context: Context) -> WKWebView  {
        view.navigationDelegate = context.coordinator
        let request = URLRequest(url: URL(string:
"https://www.google.com")!)
        self.view.load(request)
```

Chapter 16 - Framework Integration

```
            return view
        }
    func updateUIView(_ uiView: WKWebView, context: Context) {}

    func loadWeb(loadWeb: String) {
        let dataURL = loadWeb.data(using: String.Encoding.utf8,
allowLossyConversion: false)
        if let webURL = URL(dataRepresentation: dataURL!, relativeTo: nil,
isAbsolute: true) {
            let request = URLRequest(url: webURL)
            view.load(request)
        }
    }
    func goBack(){
        view.goBack()
    }
    func goForward(){
        view.goForward()
    }
    func refresh(){
        view.reload()
    }
    func makeCoordinator() -> CoordinatorWebView {
        return CoordinatorWebView(input: $inputURL, back: $backDisabled,
forward: $forwardDisabled)
    }
}
class CoordinatorWebView: NSObject, WKNavigationDelegate {
    var inputURL: Binding<String>
    var backDisabled: Binding<Bool>
    var forwardDisabled: Binding<Bool>

    init(input: Binding<String>, back: Binding<Bool>, forward:
Binding<Bool>) {
        self.inputURL = input
        self.backDisabled = back
        self.forwardDisabled = forward
    }
    func webView(_ webView: WKWebView, didCommit navigation:
WKNavigation!) {
        if let webURL = webView.url {
            self.inputURL.wrappedValue = webURL.absoluteString
            self.backDisabled.wrappedValue = !webView.canGoBack
            self.forwardDisabled.wrappedValue = !webView.canGoForward
        }
    }
}
```

Listing 16-30: Navigating back and forward in the navigation history

The code in Listing 16-30 adds three methods to the `WebView` structure to perform the actions selected by the user (moving backward, forward, or refreshing the page). In the `webView(WKWebView, didFinish:)` method, we update the URL in the text field, as before, but also modify the state of the buttons from the values of the `canGoBack` and `canGoForward` properties, so they are only enabled when there is a page to go to.

Figure 16-10: *Buttons for navigation*

 Do It Yourself: Update the ContentView.swift file with the code in Listing 16-29 and the WebView.swift file with the code in Listing 16-30. Run the application. Search a term in Google. Click on a link and press the back button. The view should go back to the previous page.

 IMPORTANT: The WebKit framework also offers tools to process cookies and JavaScript code, which allow you to interact with the web page's content. The topic is beyond the scope of this book. For more information, visit our website and follow the links for this chapter.

(Basic) Web Content

The Safari view controller and WebKit views were designed to show content to the user, but the capacity to integrate that content with our app is limited. Sometimes all we need is to extract a piece of information from the document or process its data instead of showing the entire content as it is. In cases like this, we must load the document in the background and analyze it to extract only what we need. Foundation includes a group of classes to get content referenced by a URL. The main class is called `URLSession`. This class creates a session that manages an HTTP connection to obtain data, and download, or upload files. The following are some of the properties and initializers provided by the class to create the session.

shared—This type property returns a standard session with a configuration by default that is suitable to perform basic requests.

URLSession(configuration: URLSessionConfiguration)—This initializer creates a new session with the configuration set by its attribute. The **configuration** attribute is an object that specifies the session's behavior.

The session sets up the connection, but it does not perform any task. To download data, we must create a `URLSessionTask` object with a specific task and add it to the session. The `URLSession` class includes the following method to create a task to download data. The method returns a publisher to emit the result.

dataTaskPublisher(for: URLRequest)—This method creates a task to download data from the URL specified by the request and returns a publisher that emits the result.

When the task is finished, the publisher emits the result. The result includes the data returned by the server and an object of type `HTTPURLResponse` with the status of the request. This status is determined by a code returned by the `statusCode` property. There are several values available to determine things like the success of the request (200) or more drastic situations like when the website has been moved to a different address (301). If all we want is to make sure that the data was downloaded correctly, we must check if the value of the `statusCode` property is equal to 200 before processing the response. In the following example, we use the `tryMap()` operator for this purpose. If the value of the `statusCode` property is equal to 200, we emit the data, otherwise, we emit the value `nil`.

```
import SwiftUI
import Combine

class AppData: ObservableObject {
    @Published var webContent: String = ""
    @Published var buttonDisabled: Bool = false

    var publisherWeb: AnyCancellable?

    func loadWeb() {
        self.buttonDisabled = true

        let webURL = URL(string: "https://www.yahoo.com")
        let request = URLRequest(url: webURL!)

        let session = URLSession.shared
        publisherWeb = session.dataTaskPublisher(for: request)
            .tryMap({ data, response -> Data? in
                if let resp = response as? HTTPURLResponse {
                    if resp.statusCode == 200 {
                        return data
                    }
                }
                return nil
            })
            .assertNoFailure()
            .receive(on: RunLoop.main)
            .sink(receiveValue: { data in
                if let webData = data {
                    if let content = String(data: webData, encoding:
String.Encoding.ascii) {
                        self.webContent = content
                        self.buttonDisabled = false
                        print(content)
                    }
                }
            })
    }
}
```

Listing 16-31: Loading a remote document

The model in Listing 16-31 loads the content of the website at www.yahoo.com and assigns it to the `webContent` property. The process is performed by the `loadWeb()` method. The method defines the request with the URL https://www.yahoo.com, and then gets a reference to the standard session to call the `dataTaskPublisher()` method and download the document (Because we are just loading a single web page, the standard session returned by the `shared` property is more than enough).

Notice that the publisher is stored outside the method, in a property called `publisherWeb`. When working with publishers, we must make sure that the publisher is not destroyed soon after it is created. Storing the publisher in this property keeps the publisher alive after the execution of the method is over.

To process the data emitted by the publisher, we apply multiple operators. First, the `tryMap()` operator checks the status of the response and emits the data if the status is 200 or the value `nil` otherwise. Next, we stop the publisher if there is an error or send the data downstream with the **assertNoFailure()** operator. The **receive()** operator makes sure the results are received in the main queue. And finally, the **sink()** operator decodes the data into a string and assigns it to the **webContent** property to make it available for the view. The following is a simple view to work with this value.

```
import SwiftUI

struct ContentView: View {
   @EnvironmentObject var appData: AppData

   var body: some View {
      VStack {
         Button("Load Web") {
            self.appData.loadWeb()
         }.disabled(self.appData.buttonDisabled)
            Text("Total Characters: \(self.appData.webContent.count)")
               .padding()
            Spacer()
      }.padding()
   }
}
```

Listing 16-32: Displaying the document's content

The content of the www.yahoo.com web page is extensive. For didactic purposes, the **sink()** operator prints the content on the console and the view counts the number of characters in the string and displays the value on the screen, but a professional application usually process the content to extract information.

 Do It Yourself: Create a SwiftUI project. Update the AppDelegate.swift file with the code in Listing 7-14 and the SceneDelegate.swift file with the code of Listing 7-20 to instantiate the model and insert it in the environment. Create a Swift file with the name AppData.swift and the code of Listing 16-31. Update the **ContentView** structure with the code in Listing 16-32. Run the application and press the Load Web button. After a few seconds you should see the document downloaded from www.yahoo.com printed on the console and the number of characters on the screen.

Web documents, like the one returned by www.yahoo.com, are written in HTML. This is a simple programming language used by every website to organize information. Extracting data from these documents can be tedious and error prone. That is why websites usually provide additional services to share data in JSON format. These JSON documents are dynamically generated and contain only the information requested by the application. For instance, the website www.openweathermap.org offers a service that generates JSON documents with information about the weather (https://openweathermap.org/api).

To illustrate how to access and process the documents produced by these services, we are going to read posts from a website called JSONPlaceholder that generates phony documents. The process doesn't require anything new. We must load the document with a **URLSession**, as we did in the previous example, and then decode it with a **JSONDecoder** object, as we did in the examples in Chapter 14.

```
import SwiftUI
import Combine
```

```
struct Post: Codable, Identifiable {
    var id: Int
    var userId: Int
    var title: String
    var body: String
}
class AppData: ObservableObject {
    @Published var listOfPosts: [Post] = []

    var publisherWeb: AnyCancellable?

    init() {
        let webURL = URL(string:
"https://jsonplaceholder.typicode.com/posts")
        let request = URLRequest(url: webURL!)

        let session = URLSession.shared

        publisherWeb = session.dataTaskPublisher(for: request)
            .tryMap({ data, response -> Data? in
                if let resp = response as? HTTPURLResponse {
                    if resp.statusCode == 200 {
                        return data
                    }
                }
                return nil
            })
            .assertNoFailure()
            .receive(on: RunLoop.main)
            .sink(receiveValue: { data in
                let decoder = JSONDecoder()
                if let webData = data, let posts = try?
decoder.decode([Post].self, from: webData) {
                    self.listOfPosts = posts
                }
            })
    }
}
```

Listing 16-33: *Loading a JSON document*

As we have learned in Chapter 14, to decode a JSON document we must define a structure that matches the JSON values one by one. The https://jsonplaceholder.typicode.com/posts URL returns a list of posts, each one with four values: an integer with the user's identifier, another integer with the identifier of the post, a string with the title, and a string with the message. To store these values, the model in Listing 16-33 defines the `Post` structure. The structure conforms to the `Codable` protocol to be able to decode it, and to the `Identifiable` protocol to be able to list the instances with a `List` view without having to specify the id.

The process to download the document is the same as before. We define the request, get the session, call the `dataTaskPublisher()` method on it, and then apply the operators to process the response. In the `sink()` operator, we check if there is data available, then decode it into an array of `Post` structures with a `JSONDecoder` object, and store the values in the `listOfPosts` property to update the view. Because the document is downloaded in the object's initializer, all we have to do in the view is to list the values.

```
import SwiftUI

struct ContentView: View {
    @EnvironmentObject var appData: AppData
```

```
var body: some View {
    VStack {
        List {
            ForEach(self.appData.listOfPosts) { post in
                VStack(alignment: .leading) {
                    Text(post.title).bold()
                    Text(post.body)
                }.padding(5)
            }
        }
    }.padding()
}
}
```

Listing 16-34: Listing the values from the document

 Do It Yourself: Update the AppData.swift file from the previous project with the code of Listing 16-33 and the `ContentView` structure with the code in Listing 16-34. Run the application. You should see 100 messages on the screen. To see the structure of the JSON file returned from https://jsonplaceholder.typicode.com/posts, insert the URL in your browser.

(Basic) 16.4 MapKit

Often, users need to visualize their location or the places they want to go on a map to position themselves in the world. For these kinds of applications, Apple offers the MapKit framework. The framework includes all the tools necessary to create and configure maps that users can interact with to look for places and get information.

Maps are presented on the screen with a view created from a subclass of `UIView` called `MKMapView`. The view takes care of loading the map, managing user interaction, and displaying custom content generated by our application. As always, to include this view in a SwiftUI interface, we must define a representable view with the `UIViewRepresentable` protocol.

(Basic) Configuring the Map

A MapKit view offers different styles of maps and can also let the user zoom in and out, pan, or rotate the map to find a location. The `MKMapView` class includes the following properties to configure these features.

mapType—This property sets or returns a value that determines the style of the map. It is an enumeration of type `MKMapType` with the values `standard` (by default), `mutedStandard`, `satellite`, `hybrid`, `satelliteFlyover`, and `hybridFlyover`.

isZoomEnabled—This property sets or returns a Boolean value that determines if the user can zoom the map (`true` by default).

isScrollEnabled—This property sets or returns a Boolean value that determines if the user can scroll the map (`true` by default).

isRotateEnabled—This property sets or returns a Boolean value that determines if the user can rotate the map (`true` by default).

isPitchEnabled—This property sets or returns a Boolean value that determines if the camera's pitch angle is considered to render the map (`true` by default).

Chapter 16 - Framework Integration

To modify the map, we must import the MapKit framework and then change the map's properties. The following view defines the style of the map and disables rotation.

```
import SwiftUI
import MapKit

struct MapView: UIViewRepresentable {
   func makeUIView(context: Context) -> MKMapView {
      let map = MKMapView()
      map.mapType = .satellite
      map.isRotateEnabled = false
      return map
   }
   func updateUIView(_ uiView: MKMapView, context: Context) {}
}
```

Listing 16-35: *Configuring the map*

The representable view in Listing 16-35 creates an instance of the **MKMapView** class and configures the map to show the satellite image and not allow rotation. To show the view in our interface, we instantiate it as any other SwiftUI view.

```
import SwiftUI

struct ContentView: View {
   var body: some View {
      MapView()
   }
}
```

Listing 16-36: *Showing a map*

The representable view is a flexible view by default, so the map is extended to occupy the whole screen, as illustrated in Figure 16-11.

Figure 16-11: *Satellite map*

 Do It Yourself: Create a SwiftUI project. Create a Swift file called MapView.swift with the code in Listing 16-35. Update the **ContentView** structure with the code in Listing 16-36. Run the application on a device. You should see a satellite map of the world, as shown in Figure 16-11.

Users can zoom in and out to find a specific place on the map, but we can also do it from code. To determine locations in the map, the MapKit framework implements values defined in a framework called *Core Location*. The most important is the `CLLocation` class, designed to store information about a location. The class includes an initializer to create the object and a few properties to retrieve the values.

CLLocation(latitude: CLLocationDegrees, longitude: CLLocationDegrees)—This initializer creates a `CLLocation` object with the location determined by the attributes. The `CLLocationDegrees` data type is a typealias of `Double`.

coordinate—This property returns the coordinates of the location. It is a structure of type `CLLocationCoordinate2D` with the `latitude` and `longitude` properties.

horizontalAccuracy—This property returns a value that determines the accuracy of the location's latitude and longitude. It is of type `CLLocationAccuracy` (a typealias of `Double`).

verticalAccuracy—This property returns a value that determines the accuracy of the location's altitude. It is of type `CLLocationAccuracy` (a typealias of `Double`).

altitude—This property returns the altitude of the location in meters. It is of type `CLLocationDistance` (a typealias of `Double`).

The `CLLocation` class also includes a practical method to calculate the distance between one `CLLocation` object and another.

distance(from: CLLocation)—This method returns a value that determines the distance between the location in the `CLLocation` object and the location determined by the attribute. The **from** attribute is another object of type `CLLocation` with the location we want to compare. The value returned is of type `CLLocationDistance` (a typealias of `Double`).

These values define the location, but the map is set in those locations by properties and methods of the `MKMapView` class. The following are the ones available to get the values of the area currently displayed on the screen or set a new one.

region—This property returns an `MKCoordinateRegion` structure with values that determine the area currently displayed on the screen.

centerCoordinate—This property returns a `CLLocationCoordinate2D` structure with the coordinates at the center of the visible area.

setRegion(MKCoordinateRegion, animated: Bool)—This method sets the map's visible region. The first attribute is a structure that contains a `CLLocationCoordinate2D` value to determine the region's center coordinates, and a value of type `MKCoordinateSpan` to determine the region's size in degrees. The **animated** attribute determines if the process will be animated.

setCenter(CLLocationCoordinate2D, animated: Bool)—This method sets the region's coordinates. The first attribute specifies the latitude and longitude, and the **animated** attribute determines if the process will be animated.

The `MKCoordinateRegion` structure, required to set the region, is created from a `CLLocationCoordinate2D` structure that contains the properties `latitude` and `longitude` to return the latitude and longitude of the location, and an `MKCoordinateSpan` structure that contains the size of the region in degrees. Because the degrees of an area can be difficult to calculate, the framework defines an initializer for this structure that allows us to set the size of the region in meters.

MKCoordinateRegion(center: CLLocationCoordinate2D, **latitudinalMeters:** CLLocationDistance, **longitudinalMeters:** CLLocationDistance)—This initializer creates an `MKCoordinateRegion` structure with the values determined by its attributes. The first attribute specifies the region's coordinates, and the second and third attributes determine the vertical and horizontal size of the region in meters (The `CLLocationDistance` is a typealias of `Double`).

The following example implements this initializer to show an area of 2000 meters around the location of one of the Apple Stores in New York.

```
import SwiftUI
import MapKit

struct MapView: UIViewRepresentable {
    func makeUIView(context: Context) -> MKMapView {
        let map = MKMapView()
        map.mapType = .satellite
        map.isRotateEnabled = false

        let location = CLLocation(latitude: 40.7637825011971, longitude: -73.9731328627541)
        let region = MKCoordinateRegion(center: location.coordinate,
latitudinalMeters: 2000, longitudinalMeters: 2000)
        map.setRegion(region, animated: false)

        return map
    }
    func updateUIView(_ uiView. MKMapView, context: Context) {}
}
```

Listing 16-37: Displaying a specific region

The code of Listing 16-37 creates a `CLLocation` object with the coordinates of the Apple Store, defines a region around that area with an `MKCoordinateRegion` structure, and finally sets the map's visible region with the `setRegion()` method. This time, instead of the entire world, the MapKit view shows the area of New York where the store is located.

Figure 16-12: Apple store

 Do It Yourself: Update the `MapView` structure with the code of Listing 16-37. Run the application on a device. You should see an area of New York City with the Apple store at the center (Figure 16-12).

Basic Annotations

The previous example establishes the visible area of the map and sets the center to be the location of the Apple Store, but the store is not marked on the map. To mark a location, the framework offers the possibility to add annotations. Annotations provide additional information of a location. They are associated with a view that can show an image to represent them, such as a pin, the title and subtitle of the location, and a view, called *Callout*, to show more information. Figure 16-13 illustrates how an annotation may look like on a standard map.

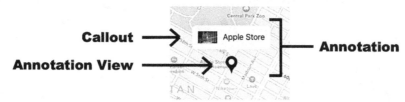

Figure 16-13: Annotation on the map

What the framework describes as annotations are objects that define the basic aspects of an annotation, like the coordinates in which the annotation view will appear, the image that will represent the location, and the title and subtitle to show along with it. To provide this information, the objects must conform to the `MKAnnotation` protocol provided by the MapKit framework. The protocol defines the following properties.

coordinate—This property sets or returns a `CLLocationCoordinate2D` structure that determines the annotation's latitude and longitude.

title—This property sets or returns a string with the annotation's title.

subtitle—This property sets or returns a string with the annotation's subtitle.

To create annotations, we must define a class that conforms to this protocol and implements at least these three properties, as shown next.

```
import MapKit

class MyAnnotation: NSObject, MKAnnotation {
    var coordinate: CLLocationCoordinate2D
    var title: String?
    var subtitle: String?

    init(coordinate: CLLocationCoordinate2D) {
        self.coordinate = coordinate
    }
}
```

Listing 16-38: Defining an annotation

Annotations are created from our custom class and then added to the map. The `MKMapView` class offers the following properties and methods to add, remove, and manage annotations.

annotations—This property returns an array of `MKAnnotation` objects that represent the annotations already added to the map.

addAnnotation(MKAnnotation)—This method adds an annotation to the map. The attribute is an object of a class that conforms to the `MKAnnotation` protocol.

addAnnotations([MKAnnotation])—This method adds multiple annotations to the map. The attribute is an array of objects of a class that conforms to the `MKAnnotation` protocol.

removeAnnotation(MKAnnotation)—This method removes an annotation. The attribute is a reference to the object that represents the annotation.

removeAnnotations([MKAnnotation])—This method removes multiple annotations. The attribute is an array of objects that represent the annotations we want to remove.

showAnnotations([MKAnnotation], animated: Bool)—This method sets a region that includes the annotations specified by the first attribute to make them visible to the user. The **animated** attribute indicates if the process will be animated.

selectAnnotation(MKAnnotation, animated: Bool)—This method selects an annotation (it shows it, as if the user had tapped on the annotation view). The first attribute is an object that represents the annotation we want to select, and the **animated** attribute indicates if the process will be animated.

deselectAnnotation(MKAnnotation?, animated: Bool)—This method deselects an annotation. The first attribute is an object that represents the annotation we want to deselect, and the **animated** attribute indicates if the process will be animated.

The following code expands the `MapView` structure from the previous example to create an annotation from our `MyAnnotation` class and adds it to a standard map.

```
import SwiftUI
import MapKit

struct MapView: UIViewRepresentable {
    func makeUIView(context: Context) -> MKMapView {
        let map = MKMapView()
        map.mapType = .standard
        map.isRotateEnabled = false

        let location = CLLocation(latitude: 40.7637825011971, longitude: -
73.9731328627541)
        let region = MKCoordinateRegion(center: location.coordinate,
latitudinalMeters: 2000, longitudinalMeters: 2000)
        map.setRegion(region, animated: false)

        let annotation = MyAnnotation(coordinate: location.coordinate)
        annotation.title = "Apple Store"
        annotation.subtitle = "Think Different"
        map.addAnnotation(annotation)

        return map
    }
    func updateUIView(_ uiView: MKMapView, context: Context) {}
}
```

Listing 16-39: Adding an annotation

By default, the MapKit view generates a view to show the annotation on the map. The view contains an image that represents a pin, pointing to the annotation's location, and the title below. When the annotation is selected, the view shows a bigger image and includes the subtitle, as illustrated in Figure 16-14.

Figure 16-14: Annotation with a view by default

 Do It Yourself: Create a Swift file called MyAnnotation.swift for the code of Listing 16-38. Update the `MapView` structure with the code of Listing 16-39. Run the application on a device and tap on the pin. You should see something similar to Figure 16-14.

 IMPORTANT: The MapKit framework includes the `MKPointAnnotation` class to create basic annotations. If your annotations only require the values of the `coordinate`, `title`, and `subtitle` properties, you can create them from this class instead of defining your own (see Listing 16-48).

As we already mentioned, an annotation object determines where the annotation is located, but the annotation view is the element responsible for displaying the graphic pointing to the annotation's coordinates on the map. If we do not provide a view for the annotation, the system creates one by default from a class called `MKMarkerAnnotationView`. The views created from this class include the balloon shown in Figure 16-14, always with the same icon and in the same color. If we want to change the configuration of the view, we must create our own objects and modify their properties. For this purpose, the `MKMarkerAnnotationView` class includes the following initializer and properties.

MKMarkerAnnotationView(annotation: MKAnnotation?, **reuseIdentifier: String?)**—This initializer creates an annotation view of type marker for the annotation specified by the **annotation** attribute. The **annotation** attribute is a reference to the annotation object we want to associate with the view, and the **reuseIdentifier** attribute is a string the MapKit view needs to be able to reuse the view to display multiple annotations.

glyphText—This property sets or returns the text displayed in the balloon.

markerTintColor—This property sets or returns a `UIColor` value that determines the color of the balloon.

glyphTintColor—This property sets or returns a `UIColor` value that determines the color of the text in the balloon.

glyphImage—This property sets or returns a `UIImage` object with the image displayed in the balloon. The image must be of a size of 20 x 20 points.

selectedGlyphImage—This property sets or returns a `UIImage` object with the image displayed in the balloon when it is selected. The image must be of a size of 40 x 40 points.

titleVisibility—This property sets or returns a value that determines whether the title will be visible or not. It is an enumeration of type `MKFeatureVisibility` with the values `adaptive`, `hidden`, and `visible`.

subtitleVisibility—This property sets or returns a value that determines whether the subtitle will be visible or not. It is an enumeration of type `MKFeatureVisibility` with the values `adaptive`, `hidden`, and `visible`.

Chapter 16 - Framework Integration

Annotations are added to the map and then the MapKit view checks which ones are inside the visible area and requests the views to display. To get these views, the MapKit view calls a delegate method. The method is defined in the `MKMapViewDelegate` protocol.

mapView(MKMapView, **viewFor:** MKAnnotation)—This method is called on the delegate when the MapKit view needs a view to show an annotation. The **viewFor** attribute is a reference to the object that represents the annotation the map has to show.

Annotation views are reusable. We must create the view inside the delegate method, assign an identifier to it, and then use the same view again for other annotations. The `MKMapView` class includes the following method to get a reusable view.

dequeueReusableAnnotationView(withIdentifier: String)—This method returns an `MKAnnotationView` object with the view identified by the **withIdentifier** attribute. The attribute is the same string declared when the view was created.

As we did in previous examples, to conform to the protocol we must define a coordinator. The following example defines the coordinator and implements the delegate method to create a custom view for our annotation.

```
import SwiftUI
import MapKit
struct MapView: UIViewRepresentable {
    func makeUIView(context: Context) -> MKMapView {
        let map = MKMapView()
        map.mapType = .standard
        map.isRotateEnabled = false
        map.delegate = context.coordinator

        let location = CLLocation(latitude: 40.7637825011971, longitude: -73.9731328627541)
        let region = MKCoordinateRegion(center: location.coordinate,
latitudinalMeters: 2000, longitudinalMeters: 2000)
        map.setRegion(region, animated: false)

        let annotation = MyAnnotation(coordinate: location.coordinate)
        annotation.title = "Apple Store"
        annotation.subtitle = "Think Different"
        map.addAnnotation(annotation)

        return map
    }
    func updateUIView(_ uiView: MKMapView, context: Context) {}

    func makeCoordinator() -> MapViewCoordinator {
        return MapViewCoordinator()
    }
}
class MapViewCoordinator: NSObject, MKMapViewDelegate {
    func mapView(_ mapView: MKMapView, viewFor annotation: MKAnnotation) -> MKAnnotationView? {
        if let temp = annotation as? MyAnnotation {
            var view = mapView.dequeueReusableAnnotationView(withIdentifier:
"Pins") as? MKMarkerAnnotationView
            if view == nil {
                view = MKMarkerAnnotationView(annotation: temp,
reuseIdentifier: "Pins")
                view?.glyphText = "Place"
                view?.markerTintColor = UIColor.blue
```

```
                view?.titleVisibility = .hidden
        } else {
                view?.annotation = annotation
        }
        return view
    }
    return nil
  }
}
```

Listing 16-40: Configuring the annotation view

The code of Listing 16-40 sets the region we want to show, adds an annotation to the map for the coordinates where the Apple Store is located, and finally defines the coordinator and declares it as the MapKit view's delegate. The protocol method is implemented in the coordinator to provide a custom view for this annotation. When the MapKit view is showing the selected area, it detects that there is an annotation inside and calls the `mapView(MKMapView, viewFor:)` method to get its view. This method checks whether the annotation is one of our custom annotations, looks for a view with the "Pins" identifier, and if there is no view, it creates a new one. Notice that the `dequeueReusableAnnotationView()` method returns a view that was previously used for another annotation, so we must assign the new annotation to it before returning it (`view?.annotation = annotation`).

The configuration defined for our annotation view includes a title for the balloon, the color blue for its background, and it does not show the annotation's title (`view?.subtitleVisibility = .hidden`). The result is shown in Figure 16-15.

Figure 16-15: Custom balloon

If we want to replace the balloon altogether, instead of using an object of the `MKMarkerAnnotationView` class, we must define our own annotation view with an object of a class called `MKAnnotationView` (this is the superclass of the `MKMarkerAnnotationView` class). The class includes the following initializer and properties to create and configure the view.

MKAnnotationView(annotation: MKAnnotation?, **reuseIdentifier:** String?)—This initializer creates an annotation view for the annotation specified by the **annotation** attribute. The **annotation** attribute is a reference to the annotation object we want to associate with the view, and the **reuseIdentifier** attribute is a string the MapKit view needs to be able to reuse the view to display multiple annotations.

image—This property sets or returns the image for the view. It is an object of type `UIImage`.

leftCalloutAccessoryView—This property sets or returns the view displayed on the left side of the callout bubble.

rightCalloutAccessoryView—This property sets or returns the view displayed on the right side of the callout bubble.

displayPriority—This property sets or returns a value that determines the annotation's priority. It is a structure of type `MKFeatureDisplayPriority` that can be initialized

Chapter 16 - Framework Integration

with a **Float** value from 0 to 1000. The structure defines three static properties to return an object with standard values: **required** (1000), **defaultHigh** (750), and **defaultLow** (250).

clusteringIdentifier—This property sets or returns a string with the name of the group the annotation belongs to. This identifier is used to cluster annotations when they are too close to each other.

isEnabled—This property sets or returns a Boolean value that determines if the view can be selected.

The process to create a custom view is the same as before, but instead of using the **MKMarkerAnnotationView** class to create the view we must use the **MKAnnotationView** class. Also, these custom views present the information in a bubble on top of the icon when the annotation is selected, so we must assign the value **true** to the **canShowCallout** property if we want the user to be able to see it. The delegate method defined in the following coordinator creates a view with a custom image and a bubble to display the title and subtitle (the iconmap.png file is available on our website).

```
class MapViewCoordinator: NSObject, MKMapViewDelegate {
   func mapView(_ mapView: MKMapView, viewFor annotation: MKAnnotation) -
> MKAnnotationView? {
      if let temp = annotation as? MyAnnotation {
         var view = mapView.dequeueReusableAnnotationView(withIdentifier:
"Pins")
         if view == nil {
            view = MKAnnotationView(annotation: temp, reuseIdentifier:
"Pins")
            view?.image = UIImage(named: "iconmap")
            view?.canShowCallout = true
         } else {
            view?.annotation = annotation
         }
         return view
      }
      return nil
   }
}
```

Listing 16-41: Defining a custom annotation

Our image replaces the balloon, and now the information is shown in a callout bubble when the annotation is selected, as shown in Figure 16-16.

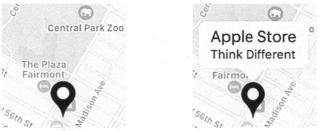

Figure 16-16: Custom annotation view

Do It Yourself: Download the iconmap.png image from our website and add it to the Assets Catalog. Update the `MapViewCoordinator` class from the previous example with the code of Listing 16-41. Run the application on a device and tap on the icon. You should see something similar to Figure 16-16.

The annotation view is responsible for the view that presents the annotation's callout bubble. Besides the title and the subtitle provided by the annotation, this view can also include two small views or controls on the sides. Because these views usually contain information specific for each annotation, we must define the data required to create the views in the annotation object. These may be images, text, decoration views, etc. For example, we might add a property to the `MyAnnotation` class to include a thumbnail that helps the user identify the location.

```
import MapKit

class MyAnnotation: NSObject, MKAnnotation {
   var coordinate: CLLocationCoordinate2D
   var title: String?
   var subtitle: String?
   var picture: UIImage?

   init(coordinate: CLLocationCoordinate2D) {
      self.coordinate = coordinate
   }
}
```

Listing 16-42: Adding custom data to an annotation

Now, besides the title and subtitle, we can also define a thumbnail for each annotation and then display that image in the callout bubble. Depending on which side we want the thumbnail to appear, we assign it to the `leftCalloutAccessoryView` or the `rightCalloutAccessoryView` properties, as shown next.

```
import SwiftUI
import MapKit

struct MapView: UIViewRepresentable {
   func makeUIView(context: Context) -> MKMapView {
      let map = MKMapView()
      map.mapType = .standard
      map.isRotateEnabled = false
      map.delegate = context.coordinator

      let location = CLLocation(latitude: 40.7637825011971, longitude: -
73.9731328627541)
      let region = MKCoordinateRegion(center: location.coordinate,
latitudinalMeters: 2000, longitudinalMeters: 2000)
      map.setRegion(region, animated: false)

      let annotation = MyAnnotation(coordinate: location.coordinate)
      annotation.title = "Apple Store"
      annotation.picture = UIImage(named: "appstore")
      annotation.subtitle = "Think Different"
      map.addAnnotation(annotation)

      return map
   }
   func updateUIView(_ uiView: MKMapView, context: Context) {}
```

```
    func makeCoordinator() -> MapViewCoordinator {
        return MapViewCoordinator()
    }
}
class MapViewCoordinator: NSObject, MKMapViewDelegate {
    func mapView(_ mapView: MKMapView, viewFor annotation: MKAnnotation) -
> MKAnnotationView? {
        if let temp = annotation as? MyAnnotation {
            var view = mapView.dequeueReusableAnnotationView(withIdentifier:
"Pins")
            if view == nil {
                view = MKAnnotationView(annotation: temp, reuseIdentifier:
"Pins")
                view?.image = UIImage(named: "iconmap")
                view?.canShowCallout = true

                let leftImage = UIImageView(image: temp.picture)
                view?.leftCalloutAccessoryView = leftImage
            } else {
                view?.annotation = annotation
            }
            return view
        }
        return nil
    }
}
```

Listing 16-43: Configuring the callout bubble

The delegate method of Listing 16-43 adds a small image to the callout's left side called appstore.png with a picture of the Apple Store (the image is available on our website).

Figure 16-17: Callout bubble with a thumbnail

 Do It Yourself: Update the `MyAnnotation` class with the code of Listing 16-42 and the MapView.swift file with the code of Listing 16-43. Download the appstore.png image from our website and add it to the Assets Catalog. Run the application on a device and tap on the pin to open the callout bubble.

(Basic) **User Location**

Displaying the user's location on a map is easy with MapKit views, we just have to set the following properties provided by the `MKMapView` class and the MapKit view takes care of detecting the user's current location and return it.

showsUserLocation—This property sets or returns a Boolean value that determines if we want the MapKit view to determine the user's location.

isUserLocationVisible—This property returns a Boolean value that determines if the user's location is currently visible on the map.

userLocation—This property returns an object of the `MKUserLocation` class with the user's location.

To get the MapKit view to determine the user's current location and show it on the map, we just have to set the `showsUserLocation` property to `true`, but before, we must ask permission to the user. There are two types of authorization we may request. We can ask permission to get updates only while the app is active (the app is being used by the user at the time), or all the time (even when the app moves to the background). The Core Location framework defines the `CLLocationManager` class to manage locations and the following methods to process the authorization.

requestWhenInUseAuthorization()—This method asks authorization to get the location while the app is in use.

requestAlwaysAuthorization()—This method asks authorization to get the location when the app is active or in the background (when it was closed or the user switched to another app).

authorizationStatus()—This type method returns the current authorization status. The value is an enumeration of type `CLAuthorizationStatus` with the values `notDetermined`, `restricted`, `denied`, `authorizedAlways`, and `authorizedWhen-InUse`.

If the app is authorized to access the user's location, the MapKit view shows a circle to indicate the location, but the configuration of the map doesn't change. If we want the map to show the area around the location, we have to set the visible region with the `setRegion()` method, as we did before. The following view includes a button to let the user zoom in to his or her location after permission is granted.

```
import SwiftUI

struct ContentView: View {
    var map = MapView()

    var body: some View {
        VStack {
            HStack {
                Spacer()
                Button("Home") {
                    self.map.showHome()
                }
            }.padding()
            map
        }
    }
}
```

Listing 16-44: Defining an interface to interact with the map

In this example, we instantiate the representable view and assign the instance to a constant to be able to call methods on it, as we did in previous projects in this chapter. When the button is pressed, we execute a method called `showHome()` on the view to zoom in to the user's location. All this logic must be implemented in the `MapView` view, as shown next.

```
import SwiftUI
import MapKit

struct MapView: UIViewRepresentable {
    var map = MKMapView()
    var locationManager: CLLocationManager!
```

Chapter 16 - Framework Integration

```
init() {
    locationManager = CLLocationManager()
    locationManager.requestWhenInUseAuthorization()
}
func makeUIView(context: Context) -> MKMapView {
    map.mapType = .standard
    map.isRotateEnabled = false
    map.showsUserLocation = true
    return map
}
func updateUIView(_ uiView: MKMapView, context: Context) {}

func showHome() {
    let location = map.userLocation
    let region = MKCoordinateRegion(center: location.coordinate,
latitudinalMeters: 1000, longitudinalMeters: 1000)
    map.setRegion(region, animated: true)
}
}
```

Listing 16-45: Getting the user's location

The first thing we do in the view of Listing 16-45 is to ask permission to the user. The instance of the **CLLocationManager** object has to remain in memory, so we store it in a property called **locationManager** and then call the **requestWhenInUseAuthorization()** method to ask permission. To get the location, we set the MapKit view's **showsUserLocation** property to **true**. The process is automatic, but we have to define an option in the info.plist file called "Privacy - Location When In Use Usage Description" with a string that explains to the user why we need to access his or her location (see Figure 5-38). After the location is determined, it is shown on the map represented by a view with a small icon, as shown in Figure 16-18.

Figure 16-18: User's location on the map

Do It Yourself: Update the **ContentView** structure with the code in Listing 16-44 and the **MapView** structure with the code in Listing 16-45. Click on the info.plist file to open it in the Editor Area. Press the + button at the top to add an option. Select the option "Privacy - Location When In Use Usage Description". Double click on the value to change it. Insert the text you want to show to the user when authorization is requested (see Figure 5-38 for more information). Run the application on a device. The first time, the system will ask you permission to access your location. Press the Allow While Using App button. After that, you may see an icon indicating your location. Press the Home button to zoom in.

The location is returned as an object of the **MKUserLocation** class. This class defines a special type of annotation to represent the user's location. As any other annotation class, it includes the **title**, **subtitle**, and **coordinate** properties that we can read to get the annotation's values, but also the following specific properties.

location—This property returns a `CLLocation` object with the user's location. If the location was not determined yet, the property returns `nil`.

isUpdating—This property returns a Boolean value that indicates if the MapKit View is currently in the process of determining the user's location.

heading—This property returns a value that determines where the user is heading. It is an object of the `CLHeading` class, which, among others, includes the `magneticHeading` and `trueHeading` properties to return a value in degrees that determines the cardinal point to which the user is heading (0 = north, 90 = east, 180 = south and 270 = west).

Using these properties, we can respond to the location's current value or configure the annotation to show information that helps the user identify the location, as we do in the following example.

```
func makeUIView(context: Context) -> MKMapView {
   map.mapType = .standard
   map.isRotateEnabled = false
   map.showsUserLocation = true
   map.userLocation.title = "You are here"
   return map
}
```

Listing 16-46: Defining a title for the user's location

The MapKit view constantly updates the user's location. To help us keep track of these changes over time and detect errors, the `MKMapViewDelegate` protocol defines the following methods.

mapView(MKMapView, didUpdate: MKUserLocation)—This method is called on the delegate every time a new location is determined. The **didUpdate** attribute is an object with the user's current location.

mapView(MKMapView, didFailToLocateUserWithError: Error)—This method is called on the delegate when the MapKit view cannot determine the user's location.

When the MapKit view detects a new location, it calls the `mapView(MKMapView, didUpdate:)` method to report the result. Inside this method, we can displace the center of the region to the new location or perform any other task necessary. For instance, the following view uses a coordinator to update the location of the user when a change is detected. Notice that we pass a reference to the `MKMapView` view to the coordinator object to be able to call the `setCenter()` method on it.

```
import SwiftUI
import MapKit

struct MapView: UIViewRepresentable {
   var map = MKMapView()
   var locationManager: CLLocationManager!

   init() {
      locationManager = CLLocationManager()
      locationManager.requestWhenInUseAuthorization()
   }
   func makeUIView(context: Context) -> MKMapView {
      map.mapType = .standard
      map.isRotateEnabled = false
```

```
        map.showsUserLocation = true
        map.userLocation.title = "You are here"
        map.delegate = context.coordinator
        return map
    }
    func updateUIView(_ uiView: MKMapView, context: Context) {}

    func showHome() {
        let location = map.userLocation
        let region = MKCoordinateRegion(center: location.coordinate,
latitudinalMeters: 1000, longitudinalMeters: 1000)
        map.setRegion(region, animated: true)
    }
    func makeCoordinator() -> MapViewCoordinator {
        return MapViewCoordinator(map: map)
    }
}
class MapViewCoordinator: NSObject, MKMapViewDelegate {
    let map: MKMapView

    init(map: MKMapView) {
        self.map = map
    }
    func mapView(_ mapView: MKMapView, didUpdate userLocation:
MKUserLocation) {
        map.setCenter(userLocation.coordinate, animated: true)
    }
}
```

Listing 16-47: Keeping track of the user's location

(Basic) **Search**

The MapKit framework incorporates a service to translate addresses into locations and find places of interest. The service is called *Local Search* and can take a freeform query string and return an array with the results. The query is created from the **Request** class included in the **MKLocalSearch** class. The following are the properties available for configuration.

naturalLanguageQuery—This property sets or returns a string with the term or address we want to search.

region—This property sets or returns an **MKCoordinateRegion** structure that determines the region in which the search is performed.

To perform the search, the framework defines the **MKLocalSearch** class. The class includes the following initializer and method.

MKLocalSearch(request: MKLocalSearchRequest)—This initializer creates an **MKLocalSearch** object to perform a search request.

start(completionHandler: CompletionHandler)—This method performs the search and sends the results to the closure specified by the attribute. The **completionHandler** attribute is a closure that receives two values, a **Response** object with the results, and an **Error** object with the errors found.

The search returns an object of a class called **Response** included in the **MKLocalSearch** class that contains the following properties.

mapItems—This property returns an array of `MKMapItem` objects that represent the results returned by the search.

boundingRegion—This property returns an `MKCoordinateRegion` structure that determines the region occupied by the results returned by the search.

The Local Search service was designed to find all the places that match the query. The framework defines the `MKMapItem` to represent each place. The following are some of the properties included by this class to return the data from the place.

name—This property sets or returns a string with the place's name.

phoneNumber—This property sets or returns a string with the place's phone number.

url—This property sets or returns a `URL` value with the URL of the place's website.

placemark—This property sets or returns an `MKPlacemark` object with additional information about the place.

There are different ways an app can perform a search and display the places returned. As an example, we have decided to use the Home button introduced before to the interface to set the region around the user's location, find places that sell pizza, and create the annotation to show them on the map.

```
import SwiftUI
import MapKit

struct MapView: UIViewRepresentable {
    var map = MKMapView()
    var locationManager: CLLocationManager!

    init() {
        locationManager = CLLocationManager()
        locationManager.requestWhenInUseAuthorization()
    }
    func makeUIView(context: Context) -> MKMapView {
        map.mapType = .standard
        map.showsUserLocation = true
        map.userLocation.title = "You are here"
        return map
    }
    func updateUIView(_ uiView: MKMapView, context: Context) {}

    func showHome() {
        let location = map.userLocation
        let region = MKCoordinateRegion(center: location.coordinate,
latitudinalMeters: 2000, longitudinalMeters: 2000)
        map.setRegion(region, animated: true)

        let request = MKLocalSearch.Request()
        request.naturalLanguageQuery = "Pizza"
        request.region = map.region

        let search = MKLocalSearch(request: request)
        search.start(completionHandler: { (results, error) in
            if let items = results?.mapItems {
                self.map.removeAnnotations(self.map.annotations)
```

```
            for item in items {
                if let coordinates = item.placemark.location?.coordinate {
                    let annotation = MKPointAnnotation()
                    annotation.coordinate = coordinates
                    annotation.title = item.name
                    annotation.subtitle = item.phoneNumber
                    self.map.addAnnotation(annotation)
                }
            }
        }
    })
}
}
```

Listing 16-48: Searching for pizza places

The code of Listing 16-48 modifies the `showHome()` method to search for places associated with the term "Pizza" and set the annotations for each location found. When the `start()` method returns the results, we remove the current annotations, get the coordinates of the location for each place, and set the new annotations with the place's name and phone number as the title and subtitle.

 Do It Yourself: Update the `MapView` structure with the code in Listing 16-48. Run the application on a device and press the Home button. You should see your location and the pizzerias in the area.

(Medium) **Directions**

Maps are not only used to find places but also to find routes to go from one place to another. The MapKit framework includes a set of classes to calculate a route and generate the graphics to show it on the map. The first class we need to implement is called `Request`, which is defined in the `MKDirections` class. This class generates a request for a route between two locations. The following are the properties available in this class to configure the request.

source—This property sets or returns the route's starting point. It is of type `MKMapItem`.

destination—This property sets or returns the route's destination. It is of type `MKMapItem`.

requestsAlternateRoutes—This property sets or returns a Boolean value that determines whether multiple routes will be returned when available or not.

transportType—This property sets or returns a value that determines the type of transportation used to travel the route. It is an `MKDirectionsTransportType` structure with the `automobile`, `walking`, `transit`, and `any` properties.

departureDate—This property sets or returns a `Date` structure that determines the date of departure and helps the system estimate the better route.

arrivalDate—This property sets or returns a `Date` structure that determines the date of arrival and helps the system estimate the better route.

The request has to be sent to Apple servers for processing. The functionality required to perform the request and process the results is provided by the `MKDirections` class. The class includes the following initializer and method.

MKDirections(request: Request**)**—This initializer creates an `MKDirections` object with the specified request.

calculate(completionHandler: DirectionsHandler**)**—This method performs the request and sends the results to the closure specified by the attribute. The closure receives two values, an `MKDirections.Response` object with the routes found, and an `Error` value to report errors.

The routes are returned as objects of the `MKRoute` class. The class includes the following properties to get the route's information.

polyline—This property sets or returns the route's geometry that we can use to draw the route on the map. It is an object of the `MKPolyline` class.

steps—This property sets or returns an array of `MKRoute.Step` objects that describe every step the user has to take to reach the destination, including instructions on how to follow the route.

advisoryNotices—This property sets or returns an array of strings with additional information that the user may need to travel the route, such as traffic jams or interruptions.

distance—This property sets or returns a `CLLocationDistance` value (a typealias of `Double`) with the route distance in meters.

expectedTravelTime—This property sets or returns a `TimeInterval` value with the expected travel time in seconds.

After the server returns the `MKRoute` object describing the route, we must present its values to the user. There are different types of information we can extract from these objects, but the most interesting is the route's geometry provided by the `polyline` property, which allows us to draw the route on the map.

The MapKit view displays the graphics in layers. There is a layer for the map, another for the labels and roads, and we can also add custom layers to display our own graphics, including the route. The value returned by the `polyline` property contains all the information required to create a layer that we can add to the MapKit view to draw the route. The `MKMapView` class offers several methods to add and remove layers. The following are the most frequently used.

addOverlay(MKOverlay, level: MKOverlayLevel**)**—This method adds a layer to the MapKit view. The first attribute is an object that conforms to the `MKOverlay` protocol and defines the layer, and the **level** attribute is an enumeration of type `MKOverlayLevel` that defines the level in which the layer will be placed. The possible values are `aboveRoads` (places the layer above roads but below labels) and `aboveLabels` (places the layer above roads and labels).

removeOverlay(MKOverlay)—This method removes a layer from the MapKit view.

Adding the layer to the MapKit view is like adding an annotation. As with annotations, the MapKit view calls a delegate method to get the information necessary to draw the layer. The following is the method defined in the `MKMapViewDelegate` protocol for this purpose.

mapView(MKMapView, rendererFor: MKOverlay**)**—This method is called on the delegate when the MapKit view needs a renderer to draw a layer. The method has to return an object of the `MKOverlayRenderer` class (or any of its subclasses) with the renderer we want to use to render the graphics. The **rendererFor** attribute is a reference to the object that represents the layer we want to draw.

This method must return a renderer that we have to configure according to how we want the layer to be drawn. The framework defines the `MKPolylineRenderer` class (a subclass of a subclass of the `MKOverlayRenderer` class) to create a renderer for a polyline overlay. The class includes the following initializer.

MKPolylineRenderer(polyline: MKPolyline)—This initializer creates a renderer for a polyline overlay.

The `MKPolylineRenderer` class inherits from its superclasses a set of properties we can use to configure the renderer.

fillColor—This property sets or returns a `UIColor` object with the color to fill the path.

strokeColor—This property sets or returns a `UIColor` object with the color of the stroke.

lineWidth—This property sets or returns a `CGFloat` value that determines the path's width.

lineJoin—This property sets or returns a value that determines the style of the path's corners. It is an enumeration of type `CGLineJoin` with the values `miter` (joins the lines with a sharp end), `round` (joins the lines with a rounded end), and `bevel` (joins the lines with a square end).

lineCap—This property sets or returns a value that determines the style for the ending of the lines. It is an enumeration of type `CGLineCap` with the values `butt` (squared end), `round` (round end), and `square` (squared end extended half the width of the line).

miterLimit—This property sets or returns a value of type `CGFloat` that determines how long the lines in the corners will extend.

lineDashPhase—This property sets or returns a `CGFloat` value that determines the offset at which the renderer starts drawing a dashed line.

lineDashPattern—This property sets or returns an array of numbers that specify the pattern used to create a dashed line.

The route's origin and destination are set with `MKMapItem` objects (the same type of objects we receive when we perform a search). The class includes the following initializer to create an `MKMapItem` object from an `MKPlacemark` object.

MKMapItem(placemark: MKPlacemark)—This initializer creates an `MKMapItem` object with the information provided by the attribute. The **placemark** attribute is an object with the information about the place (location, name, etc.).

The `MKPlacemark` class offers its own initializer to create the `MKPlacemark` object we need to initialize the `MKMapItem` object.

MKPlacemark(coordinate: CLLocationCoordinate2D)—This initializer creates an `MKPlacemark` object with the coordinates specified by the **coordinate** attribute. The **coordinate** attribute is a `CLLocationCoordinate2D` structure with the place's latitude and longitude.

A route requires two `MKMapItem` objects, one for the starting point and another for the destination. Once we have these locations, we can zoom in the map to the visual region around them, and then define the request to ask Apple servers to calculate the route, as in the following example.

```
import SwiftUI
import MapKit

struct MapView: UIViewRepresentable {
   var map = MKMapView()

   func makeUIView(context: Context) -> MKMapView {
      map.mapType = .standard
      map.delegate = context.coordinator
      return map
   }
   func updateUIView(_ uiView: MKMapView, context: Context) {}

   func showHome() {
      let coordOrigin = CLLocationCoordinate2D(latitude:
40.7637825011971, longitude: -73.9731328627541)
      let placeOrigin = MKPlacemark(coordinate: coordOrigin)
      let origin = MKMapItem(placemark: placeOrigin)

      let coordDestination = CLLocationCoordinate2D(latitude:
40.7523809365088, longitude: -73.9778321046893)
      let placeDestination = MKPlacemark(coordinate: coordDestination)
      let destination = MKMapItem(placemark: placeDestination)

      let region = MKCoordinateRegion(center: coordOrigin,
latitudinalMeters: 2000, longitudinalMeters: 2000)
      map.setRegion(region, animated: false)

      let request = MKDirections.Request()
      request.source = origin
      request.destination = destination
      request.requestsAlternateRoutes = false

      let directions = MKDirections(request: request)
      directions.calculate(completionHandler: { (results, error) in
         if let routes = results?.routes {
            let route = routes.first!
            self.map.addOverlay(route.polyline, level: .aboveRoads)
         }
      })
   }
   func makeCoordinator() -> MapViewCoordinator {
      return MapViewCoordinator()
   }
}
class MapViewCoordinator: NSObject, MKMapViewDelegate {
   func mapView(_ mapView: MKMapView, rendererFor overlay: MKOverlay) ->
MKOverlayRenderer {
      let render = MKPolylineRenderer(overlay: overlay)
      render.strokeColor = UIColor.red
      return render
   }
}
```

Listing 16-49: Calculating and showing a route

The code in Listing 16-49 implements the functionality in the `showHome()` method. When the Home button in the interface is pressed, the method defines the origin and destination from the coordinates of two places in New York, the Apple Store and Grand Central Terminal, and then sets the map to show the visible region around that area.

After the map is ready, the `showHome()` method defines the request with the two locations and creates the `MKDirections` object to process it. The `calculate()` method returns the results in an `MKDirectionsResponse` object, which contains the `routes` property with the `MKRoute` object for the route. Because we set the `requestsAlternateRoutes` property to `false`, the array returned by this property only contains one route object. If the array contains a route, we get the first element and add its polyline overlay to the map.

The route is not drawn until the renderer is defined. For this purpose, we implement the `MKMapViewDelegate` protocol method in the coordinator. The method creates an `MKPolylineRenderer` object for each layer with a red stroke. As a result, the renderer draws a red line between locations, as illustrated in Figure 16-19.

Figure 16-19: Route on the map

 Do It Yourself: Update the MapView.swift file with the code in Listing 16-49. Run the application on the simulator or a device. You should see the route shown in Figure 16-19.

If the route is too long, the user may not be able to see it in its entirety on the screen without zooming out or scrolling. There are several things we can do to improve our application, but it always depends on what we want to achieve and how the application is organized. One interesting alternative is to define the annotations for the starting point and destination and then call the `showAnnotations()` method provided by the MapKit View to set a visible region that includes both annotations. In this way, not only will the entire route be visible, but we will also ensure that the user can identify the places where the trip begins and ends.

```
func showHome() {
    let coordOrigin = CLLocationCoordinate2D(latitude: 40.7637825011971,
longitude: -73.9731328627541)
    let placeOrigin = MKPlacemark(coordinate: coordOrigin)
    let origin = MKMapItem(placemark: placeOrigin)

    let coordDestination = CLLocationCoordinate2D(latitude:
40.7523809365088, longitude: -73.9778321046893)
    let placeDestination = MKPlacemark(coordinate: coordDestination)
    let destination = MKMapItem(placemark: placeDestination)

    let region = MKCoordinateRegion(center: coordOrigin,
latitudinalMeters: 2000, longitudinalMeters: 2000)
    map.setRegion(region, animated: false)

    let request = MKDirections.Request()
    request.source = origin
```

```
request.destination = destination
request.requestsAlternateRoutes = false

let directions = MKDirections(request: request)
directions.calculate(completionHandler: { (results, error) in
   if let routes = results?.routes {
      let route = routes.first!
      self.map.addOverlay(route.polyline, level: .aboveRoads)

      let annotation1 = MKPointAnnotation()
      annotation1.coordinate = origin.placemark.coordinate
      annotation1.title = "Apple Store"
      self.map.addAnnotation(annotation1)

      let annotation2 = MKPointAnnotation()
      annotation2.coordinate = destination.placemark.coordinate
      annotation2.title = "Grand Central Terminal"
      self.map.addAnnotation(annotation2)

      self.map.showAnnotations([annotation1, annotation2], animated:
true)
   }
})
}
```

Listing 16-50: Zooming out to show the route

In Listing 16-50, the annotations are added to the map when results are received from the server. Because of this, the annotations and the route are shown at the same time and the map zooms in or out to show the full route on the screen.

 Do It Yourself: Update the `showHome()` method with the code of Listing 16-50. Run the application and press the Home button. You should see the entire route on the screen, from the Apple Store to Grand Central Terminal.

There are two more methods defined in the `MKMapViewDelegate` protocol that could be useful when working with routes and destinations.

mapView(MKMapView, didSelect: MKAnnotationView)—This method is called on the delegate when an annotation view is selected.

mapView(MKMapView, didDeselect: MKAnnotationView)—This method is called on the delegate when an annotation view is deselected.

Using these methods, we can draw the route to the destination selected by the user. The following example looks for coffee shops nearby the Apple Store in New York City and implements the `mapView(MKMapView, didSelect:)` method to get the route between the Apple Store and the selected coffee shop.

```
import SwiftUI
import MapKit

struct MapView: UIViewRepresentable {
   var map = MKMapView()

   func makeUIView(context: Context) -> MKMapView {
      map.mapType = .standard
      map.delegate = context.coordinator
      return map
   }
```

Chapter 16 - Framework Integration

```swift
    func updateUIView(_ uiView: MKMapView, context: Context) {}

    func showHome() {
        let appleCoord = CLLocationCoordinate2D(latitude: 40.7637825011971,
longitude: -73.9731328627541)
        let region = MKCoordinateRegion(center: appleCoord,
latitudinalMeters: 2000, longitudinalMeters: 2000)
        map.setRegion(region, animated: false)

        let request = MKLocalSearch.Request()
        request.naturalLanguageQuery = "Coffee"
        request.region = region

        let search = MKLocalSearch(request: request)
        search.start(completionHandler: { (results, error) in
            if let items = results?.mapItems {
                for item in items {
                    if let coordinates = item.placemark.location?.coordinate {
                        let annotation = MKPointAnnotation()
                        annotation.coordinate = coordinates
                        annotation.title = item.name
                        annotation.subtitle = item.phoneNumber
                        self.map.addAnnotation(annotation)
                    }
                }
            }
        })
    }
    func makeCoordinator() -> MapViewCoordinator {
        return MapViewCoordinator(map: map)
    }
}
class MapViewCoordinator: NSObject, MKMapViewDelegate {
    var map: MKMapView
    var route: MKRoute?

    init(map: MKMapView) {
        self.map = map
    }
    func mapView(_ mapView: MKMapView, didSelect view: MKAnnotationView) {
        if let destinationCoord = view.annotation?.coordinate {
            let appleCoord = CLLocationCoordinate2D(latitude:
40.7637825011971, longitude: -73.9731328627541)
            let placeOrigin = MKPlacemark(coordinate: appleCoord)
            let origin = MKMapItem(placemark: placeOrigin)
            origin.name = "Apple Store"

            let placeDestination = MKPlacemark(coordinate: destinationCoord)
            let destination = MKMapItem(placemark: placeDestination)
            destination.name = view.annotation?.title!

            let request = MKDirections.Request()
            request.source = origin
            request.destination = destination
            request.transportType = .walking
            request.requestsAlternateRoutes = false

            let directions = MKDirections(request: request)
            directions.calculate(completionHandler: { (results, error) in
                if let routes = results?.routes {
                    if let oldRoute = self.route {
                        self.map.removeOverlay(oldRoute.polyline)
                        self.route = nil
                    }
```

```
            self.route = routes.first!
            self.map.addOverlay(self.route!.polyline, level:
.aboveRoads)
            }
         })
      }
   }
   func mapView(_ mapView: MKMapView, rendererFor overlay: MKOverlay) ->
MKOverlayRenderer {
      let render = MKPolylineRenderer(overlay: overlay)
      render.strokeColor = UIColor.red
      return render
   }
}
```

Listing 16-51: Calculating routes to the destinations selected by the user

The code of Listing 16-51 does not introduce anything new. We search for places related to the word "Coffee" around the Apple Store, create annotations for every place found, and add them to the map. When the user selects a pin, the delegate method is executed, and we use the pin's location to get the route between the Apple Store and the selected place. Because the user can select a different place after a route was added to the map, we store a reference to the route in the **route** property to be able to remove the overlay later.

 Do It Yourself: Update the MapView.swift file with the code in Listing 16-51. Run the application and press the Home button. You should see pints showing the coffee shops around the Apple store in New York. Tap on a pin. You should see the route from the Apple Store to the selected place.

Basic **16.5 Media**

These days, personal devices are primarily used to process pictures, videos and sound, and Apple devices are no exception. SwiftUI can display an image with an **Image** view, but it requires the assistance of other frameworks to process the image, present a video on the screen, or play sounds. In this section, we introduce some of the tools provided by Apple for this purpose.

Basic **Camera**

One of the most common uses of mobile devices is to take and store photos, and that is why no device is sold without a camera anymore. Because of how normal it is for an application to access the camera and manage pictures, UIKit offers a controller with built-in functionality that provides all the tools necessary for the user to take pictures and videos or select them from storage. The class to create this controller is called **UIImagePickerController**. The following are the properties included in this class for configuration.

sourceType—This property sets or returns a value that determines the type of source we want to use to get the pictures. It is an enumeration called **SourceType** included in the **UIImagePickerController** class. The values available are **camera** (for the camera), **photoLibrary** (for all the photos available on the device), and **savedPhotosAlbum** (for the photos taken by the camera).

mediaTypes—This property sets or returns a value that determines the type of media we want to work with. It takes an array of strings with the values that represent every media we want to use. The most common values are public.image for pictures and public.movie for videos (these values can be represented by the constants **kUTTypeImage** and **kUTTypeMovie**).

Chapter 16 - Framework Integration

cameraCaptureMode—This property sets or returns a value that determines the capture mode used by the camera. It is an enumeration called `CameraCaptureMode` included in the `UIImagePickerController` class. The values available are `photo` and `video`.

cameraFlashMode—This property sets or returns a value that determines the flash mode used by the camera. It is an enumeration called `CameraFlashMode` included in the `UIImagePickerController` class. The values available are `on`, `off`, and `auto`.

allowsEditing—This property sets or returns a Boolean value that determines if the user is allowed to edit the image.

videoQuality—This property sets or returns a value that determines the quality of the recorded video. It is an enumeration called `QualityType` included in the `UIImagePickerController` class. The values available are `typeHigh`, `typeMedium`, `typeLow`, `type640x480`, `typeIFrame960x540`, and `typeIFrame1280x720`.

The `UIImagePickerController` class also offers the following type methods to detect the source available (Camera or Photo Library) and the type of media the sources can manage.

isSourceTypeAvailable(SourceType**)**—This type method returns a Boolean value that indicates if the source specified by the attribute is supported by the device. The attribute is an enumeration called `SourceType` included in the `UIImagePickerController` class. the values available are `camera` (for the camera), `photoLibrary` (for all the photos available on the device), and `savedPhotosAlbum` (for the photos taken by the camera).

availableMediaTypes(for: SourceType**)**—This type method returns an array with strings that represent the media types available for the source specified by the attribute. The attribute is an enumeration called `SourceType` included in the `UIImagePickerController` class. The values available are `camera` (for the camera), `photoLibrary` (for all the photos available on the device), and `savedPhotosAlbum` (for the photos taken by the camera).

isCameraDeviceAvailable(CameraDevice**)**—This type method returns a Boolean value that indicates if the camera specified by the attribute is available on the device. The attribute is an enumeration called `CameraDevice` included in the `UIImagePickerController` class. The values available are `rear` and `front`.

The `UIImagePickerController` class creates a new view where the user can take pictures or select old ones from storage (depending on how we have configured the controller). After the image is created or selected, the view controller has to be dismissed and the selected image processed. The way our code gets access to this image and is able to know when to dismiss the view controller is through a delegate that conforms to the `UIImagePickerControllerDelegate` protocol. The protocol includes the following methods.

imagePickerController(UIImagePickerController, **didFinishPickingMediaWith-Info:** Dictionary**)**—This method is called on the delegate when the user finishes taking or selecting the image or video. The second attribute contains a dictionary with the information about the media. The values in the dictionary are identified with properties of the `InfoKey` structure included in the `UIImagePickerController` class. The properties available are `cropRect`, `editedImage`, `imageURL`, `livePhoto`, `mediaMetadata`, `mediaType`, `mediaURL`, `originalImage`, and `phAsset`.

imagePickerControllerDidCancel(UIImagePickerController**)**—This method is called on the delegate when the user cancels the process.

An image picker can be presented with a sheet or a popover, but if we want the view to occupy the entire screen, we can embed it in a `NavigationView` view and present it with a `NavigationLink`. This is the approach we are going to take in the following example. The interface includes a button to open the image picker and an `Image` view to display the picture taken by the user.

Figure 16-20: Interface to work with the camera

 IMPORTANT: To access the camera, you must ask authorization to the user. The process is automatic, but you have to add the "Privacy - Camera Usage Description" option to the info.plist file with the message you want to show to the user when permission is requested (see Figure 5-38 for more information).

The image picker controller is a view controller and therefore it has to be incorporated into the SwiftUI interface with a representable view controller. To be able to process the image taken or selected by the user, we need to include a coordinator and implement the delegate methods. This coordinator must conform to two protocols: `UINavigationControllerDelegate` and `UIImagePickerControllerDelegate`, as shown in the following example.

```
import SwiftUI

struct ImagePicker: UIViewControllerRepresentable {
    @Binding var openImagePicker: Bool
    @Binding var picture: UIImage?

    func makeUIViewController(context: Context) -> UIImagePickerController{
        let mediaPicker = UIImagePickerController()
        mediaPicker.delegate = context.coordinator
        if UIImagePickerController.isSourceTypeAvailable(.camera) {
            mediaPicker.sourceType = .camera
            mediaPicker.mediaTypes = ["public.image"]
            mediaPicker.allowsEditing = false
            mediaPicker.cameraCaptureMode = .photo
        } else {
            print("The media is not available")
        }
        return mediaPicker
    }
    func updateUIViewController(_ uiViewController:
UIImagePickerController, context: Context) {}
```

```
func makeCoordinator() -> ImagePickerCoordinator {
    ImagePickerCoordinator(open: $openImagePicker, picture: $picture)
}
}
class ImagePickerCoordinator: NSObject, UINavigationControllerDelegate,
UIImagePickerControllerDelegate {
    var openImagePicker: Binding<Bool>
    var picture: Binding<UIImage?>

    init(open: Binding<Bool>, picture: Binding<UIImage?>) {
        self.openImagePicker = open
        self.picture = picture
    }
    func imagePickerController(_ picker: UIImagePickerController,
didFinishPickingMediaWithInfo info: [UIImagePickerController.InfoKey :
Any]) {
        if let newpicture = info[.originalImage] as? UIImage {
            self.picture.wrappedValue = newpicture
        }
        self.openImagePicker.wrappedValue = false
    }
    func imagePickerControllerDidCancel(_ picker: UIImagePickerController)
{
        self.openImagePicker.wrappedValue = false
    }
}
```

Listing 16-52: Creating the image picker controller to take pictures

The representable view controller of Listing 16-52 creates an instance of the
UIImagePickerController class and assigns the **ImagePickerCoordinator** object as its
delegate. Next, it checks if the camera is available and configures the controller in case of success
or shows a message on the console otherwise. The value **camera** is assigned to the **sourceType**
property to tell the controller that we are going to get the picture from the camera, the
mediaTypes property is assigned an array with the value public.image to set images as the
media we want to retrieve, the **allowEditing** property is set as **false** to not let the user edit
the image, and the value **photo** is assigned to the **cameraCaptureMode** property to allow the
user only take pictures.

The camera's interface includes buttons to control the camera and take the picture. After the
user takes the picture, a new set of buttons is shown to let the user select the picture or take
another one. If the user decides to use the current picture, the controller calls the
imagePickerController(didFinishPickingMediaWithInfo:) method on its delegate to
report the action. This method receives a parameter called **info** that we can read to get the
media returned by the controller and process it (stores it in a file, Core Data, or show it on the
screen). In our example, we read the value of the **originalImage** key to get a **UIImage** object
that represents the image taken by the user and assign this object to a **Binding** property to
make it available for the view. Notice that we have also implemented the
imagePickerControllerDidCancel() method in the coordinator to dismiss the controller
when the user presses the Cancel button.

The view includes a button to open the image picker controller and an **Image** view to show
the picture taken by the user.

```
import SwiftUI

class ContentData: ObservableObject {
    @Published var openImagePicker: Bool = false
    @Published var picture: UIImage?
}
struct ContentView: View {
    @ObservedObject var contentData = ContentData()
    var imagePicker: ImagePicker!

    init() {
        imagePicker = ImagePicker(openImagePicker:
self.$contentData.openImagePicker, picture: self.$contentData.picture)
    }
    var body: some View {
        NavigationView {
            VStack {
                HStack {
                    Spacer()
                    NavigationLink(
                        destination: imagePicker
                            .navigationBarTitle("")
                            .navigationBarHidden(true)
                            .edgesIgnoringSafeArea(.all),
                        isActive: $contentData.openImagePicker, label: {
                            Text("Get Picture")
                        })
                }
                Image(uiImage: contentData.picture ?? UIImage(named:
"nopicture")!)
                    .resizable()
                    .scaledToFill()
                    .frame(minWidth: 0, maxWidth: .infinity, minHeight: 0,
maxHeight: .infinity)
                    .clipped()
                Spacer()
            }.padding()
            .navigationBarTitle("")
            .navigationBarHidden(true)
        }.statusBar(hidden: true)
    }
}
```

Listing 16-53: Defining the interface to take pictures

The view in Listing 16-53 creates an instance of the **ImagePicker** structure and declares it as the destination of a **NavigationLink** button. When the button is pressed, the view is opened full screen (the modifiers applied to the view remove the navigation bar and extends the view over the safe area). If the user takes a picture and decides to use it, the picture is assigned to the **picture** property by the delegate method and the **Image** view is updated to display the image on the screen.

 Do It Yourself: Create a SwiftUI project. Create a Swift file called ImagePicker.swift with the code in Listing 16-52. Update the ContentView.swift file with the code in Listing 16-53. Download the image nopicture.png from our website and add it to the Assets Catalog. Add the "Privacy - Camera Usage Description" option to the info.plist file with the text you want to show to the user. Run the application on a device and press the button. Take a picture and press the button to use it. You should see the photo on the screen. At the time of writing, Image views do not process the image correctly. If you find any issues, you can modify the image with an image renderer before assigning it to the view, as we do later in Listing 16-58.

(Basic) ## Photo Library

Except for the value of the `sourceType` property, the rest of the configuration values used in the previous example are the ones defined by default, so if all we want to do is to let the user take a picture, we don't need to declare anything else. The same goes for the Photo Library. If we want to let the user select a picture from the list of images available on the device, we just have to indicate the source changing the value of the `sourceType` property, as shown in the following example.

```
func makeUIViewController(context: Context) -> UIImagePickerController {
   let mediaPicker = UIImagePickerController()
   mediaPicker.delegate = context.coordinator
   if UIImagePickerController.isSourceTypeAvailable(.photoLibrary) {
      mediaPicker.sourceType = .photoLibrary
   } else {
      print("The media is not available")
   }
   return mediaPicker
}
```

Listing 16-54: *Selecting a picture from the Photo library*

There are two values we can assign to the `sourceType` property to load photos: `photoLibrary` and `savedPhotosAlbum`. The `photoLibrary` option shows all the photos organized in a list of albums, and the `savedPhotosAlbum` option gives priority to the photos in the camera roll. In Listing 16-54 we choose the first option. With this simple change, instead of showing a view with an interface to operate the camera, the system opens a view with a list of pictures available. When the user selects a picture, the `imagePickerController(didFinishPickingMediaWithInfo:)` method is called on the controller's delegate and the picture is shown on the screen.

Figure 16-21: *Photo Library's interface*

The Photo Library may contain images and videos. We can define the type of media we want the controller to display assigning a new value to the **mediaTypes** property and then read the value associated to the **mediaType** key to select the media we want.

```swift
import SwiftUI

struct ImagePicker: UIViewControllerRepresentable {
    @Binding var openImagePicker: Bool
    @Binding var picture: UIImage?

    func makeUIViewController(context: Context) -> UIImagePickerController{
        let mediaPicker = UIImagePickerController()
        mediaPicker.delegate = context.coordinator
        if UIImagePickerController.isSourceTypeAvailable(.photoLibrary) {
            mediaPicker.sourceType = .photoLibrary
            mediaPicker.mediaTypes = ["public.image", "public.movie"]
        } else {
            print("The media is not available")
        }
        return mediaPicker
    }
    func updateUIViewController(_ uiViewController:
UIImagePickerController, context: Context) {}

    func makeCoordinator() -> ImagePickerCoordinator {
        ImagePickerCoordinator(open: $openImagePicker, picture: $picture)
    }
}
class ImagePickerCoordinator: NSObject, UINavigationControllerDelegate,
UIImagePickerControllerDelegate {
    var openImagePicker: Binding<Bool>
    var picture: Binding<UIImage?>

    init(open: Binding<Bool>, picture: Binding<UIImage?>) {
        self.openImagePicker = open
        self.picture = picture
    }
    func imagePickerController(_ picker: UIImagePickerController,
didFinishPickingMediaWithInfo info: [UIImagePickerController.InfoKey :
Any]) {
        let media = info[.mediaType] as! String
        if media == "public.image" {
            if let newpicture = info[.originalImage] as? UIImage {
                self.picture.wrappedValue = newpicture
            }
        }
        self.openImagePicker.wrappedValue = false
    }
    func imagePickerControllerDidCancel(_ picker: UIImagePickerController){
        self.openImagePicker.wrappedValue = false
    }
}
```

Listing 16-55: Selecting images or videos

In this example, we let the user select pictures or videos, but only process images, as we did before. We will see how to play videos later.

Do It Yourself: Update the ImagePicker.swift file with the code in Listing 16-55. Run the application on a device and press the Get Picture button. Select a picture from your library. You should see the picture on the screen.

In the previous examples, we show the picture on the screen, but we can store it in a file or in Core Data. An alternative, sometimes useful when working with the camera, is to store the picture in the device's Photo Library to make it accessible for other applications. The UIKit framework offers two functions to store images and videos.

UIImageWriteToSavedPhotosAlbum(UIImage, Any?, Selector?, Unsafe-MutableRawPointer?**)**—This function adds the image specified by the first attribute to the camera roll. The second attribute is a reference to the object that contains the method we want to execute when the process is over, the third attribute is a selector that represents that method, and the last attribute is an object with additional data to pass to the method.

UISaveVideoAtPathToSavedPhotosAlbum(String, Any?, Selector?, Unsafe-MutableRawPointer?**)**—This function adds the video at the path indicated by the first attribute to the camera roll. The second attribute is a reference to the object that contains the method we want to execute when the process is over, the third attribute is a selector that represents that method, and the last attribute is an object with additional data for the method.

 IMPORTANT: When we get media from the Photo Library, the system takes care of the security aspects for us, but when we try to store new pictures or videos in the device, we must ask the user's authorization. As always, this is done from the info.plist file. In this case, we must add the "Privacy - Photo Library Additions Usage Description" option with the message we want to show to the user when authorization is requested.

These functions store the picture or video taken by the camera in the Photo Library and then call a method to report the result of the operation. We can declare the target object and the selector as `nil` if we don't want to know what happened or define a method in our view controller to handle the response. This method can have any name we want, but it is required to have a specific definition that includes three attributes. For images, the attributes are (`image: UIImage, didFinishSavingWithError error: NSError?, contextInfo: UnsafeRawPointer`) and for videos the attributes are (`video: String, didFinishSavingWithError error: NSError?, contextInfo: UnsafeRawPointer`). In the following example, we show the picture taken with the camera on the screen, store it in the Photo Library, and open an Alert view in case of success to inform to the user that the picture is available with the rest of the photos. For this purpose, we need to update the view to include a `@State` property to indicate whether the Alert view is open or not, and an `alert()` modifier.

```
import SwiftUI

class ContentData: ObservableObject {
    @Published var showAlert: Bool = false
    @Published var openImagePicker: Bool = false
    @Published var picture: UIImage?
}
struct ContentView: View {
    @ObservedObject var contentData = ContentData()
    var imagePicker: ImagePicker!
```

```
    init() {
        imagePicker = ImagePicker(showAlert: $contentData.showAlert,
openImagePicker: $contentData.openImagePicker, picture:
$contentData.picture)
    }
    var body: some View {
        NavigationView {
            VStack {
                HStack {
                    Spacer()
                    NavigationLink(
                        destination: imagePicker
                            .navigationBarTitle("")
                            .navigationBarHidden(true)
                            .edgesIgnoringSafeArea(.all),
                        isActive: $contentData.openImagePicker, label: {
                        Text("Get Picture")
                    })
                }
                Image(uiImage: contentData.picture ?? UIImage(named:
"nopicture")!)
                    .resizable()
                    .scaledToFill()
                    .frame(minWidth: 0, maxWidth: .infinity, minHeight: 0,
maxHeight: .infinity)
                    .clipped()
                Spacer()
            }.padding()
            .navigationBarTitle("")
            .navigationBarHidden(true)
            .alert(isPresented: $contentData.showAlert) {
                Alert(title: Text("Picture Saved"), message: Text("The
picture was added to your photos"), dismissButton: .default(Text("OK")))
            }
        }.statusBar(hidden: true)
    }
}
```

Listing 16-56: Showing an Alert view when a picture is saved

The **ImagePicker** structure has to include an additional **@Binding** property to modify the value of the **showAlert** property, save the picture with the **UIImageWriteToSaved-PhotosAlbum** function, and implement the method required to activate the Alert view.

```
import SwiftUI

struct ImagePicker: UIViewControllerRepresentable {
    @Binding var showAlert: Bool
    @Binding var openImagePicker: Bool
    @Binding var picture: UIImage?

    func makeUIViewController(context: Context) -> UIImagePickerController{
        let mediaPicker = UIImagePickerController()
        mediaPicker.delegate = context.coordinator
        if UIImagePickerController.isSourceTypeAvailable(.camera) {
            mediaPicker.sourceType = .camera
        } else {
            print("The media is not available")
        }
        return mediaPicker
    }
```

Chapter 16 - Framework Integration

```
    func updateUIViewController(_ uiViewController:
UIImagePickerController, context: Context) {}

    func makeCoordinator() -> ImagePickerCoordinator {
        ImagePickerCoordinator(alert: $showAlert, open: $openImagePicker,
picture: $picture)
    }
}
class ImagePickerCoordinator: NSObject, UINavigationControllerDelegate,
UIImagePickerControllerDelegate {
    var showAlert: Binding<Bool>
    var openImagePicker: Binding<Bool>
    var picture: Binding<UIImage?>

    init(alert: Binding<Bool>, open: Binding<Bool>, picture:
Binding<UIImage?>) {
        self.showAlert = alert
        self.openImagePicker = open
        self.picture = picture
    }
    func imagePickerController(_ picker: UIImagePickerController,
didFinishPickingMediaWithInfo info: [UIImagePickerController.InfoKey :
Any]) {
        if let newpicture = info[.originalImage] as? UIImage {
            self.picture.wrappedValue = newpicture
            UIImageWriteToSavedPhotosAlbum(newpicture, self,
#selector(confirmImage(image:didFinishSavingWithError:contextInfo:)),
nil)
        }
        self.openImagePicker.wrappedValue = false
    }
    @objc func confirmImage(image: UIImage, didFinishSavingWithError
error: NSError?, contextInfo: UnsafeRawPointer) {
        if error == nil {
            self.showAlert.wrappedValue = true
        } else {
            print("Error")
        }
    }
}
```

Listing 16-57: *Storing pictures in the Photo Library*

The process is the same as before. The image picker controller allows the user to take a picture and then calls the delegate method to process it. The picture is assigned to the `picture` property to display it on the screen, but now we also call the `UIImageWriteToSavedPhotosAlbum` function to store it in the Photo library. When the function finishes the task, it calls a method using a selector (see Chapter 9, Listing 9-61). In this method, we assign the value `true` to the `showAlert` property to open the Alert view and let the user know that the picture was successfully stored in the Photo library.

 Do It Yourself: Update the `ContentView` structure with the code of Listing 16-56 and the ImagePicker.swift file with the code of Listing 16-57. Add the "Privacy - Photo Library Additions Usage Description" option to the info.plist file to get access to the Photo Library (you also need the "Privacy - Camera Usage Description" option to access the camera, as before). Run the application and take a picture. You should see an Alert view with the message "Picture Saved" and the picture should be available in your device's Photo Library.

Medium Modifying Pictures

Due to the limited capacity of mobile devices, we cannot work with multiple images in their original size at the same time. Pictures must be immediately stored and, in some cases, reduced in size for future use. SwiftUI does not include any tools to resize or clip an image, but we can use those provided by UIKit. The list of tools is extensive, but usually all we need is to create an image context to draw the graphics into an image and then store the image, process it, or show it to the user. For this purpose, the framework includes the `UIGraphicsImageRenderer` class to create and manage an image renderer. The class includes initializers to create the renderer and methods to render the image. The following are the most frequently used.

UIGraphicsImageRenderer(size: CGSize**)**—This initializer creates a renderer to manage an image of the size determined by the **size** attribute.

UIGraphicsImageRenderer(size: CGSize, **format:** UIGraphicsImageRenderer-Format**)**—This initializer creates a renderer to manage an image with a size and a format determined by its attributes. The **size** attribute determines the image's size, and the **format** attribute defines the characteristics of the renderer. To specify the values, the class includes the properties `opaque` (`Bool`), `prefersExtendedRange` (`Bool`), and `scale` (`CGFloat`).

image(actions: Block**)**—This method generates the image context and sends it to the closure assigned to the **actions** attribute. The value received by the closure is an object of type `UIGraphicsRendererContext` with the renderer's image context that we can use to create the image.

An image context is represented by an object of the `UIGraphicsImageRendererContext` class (a subclass of `UIGraphicsRendererContext`). This object offers the following properties.

cgContext—This property returns a **CGContext** object representing the drawing context.

currentImage—This property returns a `UIImage` object with the image in the context.

The UIKit framework also defines a set of functions to manage the contexts. The following is the one we need to set a new context as the current one.

UIGraphicsPushContext(CGContext**)**—This function sets a new context as the current context. The contexts are added to a stack. The current context is considered to be the last one added to the stack.

The `UIImage` class also offers methods to draw an image onto the context. The following are the most frequently used.

draw(at: CGPoint**)**—This method draws the image at the location specified by the **at** attribute.

draw(in: CGRect**)**—This method draws the image inside the rectangle determined by the **in** attribute.

A common practice is to store the original picture along with a thumbnail to use as preview. The following example creates a thumbnail of the picture taken by the camera.

```swift
import SwiftUI

struct ImagePicker: UIViewControllerRepresentable {
    @Binding var showAlert: Bool
    @Binding var openImagePicker: Bool
    @Binding var picture: UIImage?

    func makeUIViewController(context: Context) -> UIImagePickerController{
        let mediaPicker = UIImagePickerController()
        mediaPicker.delegate = context.coordinator
        if UIImagePickerController.isSourceTypeAvailable(.camera) {
            mediaPicker.sourceType = .camera
        } else {
            print("The media is not available")
        }
        return mediaPicker
    }
    func updateUIViewController(_ uiViewController:
UIImagePickerController, context: Context) {}

    func makeCoordinator() -> ImagePickerCoordinator {
        ImagePickerCoordinator(alert: $showAlert, open: $openImagePicker,
picture: $picture)
    }
}
class ImagePickerCoordinator: NSObject, UINavigationControllerDelegate,
UIImagePickerControllerDelegate {
    var showAlert: Binding<Bool>
    var openImagePicker: Binding<Bool>
    var picture: Binding<UIImage?>

    init(alert: Binding<Bool>, open: Binding<Bool>, picture:
Binding<UIImage?>) {
        self.showAlert = alert
        self.openImagePicker = open
        self.picture = picture
    }
    func imagePickerController(_ picker: UIImagePickerController,
didFinishPickingMediaWithInfo info: [UIImagePickerController.InfoKey :
Any]) {
        if let newpicture = info[.originalImage] as? UIImage {
            let scale = UIScreen.main.scale
            let maximum: CGFloat = 80
            var width = newpicture.size.width / scale
            var height = newpicture.size.height / scale

            if width > height {
                height = height * maximum / width
                width = maximum
            } else {
                width = width * maximum / height
                height = maximum
            }
            let render = UIGraphicsImageRenderer(size: CGSize(width: width,
height: height))
            render.image(actions: { (renderContext) in
                let context = renderContext.cgContext
                UIGraphicsPushContext(context)
                newpicture.draw(in: CGRect(x: 0, y: 0, width: width, height:
height))

                self.picture.wrappedValue = renderContext.currentImage
```

```
        })
        self.openImagePicker.wrappedValue = false
    }
  }
}
```

Listing 16-58: Creating a thumbnail

The code of Listing 16-58 takes the picture returned by the camera, calculates the width and height considering a maximum size of 80 points, and creates a new image with this information. Notice that the `UIImage` returned by the `originalImage` key is defined in pixels, so we must calculate its size in points dividing the width and height by the scale of the device. Because we are using the `draw()` method of the `UIImage` class to draw the image, we turn the graphic context into the current context by adding it to the stack with the `UIGraphicsPushContext()` function. After the current context is set, we draw the image and then retrieve the result with the `currentImage` property and assign it to the `picture` property, as always.

Do It Yourself: Update the ImagePicker.swift file with the code of Listing 16-58. This view returns an image 80 points wide that the `Image` view in our interface will stretch to fill the space available. To see the image in its original size, remove all the modifiers for the `Image` view and assign the `fixedSize()` modifier instead. Run the application and take a picture. You should see a small image on the screen.

(Medium) **Custom Camera**

The `UIImagePickerController` controller is built from classes defined in two frameworks: AV Foundation and Photos. The AV Foundation framework provides the codes necessary to process media and control input devices, like the camera and the microphone, and the Photos framework provides access to the user's photos in the device. We can use the classes in these frameworks directly to build our own controller and customize the process and the interface.

Creating our own controller to access the camera and retrieve information from that device demands the manipulation and coordination of several systems. We need to configure the input from at least two devices, the camera and the microphone, process the data received from this input, show a preview to the user, and generate the output in the form of an image, live photo, video, or audio. Figure 16-22 illustrates all the elements involved.

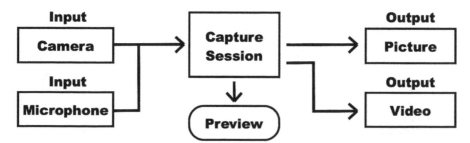

Figure 16-22: System to capture media

The first thing we need to do to build this structure is to determine the input devices. The AV Foundation framework defines the `AVCaptureDevice` class for this purpose. An instance of this class can represent any type of input device, including cameras and microphones. The following are the type methods included in the class to access and manage a device.

Chapter 16 - Framework Integration

default(for: AVMediaType)—This type method returns an `AVCaptureDevice` object that represents the default capture device for the media specified by the attribute. The **for** attribute is a structure of type `AVMediaType` with properties to define the type of media. The properties available to work with the cameras and microphones are `video` and `audio`.

devices(for: AVMediaType)—This type method returns an array of `AVCaptureDevice` objects that represent the devices of the type specified by the attribute. The **for** attribute is a structure of type `AVMediaType` with properties to define the type of media. The properties available to work with the cameras and microphones are `video` and `audio`.

requestAccess(for: AVMediaType, **completionHandler:** Closure)—This type method asks permission to the user to access the device. The **for** attribute is a structure of type `AVMediaType` with properties to define the type of media. The properties available to work with the cameras and microphones are `video` and `audio`. The **completionHandler** attribute is a closure with the statements we want to execute after the request is completed.

authorizationStatus(for: AVMediaType)—This type method returns a value that determines the status of the authorization to use the device. The **for** attribute is a structure of type `AVMediaType` with properties to define the type of media. The properties available to work with the cameras and microphones are `video` and `audio`. The method returns an enumeration of type `AVAuthorizationStatus` with the values `notDetermined`, `restricted`, `denied`, and `authorized`.

An instance of the `AVCaptureDevice` class represents a capture device. To define this device as an input device, we must create an object that controls the ports and connections of the input. The framework defines the `AVCaptureDeviceInput` class for this purpose. The class includes the following initializer to create the input object for the device.

AVCaptureDeviceInput(device: AVCaptureDevice)—This initializer creates an input for the device specified by the **device** attribute.

As well as inputs, we also have to define outputs to process the data captured by the device. The framework defines subclasses of a base class called `AVCaptureOutput` to describe the outputs. There are several subclasses available, such as `AVCaptureVideoDataOutput` to process the frames of a video, and `AVCaptureAudioDataOutput` to get the audio, but the most frequently used is the `AVCapturePhotoOutput` to capture a single video frame (take a picture). This class works with a delegate that conforms to the `AVCapturePhotoCaptureDelegate` protocol, which among other methods defines the following to return an image.

photoOutput(AVCapturePhotoOutput, **didFinishProcessingPhoto:** AVCapturePhoto, **error:** Error?)—This method is called on the delegate after the image is captured. The **didFinishProcessingPhoto** attribute is a container with information about the image, and the **error** attribute is used to report errors.

To control the flow of data from input to output, the framework defines the `AVCaptureSession` class. From an instance of this class, we can control the inputs and outputs and when the process begins and ends. The following are some of its properties and methods.

isRunning— This property returns a Boolean value that determines whether the session is currently running or not.

isInterrupted—This property returns a Boolean value that determines if the session was interrupted.

sessionPreset—This property sets or returns a value of type `AVCaptureSession.Preset` that determines the quality of the output. The `Preset` structure includes the following constants for this purpose: `cif352x288`, `hd1280x720`, `hd1920x1080`, `hd4K3840x2160`, `high` (default), `iFrame1280x720`, `iFrame960x540`, `inputPriority`, `low`, `medium`, `photo`, `qHD960x540`, `qvga320x240`, and `vga640x480`.

addInput(AVCaptureInput)—This method adds an input to the capture session. The attribute represents the input device we want to add.

addOutput(AVCaptureOutput)—This method adds an output to the capture session. The attribute represents the output we want to generate from the capture session.

startRunning()—This method starts the capture session.

stopRunning()—This method stops the capture session.

The framework also defines the `AVCaptureVideoPreviewLayer` class with the purpose of showing a preview to the user. The class includes the following initializer and properties to create and manage the preview layer.

AVCaptureVideoPreviewLayer(session: `AVCaptureSession`**)**—This initializer creates an `AVCaptureVideoPreviewLayer` object with a preview layer connected to the capture session defined by the **session** attribute.

videoGravity—This property defines how the video adjusts its size to the size of the preview layer. It is an enumeration of type `AVLayerVideoGravity` with the values `resizeAspect`, `resizeAspectFill`, and `resize`.

connection—This property returns an object of type `AVCaptureConnection` that defines the connection between the capture session and the preview layer.

The input, output, and preview layers are connected to the capture session by objects of the `AVCaptureConnection` class. The class manages the information of the connection, including ports and data. The following are its most frequently used properties.

videoOrientation—This property sets or returns the orientation of the video. It is an enumeration of type `AVCaptureVideoOrientation` with the values `portrait`, `portraitUpsideDown`, `landscapeRight`, and `landscapeLeft`.

isVideoOrientationSupported—This property returns a Boolean value that determines whether it is allowed to set the video's orientation or not.

The interface we are going to create for this example is similar than before. We need a button to open the view that allows the user to take a picture with the camera, and an Image view to show it on the screen.

Figure 16-23: Interface for a custom camera

The process to activate the camera and get the picture taken by the user is independent of the interface, but if we want to let the user see the image coming from the camera, we must create a preview layer and add it to a UIKit view. UIKit views are created from the `UIView` class, so we need to define a representable view. For this example, we are going to manage all the logic for the camera in this view. The following are the basic elements we need to set up the view.

```swift
import SwiftUI
import AVFoundation
class ViewData {
    var captureSession: AVCaptureSession!
    var stillImage: AVCapturePhotoOutput!
    var previewLayer: AVCaptureVideoPreviewLayer!
    var imageOrientation: UIImage.Orientation!
    var coordinator: ViewCoordinator!
}
struct CustomView: UIViewRepresentable {
    @Binding var openCamera: Bool
    @Binding var picture: UIImage?
    var viewData = ViewData()
    let view = UIView()

    init(openCamera: Binding<Bool>, picture: Binding<UIImage?>) {
        self._openCamera = openCamera
        self._picture = picture
    }
    func makeUIView(context: Context) -> UIView {
        return view
    }
    func updateUIView(_ uiView: UIView, context: Context) {
        let main = OperationQueue.main
        main.addOperation {
            if self.viewData.captureSession != nil {
                self.viewData.previewLayer?.frame = self.view.bounds
                let connection = self.viewData.previewLayer.connection
                connection?.videoOrientation = self.getCurrentOrientation()
            }
        }
    }
}
```

Listing 16-59: Defining a `UIView`

The code in Listing 16-59 is only part of the representable view, we still need to add a few methods to activate and control the camera, but it provides the set of properties we need to store references to every element of the system and instantiate the `UIView` view we need to show the preview layer. Because these properties are required by multiple methods, we declare them in a separate object called `ViewData`. The `UIView` is created and then returned by the `makeUIView()` method, as we did for other views, but this time we also implement the `updateUIView()` method to update the orientation of the preview layer every time the device is rotated. We will see how the orientation is determined later.

The next step is to define a method to ask for the user's permission to use the camera. This is done automatically when we use a `UIImagePickerController` controller, but we have to do it ourselves in a custom controller using the type methods provided by the `AVCaptureDevice` class. The following is the method we must add to the `CustomView` structure for this purpose.

```
func getAuthorization() {
    let status = AVCaptureDevice.authorizationStatus(for: .video)
    if status == .authorized {
        let main = OperationQueue.main
        main.addOperation({
            self.prepareCamera()
        })
    } else if status == .notDetermined {
        AVCaptureDevice.requestAccess(for: .video, completionHandler: {
(granted: Bool) in
            let main = OperationQueue.main
            main.addOperation({
                if granted {
                    self.prepareCamera()
                } else {
                    print("Not Authorized")
                }
            })
        })
    } else {
        print("Not Authorized")
    }
}
```

Listing 16-60: Asking permission to use the camera

The `authorizationStatus()` method returns an `AVAuthorizationStatus` value to inform the current status of the authorization. If the value is `authorized`, it means that were already authorized and we can use the camera, but if the value is `notDetermined`, we have to call the `requestAccess()` method to ask permission. This method includes a closure as the second parameter that is executed after the user responds to the request. The closure includes an attribute of type `Bool` to report the user's decision. If the user grants access, the `prepareCamera()` method is executed. This method is where we begin to build the network of objects introduced in Figure 16-22. This method gets a reference to the current capture device for video and creates the inputs and outputs we need to capture a still image (to take a picture).

```
func prepareCamera() {
    viewData.captureSession = AVCaptureSession()
    viewData.captureSession.sessionPreset = .photo

    if let device = AVCaptureDevice.default(for: AVMediaType.video) {
        if let input = try? AVCaptureDeviceInput(device: device) {
```

```
        viewData.captureSession.addInput(input)
        viewData.stillImage = AVCapturePhotoOutput()
        viewData.captureSession.addOutput(viewData.stillImage)
        self.showCamera()
      } else {
        print("Not Authorized")
      }
    } else {
      print("Not Authorized")
    }
}
```

Listing 16-61: Initializing the camera

We can create and add to the session all the inputs and outputs we need, in any order, but because the **AVCaptureDeviceInput()** initializer throws an error, we use it first. This initializer creates an object that manages the input for the capture device. If the initializer is successful, we add it to the capture session with the **addInput()** method and then create the output. For this example we have decided to use the session to capture a still image, so we use the **AVCapturePhotoOutput** class to create the output and add it to the session with the **addOutput()** method.

After adding the inputs and outputs to the capture session, the **prepareCamera()** method executes an additional method called **showCamera()** to generate the preview layer and show the video coming from the camera on the screen. In this method, we must create the layer and set its size and orientation.

```
func showCamera() {
    let width = view.bounds.size.width
    let height - view.bounds.size.height

    viewData.previewLayer = AVCaptureVideoPreviewLayer(session:
viewData.captureSession)
    viewData.previewLayer.videoGravity = .resizeAspectFill
    viewData.previewLayer.frame = CGRect(x: 0, y: 0, width: width, height:
height)

    let connection = viewData.previewLayer.connection
    connection?.videoOrientation = getCurrentOrientation()

    let layer = view.layer
    layer.addSublayer(viewData.previewLayer)
    viewData.captureSession.startRunning()
}
```

Listing 16-62: Showing the video from the camera on the screen

The **AVCaptureVideoPreviewLayer()** initializer creates a layer that we have to adjust to the size of its view and add as a sublayer of the current view's layer. But setting the position and size of the layer does not determine how its content is going to be shown. The video coming from the camera could have a different size and orientation. How the video is going to adjust to the size of the layer is determined by the value of the layer's **videoGravity** property, and the orientation is set from the connection established between the capture session and the preview layer. That is why, after setting the value of the **videoGravity** property and the layer's frame, we get a reference to the connection from the layer's **connection** property. By modifying the **videoOrientation** property of the connection, we can adjust the orientation according to the device's orientation and finally add the sublayer to the view's layer with the **addSublayer()**

method (In this example we assume that the device is always in portrait mode). When the sublayer is ready, the capture session can be initiated with the **startRunning()** method.

The value of the **videoOrientation** property is determined by a method called **getCurrentOrientation()**. We not only need to know the device's orientation to define the orientation of the preview layer, but also to define the orientation of the image taken by the camera. This method returns the **AVCaptureVideoOrientation** value we need to set the orientation of the preview layer and stores a **UIImage.Orientation** value in the **imageOrientation** property to set the orientation of the image later.

```
func getCurrentOrientation() -> AVCaptureVideoOrientation {
    var orientation: AVCaptureVideoOrientation = .portrait
    let device = UIDevice.current
    switch device.orientation {
        case .portrait:
            orientation = .portrait
            viewData.imageOrientation = .right
        case .landscapeRight:
            orientation = .landscapeLeft
            viewData.imageOrientation = .down
        case .landscapeLeft:
            orientation = .landscapeRight
            viewData.imageOrientation = .up
        default:
            break
    }
    return orientation
}
```

Listing 16-63: Detecting the device's orientation

 IMPORTANT: The camera always encodes the image in its native orientation, which is landscape-right. In consequence, when the device is in portrait mode, we have to set the orientation of the image to right, when it is in landscape-left mode, we have to set the image's orientation to down, and when it is in landscape-right mode, we have to set it to up. Also, the landscape orientation of the video is the opposite of the device, therefore when the device is in the landscape-right orientation, the video orientation is landscape-left, and vice versa.

At this point, the video is playing on the screen and the system is ready to perform a capture. The process to capture an image is initiated by the output object. The **AVCapturePhotoOutput** class we use to capture a still image offers the following method for this purpose.

capturePhoto(with: AVCapturePhotoSettings, **delegate:** AVCapturePhoto-CaptureDelegate)—This method initiates a photo capture with the settings specified by the **with** attribute. The **delegate** attribute is a reference to the object that implements the methods of the **AVCapturePhotoCaptureDelegate** protocol to receive the data generated by the output.

The type of photo captured by the output is determined by an **AVCapturePhotoSettings** object. The class includes multiple initializers. The following are the most frequently used.

AVCapturePhotoSettings()—This initializer creates an **AVCapturePhotoSettings** object with the format by default.

AVCapturePhotoSettings(format: Dictionary)—This initializer creates a `AVCapturePhotoSettings` object with the format specified by the **format** attribute. The attribute is a dictionary with keys and values to set the characteristics of the image. Some of the keys available are **kCVPixelBufferPixelFormatTypeKey** (uncompressed format), **AVVideoCodecKey** (compressed format), **AVVideoQualityKey** (compression quality).

The following are the properties available in this class to configure the image and the preview.

previewPhotoFormat—This property sets or returns a dictionary with keys and values that determine the characteristics of the preview image. The keys available are **kCVPixelBufferPixelFormatTypeKey** (uncompressed format), **kCVPixelBufferWidthKey** (maximum width) and **kCVPixelBufferHeightKey** (maximum height).

flashMode—This property sets or returns the flash mode used when the image is captured. It is an enumeration of type **FlashMode** with the values **on**, **off**, and **auto**.

isAutoStillImageStabilizationEnabled—This property is a Boolean value that determines if automatic image stabilization is enabled or not.

isHighResolutionPhotoEnabled—This property is a Boolean value that determines if the image is going to be taken in high resolution.

To capture an image, we have to define the settings with an **AVCapturePhotoSettings** object, call the **capturePhoto()** method of the **AVCapturePhotoOutput** object, and define the delegate method that is going to receive the image. Let's see first the methods we need to add to the **CustomView** structure to take the picture.

```
func takePicture() {
    let settings = AVCapturePhotoSettings()
    viewData.stillImage.capturePhoto(with: settings, delegate:
viewData.coordinator)
}
func makeCoordinator() -> ViewCoordinator {
    viewData.coordinator = ViewCoordinator(picture: $picture, open:
$openCamera, viewData: viewData)
    return viewData.coordinator
}
```

Listing 16-64: Taking a picture

When the user presses the button to take the picture, the **takePicture()** method is executed and the **capturePhoto()** method is called to ask the output object to capture an image. After the image is captured, this object sends the result to the delegate method. Notice that the delegate object is the view's coordinator. To be able to assign this delegate, we store a reference to the coordinator in a property of the **viewData** object called **coordinator** when the coordinator object is created.

The **CustomView** structure is finished. Now, it is time to define the coordinator and implement the delegate method to process the image.

```
class ViewCoordinator: NSObject, AVCapturePhotoCaptureDelegate {
    var picture: Binding<UIImage?>
    var openCamera: Binding<Bool>
    var viewData: ViewData

    init(picture: Binding<UIImage?>, open: Binding<Bool>, viewData:
ViewData) {
        self.picture = picture
        self.openCamera = open
        self.viewData = viewData
    }
    func photoOutput(_ output: AVCapturePhotoOutput,
didFinishProcessingPhoto photo: AVCapturePhoto, error: Error?) {
        let scale = UIScreen.main.scale
        if let imageData = photo.fileDataRepresentation() {
            self.picture.wrappedValue = UIImage(data: imageData, scale:
scale)
            self.openCamera.wrappedValue = false
        }
    }
}
```

Listing 16-65: Processing the image

The coordinator in Listing 16-65 conforms to the `AVCapturePhotoCaptureDelegate`
protocol and implements the `photoOutput(AVCapturePhotoOutput, didFinish-`
`ProcessingPhoto:)` method to receive the picture produced by the camera. The value
received by this method is an object of type `AVCapturePhoto`, which is a container with
information about the image. The class includes two convenient methods to get the data
representing the image.

fileDataRepresentation()—This method returns a data representation of the image that
we can use to create a `UIImage` object.

cgImageRepresentation()—This method returns the image as a `CGImage` object.

In our example, we have implemented the `fileDataRepresentation()` method to create
a `UIImage` object and assign it to the `picture` property to update the view. The view receives
this value and displays the image on the screen, as shown next.

```
import SwiftUI

struct ContentView: View {
    @State private var openCamera: Bool = false
    @State private var picture: UIImage?

    var body: some View {
        NavigationView {
            VStack {
                HStack {
                    Spacer()
                    NavigationLink(destination: CustomCameraView(openCamera:
$openCamera, picture: $picture), isActive: $openCamera, label: {
Text("Take Picture") })
                    }
                Image(uiImage: picture ?? UIImage(named: "nopicture")!)
                    .resizable()
                    .scaledToFill()
```

```
                .frame(minWidth: 0, maxWidth: .infinity, minHeight: 0,
maxHeight: .infinity)
                    .clipped()
                Spacer()
            }.padding()
            .navigationBarTitle("")
            .navigationBarHidden(true)
        }.statusBar(hidden: true)
    }
}
```

Listing 16-66: Showing the image

There is nothing new in this view, with the exception that now instead of opening a **UIImagePickerController** with a standard interface, we open a view that has to provide the buttons and custom controls required for the user to take a picture. The following is our implementation of this view.

```
import SwiftUI

struct CustomCameraView: View {
    @Binding var openCamera: Bool
    @Binding var picture: UIImage?
    var customView: CustomView!

    init(openCamera: Binding<Bool>, picture: Binding<UIImage?>) {
        self._openCamera = openCamera
        self._picture = picture
        customView = CustomView(openCamera: openCamera, picture: picture)
    }
    var body: some View {
        ZStack {
            customView
                .onAppear(perform: {
                    self.customView.getAuthorization()
                })
            VStack {
                Spacer()
                HStack {
                    Button("Cancel") {
                        self.openCamera = false
                    }
                    Spacer()
                    Button("Take Picture") {
                        self.customView.takePicture()
                    }
                }.padding()
                .frame(height: 80)
                .background(Color(red: 0.9, green: 0.9, blue: 0.9, opacity:
0.8))
            }
        }
        .edgesIgnoringSafeArea(.all)
        .frame(minWidth: 0, maxWidth: .infinity, minHeight: 0, maxHeight:
.infinity)
        .navigationBarTitle("")
        .navigationBarHidden(true)
    }
}
```

```
struct CustomCameraView_Previews: PreviewProvider {
    static var previews: some View {
        CustomCameraView(openCamera: .constant(false), picture:
.constant(nil))
    }
}
```

As illustrated in Figure 16-23, this view includes our custom `UIView` to show the video coming from the camera and another view on top to provide two buttons, one to cancel the process and dismiss the view, and another to take a picture. The `UIView` is instantiated first and then we call the `getAuthorization()` method on it when the view appears to start the process. If the user presses the Take Picture button, we call the `takePicture()` method on the representable view to capture the image. Once the image is processed, the view is dismissed by the delegate method, and the picture is shown on the screen.

 Do It Yourself: Create a SwiftUI project. Download the nopicture.png image from our website and add it to the Assets Catalog. Create a Swift file called CustomView.swift and insert the code in Listing 16-59. Add to this structure the methods of Listings 16-60, 16-61, 16-62, 16-63, and 16-64. Add the code in Listing 16-65 at the bottom of the CustomView.swift file. Update the `ContentView` structure with the code in Listing 16-66. Create a Swift file called CustomCameraView.swift for the code in Listing 16-67. Remember to add the option "Privacy - Camera Usage Description" to the info.plist file. Run the application and take a picture.

(Basic) AVKit Framework

The same way we can create a view with the `UIImagePickerController` class that provides standard controls to take a picture, we can also create a view with standard controls for playing videos. The framework that provides this view is called *AVKit*, and the class is called `AVPlayerViewController`. This class creates a player with all the controls necessary for the user to play a video. The following are some of the properties it provides to define and configure the player.

player—This property sets the player that provides the media for the controller to play. It is an object of type `AVPlayer`.

showsPlaybackControls—This property is a Boolean value that determines whether the player is going to show the controls or just the video.

The controller defines the player and presents the interface for the user to control the video, but the video is played by an object of the `AVPlayer` class. The class includes the following initializer to use with AVKit.

AVPlayer(url: URL)—This initializer creates an `AVPlayer` object to play the media in the URL indicated by the attribute.

The `AVPlayer` class also includes properties and methods to control the playback.

volume—This property sets or returns a value that determines the player's volume. It is a value of type `Float` between 0.0 and 1.0.

isMuted—This property is a Boolean value that determines whether the player's audio is muted or not.

rate—This property sets or returns a `Float` value that determines the rate at which the media is being played. A value of 0.0 pauses the video and 1.0 sets the normal rate.

play()—This method begins playback.

pause()—This method pauses playback.

addPeriodicTimeObserver(forInterval: CMTime, **queue:** DispatchQueue?, **using:** Closure)—This method adds an observer that executes a closure repeatedly every certain period of time. The **forInterval** attribute determines the time between executions, the **queue** attribute is the queue in which the closure should be executed (the main queue is recommended), and the **using** attribute is the closure we want to execute. The closure receives a value of type `CMTime` with the time at which the closure was called.

The following is the representable view controller required to create an `AVPlayerViewController` controller.

```
import SwiftUI
import AVFoundation
import AVKit

struct PlayerView: UIViewControllerRepresentable {
    let player: AVPlayer?

    init() {
        let bundle = Bundle.main
        let videoURL = bundle.url(forResource: "videotrees", withExtension:
"mp4")
        player = AVPlayer(url: videoURL!)
    }
    func makeUIViewController(context: Context) -> AVPlayerViewController
{
        let controller = AVPlayerViewController()
        controller.player = player
        return controller
    }
    func updateUIViewController(_ uiViewController:
AVPlayerViewController, context: Context) {}

    func playVideo() {
        player?.play()
    }
    func stopVideo() {
        player?.pause()
    }
}
```

Listing 16-68: Creating a standard video player

Because we use classes from `AVFoundation` and `AVKit`, we must import both frameworks. The structure defines a property to store a reference to the `AVPlayer` object and then creates an instance of this class with the URL of a video in the bundle (videotrees.mp4). The `makeUIViewController()` method creates the controller and assigns the `AVPlayer` object to its `player` property. This configures the player, but if we want the video to start playing as soon as the controller is opened, we have to call the `play()` method on the `AVPlayer` object. For this purpose, we add the `playVideo()` method at the end and also a method called `stopVideo()` to pause it. These methods are called by the view when it appears or disappears from the screen, as shown next.

```
import SwiftUI

struct ContentView: View {
    @State private var showPlayer: Bool = false
    let videoPlayer = PlayerView()

    var body: some View {
        VStack {
            Button("Play Video") {
                self.showPlayer = true
            }
            Spacer()
        }.padding()
        .sheet(isPresented: $showPlayer) {
            self.videoPlayer
                .onAppear(perform: {
                    self.videoPlayer.playVideo()
                })
                .onDisappear(perform: {
                    self.videoPlayer.stopVideo()
                })
        }
    }
}
```

Listing 16-69: *Opening the video player*

The view in Listing 16-69 creates the instance of the `PlayerView` structure and then calls the `playVideo()` method on it when the view appears. The view is presented with a sheet, but it can also be embedded in a `NavigationView` view, as we did with the image picker controller.

Figure 16-24: *AVKit video player*

 Do It Yourself: Create a SwiftUI project. Download the videotrees.mp4 file from our website and add it to your project (make sure that the target is selected). Create a Swift file called PlayerView.swift for the code in Listing 16-68. Update the `ContentView` structure with the code in Listing 16-69. Run the application and press the Play Video button to play the video.

(Medium) **Custom Video Player**

In addition to the video player provided by AVKit, the AVFoundation framework also offers classes to create the structure necessary to play media. There is a class in charge of the asset (video or audio), a class in charge of providing the media to the player, a class in charge of playing the media, and a class in charge of displaying the media on the screen. Figure 16-25 illustrates this structure.

Chapter 16 - Framework Integration

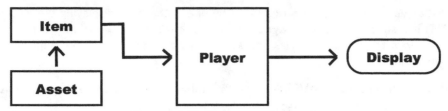

Figure 16-25: System to play media

Let's see the elements one by one, starting from the asset. This is how the information related to the media is called. An asset is composed of one or more tracks of media, including video, audio, subtitles, etc. The AVFoundation framework defines a class called **AVAsset** to load an asset and a subclass called **AVURLAsset** to create an asset object from the contents of a URL. This last subclass includes the following initializer.

AVURLAsset(url: URL)—This initializer creates an **AVURLAsset** object with the media in the location indicated by the **url** attribute. The attribute is a **URL** structure with the location of a local or remote resource.

An asset contains static information and cannot manage its state when it is being played. To control the asset, the framework defines the **AVPlayerItem** class. With this class, we can reference an asset and manage its timeline. The class includes multiple initializers. The following is the most frequently used.

AVPlayerItem(asset: AVAsset)—This initializer creates an **AVPlayerItem** object to represent the asset defined by the **asset** attribute.

The **AVPlayerItem** class also includes properties and methods to control the state of the asset. The following are the most frequently used.

status—This property returns a value that indicates the status of the player item. It is an enumeration called **Status** included in the **AVPlayerItem** class. The values available are **unknown**, **readyToPlay**, and **failed**.

duration—This property returns a value that indicates the duration of the player item. It is a structure of type **CMTime**.

currentTime()—This method returns a **CMTime** value with the current time of the player item.

seek(to: CMTime, completionHandler: Closure)—This method moves the playback cursor to the time specified by the **to** attribute. The **completionHandler** attribute is a closure to be executed after the process is over. The closure receives a Boolean value that determines whether the seek operation is finished or not.

The **AVPlayerItem** object manages the information necessary for playback but it does not play the media; this is done by an instance of the **AVPlayer** class. This is the same class we used with the **AVPlayerViewController** object to play videos. The class includes the following initializer to create a player from an **AVPlayerItem** object.

AVPlayer(playerItem: AVPlayerItem?)—This initializer creates an **AVPlayer** object to play the media represented by the **playerItem** attribute.

The last object required by the structure is the one in charge of displaying the media on the screen. This is a subclass of the `CALayer` class called `AVPlayerLayer` that provides the code necessary to draw the frames. The class includes the following initializer and property to create and configure the layer.

AVPlayerLayer(player: AVPlayer?)—This initializer creates an `AVPlayerLayer` object associated with the player specified by the **player** attribute.

videoGravity—This property defines how the video adjusts its size to the preview layer's size. The framework defines the following constants to assign to this property: `AVLayerVideoGravityResizeAspect`, `AVLayerVideoGravityResizeAspectFill`, and `AVLayerVideoGravityResize`.

These classes define the system we need to play media, but we also need a way to control time. Because the precision of floating-point values is not appropriate for media playback, the framework adopts, among other things, the `CMTime` structure from an old framework called Core Media. The structure contains multiple values to represent time as a fraction. The most important are `value` and `timescale`, which represent the numerator and denominator, respectively. To determine the time, we must specify at least these two values. For example, if we want to create a `CMTime` structure to represent 0.5 seconds, we may declare 1 as the numerator and 2 as the denominator (1 divided by 2 is equal to 0.5). The class includes initializers and type properties to create these values. The following are the most frequently used.

CMTime(value: CMTimeValue, timescale: CMTimeScale)—This initializer creates a `CMTime` structure with the values specified by the **value** and **timescale** attributes. The attributes are integers of type `Int64` and `Int32`, respectively.

CMTime(seconds: Double, preferredTimescale: CMTimeScale)—This initializer creates a `CMTime` structure from a floating-point value that represents the seconds and a timescale. The **seconds** attribute determines the seconds we want to assign to the structure, and the **preferredTimescale** attribute determines the scale we want to use. A value of 1 preserves the value in seconds assigned to the first attribute.

zero—This type property returns a `CMTime` structure with a value of 0.

The `CMTime` structure also includes multiple properties to set and retrieve the values. The following are the most frequently used.

seconds—This property returns the time of a `CMTime` structure in seconds. It is of type `Double`.

value—This property returns the value of a `CMTime` structure.

timescale—This property returns the time scale of a `CMTime` structure.

The process to create a player is straightforward. As with the custom camera developed in previous examples, creating a custom video player requires a `UIView` object. Once we have this object, we must load the asset (`AVURLAsset`), create the item to manage the asset (`AVPlayerItem`), add the item to the player (`AVPlayer`), and associate the player to a layer to display the media on the screen (`AVPlayerLayer`). But playing the media requires an additional step. The media does not become immediately available, it has to be loaded and prepare for playback, so we cannot play it right away, we have to wait until its ready. The status is reported by the `status` property of the `AVPlayerItem` object, so we must add an observer for this property to start playing the media only after the property returns the value `readyToPlay`. This is a technique called KVO (Key-Value Observing). It was developed in Objective-C and it is used to turn an object into an observer of a property. When the value of that property changes, the object executes a method to report the change. The methods to add, remove, and respond to an observer are defined in the **NSObject** class. The following are the three methods involved in the process.

addObserver(NSObject, **forKeyPath:** String, **options:** NSKeyValueObserving-Options, **context:** UnsafeMutableRawPointer?**)**—This method adds an observer to the object. The first attribute is the object that responds to the notification, the **forKeyPath** attribute is a string with the name or the path to the property, the **options** attribute is an enumeration that determines the values that are going to be sent to the method that responds to the notification (possible values are **new**, **old**, **initial**, and **prior**), and the **context** attribute is a generic value that identifies the observer (used when a class and its subclasses observe the same property).

removeObserver(NSObject, **forKeyPath:** String**)**—This method removes an observer. The attributes are the same values specified in the **addObserver()** method when the observer was added.

observeValue(forKeyPath: String?, **of:** Any?, **change:** Dictionary?, **context:** UnsafeMutableRawPointer?**)**—This method is called by the observer to report a change in the value of the observed property.

The following example implements these methods to listen to the **status** property of the **AVPlayerItem** object. We create the representable view, build the video player, and then call the **play()** method from the **observeValue()** method to start playing the video as soon as it is ready.

```
import SwiftUI
import AVFoundation

class ViewData: NSObject {
    var playerItem: AVPlayerItem!
    var player: AVPlayer!
    var playerLayer: AVPlayerLayer!

    func setObserver() {
        playerItem.addObserver(self, forKeyPath: "status", options: [],
context: nil)
    }
    override func observeValue(forKeyPath keyPath: String?, of object:
Any?, change: [NSKeyValueChangeKey : Any]?, context:
UnsafeMutableRawPointer?) {
        if playerItem.status == .readyToPlay {
            playerItem.removeObserver(self, forKeyPath: "status")
            player.play()
        }
    }
}
struct CustomView: UIViewRepresentable {
    var view = UIView()
    var viewData = ViewData()

    func makeUIView(context: Context) -> UIView {
        let bundle = Bundle.main
        let videoURL = bundle.url(forResource: "videotrees", withExtension:
"mp4")
```

```
        let asset = AVURLAsset(url: videoURL!)
        viewData.playerItem = AVPlayerItem(asset: asset)
        viewData.player = AVPlayer(playerItem: viewData.playerItem)

        viewData.playerLayer = AVPlayerLayer(player: viewData.player)
        let layer = view.layer
        layer.addSublayer(viewData.playerLayer)
        viewData.setObserver()

        return view
    }
    func updateUIView(_ uiView: UIView, context: Context) {
        let main = OperationQueue.main
        main.addOperation {
            if self.viewData.playerItem != nil {
                self.viewData.playerLayer.frame = uiView.bounds
            }
        }
    }
}
}
```

Listing 16-70: Building a video player

Because the observer methods are defined in the **NSObject** class, they can only be implemented in a class that inherits from **NSObject**. For this reason, we set up and respond to the observer in the **ViewData** class we use to store the objects required by the video player. First, we define the three properties we need to store the player item, the player, and the layer, then we define a method that sets an observer for the **status** property of the **AVPlayerItem** object, and finally we respond to that observer with the **observeValue()** method. If the current status is **readyToPlay**, we remove the observer (the method is not going to be called anymore) and play the video.

To set up the video player, we load the video from the bundle and create the player structure, as mentioned before. The player is associated with an **AVPlayerLayer** layer and the layer is added as a sublayer of the **UIView** view. The size of this layer is defined according to the size of the view every time the view is updated (either because it was just created, or the device was rotated).

In the interface, we only need to instantiate the representable view. The video is shown full screen, it adapts to the screen orientation, and it is played as soon as the view is loaded.

```
import SwiftUI

struct ContentView: View {
    var body: some View {
        CustomView()
    }
}
```

Listing 16-71: Showing a video

Do It Yourself: Create a SwiftUI project. Download the videotrees.mp4 file from our website and add it to your project (remember to check the option Add to Target). Create a Swift file with the name CustomView.swift for the code in Listing 16-70. Update the **ContentView** structure with the code in Listing 16-71. Run the application. The video should start playing as soon as the application is launched.

The previous example plays the video, but it does not provide any tools for the user to control the process. The **AVPlayer** class includes methods to play, pause, and check the state of the media, but we are responsible for creating the interface. For the following example, we are going to create an interface that provides a button and a progress bar to let the user play and pause the video and see its progression.

Figure 16-26: *Controls for a custom video player*

How we control the process and respond to the interface depends on the requirements of our application. For this example, we have decided to define two states, one to indicate if the video is playing or not, and another to determine the size of the progress bar. The following are the changes we must introduce to our representable view to let the user play or pause the video and to update the progress bar.

```
import SwiftUI
import AVFoundation

class ViewData: NSObject {
    var playerItem: AVPlayerItem!
    var player: AVPlayer!
    var playerLayer: AVPlayerLayer!
}
struct CustomView: UIViewRepresentable {
    @Binding var playing: Bool
    @Binding var progress: CGFloat
    var view = UIView()
    var viewData = ViewData()

    func makeUIView(context: Context) -> UIView {
        let bundle = Bundle.main
        let videoURL = bundle.url(forResource: "videotrees", withExtension:
"mp4")

        let asset = AVURLAsset(url: videoURL!)
        viewData.playerItem = AVPlayerItem(asset: asset)
        viewData.player = AVPlayer(playerItem: viewData.playerItem)
        viewData.playerLayer = AVPlayerLayer(player: viewData.player)
        let layer = view.layer
        layer.addSublayer(viewData.playerLayer)

        let main = DispatchQueue.main
        let interval = CMTime(value: 1, timescale: 2)
        viewData.player.addPeriodicTimeObserver(forInterval: interval,
queue: main, using: { time in
            let duration = self.viewData.playerItem.duration
            let position = time.seconds / duration.seconds
            self.progress = CGFloat(position)
        })
```

```
            return view
    }
    func updateUIView(_ uiView: UIView, context: Context) {
        let main = OperationQueue.main
        main.addOperation {
            if self.viewData.playerItem != nil {
                self.viewData.playerLayer.frame = uiView.bounds
            }
        }
    }
}
    func playVideo() {
        if viewData.playerItem.status == .readyToPlay {
            if self.playing {
                viewData.player.pause()
                self.playing = false
            } else {
                viewData.player.play()
                self.playing = true
            }
        }
    }
}
}
```

Listing 16-72: Preparing the video player

The structure in Listing 16-72 includes a method called `playVideo()`. This is the method we are going to call from the interface when the user presses the Play button. The method checks whether the media can be played or not, and then performs an action according to the value of the `playing` property. If the video is playing, we pause it, and if it is paused, we play it. Either case, we update the value of the `playing` property to reflect the new state.

To calculate the size of the progress bar, we must implement an observer. But this is not a KVO observer like the one we used before. Normal observers are not fast enough, so the AVFoundation framework offers the `addPeriodicTimeObserver()` method to create an observer that provides a more accurate response. The method requires a `CMTime` value to determine the frequency in which the code will be executed, a reference to the main queue, and a closure with the code we want to execute every time the observer is triggered. In this example, we create a `CMTime` value to represent a time of 0.5 seconds, and then use it in the call of the `addPeriodicTimeObserver()` method to register the observer. After this, the closure provided to the observer will be executed every 0.5 seconds during playback. In this closure, we get the current time and the duration of the video in seconds and calculate the progression by turning seconds into a value between 0.0 and 1.0 that we can later convert into points to present the progress bar on the screen.

The player is ready. It is time to define the interface. To incorporate the representable view, we are going to use the same technique as before. The properties are declared in an observable object, a reference to the view is stored in a property, and the view is instantiated in the structure's initializer. This way, the structure is created only once and we can call the `playVideo()` method when the user presses the button.

```
import SwiftUI

class ContentData: ObservableObject {
    @Published var playing: Bool = false
    @Published var progress: CGFloat = 0
}
struct ContentView: View {
    @ObservedObject var contentData = ContentData()
    var videoPlayer: CustomView!
```

```
init() {
    videoPlayer = CustomView(playing: $contentData.playing, progress:
$contentData.progress)
    }
    var body: some View {
        ZStack {
            videoPlayer
            VStack {
                Spacer()
                HStack {
                    Button(contentData.playing ? "Stop" : "Play") {
                        self.videoPlayer?.playVideo()
                    }.foregroundColor(Color.black)
                    GeometryReader { geometry in
                        HStack {
                            Rectangle()
                                .fill(Color(red: 0, green: 0.4, blue: 0.8,
opacity: 0.8))
                                .frame(width: geometry.size.width *
self.contentData.progress, height: 20)
                            Spacer()
                        }
                    }
                }
                .padding([.leading, .trailing])
                .frame(height: 50)
                .background(Color(red: 0.9, green: 0.9, blue: 0.9, opacity:
0.8))
            }
        }
    }
}
```

Listing 16-73: Playing and pausing the video

The video and the toolbar are embedded in a `ZStack` view, so the bar appears on top of the video. The tool bar includes a button and a `Rectangle` view that represents the progress bar. The label for the button depends on the value of the `playing` property. If the video is playing, we show the text "Stop" and when it is paused, we show the text "Play". To calculate the size of the `Rectangle` view that represents the progress bar, we embedded the view in a `GeometryReader` and then multiply its width by the value of the `progress` property. Because this property contains a value between 0.0 and 1.0, the operation returns the value we need to set the width of the bar and show the progression on the screen.

 Do It Yourself: Update the CustomView.swift file with the code in Listing 16-72 and the ContentView.swift file with the code in Listing 16-73. Run the application. You should see the video player illustrated in Figure 16-26.

The observer added by the `addPeriodicTimeObserver()` method is not the only way to get information from the player over time. The `AVPlayerItem` class also defines several notifications to report events that happened during playback. For example, we can define a publisher for the `AVPlayerItemDidPlayToEndTime` notification to know when the video finishes playing. The following is the code we need to add to the `CustomView` structure to set up the publisher and define the method to respond to it.

```
var publisherPlayer = NotificationCenter.Publisher(center: .default,
name: NSNotification.Name.AVPlayerItemDidPlayToEndTime)
   .receive(on: RunLoop.main)
func rewindVideo() {
   self.viewData.playerItem.seek(to: CMTime.zero, completionHandler:
{(finished) in
      if finished {
         let main = OperationQueue.main
         main.addOperation {
            self.playing = false
            self.progress = 0
         }
      }
   })
}
```

Listing 16-74: Adding a publisher to detect the end of the video

The code in Listing 16-74 defines a new property for the `CustomView` structure and a new method. The property defines a publisher that emits a value when the `AVPlayerItemDidPlayToEndTime` notification is posted, and the method prepares the video to be played again. For this purpose, the `AVPlayerItem` class offers the `seek()` method. This method moves the playback to the time specified by the attribute and executes a closure after the process is over. In this case, we use a `CMTime` value of 0 to mode the playback to the beginning of the video and then reset the `playing` and `progress` properties to let the user play the video again.

The `rewindVideo()` must be executed from the view every time we need to reset the video player. In this example, we ought to do it when the publisher emits a value. The following is the `onReceive()` modifier we must add to the view for this purpose.

```
.onReceive(videoPlayer.publisherPlayer, perform: { _ in
   self.videoPlayer.rewindVideo()
})
```

Listing 16-75: Responding to the publisher when the video is over

 Do It Yourself: Add the property and method defined in Listing 16-74 to the `CustomView` structure. Apply the modifier in Listing 16-75 to a view in the interface. Run the application. Press play and wait until the video is over. The player should reset itself and you should be able to play the video again.

If we want to play multiple videos in sequence, we could use this notification to assign a new asset to the `AVPlayer` object, but the framework offers a subclass of the `AVPlayer` class called `AVQueuePlayer` designed specifically to manage a list of videos. The class creates a playlist from an array of `AVPlayerItem` objects. The following are the initializer and some of its methods.

AVQueuePlayer(items: [AVPlayerItem])—This initializer creates a play list with the items specified by the **items** attribute.

advanceToNextItem()—This method advances the playback to the next item on the list.

insert(AVPlayerItem, **after:** AVPlayerItem?**)**—This method inserts a new item on the list.

remove(AVPlayerItem**)**—This method removes an item from the list.

Chapter 16 - Framework Integration

An `AVQueuePlayer` object replaces the `AVPlayer` object used to represent the media. All we have to do to play a sequence of videos is to create the `AVPlayerItem` objects for each video and create an `AVQueuePlayer` object to replace the `AVPlayer` object we have used so far, as in the following example.

```
import SwiftUI
import AVFoundation
class ViewData: NSObject {
    var playerItem1: AVPlayerItem!
    var playerItem2: AVPlayerItem!
    var player: AVQueuePlayer!
    var playerLayer: AVPlayerLayer!

    func setObserver() {
        playerItem1.addObserver(self, forKeyPath: "status", options: [],
context: nil)
    }
    override func observeValue(forKeyPath keyPath: String?, of object:
Any?, change: [NSKeyValueChangeKey : Any]?, context:
UnsafeMutableRawPointer?) {
        if playerItem1.status == .readyToPlay {
            playerItem1.removeObserver(self, forKeyPath: "status")
            player.play()
        }
    }
}
struct CustomView: UIViewRepresentable {
    var view = UIView()
    var viewData = ViewData()

    func makeUIView(context: Context) -> UIView {
        let bundle = Bundle.main
        let videoURL1 = bundle.url(forResource: "videotrees",
withExtension: "mp4")
        let videoURL2 = bundle.url(forResource: "videobeaches",
withExtension: "mp4")

        let asset1 = AVURLAsset(url: videoURL1!)
        let asset2 = AVURLAsset(url: videoURL2!)
        viewData.playerItem1 = AVPlayerItem(asset: asset1)
        viewData.playerItem2 = AVPlayerItem(asset: asset2)
        viewData.player = AVQueuePlayer(items: [viewData.playerItem1,
viewData.playerItem2])

        viewData.playerLayer = AVPlayerLayer(player: viewData.player)
        let layer = view.layer
        layer.addSublayer(viewData.playerLayer)
        viewData.setObserver()

        return view
    }
    func updateUIView(_ uiView: UIView, context: Context) {
        let main = OperationQueue.main
        main.addOperation {
            if self.viewData.playerItem1 != nil {
                self.viewData.playerLayer.frame = uiView.bounds
            }
        }
    }
}
```

Listing 16-76: Playing a list of videos

Chapter 16 - Framework Integration

This example assumes that we are using the simple interface of Listing 16-71. The code loads two videos, videotrees.mp4 and videobeaches.mp4, and then creates two `AVURLAsset` objects and two `AVPlayerItem` objects to represent the videos. The `AVQueuePlayer` object is define next to play both videos in sequence. Notice that because the interface we are using for this example does not include a button to play the videos, we add an observer to the first video and call the `play()` method as soon as it is ready.

 Do It Yourself: Update the CustomView.swift file with the code in Listing 16-76 and the `ContentView` structure with the code in Listing 16-71. Download the videobeaches.mp4 and videotrees.mp4 videos from our website and add them to your project (remember to check the option Add to Target). Run the application. The videos should be played one after another.

(Basic) **16.6 Collection Views**

With the introduction of the iPad and its larger screen it became evident to Apple that the single column layout provided by list views was not enough to create good user interfaces. Developers needed a flexible way to organize data on the screen and that is how Collection Views were born. Collection Views take a list of views and present them on the screen using a predefined layout. They come with a grid-like layout by default, but we can customize it to present the views any way we want.

Figure 16-27: Collection View

(Basic) **Collection View**

Collection Views are created from multiple objects. There is a class to create the view, a class to create the cells that present each item on the list, a class to define how those cells are going to be laid out, a class to provide the data each cell is going to display, and a class to merge the changes and update the view. First, let's see how to create and configure the view. This class is called `UICollectionView` and provides the following initializer.

UICollectionView(frame: CGRect, **collectionViewLayout:** UICollectionView-Layout)—This initializer creates a `UICollectionView` view configured with the size and layout determined by the attributes. The **frame** attribute determines the view's position and size, and the **collectionViewLayout** attribute is an object that inherits from the `UICollectionViewLayout` class and determines how the cells are going to be laid out.

The following are some of the properties and methods included in the `UICollectionView` class for configuration.

Chapter 16 - Framework Integration

allowsSelection—This property is a Boolean value that determines whether the selection of cells is allowed or not.

allowsMultipleSelection—This property is a Boolean value that determines whether multiple selection of cells is allowed or not.

backgroundView—This property sets or returns the view for the background of the cell. It is an optional value of type `UIView`.

collectionViewLayout—This property sets or returns the layout object in charge of setting the layout for the cells. It is an object of a subclass of the `UICollectionViewLayout` class.

indexPathsForSelectedItems—This property returns an array of `IndexPath` structures with the indexes of the selected cells.

selectItem(at: IndexPath?, **animated:** Bool, **scrollPosition:** ScrollPosition)—This method selects the cell at the position indicated by the **at** attribute. The **animated** attribute indicates if the process is going to be animated, and the **scrollPosition** attribute is a property of a structure called `ScrollPosition` included in the `UICollectionView` class that indicates how the Collection View is going to scroll to show the cell on the screen. The properties available are `top`, `bottom`, `left`, `right`, `centeredVertically`, and `centeredHorizontally`.

deselectItem(at: IndexPath, **animated:** Bool)—This method deselects the cell at the position indicated by the **at** attribute. The **animated** attribute indicates if the process is going to be animated.

scrollToItem(at: IndexPath, **at:** ScrollPosition, **animated:** Bool)—This method scrolls the Collection View to show on the screen the cell at the position indicated by the first **at** attribute. The second **at** attribute is a property of a structure called `ScrollPosition` included in the `UICollectionView` class that indicates how the Collection View is going to scroll. The properties available are `top`, `bottom`, `left`, `right`, `centeredVertically`, and `centeredHorizontally`. And the **animated** attribute is a Boolean value that indicates if the process is going to be animated

indexPath(for: UICollectionViewCell)—This method returns an `IndexPath` structure indicating the position of the cell referenced by the **for** attribute.

cellForItem(at: IndexPath)—This method returns the `UICollectionViewCell` object that represents the cell at the position indicated by the **at** attribute.

numberOfItems(inSection: Int)—This method returns an integer with the number of cells in the section specified by the **inSection** attribute.

(Basic) **Collection View Cells**

The views to present each item in the Collection View are created from subclasses of the `UICollectionViewCell` class. The cell is created from three empty views. There is a view to present the content, a view for the background, and a second background view that is shown when the cell is selected. The following are the properties to access these views.

contentView—This property returns the content view of the cell. All the view added to customize the cell are incorporated as subviews of this view.

backgroundView—This property sets or returns the view for the background of the cell. It is an optional of type `UIView`.

selectedBackgroundView—This property sets or returns the view for the background when the cell is selected. It is an optional of type `UIView`.

The cells are generated on demand. The Collection View creates only the cells the interface needs, and when new cells are required, it reuses those that are not visible anymore. For this reason, we do not create the cells directly, we must register the classes we want to use to generate the cells and when we need to display new content, we ask the view to create or reuse one of those cells. The `UICollectionView` class includes the following methods for this purpose.

register(AnyClass?, forCellWithReuseIdentifier: String**)**—This method tells the Collection View which class to use to create a cell. The first attribute is the subclass of the `UICollectionViewCell` class we are using to present the content, and the **forCellWithReuseIdentifier** attribute is a string that identifies these types of cells.

dequeueReusableCell(withReuseIdentifier: String, **for:** IndexPath**)**—This method returns a `UICollectionViewCell` object to represent a cell. The object is created from the class registered with the identifier specified by the **withReuseIdentifier** attribute. The for attribute is an `IndexPath` structure with the location of the cell.

(Basic) Index Paths and Identifiers

Cells and sections are identified by their position in the Collection View. Sections are assigned a consecutive index starting from 0, and then the cells inside each section are also identified with a consecutive index starting from 0. Therefore, to identify a cell, we need the index of the cell and the index of the section the cell belongs to. Collection Views store this information in a structure of type `IndexPath`. The values are returned by the following properties.

section—This property returns the index of the section where the cell is located.

item—This property returns the index of the cell (usually called *item*).

The `IndexPath` structures are automatically defined by the Collection View, but there are situations in which we must create them ourselves. The structure includes the following initializer.

IndexPath(item: Int, **section:** Int**)**—This initializer creates an `IndexPath` structure with the values provided by the attributes.

Collection Views get the data to display from a diffable source (a source that can update itself by comparing previous and future data). Diffable data sources work with their own identification system. They use the identification value provided by the data. Because we are presenting the Collection View with a representable view and still working with old delegate methods, we will have to process `IndexPath` values most of the time, but in case we need to convert one value into another, the `UICollectionViewDiffableDataSource` class includes the following methods.

indexPath(for: ItemIdentifierType**)**—This method returns an `IndexPath` structure with the location of the item with the data source identifier specified by the attribute.

itemIdentifier(for: IndexPath**)**—This method returns the item at the index path specified by the attribute.

Chapter 16 - Framework Integration

Flow Layout

The `IndexPath` structure determines the order of the cells in the Collection View, but how they are laid out on the screen is determined by a layout object. This object is created from a subclass of the `UICollectionViewLayout` class. Although we can create our own subclass to provide any layout we want, Collection Views include by default a subclass called `UICollectionViewFlowLayout` that provides a very customizable grid-like layout that is usually more than enough for our projects. The layout is called *Flow*, and it includes the following properties for configuration.

scrollDirection—This property sets or returns the direction of the scroll. It is an enumeration called `ScrollDirection` included in the `UICollectionView` class. The values available are `vertical` and `horizontal` (with `vertical` set by default).

minimumInteritemSpacing—This property sets or returns a `CGFloat` value that determines the space between cells. In vertical scrolling, the value determines the space between cells in the same row, but in horizontal scrolling it determines the space between items in the same column.

minimumLineSpacing—This property sets or returns a `CGFloat` value that determines the space between cells. In vertical scrolling, the value determines the space between rows, but in horizontal scrolling it determines the space between columns.

sectionInset—This property sets or returns the margins for the sections. Its value is a structure of type `UIEdgeInsets` with the properties `top`, `bottom`, `left`, and `right`.

itemSize—This property sets or returns the size of the cells. It is a value of type `CGSize`.

Collection View Delegate

Collection Views can designate a delegate to respond to user interaction. UIKit includes the `UICollectionViewDelegate` protocol to define this delegate object. The following are the methods we need to respond to the selection of a cell.

collectionView(UICollectionView, **didSelectItemAt:** IndexPath**)**—This method is called by the Collection View on its delegate when a cell is selected.

collectionView(UICollectionView, **didDeselectItemAt:** IndexPath**)**—This method is called by the Collection View on its delegate when a cell is deselected.

Data Source

The data is provided to the Collection View by two objects: an object of the `UICollectionViewDiffableDataSource` class that takes care of defining the cells and an object of the `NSDiffableDataSourceSnapshot` class that manages the data and is responsible of merging new values with old ones. The `UICollectionViewDiffableDataSource` class provides the following initializer and method to generate the cells and apply changes.

UICollectionViewDiffableDataSource(collectionView: UICollectionView, **cellProvider:** Closure**)**—This initializer creates a data source for the Collection View specified by the **collectionView** attribute. The **cellProvider** attribute is a closure that is called every time a cell is required. The closure receives three values: a reference to the Collection View, the cell's index path, and a reference to the data that is going to be shown in that cell.

snapshot()—This method returns a reference to the current snapshot used by the data source to get the data.

apply()—This method applies a snapshot with the most updated data to the data source object. It is used to update the Collection View with new values.

The `UICollectionViewDiffableDataSource` object generates the cells from a snapshot of the data created by a `NSDiffableDataSourceSnapshot` object. This class includes some properties and methods to process the values. The following are the most frequently used.

numberOfItems—This property returns the number of values managed by the snapshot.

numberOfSections—This property returns the number of sections managed by the snapshot.

appendItems([ItemIdentifierType], toSection: SectionIdentifierType?)—This method adds to the snapshot the items specified by the first attribute in the section specified by the **toSection** attribute. If there is only one section, the second attribute may be ignored.

appendSections([SectionIdentifierType])—This method adds to the snapshot the sections specified by the attribute.

insertItems([ItemIdentifierType], afterItem: ItemIdentifierType)—This method inserts the items specified by the first attribute after the item specified by the **afterItem** attribute. The class also includes a method to insert items before another item (**insertItems([ItemIdentifierType], beforeItem: ItemIdentifierType)**) and two more methods to insert sections (`insertSections([SectionIdentifierType], afterSection: SectionIdentifierType)` and `insertSections([SectionIdentifierType], beforeSection: SectionIdentifierType)`).

deleteItems([ItemIdentifierType])—This method removes from the snapshot the items specified by the attribute. The class also includes a method to remove sections (`deleteSections([SectionIdentifierType])`).

moveItem(ItemIdentifierType, afterItem: ItemIdentifierType)—This method moves the item specified by the first attribute to the position after the item specified by the **afterItem** attribute. The class also includes a method to move an item to the position before another item (`moveItem(ItemIdentifierType, beforeItem: ItemIdentifierType)`) and two more methods to move sections (`moveSection(SectionIdentifierType, afterSection: SectionIdentifierType)` and `moveSection(SectionIdentifierType, beforeSection: SectionIdentifierType)`).

(Basic) **Implementing Collection Views**

Collection Views are subclasses of the `UIView` class and therefore they must be wrapped with a representable view to include them in a SwiftUI interface. Because of all the logic required to provide the data and configure a Collection View, there are many ways to implement them. For the examples in this book we are going to concentrate most of the logic of our app in our model.

As always, the model must include a data model to store the values and an observable object to provide those values to the views. The following are the minimum requirements to create a Collection View like the one in Figure 16-27, above.

```
import SwiftUI

enum Sections {
    case main
}
struct Food: Hashable {
    var id: UUID = UUID()
    var name: String
    var picture: String

    func hash(into hasher: inout Hasher) {
        hasher.combine(id)
    }
}
class AppData: ObservableObject {
    @Published var listOfFood: [Food] = []
    @Published var selectedItem: Int?

    var collectionView: UICollectionView!
    var dataSource: UICollectionViewDiffableDataSource<Sections, Food>!

    init() {
        let layout = UICollectionViewFlowLayout()
        layout.scrollDirection = .vertical
        layout.itemSize = CGSize(width: 150, height: 100)
        layout.sectionInset = UIEdgeInsets(top: 20, left: 5, bottom: 20,
right: 5)

        collectionView = UICollectionView(frame: CGRect.zero,
collectionViewLayout: layout)
        collectionView.backgroundColor = .white
        collectionView.register(FoodCell.self, forCellWithReuseIdentifier:
"FoodCell")

        dataSource = UICollectionViewDiffableDataSource<Sections,
Food>(collectionView: collectionView) { collectionView, indexPath, food
in
            let cell =
collectionView.dequeueReusableCell(withReuseIdentifier: "FoodCell", for:
indexPath) as! FoodCell
            cell.picture.image = UIImage(named: food.picture)
            return cell
        }
        listOfFood = [
            Food(name: "Bagels", picture: "bagels"),
            Food(name: "Brownies", picture: "brownies"),
            Food(name: "Butter", picture: "butter"),
            Food(name: "Cheese", picture: "cheese"),
            Food(name: "Coffee", picture: "coffee"),
            Food(name: "Cookies", picture: "cookies"),
            Food(name: "Donuts", picture: "donuts"),
            Food(name: "Granola", picture: "granola"),
            Food(name: "Juice", picture: "juice"),
            Food(name: "Lemonade", picture: "lemonade"),
            Food(name: "Lettuce", picture: "lettuce"),
            Food(name: "Milk", picture: "milk"),
            Food(name: "Oatmeal", picture: "oatmeal"),
            Food(name: "Onions", picture: "onions"),
            Food(name: "Potato", picture: "potato"),
            Food(name: "Tea", picture: "tea"),
            Food(name: "Tomato", picture: "tomato"),
            Food(name: "Yogurt", picture: "yogurt")
        ]
```

```
            self.generateSnapshot()
    }
    func generateSnapshot() {
        var snapshot = NSDiffableDataSourceSnapshot<Sections, Food>()
        snapshot.appendSections([.main])
        snapshot.appendItems(listOfFood)
        dataSource.apply(snapshot)
    }
}
```

Listing 16-77: Defining the Collection View

Collection Views have a few requirements we must comply to. First, we must provide a hashable value to identify the sections. Enumeration are hashable by default, so this is the data type recommended for this purpose. In Listing 16-77, we create an enumeration called **Sections** with one value called **main** to identify the only section we are going to work with in this example. Another requirement is to also make our data model hashable and provide a unique identifier for it. In this example, we define a structure called **Food** to store the names and pictures of food, we make it conform to the **Hashable** protocol and designate the **id** property as the hashable value (see Listings 3-181 and 3-182). Now, the value of the **id** property is going to be used to identify each instance.

The observable object includes two properties to store references to the Collection View and the data source and then the values are defined in the initializer. First, we create and configure an instance of the **UICollectionViewFlowLayout** class to determine the layout. In this case, we have decided to use a vertical scrolling, give the cells a size of 150 by 100 points, and assign a padding of 5 points for the sides and 20 points for the top and bottom of the Collection View. Next, we create the **UICollectionView** object with this layout (the size determined by the frame attribute is ignored in SwiftUI), configure its background with the color white, and register a cell with the **FoodCell** class and the "FoodCell" identifier (we will define this class later).

The next step is to provide the data source. This is the object that takes care of creating the cells with the values from the model every time the Collection View requires them. The **UICollectionViewDiffableDataSource** class used to create this object is generic, so we must specify the data type used to identify the sections and the data type of the values used to populate the cells. In our example, these data types are **Sections** and **Food**. In the closure provided to the class' initializer, we get a cell with the **dequeueReusableCell()** method and then modify its values with the ones we want to show. In this case, our cell includes a property called **picture** to show the image of a meal or a beverage, so we create a **UIImage** object with the value of the **picture** property of the **Food** instance received by the closure and assign it to the cell (the closure receives the index path of the cell and the instance of the **Food** structure we should show in that cell).

Once the layout, the Collection View, and the data source are ready, we populate the model with some values and call the **generateSnapshot()** method to provide the data to the data source. This method creates an instance of the **NSDiffableDataSourceSnapshot** class adds the sections and all the values to the snapshot and apply it to the data source. This is a required process. The Collection View shows the cells on the screen, the data source configures the cells with the data, but the snapshot is the object that provides that data. If later we add, remove, of modify values, we must update or recreate the snapshot and apply it again to the data source to see those changes on the screen.

In this model, we use the **FoodCell** class to create the cells. This is a subclass of the **UICollectionViewCell** class that defines the structure of the cell and the information that is going to contain. This subclass must also comply with a few requirements. The views that determine the content of the cell must be defined with UIKit views and those views have to be assigned as subviews of the cell's content view, provided by the **contentView** property. To configure the cell, we need to override the `UICollectionViewCell` class initializer, and when we do this, we must provide an additional initializer that is required by the `NSCoding` protocol adopted by `UIView` views, as shown in the following example.

```
import UIKit

class FoodCell: UICollectionViewCell {
   var picture: UIImageView = UIImageView(frame: CGRect(x: 0, y: 0,
width: 150, height: 100))

   override init(frame: CGRect) {
      super.init(frame: frame)
      picture.contentMode = .scaleAspectFit
      contentView.addSubview(picture)
   }
   required init?(coder: NSCoder) {
      fatalError("Error")
   }
}
```

Listing 16-78: Defining the cell

UIKit views are subclasses of the `UIView` class and they all provide their own initializers and properties for configuration. For instance, images in UIKit are loaded with an `UIImage` object, as we have seen before, but these images are displayed on the screen with an object of the `UIImageView` class. The following is the class' initializers and some of its properties.

UIImageView(frame: CGRect)—This initializer creates a `UIImageView` object with a position and size determined by the **frame** attribute.

UIImageView(image: UIImage?)—This initializer creates a `UIImageView` object with the image provided by the **image** attribute. The view's frame is defined at the position 0, 0 and with the size of the image.

image—This property sets or returns the image for the view. It is an optional of type `UIImage`.

contentMode—This property sets or returns a value that determines the mode used by the view to lay out its content. It is an enumeration of type `ContentMode` with the values available are `scaleToFill`, `scaleAspectFit`, `scaleAspectFill`, `redraw`, `center`, `top`, `bottom`, `left`, `right`, `topLeft`, `topRight`, `bottomLeft`, and `bottomRight`.

In Listing 16-78, we create an `UIImageView` view with a size of 150 by 100 points. This is the same size of the cell, determined by the layout object in Listing 16-77, and therefore the image is going to occupy the whole cell. In the initializer, we configure the image with a content mode of type `scaleAspectFit` and add the view to the cell's content view with the `addSubview()` method provided by the `UIView` class.

Now the cell is ready, but we still haven't defined the representable view. Because the Collection View and all the objects required to provide the data to display by the view are defined in the model, all the representable view has to do is to return the value of the `collectionView` property of the model.

```
import SwiftUI

struct CollectionView: UIViewRepresentable {
    @EnvironmentObject var appData: AppData

    func makeUIView(context: Context) -> UICollectionView {
        return appData.collectionView
    }
    func updateUIView(_ uiView: UICollectionView, context: Context) {}
}
```

Listing 16-79: Creating the representable view for the Collection View

Finally, with the Collection View, the cell, and the representable view ready, we can build our SwiftUI interface.

```
import SwiftUI

struct ContentView: View {
    var body: some View {
        NavigationView {
            CollectionView()
                .navigationBarTitle("Food", displayMode: .inline)
        }
    }
}
```

Listing 16-80: Including a Collection View in a SwiftUI interface

The view in Listing 16-80 instantiates a `CollectionView` structure within a `NavigationView` view to provide a title. The result is the same shown in Figure 16-27, above.

 Do It Yourself: Create a SwiftUI project. Download the food pictures from our website and add them to the Assets Catalog. Create a Swift file called AppData.swift for the model of Listing 16-77. Update the AppDelegate.swift file with the code in Listing 7-14 and the SceneDelegate.swift file with the code of Listing 7-20 to instantiate the model and insert it in the environment. Create a Swift file called FoodCell.swift for the cell of Listing 16-78 and a file called CollectionView.swift for the representable view of Listing 16-79. Update the `ContentView` structure with the code in Listing 16-80 and run the application on a device. You should see the list of pictures as shown in Figure 16-27.

(Basic) Scroll Direction

The Flow layout offers two directions for scrolling: horizontal and vertical. The number of columns and rows generated by the layout always depend on the space available, the size of the cells, and the scrolling direction. For example, if we reduce the size of the representable view in the SwiftUI interface to a height of 200 points and assign the value `horizontal` to the `scrollDirection` property of the layout object, we get a Collection View with only one row.

```
import SwiftUI

struct ContentView: View {
    var body: some View {
        NavigationView {
            CollectionView()
```

```
            .frame(height: 200, alignment: .center)
            .navigationBarTitle("Food", displayMode: .inline)
      }
   }
}
```

Listing 16-81: Modifying the content of the Collection View from SwiftUI

Every change made in the representable view affects the content of the Collection View. In this example, the view presents only one row.

Figure 16-28: Custom Collection View

(Basic) **Adding Items**

When an item is added, removed, or modified in the model, the changes must be reproduced in the snapshot and applied to the data source. Depending on what we want to achieve, there are different ways to do it. For instance, if we are adding an item to the model, we can recreate the snapshot from scratch (in our model this means to execute the `generateSnapshot()` method again), or we can append the new item to the current snapshot. In this example, we follow the last approach.

```
func addItem(name: String) {
   let food = Food(name: name, picture: "nothumbnail")
   listOfFood.append(food)

   var snapshot = dataSource.snapshot()
   snapshot.appendItems([food])
   dataSource.apply(snapshot)
}
```

Listing 16-82: Adding items to the snapshot

The `UICollectionViewDiffableDataSource` class offers the `snapshot()` method to get a reference to the current snapshot, and the `appendItems()` method used before to define the items for the `NSDiffableDataSourceSnapshot` object can also be used to add more items to the snapshot. In the method in Listing 16-82, we create a new `Food` instance with the name inserted by the user, store the value in the `listOfFood` array, and then use the methods provided by these classes to also add it to the snapshot. After the updated snapshot is applied to the data source, the Collection View is updated, and the change is shown on the screen.

To let the user insert a new value and store it, we can include the following view into our project.

```
import SwiftUI

struct AddItem: View {
   @EnvironmentObject var appData: AppData
   @Environment(\.presentationMode) var presentation
   @State private var inputName: String = ""

   var body: some View {
      VStack {
         HStack {
            Text("Name: ")
            TextField("Inser Name", text: $inputName)
               .textFieldStyle(RoundedBorderTextFieldStyle())
         }
         HStack {
            Spacer()
            Button("Save") {
               let text = self.inputName.trimmingCharacters(in:
.whitespaces)
               if !text.isEmpty {
                  self.appData.addItem(name: text)
                  self.presentation.wrappedValue.dismiss()
               }
            }
         }
         Spacer()
      }.padding()
   }
}
struct AddItem_Previews: PreviewProvider {
   static var previews: some View {
      AddItem().environmentObject(AppData())
   }
}
```

Listing 16-83: Adding a new item to the model

There is nothing new in this view, just a **TextField** view and a button. When the button is pressed, we check that the value inserted by the user is not empty and call the **addItem()** method in the model to save it.

Finally, the initial view must include a **NavigationLink** button to navigate to this view.

```
import SwiftUI

struct ContentView: View {
   var body: some View {
      NavigationView {
         CollectionView()
            .navigationBarTitle("Food", displayMode: .inline)
            .navigationBarItems(trailing: NavigationLink(destination:
AddItem(), label: {
               Image(systemName: "plus.circle")
                  .font(.title)
            }))
      }
   }
}
```

Listing 16-84: Letting the user navigate to the AddItem *view*

Chapter 16 - Framework Integration

The interface built by these views is the same used in previous examples. We include a button in the navigation bar to open a view with a text field, and when the user inserts a value and presses the Save button, the item is saved in the model and shown on the screen.

Figure 16-29: New item

 Do It Yourself: Download the nothumbnail.png image from our website and add it to the Assets Catalog along with the rest. Add the method in Listing 16-82 to the observable object (below the `generateSnapshot()` method). Create a Swift file called AddItem.swift for the view in Listing 16-83. Update the `ContentView` structure with the code in Listing 16-84. Run the application in a device. Press the + button in the navigation bar. Insert a name and press the Save button. You should see a new item in the Collection View represented by the nothumbnail.png image, as illustrated in Figure 16-29.

(Basic) ## Selection

Collection View's cells show their selected background view when they are selected. The property containing this view is set to `nil` by default, so it is our responsibility to provide one. In the following example, we assign a new `UIView` object to the `selectedBackgroundView` property of each cell as soon as the cell is created.

```
import UIKit

class FoodCell: UICollectionViewCell {
   var picture: UIImageView = UIImageView(frame: CGRect(x: 0, y: 0,
width: 150, height: 100))

   override init(frame: CGRect) {
      super.init(frame: frame)
      picture.contentMode = .scaleAspectFit
      contentView.addSubview(picture)

      selectedBackgroundView = UIView()
      selectedBackgroundView?.backgroundColor = UIColor(red: 0.9, green:
0.9, blue: 0.9, alpha: 1)
   }
   required init?(coder: NSCoder) {
      fatalError("Error")
   }
}
```

Listing 16-85: Adding the selected background view to the cell

The new `FooCell` class of Listing 16-85 assigns an instance of the `UIView` class to the cell's `selectedBackgroundView` property and then changes its background color to gray. The view is automatically expanded to occupy the entire cell, so every time the user taps on a cell, the background becomes visible.

The selection is reported by the Collection View through the delegate. The method we must implement is `collectionView(UICollectionView, didSelectItemAt: IndexPath)`. The following is the representable view we need for this example. The view defines a coordinator, implements the delegate method, and assigns the coordinator as the Collection View's delegate.

```
import SwiftUI

struct CollectionView: UIViewRepresentable {
   @EnvironmentObject var appData: AppData

   func makeUIView(context: Context) -> UICollectionView {
      appData.collectionView.delegate = context.coordinator
      return appData.collectionView
   }
   func updateUIView(_ uiView: UICollectionView, context: Context) {}

   func makeCoordinator() -> CollectionViewCoordinator {
      return CollectionViewCoordinator(data: self.appData)
   }
}
class CollectionViewCoordinator: NSObject, UICollectionViewDelegate {
   var appData: AppData!

   init(data: AppData) {
      self.appData = data
   }
   func collectionView(_ collectionView: UICollectionView,
didSelectItemAt indexPath: IndexPath) {
      appData.selectedItem = indexPath.item
   }
}
```

Listing 16-86: Processing the selection of a cell

There are different ways to manage a selection. In this example, we keep it simple and assign the index of the selected cell to a `@Published` property in the model called `selectedItem` (see Listing 16-77). Because the selection is processed in the coordinator of the representable view, we need a `NavigationLink` in the initial view that will navigate to a detail view when the value of this property changes, as shown next.

```
import SwiftUI

struct ContentView: View {
   @EnvironmentObject var appData: AppData

   var body: some View {
      NavigationView {
         VStack {
            CollectionView()
               .navigationBarTitle("Food", displayMode: .inline)
               .navigationBarItems(trailing: NavigationLink(destination:
AddItem(), label: {
                  Image(systemName: "plus.circle")
                     .font(.title)
               }))
```

```
            NavigationLink(destination: ItemDetailView(), tag:
appData.selectedItem ?? 0, selection: $appData.selectedItem, label: {
                EmptyView()
            })
        }
        .onAppear(perform: {
            if let paths =
self.appData.collectionView.indexPathsForSelectedItems {
                for path in paths {
                    self.appData.collectionView.deselectItem(at: path,
animated: true)
                }
            }
        })
    }
}
}
```

Listing 16-87: Responding to the selection of a cell

The **NavigationLink** view added to the **ContentView** view in Listing 16-87 is not visible (it contains an **EmptyView** view for the label), but it responds to the value of the **selectedItem** property. If the property is **nil**, the link is inactive, but when the value of the property changes, the link becomes active and the **ItemDetailView** view is opened. In this view, we must get the **Food** instance from the **listOfFood** array using the index stored in the **selectedItem** property and show its values on the screen.

```
import SwiftUI

struct ItemDetailView: View {
    @EnvironmentObject var appData: AppData

    var body: some View {
        let food = appData.listOfFood[appData.selectedItem ?? 0]

        return VStack(alignment: .center, spacing: 20) {
            Text(food.name)
                .font(.title)
            Image(food.picture)
        }.padding()
        .navigationBarItems(trailing: Button("Remove") {
            if let selected = self.appData.selectedItem {
                self.appData.removeItem(index: selected)
                self.appData.selectedItem = nil
            }
        })
    }
}
```

Listing 16-88: Showing the value of the selected item

This view gets the **Food** structure from the **listOfFood** array and shows its name and picture on the screen. As a result, when the user taps on an item in the Collection View, the delegate method assigns the index of that item to the **selectedItem** property, the **NavigationLink** view opens the **ItemDetailView**, and this view shows the values of the selected food on the screen.

Chapter 16 - Framework Integration

Figure 16-30: Selected item

These new views, the `ContentView` view and the `ItemDetailView` view, include two more features. The `onAppear()` modifier was applied to the `CollectionView` view in Listing 16-87 to deselect the selected cells when the view appears. This is to avoid having a cell always selected. The closure assigned to this modifier goes through the items in the Collection View's `indexPathsForSelectedItems` property and deselects each cell with the `deselectItem()` method. On the other hand, the `ItemDetailView` view in Listing 16-88 includes a button in the navigation bar to remove the item from the model. When the button is pressed, the code makes sure that the `selectedItem` property contains a value and then executes a method in the model called `removeItem()` to remove the item in that index. The following is a possible implementation of this method.

```
func removeItem(index: Int) {
   var snapshot = dataSource.snapshot()
   snapshot.deleteItems([listOfFood[index]])
   dataSource.apply(snapshot)

   listOfFood.remove(at: index)
}
```

Listing 16-89: Deleting an item from the model and the snapshot

The `removeItem()` method deletes the item from the snapshot first with the `deleteItems()` method and then removes it from the `listOfFood` array so it doesn't appear next time the snapshot is recreated.

 Do It Yourself: Update the `FoodCell` class with the code in Listing 16-85. Update the CollectionView.swift file with the representable view of Listing 16-86. Update the `ContentView` structure with the code in Listing 16-87. Create a SwiftUI file called ItemDetailView.swift for the view in Listing 16-88. Add the method in Listing 16-89 to the observable object (below the `addItem()` method). Run the application on a device, tap on an item, and press the Remove button to delete it.

Basic | **Supplementary Views**

Besides cells, Collection Views use other views to include additional content. These views are called *Supplementary Views* and are managed by the layout object. The Flow layout includes two supplementary views, one for the header and another for the footer of every section. Like cells, these views are also reusable. The `UICollectionView` class includes the following methods to register and reuse a supplementary view.

register(AnyClass?, forSupplementaryViewOfKind: String, withReuse-Identifier: String)— This method tells the Collection View which class to use to create a supplementary view. The first attribute is the subclass of the `UICollectionReusableView` class we are using to define the view. The **forSupplementaryViewOfKind** attribute is a string that represents the kind of view created by the class. The `UICollectionView` class includes two type properties to specify this value: `elementKindSectionHeader` to declare the view as a header, and `elementKindSectionFooter` to declare the view as a footer. Finally, the **withReuseIdentifier** attribute is the view's identifier.

dequeueReusableSupplementaryView(ofKind: String, withReuseIdentifier: String, for: IndexPath)—This method returns a `UICollectionReusableView` object to represent additional views like headers and footers. The object is created from the prototype view with the identifier defined by the **withReuseIdentifier** attribute. The **ofKind** attribute is a string that represents the kind of view to create. The `UICollectionView` class includes two type properties to specify this value: `elementKindSectionHeader` to declare the view as a header, and `elementKindSectionFooter` to declare the view as a footer.

The Flow layout object defines the following properties to set the size for headers and footers.

headerReferenceSize—This property sets the size by default for headers. It is a value of type `CGSize`. The value perpendicular to the direction of the scroll is ignored (The height is considered in a vertical scroll, and the width is considered in a horizontal scroll).

footerReferenceSize—This property sets the size by default for footers. It is a value of type `CGSize`. The value perpendicular to the direction of the scroll is ignored (The height is considered in a vertical scroll, and the width is considered in a horizontal scroll).

Like cells, supplementary views are reusable. They are not created from the `UIView` class but from a subclass called `UICollectionReusableView`, but the rest of the process is the same. The following is the subclass we have created for the header of our example. It is called `HeaderView` and it contains a property with an `UIImageView` view to present the image gradientTop.png.

```
import UIKit

class HeaderView: UICollectionReusableView {
   var headerImage = UIImageView(frame: CGRect(x: 0, y: 0, width: 458,
height: 50))

   override init(frame: CGRect) {
      super.init(frame: frame)
      headerImage.image = UIImage(named: "gradientTop")
      self.addSubview(headerImage)
   }
   required init?(coder: NSCoder) {
      fatalError("Error")
   }
}
```

Listing 16-90: Creating a subclass for the header view

The footer view also requires a subclass. We call this one `FooterView` and include an object of type `UILabel` to display a text.

```
import UIKit

class FooterView: UICollectionReusableView {
   var footerTitle = UILabel(frame: CGRect(x: 20, y: 0, width: 320,
height: 50))

   override init(frame: CGRect) {
      super.init(frame: frame)
      footerTitle.text = "My Footer"
      footerTitle.font = UIFont.systemFont(ofSize: 24)
      footerTitle.textColor = UIColor.systemGreen
      self.addSubview(footerTitle)
   }
   required init?(coder: NSCoder) {
      fatalError("Error")
   }
}
```

Listing 16-91: Creating a subclass for the footer view

The `UILabel` class implemented in the footer view is another useful UIKit class. It is used to display text on the screen, like the SwiftUI's `Text` view. The content produced by the `UILabel` class, as any other subclass of `UIView`, is contained inside a view. Therefore, the `UILabel` class implements the `UIView` class initializer to specify the position and size of the view's area.

UILabel(frame: CGRect)—This initializer creates a `UILabel` view with a position and size specified by the **frame** attribute.

The following are some of the properties defined by the class to configure the view and format the text.

text—This property sets or returns the text displayed by the label.

font—This property sets or returns the font used to display the label. It is of type `UIFont`.

textColor—This property sets or returns the color of the text. It is of type `UIColor`.

textAlignment—This property sets or returns the alignment of the text. It is an enumeration of type `NSTextAlignment` with the values `left` (to the left side of the view), `center` (to the center of the view), `right` (to the right side of the view), `justified` (the last line of the paragraph is aligned), and `natural` (uses the alignment associated with the text).

numberOfLines—This property sets or returns the number of lines allowed for the text. If the text requires more lines than those set by this property, it is truncated according to the mode selected by the `lineBreakMode` property. A value of 0 declares unlimited lines.

After the views are defined, we can add them to the Collection View. First, we must specify their size by default with the `headerReferenceSize` and `footerReferenceSize` properties. Once these properties are set, the Collection View executes a closure to configure the views and show them on the screen. The following is the property included in the `UICollectionViewDiffableDataSource` class to provide this closure.

supplementaryViewProvider—This property sets a closure that the Collection View executes to get the supplementary views. The closure receives three values: a reference to the Collection View, a string that describes the kind of view required, and the index path with the location of the view.

Like cells, supplementary views should be defined when the Collection View and the data source object are initialized. The following are the changes we need to introduce to the initializer of our observable object to include a header and a footer in our Collection View.

```
init() {
    let layout = UICollectionViewFlowLayout()
    layout.scrollDirection = .vertical
    layout.itemSize = CGSize(width: 150, height: 100)
    layout.headerReferenceSize = CGSize(width: 0, height: 50)
    layout.footerReferenceSize = CGSize(width: 0, height: 50)
    layout.sectionInset = UIEdgeInsets(top: 20, left: 5, bottom: 20, right: 5)

    collectionView = UICollectionView(frame: CGRect.zero,
collectionViewLayout: layout)
    collectionView.backgroundColor = .white
    collectionView.register(FoodCell.self, forCellWithReuseIdentifier:
"FoodCell")
    collectionView.register(HeaderView.self, forSupplementaryViewOfKind:
UICollectionView.elementKindSectionHeader, withReuseIdentifier: "Header")
    collectionView.register(FooterView.self, forSupplementaryViewOfKind:
UICollectionView.elementKindSectionFooter, withReuseIdentifier: "Footer")

    dataSource = UICollectionViewDiffableDataSource<Sections,
Food>(collectionView: collectionView) { collectionView, indexPath, food
in
        let cell = collectionView.dequeueReusableCell(withReuseIdentifier:
"FoodCell", for: indexPath) as! FoodCell
        cell.picture.image = UIImage(named: food.picture)
        return cell
    }
    dataSource.supplementaryViewProvider = { collectionView, kind,
indexPath in
        if kind == UICollectionView.elementKindSectionHeader {
            let header =
collectionView.dequeueReusableSupplementaryView(ofKind: kind,
withReuseIdentifier: "Header", for: indexPath) as! HeaderView
            return header
        } else {
            let footer =
collectionView.dequeueReusableSupplementaryView(ofKind: kind,
withReuseIdentifier: "Footer", for: indexPath) as! FooterView
            return footer
        }
    }
    listOfFood = [ Food(name: "Bagels", picture: "bagels"), Food(name:
"Brownies", picture: "brownies"), Food(name: "Butter", picture:
"butter"), Food(name: "Cheese", picture: "cheese"), Food(name: "Coffee",
picture: "coffee"), Food(name: "Cookies", picture: "cookies"), Food(name:
"Donuts", picture: "donuts"), Food(name: "Granola", picture: "granola"),
Food(name: "Juice", picture: "juice"), Food(name: "Lemonade", picture:
"lemonade"), Food(name: "Lettuce", picture: "lettuce"), Food(name:
"Milk", picture: "milk"), Food(name: "Oatmeal", picture: "oatmeal"),
Food(name: "Onions", picture: "onions"), Food(name: "Potato", picture:
```

```
"potato"), Food(name: "Tea", picture: "tea"), Food(name: "Tomato",
picture: "tomato"), Food(name: "Yogurt", picture: "yogurt") ]
    self.generateSnapshot()
}
```

Listing 16-92: Creating the supplementary views

The code in Listing 16-92 assigns a height of 50 points to the header and the footer (in a vertical scroll, the width is ignored), and then registers the views. The header view is registered with the **HeaderView** class and the identifier "Header", and the footer view is registered with the **FooterView** class and the identifier "Footer". To tell which view is which, we use the type properties defined in the **UICollectionView** class (**elementKindSectionHeader** and **elementKindSectionFooter**). Next, the views are created in the closure assigned to the **supplementaryViewProvider** property. This closure is executed every time the Collection View needs to present a supplementary view on the screen. If the view is of kind **elementKindSectionHeader**, we create or reuse a **HeaderView** view, otherwise, we create or reuse a **FooterView** view.

Figure 16-31: Headers and Footers

 Do It Yourself: Create a Swift file called HeaderView.swift for the view in Listing 16-90 and another called FooterView.swift for the view in Listing 16-91. Update the initializer of the **AppData** class with the code in Listing 16-92. Download the gradientTop.png image from our website and add it to the Assets Catalog. Run the application. You should see a Collection View with the header and footer shown in Figure 16-31.

(Basic) Constraints

The **UIImageView** view used to define the content of the header view in the previous section was created with a width of 458 points. This covers the width of every iPhone in portrait mode, but if the iPhone is rotated or the app runs in another device, the image will not be long enough to cover the whole area. We could assign a greater value to the width parameter to cover every scenario, but in most cases that is not the optimal solution. We are creating a view that exceeds the limits of the screen in small devices and could still be short in large screens, like computer monitors, for example. To set the position and size of a view according to the space available, UIKit uses constraints.

Constraints are rules that determine how a view should be positioned and sized in relation to other views and their container. For instance, a constraint can tell the system that a view should be 20 points from the top and 20 points from the bottom of its container, or that a button should always be 10 points from the left side of an image view. Defining the position and size of the views with rules like these makes them flexible, which allows the interface to adapt to any screen and device.

Constraints are created from objects of the `NSLayoutConstraint` class and are applied using different systems. The most popular these days is a system of layout anchors that allow us to attach a constraint to anchors assigned to each view or layout guide. The system adds the constraints from one view to another using properties. The following are the properties provided by the `UIView` class for this purpose.

topAnchor—This property returns an object that represents the view's top edge.

bottomAnchor—This property returns an object that represents the view's bottom edge.

leadingAnchor—This property returns an object that represents the view's leading edge.

trailingAnchor—This property returns an object that represents the view's trailing edge.

widthAnchor—This property returns an object that represents the view's width.

heightAnchor—This property returns an object that represents the view's height.

centerXAnchor—This property returns an object that represents the view's horizontal center.

centerYAnchor—This property returns an object that represents the view's vertical center.

leftAnchor—This property returns an object that represents the view's left edge.

rightAnchor—This property returns an object that represents the view's right edge.

firstBaselineAnchor—This property returns an object that represents the baseline of the top line of text in the view.

lastBaselineAnchor—This property returns an object that represents the baseline of the last line of text in the view.

The properties return objects defined by subclasses of the `NSLayoutAnchor` class called `NSLayoutXAxisAnchor`, `NSLayoutYAxisAnchor`, and `NSLayoutDimension`. The following are the most frequently used methods included in these classes to add the constraints.

constraint(equalTo: NSLayoutAnchor, constant: CGFloat)—This method returns a `NSLayoutConstraint` object with a constraint that defines one anchor as equal to the other anchor, and with an offset determined by the **constant** attribute.

constraint(greaterThanOrEqualTo: NSLayoutAnchor, constant: CGFloat)—This method returns a `NSLayoutConstraint` object with a constraint that defines one anchor as greater than or equal to the other anchor, and with an offset determined by the **constant** attribute.

constraint(lessThanOrEqualTo: NSLayoutAnchor, constant: CGFloat)—This method returns a `NSLayoutConstraint` object with a constraint that defines one anchor as less than or equal to the other anchor, and with an offset determined by the **constant** attribute.

constraint(equalTo: NSLayoutDimension, multiplier: CGFloat)—This method returns a `NSLayoutConstraint` object with a constraint that defines the size attribute of the view equal to the specified anchor multiplied by the value of the **multiplier** attribute (used to defined equal widths and heights or to create Aspect Ratio constraints).

constraint(equalToConstant: CGFloat)—This method returns a `NSLayoutConstraint` object with a constraint that defines the size attribute of the view equal to the value of the attribute.

constraint(greaterThanOrEqualToConstant: CGFloat)—This method returns a `NSLayoutConstraint` object with a constraint that defines the size attribute of the view greater than or equal to the value of the attribute.

constraint(lessThanOrEqualToConstant: CGFloat)—This method returns a `NSLayoutConstraint` object with a constraint that defines the size attribute of the view less than or equal to the value of the attribute.

These methods return `NSLayoutConstraint` objects, but they do not add the constraints to the view. The constraints are added and managed by the following methods of the `UIVIew` class.

addConstraint(NSLayoutConstraint)—This method adds a constraint to the view.

addConstraints([NSLayoutConstraint])—This method adds an array of constraints to the view.

removeConstraint(NSLayoutConstraint)—This method removes a constraint from the view.

removeConstraints([NSLayoutConstraint])—This method removes multiple constraints from the view.

Depending on the types of constraints we need, we may use one method or another. For example, the following code applies constrains to the image in the header view to make it flexible.

```
import UIKit

class HeaderView: UICollectionReusableView {
    var headerImage = UIImageView(frame: CGRect.zero)

    override init(frame: CGRect) {
        super.init(frame: frame)
        headerImage.image = UIImage(named: "gradientTop")
        headerImage.translatesAutoresizingMaskIntoConstraints = false
        self.addSubview(headerImage)

        let constraint1 = headerImage.leadingAnchor.constraint(equalTo:
self.leadingAnchor, constant: 0)
        let constraint2 = headerImage.trailingAnchor.constraint(equalTo:
self.trailingAnchor, constant: 0)
        let constraint3 = headerImage.topAnchor.constraint(equalTo:
self.topAnchor, constant: 0)
        let constraint4 = headerImage.bottomAnchor.constraint(equalTo:
self.bottomAnchor, constant: 0)
        self.addConstraints([constraint1, constraint2, constraint3,
constraint4])
    }
    required init?(coder: NSCoder) {
        fatalError("Error")
    }
}
```

Listing 16-93: Attaching constraints to a view's anchors

In addition to the constraints, there are two more changes introduced to this view. The first one is the `UIImageView` view's frame. Instead of defining a fixed size, we declare it with zero values (`CGRect.zero`). Because we are defining its position and size with constraints, the size of the view by default is ignored. The second modification has to do with how constraints are assigned by the system. When elements are introduced to the interface without constraints, Xcode uses an old system called *Autoresizing* to position and size them (see Launching Screen in Chapter 5). The information generated by this system is later applied to create constraints for the elements and present the interface on the screen. If the constraints are added from code though, the system doesn't know that there are constraints available and tries to generate its own. To tell the system that we are going to define the constraints ourselves, we must set the view's `translatesAutoresizingMaskIntoConstraints` property to `false`. Assigning the value `false` to this property avoids the creation of automatic constraints and ensures that those we define in code will not conflict with those defined by the system.

After the view is set, we declare the constraints. The first one connects the image's left anchor (leading) with the view's left anchor. The following does the same for the right side (trailing). And the last two connect the top and the bottom of the image to the top and the bottom edge of the view. This makes the image expands to occupy the header view's whole area. At the end, we add the four constrains to the header view with the `addConstraints()` method and the view is ready (constraints involving two views are applied to the parent view). Now the image extends to the sides of the header view and therefore it adapts to the space available.

Figure 16-32: *Flexible UIKit views*

With constraints, we can develop more complex views for the cells and the supplementary views. For instance, we can introduce multiple views to the footer view.

```
import UIKit

class FooterView: UICollectionReusableView {
    var footerImage = UIImageView(frame: CGRect.zero)
    var footerTitle = UILabel(frame: CGRect.zero)

    override init(frame: CGRect) {
        super.init(frame: frame)
        footerImage.image = UIImage(named: "gradientBottom")
        footerImage.translatesAutoresizingMaskIntoConstraints = false
        self.addSubview(footerImage)

        footerTitle.text = "My Footer"
        footerTitle.font = UIFont.systemFont(ofSize: 24)
        footerTitle.textColor = UIColor.black
        footerTitle.textAlignment = .center
        footerTitle.translatesAutoresizingMaskIntoConstraints = false
        self.addSubview(footerTitle)

        let constraintImage1 =
footerImage.leadingAnchor.constraint(equalTo: self.leadingAnchor,
constant: 0)
        let constraintImage2 =
footerImage.trailingAnchor.constraint(equalTo: self.trailingAnchor,
constant: 0)
```

```
    let constraintImage3 = footerImage.topAnchor.constraint(equalTo:
self.topAnchor, constant: 0)
    let constraintImage4 = footerImage.bottomAnchor.constraint(equalTo:
self.bottomAnchor, constant: 0)
    self.addConstraints([constraintImage1, constraintImage2,
constraintImage3, constraintImage4])

    let constraintLabel1 =
footerTitle.leadingAnchor.constraint(equalTo: self.leadingAnchor,
constant: 0)
    let constraintLabel2 =
footerTitle.trailingAnchor.constraint(equalTo: self.trailingAnchor,
constant: 0)
    let constraintLabel3 =
footerImage.centerYAnchor.constraint(equalTo: self.centerYAnchor,
constant: 0)
    self.addConstraints([constraintLabel1, constraintLabel2,
constraintLabel3])
  }
  required init?(coder: NSCoder) {
    fatalError("Error")
  }
}
```

Listing 16-94: Adding constraints to the footer view

This time, the footer view contains two views, a `UIImageView` view to display the gradientBottom.png image, and a `UILabel` view to display a text. Because the image is added to the view first, is going to be displayed behind the text. The constraints for the image are the same used for the header view, but the label includes three constraints, two to pin the view to the left and right side of the footer, and one constraint to center the label vertically. In consequence, the label is going to be as wide as the footer and placed at the center. This determines the vertical alignment, but we still need to define the horizontal alignment. By default, the text in a `UILabel` view is aligned to the left, so we change the value of the `textAlignment` property to `center` to move it to the center.

Figure 16-33: Flexible label

Do It Yourself: Update the `HeaderView` class with the code in Listing 16-93 and the `FooterView` class with the code in Listing 16-94. Download the gradientBottom.png image from our website and add it to the Assets Catalog. Run the application. You should see the interface in Figures 16-32 and 16-33.

(Medium) ## Custom Layout

With the Flow layout, we can specify many things, like the margins of the sections with the `sectionInset` property, or the minimum space between cells with the `minimumInteritem-`

`Spacing` property, but the number of cells displayed in a row or column is always determined by the layout according to the space available. Flow layout gets the dimensions of the Collection View, subtracts the margins and the space between cells, and then positions the cells that fit in the remaining space. If, for example, we set the `minimumInteritemSpacing` property to a value too big to fit two cells in the same row, Flow layout will show only one cell and move the second cell to a new row. But as soon as we rotate the device and the space available becomes wider, the layout positions both cells back in the same row. The only way to make sure that the cells are organized the way we want, is by defining a fixed size for the representable view, as we did in Listing 16-81, but this not always solves all our problems. The solution is to define a custom layout object.

Although we can create our own subclass of the `UICollectionViewLayout` class to define a custom layout, the framework includes a flexible alternative called *Compositional Layouts*. Compositional layouts are defined with the `UICollectionViewCompositionalLayout` class and can organize (compose) a layout from smallest layouts and parts. There are three main parts in a compositional layout, the item (a single cell), the group (a group of cells), and the section (a subdivision of the layout that can include one or multiple groups). Figure 16-34, below, illustrates these parts in a simple layout.

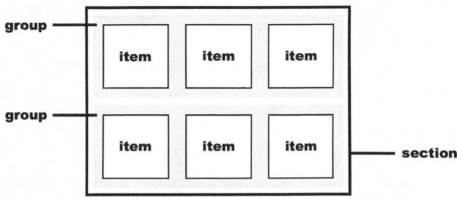

Figure 16-34: Compositional layout

The items are grouped horizontally, as in this example, or vertically, the groups repeat over and over again to show all the items available, and one or multiple sections can be used to present these groups. Each part is highly configurable and flexible, starting with the layout itself. The following are the initializers included in the `UICollectionViewCompositionalLayout` class to create the layout.

UICollectionViewCompositionalLayout(section: NSCollectionLayoutSection)—
This initializer creates a compositional layout with the section specified by the attribute.

UICollectionViewCompositionalLayout(section: NSCollectionLayoutSection, **configuration:** UICollectionViewCompositionalLayoutConfiguration)—This initializer creates a compositional layout with the section specified by the **section** attribute and with the configuration specified by the **configuration** attribute.

UICollectionViewCompositionalLayout(sectionProvider: UICollectionView-CompositionalLayoutSectionProvider)—This initializer creates a compositional layout with the section returned by the closure specified by the **sectionProvider** attribute.

UICollectionViewCompositionalLayout(sectionProvider: UICollectionView-CompositionalLayoutSectionProvider, **configuration:** UICollectionView-CompositionalLayoutConfiguration)—This initializer creates a compositional layout with the section returned by the closure specified by the **sectionProvider** attribute and with the configuration specified by the **configuration** attribute.

The layout is configured with an object of the `UICollectionViewCompositionalLayout-Configuration` class. The class includes the following property to configure the layout.

interSectionSpacing—This property sets or returns a `CGFloat` value that determines the space between sections.

scrollDirection—This property sets or returns a value that determines the orientation of the scroll. It is an enumeration of type `ScrollDirection` with the values `vertical` and `horizontal`.

Once we have the layout, we must define the parts. The items are defined by the `NSCollectionLayoutItem` class. The class includes the following initializers.

NSCollectionLayoutItem(layoutSize: NSCollectionLayoutSize)—This initializer creates an item of the size specified by the **layoutSize** attribute.

NSCollectionLayoutItem(layoutSize: NSCollectionLayoutSize, **supplementary-Items:** [NSCollectionLayoutSupplementaryItem])—This initializer creates an item of the size specified by the **layoutSize** attribute for the supplementary views specified by the **supplementaryItems** attribute.

The class includes the following properties to configure the items.

contentInsets—This property sets or returns a structure of type `NSDirectionalEdgeInsets` with the inset for the left, right, top and bottom sides of the content. These values are defined from the structure's initializer (`NSDirectionalEdgeInsets(top: CGFloat, leading: CGFloat, bottom: CGFloat, trailing: CGFloat)`).

edgeSpacing—This property sets or returns an object of type `NSCollectionLayout-EdgeSpacing` that defines the space on the sides of the layout. The space is defined with an object of type `NSCollectionLayoutSpacing`, which includes the type methods `fixed(CGFloat)` for fixed values, and `flexible(CGFloat)` for flexible values. The values for each side are declared by the `NSCollectionLayoutEdgeSpacing` class' initializer (`NSCollectionLayoutEdgeSpacing(leading: NSCollectionLayout-Spacing?, top: NSCollectionLayoutSpacing?, trailing: NSCollection-LayoutSpacing?, bottom: NSCollectionLayoutSpacing?)`).

The items are organized in groups. The framework includes the `NSCollectionLayoutGroup` class to create these groups. The class includes the following type methods to define and configure a group.

horizontal(layoutSize: NSCollectionLayoutSize, **subitems:** [NSCollection-LayoutItem])—This method returns a group with the items in horizontal order. The **layoutSize** attribute determines the size of the group, and the **subitems** attribute determines the type of items the group is going to contain. The number of items in the group is determined by the space available.

horizontal(layoutSize: NSCollectionLayoutSize, **subitem:** NSCollectionLayout-Item, **count:** Int)—This method returns a group with the items in horizontal order. The **layoutSize** attribute determines the size of the group, the **subitem** attribute determines the type of items the group is going to contain, and the **count** attribute specifies how many.

vertical(layoutSize: NSCollectionLayoutSize, **subitems:** [NSCollectionLayout-Item])—This method returns a group with the items in vertical order. The **layoutSize** attribute determines the size of the group, and the **subitems** attribute determines the type of items the group is going to contain. The number of items in the group is determined by the space available.

vertical(layoutSize: NSCollectionLayoutSize, **subitem:** NSCollectionLayout-Item, **count:** Int)—This method returns a group with the items in vertical order. The **layoutSize** attribute determines the size of the group, the **subitem** attribute determines the type of items the group is going to contain, and the **count** attribute specifies how many.

custom(layoutSize: NSCollectionLayoutSize, **itemProvider:** NSCollection-LayoutGroupCustomItemProvider)—This method returns a group with the size determined by the **layoutSize** attribute and the item returned by the closure assigned to the **itemProvider** attribute.

The `NSCollectionLayoutGroup` class also includes a property to specify the space between items.

interItemSpacing—This property sets or returns an object of type `NSCollectionLayoutSpacing` to define the space between items. The class includes the type methods `fixed(CGFloat)` for fixed values, and `flexible(CGFloat)` for flexible values.

Groups are the components of sections and sections are defined with the `NSCollectionLayoutSection` class. The class includes the following initializer.

NSCollectionLayoutSection(group: NSCollectionLayoutGroup)—This initializer creates a section with the type of groups specified by the **group** attribute.

To configure the section, the class includes the following properties.

contentInsets—This property sets or returns a structure of type `NSDirectionalEdgeInsets` with the inset for the left, right, top and bottom sides of the section. These values are defined from the structure's initializer (`NSDirectionalEdgeInsets(top: CGFloat, leading: CGFloat, bottom: CGFloat, trailing: CGFloat)`).

interGroupSpacing—This property sets or returns a `CGFloat` value that determines the space between groups.

orthogonalScrollingBehavior—This property sets or returns a value that determines the section's scrolling behavior. When it is declared, the section scrolls perpendicular to the layout. It is an enumeration of type `UICollectionLayoutSectionOrthogonal-ScrollingBehavior` with the values `continuous`, `continuousGroupLeading-Boundary`, `groupPaging`, `groupPagingCentered`, `paging`, and `none`.

The size of items and groups is determined by objects of type `NSCollectionLayoutSize`. The class includes the following initializer.

NSCollectionLayoutSize(widthDimension: NSCollectionLayoutDimension, **heightDimension:** NSCollectionLayoutDimension)—This initializer creates an `NSCollectionLayoutSize` object with the dimensions determined by the attributes. The attributes are objects of type `NSCollectionLayoutDimension`. This class includes the type methods **absolute(CGFloat)** to provide absolute values, **estimated(CGFloat)** to provide an estimate of what the size could be, **fractionalWidth(CGFloat)** to calculate the value from the width of the container, and **fractionalHeight(CGFloat)** to calculate the value from the height of the container. The fractional values are specified with numbers from 0.0 to 1.0.

It is time to see an example of how to compose a complex layout with these tools. The first step is to prepare the Collection View to work with this layout. This is easy. Instead of instantiating the **UICollectionView** object with a Flow layout, we do it with our custom layout. The following are the changes required in the initializer of our observable object.

```
init() {
    let layout = createLayout()
    collectionView = UICollectionView(frame: UIScreen.main.bounds,
collectionViewLayout: layout)
    collectionView.backgroundColor = .white
    collectionView.register(FoodCell.self, forCellWithReuseIdentifier:
"FoodCell")

    dataSource = UICollectionViewDiffableDataSource<Sections,
Food>(collectionView: collectionView) { collectionView, indexPath, food
in
        let cell = collectionView.dequeueReusableCell(withReuseIdentifier:
"FoodCell", for: indexPath) as! FoodCell
        cell.picture.image = UIImage(named: food.picture)
        return cell
    }
    listOfFood = [ Food(name: "Bagels", picture: "bagels"), Food(name:
"Brownies", picture: "brownies"), Food(name: "Butter", picture:
"butter"), Food(name: "Cheese", picture: "cheese"), Food(name: "Coffee",
picture: "coffee"), Food(name: "Cookies", picture: "cookies"), Food(name:
"Donuts", picture: "donuts"), Food(name: "Granola", picture: "granola"),
Food(name: "Juice", picture: "juice"), Food(name: "Lemonade", picture:
"lemonade"), Food(name: "Lettuce", picture: "lettuce"), Food(name:
"Milk", picture: "milk"), Food(name: "Oatmeal", picture: "oatmeal"),
Food(name: "Onions", picture: "onions"), Food(name: "Potato", picture:
"potato"), Food(name: "Tea", picture: "tea"), Food(name: "Tomato",
picture: "tomato"), Food(name: "Yogurt", picture: "yogurt") ]
    self.generateSnapshot()
}
```

Listing 16-95: Instantiating the Collection View with a compositional layout

The code in Listing 16-95 executes a method called **createLayout()** and then instantiates the **UICollectionView** object with the layout returned by this method. Notice that the view was declared the size of the screen (**UIScreen.main.bounds**). This is necessary because the compositional layout we are going to create uses fractional values and those values are calculated from the size of the view.

The process to define a compositional layout is declarative. We define the object that configures the items, then the object that configures the groups, then the object that configures the sections, and finally the layout object that contains these sections.

```
func createLayout() -> UICollectionViewCompositionalLayout {
    let itemSize = NSCollectionLayoutSize(widthDimension:
.fractionalWidth(0.5), heightDimension: .fractionalWidth(0.5))
    let item = NSCollectionLayoutItem(layoutSize: itemSize)
    item.contentInsets = NSDirectionalEdgeInsets(top: 10, leading: 5,
bottom: 5, trailing: 10)
```

```
    let groupSize = NSCollectionLayoutSize(widthDimension:
.fractionalWidth(1), heightDimension: .fractionalWidth(0.5))
    let group = NSCollectionLayoutGroup.horizontal(layoutSize: groupSize,
subitems: [item])

    let section = NSCollectionLayoutSection(group: group)

    let layout = UICollectionViewCompositionalLayout(section: section)
    return layout
}
```

Listing 16-96: Defining a compositional layout

We begin by defining the size of the items. To make the items adapt to the space available, we use fractional values. The width dimension was declared as half the width of the container and the same for the height. This means that the system is going to get the width of the group, divide it by half (width * 0.5), and assign the result to the item's width and height. For instance, if the screen has a width of 320 points and the group is declared of the same size, the items are going have a size of 160 by 160 points (320 * 0.5). With this size, we instantiate the **NSCollectionLayoutItem** object and then assign a new value to the **contentInsets** property to separate the items from each other and the edges of the container.

With the items configured, we can now define the group that is going to contain those items. First, the size of the group is declared with fractional values. This time, we assign a width that is 100% the size of the group's container (`.fractionalWidth(1)`) and a height that is half the width. Again, if the screen is 320 points wide, the group is going to have a width of 320 points and a height of 160. Next, we use the **horizontal()** type method to create the group using the size we just calculated and an array with the **NSCollectionLayoutItem** objects defined before. This tells the layout to align the items in the group horizontally and to fit as many as possible. Finally, the section is defined with this group and the layout is defined with this section.

This example creates a simple layout, like the one built with a Flow layout before, but with the difference that the size of the items adapts to the space available. To take advantage of this flexibility, we must define the content of the cell with constraints to also make it flexible, as in the following example.

```
import UIKit

class FoodCell: UICollectionViewCell {
    var picture: UIImageView = UIImageView(frame: CGRect.zero)

    override init(frame: CGRect) {
        super.init(frame: frame)
        picture.contentMode = .scaleAspectFit
        picture.translatesAutoresizingMaskIntoConstraints = false
        contentView.addSubview(picture)

        selectedBackgroundView = UIView()
        selectedBackgroundView?.backgroundColor = UIColor(red: 0.9, green:
0.9, blue: 0.9, alpha: 1)

        let constraint1 = picture.leadingAnchor.constraint(equalTo:
self.leadingAnchor, constant: 0)
        let constraint2 = picture.trailingAnchor.constraint(equalTo:
self.trailingAnchor, constant: 0)
        let constraint3 = picture.topAnchor.constraint(equalTo:
self.topAnchor, constant: 0)
        let constraint4 = picture.bottomAnchor.constraint(equalTo:
self.bottomAnchor, constant: 0)
```

```
      self.addConstraints([constraint1, constraint2, constraint3,
constraint4])
   }
   required init?(coder: NSCoder) {
      fatalError("Error")
   }
}
```

Listing 16-97: Laying out the content of the cell with constraints

The layout is ready, and the content of the cell adapts to the size of the items, but there is one more change we need to introduce for the Collection View to be ready. At the time, the **bounds** property of the **UIScreen** object always returns the values in portrait mode. To make sure that the layout is always calculated with the size of the Collection View determined by the orientation of the screen and the current size of the representable view, we must recreate it before returning the **UICollectionView** object from the **makeUIView()** method of the representable view. For this purpose, the **UICollectionView** class offers the **collectionViewLayout** property to return a reference to the layout, and the **UICollectionViewLayout** class defines the **invalidateLayout()** method to invalidate the layout and force it to recalculate the positions and sizes of its content.

```
struct CollectionView: UIViewRepresentable {
   @EnvironmentObject var appData: AppData

   func makeUIView(context: Context) -> UICollectionView {
      appData.collectionView.delegate = context.coordinator
      appData.collectionView.collectionViewLayout.invalidateLayout()
      return appData.collectionView
   }
   func updateUIView(_ uiView: UICollectionView, context: Context) {}

   func makeCoordinator() -> CollectionViewCoordinator {
      return CollectionViewCoordinator(data: self.appData)
   }
}
```

Listing 16-98: Recalculating the layout

With this final adjustment, the app is ready. The layout organizes the items in one section and one group, and because the size of each item was specified as half the width of the container, only two are included per group.

Figure 16-35: Compositional layout

Chapter 16 - Framework Integration

Do It Yourself: Update the initializer of the observable object from the previous example with the code in Listing 16-95. Add the `createLayout()` method of Listing 16-96, to the `AppData` class. Update the `FoodCell` class with the code of Listing 16-97. Update the `CollectionView` structure from the CollectionView.swift file with the code of Listing 16-98. Run the application and rotate the device. You should see the cells adapt to the space available.

Designing the perfect layout for our application is easy with a compositional layout. For instance, we can include five columns of items by assigning a fractional size of 0.2 to the items.

```
func createLayout() -> UICollectionViewLayout {
    let itemSize = NSCollectionLayoutSize(widthDimension:
.fractionalWidth(0.2), heightDimension: .fractionalWidth(0.2))
    let item = NSCollectionLayoutItem(layoutSize: itemSize)
    item.contentInsets = NSDirectionalEdgeInsets(top: 10, leading: 5,
bottom: 5, trailing: 10)

    let groupSize = NSCollectionLayoutSize(widthDimension:
.fractionalWidth(1), heightDimension: .fractionalWidth(0.2))
    let group = NSCollectionLayoutGroup.horizontal(layoutSize: groupSize,
subitems: [item])

    let section = NSCollectionLayoutSection(group: group)

    let layout = UICollectionViewCompositionalLayout(section: section)
    return layout
}
```

Listing 16-99: Generating more rows

The width and height of the items were declared as 20% the width of the container, which means that a total of five items will fit in a group. Notice that the height of the group was also defined as the 20% of the width of the container, so it matches the size of the items.

Figure 16-36: Compositional layout with five columns

 IMPORTANT: A compositional layout can include multiple sections with different groups, items, and scroll orientations. With these types of layouts, you can order the items any way you want and add as much complexity as your app requires. The topic goes beyond the scope of this book. For more information, visit our website and follow the links for this chapter.

(Basic) **Collection Views and Core Data**

So far, the data for the Collection View has been defined with temporary values. The testing values included in the `AppData` class' initializer were stored in an array and regenerated every time the app was launched. Of course, we could store the values inserted by the user in a file, as we did in previous chapters, but Collection Views were designed to work with thousands of values, and the best way to store and managed indexed values is with Core Data. The problem is that we are combining three disparate systems. Core Data was developed in the days of Objective-C, Collection Views were developed in the days of UIKit, and now we are trying to integrate these old systems with SwiftUI. The main issue is that SwiftUI tools, like the `@FetchRequest` property wrapper, were designed to work with SwiftUI views, like the `List` view. Although we could find a way to integrate these tools with a Collection View wrapped in a representable view, it is not the right solution. A more reasonable approach is to define these elements manually, as we used to do before SwiftUI arrived.

Collection Views, like `List` views, can handle thousands of values, but we cannot load them all at once or the device will run out of memory. The `@FetchRequest` property wrapper provided by SwiftUI solves this problem by creating a structure that takes care of loading from Core Data only the objects that are required. If we want to recreate this feature for Collection Views, we must implement the tools provided by the Core Data framework. We already learned how to define a request with the `NSFetchRequest` class to get objects from the persistent store (see Listing 14-64), but to get only the objects the interface needs at any given moment, we must use an `NSFetchedResultsController` object. This class provides highly optimized code that intermediates between the Collection View and the persistent store; taking care of fetching the objects the view needs and updating the list of objects available when some are modified, added, or removed. To create the controller, the class provides the following initializer.

NSFetchedResultsController(fetchRequest: NSFetchRequest, **managed-ObjectContext:** NSManagedObjectContext, **sectionNameKeyPath:** String?, **cacheName:** String?)—This initializer creates an `NSFetchedResultsController` object that fetches `NSManagedObject` objects from the persistent store. The **fetchRequest** attribute is an `NSFetchRequest` object with the request we want the controller to use to get the objects, the **managedObjectContext** attribute is a reference to the Core Data context, the **sectionNameKeyPath** attribute identifies the name of the property used to create the view's sections, and the **cacheName** attribute defines the name of the file the controller uses to cache the objects returned by the request.

When we work with an `NSFetchedResultsController` object, we must ask this object for any information we need about the request. The following are some of the properties and methods offered by the class for this purpose.

fetchedObjects—This property returns an array with objects currently fetched by the controller.

performFetch()—This method executes the fetch request set for the controller. The controller does not return any value until this method is called.

object(at: IndexPath)—This method returns the object corresponding to the index path specified by the **at** attribute.

indexPath(forObject: ResultType)—This method returns the index path of the object specified by the **forObject** attribute. The value returned is an `IndexPath` structure.

After the `NSFetchedResultsController` object is initialized, we have to call its `performFetch()` method to execute the request. The results produced by the request are stored in a temporal container and automatically updated by the `NSFetchedResultsController` object every time a modification is introduced to the context (an object is modified, deleted, moved, or new objects are added). Because of the close relationship between this controller and the Collection View, it is important to make sure that all the changes are immediately reflected on the view. Core Data simplifies this task with the addition of the `NSFetchedResultsControllerDelegate` protocol. The protocol defines methods that are called every time a change occurred in the objects managed by the `NSFetchedResultsController` object, and therefore we can implement them to update the snapshot. The following are the most frequently used.

controllerWillChangeContent(NSFetchedResultsController**)**—This method is called on the delegate when the controller is going to start processing changes.

controller(NSFetchedResultsController, **didChange:** AnyObject, **at:** IndexPath?, **for:** NSFetchedResultsChangeType, **newIndexPath:** IndexPath?**)**— This method is called on the delegate when an object managed by the controller changed. The **didChange** attribute is a reference to the object that changed, the **at** and **newIndexPath** attributes are `IndexPath` structures that represent the old and the new index path of the object, and the **for** attribute is an enumeration that indicates the type of change. The possible values are `insert`, `delete`, `move`, and `update`.

controllerDidChangeContent(NSFetchedResultsController**)**—This method is called on the delegate when the controller finished processing changes.

With these tools, we can finally integrate Core Data, Collection Views and SwiftUI. But first, we need a Core Data model. For this example, we are going to use an entity called Foods with two attributes called name (String) and picture (Binary Data), as illustrated in Figure 16-37.

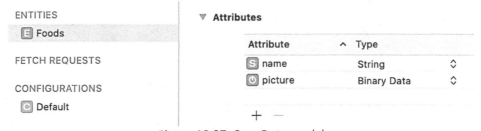

Figure 16-37: Core Data model

Next, we need a Core Data stack. As before, we define it in the `AppDelegate` class with a computer property. The class also has to include the initialization of our data model (the `AppData` class).

```
import UIKit
import CoreData

@UIApplicationMain
class AppDelegate: UIResponder, UIApplicationDelegate {
    var myData: AppData!

    func application(_ application: UIApplication,
didFinishLaunchingWithOptions launchOptions:
[UIApplication.LaunchOptionsKey: Any]?) -> Bool {
        myData = AppData()
        return true
    }
    func application(_ application: UIApplication,
configurationForConnecting connectingSceneSession: UISceneSession,
options: UIScene.ConnectionOptions) -> UISceneConfiguration {
```

```
        return UISceneConfiguration(name: "Default Configuration",
sessionRole: connectingSceneSession.role)
    }
    lazy var persistentContainer: NSPersistentContainer = {
        let container = NSPersistentContainer(name: "TestCollectionView")
        container.loadPersistentStores(completionHandler: {
(storeDescription, error) in
            if let error = error as NSError? {
                fatalError("Unresolved error \(error), \(error.userInfo)")
            }
        })
        return container
    }()
}
```

Listing 16-100: Initializing Core Data

In the `SceneDelegate` class, we need to inject two values into the environment, our data model and the Core Data context.

```
import UIKit
import SwiftUI

class SceneDelegate: UIResponder, UIWindowSceneDelegate {
    var window: UIWindow?

    func scene(_ scene: UIScene, willConnectTo session: UISceneSession,
options connectionOptions: UIScene.ConnectionOptions) {
        let app = UIApplication.shared
        let delegate = app.delegate as! AppDelegate
        let dbContext = delegate.persistentContainer.viewContext
        let contentView = ContentView()
            .environmentObject(delegate.myData)
            .environment(\.managedObjectContext, dbContext)

        if let windowScene = scene as? UIWindowScene {
            let window = UIWindow(windowScene: windowScene)
            window.rootViewController = UIHostingController(rootView:
contentView)
            self.window = window
            window.makeKeyAndVisible()
        }
    }
}
```

Listing 16-101: Injecting the values in the environment

Following the approach of previous examples, we are going to concentrate all the logic in our observable object. To illustrate how to work with Core Data, we will use a simple Collection View with a Flow layout and cells of a fixed size.

```
import SwiftUI
import CoreData

enum Sections {
    case main
}
class AppData: NSObject, ObservableObject,
NSFetchedResultsControllerDelegate {
    @Published var selectedItem: Int?
```

Chapter 16 - Framework Integration

```
    var collectionView: UICollectionView!
    var dataSource: UICollectionViewDiffableDataSource<Sections, Foods>!
    var fetchedController: NSFetchedResultsController<Foods>!
    var dbContext: NSManagedObjectContext!

    override init() {
        super.init()
        let app = UIApplication.shared
        let delegate = app.delegate as! AppDelegate
        dbContext = delegate.persistentContainer.viewContext

        let layout = UICollectionViewFlowLayout()
        layout.scrollDirection = .vertical
        layout.itemSize = CGSize(width: 150, height: 100)
        layout.sectionInset = UIEdgeInsets(top: 20, left: 5, bottom: 20,
right: 5)

        collectionView = UICollectionView(frame: CGRect.zero,
collectionViewLayout: layout)
        collectionView.backgroundColor = .white
        collectionView.register(FoodCell.self, forCellWithReuseIdentifier:
"FoodCell")

        dataSource = UICollectionViewDiffableDataSource<Sections,
Foods>(collectionView: collectionView) { collectionView, indexPath, food
in
            let cell =
collectionView.dequeueReusableCell(withReuseIdentifier: "FoodCell", for:
indexPath) as! FoodCell
            if let data = food.picture {
                cell.picture.image = UIImage(data: data, scale:
UIScreen.main.scale)
            } else {
                cell.picture.image = UIImage(named: "nothumbnail")
            }
            return cell
        }
        self.generateFetchResult()
    }
}
```

Listing 16-102: Initializing the model

The code in Listing 16-102 includes only the initialization of the Collection View, but it defines two properties to store a reference to the **NSFetchedResultsController** object we need to fetch objects of type **Food**, and another to keep a reference to the Core Data context. The context is retrieved from the **AppDelegate** class as soon as the class is initialized, but the **NSFetchedResultsController** object is created by the **generateFetchResult()** method executed at the end. The following is our implementation of that method.

```
func generateFetchResult() {
    let request: NSFetchRequest<Foods> = Foods.fetchRequest()
    let sort = NSSortDescriptor(key: "name", ascending: true)
    request.sortDescriptors = [sort]
    fetchedController = NSFetchedResultsController(fetchRequest: request,
managedObjectContext: self.dbContext, sectionNameKeyPath: nil, cacheName:
nil)
    fetchedController.delegate = self
```

```
do {
    try fetchedController.performFetch()
    self.generateSnapshot()
} catch {
    print("Error fetching")
}
}
```

Listing 16-103: Initializing the fetched controller

The method creates a fetch request for the entity Foods, sorts the objects by name in ascending order, and then defines the **NSFetchedResultsController** object with this request. After we get this controller, we call the **performFetch()** method on it to start fetching objects from the persistent store and then execute the **generateSnapshot()** method to update the snapshot with these new objects. The following code illustrates how to implement this method and how to create a snapshot from the objects fetched by the controller.

```
func generateSnapshot() {
    var snapshot = NSDiffableDataSourceSnapshot<Sections, Foods>()
    snapshot.appendSections([.main])
    snapshot.appendItems(self.fetchedController.fetchedObjects ?? [])
    dataSource.apply(snapshot)
}
```

Listing 16-104: Creating a snapshot with objects fetched by a fetched controller

The **NSDiffableDataSourceSnapshot** object is created as before, but to get the items to append to it we read the **fetchedObjects** property of the fetched controller. If the property returns **nil**, we provide an empty array, otherwise, the object currently fetched by the controller are assigned to the snapshot and shown on the screen.

The **generateSnapshot()** method has to be called two times, one after the **performFetch()** method is executed, and another when the controller is updated, either because the user added, removed, or modified an object. To be able to respond to these changes, we make the **AppData** class conform to the **NSFetchedResultsController-Delegate** protocol, declare the **AppData** object as the controller's delegate (see the **generateFetchResult()** method in Listing 16-103), and finally implement the following method.

```
func controllerDidChangeContent(_ controller:
NSFetchedResultsController<NSFetchRequestResult>) {
    self.generateSnapshot()
}
```

Listing 16-105: Updating the snapshot when the controller changes

The **controllerDidChangeContent()** method is called on the delegate every time a change is introduced in the objects managed by the controller. Therefore, when we add or remove objects from the persistent store, the fetched controller is automatically updated, without us having to do anything. To illustrate how this works, we are going to add the following methods to add and remove objects.

```
func addItem(name: String) {
    let newFood = Foods(context: self.dbContext)
    newFood.name = name
    newFood.picture = UIImage(named: "nothumbnail")?.pngData()
```

```
    do {
       try self.dbContext.save()
    } catch {
       print("Error creating Foods object")
    }
}
func removeItem(index: Int) {
    let path = IndexPath(item: index, section: 0)
    let food = fetchedController.object(at: path)
    self.dbContext.delete(food)
    do {
       try self.dbContext.save()
    } catch {
       print("Error deleting object")
    }
}
}
```

Listing 16-106: Adding and removing objects

Although the process is the same we used in the Core Data examples in previous chapters, the `removeItem()` method has to get the object to be removed from the fetched controller. For this purpose, we use the `object(at:)` method provided by the controller. We create an `IndexPath` structure with the object's index received by the method, then get the object at that path, and remove it from the persistent store with the `delete()` method, as always.

The main code is ready, but we still have to provide the views to show the values produced by it. First, we are going to extend the `Foods` class created by Xcode for the Foods entity to convert the data of the picture stored by each object into an `UIImage` object and unwrap the `name` property.

```
import SwiftUI
import CoreData

extension Foods {
    var foodThumbnail: UIImage {
        if let pic = picture, let image = UIImage(data: pic, scale:
UIScreen.main.scale) {
            return image
        } else {
            return UIImage(named: "nothumbnail")!
        }
    }
    var foodName: String {
        return name ?? "Undefined"
    }
}
```

Listing 16-107: Extending the `Foods` class to format the values for the views

This, of course, is just to simplify the code for the views. Next, is time to define the representable view to include the Collection View in our SwiftUI interface.

```
import SwiftUI

struct CollectionView: UIViewRepresentable {
    @EnvironmentObject var appData: AppData

    func makeUIView(context: Context) -> UICollectionView {
        appData.collectionView.delegate = context.coordinator
```

```
        return appData.collectionView
    }
    func updateUIView(_ uiView: UICollectionView, context: Context) {}

    func makeCoordinator() -> CollectionViewCoordinator {
        return CollectionViewCoordinator(data: self.appData)
    }
}
class CollectionViewCoordinator: NSObject, UICollectionViewDelegate {
    var appData: AppData!

    init(data: AppData) {
        self.appData = data
    }
    func collectionView(_ collectionView: UICollectionView,
didSelectItemAt indexPath: IndexPath) {
        let index = indexPath.item
        appData.selectedItem = index
    }
}
```

Listing 16-108: Defining the representable view for the Collection View

Nothing new here, but we had to implement the protocol method to respond every time an item is selected. The initial view is also the same as before.

```
import SwiftUI

struct ContentView: View {
    @EnvironmentObject var appData: AppData

    var body: some View {
        NavigationView {
            VStack {
                CollectionView()
                    .navigationBarTitle("Food", displayMode: .inline)
                    .navigationBarItems(trailing: NavigationLink(destination:
AddItem(), label: {
                        Image(systemName: "plus.circle")
                            .font(.title)
                    }))
                NavigationLink(destination: ItemDetailView(), tag:
appData.selectedItem ?? 0, selection: $appData.selectedItem, label: {
                    EmptyView()
                })
            }
            .onAppear(perform: {
                if let paths =
self.appData.collectionView.indexPathsForSelectedItems {
                    for path in paths {
                        self.appData.collectionView.deselectItem(at: path,
animated: true)
                    }
                }
            })
        }
    }
}
```

Listing 16-109: Defining the initial view

The view opens the `AddItem` view when the + button is pressed to let the user add a new object, and when an item is selected, it opens the `ItemDetailView` view to show information about it. The `AddItem` view just has to call the `addItem()` method implemented before in the model to add an item with the name inserted by the user.

```
import SwiftUI

struct AddItem: View {
    @EnvironmentObject var appData: AppData
    @Environment(\.presentationMode) var presentation
    @State private var inputName: String = ""

    var body: some View {
        VStack {
            HStack {
                Text("Name: ")
                TextField("Inser Name", text: $inputName)
                    .textFieldStyle(RoundedBorderTextFieldStyle())
            }
            HStack {
                Spacer()
                Button("Save") {
                    let text = self.inputName.trimmingCharacters(in:
.whitespaces)
                    if !text.isEmpty {
                        self.appData.addItem(name: text)
                        self.presentation.wrappedValue.dismiss()
                    }
                }
            }
            Spacer()
        }.padding()
    }
}
```

Listing 16-110: Defining the view to add an item

And finally, we implement the view that is going to be opened when an item is selected. This is the only view that introduces something different from previous examples. The process we use to determine which object was selected is the same, but now the view has to get that object from the controller with the `object(at:)` method.

```
import SwiftUI

struct ItemDetailView: View {
    @EnvironmentObject var appData: AppData

    var body: some View {
        let path = IndexPath(item: appData.selectedItem ?? 0, section: 0)
        let food = appData.fetchedController.object(at: path)

        return VStack(alignment: .center, spacing: 20) {
            Text(food.foodName)
                .font(.title)
            Image(uiImage: food.foodThumbnail)
        }.padding()
        .navigationBarItems(trailing: Button("Remove") {
            if let selected = self.appData.selectedItem {
                self.appData.removeItem(index: selected)
```

```
                    self.appData.selectedItem = nil
            }
        })
    }
}
```

Listing 16-111: Defining the view to show the details of the selected item

And the application is finished. We only miss the cell, but we can use any `FoodCell` class introduced before. Because we didn't store any data for testing, the Collection View is empty at first, but then is populated by the items inserted by the user.

Figure 16-38: Collection View populated with Core Data objects

Do It Yourself: Create a SwiftUI project. Download the nothumbnail.png image from our website and add it to the Assets Catalog. Create a Core Data Model file and call it TestCollectionView. Add an entity called Foods with two attributes called name (String) and picture (Binary Data). Select the picture attribute and check the option Allows External Storage from the Data Model Inspector panel on the right (see Figure 14-20). Update the AppDelegate.swift file with the code in Listing 16-100 and the SceneDelegate.swift file with the code in Listing 16-101. Create a Swift file called AppData.swift for the model in Listing 16-102. Add the methods of Listings 16-103, 16-104, 16-105, and 16-106 to the `AppData` class (below the initializer). Create a Swift file called Extensions.swift for the extension in Listing 16-107. Create a Swift file called CollectionView.swift for the representable view in Listing 16-108. Update the ContentView.swift file with the code in Listing 16-109. Create a SwiftUI file called AddItem.swift for the view in Listing 16-110 and a SwiftUI file called ItemDetailView.swift for the view in Listing 16-111. Create a Swift file with the name FoodCell.swift for the class of Listing 16-97. Run the application and press the + button to add an item. You should see something similar to Figure 16-38.

Chapter 16 - Framework Integration

Basic | **17.1 Publishing**

At the beginning of this book we talked about Apple's strict control over the applications the users have access to. Because of Apple's policies, we cannot sell mobile applications on our own; we must publish them in the App Store. The process is performed from Xcode, but there are a series of requirements we need to satisfy for our app to be published and become available to the users.

- We need an Apple Developer Program membership.
- We need a Distribution Certificate.
- We need a Provisioning Profile for distribution.
- We need an App ID for each application.
- We must register the app in the App Store Connect website.
- We must create an archive with our app to send to Apple's servers.
- We must upload the archive to App Store Connect for review.

Basic | **Apple Developer Program**

Developing and testing can be done with a free account, but publishing our app requires a membership to the Apple Developer Program. The option to enroll in this program is available on the **developer.apple.com** website. We must click on the Discover/Program options at the top of the screen, press the Enroll button, and follow the instructions to register an account for an Individual or an organization. At the time of writing, the membership costs 99 USD a year.

Basic | **Certificates, Provisioning Profiles, and Identifiers**

Apple wants to make sure that only authorized apps are running on its devices, so it requests developers to add a cryptographic signature to each application. There are three values that are necessary to authorize the app: certificates, provisioning profiles, and identifiers. Basically, a certificate identifies the developer that publishes the application, the provisioning profile identifies the device that is allowed to run the application, and an identifier, called *App ID*, identifies the application. These values are packed along with the application's files and therefore Apple always knows who developed the app, who is authorized to run it, and in which devices.

Xcode automatically generates these values for us, so we do not have to worry about them, but Apple offers a control panel in our developer account in case we need to do it manually (the option is not available for free members). Figure 17-1 shows the menu we see after we go to developer.apple.com, click on Account, and select the option Certificates, IDs & Profiles.

Certificates, Identifiers & Profiles

Certificates

Certificates	Certificates ⊕				Q All Types ⌄
Identifiers	NAME ⌄	TYPE	PLATFORM	CREATED BY	EXPIRATION
Devices					
Profiles					
Keys					

Figure 17-1: Web page to manage certificates, provisioning profiles, and identifiers

In this page, we can create, edit, or remove certificates, provisioning profiles and identifiers. The page contains two panels, the left panel offers a list of options to select the type of values we want to work with, and the right panel shows the list of values available and buttons to create new ones. When a value is selected, a new panel opens with tools to edit it.

(Basic) App Store Connect

The first step to submit our app is to create a record on Apple's servers. Apple has designated a special website for this purpose, available at **appstoreconnect.apple.com**. This website is integrated with Apple's developing system and therefore it already contains information of our developer account. To login, we must use the same Apple ID and password we use to access our account at developer.apple.com. Figure 17-2 illustrates the options available.

Figure 17-2: App Store Connect menu

From this panel, we can insert our financial information required to put our apps on the market (Agreements, Tax, and Banking), publish our apps (My Apps), and see how the business is going (Sales and Trends). The first step is to create a record of the app we want to publish from the My Apps option. When we click on this icon, a new window shows the list of our apps and a + button at the top to add new ones.

Figure 17-3: Menu to add apps to our account

To add a new app, we must click the New App button and insert the app's information. The first window asks for the platform, the application's name, the primary language, the bundle ID, and a custom ID (SKU) that can help us identify the app. The name and language are values we already have, and the SKU is a custom string, but the Bundle ID is a value generate by Xcode. Xcode creates a Bundle ID and submit it to Apple servers when we enable services from the capabilities panel. If our app does not use any of these services, we will not find its ID on this list. In this case, we must select the option "Xcode iOS Wildcard App ID - *" and insert the app's Bundle Identifier (available in the app's Settings panel). Figure 17-4 shows the information we must insert to register an app called Test that was created with the Bundle Identifier com.formasterminds.Test.

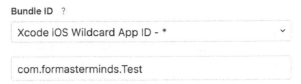

Figure 17-4: Bundle ID

After these values are inserted, we can press the Create button and complete the rest of the required information. This includes the app's description, screenshots, and personal information. We also must select the option Pricing and Availability on the left to set the price and where the application will be available. Once all the information is provided, we can finally press the Save button and go back to Xcode to prepare the files for uploading.

(Basic)   **Submitting the Application**

The application and resources must be compiled in a single archive and then submitted to App Store Connect. The option is available on the Xcode's Product menu. The option is only available when a device is selected on the Schemes, so we have to select a device and then click on the Archive option inside the Product menu (we may use the Generic iOS Device option, or the device currently connected to the computer).

Figure 17-5: Archive option

After we click on this option, Xcode compiles the application and creates the archive. The next window shows the archive and offers buttons to validate and submit the app.

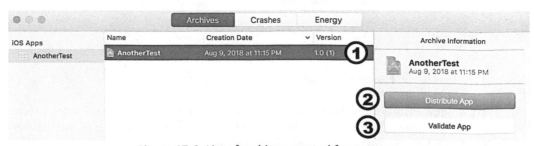

Figure 17-6: List of archives created for our apps

Figure 17-6 shows an archive created for an application called AnotherTest (number 1). The item representing the archive includes the date it was created, the app's version, and the number of the archive (we can send multiple archives to App Store Connect and later decide which one we want to be reviewed by Apple).

 The Basics: The app's version is determined from the app's settings editor (by default it is set as 1.0). If we want to specify a different version, we must declare the numbers separated by one or two periods (e.g., 1.0 or 1.2.5). The values represent different revisions of our app, with the order of relevance from left to right. The actual meaning of the value is arbitrary, but we are required to change it every time an update is published to the App Store to reflect how big the update was.

Although it is not required, we should always validate the archive before submitting the app to App Store Connect. The process allows Xcode to detect errors and suggest how to fix them. To begin the validation process, we can press the Validate button (Figure 17-6, number 3). The first window presents three options to tell Xcode how to configure the archive and what to include.

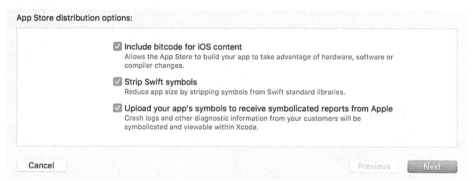

Figure 17-7: *Options to configure the archive*

All these options are recommended. The first one tells Xcode to include code that improves the app's performance, the second includes symbols that represent code from the Swift Standard Library, which reduces the size of the app, and the last option uploads the necessary information for Apple to be able to report errors and perform diagnostics.

The next window lets us select how we want to sign the app. With automatic signing, we let Xcode take care of everything for us (recommended).

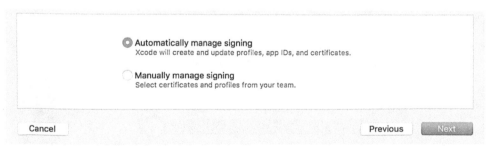

Figure 17-8: *Option to select automatic signing*

The last window displays a summary and provides a button to initiate the validation process. Once this process is over, if no errors are found, we can finally submit our app to Apple servers by pressing the Distribute App button (Figure 17-6, number 2).

Chapter 17 - App Store

As we already mentioned, we may submit multiple archives to the server. For this reason, we must go back to the App Store Connect website, open the description of our application, and select the archive we just uploaded (it may take a few minutes to be available). Figure 17-9 shows the option with the archive (build) we just uploaded for the AnotherTest application.

Build

Build	Upload Date
 2.1 (7)	Oct 1, 2015 at 6:20 AM

Figure 17-9: *Selecting the build to send to the App Store*

After the archive is selected, we can press the Save button to save the app's description. If all the required information was provided, we can finally press the Submit for Review link at the top of the page to submit the application. The system asks us a few questions and then the application is sent for review (the message Waiting for Review is shown below the app's title).

The process takes a few days to be completed. If everything is correct, and the app is accepted, Apple sends us an email to let us know that the app has become available in the App Store.

Chapter 17 - App Store

Index

Z

CPSIA information can be obtained
at www.ICGtesting.com
Printed in the USA
LVHW101145191020
669132LV00009B/468